TOWARDS A NON-BRAHMIN MILLENNIUM

TOWARDS A NON-BRAHMIN MILLENNIUM

From Iyothee Thass to Periyar

V. GEETHA and S. V. RAJADURAI

Samya

TOWARDS A NON-BRAHMIN MILLENNIUM:
FROM IYOTHEE THASS TO PERIYAR
first published in June 1998 by
SAMYA, an imprint of Bhatkal and Sen
16 Southern Avenue, Calcutta 700 026
in association with
THE BOOK REVIEW LITERARY TRUST

First reprint 1999
Second as revised edition, 2008
Third reprint 2011
Fourth reprint 2023 with
Tamil Nadu Textbook and Educational Services Corporation
and the Adi Dravidar & Tribal Welfare Department.
Fifth reprint, Samya, December 2024

ISBNs hardback 978-81-85604-37-4
paperback 978-93-81345-89-4

Rs. 1399.00

Typesetting and design by Sonal Mansata,
85 Park St, Calcutta 700 016, and printed by
Sarat Impressions Pvt Ltd,
18B Shyama Charan Dey Street, Kolkata 700073

Published by Mandira Sen for SAMYA,
an imprint of Bhatkal and Sen
16 Southern Avenue, Calcutta 700 026

To the memory
of those wonderful Self-Respect years

Contents

APPENDICES

Acknowledgements

AT THE OUTSET, we would like to acknowledge our debt to V. Anaimuthu and his three-volume edition of Periyar's speeches and writings, which served us as a veritable archive. We thank the librarian and staff of the Adyar Library and Research Centre for letting us see and use old and precious issues of—*New India*. We are also grateful to the librarian and staff at the Periyar Rationalist Library and Research Centre where we spent many long days, pouring over newspapers and periodicals. Our special thanks in this instance are to 'Viduthalai' K. Rajendran whose kind help and encouragement smoothened our work at the library. We would also like to thank M. Ashok, who let us take photocopies of the collection put together by his father, the late Munusamy Parayar, of publications by Iyothee Thass and other dalit intellectuals.

If it had not been for Kuruvikarambai Velu, we would not have been able to remember and record the work of Kuthoosi Gurusamy. The late 'Noble' Govindarajulu of Trichy put aside the exhaustion of age and personal tragedy to share with us his memories of the Self-Respect movement and allowed us to photocopy rare publications. Professor Sunderraj Manickam of the department of history, Madurai-Kamaraj University, shared with us his views and ideas on dalit history, struggles and liberation. K. Thirunavukarasu and Pon. K. Kothandapani lent us valuable books and journals for which we are grateful.

R. Vidyasagar, Jayashree Nambiar, M. Vijayabhaskar, Millie Nihila and Padmini Swaminathan checked out books for us from various libraries and we cannot thank them enough. S. S. Kannan of Karl Marx Library, Madras, was patient with us as we borrowed several of his fine volumes. Meena Gopal, P. A. Ambedkar and G. Aloysius took care of things we needed from Delhi. Ravi G. and Madhav Sathe helped arrange fruitful discussions with Sandip Pendse, Arjun Dangle and Daya Pawar in Mumbai.

The writing of the text has been an arduous affair. Jayanthi who worked with us at the Adyar Library, Kalaichelvi, who helped copy things down from Self-Respect journals, deserve our very special thanks. Of course this book would not have read the way it does now, if it had not been for Smriti whose timely suggestions made us re-write huge chunks of it. This manuscript was written, re-written, lost and retreived from a temperamental computer. We are grateful to Gita Wolf for sparing us her office computer to finish the book and for all the good cheer which lightened a hard day's work. J. S. Prakash, Helmut Wolf, Priya, Saraswathi Ananth and C. Arumugam were there when we needed them to help us fix a difficult text. Gopal Guru, Nalini Pandit, M. S. S. Pandian, Smriti Srinivas and S. T. Baskaran read portions of the manuscript and we are happy that they took time off to do so.

When it seemed that we would not be able to finish the book because of financial constraints, Ravi Shankar and Nirmala were helpful in putting us in touch with people who would support us. Anupama Rao, M. Sundaramourthy, Kumar N. Kumarappan, Jaya Tirumalai and Jayanth and Saroj Tirumalai were there to help. Palladam Manickam, Kavithasaran, Kurinji, 'Nirapirigai' D. Ravikumar, P. Sivagnanam, Ranjini and Ravi (from Switzerland), Aranamuruval, Inquilab, V. Raghavan (Rayan), Subaveerapandiyan, Senthil, Anuradha, Subha De, D. Geetha, the late Fr. Poornam de Mel, Fr. Manuel Alphonse, D. L. Sheth, Sudarshan and Veli Rangarajan: we thank them for their faith in our work and their consistent support.

None of this would have been possible without the support of Pradip Thomas and World Association for Christian Communication who were there at the very beginning, and who enabled us to begin work. As for Sagu, Varadarajan and Suseela, who put up with five years of 'Periyar-talk' and with all those demands we made on their time and energy, we cannot thank them enough. And, finally, Mandira and others at Samya who offered to publish our text: this has been a fruitful partnership.

We also thank the Tamil Nadu Textbook and Educational Services Corporation and the Adi Dravidar & Tribal Welfare Department for bringing out this edition and we appreciate Mini Krishnan's unstinting support and guidance in this endeavour.

Introduction to the New Edition

S. V. Rajadurai and I began to work on this book more than 25 years ago, in 1991-92. The decade witnessed the unfolding of unquiet politics. Upper caste students across the country protested against the Mandal Commission's recommendations: the Commission had prepared a rational and comprehensive case for reservation for the Other Backward Classes (OBCs) in the services and education. These years also saw the Hindu Right insisting that a temple to the god Ram be built in the precincts of the Babri Masjid in Ayodhya on the argument that the mosque was once a temple. The hostility displayed by the dominant castes to the Mandal Commission's suggestions was dramatic and frightening. Meanwhile, a trail of blood and gore snaked its way into the nation-wide yatra that the Hindu Right undertook to gather support for its temple demand. But there was hope in the air as well: a resistant and assertive dalit movement in alliance with a broad coalition of democratic and feminist groups challenged this casteist rancour as well as the Hindu Right that endorsed and justified it. A host of political parties and groups opposed the yatris' call for a temple.

In Tamil Nadu, there was no great opposition to the Mandal Commission, nor much enthusiasm for a Ram temple. But the moment proved decisive for other reasons: since caste-based justice was being argued out, it appeared an opportune time to examine the histories that had made positive discrimination in favour of dalits and the so-called backward and most backward castes a given in this southern state. On the one hand, it led to an interrogation of the Periyar-inspired Dravidian movement's politics, with regard to dalit claims and rights and on the other hand, made for a lively and critical examination of E. V. Ramasami Periyar's thought world, and his ideological legacy. Much was said on both sides, and yet the spirit was essentially dialogic even, if at times, acrimonious. It was in view of the energetic arguments that we were privy to, in the Tamil public sphere, that we decided to enquire further into the histories that shaped Periyar and his contemporaries.

Rajadurai (b.1940) had a longstanding association with the Left as well as anti-caste movements in the state. In his boyhood, he was drawn to the Dravida Munnetra Kazhagam (DMK), but in his twenties became part of the Left. He took the part of the CPI(M) when the CPI split. Subsequently, along with some others, he urged forth a radical Left politics, which aligned itself with the Marxism-Leninism, advocated by Charu Mazumdar. Yet Rajadurai retained his admiration for and interest in Periyar and anti-caste thought: years spent in the Nilgiris, in the company of plantation workers and labourers from sundry castes had demonstrated to him the manner in which class and caste relationships were enmeshed. Further, while he remained within the Left fold, he was critical of Soviet socialism, and while admiring of Mao's China, did not let the politics of Beijing entirely define his political understanding: he read widely in European and American Marxism and published a pioneering Tamil study of the Marxist category of Alienation in 1979.

Given his complex understanding of two different political traditions, and the practical work he undertook with respect to both—from mobilizing workers into unions, to writing and publishing on a range of progressive issues—he was well positioned to undertake a review of Periyar's life, work and ideas. In view of the many questions that came to be posed, with regard to communist politics in India, by a range of actors—from those committed to a politics of national self-determination to those who wished to annihilate caste, from feminists to those who were part of the new social movements—he was drawn to a project, which held the promise of opening up a dialogue between the Left and anti-caste movements in the state.

I came to this project from another perspective: from the late 1980s, in a day-to-day sense, I was involved in feminist politics, which in the Tamil context, was shaped by an active bahujan-dalit constituency of women, some politicized by Christian social work, others by socialism, and yet others by individual experiences of discrimination and violence. This had brought home to me, as it did to others, the manner in which the caste and gender questions were intertwined, a fact that was all too evident in the manner dalit women's lives and deaths underwrote the continuous violence that dalits in Tamil Nadu endured, and which appeared a given in the 1980s and 1990s. Meanwhile, other influences shaped my sense of history and politics as well. Since my student days, I had read widely in socialist thought and politics, which is how I met Rajadurai, in the first place. Given our converging interests, we wrote three introductory texts, in the early 1990s on western Marxism in Tamil: on Althusser, the Frankfurt School and Antonio Gramsci. While working on these projects we decided that we ought to turn our attention to more immediate and local matters and so began to write articles on the caste and gender questions in contemporary Tamil Nadu for the *Economic & Political Weekly*.

Rajadurai's longstanding critique of the DMK's populism, my anguish at the misogyny that party leaders routinely displayed, and our dismay over the continuing violence against dalits shaped our understanding of the Dravidian movement of our times. From this sense of unease, and yet convinced, at the time, that only a unity of bahujan and dalit communities could secure social and economic justice, and keep the Hindu Right, and its constitutive Brahminism at bay, we committed ourselves to rethinking Periyar's legacy.

It seemed to us that it was necessary to bring back into focus the discursive richness of the movements that Periyar and his comrades founded, starting from 1925. Whether this had to do with new and radical ideas on with sexual and gender equality or critical thought that sought to deconstruct the brahminical pieties which justified the caste order and untouchability, the Self-Respect movement, as well as the Dravidar Kazhagam, came to house these in the Tamil language, through a remaking of idiom, metaphor and argument. The ideas and expressions which pushed the limits of public thought and debate constituted a new and reckless counter-public, whose contours were mobile and open to redrawing, in any given instance. Set against uncritical political nationalism, these counterviews gestured towards a universal culture of equality and fraternity. Equally, these words and views impinged on, and unsettled, intimate and familial lives, leading to astonishing expressions to do with love, conjugality and motherhood.

We also wanted to frame Periyar's writings within the histories that shaped them, and which they reflected but also sought to transcend.

While his speeches, editorials and occasional articles had been collected into three volumes by Ve. Anaimuthu, the ways in which his ideas evolved over time, the play of the contingent and the normative in his reasoning, and his millenarian commitment to upend the caste order had not been attended to with the acuity they deserved.

We took on board existing scholarship, in English and Tamil and in addition examined a range of histories and sociological writings: of caste and land, labour migration, missionary presence and activity in the Madras province, and of anti-caste assertion in other parts of British India. We were inspired by Gail Omvedt's pioneering study of Mahatma Phule and the Satyashodhak Samaj as we were by Rosalind O'Hanlon's subtle and admiring analysis of Phule's thought world. This decade opened up another world for us: of dalit intellectual histories and texts, especially the writings and ideas associated with Pandit Iyothee Thass and his Buddhist contemporaries. Essays on Thass by popular Tamil scholars, Pe. Su. Mani and Thirunavukkarasu enthused us to seek out Thass' writings. Eventually we got to discover a very distinctive archive of texts, which was unlike anything that we had known, until then. Iyothee Thass' *Tamizhan*, as well as other publications by Thass' publishing house, the Siddhartha Puthagasalai, opened up a new world of critique and creativity, which had come to claim its place besides modern brahminical thought, as well as an emergent Non-Brahminism.

For our part, we claimed Thass' work for a broad Non-Brahminism, given his assertion of what he, at times, termed a non-caste Dravidian worldview. While he differed from the dominant strands of Dravidian thought, he anticipated the relentless critique of Brahminism that ideologues of the Justice party and the Self-Respect movement would put forth. He was a pioneer in other ways as well, especially with regard to his writings on the Buddha and what he termed 'Living Buddhism', a fact that we took note of, but did not explicate further. Contemporary writings on Dalit intellectual traditions and histories, which emerged with force in the last decades of the twentieth century, have opened up research into dalit thought worlds and it is evident that the history of Dravidian politics ought to perhaps be traced to the ideas that animated an earlier generation of dalit thinkers and legislators.

Another archive that we assembled had to do with the Justice party, the first Non-Brahmin party in the Madras Presidency. Since the weeklies produced by the latter were unavailable, we looked to understand their times and labour through the eyes of their mostly brahmin critics, many of whom wrote in Annie Besant's *New India*. This also helped us grasp the nature and content of brahmin self-making, as it unfolded in the early twentieth century, and pushed us to speculate on the usefulness of designating modern Brahminism as a structure of feeling.

Our concerted archival efforts were undertaken with regard to the Self-Respect movement: we read and learnt a great deal from the rich repository of weeklies and other publications that the movement had put out. We worked our way through thousands of pages, all of which bore witness to the making of an exciting social radicalism, crucial aspects of which had slipped out of public memory. We also scoured through early Left weeklies, as were available to us, such as *Samadharmam*. Besides these textual efforts, we spoke to a number of men and women, associated, in different ways, with the fight against caste, Brahminism and Untouchability. We worked for many years, and amidst busy workaday and political lives, to marshal our rich source material into two books, one in Tamil and the other in English.

We were enthusiastic and excited by the archives we had assembled for ourselves, and, equally by the widespread debates around caste that had come to be. Working with Iyothee Thass' writings, and also with work by other dalits of his time, we were made aware of a world of ideas that was novel and startling, and which appeared apposite to the rich literary and political writings by dalits that had begun to appear from the early 1990s. Located as we were in this charged social context, we chose to be receptive to the limited yet effective Non-Brahminism of the Justice Party, which, otherwise, we might have marked as cautious and modestly liberal. And so, we ended up writing a critical yet engaged history of its time in politics. Equally, our research helped us value the incipient and distinctive socialist possibilities that lay immanent in anti-caste movements and histories, and this was something that we were determined to foreground, given our contentious yet comradely relationship with various strands of the Tamil Left. Lastly, we were thrilled by the feminisms of the time, ably articulated by women in the Self-Respect movement, and which S Anandhi had pointed to earlier. We sought to frame this feminism within the wider ideological and political contexts that had helped constitute Self-Respect thought.

The Tamil book that we wrote, *Suyamariyathai Samadharmam*, was published in 1996 and has since seen several editions. Its publishing proved consequential, in that Left groups had to grapple with their silences to do with caste, while Dravidian enthusiasts had to reflect on a radical legacy, whose crucial aspects had to do with gender and the situation of dalits, but which, had been either ignored or reduced to political pieties. The English volume that we wrote, which is this book, was published in 1998, thanks to Mandira Sen's willingness to risk publishing two unknown non-academic writers, on a subject that was yet to command sufficient interest in English social science publishing; or for that matter, in the domain of history.

We are all too aware of the limits of what we had attempted: Sumit Sarkar, an early reader of the book, pointed out that we might want to think of the political economy of Self-Respect. Young Dalit readers have wondered if we did not overstate our case for bahujan-dalit solidarity, and if our arguments would have been differently made, had we been aware of the relative autonomy of dalit intellectual history. We have asked ourselves if we ought to have written yet another volume in English that critically reckoned with the transformation of Self-Respect thought into a putative Dravidian nationalism (Rajadurai in fact wrote such a volume in Tamil). Clearly more needs to be done, and might well be attempted in the decades to come—as a younger generation seeks to house Periyar and his cohort in the world of academia and global intellectual thought.

We have not added or altered our text of 1998, which was revised in 2008. But we thought a new introduction was in order that explains why we came to write this book. We thought that this back story would be of interest to a new generation of scholars and readers, most of whom work in a context that associates research and writing with universities, grants, time taken off from regular study or work We wanted to indicate to them how, shaped by the anxieties of the times and history, some of us undertake non-scholastic yet rigorous intellectual labour. In doing so, we align ourselves with lineages of thought that have to do with collective traditions of knowledge-making, safeguarding and transmission.

Our book, we are all too aware, would not have been possible, without the affectionate and critical support lent to it by several political and cultural critics, activists, individual archivists, librarians, and a large host of memory-keepers, who shared their generational insights with us. We might not agree with all that we were told, or read, but the experience of heeding diverse memories and texts produced in the melee of everyday politics and struggle was educative: we learnt to value transformative political and cultural work undertaken by volunteer citizens, intellectuals, many of whom are from very modest if not marginal social backgrounds.

The challenge for us, as for several others, who write in tandem with what inspires them, is to retain critical thought and reflection, while doing so—a practice that is not easy, is always and already fraught, and yet one that has to be risked.

Chennai, 2023 V. GEETHA

Authors' Note

IN THIS BOOK we have used 'proportional representation' and 'communal representation' interchangeably, following the practice of several leaders and cadres of the Non-Brahmin movement. We have not capitalized varna terms like 'shudra' or 'dalit' or 'adi dravidas', but we have capitalized the names of castes, for example, Nadars. We have used terms such as 'Paraiah' or 'panchama' and 'shudra' in a purely descriptive sense. Given today's context of dalit militancy, we would have liked to use the word 'dalit' but this would be clearly anachronistic. Wherever we have spoken in our own voices, we have preferred the term 'adi dravida'. We have capitalized 'Paraiah' and 'Palla' to distinguish these distinct castes from the generic 'panchama'.

We have referred to the journals and newspapers extensively and have cited them within the chapters themselves. Those newspapers or journals that have been cited infrequently have not been abbreviated. But we have provided the following abbreviations for those that have been cited frequently:

New India NI; *Swadharma* SWD; Desabandhu Db; *Kudi Arasu* KA; Nagara Thoothan NT; *Oru Paisa Tamizhan* Tamizhan; *Pagutharivu* Pa; *Puduvai Murasu* PM; *Puratchi* Pu; *Revolt* R; *Samadharman* Sd; *Viduthalai* Vi.

The Tamil script used on the book jacket and on the chapter openings refers to '*Suyamariathai*' or self-respect, representing the key symbol of this period.

CHAPTER 1

The Brahmin in the Tamil Country in the Early Twentieth Century

WHEN THE NON-BRAHMIN MANIFESTO was released for public debate and scrutiny in December 1916, Annie Besant, editor of *New India* (NI) and patron saint of the Home Rule movement denounced its contents and stated intentions in strident terms. She characterized the Manifesto as 'mischievous and unpatriotic' and claimed it had been authored by 'short-sighted narrow-minded people' whose chief objective was 'to denounce the work of the National Congress and the Home Rule Movement':

> In our midst there are some who are our brothers, the sons of the Mother who are short-sighted and [who] fall prey to the divide-and-rule policies of the enemies of national regeneration and are so childish so as not to see that in the matter of the country's progress personal freedom should be put aside.

The signatories to the Manifesto had sought to provoke 'disharmony and disunion' and engaged in a veritable 'crusade of hate' that bode no good. For,

> As long as India gains Home Rule it is but of secondary importance whether brahmanas or non-brahmana Hindus or Muslims gain prominence. We are children of one Mother and our interest as those of our country in the first instance is to our sense of unity (NI 20.12.16).

Annie Besant's close associate in the Home Rule movement and a prominent Madras notable, C. P. Ramaswamy Iyer, was also inclined to dismiss the Non-Brahmin Manifesto as unworthy of serious political consideration. He objected chiefly to the Manifesto's pointed antipathy towards brahmins and argued that the authors of the Manifesto ought to have desisted from thus vilifying a particular community and, instead, spent their energies in a 'more profitable way' such as 'sending out a large number of lads to foreign countries and equipping them educationally' (NI 1.11.20). Ramaswamy Iyer observed:

> Everyone of us, whether brahmana or non-brahmana, must admit that to the extent we are lacking in our efforts to develop that sense of social equality to that extent we are falling short of truly democratic ideals.

The brahmin could not be called an enemy of democracy nor could the caste system be termed inherently inegalitarian. For, argued Ramaswamy Iyer, the caste order in its constitutive phase was founded on principles of comradeship and brahmins had never quite forgotten that this comradeship was the 'fundamental basis of the caste system' (NI 1.11.20). He had remarked on another occasion,

> There is not [today] a single person [brahmana] throughout the length and breadth of this country who would not say [to the non-brahmana), 'By all means take your share in the country. You are blood of our blood, bone of our bone' (NI 7.11.19).

S. Subramania Iyer, another Home Rule enthusiast (and theo-sophist) insisted that non-brahmins and panchamas were profoundly misguided in their hatred of brahmins and caste. For though the varna principle, at times, may seem to subserve brahmin concerns, it yet allowed 'the low to be brought to the level of the high'. Brahmins were open to change in these modern times and ready to repent for the sins of their ancestors and do their duty by the panchamas. The columns of The Hindu, for instance, were now open to all, including panchamas, and the latter had come to enjoy 'equality and fraternity in the eyes of the law' (NI 22.8.17).

New India's non-brahmin readers, many of whom were also in the

Home Rule League, found the Non-Brahmin Manifesto objectionable for other reasons. The Manifesto had observed, that in the present circumstances of India, it was the British alone who could 'hold the scales even between creed and class and ... develop that sense of solidarity and unity without which India will continue to be a group of mutually exclusive and warring groups without common purpose and a common patriotism' (Varadarajulu Naidu 1932: vol 1, 6). P. Kesava Pillay, Home Ruler and Congressman, confessed himself 'pained and humiliated' by this admission of dependence on the British by his fellow non-brahmins:

> As a member of the Congress since 1885, as a humble worker in the rural parts, sharing in the fears and hopes of the people; as a people's representative who had laboured long in the Madras Legislative Council, as a British subject with feelings of sincere loyalty and as a self-respecting non-brahmana Hindu, I feel it my duty to respectfully dissociate myself from the Manifesto (NI 22.12.16).

Kesava Pillay, like Ramaswamy Iyer, disapproved of the Manifesto's pronounced anti-Brahminism and observed that brahmins cannot be blamed for observing caste, for 'the east coast Vellalas or the west coast Nairs and the midland Reddis ... were more contemptuous than brahmins of the Paraiahs, Malas, Thiyas and Pulayas' (ibid).

Kesava Pillay was not the only 'self-respecting non-brahmana' whose views were eagerly and enthusiastically reported in *New India*. On 30 December 1916, *New India* carried a statement by one Venkataranga Reddy, landholder, High Court vakil and non-official president of the Kurnool Taluk Board, which noted that the community of Reddys, who were mainly landholders, were in favour of the Congress proposal for reform in government and entirely opposed to the sentiments expressed in the Non-Brahmin Manifesto. The 9 January 1917 issue of *New India* reproduced the letter of M. Subbiah, General Secretary of the Vokkaliga Sabha. The letter writer noted, 'Aren't we all Hindus and has not a great Congress leader who is a brahmana remarked, "Let everybody even Paraiahs get what we are fighting for; I shall be satisfied."'

An anonymous reader commended the patriotic stance of the

Vokkaliga Sabha and clarified that 'the term "brahmana" represents not merely a small caste but also an entire civilization. To call oneself a Hindu and yet denounce the brahmana and all that is brahmanical is worthy of gross ingratitude' (From *Karnataka*, quoted in NI 9.1.17). A Vokkaliga conference held in Malanad supported these views and its chairman, Hossappa Krishna Rao, observed that one was first of all an Indian and only then a brahmana or non-brahmana (NI 25.1.17).

There were others who objected to the sentiments expressed in the Non-Brahmin Manifesto because they were puzzled and bewildered by what seemed to them incomprehensible and erroneous notions of brahmin autocracy and non-brahmin ineptitude. The *Tribune of Lahore*, for instance, stated:

> To our knowledge there is no such community as non-brahmana or non-Buddhist or non-Hindus or non-Jews and nothing can be more ludicrous than to form a new community on the basis of excluding a small community...the one small but important caste of brahmins (quoted in NI 30.12.16).

The *Times of India* rejected the possibility of a non-brahmin community functioning as a 'single homogenous group, capable of common or united action' (quoted in NI 2.1.17). The *Ceylonese* rebuked those non-brahmins who sought to better their lot by 'girding at the brahmanas' and urged the former to tread the path of 'organised self-help' (quoted in NI 19.1.17).

The hostile reception accorded the Non-Brahmin Manifesto was not entirely capricious or even unexpected. It represented, in fact, the outrage of a class which had come to take its hegemony for granted. Since the last quarter of the nineteenth century, intellectuals in Madras, especially those who in 1916 supported the cause of Home Rule, had worked hard to present themselves as respectful and humble purveyors of the commonweal; as an honourable community of civic-minded citizens who could effectively mediate native concerns and represent native interests to an essentially alien government. As early as 1884 these men of Madras city—lawyers, merchants, publicists and administrators—had sought to legitimize their representative status. At the First Provincial Conference of the Madras Mahajana Sabha, of which almost all Madras notables were members, it was proposed that Indian public opinion be taken seriously and granted credence by the government, for Indians were 'no longer a stationary people' and had 'outgrown the conditions of the past' when they had to be contained and ruled (Suntharalingam 1974: 221). The time had come to recognize the importance of the ideal of popular representation and work to transform the existing legislatures which, at present provide 'little room for the successful expression of popular opinion and fail to command that degree of confidence which is so needful for their efficient working' (ibid: 222).

Madras's distinguished citizenry which thus sought to serve as a 'voice of the people' comprised a large number of brahmins—Tamils, Telugus, Deshastas and Niyogis—and a smattering of non-brahmins. The latter were either prominent merchants or bankers or respectable landlords who subscribed to brahminic ways and views. These men, brahmins and non-brahmins, were bound together by professional, intellectual and cultural concerns: while mercantile wealth contributed to and sustained the citizenry's civic work, a political liberalism learnt mostly in the classrooms of the Raj and articulated successfully by journals and newspapers underwrote all efforts at organizing for political change. But, perhaps, what really united these men in their endeavours was a set of cultural (and religious) preferments. They were mostly Hindus, a good number of them were theosophists and, most important of all, they were men who were ready to re-claim their history, tradition and culture with pride.

Influenced by the work of British adminstrator-scholars, Indologists and linguists, these men were quite different from their counterparts of an earlier generation who disdained all things Hindu. Conversely, these men were eager to identify themselves and their way of life with an archaic past and culture which stood to be recovered in the here and now. Eventually they came to represent their civic and political concerns and anxieties as 'nationalist' in character and were prone to locate this nationalist sentiment in a remembered and sanctified past. Deemed Aryan and Vedic in origin by European scholars and their Indian interlocutors, this past seemed particularly significant, since Max Mueller and others considered it a natural progenitor of all worthwhile civilizational and cultural progress in the Western as well as the Eastern worlds. Colonel Olcott of the Theosophical Society had enthused Madras elites in the cause of an Aryanist revival and called all Hindus to return to the ways of the 'the sages, the warriors; the great intellects of yore'. He had imagined a future time when disunity amongst men would disappear, when brahmins would no more wallow in menial professions as clerks and merchants and when all Hindus would 'feel fit to rule the world, nay meet the gods on equal terms' (ibid: 294). Writing in 1917, years after Colonel Olcott had made his ideas publicly known, S. Setlur, a Madras notable, reminded Hindus of the promises implicit in Olcott's vision. He observed it was entirely right that the 'proverbially mild Hindu' should clamour for self-rule while all others, 'though not Aryan in blood', being nurtured in Aryanism for scores of years, should also be 'saturated through and through with the Aryan love of liberty' (NI 1.9.17).

It is not to be wondered then that Madras elites, self-assured in their historic (and spiritual) patriotic mission and complacent in their sterling public virtues, should mistrust and treat with lofty contempt the Non-Brahmin Manifesto which was openly critical and scornful of that mission. Not only brahmins, but the handful of non-brahmins, who along with the former were the makers of public opinion in Madras, found it disturbing that brahmins who constituted the very warp and woof of intellectual life in this southern Presidency should thus be berated and asked to examine their actions and motives critically. After all, had not Annie Besant, Olcott's successor at the Theosophical Society and a self-professed radical thinker and social reformer, admitted to the intellectual supremacy of the brahmins and called upon them to precede and lead others in national work? Very few could forget her impassioned appeal to the 'brahmana' races that was issued in 1913 where she had counselled them to take history by its horns and make it subserve their exalted purpose. She pointed out to them that there were essentially two ways of change, 'two ways in which privileges disappear'. In the one instance, the commoners rise against the privilege-holders, outraged by a sense of injustice. In the other instance, as with the samurais of Japan, the privileged class lays aside its glory and sacrifices it for the sake of the Motherland. Annie Besant went on to note,

> I have a vision...which I hope is not only a dream of this mighty [brahmana] caste which in the past has given to India all that was greatest in her literature and arts; and of you the natural leaders of

> the people by your high education, by your brilliant intelligence, by your powers of speech—I have had a vision of your mighty caste going forward to the feet of India...the mother taking off the coronet of privilege and laying it down in sacrifice at her feet. I have dreamt that the great act of national sacrifice once accomplished, splendidly performed, India the Mother would stretch out her hands in blessing and say to her children who made the sacrifice: 'Go back to your people and take your rightful place again as leaders still in India. Give to them your splendid intellect, give to them your wonderful eloquence, give to them the power of your past and the influence of your names crowned no longer with the crown of privilege but with the deathless crown of self-sacrifice.' This is the vision I have (reproduced in NI 27.11.18).

Annie Besant had also reminded brahmins that they carried within their hearts and minds the weight of authoritative learning and had made it clear that brahmin participation in public life had been mandated by fate and was required by history:

> Millennia of studious poverty have built up a body of fine nervous development, refined, sensitive and admirably adapted for its functions and have chiselled out an incomparable brain that has not its peers as a class in the whole world...Natural Law has been utilised and the result is there before us (NI 25.6.15).

Annie Besant's unbounded energy, her imaginative and polemical vigour and her mercurial temperament rendered her an inspiring and natural leader. Madras notables, many of whom were associated with her and her work in the Theosophical Society, rallied around her enthusiastically when she founded the Home Rule League in September 1916. Annie Besant not only expressed concern for the cultural worth and salience of Brahminism but was inclined to display a personal and almost maternal concern towards brahmins. For instance, she responded angrily to an observation in the Census report, 1911, which noted that many brahmins who desired to admit relatives as voluntary boarders into the Madras Lunatic Asylum withdrew their request due to want of 'caste conveniences' for their wards. Besant not only wondered why the government had made no special provisions as demanded by 'caste scruple' but also pointed out that an extant government order enjoined the Surgeon-General to submit plans and estimates for the provision of separate accommodation for brahmana patients in the Madras asylum (NI 18.6.15).

Annie Besant exhibited great anxiety over brahmin welfare in more routine instances as well. When the Madras government raised school and college fees, she denounced the measure in no uncertain terms and bemoaned the fate of the 'ordinarily penurious brahmana student'. In 1918 she wrote:

> One of the cruelties of English rule in India is that it has made education dear and reduced those who have ever enjoyed it to beg as a favour what would be theirs by right (NI 25.6.18).

Annie Besant's benevolent interest in brahmin affairs proved immensely soothing to that community which, in spite of its much vaunted faith in its own superiority and intellectual prowess, felt beleaguered. While brahmins, after the coming of the British, came to wield enormous secular power, as administrators, lawyers, judges, journalists and teachers, and were revered for their ascriptive status as well, they yet felt scapegoated. Since the arrival of the white man, especially his missionaries of faith, they were subject to ridicule and reviled and rebuked for their lack of humanity. Not only missionaries, but British civilians and even a few amongst Hindus were now given to berating brahmin prejudice and narrow-mindedness. Men as different in their intentions and objectives as Grant-Duff, Governor of Madras, and Swami Vivekananda were harshly critical of the Southern brahmin's pretensions to purity and a superior status (Irschick 1969: 281; Vivekananda 1989: vol. 4, 296-302).

What was however most galling to brahmin self-pride was the emergence of a profound anti-brahmin sentiment amongst ordinary people. Even as early as 1870, when Muthuswamy Iyer, a Madras notable, was elevated to a judgeship in Madras, a 'shudra' and a 'Dravidian' had protested the appointment and argued that a brahmin judge was ill-suited to hold such an office. For, in all likelihood, he would be unfamiliar and even unsympathetic to the customs, mores and norms which governed the lives, thoughts and actions of vast numbers of non-brahmins (Suntharalingam: 151-52).

The last decades of the previous century witnessed a quickening of the tide of anti-brahmin anger and sections of the vernacular press in Madras were openly critical of brahminic virtues and values. The Tamil weekly, *Oru Paisa Tamizhan* (*Tamizhan*), published from 1907, carried out an unrelenting and systematic attack on brahmin attitudes to reform and their courting of the Swadeshi ideal. Satiric, vituperative and angry in turn, these criticisms anticipated the anti-Brahminism of the later Self-Respect movement in many ways. They mocked at what they considered brahminic superstitions, hypocrisy and scriptural inconsistencies and the brahmin's pursuit of worldly power in the name of an assumed and false sacrality.

The emergence of anti-Brahminism in Madras may be traced to a complex of reasons (see Chapter 2). British economic and mercantile practices had transformed the material fortunes of hitherto subaltern communities. These latter strove to translate their material gains into symbolic ones and either courted a higher varna status or converted to Christianity to pursue a life of self-contained dignity. The language and vocabulary of political liberalism opened up to these 'upstart' castes a discourse of rights and freedom. The literate amongst these castes soon came to challenge the bounded civic space carved out by brahmin elites, either by organizing caste organizations or through a recourse to a plea—which later on was transformed into a demand—for proportional representation of all castes in the civil services and in educational institutions.

What proved most enabling to these new imaginings of the self and the community was the discovery of history by non-brahmin intellectuals towards the last quarter of the nineteenth century. These men, schooled in traditional Tamil learning and having frequented the classrooms of the Raj, came to articulate a non-'Aryan' version of history in which non-brahmin shudras were proclaimed chief and valued actors while brahmins were considered alien interlopers and foreigners. Adi dravida intellectuals presented an interesting variation on this argument and held that the so-called panchamas were the original inhabitants of this vast subcontinent, who had been cast out of history and relegated to the fringes of society with the historic defeat of their Buddhist faith by Aryan-brahmin invaders.

These various strains of non-brahmin dissent and subversion proved irksome to Madras brahmins and they were naturally responsive to Annie Besant's call to their community to heed and attend to its appointed hour and fulfil its destiny. They were captivated by Besant's superb rhetoric of culture, caste and nation and came to view her ideas as so many mirrors which returned to them flattering images of themselves and fortified them in their self-appointed roles of patriots, reformers and modern Hindus who would usher in a brave new world of glory and prosperity.

To understand better that amazing self-pride and narcissism which Annie Besant's genius made resonant with patriotic fervour, we need to enquire into the making of brahmin subjectivity in colonial Madras. We are not concerned so much with those various socioeconomic and institutional processes which elevated brahmins as a caste group into positions of power and authority in colonial India. Instead, we intend looking at various instances of brahmin self-imaging in certain well-defined contexts: the realm of reform, the social sphere and political society. These three related arenas proved to be the most favoured sporting grounds of local elites and in and through the attitudes, opinions and ideas generated in these realms emerges the brahmin persona; mythic in its pretensions to power and, yet, sufficiently real in its will to consolidate that power into definitive social, cultural and political authority.

THE QUESTION OF REFORM

Social reform concerns and activity in early twentieth-century Madras were firmly focused on two issues: the status of women and the condition of the adi dravidas. The women's question was raised in the context of two interlinked debates: on the Post-Puberty Marriage (PPM) Bill, introduced in the Madras Council in 1914, and on a suitable educational curriculum for girls, a matter that gained in importance with Annie Besant's interventions in the cause of evolving a national curricula for aspiring learners.

Public opinion on these matters was expressed through debates in the press, at reform meetings and in various caste and community forums which were active during this period. *New India's* 'Vox Populi' columns carried statements, rejoinders, arguments and explications on the PPM Bill and on the question of a suitable curriculum for girls. Annie Besant brought her formidable intellectual energy to bear on these issues and initiated, provoked and annulled discussions at her discretion.

The Post-Puberty Marriage Bill

The PPM Bill provoked a considerable measure of public antipathy. Questions were raised as to the propriety of the government interfering in practices ordained by the shastras; doubts were entertained as to the wisdom of enforcing rather than enabling social change; valiant efforts were made to interpret shastraic injunctions rationally and to rationalize an ingrained conservative resistance to change.

Reader S.M.L. from Kumbakonam, writing in the 'Vox Populi' columns, argued indignantly that 'permission to do a prohibited thing' could only constitute 'an interference with the Authority from whom the prohibition proceeds'. Besides, having allowed Hindus to be governed by shastraic law, the government could hardly afford to validate post-puberty marriages which were not sanctioned by the shastras. Thus,

> In Hindu law, divorce is unknown and a man in the Christian communities is prohibited from having more than one wife at a time. Suppose a law is passed which permits divorce to the Hindus on certain grounds in the one case and for two wives in the other case, would not such a law be an interference with the Personal Law of the Hindu and Christian respectively, though there is only a permission given for divorce in the one case and for bigamy in the other case? (NI 3.11.14)

Another *New India* reader, R.N. (also from Kumbakonam), drew on the Grihayashastras, and deftly distinguished samvesana (consummation) from *kanyadana* (the actual marriage sacrament) and noted that the former could (and did) take place after puberty but the latter clearly is and must be a pre-puberty ritual (NI 3.12.14).

Others, indifferent to the government's inconsistencies and to questions of shastraic validity, observed that the problem lay neither with the proposed measure which, in itself, was worthy nor with the shastras, which upheld ideal norms that fallible mortals were not really expected to practice. The problem, instead, had to do with reform as such. Manav, adding to the points of debate on the PPM Bill in the same columns, thus, remarked:

> To my mind it seems that society as a living organism is capable of adjusting itself automatically to every kind of rude shock to which it is subjected by the spread of Western civilisation. In order to quicken this adjustment and protect society from losing its cohesion, a conscience of the community and of the individuals composing it alike have to be educated (NI 24.11.14).

Manav's characterization of society as an organic whole invokes a metaphor that was fairly common currency during this period. Several opponents of the PPM Bill would resort to such uses of language to rationalize their own studied resistance to reform. It is in such instances that we see language mediating deeply-felt prejudices and attitudes to constitute them as rational and given. T. S. Subramania Iyer commenting on the reformist approval of the PPM Bill observed:

> Government knows that if in a small organism like the human body the one water in it that comes from the eye, the nose, the mouth, the skin and the bladder differ in form, name, quantity and quality the variety in the whole world must be immense; that any attempt at reducing it to a uniformity will not only be futile but even a mistake and that therefore the best way to rule an alien country is not by ignoring natural laws and introducing into it structural changes but by helping it to advance in its own line, adjusting itself at the same time to the changed and changing conditions of things in its environment (NI 26.1.15).

The insistence on evaluating reform in the context of a 'natural' process of national and societal regeneration was echoed by several others but with this difference in emphasis. Thus, G. P. A. Sharma writing in favour of the proposed legislation, went all out to identify national resurgence with the restoration of Indian womanhood to its former arcadian glory:

> If the crying need of India is women, women virtuous...cultured, women who can influence the morals, manners and character of the nation as well as individuals...women who can build the glorious

> manhood and womanhood of India that is to be—we should raise the age of marriage and equip our girls as highly as possible before thinking of marrying them (NI 2.3.15).

S. Viswanatha Iyer, S. Srinivasa Iyengar and a host of others, who obviously spoke for the reform party, felt it important to support the bill. Srinivasa Iyengar was anxious that India live up to her 'Aryan' heritage and concurred with G. P. A. Sharma who had observed 'we should not become a laughing stock in the eyes of the world, since we are the descendants of noble, wise and courageous people as the Aryans' (ibid).

An anonymous reader summed up reform opinion with respect to the bill thus:

> The cry for self-government is heard on all sides and after the war some of us will feel ourselves aggrieved if some large amount of ruling power is not placed in our hands by Britain who stands for freedom. But we forget that British statesmen are watching us to see whether we are prepared to be trusted with power over the weak amongst ourselves. Such a test as the PPM Bill will weigh heavily against us in the minds of the plainspoken British people if it is not accepted (NI 12.4.15).

Not all were willing to grant that a mere reform of marital customs would enhance the credibility and prestige of Hindu practices in the eyes of its critics. V. A. Nagasami observed somewhat irately that there were other urgent matters which needed to be addressed if women (and men) were to be reformed into adopting more progressive attitudes. Arguing that the passing of the PPM Bill should be preceded by educating the public, he remarked:

> The brahmana lady (at least the uneducated) is the embodiment of the highest form of orthodoxy imaginable. She cannot think of any reform without great horror...the torch of education must be introduced to illumine her dark bosom. This reform is a higher, nobler and more sustained one than a hundred PPM bills and a thousand widow-remarriage bills (NI 25.2.15).

Other sorts of fears and apprehensions with regard to the brahmana lady persuaded some to dissociate themselves completely from the issue of post-puberty marriages. Ram Sharma wrote with feeling that he could not 'contemplate spinsters of seventy moving freely in our society without horror' and argued that this would emerge as an imminent possibility if girls and women 'whose social purity and welfare is in charge of their parents and brothers' were allowed to shift their age of marriage like 'work-a-day men in the modern world' (ibid).

The debates over the Post-Puberty Marriage Bill reveal the imaginative prowess of a community whose members could thus advance various and even contradictory arguments with respect to a matter that was of interest to no one really but themselves. For, as several non-brahmin readers of *New India* pointed out, post-puberty marriages were the norm rather than the exception amongst all communities other than the brahmins. Writing in support of the bill, A. Damodharan noted:

> First of all none of the opposers of the bill seem to understand that the bill is permissive and optional and does not prohibit a pre-puberty marriage. Neither do they seem to have knowledge of others outside the narrow pale of their own caste. For instance, they seldom understand that nearly all non-brahmin castes, Mudaliars, Pillays, Naidus are already having post-puberty marriages for centuries (NI 24.10.15).

To such men as these (and a few women) the debate was over a non-problem since the purported issues at stake—the validity of the shastras, the role of legislation with regard to reform, the 'Aryan' predilection for progressive customs—could not possibly affect the status of non-brahmin women or the morality of those customs which enjoined them to marry after attaining puberty. Nor could these arguments serve to evaluate a non-Aryan culture which rendered meaningful the lives of a majority of people in the southern Presidency. The only use of these debates was, as one reader pointed out in sorrow, they drew attention to and helped to establish a retrograde practice even amongst non-brahmins:

> I am sorry to say that the evil custom is spreading amongst some of the non-brahmana castes. Many take pride in imitating the

> habits of brahmanas and some have indirectly adopted their ways in marriage...In my village I saw a shudra girl of nine with a sacred tie around her neck. The girl's mother was infuriated when I expressed surprise and said, 'It is not the custom amongst us to marry after puberty like the low castes' (NI 27.1.15).

Neither the interventions of non-brahmins nor the pleas against orthodox opposition to the bill articulated by a 'woman sufferer' helped transform the nature and contents of the debate which, in the final analysis, was concerned with matters that had nothing to do with women's desires or concerns. The 'woman sufferer' pleaded that the PPM Bill was 'perfectly harmless and innocent':

> It only seeks to declare valid marriages which may possibly now be invalid in the eyes of the law; it only tries to prevent the issues of such marriages being termed illegitimate. Can Ultra-Orthodoxy deny this boon to human beings? (NI 3.12.14)

But the reformers (and their opponents) were in no position to listen to her and heed her plea. The questions which plagued their souls and intellect were different: Would a reform of this kind disturb or enhance brahmin selfhood, whose integrity, conventionally, at least, had been preserved by observance of tradition and scriptural norms? Would this reform help the brahmin accommodate change within the confines of custom? Would the brahmin emerge a worthy Aryan nationalist or would he persist in his ignorance of his noble origins that stood to be recalled and commemorated in the present hour?

It is clear that no one really feared imposition, for they knew this would not come to pass; nor did the reformers imagine that post-puberty marriages would be performed in hundreds and thousands, once the bill was passed. As C. Appanna Shastri, pleader and author of a book on Hindu Law in Tamil, remarked with disarming wit and candour:

> To say that in bringing this bill and passing it into Law it is the intention of...the Legislative Council to induce brahmanas to marry their girls only after puberty is as unreasonable and fallacious as it would be to say that it was the intention and policy of government

> in passing Act 15 of 1856 to induce all widows to re-marry and in passing Act 21 of 1856 to induce all Hindus to become Christians. This is after all a permissive and provisional measure for a contingency which need or need not happen and it is entirely left to the free will and choice of every individual to marry his girl even before the age of seven or in the cradle itself if not before she is born (NI 8.12.14).

It is in such instances that we find British pragmatism, so often mistaken for hesitancy, being acknowledged for what it was. Neither India's rulers nor their privileged subjects were deceived as to the nature of the changes either wished to advance. A sort of tacit and barely expressed 'gentlemen's agreement' existed between them and as Appana Shastri pointed out it would be 'unreasonable and fallacious' to imagine that the rulers were exemplary progressives who desired to legislate changes in customary practice or that their subjects actively desired such changes.

Educating Women

The debates over women's education further testify to the fact that reform of women's status and life possessed for the brahmin a certain rhetorical and symbolic significance. As with the PPM Bill, the problem of educating women was transfigured to represent a problem of individual (caste) honour and national identity. The matter of women's education assumed importance in the context of the debates over the PPM Bill and was considered a highly sensitive issue, the resolution of which would either retard or, alternatively, encourage the growth and development of a nationalist sentiment. Supporters of the PPM Bill argued that the deferment of women's age at marriage would enable them to educate themselves to cope with the demands of these fast-changing times. Detractors of reform took issue with the progressives over the content of this education.

Those who felt it impolitic and unnecessary to educate 'our brahmin girls' in the Western style advised that an 'elementary education on Hindu lines' be imparted so that 'our women' would be able to lead a 'peaceful and successful domestic life' (NI 3.8.15). S. V. Sharma from Kumbakonam was convinced that only an education that would foster in women those virtues conceived by Manu as ideal for her would help develop her character:

> The Indian woman until now has been brought up in an atmosphere created by the laws of Manu handed down as legacies from generation to generation . . . The virtues . . . inculcated were chastity, love, industry, love of children, harmony, cleanliness, aesthetic culture and above all skill in providing nourishing wholesome food . . . for such a consummation of character, knowledge of English, Greek or Polish language is needless luxury if not positively harmful.

Sharma further argued that Western knowledge would rudely interrupt and retard the natural development of the Hindu woman's mind. He observed, 'every organism requires a congenial environment for its proper development' and if one were to 'accelerate the growth of an organism by introducing foreign and unsuited elements of education' this would 'cripple and finally destroy the organism' (NI 13.8.15).

Supporters of Western education for women misread their opponents' resistance to the latter and concluded they were against educating women as such. Thus M. Narayanaswami who felt the orthodox were intent on keeping their daughters bound to ignorance felt impelled to caution the former:

> The eyes of her [India's] fair daughters must be opened to the degraded conditions of their motherland who is crying for the education of her daughters; but her sons are selfish and foolishly fear that education will prove detrimental to their interest, not knowing what an enormous amount of hidden forces they are bringing into active play . . . The women are the mothers of the future generation . . . It is the mother who first suckles the child with the milk of education. An ignorant mother cannot fulfil her duties as a mother (NI 5.8.15).

Ironically enough, these proponents of Western education also noted that educating women was as much an aspect of tradition as anything else and observed tirelessly that Savithri, Damayanthi, Sita and Draupadi possessed highly cultivated minds (NI 2.8.15; 3.8.15). The reformers also insisted that their pleas for women to be educated ought not to be taken to mean that they desired to see women in 'High Courts and Legislative Councils' (NI 2.8.15). As Narayanaswami observed somewhat defensively:

> I have stated that education will certainly establish a better understanding between husband and wife and will enable women to exercise better tact in the management of family affairs (NI 5.8.15).

The orthodox however were indefatigable in their resistance to these pleas for modernizing the curriculum for women and quite scornful of what they considered the reformers' pretensions. One Rajam pointed out, for instance, that Shakuntala, Damayanthi and the rest were not educated along Western lines (NI 3.8.15), while R. Nagaraja Sharma declared he was tired of reformers 'harping one string in season, out of season that... Sita and Damayanthi were educated and that women should be educated'. He remarked in exasperation:

> By all means educate your women. But what sort of education was imparted to Sita and others? Did they read Shakespeare, Keats and Chaucer?... In conclusion it appears to us that higher education along Western lines is extremely unsuited to our women. It is calculated to produce in our society all the evils from which Western society is at present suffering, evils that are every moment shaking our society to its very foundations (NI 10.8.15).

'An Indian Lady' understood very well the intents of the reformers as well as the orthodox and wrote as if she were summing up their arguments on this matter:

> For the proper training of the children women should be well educated in religious ways for they will only then appreciate beauty, truth, usefulness and gain a religious orthodox life. Thus if mothers are educated to know fully the value of their own religion they will pass it on to their children. To decide the quarrels of the household and to carry out household management women should have the impartiality and wisdom of a judge. To regulate the expenses of the household economically and properly as to make the family happy and prosperous she should have the ability of a treasurer and economist. To look after the cooked dish carefully and serve them to guests she should have practised cooking enough. To observe the hygienic rules in the home and make healthy arrangements she

> should have the training of a sanitary officer. The useful art of needlework and elevating one of music should also be learnt. To guard household property carefully she must have the capacity of a police officer. To urge good and useful things on all alike she should have the skill of a wise, patient and experienced teacher (NI. 18.8.15).

It is interesting that an 'Indian Lady' would re-imagine the family as a micro-polis in which conventional wifely duties are re-defined to represent important civic tasks but where the woman, the wife-mother, assumes a multitude of roles which transform her duties into moral and social obligations. It is in this re-creation of the family as a micro-polis that orthodox and reformist discourses on women's education played a complementary role. They endowed familial tasks and responsibilities with social and historical worth on one hand and defined woman's social worth in explicitly familial terms on the other.

It is clear that arguments and counter-arguments on the question of women's education were not about the desirability or otherwise of this measure. The orthodox and reformers were both convinced of the need to educate women. The question they sought to answer differently was, what kind of an education would suit women and be good for them? As with the arguments for and against the PPM Bill, tradition and history, custom and habit constituted the real subjects of this debate. What was, of course, left out, rendered absent in these debates around reform, whether of marital customs or learning mores, was the woman herself. Her presence, as we have seen, was invoked to signify a social wrong or a social virtue; in the one instance she had to be set right to mend the wrong whereas in the other she was to be preserved and protected from hurt to consecrate the virtue. A common and shared fear of woman's autonomy and sexuality brought the orthodox and the reformers together into a discursive ambit which possessed certain other common features. One was their conception of society, the other was their view of change.

The orthodox desired that the social organism evolve along its own given lines, while the reformers held that such changes as would enable society to transform itself along 'destined' lines would not harm its progress. For the orthodox, change was necessary but was not to be mandated or even enabled, for either would mean an imposition from without. Change would and often did occur of its own accord, out of the steady evolution of custom and tradition. For reformers, change was called for by those very norms which urged tradition to sustain itself and survive time. The customs of the past, they held, were to be viewed in their specific contexts which gave rise to them. The orthodox stressed continuity over dynamism, obedience over creativity, while the reformers defined continuity and obedience in dynamic terms. Bound by a common imperative to view themselves as ideal native citizens, and animated in their endeavours by a sense of historical mission, Madras brahmin reformers and their detractors thus practised a highly sophisticated art of self-representation. Perhaps nowhere was the subtle, self-referential nature of brahmin attempts at social reform as evident as they were in the theory and practice of reform with respect to the adi dravidas.

The Adi Dravidas

The persistent inhuman treatment meted out to adi dravidas even in these ostensibly modern times angered many a literate brahmin. Several brahmins undertook to set up schools for the children of the adi dravidas. Others were keen on instructing them to observe what seemed to them elementary cleanliness and practice abstention with respect to liquor. Some went a step further. B. Narasimha Iyer, for instance, introduced a bill in the Madras Council to abolish the cruel custom of putting an offending adi dravida—however petty the crime he had committed—in stocks. In a long letter to New India, one Israel Nallappan, expressed his thanks to Narasimha Iyer for the favour done his community.

Noting that 'a village magistrate can confine a man of the depressed classes any time that he likes', he went on to say that even such things as 'laziness in tending the cattleshed, disobedience to the order of the landowner can bring the depressed brother the punishment of confinement in stocks'. In 1913, the Fourth Depressed Classes Conference held at Mayavaram had resolved to entreat the government to remove this obnoxious practice. Narasimha Iyer, acting on this resolution, had gone on to introduce a bill calling for the abolition of the use of stocks as punishment (NI 27.5.15).

Some brahmin reformers were concerned that the attitudes of the orthodox Hindus were driving adi dravidas away from Hinduism and into the welcoming arms of Christianity:

> A little sympathy with their condition, some simple medicine, a little knowledge of the love and affection of the white man's God, a studied comparative statement of his state and the state of the higher classes in the same town or village, the peculiar freedom of access to a civilised important white Dorai and the semi-contemptuous behaviour of the aristocrats of their own religion—these are things by which missionaries succeed.

It was argued that brahmins should 'wake up' and remedy the situation: 'Set down a code of conduct for these "untouchables" to follow, so that after a period of probation . . . these people might be taken into the four castes as one of the sub-castes of the shudras' (NI 12.6.15).

Annie Besant, with her reputed concern for adi dravida welfare, also expressed a desire to 'humanize' them. Responding to a letter complaining of servant intransigence from an Englishman, who felt his servants, who were of the Paraiah, an 'untouchable' caste, had discarded caste and conscience, she wrote to say the adi dravidas she knew in Adyar were good Buddhists and Hindus who had managed to 'rise to a highest level of faithful and honourable service' (NI 3.11.14; 7.11.14).

More often than not, however, Besant's attitude towards adi dravidas was paternalistic and carelessly so. Thus she would remark 'here as well as in Britain they [the lower classes] are a menace to civilisation and were undermining the fine fabric of society . . . the danger to the country was not as many imagined from educated India but from these poor miserable classes' (NI 13.9.15). Further, like her arch critics, the members of the Varnashrama Dharma Sabha, Annie Besant held that a Paraiah had to work out his karma now and in the hereafter to break free from the shackles of untouchability. The Varnashrama Dharma Sabha had argued that brahmins are only born and not made—a statement which incited an angry citizen to retort that 'a Paraiah by birth by a process of purification rises to the highest caste even in this life' (NI 3.11.16). Professor Lakshminarasu, Buddhist scholar and friend of the adi dravidas, deplored such opinions as were expressed by members of the Varnashrama Dharma Sabha but, more important, criticized Annie Besant for maintaining that a Paraiah needs to work out his karma (NI 17.11.16).

It is obvious that reform opinion was careful of caste distinctions and did not really want to level these down. Adi dravidas were problematic for yet another reason. Objectively speaking, they were outside the caste system. Yet, they existed as the polar others of brahmins, denied all and everything claimed by the latter as their ritual and spiritual prerogatives. In other words, brahmin selfhood was crucially dependent, for its existence, on the non-self of the panchama. Thus, if the brahmin desired to reconstitute himself, so as to meet the pressures and anxieties of contemporary society, of necessity, he had to re-constitute adi dravida selfhood as well.

To eradicate the social and economic basis of untouchability was, of course, impossible, for that would break down caste distinctions, which were, after all, mediated through various degrees of touchability and untouchability. Thus the ideal solution with respect to adi dravidas and one which best expressed brahmin endeavours at reform as well as their intent to maintain ancient norms was to bring the adi dravidas into the caste system and re-define them as 'shudras'. Simultaneously, efforts could be made to persuade the 'birth-shudras' to give up what was often termed by brahmins as 'their deplorable attitudes' towards adi dravidas and accept the latter as their brothers.

A speaker at a meeting organized by the Hindu Reform Association, perhaps, captured the brahmin attitude towards abolition of caste differences rather succinctly when he argued that reform measures ought to heed 'the silent voice within oneself', eschew self-interest and promote, instead, the interest of all:

> Reform did not consist in all the people of all classes eating together...it was remoulding...the caste system according to natural laws. The Law of Nature is variety and if there was variety there was also division of labour...Reform could only be brought about by love (NI 17.9.15).

This rhetoric of love was so thoroughly internalized by brahmin reformers that they could movingly speak of the essential 'one-ness' of the brahmin and the adi dravida. K. V. Sesha Iyengar, writing nearly fifteen years later and in the wake of Gandhian anti-untouchability campaigns, thus remarked:

> When the history of these eventful years comes to be written not the least conspicuous among the social phenomenon of the age will be the release for national service of the unused energy of two communities, the brahmin and the untouchable.... Both have been victims of a common self-denying ordinance which excluded them from the full social and economic life of the country.... Adi dravida and Brahmin along with other Hindus are heirs of a common heritage... we all have to work in cooperation for the enrichment and diffusion of that heritage (1932).

It is clear that even those brahmins who were critical of the inhumanity of the caste system could not bear, as we shall soon see, to abandon what they considered to be the fundamental principles of their faith.

THE IDEAL SOCIETY

Discussions on caste and the superior status the varna system conferred on the brahmins often figured in the pages of *New India*. These debates acquired a sharpened focus with the emergence of the Non-Brahmin movement. Brahmins, clearly under pressure to reconcile felt and perceived notions of their superiority to their modern liberal outlook, were driven to redefine the caste order so as to render it relevant to modern democratic tasks and objectives. Their defences of the caste system ranged from arguing its inseparability from the central tenets of Hinduism to reconstituting it to represent a functional division of labour. A *New India* reader from Masulipatnam observed that the chaturvarna lay at the very heart of the Hindu religion and warned that if the varna system was abolished, as some opined, 'materialism, agnosticism and scepticism' were bound to take its place (NI 11.12.17).

Then, there were those such as T. Narayana Shastry from Ongole who claimed 'the sublimity of Hinduism consists in the inseparability... of caste, ritual and philosophy.... Any Hindu who casts off or repudiates these three points ceases being a Hindu'. He further argued that critics and reformers who desired abolition were ignorant of the 'remarkable daily life of the orthodox brahmanas who are uncontaminated by city life' and who, 'residing in out-of-the-way interior *agraharams* (exclusively brahmin settlements), carried on a life of personal austerity and penance (NI 17.11.19).

Others, however, were less inclined to 'remember' the remarkable daily life of brahmanas and less apprehensive of materialism. They were also annoyed by what they termed 'caste spirit'. K. V. Sesha Iyengar, for instance, was troubled and annoyed by that feeling of 'self-complacency' and 'self-superiority' ascribed to itself by a 'particular community that considers itself chosen'. He was, however, confident that differences and inequalities would disappear with the growth and spread of national consciousness and social democracy (NI 5.9.19). P. S. Sivaswamy Iyer, a Madras notable and advocate-general for a time, observed that while one wished to see a destruction of the caste spirit, it would be 'unwise to blind oneself to differences and inequalities and to the operation of the laws of heredity' (ibid).

Some brahmins ventured tentative explanations and solutions that would help clarify and regulate reform with respect to caste. A. Mahadeva Shastri was convinced that at one time all were Aryans and brahmins and pointed out that a brahmin in ancient times meant one who 'is of the people, who alike believes in the divinity of Man, and whose life work consists in the gradual realization of human unity and solidarity as based on their inherent oneness with Brahmana, the one divine life'. He further opined that brahmins grew arrogant in their priesthood and allowed other castes to stray away from the path of the Brahmana. But, insisted Shastri, the brahmin alone is not to blame for this state of affairs. If non-brahmins desired to achieve a status within the caste system equal to that enjoyed by the brahmins, they ought to recognize that,

> The brahmana is what he is by his well-regulated life...his temperate habits...to maintain their supreme position in the social hierarchy brahmanas as a class have given up animal food and intoxicants to which they were accustomed in the past and as a result they possess a fine well-balanced nervous system and great power of endurance (NI 14.12.17).

To such men as these, the caste order could not be wished away and therefore reforming the order rather than destroying it was important.

Besides, they were deeply religious men, convinced of the spiritual excellence of their Hindu faith, and whether conservative like Narayana Shastri, or dynamic in their outlook like Sesha Iyengar and Mahadeva Shastri, they could not step out of the order of which they were a part and regard it as a historically evolved social order. There were certain genuine attempts made, though, to examine critically the meaning and significance of varnashrama dharma. The poet Subramania Bharathi and Justice Sadasiva Iyer managed to articulate clearly and systematically the opinions of a section of the brahmin intelligentsia who were keenly aware of the more untenable aspects of caste and critical of brahmin proneness to intellectual arrogance.

Bharathi considered caste in its contemporary form an aberration. He argued that 'the chaturvarnya, the "ordinance of the four colours"' which the Bhagavad Gita characterized as divine in origin was based on natural qualities and acts—not on birth:

> Illuminated or blind, free or bound, godly or bestial—all men and women are by nature ordained to live and work by one or the other of the following ways: (*i*) by service; (*ii*) by thrift; (*iii*) by sacrifice; (iv) by knowledge. A fifth mode of life is not possible (NI 12.3.15).

To the poet varna divisions referred to moral-spiritual categories and these categories were necessarily inclusive of all human activity and aspiration. Bharathi, of course, is not concerned here with the social effects of caste or its history, but only with the morality of chaturvarnya. Like Mahadeva Shastri, he subscribed to a certain moral-spiritual ideal of living, conventionally associated with brahmins, though to Bharathi, the actual act of living spiritually was far more important than claiming such a spirituality as one's birthright. However this may be, his re-definition of the varna principles to mean moral categories did not raise or answer the question of how certain moral acts—sacrifice, for instance—were transformed into acts of subordination and slavery or how certain qualities such as wisdom became associated with a single group.

Others, however, would raise and answer the question that Bharathi was silent about through other means. While admitting that the ideal and essential meaning of the varna divisions had become travestied in practice and through centuries of usage, they would yet attempt to justify it. Sharma, writing on the origins of the caste system, declared that 'God endowed his creations with various permutations and combinations of structure so that each permutation and combination enable a certain function being performed by its possessor but disable it from doing any other'. However this cannot be taken to mean that 'whoever may now possess a structure which is, in other words, fitness for a particular work, ... be called by the original name of the functional caste' (NI 22.9.15). That is, one may practise the profession of a priest or a trader but one cannot, on that account, aspire to be a brahmin or a vaishya!

P. V. Govindaswamy Iyer, perhaps, spoke for all when he wrote—of the past of Malabar—that the efficacy of the caste system cannot really be doubted for in spite of a fundamental division of labour,

> It is gratifying to remember that brotherly cooperation and social harmony of the best type prevailed among the peoples of the land.... The brahmanas devoted attention to religions and spiritual affairs while the kshatriyas attended to the military and material aspects of the kingdom. The vaishyas looked after the peaceful pursuits of agriculture, commerce and the dutiful shudras looked after the general duty of according facilites for social service and public benefit (NI 22.10.14).

The most sophisticated defense of varnashrama dharma was provided by Justice Sadasiva Iyer. In a three-part article published in *New India* (3-13 July 1916), he responded to various debates that had grown around the question of caste and attempted to resolve some of the more important questions which had been raised. He noted that being born into a particular caste did not imply that one possessed an inalienable right to inherit one's father's occupation. In the past it was believed that the body of a particular caste possessed a soul which could reside only in that caste and nowhere else. But such ideas were clearly irrelevant in the present time. For instance, how would society ensure 'the right of a Vellala husbandman to cultivate his father's land which the father has sold to a patnul (silk) weaver, the weaver having lost his father's occupation through the influx of cheap Manchester cloth?'

Sadasiva Iyer was particularly severe on those brahmins who claimed their rights to sacrality even after they had deserted their caste-ordained occupations to engage in worldly pursuits which fetched them profit and power. He felt the brahmins had grown rich on the fat of the land due to 'the eagerness of the people to support by gifts even nominal brahmanas and nominal sannyasis'. He advocated the abolition of all subsects within castes, the restriction of brahmin identity to those who were of good character and who are engaged in religious rites that benefit mankind, the abolition of all castes below the shudras and bringing them within the shudra fold and an increase in the number of vaishyas from nominal brahmins (such as Vishwakarmas) and shudras. Yet, Sadasiva Iyer cautioned reformers against extremism and argued the members of the Varnashrama Dharma Sabha were right to be critical of and hostile to those who wished to 'divorce social reform and religion' and base it on 'individual reason'. For westernization of this kind would, in the long run, kill national sentiment. He also attempted to answer non-brahmin criticisms of brahmins. Arguing that contemporary anti-Brahminism had adopted the doctrines associated with the later developments of Buddhism and succumbed to the preachings of Christian evangelists, Sadasiva Iyer opined that anti-brahmins were either jealous of the worldly power and prosperity of the birth brahmins (who had misused their privileges for acquiring secular honours) or were naturally indignant with brahmins who have 'continually depressed other classes'.

To contain the spread of anti-brahmin sentiment, to ensure the survival of the 'spirit' of the varna system, namely, the 'original' stress on qualities and acts, rather than birth, and to counter westernization, Sadasiva Iyer favoured, within limits, the practice of exogamous marriages. That is, he did not wish to consider such marriages which took place between men and women of different castes illegal. He also desired that brahmins bear in silent patience the attacks of 'our non-brahmana brothers' and suggested that brahmins give up 'misuse of their caste prestige' and take up social service amongst the depressed classes.

Finally, Sadasiva Iyer pointed out that he and others like him were concerned with the 'existing filth' in order that it may be cleaned. He was willing to admit that the 'nest' might have become too fouled for cleaning but on that account he could not forsake the 'Grand Tree of Sanatana Dharma'. He would rather build another nest with 'as much as can be saved from the old material and on the same branch of the same tree'. It is significant that though he favoured breaking of caste he was ambivalent on the question of exogamous marriages. Likewise, he would preserve the integrity of the brahmin caste as far as possible, while permitting a certain degree of mobility amongst the other castes. Thus adi dravidas could raise themselves into shudras and nominal brahmins be moved into the vaishya class. In other words, as far as social mobility was concerned, qualities, acts and talents mattered as long as they facilitated limited interaction amongst non-brahmin castes.

It is clear that as far as the brahmin reformer was concerned, he would not acknowledge that the caste system was an antagonistic system and that it could not be easily reformed into a more humane social order. In the face of lower caste claims, the reformer would counsel patience and urge the claimants to trust to the inexorable process of change which, by itself, would fulfil their aspirations. Thus, the Hon. S. Srinivasa Iyengar while addressing a Nadar (a near-untouchable caste till recently) conference observed that he was essentially sympathetic to their claims to temple entry, of their rights of access to village wells and tanks and to go in procession along village streets. But he was also aware of the persistence of 'restrictions', though these were really temporary. Besides,

> Caste is no longer what it was. Hindu social life has undergone a wonderful transformation....The day is not far distanced when your neighbours will readily welcome you to their ancient temples (NI 7.6.18).

Srinivasa Iyengar's exhortations to Nadars and his praise of their self-help efforts represent Nadar history as a continuous development from their toddy tapping days to their prosperous present. The long-drawn struggles Nadars waged against caste Hindus, the ignominies suffered by Nadar women during the so-called breast-cloth controversy, the social struggles that accompanied Nadar growth into wealth and prosperity—all these disjunctive moments are elided in this history (Hardgrave 1965). Fulfilment of Nadar rights to mobility and worship are conveniently pushed to a future utopia conjured out of brahmin perceptions of change and regeneration. It is noteworthy that much as Srinivasa Iyengar appreciated Nadar efforts at 'upgrading' their lives, he was uneasy with their claims on history. Thus he counselled his listeners that such efforts at re-reading history as those of Chattam Pillay, a Nadar Christian convert who argued Nadars were really kshatriyas, were really of no avail. For, 'pedigrees are well enough in their place...but greater than pride of pedigree is humility...A self-made man or a self-made caste is entitled to greater credit and admiration' (ibid).

Brahmin desire to thus regulate reform was nowhere as evident as it was in the responses brahmins offered to non-brahmin criticisms of Brahminism. When one Kittu, writing in *New India*, claimed brahmin tyranny was not as bad as that of the papacy, C. D. Nayar, an erudite non-brahmin, responded saying, that the brahmin hierarchy was tyranny itself. He also observed that brahmins might find the idea of self-government splendid but since they persisted in thinking ill of non-brahmins and considered them their slaves, self-government would only confirm them in their tyranny and, worse, legitimize it. Nayar was particularly critical of the South Indian brahmin with his 'silly and selfish' prejudices and observed that an example of brahmin ill-government was afforded by the Travancore administration where 'brahmanas are petted and pampered under religious guise and where a brahmana murderer can go scot-free without being hanged for his crime' (NI 20.12.15).

K. Swaminathan from Panruti responded angrily to Nayar with the argument that brahmins had ever done the Travancore administration proud by their intellect and industry (NI 28.12.15). An anonymous letter writer, writing in the name of 'Per Critic,' observed that Nayar had failed to appreciate the superior intellect of the South Indian brahmins and had raged against their supposed tyranny, as if the world around—and the brahmins with it—were not changing (NI 29.12.15).

In another instance, when S. Sankaran Nair, a prominent Madras notable and long-time critic of Brahminism, observed at a meeting of the Hindu Social Reform Association that the system of caste posed 'a great danger to public life in this country' and rendered harmonious cooperation impossible (NI 13.2.15), he was repudiated in no uncertain terms. An anonymous reader wrote to the 'Vox Populi' columns of *New India*, protesting this denunciation of a brahminic world-view (NI 16.2.15).

In spite of such 'reasoned' defences of brahminic virtues, criticisms of South Indian brahmins persisted. *New India* carried one such critique, voiced by a brahmin from Bangalore who expressed acute exasperation at the ways of the men of Madras. Retelling an amusing anecdote, he narrated how he once chanced to upset a vessel of water belonging to a fellow passenger—a brahmin from Madras—in a railway carriage; whereupon the latter was visibly upset. It was only after the culprit had reluctantly revealed his caste identity that the gentleman with the water jug settled to his comfort. The Bangalore brahmin confessed that 'the idea of the pollution of the inside water by the chance contact of the outside of the vessel with another clean and healthy individual would have never occurred to me who had lived in Bombay.... What then is there in the atmosphere of Madras to make such a thing a common enough feature?' (NI 15.3.16).

It is clear the Madras brahmin simply could not interrogate himself and his world-view or see himself as others saw him. Nevertheless, his commonsense, shaped as it was by prevailing popular and scholarly opinion on Hindu society and history, was a constructed one; that is, one cannot ignore the real role of brahmin agency in the making of a self-validating ideology. Whether brahmins were engaged in asserting their 'traditional' rights or were responding to a changed historical situation, they were actively involved in imagining a society—and a nation—which would preserve caste and their own privileges.

THE IMAGINED NATION

An imagined nation and the invocation of a national oneness constituted the most fitting expressions of brahmin self-consciousness and hegemony during this period. Brahmins associated with the Congress and the Home Rule League adumbrated a political philosophy which successfully transmuted felt notions of difference and exclusivity to signify lofty aims and objectives. The basic constituent of this political outlook was a belief in a sense of one-ness, in a unity that was believed to inform Hindu (Indian) religious as well as social and political life.

R. Kulasekharam writing of the teacher's role in shaping national life observed 'the central note of the evolution of religious thought in India has been striving after unity—Buddha who taught the proud Aryan to love his dark brother, Shankara the philosopher of unity,

Ramanuja, Chaitanya, Nanak, Tukaram, Ram Mohan imbued with a cosmopolitanism' had all aspired to realize such a unity (NI 8.2.15). N. P. Rama Iyer stressed the need to build on this one-ness and suggested that Congress undertake a mission to imbue the masses, the majority of whom were barely literate, with 'national ideas'. This could be done through pamphlets which contained articles on themes such as 'union, love of country, reverence for leaders and heroes of the past, brotherly feelings between the Hindus and Mohammedans, education, elevation of the depressed classes, female education, self-sacrifice, character, dignity of labour, removal of caste bias' (NI 18.12.14).

This imperative to infuse, extend and render consensual the idea of nationalism acquired great relevance with the launching of the Home Rule movement. Home Rule tracts were published, in Tamil as well as in English, and priced low to enable students to buy them. Annie Besant arranged for lectures on constitutional topics by men such as A. Rangaswamy Iyengar and C. P. Ramaswamy Iyer (Irschick: 34). *New India* interpreted Home Rule to mean not merely a political demand but a socio-spiritual ideal as well. A daily prayer was published under the column titled, 'Home Rule Is the Only Rule' that read as follows:

> King of Kings! Ruler of Nations! Deliverer of the Oppressed! Open thine Eye of Mercy on thine Ancient People of India and that thy Servant the Emperor may know the wrongs that are being committed in his name in India. Break thou the rod of the Oppressor which forbid us to claim our birthright of freedom and deliver thy people. Free thou thy servants who are unjustly imprisoned for Freedom's Sake of the Motherland, so shall thy people live in peace and safety in the Land thou has given us for our habitation.

This prayer appeared first on 12 July 1917, and was thereafter inserted almost every day in the same manner until September, when following objections from the government, a verse from the *Manusmriti* was substituted in its place, which lead a *New India* columnist to remark that 'these well-known' verses of Manu are 'better than anything that can be composed by the *New India* staff to express the main contention of the Home Ruler'. The columnist went on to observe,

> The *Manusmriti*, at least the portions relating to Aryan manners and customs, is really the old Aryan code common to all Aryans, whether European or Indian.... The text selected... contains in our opinion the basic principles on which both the branches of the Aryan family, the European and the Indian have based and moulded their civilisation (NI 1.9.17).

While Home Rule propaganda mirrored a spontaneity of feeling, it was, nevertheless, orchestrated with great skill by Annie Besant and her publicists. In June 1917, when Besant, B. P. Wadia and George Arundale were arrested and interned at Ootacamund for their political activities, *New India* undertook a systematic and impassioned campaign for their release. The paper's 'Vox Populi' columns resounded with popular ire and indignation over the fate of the 'interned' and protest meetings were held throughout the Presidency, demanding the release of the 'heroic three' (NI 1.8.17; 4.8.17). Picture postcards of the 'martyrs' were printed, pendants displaying their visages made, all of which were reverentially bought and sold. *New India's* columnists never failed to note that public antipathy to the internment was such that protest meetings drew not only the brahmanas but labourers, weavers and students (NI 4.9.17; 11.9.17).

The claims of Home Rule and nationalism were urged most vociferously and proclaimed self-evident in the face of sustained criticisms from non-brahmins who argued that the advent of Home Rule would enshrine brahmin rule. The publication of the Non-Brahmin Manifesto proved to be an extremely opportune event for Home Rulers, since it provoked them to express their political desires and will to power in and through a dazzling display of language. Defences and assertions of Home Rule were varied in character and emphasis, but in all instances, they derived their power of appeal from a condemnation of the anti-Home Rulers. Critics of Home Rule were dubbed as being misguided, ignorant, insincere (and, therefore, dishonest) and above all disloyal to the national cause. Dr. T. M. Nair, the chief author of the Non-Brahmin Manifesto, was criticized in the harshest possible terms. A *New India* editorial of 26 June 1917 was explicit in its condemnation of Dr. Nair. It accused him of political opportunism and argued that he had always sought the support of the British civilians to hold his own against local competitors in whatever institution he held office. His performance as a councillor in the Corporation of Madras was also severely criticized. It was suggested that in the past his activities were such that his present-day friend and comrade-in-arms, P. Theagoraya Chetty, had mounted a strong opposition to him. Commenting on his initial enthusiasm for the nationalist movement, the editorial remarked:

> Presiding over the Tanjore district conference he had spoken of the urgency of the immediate grant of political privileges and he had used the same cliché which now according to his revised gospel constitutes one of the seven deadly sins. The same figure of speech as to a swimmer learning to swim and need for his taking to water were then in requisition but Dr. Nair had then no vision of a separatist communal movement which may one day make him the self-constituted protagonist of dumb millions and may evolve him to the unofficial or perchance official counsellor of Government.... We have every sympathy with the genuine non-brahmana movement intended to educate and elevate the condition of the masses in this land but not with the spurious and superficial campaign of hatred which has been inaugurated recently.

P. C. Sundaram Iyengar from Triplicane was categorical in his judgement of Dr. Nair:

> Dr. Nair the public man who was loved and honoured by the people is dead; there lives a new Dr. Nair who is... working out the karma of a past evil life. Dr. Nair has survived his usefulness and his right to continue and speak on behalf of the public (NI 26.6.17).

What is interesting about this denunciation of Dr. Nair is that the ordinary citizen was struck not by his so-called opportunism but bewildered chiefly by what seemed a sudden and unexpected burst of anti-brahmin anger on the good doctor's part. To this extent it may be said that *New India's* existence, as a sort of conscience keeper of the Tamil brahmin community, had not been in vain. That is, even as Annie Besant sought to settle old political scores—her recriminations against Dr. Nair were no more than that—her habitual endorsement of brahmin self-pride and self-love endowed her opinions with a certain validity and relevance.

Theagoraya Chetty, the other important signatory to the Non-Brahmin Manifesto, was also subjected to a relentless critique. In an address to the South Indian Chamber of Commerce, he had flayed imperial trade policies and observed that Britain must grant Indians the freedom to settle their own 'commercial, industrial and economic questions ... in [our] own interest without any subordination of such interests to those of any others'. He had also demanded that 'the industrial and fiscal freedom of India must be firmly established and the economic independence of India must be ensured' (NI 2.4.17). Characterizing these aims as 'noble' and agreeable to the Home Rulers, Annie Besant nevertheless wondered how these were to be achieved:

> Our speaker asks the people to move as 'one'. But the movement lead by Rao Bahadur Theagoraya Chetty has split the Hindu community into two and he is carrying on a crusade of hate against the brahmanas who would have been invaluable helpers to him, they being a class, the bureaucracy fears (ibid).

Besides, thus drawing attention to the foibles of the non-brahmin leaders, *New India* also undertook to point out that not all non-brahmins were sympathetic to the sentiments contained in the Non-Brahmin Manifesto. Not only were the observations and statements of prominent non-brahmin notables such as Kesava Pillay carried in all their detail, but several instances of ordinary' non-brahmins criticizing the Manifesto and its authors were recounted.

Several letters by non-brahmins which endorsed the cause of Home Rule and explained brahmin power as a function of that caste's merit and industry appeared in *New India* almost daily. There were also several reports of meetings held in various parts of the Presidency to protest the arrest of Besant and others in which it was claimed several non-brahmins participated. A report of 4 July 1917 commenting on one such meeting at Behrampore observed: 'Non-Brahmanas contributed largely to the success of the meeting and were most enthusiastic to join the Home Rule League.' A report on a public protest meeting at Tiruppur recorded that many weavers and labourers were present and noted rather pointedly that the brahmins at the meeting were only six in number (NI 10.7.17).

Home Rulers—and Annie Besant—sought to further discredit the Non-Brahmin movement by casting aspersions on the non-brahmin leaders' commitment even to their stated cause. During this period, Congressmen were busy mobilizing and organizing men and campaigns in the cause of indentured labour, at work in faraway Crown colonies, often in deplorable conditions. The Anti-Indenture League, comprising several prominent Home Rulers, held regular meetings at this time in Madras and elsewhere in the Province in the early months of 1917. The leaders and spokesmen of the League often wondered why those non-brahmins who rallied against brahmin tyranny held themselves aloof from the activities of an organization that was concerned with the fate of thousands of indentured (non-brahmin) workers. *New India* reported that while a number of non-brahmins were eager to associate themselves with the League, their so-called leaders appeared disinterested and, worse, distrustful of the League's work.

A letter written by an unnamed 'non-brahmana' published in *New India* expressed deep disappointment that non-brahmin leaders, 'especially those who issued the recent Non-Brahmin Manifesto' had stayed away from an important Anti-Indenture meeting:

> It is a question in which the moral prestige and dignity of these non-brahmana coolies are concerned.... It is really wrong to have kept themselves aloof while the brahmana leaders (who formed the majority of the speakers in yesterday's meeting) are fighting for the rights of the poor non-brahmana coolies beyond the seas (NI 16.2.17).

The failure of the non-brahmin notables to serve their cause justly was explained away as an instance of their bad faith—in their brethren and in brahmins. An editorial comment of 18 April 1917 found fault with the non-brahmin newspaper *Justice* for carrying on a 'crusade of hate' against brahmins and called upon well-intentioned and right-thinking non-brahmins to dissociate themselves from *Justice's* 'guerrilla method of warfare':

> The anti-brahamana movement preaching the crusade of hate is mischievous and deplorable and is essentially foreign in spirit, not

> Indian. There is no continuing life in a movement inspired by hatred with the war cry '*Gott straffe Brahmana*' and there is little doubt that the healthy non-brahmana movement will ere long separate itself from the virulent anti-brahmin crusade.

Such sentiments were taken up eagerly by men like Kesava Pillay who, naturally enough, found themselves in a delicate position. After issuing a repudiation of the Manifesto within days of its publication, we find him, a mere four weeks later, clarifying his stand. He now claimed that he was in agreement with all but one section of the Manifesto and that he did not want the movement to appear as if it was working against a particular community (NI 22.1.17).

But even Kesava Pillay had to acknowledge the tenacity and strength of the anti-brahmin sentiment which had been prevalent for a while now and which was granted visibility by the Non-Brahmin Manifesto. Thus, at a public meeting held in Madras he was forced to admit that non-brahmin distrust of brahmins was in all likelihood provoked by the arch-revivalist 'varnashrama dharma preservers' and by those 'sins of omission and commission of old and modern brahmanas'. But Kesava Pillay felt impelled to separate the cause of Home Rule from that of brahmin supremacy and counselled his fellow non-brahmins to throw in their lot with 'liberal brahmanas', who, he claimed, were substantial in number, and work for the common cause of 'our motherland' (NI 19.3.17).

Such an ambivalence with regard to the questions of Home Rule and Manifesto, encouraged by *New India*, was not uncommon amongst non-brahmins. N. C. Ramaswamy Naidu, for instance, granted that the Non-Brahmin Manifesto was occasioned by very genuine grievances. Yet the movement had 'fallen into [the] unworthy hands of those who were swayed by selfish desires and were infuriated by failures and... [who] transform[ed] their private injuries into public wrongs. Then was brought into play the anti-brahmana feeling which found in everything which was of the brahmana and his activities ample room for hostile criticism' (NI 10.7.17).

Home Rule propaganda was at its effective best in such instances, where non-brahmins spoke in the name of Home Rule and denounced the Non-Brahmin Manifesto. A characteristic feature of this vivifying patriotic imagination which suffused alike the souls of brahmins and non-brahmin elites was its power of utterance. It drew its sting and effectiveness from an assemblage of phrases, symbols and an inner grammar which structured and directed its rhetorical energy.

Day after day, *New India* carried messages such as 'Home Rule Is the Only Rule', 'Home Rule Is Self-Rule'. The issue dated 13 September 1918 had this memorable message: 'All Other Rule Is Misery; All Self-Rule Is Bliss' (Manu). Day after day, Annie Besant or one of her many able correspondents and columnists, provided instances which would (ostensibly) show up the absurdity and invalidity of the sentiments entertained by the signatories and supporters of the Non-Brahmin Manifesto. The Non-Brahmin movement was described as a 'source of mischief' (NI 6.1.17); its leaders were referred to as 'self-constituted protagonists of dumb millions' (NI 26.6.17). Accusations made against Home Rulers by non-brahmins—that they were unmindful of caste differences and indifferent to brahmin tyranny—were termed 'ungenerous and foolish' (NI 12.9.17). The accusers were berated for their 'deplorable' stance (NI 18.4.17). Non-brahmin efforts at securing a place for themselves in the new reform scheme commensurate to their numerical strength were considered as so many instances of 'wire-pulling from behind' by 'certain misguided Indians' (NI 5.5.17). The Non-Brahmin movement was consistently referred to by *New India* staff as the 'anti-brahmana' movement and its editor remarked that non-brahmin resistance to Home Rule was but an illustration of Sri Krishna's dictum: 'All things act according to their nature' (NI 21.5.17). C. P. Ramaswamy Iyer characterized the movement as a 'festering sore', a 'wound at the foot which if left untreated could poison the entire organism' (NI 1.11.20).

The language which expressed such contempt and which dwelt long and lovingly on various instances of non-brahmin folly and ignorance often assumed the voice of commonsense and backed up its self-confident assertions by a tacit appeal to 'universal' notions of 'right and wrong' and 'sense and nonsense'. When the raja of Kurrupum, a prominent non-brahmin notable and supporter of the Manifesto, demanded why non-brahmins should consent to be governed by a microscopic minority, Annie Besant retorted: 'If you like to be tyrannised by your rulers then it is all right. But some people might prefer the tyranny of our countrymen' (NI 31.3.17).

In several other instances Annie Besant would express a similar contempt towards the claims of discrimination made by non-brahmins. She was given to treating the non-brahmin demand for proportional representation for all sections of the population in government service as a huge joke and a foolish one at that. An editorial short-note pointed out in an ironic though laboured fashion:

> As everything now must be classified as brahmin and non-brahmin a correspondent has taken the trouble to sort out the Presidents of the National Congress. There have been 9 brahmanas, but two of them were elected twice, so they count as 11, there were 17 non-brahmanas which divide up into 6 Hindus, 3 Mussalmans, 3 Parsees but one of them 3 times so that they count 5 and 4 Europeans, one of them twice counting 5 and one Christian (NI 2.4.17).

Non-brahmin efforts to forge a united community out of disparate castes also came in for sustained mockery and attack. Several ostensible instances of non-brahmin—caste Hindu—antipathy to adi dravidas were cited to indicate the absurdity of wanting to create a non-brahmin constituency. Adi dravidas themselves were not spared and were berated for their opposition to Home Rule. An editorial on adi dravidas and Home Rule noted that 'just at present for anything that goes wrong in Indian society the Home Ruler is made responsible. The case of the adi dravidas is the latest instance'. This, in spite of the fact that recent movements to uplift the depressed classes had been lead by Home Rulers and brahmins. The sin of untouchability could not therefore be laid at the feet of the brahmins alone for 'this is a sin which lies at the doors of every Indian and perhaps even more on the high class of non-brahmins' (NI 12.9.17). In a similar vein, P. M. Rangaswamy Iyengar opined that the origin of the panchama oppression could not be dated to Aryan custom and that it probably owed a great deal to the culture of the Dravidian South (NI 1.12.17).

The discursive energy that animated Home Rule utterances and made for the evocation of the ideal nation was also amazingly flexible and accommodative. Congressmen in Madras such as Kesava Pillay and Raman Menon were quick to sense that a non-brahmin consciousness, sensitive to historical wrong and mindful of its social subordination and powerlessness had come to be present at large among thinking non-brahmins and adi dravidas everywhere. These men also realized that if Home Rule was to become a reality and if nationalism was to prove a viable and attractive proposition in Madras, Congress and the Home Rule League would have to rethink and re-define the troublesome and vexed question of Brahminism. This shift in Congress thinking, as yet a subtle and qualified change of mood and political tone, was visible in an article written for *New India* by K. Vyasa Rao, from the Home Ruler's point of view. Written as a sort of general appeal to brahmins and non-brahmins alike, this article referred specifically to the importance of the first Non-Brahmin Conference of the Presidency which was to be held at Coimbatore shortly, in August 1917. Vyasa Rao noted that the proposed conference was probably the most important, far-reaching event to come out of the movement and that it was a pity that the latter had aroused such antagonism and allowed itself to be used by the British. Yet, it could not be denied that

> When men meet as men, when mind thinks with mind, when broad issues have to be faced, when a poignant situation has to be conscientiously considered and men assemble openly to render an account of themselves as natives of a country and independent and thinking citizens, official prompting if any is bound to disappear.

The non-brahmin community, as a whole, he wrote, ought to support the conference and devise ways and means to bring cohesion to a vast complex and heterogeneous group. Not only would this help non-brahmins see what an illusion it was to think of doing away with caste altogether, but would also help them understand 'brahmanas are no more responsible for the continuance of the present social system as non-brahmanas'. Vyasa Rao also entreated non-brahmins to think of India as 'exclusively their own country and themselves its only natives'. If this were to come to pass, non-brahmins would realize that there was a 'world of difference' between a non-brahmin 'thinking and acting for himself... [than] merely concurring in the views of his brahmana countrymen'. For, 'When a man [or a community feeling itself as a separate factor] thinks for himself or itself there is not simply a conclusion arrived at but a conviction engendered' (NI 7.8.17).

Vyasa Rao's well-meaning, yet, thoroughly political effort to win over non-brahmins to the cause of Home Rule was not without its effects. In his welcome address to the First Non-Brahmin Conference at Coimbatore, the chairman of the Reception Committee to the conference observed that though non-brahmins had decided to convene their own conference rather than hold a district political conference, the present endeavour was not, as some had hinted, motivated by a 'spirit of hatred towards any individual or community'. Non-brahmins were inspired to come together by a love of their community and by a desire to better their lot. Besides,

> We have been lethargic for too long. We have not taken advantage of Western education to the extent to which we should have with the result that those who were first in the field have taken possession of the whole field. It is now our duty to make up for lost time and put forth strenuous efforts to overtake those who are in advance (Varadarajulu Naidu 1932: vol 2, 4).

The raja of Panagal who was nominated president of the conference clarified the nature of the non-brahmin resistance to Home Rule and observed that it was not Congress as such or its policies which he and his peers abhorred. They were opposed to the Home Rule movement with its rhetoric of revivalism and caste. This new 'brahminical programme of religious, social and political reform' possessed a great deal of 'glamour and glitter' but very little substance.

> It must however be borne in mind that if India is ever to attain nationhood, the masses and especially the depressed classes have to be taken along with the more enlightened communities and as the Congress during its existence has bestowed very little thought on this aspect of great socio-political reform, those who are deeply interested in the uplift of the masses and in the development of all classes, irrespective of caste, community or creed could not but regret its indifference and apathy (ibid: 8).

The refined and carefully modulated utterances of non-brahmin leaders, their professed commitment to nation building and their principled antipathy to Brahminism prompted a sympathetic response from even *New India*. Commenting on the resolutions of the Coimbatore conference, an editorial of 24 August 1917 observed that a remarkable similarity with Congress opinions was to be found here.

Congressmen, however, were watchful of the Non-Brahmin movement's social concerns, for these determined the exact line of demarcation between Home Rulers, Congressmen and non-brahmins of the South Indian Liberal Federation, or the Justice party, as it was popularly known. Raman Menon, speaking at the Coimbatore District Conference of the Congress, observed that non-brahmins would do well to heed and mend the casteism in their own ranks and refrain from conducting antiquarian researches which proved brahmins were interlopers. He urged non-brahmins to advance their political rather than social objectives for these posed difficult problems to their perceived opponents and alienated them. Non-brahmins should also realize they would wield decisive influence under Home Rule for there would not be an electorate 'divorced from the landed interest' and non-brahmins were clearly in the majority here (NI 20.8.17).

The attempts by Raman Menon and Vyasa Rao to constitute a non-brahmin political bloc would fructify in the years to come when both Congress non-brahmins and Justicites would unite to urge the cause of proportional representation for all castes in the legislature. But in 1917, these attempts did not really achieve anything subtantial. However, they lead to the forming of the Madras Presidency Association (MPA), a forum for non-brahmins in the Congress. Brahmin Congressmen not only welcomed the move but also encouraged leading non-brahmin notables to join the MPA. Annie Besant was also supportive of the MPA which she referred to as the 'real non-brahmana movement'. In this instance, the patriotic imagination, however suffused by brahminic desire and nostalgia for an archaic past that stood to be regained in the here and now, and however underwritten by the Madras brahmin's search for an ideal self, proved itself supple and cunning. It sought to constitute a broad-based political unity, and one less likely to be criticized for its partisan basis.

Its success in this regard was however modest: this new patriotism brought many non-brahmins into Congress but these men never attained national pre-eminence. For, Madras brahmins, of whatever faction in the Congress, retained for themselves the prerogative to mediate provincial concerns at the national level. Thus the non-brahminization of the Congress in Madras remained more apparent than real, serving to remind non-brahmins that brahmin hegemony was flexible but mindful of limits that may not be crossed without affecting the supremacy of the brahmin.

Ultimately, the national one-ness which Madras Congressmen sought to create existed more as an effect of their own linguistic skills and their political will to power rather than as a tangible material reality. Their sense of the self, the language which mediated their concerns, and the ideas which structured and defined these concerns as pertinent existed together as a seamless unity; so much so that the hyper reality of words, images and ideas they created seemed at times more real and attractive—to themselves and others—than the real itself.

It is clear the brahmin persona in Madras at the beginning of our century was constituted on the basis of a complex sense of self, whose will to power and dominance was articulated through various communicative means and in diverse realms. Through their hold over the Presidency's administration and judiciary and as participants in a political and ideological process which was committed to integrate India into Queen Victoria's global empire, brahmins were particularly well situated to covet power and strive to attain positions of authority. In a context where political society responded to the dictates of an imperial logic, they practised a politics of the possible—through the successes they managed to notch up in civil society. Through their journalistic and reform work, they came to dominate the colonial public sphere and through an ingenious use of the English language appropriated all the marks and signs of the commonweal. Most important, they provided the modern upper caste Hindu with an appropriate language and symbols to articulate his desires, fears, hopes and apprehensions and secure for these a universality.

CHAPTER 2

The Emergence of Non-Brahminism

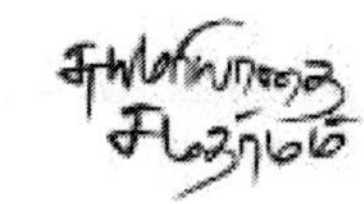

THE YEAR 1907 witnessed fairly successful Swadeshi campaigns in several parts of the Madras Presidency. The twin ideals of Swaraj and Swadeshi were invoked to signify a new phase of Congress agitations and proved persuasive in their appeal. Brahmins as well as non-brahmins joined together enthusiastically in carrying out several acts of defiance (Rajendran 1994). But there were dissenting voices, sceptical and critical of Swadeshi and Swaraj, which felt compelled to interrogate the content of these ideals. Pandit Iyothee Thass, a Buddhist by conviction and a Paraiah by birth, was one of those who pursued a relentless and sustained campaign against 'Swadeshi Reform', as he termed it, while writing in his *Oru Paisa Tamizhan*, a weekly published from Madras.

Iyothee Thass was convinced there existed a casteist edge to Swadeshi pronouncements. In an article which appeared in the 12 February 1908 issue of *Tamizhan*, he observed that in the wake of British rule,

> The brahmins... threw overboard those Vedas, Puranas, Smritis and Bashyams they had evolved over the years to enable them make a living. Now they took to the learning of those Vedic hymns that would earn them posts in the high court; they mastered those Smritis that brought them appointments in the Department of Revenue, the Upanishads which would help them find a place in the Abkari department and Bashyams that would lead them to jobs in the municipal office.

Yet, added Iyothee Thass, the brahmins, as in the days of old, continued to remain exclusive and quarrel over their caste symbols, their subsects, their distinctive modes of living and eating. While they did not consider it an embarrassment to travel, dine and interact with peoples of other races and nations, they persisted in their semantic and symbolic quibbles over questions of caste identity, if only to distinguish themselves constantly and systematically from their fellow men and women.

Nearly a decade later, in his welcome address to the First Non-Brahmin Confederation held at Madras in December 1917, Theagoraya Chetty, also drew attention to the brahmins' proclivity to remain exclusive and constitute an oligarchy which historically had successfully resisted all revolts against it.

> More than 2400 years ago the Buddhist reformation sought to unify all classes but the influence of varnashrama dharma was too strong. Ramanuja, though a brahmin, tried to mitigate the rigours of the social and religious tyranny of the brahmin priesthood and succeeded partially for some time...Basavaiaya made a similar attempt which was attended with a similar result. Thus every successive attempt to put down the brahminical tyranny ended in failure...with the result they elaborated the present system of untouchableness and pollution (Varadarajulu Naidu 1932: vol 2, 139-40).

In his presidential address to a non-brahmin conference held at Pulivendala, K. Subba Reddi, a youthful member of the Justice party, attempted to account for the durable character of the brahmin oligarchy. Referring to V. S. Srinivasa Shastri's assertion in the Imperial Legislative Council, that the non-brahmin will prefer the brahmin oligarchy to the British oligarchy, Subba Reddi pointed out that this statement 'serves us as an eye-opener and gives us a glimpse of the unknown regions of the South Indian brahmanic mind':

> While the British oligarchy touched us here and there and that too only superficially, the Brahmin oligarchy pursues us at every turn and makes itself felt in the innermost recesses of our life. While the power of the secular oligarchy is finite and can be understood that of the spiritual oligarchy is infinite and inscrutable....The Brahmins' claim of superiority by birth, their ill concealed sectarian bias... their powers of combination, their policy of mutual advancement and

> their inordinate selfishness in the past have made them dangerously formidable against the legitimate attempt at improvement made by other communities (ibid: 75).

Such an awareness of the dominance that held them in thrall and of a hegemony which willed them to life-long humiliation was widely present amongst literate non-brahmins in the early years of our century and articulated by them at opportune moments. This awareness was most evident in articles written for vernacular weeklies such as *Tamizhan* and usually expressed itself at several levels: as anti-Brahminism and anti-casteism; as anti-Aryan and anti-Sanskrit or alternately as pro-Tamil and pro-Dravidian.

Annie Besant's *New India* with its pronounced brahmin bias attracted the ire of several non-brahmin writers and publicists who engaged her and her many columnists and readers in lively and, often, indignant debates. One such debate proved to be particularly protracted and may be read as a fitting instance of a battle of words in which non-brahmins proved themselves to be no mean opponents. A veritable war of words ensued between a reader who signed himself 'Tamilian' and Annie Besant on the matter of Home Rule, non-brahmins and the Non-Brahmin Manifesto. Tamilian was pained by Annie Besant's angry editorial published in the wake of the Manifesto's release, wherein she declared her columns would henceforth be closed for discussion on the subject (NI 20-21.12.16).

Tamilian observed—in a letter that was published in *New India's* 'Vox Populi' column—that since then, attacks on the Manifesto had been published, but not defences of it. Besides, *New India* had opened up its columns for the propaganda of the Varnashrama Dharma movement which sought to uphold 'claims for privileges, both religious and secular, on the basis of birthright'. That such a movement should be allowed space for its views in *New India* was strange, especially when the latter claimed to be a nationalist organ, committed to equality and fair play. Tamilian was also puzzled by Annie Besant's refusal to see 'all the mean subterfuges adopted in all offices to keep out non-brahmanas and make them a huge monopoly of the brahmana community alone'. Admitting that the Manifesto's authors ought not to have interfered with the Home Rule movement, Tamilian went on to note that the Manifesto was otherwise sound in its observations and cannot be dismissed away as worthless especially since 'there exists a vast body of educated brahmanas who are not imbibed with...the liberal sense' (NI 28.4.17).

Annie Besant was unmoved by these charges and denied every one of them. She claimed that non-brahmins were not found in large numbers in the services because they 'preferred to seek wealth in trade and commerce than petty salaries in government offices'. She also denied she was out to kill a popular movement: 'I have praised the effort to uplift but I have opposed and shall oppose the crusade of hate.' She declared that the leaders of the Varnashrama Dharma movement constantly vilified her and she could not be accused, therefore, of being partial to them. Finally, she wondered why non-brahmins were more illiberal than the brahmins and less committed to the education of the depressed classes (ibid). Tamilian responded equally vociferously and observed that *New India's* editor was clearly 'not open to reason' and remarked that 'If the non-brahmana controversy had become acrimonious and pungent it must be understood that it was a direct result of the way the movement was received by the responsible leaders on the other side' (NI 5.5.17). Not to be outdone, Besant wrote back, accusing Tamilian of irresponsibility and rashness (ibid).

In spite of Annie Besant's hostility to their cause, non-brahmins continued to challenge and query brahminical pride and the exalted status accorded them in the caste system. *New India,* to its credit, allowed for contrary views, though its redoubtable editor reserved for herself the authority to begin and end debates. Imprecations against caste by non-brahmins—as these are found in *New India*—were usually directed against its 'foreign-ness' and therefore its illegitimacy as far as its claims on Tamil society were concerned. When a Congress stalwart such as S. Srinivasa Iyengar argued that non-brahmins were chiefly responsible for the low and despised status of the adi dravidas (NI 27.12.14), Radhakrishnan from Madras responded spiritedly. The Tamil classics, he noted, 'our sole authority for a knowledge of the historical and social conditions of the great non-brahmana communities in the South' provide no evidence as to the existence of untouchables in Tamil society. Radhakrishnan also challenged Srinivas Iyengar's views that caste was more important to the non-brahmins than to the brahmins:

> How is the existence or the perpetration of the caste system advantageous to the non-brahmana? Does he make a living out of it? The brahmanas having no other occupation than spiritual priesthood to follow had at least something to gain in getting society divided into as many units as possible thus easily domineering over all and gaining much material advantage from the situation created.

Radhakrishnan also pointed out that caste reproduced itself, not because non-brahmins continued to abide by its rules but because brahmins had come to enjoy 'great temporal power' over all others (NI 4.1.15).

In another instance, when one Pandit averred that though Vellalas (agriculturalist non-brahmin castes) had pretensions to *dwija* status, their claims cannot be upheld or validated since they were, after all, tillers of the soil and sport neither the *shika* (sacred tuft) nor the *suthra* (sacred thread) which denote *dwija* status (NI 22.4.15), Somasundaram Pillay, a Vellala himself, observed:

> The land of the Tamils had once been most democratic in spirit in more than one sense. People who attach fictitious importance to certain callings and who would fain claim superiority over others without right or merit have been more or less assertive due to ignorance and want of true piety (NI 28.4.15).

An even more pointed and consistent critique of caste as a foreign import was advanced by Iyothee Thass and his group of Buddhist Paraiahs. These men located the origins of caste and untouchability in those historical conditions which lead to the demise of Buddhism. Regular articles appeared in *Tamizhan* which celebrated the civilizational and cultural achievements of pre-brahminical, Paraiah-Buddhist people. In a particularly vivid description of the Tamil past or the 'original Dravidian culture', as he termed it, Iyothee Thass observed this latter had been integral rather than divisive, interactive rather than exclusionary and inter-communicative rather than lofty and distant (*Tamizhan* 4.11.08). M. Masilamani, another regular columnist in *Tamizhan*, writing in its 5 August 1908 issue, also testified to the glories of a forgotten past when Tamils had lived far and wide in the subcontinent and achieved a level of culture unmatched by anything that succeeded this golden age.

This antipathy to caste and to all things Aryan expressed itself most thoroughly in and through a commitment to the cause of Tamil culture and, more important, the Tamil language. Tamil existed in these oppositional discourses as the most valuable index of a 'hoary civilisation' (NI 19.11.14) and was defined in its opposition and difference from Sanskrit. When the Madras government requested the services of a Tamil pundit with a 'fair knowledge of Sanskrit' to assist in its efforts at the collection of precious manuscripts, a bewildered but angry reader responded thus:

> What has Sanskrit to do with Tamil culture and Tamil? If it has done anything it is to pollute her literature by bringing in far-fetched similes and fantastic imageries and to flood the language with all sorts of puranic legends.... Is it not an injustice to Tamil with its hoary civilisation and culture [that] it should be denied the honour of a classical language; when its sister language Sanskrit whose development does not extend far beyond the historic period should be given them (ibid).

It is noteworthy that the 'honour' accorded to Sanskrit was not merely an instance of bureaucratic misdemeanour. Not only the government, but also its most illustrious representatives and subjects, were inclined to favour Sanskrit—in academia and in polite cultural exchanges. For instance, in his convocation address to the graduates of the University of Madras, the Honourable P. S. Sivaswamy Iyer said:

> As a language which enshrines the highest ideas of Indo-Aryan civilisation, as a language in which the highest achievements of the Hindu mind in the region of philosophical speculation and religion have been recorded, as a language to which most of what is valuable in the vernacular literature of India owes its inspiration, as a language in which the ordinances which regulate our social life and institutions to the day have been written, a knowledge of it is an essential event of culture to every Hindu (ibid).

In the face of such insistent support for the study of Sanskrit, Tamil scholars and enthusiasts naturally pleaded for an active encouragement of Tamil studies. Arguing that a proper and systematic study of Tamil was absolutely indispensable for a reconstruction of the history of

South India, Radhakrishnan—whom we have encountered earlier—complained the claims of Tamil had been ignored and refused validity by the University of Madras and the Madras government (NI 5.7.15).

Such complaints as these had been voiced from the first decade of our century, from 1906, in fact, when the Madras University Senate proposed the elimination of the compulsory study of the vernaculars at the Intermediate and B.A. degree levels (Nambi Arooran 1980: 75). The language controversy continued to dominate the public imagination well into the decade starting with 1910 and when, at this juncture, the nationalist press urged forward the claims of Hindi as the national language, older debates acquired a sharper and newer edge.

The second decade of the twentieth century was witness to a concerted attempt by Congressmen in Madras to promote Hindi as the future national language of India. As early as 1907 a Madras Tamil brahmin notable, Professor Rangachari, had declared that 'Hindi would and should be the national language of India' (ibid: 79). In 1917, in a letter addressed to the press, Gandhi had stressed the importance of Hindi as a 'common language for India'. Referring to the non-Hindi South, where this 'common language' was neither spoken nor understood, he remarked that missionaries of Hindi could be sent to the South to teach the language. As for Muslims who spoke Urdu, only the written character of their language was different and it was, in other respects, like Hindi and this should therefore pose no problem (NI 29.6.17).

By 1918, *New India* had begun a special column for Hindi through which it attempted to instruct prospective learners. While a majority of its brahmin readers were keen to learn Hindi, there were a few who wished to substitute English in its place. N. M. Rama Iyer, in a letter to *New India*, remarked that 'Hindi has little chance of getting enthusiastic adherence in South India among the Hindus. From the Hindu point of view all the Dravidian languages are quite as rich as Hindi if not richer'. Therefore, he went on to say, it would be better to consider English 'which has the greatest chance of becoming the world language' as a common language for India. Besides, India had a role to play in history, 'as a spiritual saviour to the world' and English would be the handiest instrument for this purpose (NI 2.5.18).

The case for Hindi, however, aligned as it was to patriotic pride and the overriding claims of nationalism, was repeatedly upheld by Congressmen. K. G. Rangaswamy argued that 'the knowledge of Hindi not only helps to communicate with the Hindi knowing public' but also 'forms an essential medium for him who out of patriotism desires to learn first hand the needs and aspirations of struggling villagers in the remote corners of the country' (ibid). The political significance attributed to the learning of Hindi was not entirely lost on Madras' non-brahmin intellectuals who now saw all too clearly the links which obtained between knowledge of a 'chosen' language, education and dominance. Thus K. M. Panickar, a young student at the University of Oxford, in an extremely well-argued piece, 'The Educational Problems of Indian Nationalism', pointed out that every government (and class) interested in maintaining and perpetrating its hold over its populace manipulated the educational machinery of the community to suit its purpose. This had been the case with governments as different as republican France and monarchical Russia. In nearby Malabar too, such control as wielded by brahmins over educational institutions, had yielded rich dividends for members of that community who utilized their learning to mark themselves off as differently privileged than the rest. Language—in this instance, Sanskrit—became a badge of privilege and just as the British prohibited naval and military education to the natives, so had the brahmins prevented and continued to prevent shudras from the learning of the Vedas (NI 6.3.18).

The political importance of language learning was registered by the Justice party leaders as well. At several conferences held throughout the Presidency in 1917, even before *New India* had begun its Hindi columns, many leaders spoke of the unfair eulogizing of Sanskrit and the concomittant neglect of the vernaculars. Such a disregard of the spoken languages of South India, they argued, often went hand in hand with a total indifference towards primary education; for in both instances an elitist conception of learning shaped opinion. Theagoraya Chetty thus noted:

> The University of Madras encourages Sanskrit language as against the living vernaculars of the masses and chhatram funds, endowments of Dravidians, are available for the encouragement of a dead language; but for primary education which is of such real importance to the people, money cannot be found (Varadarajulu Naidu: vol 2, 136).

Theagoraya Chetty felt impelled to uphold in this context 'the genius of Dravidian civilisation' for the latter did not observe distinctions amongst peoples; nor did it seek to withhold a knowledge of its wisdom and learning from whoever wished to acquire them.

Non-brahmin critiques of caste and Aryanism, re-writings of history and assertions of a radical subjectivity were often undertaken in the context of specific instances of felt deprivation and humiliation and adumbrated into more generalized disquisitions on history, culture and society. What is noteworthy about these bursts of anti-brahmin anger and the emergence of a non-brahmin sensibility is that much of these pre-dated and, in many crucial ways, anticipated the political message of the Non-Brahmin Manifesto. This is especially true of the writings of men such as Iyothee Thass which we shall soon consider in some detail.

A number of reasons may be cited to explain the emergence of Non-Brahminism in the Tamil country. From the last quarter of the nineteenth century at least, a language of rights was available for use by all those who wished to do so. In the Tamil country, as elsewhere, not only did the schoolrooms of the Raj resonate with liberal opinions, but several other forums and spaces came to be possessed of the power and appeal of ideas of freedom and equality. Street corners where missionaries strove to attract attention by distributing pamphlets on the inconsistencies of the Hindu faith and the ingrained cunning of the brahmin priest; 'circar' or government space which the government, in its eagerness to lay claims to all wasteland now defined as its own and which, in theory, at least, was accessible to all; urban arenas such as markets (and garrisons) where, irrespective of caste, men (and women) gathered to seek work; public meeting halls, reading rooms and debating societies where a variety of people congregated to exchange ideas and opinions; caste associations in which the power of community and the strength of numbers made for hitherto unknown sodalities—the language of rights was heard in one form or another in these various sites, loud and clear in some instances, quaint and mutated beyond recognition in others.

Equality, in the service of liberty and fraternity, was proclaimed a desirable ideal, as non-brahmins of various sorts came to demonstrate and realize their rights of access to places, events and honours conventionally denied them. Notions of fraternity were invoked in pointed critiques of caste and in protests directed at various exclusionary practices. The ideal of liberty came to acquire a different resonance and emphasis and was re-defined, as non-brahmin publicists came to query the principles and practices of nationalist politics. The firm and solid presence of the British, the nature of their authority, which derived neither from the priest or from accidents of birth, but from their avowedly progressive, rational credentials, their assumptions of a 'neutrality' stance which, in some circumstances, could represent itself as fair and objective, the gifts of Western science and learning they seemed eager to disburse to all, irrespective of caste or creed, their own personal indifference to purity and pollution tenets—all these served to validate, legitimize and actualize for countless non-brahmins and adi dravidas the doctrine of rights which they eagerly learnt from their rulers.

What proved decisive, though, in non-brahmin imaginings of the self was history; a history of changed fortunes, a history that catapulted subaltern communities into positions of influence, if not power, and allowed them to negotiate fairer and more reasonable terms for themselves in the social order, in the public sphere, in the government and in the realm of culture. The new learning they now possessed provoked a flush of nostalgia amongst its adherents who came to write tales of identity and community. In all instances, non-brahmins sought to uphold their claims in the name of an unsullied Dravidian past and attempted to 'fit' that history to the secular imperatives of the present.

THE LANGUAGE OF RIGHTS

The Making of Public Space

Railway carriages and tramcars proved to be highly volatile spaces in colonial Madras during the early years of the twentieth century. So much the symbols of modernity and alien rule, they emerged as contentious sites—of interaction and confrontation—between brahmins, non-brahmins and the adi dravidas. The introduction of the tramcar in the city saw the appointment of a number of Paraiahs as conductors. This measure provoked an immediate outcry among the city's orthodox who protested that the presence of these low caste conductors would deter the orthodox from using the tramway. Paraiahs, for their part, were naturally enough incensed and looked to the British for help. In this instance, though, the colonial authorities preferred to heed the complaints of the orthodox and members of the so-called clean castes were appointed in the place of Paraiah conductors. In a letter addressed to *Tamizhan*, a Paraiah reader complained of the discrimination practised against his community and noted that not only had Paraiahs lost jobs but had been forced to bow down to caste malice. The tramway incident had served to remind his people of all the devious ways adopted by their enemies to deprive them of the means to make a honest living. Those brahmins who now held jobs in the tramcars did not obviously fear pollution that may result from accepting money from Paraiahs while dispensing tickets. It is clear they objected only to the pollution attached to a Paraiah conductor's body (4.3.08).

Railway carriages, no less than tramcars, proved hostile to the adi dravidas. Orthodox brahmins often complained that though Europeans and Eurasians had carriages reserved for themselves, no such privilege was accorded brahmins. They, thus, had to crowd into unreserved coaches where they were forced to sit, cheek by jowl, as it were, with 'dirty, smelly inferiors'. S. Narasimhan claimed that a railway carriage proved a veritable 'hell' for a brahmana who had to travel with 'dirty people... wanting in neatness and much addicted to smoking and drinking,... who emitted an evil odour' which was intolerable to one 'who was not accustomed to it'. At least, Europeans were 'free to move with all low caste peoples such as the panchamas' but brahmins were explicitly forbidden by their religion to even sit near the latter and were required to keep themselves strictly inviolate. Hence a separate coach for brahmins was in order (NI 20.10.14).

S. Narasimhan's request for a separate carriage for brahmanas angered the 'clean' non-brahmins who insisted with pride that 'among the shudras there are a good number of orthodox people who are cleaner than some of the brahmanas themselves'. M. Nagappa Chettiar, for instance, felt impelled to argue that, since it was the panchamas who were unclean, 'the railway authorities will do well to reserve compartments for panchamas alone. By doing this the authorities will remove the difficulties that are now unavoidably being experienced by the orthodox section of the Hindus' (NI 4.11.14).

But there were others from amongst the 'orthodox section of the Hindus' who thought differently. D. Ayyapillai argued that many communities, 'even among the kshatriyas and vaishyas', were still in an 'uncivilised state' and poor. Therefore,

> If the railway authorities were to allow reserved carriages ... for panchamas with special concession at half-rate how many kshatriyas and vaishyas will turn themselves to temporary panchamas for the sake of cheap conveyance? The Railway Board allows carriages to be reserved on proper notice given, so if the ablutions of the orthodox people make them strictly avoid the mere touch of panchamas (who are also God's creatures) they may quite well use the first and second class, as is frequently done (NI 16.11.14).

Writing nearly two years later, when the matter of railway travel was as contentious as ever, S. Sadasivam Pillay declared he too desired that separate carriages be allotted to panchamas. But the reasons he offered were markedly different. In a petition submitted to the government, he described a sight he had witnessed and which, he pointed out, was by no means uncommon. He spoke movingly of how four panchamas seeking entry into a coach 'visited compartment after compartment and literally fell on the knees of the passengers to gain admission. The ... train was by no means crowded and even the entreaties of the railway officials were useless and the train stealed [sic] away leaving the four panchamas on the platform' (NI 26.5.16).

Railway travel created other sorts of tensions as well. One 'Socialist' complained in a letter to *New India* that 'while we enjoy under British rule absolute freedom from religious, racial and caste prejudices, the South Indian Railway Company are acting in a way contrary to British policy.... There is set apart [in trains] a separate buffet canteen for brahmanas and brahmanas alone while all other castes are rushed into one. I do not see any wisdom in allowing a special apartment for brahmanas when I see that all passengers from orthodox brahmanas to a paraiah are obliged to travel sitting side by side in the same compartment' (NI 15.9.16). In response, S. Narasimhan observed: 'He the Socialist should understand that in all hostels attached to colleges managed by the Government, cooks of different castes are appointed; separate dining halls are also built.

What is the reason for this? The authorities never want to take the initiative in social questions and at the same time neither object to anything new' (NI 22.9.16).

Such restrictions on their mobility and the daily humiliations they were forced to endure elicited bitter and angry responses from the adi dravidas. They pointed out that those brahmins who considered them unclean were not necessarily poor or ignorant. Many of them were very well-educated but their behaviour in public places, especially railway coaches, was reprehensible. Even as they made sure panchamas could not travel with them, they saw to it that their own found a place in the carriage (*Tamizhan* 15.6.15).

Colonial Rule and the Emergence of a Notion of Rights

The fierce contesting of public space was not restricted to rail and tramcars. Streets, schools, temples and water points emerged as contentious spaces to which all sorts of people, individually, severally, and through their caste associations sought free and equal access. The dissolution of agricultural frontiers, the changed basis of agrarian relationships, the laying of roads, the coming of the railway, the rapid expansion of trade, the growth of market towns, in what were once rural hinterlands, the passage of peoples from country to town and across the oceans: these diverse and often interlocking transformations which had come to change the physical and mental worlds of the Tamils, since the advent of colonial rule, provoked new conceptual categories into existence. In earlier periods, the organization of space (which is our immediate concern), was contingent on the opinions and will of locally dominant communities, religious and sacral authority and royal dictum. These various authorities, on their own or in unison, could and often did direct and regulate the use of space (Stein 1980; Appadurai 1981). Now, with the coming of colonial rule, space was re-imagined, re-constructed and re-possessed in specific ways. For here was a ruling authority which not only arrogated to itself secular and sacral responsibilities but also showed itself to be essentially indifferent to rules of distance and purity. The British official in India observed no caste rules. He ate beef, employed adi dravidas in his household—they could even wait at his table—and fraternized with all sorts of native citizenry. Further, the authority which proceeded from his person was that of an imperial state which recognized no claims to power except its own, which it assumed as a matter of right.

Of course, the British needed help and assistance in the business of governance and they did not wish to destroy the old order entirely while imposing their own. They created a system of governance which implicated key native personnel in positions of power within an overarching framework of authority that in the final instance rested on the discretion and the will of the white man. For Madras, they envisaged a revenue system which, in principle, sought to respect the claims of the cultivator but which, in practice, served already entrenched interests in land. Meanwhile, a complex revenue bureaucracy, which respected no claims except those of its greedy coffers, had been set in place (Kumar 1965; Frykenberg 1969).

The discourse of ryotwari created a language of rights and private property which, over a period of time, allowed subaltern castes to stake upstart claims on land, on which until recently they had merely laboured. In the past, these castes had possessed particular rights on the land and its produce but such rights had gradually been abrogated as British rule came into its own in the nineteenth century. But new rights seemed a possibility now, especially since land had become a commodity that could be bought and sold. Besides, with the naturalization of the concept of private property, there emerged the notion of public property or circar space (Frykenberg 1976; Ludden 1985). Symbolized most aptly in the collector's office whose long and wide shadow fell athwart the social landscape of the village and the moffusil, this rarefied government space allowed for the generation and resolution of disputes over questions of access: to land, wells and forest.

The judicial administration created by the British proved homologous to their administration of revenue. On the whole, local custom was sought to be honoured and local opinion heeded, but the very presence of a court of law, the evolution of judicial procedures which created a body of Hindu and Mohammedan case law, and, most of all, the gradual but inevitable rationalization of legal procedure meant that new forms of adjudication were now available. The premises of the law court observed their own decorum, required their own distinctive modes of submission of evidence and represented a judicial authority, which theoretically at least, was fair, objective and keen to practise a logical interrogation of the truth claims of witnesses, irrespective of the latter's origins (Rudolph and Rudolph 1967; Cohn 1987).

With the collector's office and the courts of law housing a radically different form of authority, those sites of power and nodal points through which kingly authority mediated its needs in the past—the South Indian temples—diminished in importance. They ceased to be the privileged sites they were in earlier times, where sectarian conflicts were resolved and political worth measured. While retaining their enormous cultural and religious significance, they also came to be marked as 'public' spaces of an altogether different sort. Company and, later, Crown rule assumed responsibilities of a secular nature for the smooth conduct of temple affairs and this, in turn, robbed them of their sacral aura. They became units of a religious bureaucracy and laid themselves open to access and assailment.

The creation of circar space and the secularization of space, the freeing of wells, water points, roads and temples—from ascriptive markings—did not, of course, mean that traditional notions of purity, pollution and maintenance of appropriate social distance between members of different castes had given way or even enabled more reciprocal modes of conduct and interaction in Hindu society. More than anything else, the constitution of circar space indicated a resolve on the part of the government to redraw the boundaries of social exchange and conduct on its own terms. Fortuitously, in some instances, this resolve worked to the advantage of subaltern groups which could now lay access to forbidden domains.

If the declaration of certain spaces as public rendered them open and free in terms of approach and use to subaltern groups, a language of rights, which Western education and an acquaintance with political liberalism had provoked into existence, came to structure and direct subaltern aspirations for equality and justice. The spread of education through the second half of the nineteenth century ensured that more and more non-brahmins in Madras were brought within the ambit of Western learning. While in terms of real numbers, or in proportion to their presence in the population, non-brahmin literacy was not spectacular, and while, as yet, it was confined to a few castes, the impact of this literacy was far-reaching. It enabled non-brahmins and the adi dravidas to challenge brahmin supremacy and comprehend the changed face of brahmin power and authority in colonial Madras.

Non-brahmins came to master the discourse of rights in an unlikely context: the caste association. For it was the caste petition or memorandum addressed to government officials—census commissioners, collectors, the Governor himself—which actualized felt grievances of particular castes and gave expression to specific demands: of access to roads, wells, for a superior varna status; for equality in the eyes of the law. A fine instance of a caste memorandum which set forth particular demands and sought specific liberties and concessions was the charter prepared in 1891 by the Dravida Mahajana Sangam, an organization of Paraiahs. Here, besides, the usual list of perceived humiliations, we find a tacit appeal to the government to disallow—directly or indirectly—dominant castes from exercising their prejudices with respect to Paraiahs.

Thus, Demand No. 1 requested 'an Act may be enacted with provisions to punish that whoever expresses or addresses as paraiah to ridicule the depressed classes should be deterrently punished'. Demand No. 6 requested that 'equal respect and treatment should be given to the depressed class members in running the administration of panchayats and municipalities'. Demand No. 7 called for a repeal of Rule 464 of the Jail Manual which empowered authorities to force Paraiahs to perform 'demeaning' tasks. Demand No. 9 asked that 'the existing restriction preventing the depressed classes from entering or sitting near the premises of courts and offices where Hindus are employed should be abolished' (Kamalanathan 1985: 42-43). In each of these instances, the petitioners may be seen to display an awareness of rights that are indivisible and universally applicable. One may also discern here a sense of comparative worth and a resistance to the violation of the self by others.

The Policing of Rights: Orthodox Responses

Orthodox and, specifically, brahmin responses to the subversive possibilities which lay immanent in a changed physical and social landscape were characteristically arrogant. When a certain municipality metalled one of its roads through raising public funds, but subsequently disallowed certain castes from walking on these roads, non-brahmins in the locality protested. They pointed out that since public funds had been utilized for the metalling of the roads, these latter were really 'public' property and ought to be made available for use by all; or alternately public funds be withheld with respect to such roads, in future, if this request was not granted. A municipality notable who was a brahmin was categorical in his refusal to heed this demand:

> A street can be called a public street though it is open only to a section of the public and that the fact of vesting a street in the municipality and thereby converting it into a public street...does not throw it open to all classes (NI 3.4.15).

In another instance, when local government in Madras attempted to implement measures to improve sanitary conditions in Suparingunta *paracheri* (a 'cheri' refers to a lower caste locality. A 'paracheri' is an adi dravida 'ghetto') in north Madras, there ensued a vociferous protest against the proposed changes. Orthodox brahmins expressed their discontent over this move while Annie Besant tried to utilize the support of the famous architect and town planner Sir Patrick Geddes in this matter. The debate became somewhat acrimonious with Dr. Nair who, a year later, would publish with others the Non-Brahmin Manifesto, taking the part of the government.

Objections to improving the access roads to the paracheri stemmed chiefly from the fact that this would interfere with life and activity in and around the Tiruvateeswaran Temple that was adjacent to the *cheri*. It was argued that the changes desired by the Corporation of Madras would involve the destruction of three houses on one of the *mada* streets (streets that run around the temple in all four cardinal directions). Running a straight line from the paracheri through the houses to the temple would interfere with the sentiments of the local resident brahmins, who along with the dharmakartha of the temple disapproved of the whole business. For the new street, if it came to be, would necessarily become a 'thoroughfare for the residents of the paracheri' and 'will seriously interfere with 10 days brahmavucchavam and other festivals when the Deva Eswaran halts first in the middle of the West Mada street to allow the performance of the necessary puja which lasts for about an hour usually' (NI 13.7.15).

Annie Besant, drawing on the writings of Patrick Geddes, argued in favour of keeping intact mada streets as they were, and noted:

> The scheme . . . however desirable from the standpoint of the revolutionary social reformer should be avoided by the town planner, not only because of the necessity not to wound the religious susceptibilities of the people but also . . . of the harmful influence which such a scheme will have on the value of the property concerned. The opening of a paracheri into a street inhabited by orthodox people will surely involve the lowering of the desirability of a residential quarter and of the demand of its houses. The money value of the street in the quarter is lowered and this capital depreciation of the property of the city (with corresponding reduction of city incomes also) will usually outweigh any gain to communication (NI 15.9.15).

It is significant that the paracheri was often the object of open and contemptuous abuse and violence during these early decades of our century. Thus, Seshachari of the Madras Reformists' League thought it fit to complain that the Mylapore burial ground proved difficult of access to caste Hindu men and women since they had to cross through a paracheri before reaching the grounds. This elicited a vigorous condemnation from a *Tamizhan* columnist who wondered why brahmins should thus 'fear' panchamas, especially since such fears deserted them when it came to entering paracheris for teaching at a school. Was it because a pecuniary compensation for the latter rendered the environs and the task associated with it less demeaning and polluting? (23.9.08) *Tamizhan* also carried reports of deliberate acts of violence directed at adi dravida settlements. A letter from the dwellers of Orandur (near Madurantakam) described the ignominies inflicted on the paracheri inhabitants of the said town when they had to cross the agraharam to reach the village post office and the tahsildar's office. Brahmin residents of the agraharam would not countenance such insolence, the more so since some of the 'trespassers' had dared to acquire land and shown themselves eager to break through the ghetto lines which marked them as impure and lowly (27.1.09).

It is evident that the secularization of space brought with it problems even as it proved advantageous. As we have seen, with reference to the Suparingunta paracheri in Madras, even as men like Dr. Nair sought to de-sacralize agraharam space, Annie Besant upheld the claims to exclusivity of such spaces by bringing them under a new sign: that of capital and property. In a limited sense this rule of property aided adi dravidas and other subaltern castes to trade in and acquire land, but in the context of a city, the commercialization of space did not work in their favour. Secondly, as was evident from the Orandur incidents, adi dravidas, even if they were endowed with some wealth, were essentially vulnerable to attacks from their upper caste neighbours. The cost of freedom and equality proved exceptionally high for subaltern groups. Generally, it may be said that disputes over space proved crucial, and however ugly such disputes turned out to be in practice, they facilitated an expansion, literally and ideologically, of civil society. This was true especially of institutionalized public spaces such as schools, which became important arenas of struggle for non-brahmins and adi dravidas, as they sought to breach the limits of a civil society which had become captive to the brahmins' will and imagination.

Adi dravidas objected to the misplaced compassion of upper caste men that expressed itself in the demand for separate schools for them. Annie Besant was a great patron of such schools and was given to pointing out that while brahmin names adorned the subscription lists for setting up such schools, non-brahmin names were far and few between. Many a column in *Tamizhan* was devoted precisely to a criticism of this sort of careless benevolence. The columnists were often incensed by the fact that those who demanded separate schools for the adi dravidas were often loath to teach in them since such schools, for the most part, were located in the cheris. Thus the schools were often neglected for want of instructors and, even where there were teachers, there was, everywhere, a dearth of supervisors. The latter would not visit the schools for fear of 'pollution' and would often hold their tests in groves and commons adjacent to the cheris. Parents of such children who went to school were reluctant to send their children to be examined in such places and were afraid further that some harm may befall them if they were to leave their homes thus. Adi dravidas were also struck by brahmin hypocrisy in these matters: that they would not mind accepting money for teaching adi dravidas, but yet insist the latter were unclean and polluting (2.4.08; 17.6.08).

The language of rights, so effectively deployed with respect to conflicts in the public domain, soon acquired a generalized character and was put to fitting use by non-brahmins and adi dravidas in everyday situations and with regard to those countless quotidian habits, gestures and rituals through which caste society sustained rigid lines of distinction between brahmins and others. Such practices of daily living, however routine or absurd these may be, served to remind the practitioners and their victims of the limits to mutuality and the reality of subordination in caste society. In some instances, the more absurd and laughable the discriminatory practice, the more hurtful it could be to the victim, who in such situations, emerged as a mere accidental presence that nevertheless could bode disaster.

A description of a school celebration (in Mangalore) which appeared in *New India* (16.4.15) illustrates this rather well:

> An...unhappy incident...[at the celebration] and not from the social reformer's point of view was the touching of a coffee pot by a non brahmana...Some of the victims of pollution are very orthodox brahmanas who had been consistent opponents of even the union of subcastes. It is feared the religious head of the caste...may think it necessary to call upon the reform party in favour of the union of subcastes [lest they] may take advantage of the unhappy incident in propaganda work.

Non-brahmin tactility emerged as problematic in another peculiar instance as well. K. Srinivasa Ranga Rao wrote in protest to *New India* against the impropriety involved in appointing anyone but a brahmin to the post of *parupathiyadan* (one who examines the offering, *prasadam*, to the deity before it is distributed to the public). Ranga Rao observed with barely concealed anger that the brahmin cooks who make the prasadam 'will not stoop to such a mean service as carrying food to the house of a non-brahmana [for inspection]' (3.1.16).

Non-brahmins were angered and irritated beyond measure by such open avowals of superiority and, in their turn, drew attention to several pointed instances of brahmin arrogance. On one occasion, Theagoraya Chetty criticized the practice observed in a certain choultry where brahmin and non-brahmin travellers were fed differently. While brahmin travellers were given ghee and buttermilk, non-brahmins were shown no such consideration. Whereupon, the President of the District Board, under whose jurisdiction the management of the choultry fell, wrote a long explanatory letter that was duly published in *New India.* He said that while enquiring into the use of choultry funds it was discovered that vast sums had been spent on ghee and buttermilk for non-brahmin travellers. This was clearly an unviable practice since 'non-brahmin travellers fed in the choultry are coolies and beggars and as a rule in these parts they do not use ghee and they seldom use buttermilk'. Hence, to correct the obvious misapplication of funds, it was decided that no expenditure on ghee and buttermilk for non-brahmins would be allowed. However the District Board President hastened to add, 'the poor brahmana travellers are given ghee and buttermilk as it is their usual food. Even non-brahmin travellers are given ghee... when required but as a rule they are averse to using it and avoid it' (20.1.20).

It was this refusal to see a discriminatory practice for what it was, and the sophistry which was used to explain and legitimize such a practice which irked non-brahmins and made them rail against 'brahmana tyranny', which, some claimed, was worse and more tainted than the tyranny of the Pope himself! By drawing attention to these molecular instances through which brahminical values expressed themselves, non-brahmins and adi dravidas managed to bring into the public domain those numerous acts of discrimination which ensured brahmin exclusivity. The boundaries of the public domain thus came to be re-drawn; not only civic injustices, but even the social and ritual denial of rights were represented as public wrongs that needed redressal.

Critiques of brahminical privilege did not end with reflections on particular unjust practices. The language of rights was also utilized to mount a systematic and sharp critique of brahminical power, the brahmin's role in the modern polity and society and, most of all, his espousal of a problematic nationalism. The various addresses and presentations at the conferences held throughout the year, following the publication of the Non-Brahmin Manifesto are replete with such themes. But the earliest instances of such a critique are to be found in the columns titled 'Swadeshi Reform' that were published in *Tamizhan* from the first week of its commencement.

Iyothee Thass and the 'Swadeshi Reform' Columns

Written chiefly by Iyothee Thass, these columns, begun in the heyday of Swadeshi radicalism in Madras, interrogated the politics of Brahminism and the brahminical tenor of nationalism. For Iyothee Thass, Swadeshi activities seemed suspect and undesirable for a number of interrelated reasons. His primary objection to Swadeshi and Swaraj was directed against the conduct of the brahmin proponents of nationalism. He enumerated several instances of discrimination and prejudice exhibited, not only by the brahmin Congressman, but by the largely brahmin-owned press and the brahmin publicist who mediated and constructed public opinion. Iyothee Thass often resorted to parable-like narratives to indicate the dubious origins and associations of the nationalist idea. Recounting the story of a little boy who died while crossing a railway track in Madras, he observed that while several gathered to gape at the gory sight, only an Eurasian inspector dared lift the child and take him to a nearby hospital. Notions of touchability and untouchability defined caste Hindu behaviour and attitudes to such an extent that Hindus dared not break these norms, even to help the distressed. In a society where such a lassitude governed the human spirit and was cultivated and protected by casteist brahmins, all talk of Swadeshi and Swaraj was obviously irrelevant and, worse, insincere (25.9.07).

What seemed galling to Iyothee Thass was the brahmin's proclivity to fortify his caste status. As soon as a brahmin secured an appointment in an office, in no time at all, he would gather his own kindred folk around him, such that the office in question would be transformed into a brahmin enclave (27.5.08). A caste, so possessed of its own interests to the exclusion and forced expropriation of the interests and concerns of others, could hardly be considered representative or national. Iyothee Thass located the power of the modern, secular brahmin in the control he wielded over public opinion. On several occasions, he criticized the leading nationalist daily, *Swadesamitran*, and the reputed weekly *India* (8.4.08) for the bias they exhibited in their reporting and for their barely disguised rancour. For instance, reporting on a riot in Villupuram, *Swadesamitran* referred covertly to the proselytisation attempts by Christian missionaries amongst the Paraiahs and wrote rather disparagingly of the latter (*Tamizhan* 18.2.07). Reporting on the Tirunelveli Swadeshi agitations, *India* noted that of the five dead, one was a Mohammedan and one a Paraiah. But, while referring to the former, the report had used the customary third person plural form of address, which in Tamil denotes respect, but had contented itself with using the pejorative third person singular—used to denote familiar objects—while referring to the latter, that is, the Paraiah (*Tamizhan* 1.4.08).

Swadesamitran's condescending reformist tone also irritated Iyothee Thass and he sharply rebuked those who would write to urge the cause of panchamas but not go beyond suggesting that separate eating houses and schools be made available for them (29.4.08). Just as annoying was the daily's sentimental liberalism. It would wax eloquent on the horrors endured by prison inmates (nationalists) who were forced to carry and dispose off their urine and faecal matter, but would not spare a thought for those panchamas who, by tradition, had been condemned to perform this degrading task and, worse, were forced to clear the excreta of others (27.5.08).

India's reformism also came under attack from Iyothee Thass. When one R. N. Swamy, writing in that magazine, suggested that special panchama schools be instituted, Iyothee Thass responded rather caustically. He remarked on how caste never came in the way of the brahmin if he stood to make money through it, but caste lines were firmly drawn whenever the brahmin perceived his exclusivity to be under threat. The demand for special panchama schools thus reflected on the brahmin's fundamental reluctance to allow a free mingling of castes (17.6.08).

Adumbrating at length on the 'inner spirit' of Swadeshi and Swaraj, Iyothee Thass observed that it was animated by four sorts of pride: caste pride, religious pride, the pride of knowledge and the pride that comes from being wealthy (9.10.07). It was this ingrained and uncritical pride in one's self and castehood that informed Swadeshi notions of boycott. In reality, the boycott of foreign goods was a call to preserve all things Indian and to abjure all things associated with the 'white Paraiah'. (Iyothee Thass refers here to the rabble-rousing talents of a Swadeshi publicist who was wont to hold meetings near temples and urge his listeners to give up covering their corpses with the white Paraiah's coarse cloth.) This invariably led to a celebration of the arcane, and, since the caste-spirit permeated the arcane, this inevitably meant an extollation of the virtues and uses of caste (16.10.07).

Having thus identified the 'brahminical' core of Swadeshi ideology,

Iyothee Thass proceeded to interrogate the idea of 'boycott'. What needed to be boycotted, he observed, was not foreign cloth but caste hatred, the kind of prejudice that could burn the houses of the poor and damn and destroy their gods and rituals. Iyothee Thass pointed at the vast gap which separated the actions of those who lustily chanted 'Vande Mataram', from their passionate espousals of the cause of their motherland. To insist that 'lowly' Gods cannot be carried through the 'hallowed' streets in which the 'twice-born' resided and to proclaim that pure brahminical deities cannot pass through a paracheri and yet declare one's love for one's motherland was not only inconsistent but hypocritical as well. The pertinent, but unasked question, whose significance Iyothee Thass nevertheless articulates through his critiques of nationalism, was simply this: Was a paracheri a part of the motherland? If not, what could be the relevance or usefulness of the nationalist credo to his people? (25.12.07)

Writing on different occasions, Iyothee Thass observed that even those self-professed champions of the poor and the deprived were motivated by material considerations and moved by false sentiment. He was particularly severe on those who protested the plight of indentured labour and demanded an end to this practice of forced out-migration to distant lands. He characterized those caste norms which prevented a Paraiah from wielding the plough (that is, owning and working on his own land) as pernicious and noted that, to protest the migration of these miserable abject slaves, who moved away to escape the rigours and humiliations of farm slavery, seemed an instance of a perverse and entirely misplaced charity. Such protests over the fate of the indentured arose from purely selfish motives, for who would work on the land of the rich and the 'twice-born' were the Paraiahs to leave thus? (20.10.09)

Iyothee Thass also found it hypocritical that Congressmen would rage against the unfair treatment meted out to Indians in Natal and elsewhere in South Africa and yet remain silent with respect to their own inhumanity towards the panchamas (6.1.09). He pointed out that Congress' outcry in favour of the lowly-born, expressed but rarely, was seldom innocent or spontaneous and often signified barely disguised political intentions and apprehensions. It seemed to him somewhat ironical that those who customarily shunned toil and refrained from labouring on their own land should thus concern themselves with the plight of those who did, and only in those times when the labourers languished in misery due to famine and want. Such times of misery served the nationalists well as they could blame the imperial rulers and, more important, gloss over their own complicity in creating the conditions leading to famine. For had they not contributed to the decline in production of grains by resorting to cash crop cultivation which promised rich returns? (26.2.08) Nationalist 'tears' in this respect seemed suspect on another account as well: since, even in good times, those nationalists who owned land had never paid their workmen enough nor sought to lessen the burden of additional customary labour imposed on the farm slaves, due to the latter's caste status (3.6.08).

The un-representative nature and content of Swadeshi and Swaraj ideologies were attributed by Iyothee Thass to a flawed epistemology and a jaundiced world-view. Characterizing all brahminical learning as unproductive and passive in that it encouraged laziness and reduced knowledge to a concern with the superficial, Iyothee Thass went on to delineate the various implications of this mode of knowing the world (26.2.08). Firstly, the brahmin's contemplative knowledge deterred him from aligning that knowledge to work and action. Intellectual energy was thereby expended on thoroughly gratuitous tasks such as the defining of rules of touchability, seeability and approachability. Secondly, through the centuries, the arts of religious enquiry, useless and irrelevant as they were, had been developed in all their subtlety and differences; such that there existed a plethora of creeds, each advancing its own claims on truth and wisdom. In addition to the creeds of the past, there had come to be new ones, the Brahmo Samaj, being one of them (28.10.08).

Thirdly, even modern degrees such as the B.A., the F.A. and the M.A. had added nothing to the brahmin's archive. Instead, the new learning had created a vast constituency of disaffected and restless intellectuals: on one hand, these young men were anxious to turn their knowledge to practical use to make a honest living. But, on the other hand, in the face of repeated failures to find jobs, they were led to agitate, hold meetings and show off their learning, especially their knowledge of English. On such occasions, they were enraptured by their familiarity and mastery over an alien tongue (of command) and would rather proudly observe rules of grammar than express a single, intelligible, useful and relevant thought or idea (26.2.08). In other words, they expressed a will to power, configured in their felicitous use of language, rather in those principles of liberalism which lay embedded in it.

The 'really useless' knowledge systems of the brahmins, impractical and internally inconsistent, had lead to a consequent underdevelopment of the practical arts of agronomy, irrigation and transport (28.10.08). Besides, the labouring Paraiahs and others who could have contributed to the making of such a needs-based knowledge had been prevented from doing so by a system that allowed them no access to learning. In these modern times, Paraiahs and others were further handicapped because all deliberations on matters of the commonweal, such as those debated in Congress forums and in organizations such as the Madras Mahajana Sabha, were carried on in English (26.2.08).

The political ideal produced by the inhibited and grotesque epistemology of the brahmins seemed as problematic as the knowledge which informed it. Not only was the nationalism of the Swadeshis remarkably opaque to the needs of the poor but seemed to be wary of admitting the influence of ideas and opinions which the poor or their spokespersons may express. For instance, Iyothee Thass was called to ratify the setting up of the Indian National Industrial Fund by a group of Madras financiers and elites; but when he suggested that the Fund be administered by a representative and multicaste body and that it be spent to ensure the welfare of all communities, the notables in charge of the fund had ignored him (21.10.08).

Further, Swadeshi nationalism, de-linked as it was from labour, had no viable alternatives to propose to economic misery (2.2.08). It was patently clear to Iyothee Thass that unless Swadeshi nationalism heeded the concerns and anxieties of artisans, traders and workers and until it learnt to express itself in the vernacular, it could neither be consensual nor effective. What appeared most irksome and destructive—to Iyothee Thass—in Swadeshi practice was its tendency to deviate into militancy. In the intense years of boycott in the Tamil country, sporadic troubles and rioting broke out in many places but, perhaps, Tirunelveli was the worst affected. Swadeshi propaganda, the activities of V. O. Chidambaram Pillay's Indian National Steam Navigation Company, the textile workers' strike at Tuticorin and the distress of weavers combined together to create an explosive situation

(Rajendran). Iyothee Thass was critical of Swadeshi involvement in these agitations since he feared the nationalists would incite the unlettered and the frustrated to furious action and then withdraw from the scene. While he was keenly sensitive to the grievances that lead to the unrest and did not doubt their validity, he was not convinced of the need or the imperative to collide head-on with India's rulers. Neither was he prepared to accept the nationalist argument, that their agitations were provoked by Lord Curzon's move to partition Bengal. He argued that the decision to partition Bengal was only a functional administrative measure and that Curzon had incurred the wrath of nationalists because he desired to better the conditions of existence of all classes and castes (*Tamizhan* 2.11.08).

Iyothee Thass' mistrust of Swadeshi militancy was such that he lent his support to those repressive measures launched by the government to curb seditious meetings and activities. It was not that he was unmoved by the effects of repression unleashed by the British and the travails that V. O. Chidambaram Pillay and Subramania Siva were forced to endure. But for him these troubles, in a sense, had been invited by the agitators who tried the patience of the British sorely. The Swadeshis, he argued, unmindful of the good wrought by the British, dared to undermine its prestige and legitimacy for nothing more substantial than personal gain—this, with reference to V. O. Chidambaram Pillay's navigation attempts, which Iyothee Thass felt were motivated by competitive envy (*Tamizhan* 22.7.08). Iyothee Thass criticisms of Swadeshi grew out of his conviction that the brahmin's engagement with the secular world of modern politics boded ill for all non-brahmins. His rejection of Swadeshi nationalism represented a plea for a political ideal that embraced social reform and democratic political activity, for this would ensure that not only brahmins but a host of others would come to wield power and represent the commonweal.

It must be pointed out here that Iyothee Thass did not desist from seeking to press his agenda with the Swadeshis. As early as 1892, he and others of the Dravida Mahajana Sangam, of which he was the founder, had sent memorials to the Congress on a number of issues pertinent to Paraiah welfare. The Congress had not responded directly but suggested these matters be forwarded to the Madras Mahajana Sabha that was a more appropriate forum to discuss such concerns.

When Iyothee Thass approached the Sabha with diverse demands, the latter were accorded a mixed reception. His plea that panchamas be allowed to worship at caste Hindu temples was cried down by the Sabha as a whole. The Sabha's Thanjavur representative, Sivarama Sharma, argued that since panchamas had their own Gods, their Madurai Veerans, Katterisamis and Karuppannasamis, they could not hope to nor needed to worship at the temples of Siva and Vishnu. Iyothee Thass let that pass but insisted that panchamas be allowed to study and go to school and that they be assigned *poromboke* (waste) lands. These demands were supported and endorsed by Elluru Sankaran and Savalai Ramasamy Mudaliar who also suggested resolutions be passed on these matters (*Tamizhan* 16.12.08).

Iyothee Thass' encounters with the Congress thus did not prove to be very fruitful. In later years, he bemoaned the gracelessness which characterized the behaviour of Congressmen during the Moderates-Extremist split and the lack of unity that pervaded that party. He was shocked that differences such as those that had surfaced at the Surat Congress were sought to be resolved along caste lines, for it had been suggested that troublemakers be denied caste rites, rituals and concessions! (*Tamizhan* 15.1.08) It is in the context of Iyothee Thass' failed engagement and dissatisfaction with Congress and nationalism that we should locate his guarded and qualified endorsement of even the Morley-Minto proposals (*Tamizhan* 30.12.08).

Iyothee Thass' well-voiced and subtly argued criticisms of Swadeshi dovetail neatly into a set of fundamental premises on reform, liberty and governance which may be seen to underwrite the political philosophy of non-brahmins in Madras, then and subsequently. Firstly, the idea and practice of political reform, of necessity, ought to lead the reformer into thinking through and acting on principles of social reform. Iyothee Thass imaged civil society or the sphere of social and economic relationships and interaction as 'the people' and political society as 'the nation' and argued that national reform and progress would only be achieved when peoples' lives were transformed. Secondly, political liberty or Swaraj was re-defined to signify not merely an ideal of self-government but a state of social and economic well-being as well. Thus, true liberty could be possible only when differences in caste disappeared and labouring classes attained a measure of good living and came to impress upon political life their particular concerns. Lastly, good governance, for Iyothee Thass, was possible in India only under a benign outsider. Indians might participate in this rule but, until and unless diverse communities were represented in the processes and institutions of the government, all of Britain's efforts to govern justly would be thwarted by self-seeking and ambitious brahmins.

THE BRITISH PRESENCE

The Goodness of British Rule

The successful deployment of a language of rights by non-brahmins and adi dravidas was often contingent on the attitudes struck by the British in any particular instance. Generally speaking, it was the presence of the British and all that it implied which enabled subaltern groups to attempt and succeed in their challenges to and defiance of social and religious creed and custom. Pax Brittanica and the rule of law, the promises—of equality and freedom—implicit in Western learning, the exciting knowledge contained in Western views of the world, history, society and culture and the notion that the white man stood in the forefront of history and progress worked to render British rule enabling and attractive. It was not only the subalterns who felt thus. The subcontinent's elites, brahmins and others who saw themselves as the natural and chosen leaders of their people, were also convinced that white rule represented the working out of historical destiny, of an inevitable law of progress. While grateful to the white man for bringing India on to the stage of a universal history, the native elite felt the time had come for its own representatives to participate in the workings of this ordained fate.

As the Memorandum of the Nineteen, submitted to the government on the eve of the announcement of the Montagu-Chelmsford (Montford) reforms, put it:

> The people of India have good reasons to be grateful to England for the great progress in her material resources and the widening of her political outlook under British rule and for the steady if slow advance up to date... There is no doubt that the termination of war will see a great advance in the ideals of Government all over the

> civilised world and especially in the British empire which entered into the struggle in defence of the liberties of the weak and small nationalities.... India has borne her part in the struggle and cannot remain unaffected by the new spirit of change for a better state of things.

The Memorandum went on to list the proposals for such reform as its signatories desired. These included the inclusion of greater numbers of Indians in the imperial and provincial executives; an increase in the number of elected representatives in all legislative councils; the granting of fiscal autonomy to Indians; the expansion of subjects on which Indians could legislate; provincial autonomy and, finally, a full measure of local self-government (Varadarajulu Naidu 1991: vol 2: 31-35).

The expectations of non-brahmins and adi dravidas, elites or not, with a few exceptions, were very different, as was their perception of British rule and their own relationship to their rulers. The raja of Panagal perhaps summed up non-brahmin opinion on the significance of British rule when he remarked:

> When... the English first came to India, they found our ancestors in a condition of hopeless ignorance and superstition. Gradually... our rulers were awakened to the necessity of instructing the people in those ideas and truths which would emancipate them from priestly bondage and degrading superstition (ibid: 6).

Iyothee Thass was as euphoric in his admiration of the British and as convinced of the immense and liberative possibilities of their continued rule. He observed, that for him and his people, the coming of the white man had proved fortuitous and emancipatory. The British brought with them a learning that was available to all. Innovations such as the tramcar and the railway broke, once and for all, the insularity of rural life and made nonsense of the rituals which enjoined observance of norms of purity, pollution and distance. Like their learning, the medicine the white man brought was given to all (*Tamizhan* 1.7.08). Even British trade practices held lessons for adi dravidas. They signified an openness—to traffic in goods and ideas. In contrast to the sedentary lives led by many an Indian, English lives seemed exciting, adventurous and above all free (*Tamizhan* 22.7.08).

It is surely significant that Iyothee Thass included traders and merchants along with peasants, agricultural labourers and artisans in the nuclei he felt ought to constitute the core of worthwhile Swadeshi activity in India. For a community such as the adi dravidas, condemned to a ghettoized existence, it was not only the liberal rule of law in British India, which granted them the status of persons and the right to a hearing by a neutral arbitrative body—the law courts—but the very principles of free trade, property and work which underwrote and justified that rule which seemed attractive (*Tamizhan* 1.7.08).

Iyothee Thass was also convinced that the coming of the British had ended centuries of misrule and tyranny. He held that Ancient India had known humane governance under Buddhist monarchs and had been prosperous and cultured. The ousting of Buddhist rulers by brahmin invaders enshrined the tyranny of caste and resulted in the marginalization of the former Buddhists—rulers and subjects—who were cast out and considered low, unclean and untouchable. The Muslim interregnum had proved itself no less indifferent to the former Buddhists who now sank into narrow barbarity and began to observe such regressive customs as child marriage and ritual widowhood. These latter had become the order of the day with the populace living in fear of abduction of their women by Muslim warriors, to forestall which they got their girls married off early and de-feminized the widows in their community (*Tamizhan* 10, 17, 24, 31.6.08; 8.7.08).

It is clear from the pages of *Tamizhan* that Iyothee Thass was not alone in his admiration for the British. Several intellectuals and leaders of the community evinced a similar faith in the goodwill of their rulers. Apart from the ameliorative effects produced by particular changes ushered in by the British, certain transformations in the quotidian aspects of living—the mode of dress, form of address—proved to be enormously important for adi dravida self-perceptions. For instance, the recruitment of adi dravidas in large numbers into the army, the fashioning of a martial self through the rituals and drill observed in the barracks, the award of the King Emperor's uniform, wearing which, the adi dravidas were told, they could freely walk down the brahmin's street and spit there if they so wished, provoked mutations in adi dravidas' sense of the self (Manickam, personal communication, 1991).

Non-brahmin life and consciousness too underwent fundamental transformations in the wake of colonial rule, as the raja of Pangal observed, and as we shall soon see. These transformations enabled the making of a non-brahmin sodality which would cut across castes and subcastes to posit a new vision of community. It was in the name of this community that men like Dr. Nair, one of the original signatories of the Non-Brahmin Manifesto, came to query the demand for reform which was being raised by brahmin legislators and Congressmen. In a lengthy critique of the Memorandum of the Nineteen, Dr. Nair pleaded against the granting of Home Rule, except through a series of gradual constitutional measures (Varadarajulu Naidu: vol 1, 36-59). He noted that, like the authors of the Memorandum, he was for the removal of disabilities currently endured by Indians, for instance, with regard to the Arms Act, volunteering and commissions in the army. But he could not, without a sense of apprehension, countenance the transformation of a 'highly centralised bureaucracy into a set of de-centralised self-government systems in the passing of a night'. For,

> A British Government which in a nervous spirit and deference to an agitation gives into the demand of immediate Home Rule for India will not only betray its trust to the British nation but also betray the many millions in India who will be handed over the care of a close and relentless oligarchy and whose only fault has been their placing too great a confidence in Government....The withdrawal or weakening of British power in India at the present time must certainly destroy all the forces of civilised Government that have been brought into existence in India by its British administrators (ibid: 59).

The Rulers' Vocation

While brahmins, non-brahmins and adi dravidas, each for their own set of reasons, welcomed British rule, the rulers were quite clear as to the import and usefulness of their vocation in India. They regarded their rule as not only just and fair but an improvement on all previous regimes. However, the exigencies of keeping a subject population in control and at peace, made the British evolve a relationship with their subjects, particularly its elite segment, which would persuade the latter to see and accept the wisdom of alien governance. This arrangement worked well until the last quarter of the nineteenth century, when the elite segment, especially its brahmin element, began to claim rights and privileges, coeval with the British.

Here was a problem the British had to address in all its nuances. The brahmin—as nationalist, social reformer and publicist—was necessary to essay such roles and functions as would allow the imperial scheme of things to succeed. Yet, he needed to be contained and shown his place. To countenance his impudence, the British had to set themselves up as superior, which they promptly did in two ways: by expanding the space of political society to accommodate their subjects' needs and by formulating a judicious policy of social reform. As 'benevolent' rulers, they decided to carry out reforms in the mode of governance: in local self-government, in the elections to the provincial and imperial legislature and in the matter of nomination of Indian members to the Viceroy's Council. Initially, the resident white populace, especially the civilians, who guarded their authority rather jealously, were extremely hostile to the idea of political reform. Grant-Duff, Governor of Madras, attempted to persuade Lord Ripon to abandon his schemes for enlisting the service of Indians in the government and noted that it was only the 'small clique of wire pullers in the Presidency and some of the big towns' who clamoured for reform whereas the rest of India was content with 'sensible things, bridges, roads, railways and so on' (Suntharalingam 1974: 179). Ripon, in turn, noted somewhat wryly:

> I believe that to rely upon force alone to keep down the aspirations and curb the ambitions of men like these is to trust to a reed which will break under our hand; and that if we do not by timely foresight take steps to supply legitimate outlets for these aspirations in a manner consistent with the maintenance of our authority we shall find in a few years that we have raised up a power we cannot control (ibid: 79).

What were to be the limits to such reform? Allan Octavian Hume spoke for the Viceroy and revealed the latter's intent when he wrote that the announcement of reforms had achieved their purpose, for now 'universal sullen discontent' had given way to 'enthusiastic loyalty'. The reforms had restored the people's waning faith in 'British honesty of purpose and good faith' and made 'the whole country once more wholly amenable to the intellectual guides' (ibid: 241).

British interventions in the realm of civil society proved to be much more complex and ambiguous than their interventions in the political realm. Civil society seemed to them a fit arena to demonstrate their moral superiority. They did this by invoking a morality independent of and, in some material respects, different from the standard set up by caste (*Babasaheb Ambedkar Writings and Speeches*: vol 12, 137). However they were careful not to overreach their efforts in this regard. The rule of law, which they instituted, functioned almost always in tandem with the rules of caste and convention.

Even as legality came to direct and define activities in the public sphere—with respect to property, acts of crime, rights and privileges of various sections of the native citizenry—customary practices and revivified traditions were allowed to structure and determine familial and community behaviour. The 1858 Proclamation had already indicated that law in British India would be fundamentally and constitutively schizoid and in the late nineteenth century, the double-facedness of legal authority was particularly evident. Replying to the various debates which had been provoked by the Age of Consent Bill, the government explained:

> When caste or custom enjoins a practice which involves a breach of ordinary criminal law the State will enforce the law. When a caste or custom lays down a rule which is of its nature enforceable in the civil courts but which is clearly opposed to morality or public policy, the State will decline to enforce it. When caste and custom lays down a rule which deals with such matters as are usually left to the opinions of citizens and which does not need the aid of civil or criminal courts for its enforcement State interference is not considered either desirable or expedient. In the application of such general principles to particular cases there is doubtless room for differences of opinion: but there is one common sense test which may often be applied with advantage in considering whether the State should or should not interfere in its legislative or executive capacity with social and religious questions of the kind now under consideration. The test is 'Can the State give effect to its commands by the ordinary machinery at its disposal?' If not it is desirable that the State should abstain from making a rule which it cannot enforce

without a departure from its usual practice or procedure (ibid).

The government's power of enforceability was limited by two crucial factors: its fear of rebellion and its awareness of the immense distance which separated the rulers from the ruled. It did not wish to compromise its imperial authority, and because it was imperial in intent it was not in touch with the pressures and anxieties which moved the masses of the people, and hence could not enforce even such legislation as it assumed was in keeping with its moral concerns. However, the government often resolved the matter rather neatly, as is evident from its pronouncements in a particular instance:

> It is our business until the legislature has otherwise ordained to administer the Hindu Civil Law as it stands and to every class its rights as we find them established—whatever may be the bad effects of the distribution of people in this class; this good results . . . that it will always prevent any general combination hostile to our interest (Wagle 1980: 140).

Invariably, of course, the government was forced to abandon its spurious neutrality and take up positions in local disputes. After all, throughout the period leading up to Crown rule and even after, government officials, men of the army and various others, had graced local events—in temple festivals, for instance—and even enforced ritual labour such as those of the Paraiahs' for pulling the temple car. Besides the government found itself debating and arguing the nature of custom itself: was it to be understood in its literal, local, contextual sense or was it to be understood in its shastraic form: as injunction and rule?

The phenomenal growth of law courts during the second half of the nineteenth century which led to a certain uniformity in legal procedure and practice, the professionalization of legal education and the preponderance of brahmin officials at the lower levels of the judiciary created the conditions for the evolution of a jurisprudence that was not only abstract and uniform but brahminic as well. If, on the one hand, the learning and practice of brahmin advocates and pleaders served to actualize brahminic norms, the dissociation of law from temporality and its textualization rendered these norms prescriptive and universal. This brahminization of law represented a conciliation between the demands of custom and the imperative to rationalize judicial activity. While the shastras would lend the law a certain validity, the law could also function on the basis of its own rationality, as constituted by precedents and practices which bespoke a certain authority that could not be easily countered (Aiyar; 1950).

The creation and establishment of brahminic norms was however a process in that it was rarely coherent and allowed ample room for interpretative differences and the prerogatives of local custom. Besides, the British retained overall judicial authority in their hands and, with court procedures allowing for the contesting and re-contesting of claims, the law courts attracted litigation from all sorts of people. The courts may be seen as representing colonial authority in every sense of the term: they heeded the claims of custom and convention, they gave a 'fair' hearing to all parties in the dispute and, most important, the British judicial officer pronounced the final verdict, in keeping with his notions of morality and justice.

British attitudes towards their non-brahmin and adi dravida subjects were of a part with their overall logic of governance. Here, too, they wished to appear fair and morally right. They did not mind playing one segment of the populace against the other for political gains, in this instance, non-brahmins against brahmins and adi dravidas against both, as we shall soon see.

The Nature of British Benevolence

The hiatus between government precept and practice with respect to the public morality it wished to promote and uphold was particularly evident in its attitudes towards the adi dravidas. For instance, the British clearly regarded slavery, that is, agrestic servitude as it existed in Madras (and elsewhere), as a great social evil. But their practice with respect to the abolition of this evil was motivated not so much by highfalutin moral rhetoric as it was by the exigencies of their revenue policy. On the one hand, the condition of bondsmen, often attached to great farmhouses into whose authority they were born and reared, was pathetic and clearly needed redressal. On the other hand, having stated, in and through the terms of ryotwari, that the ryot's claims to his property would be respected, the government could not very well tamper with that holy of holies: the ideal of private property. In 1819, the Board of Revenue observed it was averse to slavery as such but felt 'it would be obviously unjust to interfere with the private property which...the raiyats at present possess in their slaves'. Besides, 'it must be dangerous to disturb the long established relations subsisting between these two orders' (Kumar: 69).

In the years that followed, though, this 'aversion' to slavery leaked into judicial decisions and it was now held that slavery violated those (natural) principles which governed the free exchange of labour. But, as late as 1836, decades after this pronouncement, Vellala and brahmin landholders continued to maintain slaves (ibid: 43-44). It was in such a context, defined by revenue imperatives and marked by a faint twinge of conscience, that the Slavery Abolition Act of 1843 was framed. The act made it impossible to uphold in court the claims by landlords to the bound and continual services of their labourers but did little to alter the actual practice of agrestic servitude which survived in other forms. This act was embodied in the Indian Penal Code 1861. It merely facilitated the passage of labourers from slavery into a bondage system ratified by a contract. For, stripped of their customary status (and entitlements), the former slaves had no recourse other than to enter into written agreements with their masters; thus, they often agreed to sell their labour power for a meagre cash loan which, of course, bound them to lifelong toil on their masters' lands. Moreover, now, they came to be governed by the Workmen's Breach of Contract Act (1859) which rendered any violation of contract terms legally punishable and disallowed them from leaving their work premises and their master unless they had repaid the amount for which they may have originally pledged their labour. There also came into existence during this time a system of 'man mortgage', whereby a labourer could pledge himself or his family for a loan incurred by him (Sarkar 1985: 110-11).

If, in spite of this tragic sequence of events, that was set in motion by the 1843 Act, adi dravida intellectuals continued to believe the British abolished slavery and returned to them their long lost freedom, this was because, apart from being truly grateful to the white man for what they perceived as his benevolence towards them, they rarely associated colonial rule, policy or presence with whatever befell them in their villages. Iyothee Thass, for instance, in an article on the wide incidence of famine in Madras during the nineteenth century, argued that the cultivation of cash crops had brought about this disaster. But, he warned, the situation could not be remedied by merely berating British policy. For it was the greed of the landlord and the merchant and the indifference of the brahmin who would not give any portion of his earnings towards famine relief that had brought about hunger and misery. The British presence, argued Iyothee Thass, had proved useful, for it was the roads they laid and the railways they built which facilitated the easy passage of grain to famine-ridden areas (*Tamizhan* 26.2.08; 3 and 10.6.08).

Not only did Iyothee Thass not link up the practices of imperial trade and the new found fashion of cash crop cultivation, but he also failed to interrogate the revenue administration for its various sins of exaction which, in part, added to the miseries of famine. For him, as for many other adi dravidas, such problems and crises as arose in rural life, were due to the caste rancour of dominant communities whose arrogance knew no limit. Even in those instances when Iyothee Thass blamed the administration for its chicanery, corruption and its deep-seated prejudices towards the adi dravidas, he refrained from criticizing the higher rank of the bureaucracy which comprised almost entirely British. Thus the local karnam or tahsildar may be wrong, but the collector was above blame. He represented an authority that was above local feeling and could be addressed in good faith for the redressal of adi dravida grievances (*Tamizhan* 15 and 22.4.08).

The good faith the adi dravidas reposed in British rule signified the triumph of a certain ideology of rule. This ideology defined British presence in India—in itself—as inevitable, destined and calculated to work for the good of all Indians. For adi dravidas, the availability of an arbiter who would hear out their point of view proved important. It is noteworthy that Iyothee Thass' critique of Swadeshi reform was often resonant with a rhetoric of faith, treason and betrayal. The proponents of Swadeshi were branded as traitors and their cause a betrayal of British goodwill. The repetitive use of this rhetoric not only constituted the British as rightful heroes in history but also cast the adi dravidas in the role of a loyal vanguard that would stand by and strengthen the authority of its rulers.

Likewise, with the Madras non-brahmins, the solidity of the British presence proved reason enough for them to want their rulers to rule on. As the raja of Panagal remarked in his presidential address to the

First Non-Brahmin Conference held in Coimbatore in 1917:

> Thanks to the British government we are just emerging into the dawn of a brighter and clearer day than was ever known in this ancient land. Let us no more allow the siren voice to lure us back into our former state of bondage.... We have a Government deeply interested in our welfare and ready to help us on when and where their help is needed. Let us then under the fostering care of this benign Government and under the leadership of the best and wisest amongst us march steadily onward (Varadarajulu Naidu: vol 2, 17-18).

The zamindar of Telarpole defended the British and their work from charges of ineptitude and arrogance and noted:

> The European official in India may have his defects. He may be too much the slave of routine, too impatient of criticism and too apt to believe that his way of doing things is the only way....As for the non-official European...he has served as a pioneer and as an example of patient enterprise from whom our Indian business men have learned a good deal and must learn a good deal more. It is true he has not been a pure altruist: What man of business is? (ibid: 107)

Such a sense of gratitude towards the British for merely being there clearly overrode all other considerations. Though non-brahmins admitted that British rule and education had catapulted brahmins to positions of supremacy, and though men like Theagoraya Chetty were critical of the protectionist policies of the imperial government with respect to trade and manufacture, non-brahmin notables everywhere in Madras proclaimed they did not wish to see their brahmin peers rule in place of their British overlords. The raja of Panagal declared that the non-brahmins were not opposed to Home Rule as such, but felt it would 'push back the non-brahmin communities to their original state of dependence and enslavement and re-install in the place of our British rulers the very priestly class who were responsible for the unenviable state in which the non-brahmin communities were stagnating before the advent of British rule' (ibid: 7-8).

Just where did the benevolence of the British lie, when by their own admission, they were cautious of affecting such changes as would transform the lives of non-brahmin communities and the adi dravidas and free them from the rigours of caste?

The Productive Contradictions of Colonial Rule

The dynamic of colonial rule, in spite of its stated economic and social intentions, produced remarkable transformations in the lives and fortunes of many subaltern communities. When tea and coffee estates were opened in Malabar and Ceylon in the 1840s large numbers of Paraiahs and Pallas (another untouchable caste) went to work there. The expansion of the plantation economy into Wynad, Coorg, Nilgiris, Mysore and Annamalais and the construction of roads and railways which accompanied this expansion attracted a further number of adi dravidas. Migration to the Strait settlements and Malaya had begun as early as 1833 and by 1837 the system of indentured labour was in place (Sarkar: 110; 116). Migration intensified by the last quarter of the nineteenth century and by the twenties there was in any one year about a million and a half Tamils working overseas and nearly one third of them were from the rich valleys of Thanjavur, amongst whom were a substantial number of former bondsmen and their families (Baker 1984: 179-80).

Migration proved a hazardous process: the passage across the seas was rough and the condition of existence and work on the plantations invariably harsh but the enhanced income which accrued from the long hours of gruelling work and the relative freedom from ritual humiliation seemed compensation enough. Though caste relationships amongst plantation workers survived their pre-plantation days to reproduce themselves in alien soils, there was this important difference. Discrimination and prejudice arising out of caste inequality and underwritten by ritual status could not express themselves as forcefully or with complete authority as at home. For one thing, workers in the plantations received the same wages, lived in labour lines and were granted (or denied) the same set of benefits. Besides, one's ascriptive status did not entail one to special concessions and life on the plantations often brought the ritually superior castemen 'down' to the habitual level of existence of the ritually impure Paraiah or Palla, since wretchedness was their common lot now.

This enforced fraternity of workers, bound together by a shared destiny of suffering, instilled a measure of self-worth and confidence in Pallas and Paraiahs who were also earning more now than they did at home. For instance the prevailing wage rates in most Madras districts—during this time—was between seven and four annas a day. But in Burma, the average monthly income of a Tamil was twenty-four rupees, four annas and nine pice (Report of the Royal Commission on Labour [RRCL] 1931: 439). Those who managed to successfully complete their contract and find a passage home often brought back with them modest but useful sums of money.

The Palla or Paraiah migrant on his return invariably sought to buy land and several of them established themselves as small time farmers in Madurai, South Arcot and Chinglepet. Land was available aplenty in the market, what with non-cultivating elites migrating to towns and leaving behind not only cultivable tracts, but also forest and waste land to which claims of ownership could be and were advanced. Pallas and Paraiahs, though small players in the land market, nevertheless worked it to secure ownership titles for themselves, often braving prejudiced and treacherous tahsildars, corrupt revenue officers and scheming mirasidars (Baker: 182-83). The actual number of cultivating outcaste men who purchased land and of those who made a success of their subversive claims was, in all probability, very small but the impact of these success stories was considerable. It must be noted here that a few adi dravida families also acquired modest fortunes in trade and, on their return to India, like Madurai Pillay and others, assumed the role of philanthropists and leaders of their communities.

Migration helped raise Palla and Paraiah fortunes in other ways as well. As large numbers of men and women left their homes and their landlords' fields to seek their fortunes elsewhere, those left behind managed to command a higher price for their labour. While this was not a substantially higher claim, the fact that there had emerged a market in labour helped workers negotiate better service and work conditions for themselves (ibid: 180-81).

Perhaps what proved to a particularly enabling factor in the transformation of Paraiah and, more generally, adi dravida fortunes was the work of Protestant missionaries. By the mid-nineteenth century Protestant missions in the Tamil country had evolved a consensus on their future attitude and approach to evangelization and the problem of caste. In the past, differences had existed amongst the various Protestant denominations as to the desirability or otherwise of interfering with the institution of caste. Was caste to be considered a civic matter, representing a functional ordering of society and, therefore, religiously 'neutral', or was it be considered an abominable practice of distinctions amongst peoples who were, essentially, equal in the eyes of Christ? By refusing to assent to the persistence of caste divisions within the church, missionaries would run the risk of incurring the displeasure of upper caste converts. On the other hand, the principle of caste was clearly un-Christian and by allowing the retention of caste distinctions and privileges within the church, missionaries would have to suffer a loss of good faith and sincerity (Manickam 1988: 47-53). Ultimately, Christian faith and doctrine prevailed over the imperative to convert and by 1850 all Protestant missions with the exception of the Leipzig mission in South India were in agreement that 'caste was a great evil that must be ruthlessly uprooted from the Christian Church in India' (ibid: 53).

For the adi dravidas, the church and its zealots were attractive for a complex of material and spiritual reasons. The church recognized that the adi dravidas' physical distress often led him to the pastor's doorstep. William Goudie, who carried out evangelical work in Chinglepet, noted that 'almsgiving cannot be used as a means of winning converts. Missionaries should as a general rule have nothing to do... with those who expected missionaries to pay their debts or lend them money or buy them bullocks and land' (Houghton 1983: 115). Yet, Goudie was also conscious of the fact that physical misery could not be wholly ignored and observed 'No one has a right to call himself a Christian whose eyes and ears are closed to the common physical hardships of those around him'. The church found itself involved with famine relief work through the second half of the nineteenth century and, despite adverse criticism from sections of the caste Hindu population, persisted in its efforts (ibid: 114-15).

It is certain the adi dravida convert acquired self-respect and pride in the course of his sojourn in the church even if, at times, he considered the latter a mere material benefactor. Christianity regarded him first and foremost as a 'brother in Christ' and as the Bishop of Madras noted, the effects of a religion which 'treats him [the adi dravida] as a man, tells him of the true dignity of his human nature... and proclaims to him that he in common with the Englishman and the Brahmin is a son of God and an inheritor of the Kingdom of Heaven' cannot be underestimated (ibid: 101). The fact that the religion constituted the adi dravida as one who could partake of the flesh and blood of Christ with others was of immense significance to one who, for centuries now, had been considered unclean and polluting.

Missionary activity in tandem with the good intentions of conscientious and sympathetic civil servants attempted to resolve what was being increasingly characterized as 'the Paraiah question'. Officials like Tremenheere, the collector of Chinglepet, and missionaries like A. Andrew and William Goudie, unlike their utilitarian and evangelical counterparts in England who addressed the issue of slavery from a purely moral and religious angle, sought to understand the linkages between the mirasi (and non-mirasi) systems of landholding and the persistence of agrestic servitude. They even proposed that the government assign waste land to Paraiahs (ibid: 99-112). When the Secretary of State remarked that 'there was no bar in law or practice to low caste people obtaining and cultivating waste lands on the same terms as high caste people', Tremenheere's reply was sharp in its rebuke:

> It is doubtful what meaning should be attached to the word 'practice'...[the Paraiah] can apply for it [land] but has to run the gauntlet of first the mirasidars and secondly the non-mirasi pattadars both of which classes abhor the thought of his acquiring land (Manickam: 74-75).

Tremenheere also pointed at the collusive links between these classes and the bureaucracy:

> The influence of these classes with the official world can hardly be exaggerated. Every office from the highest to the lowest is stocked with their representatives and if there is a proposal affecting their interests...they can bring a score of influences to bear upon in its course from inception to execution (ibid: 76).

Besides these obstacles that Paraiahs had to overcome there were any number of instances of the landed classes, invariably though not exclusively brahmin, foisting false cases on Paraiahs in village courts;

encroaching on waste land adjacent to the paracheri so as to impound the Paraiah's cattle that strayed into these lands or to obstruct pathways to temples and burial grounds; manipulating government records in order fraudulently to enter mirasi names against the paracheri; pulling down huts and destroying the crops raised in the kitchen gardens of the adi dravidas; denying occupational rights in subtenancies Paraiahs had conventionally held; cutting off flow of water to Paraiah fields (BAWS: vol 2, 553). That such bullying tactics continued till the twenties could be evidenced from the various resolutions passed in the conferences of the Depressed Classes Associations, Adi Dravida Mahajana Sabha and in the petitions submitted by them to the government seeking redressal.

Tremenheere and missionaries like Goudie raised the Paraiah question in London as well and succeeded in eventually attracting the attention of the British Parliament. But even as the Government of India issued two orders notifying measures to improve the lives of adi dravidas, the Board of Revenue refused to accept Tremenheere's report regarding the existence of slavery. The Board noted that 'there was no proof of the slavery alleged to exist...Although slavery is not recognised, every free man has the right to enter into a contract for the disposal of his labour and those of the members of his family, dependant on him for support and if he is cajoled into a contract of slavery it is, ipso facto, null and void and voidable at his own pleasure.' Justifying the existing bondage, the Board concluded 'the only remedy if such cases exist is the spread of education' (Houghton: 109-10).

The government, however, had not been particularly concerned in this regard either, since most of its energies were expended on furthering higher education. The 1882 Education Commission reiterated the importance of primary education and recommended the transfer of all government private schools to the control of municipalities and local bodies. While this did lead to a marked improvement in primary schooling it did not serve the cause of adi dravida education very well. The schooling of adi dravidas had been almost wholly undertaken by missionaries. Missionaries had been active in educational tasks since the early days of evangelical work in South India. When in the 1870s, there occurred mass conversions to Christianity, schools were opened up for the converts, most of whom were Shanars and adi dravidas, and their children. Subsequently some of these schools had to be closed down for lack of qualified teachers. If missionaries were to avail of the 'salary-grant system' which supplied them with funds from the government for defraying teachers' salaries, then they had to appoint qualified teachers. But these latter, as a rule, were reluctant to teach in adi dravida schools and mission schools often had to do with teachers who, in some instances, did not possess a 'teacher certificate'. Another major difficulty faced by mission-run schools arose from the indifference of subordinate officers in the education bureaucracy.

The 1882 Education Commission had brought mission schools under the scrutiny of the government and while this did enable these schools to avail of government grants it also laid them open to government intervention. As Iyothee Thass and others pointed out, government officials at the lower levels were unwilling to enter the paracheris of adi dravidas to inspect their schools. The grants-in-aid system stipulated that the grant paid to a private school would be in proportion to the number of students who passed; which, in turn, depended a great deal on the goodwill of the school inspector. These inspectors, who were mostly brahmins, were hostile to mission-run schools on two counts: that they were run by missionaries and that they catered to adi dravida needs.

Yet, in spite of these problems, mission schools helped many an adi dravida acquire some learning, equipped them to compete on more favourable terms—with brahmins—for jobs in the services and enhanced their claims for a more equal political participation. The government, for its part, attempted to address the problem of education with a greater degree of seriousness in the face of the sustained campaign by missionaries for the cause of adi dravida liberty and education. Government Order 68 issued in February 1893 announced a series of concessions for adi dravida students and while these were of limited use, given the vagaries in government policy with respect to primary education as a whole, they signified the triumph of missionary will and work with respect to the schooling of the adi dravida (Manickam: 80-102).

It must be mentioned here that not all adi dravidas were euphoric with the conduct and relevance of missionary work. Iyothee Thass, for instance, was ever watchful of the activities of Catholic priests and addressed a series of missives to the Catholic clergy in Madras in which he warned against the attractions and power of caste. Iyothee

Thass also urged missionaries to interpret the spirit of the Word of God and not its letter (*Tamizhan* 16, 23.12.08; 13, 27.1.09).

Adi dravidas were not the only subaltern group whose lives were significantly transformed due to colonial rule. Imperial trade implicated traditional mercantile groups such as the Komatis as well as the near-untouchable Shanars in an economic process that generated considerable material gain for the English as well as their local agents.

Shanars, originally a caste of tree climbers, well-diggers and itinerant agriculturists who lived and moved in the sandy palmyra-infested regions of southern Madras and in parts of the Travancore state, came into their own in the nineteenth century. During this time several of them moved northwards, settling on the fringes of wet lands adjacent to the Tamarabarani basin where they came to advance and retain subversive claims against their Vellala landlords. Others migrated outwards to the plantations in Malabar and Ceylon while those who had followed the route of the cotton trade northwards and beyond came to own and maintain trade entrepots along the routes of the cotton belt. Eventually they came to wield almost complete control over the movement of cotton in Madras. While mercantile Shanars became a very powerful and contentious status group their brethren in the South did not witness as rapid a rise in their fortunes. What they did witness was the work wrought by Christian missionaries which, as in the case of adi dravidas, transformed their lives, perceptions of the self and attitudes towards other castes.

While uptown mercantile Shanars sought and won symbolic honours, appropriated forbidden rights—such as the wearing of the sacred thread, the sporting of a tuft, entering temples—and came to proclaim a proud corporate identity, southern Shanars, from whom the former sought to distance themselves, were caught up in a different sort of conflict over identity. While Christianity marked Shanars, along with others, as being equal and worthy as any other in the eyes of Christ, missionary polemics recognized and inscribed a distance within Christianity between the preacher-saviour and his potential convert, the to-be-saved heathen. On the one hand, missionaries would despair at the inequities of caste and its fundamental inhumanity. On the other hand, as Bishop Caldwell's descriptions of Shanars indicate, missionaries were themselves given to describing the heathen in unflattering terms that barely concealed their distaste for the object of their conversion work. The heathen, the Shanars, in this regard, were none too happy with missionary ambivalence. Thus we find a section of Shanar converts, in the late nineteenth century, confounding missionary polemics with their own; whereby missionary knowledge with respect to the Shanars' lowly origins and status was stood on its head and transmuted into a highly flattering history of Shanars (Hardgrave 1969; Ludden 1985: 191-96).

Not all subaltern castes experienced such a break in consciousness or such a disruption in their modes of work and existence. But all non-brahmin castes, high or low, suffered disjunctions of various sorts: in their economic status, social standing and cultural consciousness. For castes such as the mercantile Chettiars and the agriculturist Vellalas, the British presence constituted a norm of power and authority against which rank and status amongst local elites could be measured and reconstituted. The brahmin, by his early association with the British had, inadvertently, de-sacralized himself in the eyes of local society, and locally dominant groups, whose relationship with the brahmins was at best competitive, and at worst, underwritten by a kind of resentment, now discovered a means to rebuke and thereby reject the latter's claims to exclusivity. Theagoraya Chetty could thus remark ironically:

> Thanks to the British government...our brahmin friends have given up their pious occupations and turned to worldliness. The great veneration in which the people held them for their piety, learning and austerity of life is dying out, the great disillusionment has begun and this is the most opportune moment for the social reformer to knock down all barriers of caste and uplift the depressed classes (Varadarajulu Naidu: vol 2, 140).

For Vellalas, the brahmin now seemed a veritable outsider. His proclaimed pride in being Aryan made it easy for Vellala elites, many of whom were famed for their Tamil learning, to reject the brahminical element in Tamil culture and civilization. For mercantile communities, such as the Komatis, who had all along built choultries and fed brahmin priests and travellers, the British obsession with classifying castes and communities along a varna axis proved immensely useful. While remaining conservative in most respects—for instance, their caste organization, the Arya Vaishya Mahasabha, opposed the PPM Bill and its members were even reluctant to advance the cause of female education—Komati publicists nevertheless demonstrated their will to power in local society. The Arya Vaishya Mahasabha formed in 1906 thus petitioned the government to classify Komatis as vaishyas and battled with brahmin pundits for their rights to a dwija status (Washbrook 1975).

Artisan castes such as the Kammalas also sought to enhance their ritual rank using the good offices of the Census Commissioner; in fact a whole host of communities including the labouring Vanniars and untouchable Pallas demanded a higher varna ranking. The former desired to be referred to as 'Vanniakula Kshatriyas' and the latter claimed descent from an exalted ancestor and asked to be called 'Devendrakula Vellalas'(ibid).

Other locally dominant groups which benefited directly from the colonial presence, that is, which reaped to advantage the uses of colonial rule were the Vellala Gounders and Kamma Naidus of the Kongu country. Their economic powers were enhanced and re-affirmed, with the cultivation of cash crops in the region and due to the cotton trade. Both communities attained political prominence beyond the locality as several elites amongst them threw in their lot with nationalist politics or with the Justice party (Baker: 200-14; 255).

In almost all non-brahmin communities there emerged new men of learning, who, as teachers, lawyers or as publicists made available to their respective constituencies a discourse of rights with which caste ranking could be questioned, privileges of higher castes criticized and a corporate caste identity established. Thus supralocal sodalities emerged, an imagined fraternity of disparate subcastes was forged. Since caste solidarity was largely a constructed affair, responsive to the pressure of local society, yet broad-based and evocative in its appeal, it remained flexible rather than a rigid marking of identity. Castes could thus simultaneously view themselves as particular, as constituting, say, a subcaste, or as larger blocks which would function as the constituent units of a larger community. When Non-Brahminism as political ideology came to be propounded, different and often antagonistic castes found it appealing since the basis for horizontal comradeship had already been established. (Also nearly 25 years of nationalist propaganda had created the possibilities for trans-caste interaction and banding together. It must be pointed out though the Madras Congress remained largely brahmin for the first twenty years or so of its existence and only after the Swadeshi agitations got under way did the nationalist message prove attractive to non-brahmins.)

It is clear that with the coming of the British, or more specifically, the onset of colonialism, the political economy of agriculture and trade which, until then, had interlocked and functioned in tandem with the moral economy of the caste order suffered a dislocation. Political and economic relationships and caste hierarchies were now pushed into patterns of uneasy alignment. While caste continued to remain a significant marker of identity, it was also being simultaneously absorbed into a new discursive space. Created largely out of the findings of colonial adminstrator-historians and their brahmin informants, this new discourse of caste rendered it a contested category in a very specific sense. Caste now came to mark not merely high or low, but levels of oppression and subordination, wealth and deprivation, learning and forced ignorance. Along with caste, the category of work was also subject to semantic changes. Work was now construed as labour and certain castes were deemed to be productive and others parasitic. While this did not transform the conditions of labour or the nature of the labourer's existence, it created a new vocabulary of work and worth which non-brahmin and adi dravida publicists put to good use. In the shaking up of the moral order of caste and the order of production, and, in the interstices of a disaligned economy and society, there emerged new modes of perception, new structures of feeling and new imaginings of the self.

CHAPTER 3

Narratives of Identity

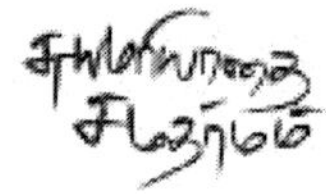

THE EXAMPLE OF THE CASTE DIFFERENCE

A tract titled *The Example of the Caste Difference* by M. Masilamani published by the Sri Siddhartha Puthagasalai in Kolar was warmly recommended as a worthy and useful anti-caste work by E. V. Ramasamy Periyar in his journal *Kudi Arasu* (KA 3.3.35). Obviously re-issued that year, the tract as its contents indicate, was written in the last years of the nineteenth century. Sri Siddhartha Puthagasalai published many such tracts in the thirties: on the condition of the Paraiahs, their forgotten history, their lost Buddhist faith, on the arrival of Aryan impostors and their various intrigues which gained them power over local Paraiah society and culture, and on ancient Tamil texts whose Buddhist origins had been successfully erased through time and due to the deliberate distortions in interpretation by brahmin scholars of a later generation. Most of these tracts were composed in the early years of our century and the concerns they expressed were those of a group of men, including Masilamani, who felt the need to interrogate and re-write history, especially the history of the Paraiahs and other despised castes.

Masilamani also wrote regularly for *Tamizhan* and, while not a Paraiah by birth, was a Buddhist by conviction. His faith obviously compelled him to take the part of the so-called untouchables. His association with Iyothee Thass proved to be an extremely fruitful one and, taken together, their various writings comprise an extraordinary corpus: part history, part polemic, they represent a 'Buddhist' vision of the past; one that anticipated, in many ways, the historiographical writings of Dr. Ambedkar. More important, they pre-figured and, to an extent, overlapped with an emergent Dravidianism which, as we shall soon show, provoked a wholly new historiographical tradition into existence. Directed against the Aryanist version of history, this latter came to articulate a historical sensibility that was assertive in its Tamilness and scornful of what it considered the Aryan element in India's culture.

The neo-Buddhist tracts of Masilamani, Iyothee Thass, Narayanasami Pillay, Periyasami Pulavar and others who wrote regularly for *Tamizhán* were concerned chiefly with the problem of Paraiah and, to an extent, non-brahmin identity and history. This search for a history which seemed discontinuous, elusive and ever-mysterious, produced serious reflections on the nature of caste society, the persistence of inequality and the treacherous nature of language which could lie, deceive and distort received meaning.

The Example of the Caste Difference was concerned with the inconsistencies and contradictions which sustained and informed a brahminical view of caste. This remarkable text contained several intertwined themes: the coming of the Aryans and the decline of the Buddhist way of life; the rise to dominance of an Arya-brahmin clergy; the birth of the fourfold varna divisions; the ideal of purity and the strictures against pollution and finally the 'caste' of women. Aryans and brahmins, argued Masilamani, often using these terms interchangeably, were invaders from afar who intruded and later imposed themselves on a civilization of great antiquity. This ancient civilization was found throughout the subcontinent at one time. It eschewed violence, was pacific in character, forbade the taking of alcohol and adhered to the creed preached by the Buddha. Architecture, metal work and sculpture were much advanced in those times. Subsequently, these arts (and artisans) were appropriated by Aryan brahmins who, claimed Masilamani, never had a good word to say about anybody's faith and culture but their own. Though this pre-Aryan civilizational impulse more or less disappeared, as a consequence of the Aryan interregnum, its creations had survived, albeit, in symbolic form. For instance, the lingam and the orthography of temple inscriptions were clearly the marks of an earlier culture which had since been supplanted and re-defined.

Masilamani pointed out that, no sooner had the Aryan brahmins established their dominance, by conspiring against the pre-Aryan kshatriyas and deceiving them, they came to erase the history of the conquered. They wrote their own histories in the form of implausible and fanciful tales and inscribed themselves into these texts of their own creation: so that all history seemed to exist only to gratify and confirm them in their dominance. Masilamani also wrote of how brahmins came to reign supreme. Firstly, they cheated and coopted the rulers of the land and, secondly, they made themselves indispensable not only as ministers and advisers at court, but as self-ordained prophets, soothsayers, medicine men and law givers. Further, they made sure that the humane rulers of pre-Aryan times such as Hiranya and Ravana were remembered, not as the good and selfless kings that they were, but as anti-brahminical fiends. Masilamani recalled, in this context, the tale of Parasurama and noted that his triumph over kshatriyas signified the symbolic victory of the Aryan-brahmins over the native rulers, some of whom had valiantly resisted the intruders.

The brahmin, however, did not triumph by force and guile alone. He created new forms of social organization and a new culture of the self which proved attractive and persuasive in the long run to even native rulers and their minions. The fourfold division of castes thus came to be in place and strict ordinances, which specified conduct and labour for various castes and which set the norms of social interaction between discrete caste groups, came to be instituted. All castes were, of course, to defer to the brahmin and work to fulfil his needs and consider such a task the highest virtue they could practise. Thus vaishyas and shudras were enjoined to hand over their best grains to the brahmins and make do with coarser grains for themselves. The brahmin's diet was deemed superior while that of the other castes was considered an index and source of their always already polluted status.

Masilamani found the fourfold division of castes unjust and arbitrary. He observed that elsewhere in the world a division of labour, even where it exists, does not necessarily congeal into a stratified and rigid system of social organization and interaction. Yet this system was contradictory and inconsistent in its workings. Masilamani pointed out that men like Vyasa and Viswamitra, revered as the greatest of sages, were not born into brahminhood but had attained it through their deeds. On the other hand, sages born into brahminhood, like Vamadeva had flouted brahminical norms (he ate the carcass of a dog). If, therefore, non-brahmins could grow into brahminhood through good deeds, would brahmins, then, grow out of brahminhood through their transgressions?

Masilamani tested the creed of brahmin purity and difference by systematically interrogating the so-called brahminical virtues. He observed that brahmins claimed they were pacific in nature, and abhorred injury to any living creature and did not eat meat. But, yet, they did not refrain from subduing and chastening animals for domestic use. Brahmins would argue they attained brahminhood through a rite of passage deemed essential for them, the *upanayanam* ceremony, where the brahmin boy was invested with the sacred thread. The sacred thread, rather the investiture of it, was considered an act which facilitated their passage from shudrahood to brahmin status. Masilamani likened this passage into superiority to a grafting operation, wherein part of a plant is grafted onto another, so that it would bear better and more luscious fruit. But in the case of the sacred thread, the graft obviously did not work at all times, for it did not enable castes such as the Kammalas, the Chettys and Valluvans, all of whom sported such a thread, to attain brahminhood.

Masilamani was also skeptical of the brahmin's conventional defence of his superior status. Brahmins often claimed they were different and superior on account of their scriptural learning, their dietary habits, their Aryan origins, their obviously exceptional conduct and, of course, on account of their birth—from the forehead of the creator himself. Masilamani queried these claims and showed them to be false and inconsistent in their assumptions. As far as the brahmin's sacral learning was concerned, there could be nothing unusual about it, given present circumstances, when not only Paraiahs, but also the alien white men, had access to and, in many instances, were well-versed in the sacred texts of Hinduism. Secondly, the brahmins' claim that their diet was pure and non-polluting very conveniently overlooked the origins of such a diet. The food the brahmin ate was originally grown, processed and cleaned by unclean shudras and Paraiahs. Thirdly, as far as racial superiority was concerned, the brahmins of South India, at least, were as dark-skinned as the shudras and panchamas. Fourthly, brahmin conduct was neither exceptional nor particularly different from that exhibited by other men. Brahmins were not different from others in respect of their mortal and human needs. They were subject to the same fears, expectations and travails of the flesh and to the universal process of birth, decay and death as any other mortal creature. Besides, brahmins were known for their practice of guile and deception and their conduct could not really be considered exemplary.

Masilamani was also scathingly critical of the argument that a 'sacred birth' was the basis of the brahmin's superior status. He wondered if the birth of a brahmin child was any less painful and traumatic to its mother, on account of the child being a sacred creature. If, indeed, brahmins were sacred, then why was the brahmin widow, in custom and practice, made to endure untold suffering? Did brahmin women suffer less, being brahmin? Were they spared all those tribulations their sex was routinely subjected to?

Having thus demolished brahmin claims to a superior status, Masilamani went on to examine the dynamics of the purity-pollution idea. Brahmins, he remarked, were not averse to standing with shudras and panchamas at a ticket counter in a railway station, but would protest sharing a railway coach with them. They would not mind working in a hospital run by missionaries where they had to work with and even minister to Paraiahs, but outside the hospital premises they would take offence if a Paraiah so much as dared to offer them a glass of water. Not only did such practices of a flexible orthodoxy seem hypocritical to Masilamani but also extremely arbitrary. An object was deemed pure or otherwise solely on the basis of the brahmins' felt needs and brahmins 'fixed' the quantum of purity that was thought to reside in any object. Thus a mud pot was seen as being rendered unclean by the mere glance of a shudra and had to be broken. But copper and silver vessels were not discarded thus, in the wake of a polluting glance—the argument being that objects of pure metal did not secrete pollution as objects of baser matter did! In this scheme of things, gold and its contemporary form, currency, were considered pure and undefiled.

Masilamani found the effects of caste on women's lives particularly cruel and unjust. He observed the logic of Brahminism ordained even brahmin women to be shudras until such time as they were given away in marriage and the marriage was consummated. Just as how wearing the sacred thread was supposed to produce a brahminization of the male soul, so was consummation of marriage deemed the only means through which a woman may lose her shudrahood and become a brahmin. But, women were not considered as consistently pure as brahmin men. Since they menstruated, they were defiled at least four days in a month. Besides, the death of a husband effected a loss of brahminhood and the loss therefore required to be redeemed or at least mourned by mortificatory acts, such as the shaving of one's head. Masilamani was acutely sensitive to the sexual politics of Brahminism and wrote movingly of the wretched existence of the upper caste Hindu widow. He saw the subordination of women and the shudras and the panchamas as the real basis of brahmin power and noted that in former times, women were free to even choose their husbands, a practice that the Aryan-brahmins had distorted to their own advantage.

These various themes figured often in Masilamani's contributions to *Tamizhan* as well, where he argued, on different occasions, that the Tamils—Paraiahs and shudras—were the original inhabitants of Southern India who had since been downgraded in their status and learning. This argument was, of course, to remain a persistent concern with Iyothee Thass and one he would seek to illustrate with the help of Tamil literary and scriptural texts.

THE WRITINGS OF IYOTHEE THASS

Iyothee Thass' writings on Paraiah history and identity were woven around two major themes: historical and adumbrated in texts such as *Indirar Desa Charithram* (History of Indirar Desh [as the subcontinent was known in earlier times]) (Thass 1957). Here, the fall of Buddhism and the rise of Brahminism are treated as simultaneous events and the text sets about establishing the links between the two. The second theme had to do with the nature of the 'fall' suffered by the former Buddhists. Through a detailed re-reading of various Tamil sacral (and literary) texts, Iyothee Thass sought to demonstrate how the victory of Brahminism in the subcontinent signified a semiotic conquest, an achieved mastery over language and meaning. In subsequent centuries, this victory was perpetrated and consolidated through the use, alternately, of guile and force. Iyothee Thass also wrote at length on Buddhism: the life of the Buddha, his teachings, the dialogues he had with his disciples and on the principles of faith and action which he upheld. A regular column, 'Poorva Tamizh Olli' was devoted to this purpose in *Tamizhan*. Anecdotal and philosophical in tone and content, these various articles were subsequently collected together and published as a tract in 1912.

The Decline of the Paraiah Caste

The tracts, *Indirar Desa Charithram, Yathartha Brahmana Vedanta Vivaram* and *Vesha Brahmana Vedanta Vivaram* (Thass 1932) address the question of Paraiah insubordination directly. Like Masilamani, Iyothee Thass argued that the Paraiahs were, in fact, the original Tamils whose religion was Buddhism. Paraiahs were degraded and their religion systematically destroyed when Aryan invaders from the north (Iyothee Thass refers to them as Arya *mlechchas*) imposed their rule and culture on these original Tamils. Subsequently, historical development in the Tamil country, and the subcontinent as a whole, followed a pattern in which was visible the steady and gradual decline of Buddhism and the way of life it enjoined and their substitution, through the use of deception and cunning, by brahminical Hinduism. Aryan mlechchas now arrogated to themselves the power of a class of wise men who, in Buddhist society, had been the traditional custodians of ethical norms and values. These wise men had renounced the world and its joys and had dedicated themselves to the education of their people in morality and ethics. These *yathartha* (real) brahmins were of the Buddhist faith, argued Iyothee Thass, and were the original and authentic gurus whose fame, learning and wisdom were (mis) appropriated by Aryan mlechchas or Persians. These latter were thus veritable false prophets or, as Iyothee Thass described them, they were *vesha* brahmins.

In *Indirar Desa Charithram* Iyothee Thass declared that in the past, the subcontinent was known as Indirar Desam or the land of Indirar. Indirar was none other than the Buddha who had managed to control his five senses (*indiriyams*) successfully. The term 'India', thus, was but a transmuted form of the word 'Varatha', one of the names by which the Buddha is known. Iyothee Thass held that it was the vesha brahmins who had coined the word 'Hindu' and made it acceptable to even Mohammedans and Europeans, ensuring thereby its permanence as a term of reference.

How did the vesha brahmins succeed in their endeavours? Iyothee Thass contended that they practised a fine art of deception and cunning on the natives of Indirar Desam and, having succeeded in their initial attempts to acquire power and glory, sought to perpetrate the latter through falsifying texts, re-writing them in some instances and by Hinduizing Buddhist works.

> In order to acquire those honours and respect which accrued only to our spiritual teachers [the yathartha brahmanas] they [the vesha brahmanas] approached the illiterate chieftains' and citizens of Indirar Desam and claimed falsely that they were also arhats [enlightened men]. They also sent their women to the kings, distracted them into debauchery and thus corrupted them. They did all they could to pass themselves off as yathartha brahmanas, worthy of worship by all. Those who fell prey to the sophistry of the vesha brahmanas became Hindus. Those who rejected them and were degraded were the Buddhists, who came to be known, from then on, as Paraiahs (Thass 1957, 2nd ed).

Iyothee Thass insisted that the erasure of the Buddhist origins of Indian civilization and the Buddhist character of Indian culture by the vesha brahmins proved to be so successful that no one ever interrogated their seemingly self-evident claims regarding the long lost antiquity of Hindu culture and civilization and its spiritual legacies. For instance, the brahmins of his time were given to praising the glories of 'Vedic culture' and the genius of 'Indian' civilization. But what were these but the constructions of Western historians and scholars who were all too eager to accept the claims and arguments of modern vesha brahmins?

Iyothee Thass noted that in the past there existed no recognizable 'Hindu' scriptural corpus. Neither Shankara nor Ramanuja or Madhavacharya instituted such attempts as would bring the four Vedas into a cohesive and unified text. If the vesha brahmins of the present day had created one, this could only be taken to be a further instance of their habitual cunning. When the British came to India the (vesha) brahmins declared themselves to be the highest caste; whereupon the English asked to see their religious texts. The brahmins then sought to put together a religious book of the Hindus from a variety of textual sources that espoused mutually contradictory ideas. After all, noted Iyothee Thass, for the past several hundreds of years, the vesha brahmins had worked to collapse the distinction between the Buddhist faith and their own. For had they not succeeded in modifying and adopting as their own the Upanishads that were originally Buddhist creations? Therefore, when the English demanded to see the sacred books of their subjects, their definitive religious text,

> The vesha brahmans appropriated some of the Buddhist historical and moral texts and added to these the incomplete translations of the Vedic myths done by the Zoroastrian, Dara Shikoh. These were then presented to Colonel Bolier, Sir Robert Chambers, General Martin, Sir William Jones and Colebrook who, in turn, translated these manuscripts and brought them together into a single large work, which, when published, became a book that could be claimed by the Hindus as their Veda (ibid).

Iyothee Thass was critical of not only the vesha brahmins' capacity for producing a bewildering array of mismatched texts but also of Max Mueller's attempt to conflate Buddhist texts with their creations and of his granting precedence to the evidence and arguments contained in the latter:

> Max Mueller has failed to situate and judge the language that existed in the Buddha's time, has failed to place in its context his message and has not distinguished the languages that were refined by the Buddha and the Upanishads of the Buddhist sangams. Thus he does not know which came first—the Upanishads which reached his hands or the Buddha Damma. He has expressed opinions that are baseless. Are we to devalue the histories and evidences contained in copper plates and inscriptions on the basis of one man's opinion? Certainly not! (ibid)

Iyothee Thass' critical strategies reveal him to be working on several issues simultaneously. On the one hand, he reinterpreted the historical defeat of Buddhism in India at the hands of brahminical Hinduism to signify the corruption of an ethical and spiritual tradition that was inherently egalitarian and rational. On the other hand, he located this fact of corruption in the systematic marginalization and degradation of a section of society, which, ostensibly, refused to be lured by this new faith: that is, he identified the downfall of the Paraiahs with the triumph of Brahminism and the caste order. The brahminical victory was thus not merely a political act with far-reaching social implications. For him, as we have remarked before, it represented a semiotic conquest as well.

The Erasure of Paraiah Memory

In a series of remarkable tracts, Iyothee Thass established the details of this semiotic conquest. He analysed puranic and literary texts to demonstrate the various hermeneutic and textual tactics utilized by the vesha brahmins to reiterate the fact of Paraiah lowness. His explanation of a common Tamil religious and cultural practice, the worshipping of the mother goddess, Ambigai, in her various forms in the Tamil month of Aadi (15 July-15 August) merits close attention for the insight it allows us into what he distinguishes as a pre-brahminic practice.

In a tract titled, *The Significance of Meditating on Ambigai Amman in the Month of Aadi* (Thass 1929, 4th ed), Iyothee Thass narrated the tale of the Princess Ambigai of Puna Nadu who, at an early age, desired to join and serve in the Buddha Sangam; whereupon her father attempted to dissuade her on the grounds that she was neither a child nor an old woman, whose youth lay in her past but a young girl who had just attained puberty. As such she could not be admitted into the holy order. But she insisted her father find a way out of this conundrum. Thereafter, her father summoned her maternal uncle and requested him to tie the sacred yellow thread around her neck so that she would be 'ritually' married and, hence, eligible for the rite of renunciation.

Ambigai thus entered the ranks of the *bhikinis* and, in the course of time, became famous for her powers of healing. Not only did she administer herbs and potents, but enjoined and demanded of the sickly and the ill, that they be pure of heart, for otherwise diseases would abound and nature cease to be her giving bountiful self. Ambigai's presence attracted princes and commoners alike, who came to hear her speak, meditate and heal under the neem tree. Gradually, she came to be referred by various names, each of which reflected a particular attribute she possessed. To some, she was Avvai, the all-knowing; to others, she was Pachaiamman, the ever-youthful or Vadivudaiamman, of the blessed presence. She came to be associated and worshipped at the Buddha vihara at Nagapattinam and came to be called Verkanni in those parts. It was to keep her memory and remember her good deeds that the mother goddess (Amman) festival, came to be celebrated in the month of Aadi: then, men and women would observe fasts, refrain from acts of lust and anger, perform penances of various sorts and finally commemorate her glory by ritual bathing and, most important, by feeding the poor.

But this entirely Tamil ritual underwent several transformations with the coming of the vesha brahmin intruders. The vihara at Nagapattinam was all but destroyed (as was the Buddhist temple at Sri Rangam), the Buddhists were re-named Paraiahs and the beautiful Aadi ritual was distorted to represent a ritual for the appeasement of an angry goddess who demanded the sacrifice of animals at her altar. The Verkanni cult underwent another mutation with the coming of the Portuguese, who instituted a temple to Mary, mother of God in the precincts of the old Amman shrine. Elsewhere, the meaning of the Amman ritual acquired other resonances and was overlaid with other significations. The tale of the *patini* (chaste) Kannagi, who willed the city of Madurai to destruction through fire and caused the death of a 1000 goldsmiths because her husband was wrongfully accused of stealing the queen of Madurai's anklet, got mixed up with the memory and tales of Ambigai. This was because Kannagi's wrath and the destruction of the city which followed it were also remembered and commemorated—through the slaying of animals—in the month of Aadi. The patini Kannagi thus merged with one of the many forms (and names) through which Ambigai was known amongst her worshippers. In the course of time, Ambigai's antiquity, and the original grace which was invested in the rituals conducted in her memory, were all forgotten and in some instances displaced onto latter-day figures such as Kannagi.

Iyothee Thass clarified in his tract that the real Ambigai was neither the Kannagi of epic fame nor the angry goddess of the vesha brahmins. She was a benign local divinity, a *grama* (village) *devata* and a *kula* (clan) devata, a healer and guardian of her people who helped her devotees cleanse themselves of their physical and spiritual ills.

In another thought-provoking tract, *The Inquiry of the Skull*

Bearer's Story (Thass 1932, 3rd ed), Iyothee Thass demonstrated the Hinduizing of yet another Buddhist event. Quoting from ancient and medieval literary texts, he argued that present-day Mylapore in Madras was once the home of the Valluvans (Chakyars) who were Buddhists. The existing Saivite mutt in Mylapore was also once the abode of the Valluvans and had contained a reclining statue (the Buddha is sometimes portrayed in this manner). The Sivarathri festival currently celebrated in the mutt and in the temple at Mylapore (as at all Saivite places of worship) was originally meant to consecrate the day of Siddhartha's renunciation of his princely life and his leaving home, alms-bowl in hand. The Tamil word for the alms bowl, noted Iyothee Thass, is *karabol*, which Saivites at a later date twisted to mean *kabalam* or skull. Thus Karaboleeswaran (Lord with the alms-bowl in his hand) became Kabaleeswaran (Lord with skull in his hand). Along with this change of name, a new story came to be narrated as well. The vesha brahmins now conceived of the myth of Siva who, at the instigation of his consort, Parvathi, removed one of the five heads of Brahma. The detached head, it was said, got stuck onto Siva's palm and he came to be known as Kabaleeswaran. There existed more than one version of this tale for, on another ocassion and in a different context, the vesha brahmins insisted that the skull that got stuck onto Siva's hand was once the head of Brahma who was beheaded for having dared to have had sexual intecourse with his own daughter.

To Iyothee Thass, these myths were proof enough of the ingrained folly and falsehood of the religions practised by the vesha brahmins. More important, these myths served to identify, by contrast, the significance attributed to the alms bowl in the Lord's hand in Buddhism. Whereas Buddhism had sought to remember a noble and rational deed through the image of the Buddha with an alms bowl in his hand, brahminical Hinduism only served to vulgarize and erase the immense importance of the Buddha's message. Now, Sivarathri was celebrated by the faithful by going to the cremation grounds the morning after keeping vigil for Siva the previous night, and the Buddha's day of renunciation was all but forgotten.

It is significant that Iyothee Thass' re-definition of local festivals, rather his 're-discovery' of their Buddhist origins, endowed these events with a social and ethical resonance. Sivarathri, thus, becomes a memory of the Great Renunciation; a reminder of the Buddha's teachings regarding desire, suffering and salvation. The Amman festival becomes an occasion for self-purification, when men and women sought to remember and practise the art of self-healing, as enjoined by the bhikini healer of antique memory.

Iyothee Thass' most felicitous re-reading of texts and history had to do with a text that has remained the most contested, desired and revered of all ancient and modern Tamil works. The *Thirukural*, that compendium of knowledge, morality, political wisdom and romantic love and social conduct, to this day, has remained a sort of touchstone of 'Tamilness', an honoured instance of the civilization and cultural achievements of the Tamils. Iyothee Thass considered this text as Buddhist in inspiration and observed that its author was a Buddhist by faith. He argued that the text was originally known as *thiri-kural* (thiri = three) and was the first Buddhist text in a Dravidian language. The Kural in its content adhered to the three *pitakas* of the Buddha's teachings and was, hence, known as the *Thirikural* (Thass 1950, 4th ed).

It was because the *Thirikural* was such an important text, and an obviously Buddhist one, that several myths had grown around it and its author. Thiruvalluvar's parentage had evoked a lot of interest amongst scholars and as Iyothee Thass argued the matter of the Buddhist seer's origins became an important means of measuring the validity or otherwise of his work. Iyothee Thass pointed out that the most popular myth regarding Thiruvalluvar's origins, which describes him as being born to a brahmin father and a Paraiah mother, was really a nineteenth-century interpolation, invented and inscribed by partisan brahmin and caste Hindu scholars into the *Thiruvalluvar Malai*, a medieval hagiographic text on the poet's life. These scholars clearly desired to elide the fact of Thiruvalluvar's Valluvan-Buddhist origins and appropriate his Buddhist sensibility to their own Hindu creed. Within the varna scheme they lived by, a 'low' caste man could not be learned and if, therefore, such an one was to be found, then he had to be 'accounted for'. In other words, his intelligence had to be explained and, in the case of Thiruvalluvar, these scholars set themselves the task of discovering and restoring to history his ostensibly lost 'high' origins (ibid).

The Problem of Paraiah Identity

Iyothee Thass' re-readings of history and literature reflect a concern and anxiety over the semantic import of the term 'Paraiah'. His research into its origins had convinced him that the venom and distaste invoked by the word derived from a rhetorical and political strategy that had been in historical use for a long time to keep the former Buddhists ignorant of their glorious past. It seemed important to Iyothee Thass to deconstruct the term and situate it in a history of brahmin domination. In doing so, he sought to provide an ideological and historical understanding of the Paraiah's condition and, what is more important, showed the Paraiah to be in an always already antagonistic relationship to brahminical Hinduism.

It was because Iyothee Thass desired to preserve this antagonism, if only as a reminder of his people's former glory, that he refused any engagement with Christianity and Islam. In his view, these religions might help the Paraiah get out of the clutches of Brahminism but would not be able to provide them with spiritual and philosophical resources to confront the latter. Such resources, in his opinion, could only be offered by Buddhism which was not alien to the culture of his people and which had historically waged a long and ardous battle with a corrupt priesthood and its habitual deceptions.

Commenting on the efforts of nationalist social reformers to coopt Paraiahs into Hinduism, Iyothee Thass wrote: 'Not content with characterising us as Paraiahs, they now proclaim that they are going to reform the depressed classes. When asked who these depressed classes are, they say, the Paraiahs and chandalas.'

To Iyothee Thass, this shift in terms of reference from 'Paraiah' to the 'depressed classes' was indicative of rank hypocrisy; since the change in name was only a continuation of the old brahmin practice of referring to the former Buddhists by names that reified them in their lowly status and elided the all-important fact of their historical origins. Besides, even as they resorted to the use of the euphemistic 'depressed classes', nationalist reformers sought to retain their old biases through other means. They introduced the new practice of putting up signboards with words such as 'paracheri street' inscribed on them (Thass 1957, 2nd ed).

Just as Iyothee Thass desired to restore to Paraiahs their original identity, so did he wish to take away from the brahmin his assumed sacrality. His re-rendering of the meaning and import of the term 'brahmana' was undertaken in the course of another important re-defining venture: the re-definition of the fourfold varna divisions. He argued that ancient Tamil creed and custom defined the varna divisions on the basis of occupations and work and originally, at least, these definitions had nothing to do with highness or lowness. Thus, the term 'shudra', whose Tamil equivalent was 'vellala', actually referred to all those 'who, whether he be European, American, Chinese or Burmese, work the soil, cultivate it; to those whose hands and feet serve as instruments of toil; to those that create tools, build ships, railway tracks; to those who weave, sculpt and in every manner possible work for the betterment of society.'

The term 'vaishya' whose Tamil equivalent was 'vaniga' referred to those 'who, irrespective of whether they are Australian, Indian, or East Indian are engaged in trade and exchange, who buy and sell rice, sheepskins, rubies, leather, spices, liquor, perfume, fish, sweets, precious gems, crabs, gold ornaments, mutton, pearls and the like'. Kshatriya or the Arasar class (as they are refered to in Tamil) 'could be of the Mongol race. They could be Sindhis or Indians or others. Yet they were referred to as Arasar in the past, if they were strong, courageous, stout-hearted and were willing to lay down their lives for their subjects'.

Brahmanas or the class of Andanars, as the Tamil classics define them, referred to 'those who were clean and pure of body, mind and heart. They could hail from anywhere, even from the African continent and in the past were known for their compassion, selflessness and famed for the arts of healing. They knew the secrets of time and served as teachers and preceptors to the community'. Brahmins, concluded Iyothee Thass, were purveyors of learning and wisdom in the Buddhist past and were known as 'arhats'. Then, they knew no divisions, harboured no notions of 'high' and 'low' and it was for this reason that those latecomers to history, the Aryan mlecchas, sought to silence them and exile them to eternal lowness (*Tamizhan* 3 and 10.7.07). It is significant that Iyothee Thass and Masilamani never simply referred to brahmins or Paraiahs. Instead, they referred to these classes as groups of 'those who are considered brahmanas' and 'those who are considered Paraiahs'.

Most adi dravida intellectuals of this time were at one with Iyothee Thass in his criticisms of caste and Brahminism. A. P. Periyasami Pulavar, who lived in Kolar and was learned in classical Tamil literature, wrote a column for *Tamizhan* titled '*Gnanaprakasasudar*' in which he detailed, along the lines set out by Iyothee Thass, the travails endured by Paraiahs through the centuries after their forced fall from grace (6.5.08). T. C. Narayanasami Pillay, another regular columnist in *Tamizhan*, a Paraiah by birth who lived in Ootacumund, also wrote articles which contained arguments and ideas substantially similar to those advanced by Iyothee Thass and Masilamani.

What is noteworthy about these various assertions of Paraiah identity and denunciations of caste and Brahminism is their essentially social intent. That is, these researches and debates were undertaken in the service of Paraiah liberation and were geared towards fostering in the minds and hearts of Paraiahs a measure of self-worth. Iyothee Thass, as we have seen, paid as much attention to details of contemporary Paraiah life—their everyday problems, the countless and routine humiliations they were forced to endure, their lack of visibility in social and public life—as he did to their past history. Often this history and the philosophy which underwrote it were invoked in the course of present-day debates on urgent social matters.

It was not uncommon for an adi dravida intellectual to direct his polemical energies against, for instance, the preachings of Christian proselytizers who attempted to convert adi dravidas to Christianity. We also find that subtle theological investigations—as on the existence or otherwise of God, on the nature of matter—often subserved a social purpose. Narayanasami Pillay's reflections on the Theist-Atheist debates of his time—debates that were provoked by the activities of Iyothee Thass' Boudha Ashrama where he arranged for free-thinking lectures on all sorts of spiritual and moral topics—were clearly oriented towards upholding the Paraiah's right to an atheist identity. Often enough, both caste Hindus, brahmins and Christians were angered by Buddhist refutations of the existence of 'God' and divinity. To Hindus, such a rejection seemed a patent and unwarranted instance of insolence and, worse, defiance on the part of those whose birth really pre-empted them from thus conducting enquiries into spiritual matters!

Narayanasami Pillay's interventions in this matter are interesting.

He upheld atheism as an option for those who stood to gain little by theism. In a letter to the editor of *Tamizhan* he wrote of the atheist-theist debate in terms of a striking metaphor. He envisaged a mock court—especially designed to deal with social disputes—and presided over by a learned judge. To this court of hearing, come the plaintiff and the defendants. The plaintiff, an ostensible atheist, pleads he is being attacked unjustly. The defendants—Saivites, Vaishnavites and other believers—argue that their faiths are true, consistent and worthy of worship by all. The judge finally argues that in the absence of irrefutable proof, regarding the existence of God, theists have no right to impose their 'truth' on atheists (4.3.08). In an article titled '*Prakruthi*', Narayanasami Pillay dwelt at length on the nature of divinity and on why it seemed irrelevant even to refer to belief with respect to this all-pervasive presence (11.3.08). Defining the divine as *prakruthi*, he characterized it as a constellation of the five elements and their various causes and effects. Prakruthi, in this sense, was life itself and the end of life as well as its persistent existence. Prakruthi, by the nature of its being, defied naming, the attribution of qualities and thus would not, indeed, could not respond to prayers, altercations and testimonies of faith and belief.

In both these articles, Narayanasami Pillay was concerned with the right of atheists to doubt and reject faith and religious doctrine. Till the present time, such a right had not been granted his people, who had been confined to ignorance. He even argued, more generally, that all hitherto existing history was but a record of human servitude in the service of ignorance. The panchamas, particularly, had been bound in fealty to a destiny of Unknowing through the power of the King's sword and the Priest's lore. While King and Priest profited from the panchama's quiescence, they remained subjugated to a false faith. Panchamas, therefore, had to re-gain their autonomy and free themselves from intellectual and spiritual bondage and learn to know the world anew (25.3.08).

The Paraiah's right to history, then, existed as an inalienable aspect of their oft-proclaimed right to a life of equality and dignity. To these combined rights was added an other: the right of women to education. Swapaneswari, a woman of learning who edited her own journal, *Tamizhmaadhu*, often asserted this right and worked towards actualizing it. She spoke in several public forums and on varied matters, often revealing herself to be a woman of great erudition (*Tamizhan* 13.5.08).

Iyothee Thass, Masilamani, Narayanasami Pillay, Periyasami Pulavar and Swapneswari and others inaugurated and practised an art of criticism which, on the one hand, was polemical and dictated by existential needs. On the other hand, this critique demanded an alternative reading of history, in fact, asserted it and called for the coming together of all human beings on the basis of a shared comradeship. This latter was often defined in specifically cultural and civilizational terms: as Dravidian in character and Tamil by association.

It is significant that Iyothee Thass' organization for Paraiah welfare and liberation chose the appellation 'Dravida' instead of 'Adi Dravida' and that Iyothee Thass characterized his people as the '*Poorva* [original] *Tamizhar*'. As a community, Paraiahs were clearly part of the great Dravidian fraternity comprising all non-brahmin (non-Aryan) castes, but in themselves, they represented the oldest cultural segment of this fraternity. Being outcastes and exiled for their difference, as it were, which centuries of Brahminism could not subdue or domesticate, they were the historical carriers of a Tamil culture of great antiquity. Other non-brahmins, though Buddhist and Jaina once, had since been coopted into the Hindu fold and could not, therefore, be deemed 'Poorva Tamizhar'. However, both Iyothee Thass and Masilamani were insistent that non-brahmins and panchamas come together and redeem their shared Tamil past. This coming together was to be accomplished not merely on the basis of a shared linguistic identity but on the basis of a remembered way of life that was far more egalitarian and just than anything to be found in the present day. Being Dravidian, then, meant renouncing caste and embracing Buddhism; whereas, being Tamil meant acknowledging an autonomous history that belonged to all Dravidians.

DRAVIDIANISM OR A STORY OF ORIGINS

The works of the adi dravida intellectuals centred around *Tamizhan* reveal a vivid and creative historiographical imagination at work. It is clear that these men reaped to advantage the information and insights proffered by the new colonialist knowledges of the time: philology, linguistics, anthropology and a universal philosophy of history derived from Enlightenment notions of time. Such knowledges made available to bilingual and literate natives everywhere the necessary interpretative means to grapple with and make sense of a complex and distant past. Further, the findings of these new knowledges were available, from at least the mid-nineteenth century onwards, in a modular form: the Aryan theory of race—and the refutation of its premises and findings by Bishop Caldwell in 1856—provided brahmins, non-brahmins and adi dravida intellectuals with a stock of arguments they could deploy at will in their semantic and political quarrels with each other.

The Aryan-Dravidian opposition which was manifest in the realm of theory and debate by the closing decades of our century was, however, never a simple antagonism. Though Aryanism posited itself as hegemonic it was invariably contested. Its terms of reference were queried, its fundamental hypotheses challenged and its self-congratulatory tone derided, and not only by those who saw themselves as non-Aryan and non-brahmin and, therefore self-consciously Dravidian. Even a few brahmin historians, such as P. T. Srinivasa Iyengar and K. G. Sesha Iyer and brahmin Tamil scholars such as Suryanarayana Shastri refused to accept the inherent superiority of Aryan culture and the pre-eminence of the Sanskrit language.

Anti-Aryanism, in its turn, was not merely reactive. The work of Iyothee Thass and others, as we have seen, achieved an inversion of Aryanist history. It was because Iyothee Thass desired to recover the past in its own moment that he often played an amateur philologist, examining words, splitting them up, identifying their roots and reconstructing their meaning. His work and research, undertaken with the intent of endowing Paraiahs with a sense of self-worth and history, was really a part of a great historiographical adventure. Conventionally characterized as 'Dravidianist' in content, and usually identified with the 'discovery' of the Tamil classics by C. V. Damodaram Pillay and U. V. Swaminatha Iyer and with the work of Sundaram Pillay, this historiography proposed a reading of the past which saw the Tamils, a distinctive race of peoples, as agents and actors in a history which owed little or nothing to Aryan influences.

If for Iyothee Thass and others, this history was to be consciously recovered and restored to its moment of original grace, for men like Sundaram Pillay and others, their past was always already there, available in all its transparent glory in classical Tamil literature. If Iyothee Thass had been motivated by a desire to re-endow adi dravidas with a dignity that had been wilfully stolen from them, these men of Tamil learning were moved to examine their past by a passion for their language and literature. This passion was never simply a matter of individual preference. It represented for those who were moved to act on its insistence, memory, destiny and, most important of all, a consciousness of community and society that was singular and distinctive. What provoked this discovery of an 'otherness' by adi dravida and non-brahmin intellectuals? How, in other words, may we write this history of ideas?

The 'Protestant' History to Modern Tamil

This history does not begin, as is usually understood, with the publication of Robert Caldwell's *A Comparative Grammar of the Dravidian Languages* in 1856. Even before this event occurred, the sense of a difference the erudite bishop discovered and attributed to Tamil cultural and civilizational genius, had been registered for posterity by other missionary scholars. Bartholomeó Ziegenbalg, a German missionary who came to reside at Tarangambadi —a Danish settlement—was one of the earliest of those Protestant missionaries who worked to render the Bible accessible to the local populace by translating it into their own language. His translation of the Bible into Tamil, completed in 1711, drew heavily on the vernacular as the good missionary found it spoken in those parts of the Tamil country where he resided (Packiamuthu 1990: 45). Ziegenbalg was acutely sensitive to the nuances of local life and culture and observed, nearly a century before Caldwell, that the Tamils possessed a culture and a past comparable to the glories of ancient Greece. He noted that his heathen compatriots were not only literate but displayed good conduct and seemed filled with an inner grace and goodly faith which Christian preachers ought not to ignore or dismiss away as worthless or pagan (ibid: 67).

Ziegenbalg was also conscious of the dangers posed by the caste system to the spirit of Christianity and attempted valiantly to unite his multi-caste congregation (ibid: 54). It was this concern he evinced in the commonest of his converts which made him adopt a language they would understand and respond to, in his translation of the Bible. Significantly enough, this earned him the opprobrium of men like the Abbé Dubois and Father Beschi who considered it dishonourable that a Christian should thus seek to sully the word of God by disseminating it in the coarse, vulgar language of the people (ibid: 50-51; 53).

Ziegenbalg's efforts at using the vernacular for biblical translation were crowned by the work of Johann Fabricius who re-worked the former's translation to produce a literal, word-for-word translation of the original text. While it disrupted the syntactic form of Tamil, it contributed to an enriching of Tamil vocabulary. Fabricius, it seems, used to read his work out to brahmin and Vellala Tamil scholars and ask for their approval and make changes as were suggested by the native speakers. Fabricius also rendered several German hymns in Tamil that are in vogue even today (ibid: 79-81).

Protestant missionary work became somewhat more concerted and systematic towards the early decades of the nineteenth century when Bible societies were constituted in Madras and elsewhere on the model of the International Bible Society in London to regulate missionary work (ibid: 95). The impetus provided by such societies was put to good use by the German reformist missionary, Rhenius. On his arrival in India in 1814, Rhenius was asked to minister to the religious needs of the East India Company, since at that time the Church of England had not yet sent its own missionaries to work. Rhenius, however, was uneasy with the Anglican creed and opposed to its conservative stance on caste (ibid: 98). The Anglican church was not keen on disturbing the Hindu caste order and, in addition, was troubled by the zeal with which Rhenius set about re-working Fabricius' Bible to further 'Tamilize' it. Rhenius, for his part, was intent on breaking caste taboos which seemed to him most un-Christian. He encouraged co-habitation of students from different castes in the hostels under his chaperonage and permitted intercaste mingling in the schools under his control. Like Ziegenbalg, Rhenius was also anxious to render the Bible accessible to the ordinary convert and hence, preferred, much to the consternation of the Anglicans, a free translation of the holy text which would keep its meaning intact, but use popular and common modes of expression (ibid: 98-101). Further, Rhenius was convinced that a literal and unimaginative translation of the Bible into such well-developed and grammatically sophisticated languages as Tamil would only lead to much confusion and error. He considered language the very warp and woof of a people's culture and held that particular languages expressed particular cultural and historical sensibilities which had to be respected while attempting translations into them (ibid: 105-13).

Rhenius' friend and colleague at work, Bernard Schmidt, observed, in this context, that the Tamil language owed very little to Sanskrit in respect of its vocabulary, grammar and syntax (ibid: 146-47). Rhenius was also careful about his choice of register. He realized that there existed no single form of spoken Tamil, since the spoken tongue differed from caste to caste and region to region. Neither could he adopt a single literary style, since there were various forms of writing and different sets of rules which regulated the written word. Ultimately, Rhenius came to build on the Tamil prose style introduced and nurtured by his predecessors, but took great care to see that it was simple, clear and elegant in its expressions (ibid: 128-36).

Rhenius worked to render the Tamil language a supple, flexible and popular medium through other means as well. He promoted vernacular education and himself wrote books in Tamil on history, geography and the general sciences. He lived and worked at a time when the educational activities of the church and the government had touched new limits and when the number of converts in Tirunelveli, where he was resident, was rapidly increasing. Thus his democratic and egalitarian initiatives were adequate to the historical context in which they were cultivated and did much for the naturalization of a Tamil prose style which, in the years to come, would become the vehicle of secular and modern thought and consciousness. Through their publication and research efforts, Rhenius and Schmidt proved that Tamil was worthy of learning and use and could easily de-Sanskritize itself (ibid: 151-55).

Rhenius' influence was most evident in the following decades when a new experimental translation of the Bible was attempted by missionaries in Ceylon. These missionaries were aided in their efforts by the ardent Saivite and Tamil and Sanskrit scholar, Arumuga Navalar. Work on the experimental Bible was begun in 1840 and it attracted a great deal of attention and controversy. Anglicans in India such as Caldwell who were Tamil scholars themselves criticized the experimental Bible's over-Sanskritized vocabulary. Fabricius' translation, rather than that of Rhenius, had been chosen as a model and Arumuga Navalar had chosen Sanskrit equivalents for words for which Rhenius had consciously used Tamil ones (ibid: 169). This controversy clearly represented a growing awareness amidst missionaries in the Tamil country of the distinctive nature of Tamil and of the necessity of adopting its popular rather than classical forms for missionary work. Protestant missionaries had already discovered in the native (brahmin) priesthood the repugnant characteristics of obfuscation and scheming they associated with the Catholic clergy in Europe (O'Hanolan 1985: 53). It was inevitable, therefore, they would equate Sanskrit with Latin, the chosen language of the Catholic clergy and the vernaculars, in this instance, Tamil, with English (Packiamuthu: 166-68).

It is clear that when Caldwell came to write his comparative grammar, he was, in a sense, carrying forth into history an early and persistent Protestant intention to root the Christian faith in the lives of the people, their language and culture. (It is another matter that Caldwell was not always or altogether sympathetic of the heathen as Ziegenbalg and Rhenius were. The Shanars of Tirunelveli were incensed by his remarks on their barbarity.) Caldwell's genius lay in appropriating the history of Protestant lingualism to a theory of race and civilization. This resulted in transformations as well as displacements. The Protestant concern with the vernacular now came to express itself in and through a grand theory of race which served native Tamil men of learning well in their polemical skirmishes with those who upheld the claims of Sanskrit over and above that of Tamil. But it is clear this also led to a certain 'classicizing' of the Tamil language and, in some instances, promoted a kind of atavism. The early missionary desire to render the vernacular a popular medium was thus compromised.

Other developments, especially those which obtained in the political realm, helped transform Tamil into a communicable modern language. The early decades of the twentieth century witnessed a complex interaction between classical and popular Tamil, as the claims to a grand antiquity advanced by Tamil scholars came to underwrite the political and social reform concerns of non-brahmin publicists and politicians. These years also witnessed the eruption of conscious efforts to modernize Tamil and this resulted in fascinating mutations in Tamil cultural sensibility. To Tamil scholars of the last quarter of the nineteenth century, Caldwell's work proved immensely useful. It served to discipline and structure those intimations of anti-Sanskritism and anti-Aryanism which haunted the writings of several men of letters of that time. Such a felt and pronounced anti-Aryanism was, of course, not new to the Tamil country.

The Sense of a 'Difference': Tamil and a Dravidian Identity

Historically, Tamil had embodied the existential longings, historical aspirations and religious agonies of Tamils. Through significant periods of Tamil history, the language had persisted as an invaluable site for social and cultural conflicts over questions of identity. For instance, it was through a deft and delicate use of Tamil that Saivite and Vaishnavite poet-saints had resisted the hegemonic attractions of Buddhism and Jainism; while it was through a conscious 'Tamilizing' of their philosophies that these religions had initially struck root in the Tamil country. Ironically enough, Tamil had stood the imperial Cholas in good stead when they sought to legitimize their rule through an invocation and celebration of brahminical Hinduism. The two great Tamil epics of this period, Kamban's *Ramayanam* and Sekkizhar's *Periyarpuranam*, testify not only to the grandeur and suppleness of the Tamil language, but also inscribe the Chola imperial present within Sanskrit as well as Tamil pasts. These epics may be read as grand legitimizing narratives which brought together Aryan notions of kingship, rule and culture and the patently Tamil and protestant bhakthi traditions into a coherent and seamless unity. This unity was then shown to be always already present in life and culture in the Tamil country under the Cholas.

Tamil had figured as an important religious trope in the great Sri Vaishnavite debates of medieval South India when it was sought to be made the vehicle of a semi-popular, less rigid Sri Vaishnavism, subsequently associated with the *Tenkalai* (southern) school of worshippers. In the eighteenth century, when the Tamil country was rocked by intermittent wars, an anonymous poet recalled in his long poem, *Tamizh Vidu Thoothu* (Message Sent through Tamil) the glories of the Tamil language and its hoary past, constructing as it were, a poetic history of Tamil literature, the Tamil country and Tamil rulers. This poem seems a spirited response to that crisis of Tamil history and identity which had occurred due to the prolonged rule of Vijayanagara monarchs and Nayaka kings in the Tamil country. These Telugu royals had encouraged Sanskrit learning, often to the detriment of Tamil scholarship, and paved the way for a gradual marginalization of Tamil as the language of rule. Hence, the fervour and intensity of the anonymous poet, who sought to restore to Tamil culture its receding past (Krishnan 1984).

The earliest of those Tamil scholars (and historians) to write in the shadow of Caldwell's Dravidianism was Sundaram Pillay, who managed to subsume the mythic attractions of Caldwell's grand theory of race in a series of carefully researched monographs on Tamil literature and history. Sundaram Pillay learnt and then taught history in various colleges in the erstwhile Travancore state. He was also well-versed with the classical literature of Tamil Saivism, having learnt these works, in the traditional fashion, from his father at an early age. Sensitive to the changes in historiographical method which had been pioneered by Europeans and eager to put them to use in his own researches, he was, yet, keenly aware of the fundamental inadequacies of European scholarship. He granted that Europeans were sincere and painstaking in their labours but they lacked that degree of direct acquaintance with the Tamil language which was absolutely necessary for a proper and authentic reading of the Tamil past. He lamented that 'critical scholarship in Tamil has come to be regarded as not so essential to researches' and noted that as a result patent absurdities were visible in certain scholarly writings. Further, the 'oracular utterances' of such scholars were allowed to assume the status of 'axiomatic truths' which they certainly did not deserve (Sundaram Pillay 1909: 9-10).

Sundaram Pillay argued that even Caldwell, for whom he professed the highest regard, had erred in this respect. Caldwell had observed that 'Tamil writers, like Hindu writers in general hide their individuality in the shade of their writings.... They seem to have regarded individual celebrity like individual existence as worthless and absorption in the universal spirit of the classical literature of their country as the highest good to which their compositions could aspire. Their readers followed in their course, age after age. If a book was good, people admired it; but whether it was written by a man or by a divinity or whether it wrote itself, as the Vedas were commonly supposed to have done, they neither knew or cared. Still less did they care of course if the books were bad' (quoted in ibid: 27-28). Sundaram Pillay granted that a great deal of Tamil literature was of the sort that seemed to have exasperated the researcher in Caldwell. But he insisted that the same cannot be said of the 'fountains of Tamil literature' where, he declared, one met with 'well-marked individualities both in the authors and in the characters they create' (ibid: 28-29). These works may not supply any evidence as to chronology, in the sense the historian understood it, but 'they nevertheless specify the names of their patrons, sovereigns, friends and so forth, as occasion offers itself, and otherwise furnish us with much historical information which is waiting only to be gathered and collated, to yield the most reliable data for reconstructing extinct societies and social conditions' (ibid: 29).

Sundaram Pillay's own use of the Tamil classics was in keeping with his conviction that these texts could be read as carriers of historical information. He devoted a great deal of his short but eventful life to an examination of the Tamil Saivite texts, which he considered equivalent in several respects to scriptural texts in Sanskrit and as capable of yielding a coherent vision of life, culture and philosophy; only the Sanskrit texts spoke of Aryan peoples, while the Tamil ones clearly referred to those who were non-Aryan. In his *Some Milestones in the History of Tamil Literature or the Age of Tirujnana-Sambandha*, he offered a general theory of Tamil cultural and religious development. His arguments, in part, resemble those put forth by Iyothee Thass and Masilamani but his protagonists are the Tamil people as a whole and he does not regard caste as valuable a category of analysis as the former did (22-27). Yet these scholars stand united in their view of Aryans as interlopers, though, it must be said, Sundaram Pillay allows and accepts the emergence of an Aryan-Dravidian composite culture at a particular moment in Tamil history. Iyothee Thass, of course, discounts any reading of the past that is not a history of victimage and oppression. In this sense, Iyothee Thass' history transcends the ground of historiography, as we conventionally understand it, and proceeds along a hermeneutical trajectory governed more by the laws of imaginative rather than empirical enquiry.

Sundaram Pillay's history posits the existence of a primordial

Tamil past, now lost in hoary antiquity, 'when the native Dravidian religion, with its peculiar form of sacrifices, prophecies and ecstatic dances...was alone in vogue'. He goes on to argue that the 'first foreign influence brought to bear upon the primitive form of worship was that of the Vedic religion which with its usual spirit of toleration and compromise, adopted and modified the practices it then found current in the country'. This Vedic influence, it seems, grew with time and by the time the famous grammar of the Tamilians, the *Tolkappiam*, came to be written, 'the Dravidians would appear to have adopted a few of the social institutions, myths and ceremonies of the Aryan settlers'. He however hastens to add that 'it was even then only an adaptation and no copy' (ibid: 22).

Following this period came the Buddhist movement 'during which was produced the bulk of the extant Tamil classics' (ibid). Later, however, 'the mild doctrines of the Buddha seem to have undergone rapid degeneration and to have otherwise offended the followers of the original cult. Then followed the revival of Hinduism'. But he points out, Buddhism left its permanent stamp on Tamil history for 'in the course of its long contact with Buddhism the Dravido-Aryan religion was certainly modified in principles and practices and the Hinduism that was now revived was altogether a higher and more complex compound' (ibid: 22-23).

Then came the protests against Buddhism, the Saivite and Vaishnavite revivals, a prolonged and attritive war of ideas and men, which finally resulted in the defeat of the Buddhists. 'Thus was inaugurated the period of piety and miracles, which no doubt impeded for a while the cause of sound learning and culture' (ibid: 23-24). The Tamil country witnessed much temple building during this period, the end of which saw the rise of the great sectarians of Hindu theology, the three Acharyas. However, 'the dogmas of none of these Acharyas affected the forms of public worship. The temples and the professions remained, exactly as they were in the days of the fiery votaries of old, the Saiva Nayanmars and the Vaishnava Alvars'. Finally, came the Mohammedans whose arrival arrested 'all native activities in religion, literature and other walks of intellectual life then experienced' (ibid: 25).

Sundaram Pillay's narrative schema is fairly conventional in its unfolding in that it narrates a gradual fall from arcadia, redeemed somewhat by the Buddhist interregnum, the passage into medieval kingdoms and the gradual conquest of the natives by an alien ruler. It resembles the English reading of Hindu history in many crucial respects, only its judgement of time and events is tempered and nuanced by a knowledge and awareness of the distinctive claims of Tamil culture and civilization. Sundaram Pillay, it is clear, was no atavist. He was pained and annoyed by the attempts of Sanskritists to appropriate all legitimate history and culture to an Aryan past and was keen on redressing the balance of historical enquiry. His great love for his language lead him to adopt a recognizably modern, yet, self-consciously classical style of Tamil in his creative compositions. This lead to subsequent generations of scholars and writers hailing him as a predecessor, for, in his work, was visible a fruitful union of the spirit of classicism and the tenor of modern Tamil. This proved immensely attractive to those men of Tamil learning who were eager to proclaim the glories of ancient Tamil culture but who also wished to communicate their findings to a contemporary public.

In many ways, Sundaram Pillay had revealed the historical (and polemical) uses of literature and literary history and many others, who wrote during the same time and after, produced interesting disquisitions on questions of Tamil historical and cultural identity, drawing on the Tamil classics for their evidence and argument. Arnold Sadasivam Pillay, who published his *Lives of the Tamil Poets* in 1886, noted that he desired to reveal the excellence of Tamil poetry to the outside world and had sought therefore to compile a history of the innumerable poets, male and female, who had lived in the Tamil country and Ceylon. The task seemed to him a rather urgent one since such a history had never been attempted before, either in the past or present (Sivathamby 1988: 90-91). The need for history was also eloquently expressed by T. Selva Kesavaraya Mudaliar who wrote in 1894 that, in the face of taunts and disparaging comments from Sanskritists, lovers of Tamil must produce evidence of their ancient culture and its achievements. He also observed that Sanskritists were wont to argue that there were no Tamil texts that were not based on Sanskrit and that no Tamil treatises on Logic or the Vedanta existed. Such misconceptions clearly needed to be set right and it was up to Tamil scholars to undo the mischief of those who never had a good word to say about Tamil (ibid: 91-92).

The sourcing of history through an appeal to literary classics had become more or less inevitable during the early twentieth century. Throughout the last quarter of the nineteenth century, C. V. Damaodaram Pillay and U. V. Swaminatha Iyer published the Sangam manuscripts they had recovered from various collections after years of patient labour. Damodaram Pillay had published a section of the *Tolkappiam* as early as 1868 and was engaged in an almost continuous publication of manuscripts for the rest of the century. He was joined in his efforts by Swaminatha Iyer in the 1880s and the impact of their work proved to be tremendous. Since the published manuscripts conclusively established the antiquity of Tamil civilization and culture, and underscored their distinctive ethos, their appearance and circulation granted a fillip to amateur historians and serious researchers alike (ibid: 93-94).

V. Kanakasabai Pillay wrote a series of articles in the *Madras Review* on Sangam literature through the years 1895-1901. These were subsequently collected and published as *The Tamils Eighteen Hundred Years Ago*. (It is interesting to note that almost every issue of *Tamizhan* carried advertisements for Kanakasabai Pillay's book, copies of which were available for sale with Iyothee Thass himself.) This work took stock of all the literary and historical discoveries of the past decades and provided a 'definitive' history of the Tamils' Dravidian past (ibid: 94-95). The publication in 1904 of M. S. Purnalingam Pillay's *A Primer of Tamil Literature* announced that Dravidianism was here to stay. Purnalingam Pillay's pedagogical intentions expressed an intellectual confidence and maturity which, henceforth, would inform debates on the nature and content of Tamil life. Purnalingam Pillay noted modestly that his work was not without defects but, at least, he had attempted to show to the outside world the glories of Tamil literature through those texts which had been rescued from the ravages of time and which had survived the hatred of foreigners and the intellectual laziness of the Tamils themselves (ibid: 100).

The work of these scholars and the researches they pioneered and published in journals such as *Saiva Siddhantha Deepika and Tamilian Antiquary* proved immensely influential. That redoubtable Aryanist, Max Mueller in *The Six Systems of Indian Philosophy* (published in 1899) acknowledged the importance of studying non-Aryan, non-

Sanskritic texts for a more complete and nuanced understanding of Indian philosophy and noted in particular the distinctive tenor of Saiva Siddhantha (ibid: 96-97).

The game of appropriating, owning and naming history in the Tamil country attracted non-brahmins and brahmins alike. While a number of brahmins were eager to defend the antiquarian claims of Sanskrit over Tamil and argue for its superior achievements in literature and philosophy, a few brahmin scholars were emphatic in their defenses of a Dravidian culture and civilization. T. R. Sesha Iyengar in the introduction to his book *The Ancient Dravidians* wrote that his aim in writing such a treatise was to establish, once and for all, the place of Dravidians in South Indian history, record their contributions to Indian life and thought and detail the nature of their influence. Sesha Iyengar also noted that his propositions, though contrary to established views, were meant to counter Aryan fanaticism and pride and to indicate how the rich Dravidian traditions had all along amplified and enriched the content of Aryan culture. P. T. Srinivasa Iyengar, K G. Sesha Iyer and others associated with Madurai Tamil Sangam, proved to be of a similar ilk. There were others such as Suryanarayana Shastri who advocated the use of a Tamil, freed of all Sanskritisms and researchers such as Swaminatha Iyer who were convinced of the inherent worth of research in Tamil (ibid: 88-89).

What is significant about this discovery of history by Tamilians during this period is that the scholar-adventurers who ventured thus to decipher a distant past were, none of them, except for Sundaram Pillay, trained historians. The scientific study of history at the Madras University attracted and remained a preserve of brahmin scholars who, no doubt, took to a discipline which demanded superior English language skills and a knowledge of Sanskrit. One has only to think of S. Krishnaswamy Iyengar, K. A. Nilakanta Shastri and R. Satianatha Iyer, each of whom brought their formidable scholarly influence to bear on the University of Madras' department of history. Several other brahmin scholars, though not students of history, nevertheless made their mark in the field of historiography. K. V. Subramanya Iyer and T. N. Subramanyan, neither of whom were formally schooled in the study of history, were both acknowledged epigraphists (Subramanium 1988).

Thus there came to exist in the Tamil cultural universe two sorts of history: a 'soft' history, where insight and imagination held sway in equal measure, and a 'hard' history that looked to the evidence of the epigraphs, coins, inscriptions and the findings of archaeology. The practitioners of the latter, naturally enough, frowned upon the former sort of knowledge seekers. These men of Tamil letters were, meanwhile, caught up in the thrills of a distinctive kind of discursive activity—one where politics, social concerns and antiquarian enquiry intersected in an alluring fashion.

The Modernity of Dravidianism

The sense of Tamilness and the eager owning of identity which occurred in the Tamil country, during the last decades of the previous century, fructified in assertions of a Dravidian-Tamil sensibility in the early years of our own. This owning of identity was contingent on certain other transformations in the history of ideas and the organization of social and intellectual activity which occurred during this time. Significant shifts took place in the history of Tamil religious thought, which impinged upon the venturesome search for a past in crucial ways. Likewise, new uses for language, urged and articulated by Tamil intellectuals who now felt themselves to be self-conscious and purposive actors in an emergent public sphere, served to render the search for history a matter of existential import.

As we had remarked earlier, the restoration of the Tamil past revealed to the world the existence of an authentic Tamil tradition of religious thought, most systematically articulated in the writings of Saiva pietists. Referred to as Saiva Siddhantha and proposed as a Dravidian counter to Vedanta, this school of philosophical enquiry attained a contemporary relevance and importance due to the labours of, among others, Arumuga Navalar in Ceylon. Navalar was born into a Saiva Vellala family and was well-versed in Tamil and Sanskrit. He had learnt English in a mission school and came to use it adeptly. Navalar became familiar with modern conventions of prose-writing and with the polemical style adopted by the missionaries during his sojourn with the Bible translation group. Thereafter, he adopted these conventions in his talks and writings on Saivism. Provoked to act in the service of his faith by missionary diatribes against idol worship and Saivite rituals, he decided to appropriate the rhetorical and methodological skills of the missionaries to propagate the principles of Saiva Siddhantha and establish their philosophical validity. Navalar worked hard to thus 'upgrade' Saivism and render it a classical high religion. His work granted a fillip to the labour of Saiva Siddhantha adherents in Ceylon and the Tamil country and facilitated the emergence of this creed as the rightful and quintessential religious tradition of the Tamils (Packiamuthu: 167-76).

The appeal of Saiva Siddhantha during this period derived from its association with a 'Tamil' past and this, in turn, imparted to this past a philosophical and spiritual resonance. Its adherents were chiefly Vellalas who, of course, claimed it as their heritage. But there existed a heretical variant of Saivism during this period, delienated and interpreted by the mystic poet, Ramalinga Swamy (1823-74). He claimed as his own, another and equally hoary tradition of religious enquiry, that of the Siddhars, who were medieval iconoclasts, reformers and healers. His strange but remarkable life was, in many ways, symptomatic of the changes which were underway in the religious consciousness of the Tamils. Christianity and colonialism generated a general crisis of faith amongst the by now painfully self-conscious native intelligenstia everywhere. It lead men like Navalar to the defence of their faith which was transformed in the process and it caused men like Ramalinga to turn inward and contemplate anew the terms of faith, worship, divinity and the relationship of religion to lived existence.

Ramalinga claimed affiliation with the Tamil Siddhars of old and, like them, was critical of religious dogma and of the caste order. He lived the life of an itinerant preacher and healer, engaging his contemporaries in a dialogue on matters of religion and faith. In the course of a discussion with the Kanchi Shankaracharya he is believed to have upheld the spiritual and aesthetic claims of Tamil against the sacred and inviolable status of Sanskrit. Ramalinga envisioned Tamil as an expressive form of divine energy and held that the Tamil syllable, with its characteristic combination of vocalic and consonantal sounds represented, in itself, the union of life and matter, sound and its corporeal form, the creator and his creations. Tamil was thus life itself and the very form of life to this rapturous saint who was convinced that the language could express various and wide ranging emotions and truths (Krishnan: 195-96).

Ramalinga's own writing, chiefly in verse, inaugurated a conspicuously modern tradition of self-expression; one that forcefully, and unabashedly, discussed the sorrows, apprehensions and ecstasy of the writing consciousness. Ramalinga's verse was autobiographical for the most part, being a narrative of his spiritual progress and in it may be glimpsed the desire of the modern self to pronounce its particular concerns as socially pertinent and seek for them a universal validity (Balakrishnan 1991: 5-61).

Ramalinga's Tamil ardour and Saivite faith were wedded to an utopian social vision. He was fiercely critical of caste and the byzantine and endless rituals of orthodox Hindusim. Influenced by the Brahmo Samaj he desired to substitute the worship of idols with the worship of Light. He laid great emphasis on the quality of mercy, sounding almost Christian in his invocation of peace, goodwill and charity. He was deeply influenced by Islam as well and his pietistic principles were eclectic and combined aspects of these faiths along with the principles of classical Saivism. When Ramalinga founded the Samarasa Suddha Sanmarga Sangam he insisted that its purpose was not to enthrone new doctrines but to persuade people of the inherent worth of the following: the teaching and practice of mercy and love to all creations and hence the abolition of all meat eating; the discarding of temple sacrifices and other related superstitious beliefs; casting away of jati and varna differences and effecting spiritual unity amongst peoples; inculcating in peoples' minds the idea and importance of a belief in life after death (ibid: 35-46; 52-61). Ramalinga thus proposed not only a new social and religious order that may be obtained in the here and now but also articulated a wholly new vision of the body, as one that ought to be disengaged from its conventional associations with principles of purity and pollution and re-affiliated with notions of temperance, discipline and grace.

Interestingly enough, Ramalinga's life was implicated in very many ways with the institutions and public activities of his day. He often played amateur philologist, seeking to discern the root of a word and, thereby, identifying its original semantics (ibid: 25-28). He appeared in court once to defend himself against charges of religious charlatanry (ibid: 49-51). His name and work attracted the attention of British adminstrator-scholars, at least one of whom referred to him in his writings (Francis 1990: 18). His call to his disciples towards the end of his life to construct a place of worship that would be different from a conventional temple, with its tenets of approachability, purity and pollution, and his own detailed plans for such a place, reveal him to be one who was deeply sensitive to the changes which had occurred in the life of temples in the Tamil country (ibid: 83-89). A unique product of colonial society in the Tamil country, Ramalinga's life represented a creative encounter with the forces of change which had beset the latter. Eschewing atavism and yet mindful of the claims of history, Ramalinga sought to establish Tamil spiritual and social life on a radical basis. By doing so, he suggested a relationship with the past that could prove adequate to the complex demands of the existential present, marked as the latter was by multiple anxieties and concerns.

If, on the one hand, nostalgia and desire constituted the core of an imagined Tamil selfhood during this period, a stubborn faith in the modernity of Tamil and its contemporary relevance as the language of the people, in contrast to Sanskrit which was, of course, the language of the sacral literati, was also present and expressed fervently. The arrival of the Tamil novel may be considered an important index of this wish to ground language in observed reality and it is no accident that Vedanayagam Pillai, the first Tamil novelist, devoted an entire chapter in his first work of fiction, *Prataba Mudaliar Charithiram*, to discussing the importance of learning to use one's mother-tongue (Krishnan: 200-203). The modern Tamil self, with its doubts, fears, apprehensions, especially with regard to matters of faith and social reform, emerged as the protagonist of many a novel during this period. A. Madavaiah's fiction was constructed around those heroes who found themselves wandering between two worlds. Madavaiah often resolved his plots to the advantage of the reform party; but his narratives exhibited those tensions and complexities that marked the educated sensibility of that period. Caste and its effects, the plight of the upper caste Hindu widow, the salutary effects of English learning, the misery of the adi dravidas, the humaneness of Christianity—these were recurring motifs in Madavaiah's fiction that may be seen as emblematic of a new sort of narrative in the Tamil country, where sociology, history, anthropology and fiction intersected in very interesting ways (Raj Gowthaman 1995).

By the first decades of our century, the readership of Tamil papers had grown, the number of Tamil dailies was on the increase and Tamil was beginning to be widely used in the public sphere (Samy 1992: 243-44). The Swadeshi agitations of 1907-08 achieved their purpose in the Tamil country, only because a phalanx of able Tamil professional public speakers carried the Swadeshi message far and wide (Rajendran 1994). Even the theosophists conducted their deliberations, at times, in Tamil! Then there were men like the poet Subramania Bharathi, who experimented in prosody, and who sought to bring within the purview of an evolving modern sensibility, older forms of communication. Bharathi revived several folk idioms and bent their formal characteristics to accommodate the rhythms of contemporary life, with its varied concerns. Bharathi's poetry was self-conscious in its modernity and encompassed a range of contents—from the romantic to the political, from the social to the religious and from the spiritual to the philosophical.

The beginning of our century thus witnessed two distinctive but intersecting developments in the Tamil country, as far as questions of identity were concerned. The search for an authentic past facilitated the emergence of a Tamil classicism, a concern with origins and of a Tamil literati whose traditional learning was now subverted to serve the anxieties of the present. Simultaneously, however, this present historical moment demanded the transformation of Tamil into a secular tongue, one which would serve purposes of rational communication and help to carry messages of political and social reform. As a marker of identity, Tamil, thus, came to be upheld by the antiquarian as well as the non-brahmin publicist. The two, antiquarian and ideologue, joined hands when the occasion demanded it and spoke in the name of the Tamil people who were presented as engaged in a battle for the recovery of their past as well as for an establishment of their rights in the present. Together, the two created the ideological conditions which made for the emergence of political Non-Brahminism and this latter, in turn, lent to their endeavours a purposive edge.

CHAPTER 4

The Justice Party and the Advent of Political Non-Brahminism

THE FIRST CONFERENCE organized under the auspices of the Non-Brahmin Movement was held in Coimbatore in August 1917. The chairman of the Reception Committee for the conference, Dewan Bahadur M. R. Kalingarayar, the zamindar of Uttukuli, in his welcome address observed with pride: 'This is the first time in the history of our Presidency that a Non-Brahmin Conference is held' (Varadarajulu Naidu 1932: vol 2, 1-2). He went on to say that for too long brahmins had got accustomed to speak for the country and had appropriated to themselves 'whatever benefits might result from political agitation'. Therefore,

> It is now our duty to make up for lost time and put forth strenuous efforts to overcome those who are in advance. This is a question in which we have to work out our salvation and not depend on others to help us. With the awakening that is perceptible everywhere, the non-brahmin communities all over the country will, ere long, be in a position to take their rightful place in all the public movements of the country (ibid: 4).

Kalingarayar hastened to add that non-brahmins would function as 'practical men' rather than as 'professional fault-finders, as befitting our position as responsible men and our stake in the country' (ibid: 5).

Ramarayaningar, the raja of Panagal, president-elect of the conference clarified that the Non-Brahmin movement he and his peers had launched was not reactive; nor should it be construed to represent a counter-Home Rule agitation. For, 'even if the Home Rule movement had not come into being, the Non-Brahmin movement... was bound to be inaugurated by those who cherished very different ideas about Indian nation-building and about national regeneration'. To the non-brahmins, progress could not mean the 'development along modern lines of any particular class or section'. Besides, 'in a country of castes, the purely democratic idea seldom finds a place' (ibid: 7-9).

If democratic principles were to be realized in practice, continued Ramarayaningar, mere assumptions or affirmations of equality alone would not do. In a caste-bound society, the democratic idea 'requires that all members of the community must have the same chance and the same opportunities with no artificial barriers between group and group to obstruct their progress'. The time had come for non-brahmins to claim whatever was due to them by right, 'firmly and unflinchingly', for the rights to equality and social justice, which they so eagerly sought, were really rights they were entitled to 'by reason of our stake and our numerical strength' (ibid: 9-10). After all, non-brahmins constituted the 'producing communities' and in their own interest would do well actively to seek a power, adequate to their economic strength: For, 'without political power in proportion to its importance and stake in the country no community can advance' (ibid: 14-15).

At the Bikkavole Non-Brahmin Conference held two months later, 27-28 October 1917, K. V. Reddi Naidu reiterated the idea that political power must be commensurate with economic worth. In contrast to other 'civilised countries', where political power was vested in the taxpayer, in India there existed an anomaly. For here, the brahmins usurped all 'real' power, 'while the cultivators and ryots who toiled and moiled all day long in the fields and contributed substantially to the coffers of the government had not even a semblance of power in their hands'. Reddi Naidu also pointed out that since 1892, there had not been a single non-brahmin in the Madras Legislative Council (ibid: 63).

In his welcome address to the Bikkavole conference, M. Venkatratnam Naidu reminded his peers—and the non-brahmin public—that the practice of democracy required the substitution of the caste sentiment by a truly national sentiment. Quoting J. S. Mill, he observed that at present, there did not exist in India, those common sympathies and that spirit of cooperation which bound people together into a political community. Not only did there exist caste and subcaste differences, but also each of these units functioned as a complete entity in itself. That 'unity in food and blood' a clear mark of nationality was, at present, only to be found in caste groups. Besides, efforts to blend different communities into a whole, 'so as to generate that broad sympathy characteristic of nationality' had been systematically thwarted by orthodox Hindus who naturally feared such measures would deal a 'death blow' to their privileges and their doctrine of supremacy (ibid: 35-36).

Further, in the absence of that 'public spirit', which, ideally, ought to animate a community, leadership had become a matter of mere self-gratification. Thus, not one of the so-called leaders, including those who had got themselves elected to local boards and councils, had managed to attain that 'standard of character necessary for considering the wants and grievances of these innumerable communities and suggesting remedies for them from that standpoint of impartiality'. He called upon non-brahmins to make themselves into such leaders, eschew caste rigidities and work towards a time when Indians would be fit to govern themselves. Until such a day there could be no real political alternative for non-brahmins than to 'go on improving and blending these various communities into one' (ibid: 38-39).

Men like Theagoraya Chetty, Dr. Nair and others who went ahead to form the South Indian Liberal Federation or the Justice party, as it was popularly known, were confident that non-brahmins could attain a unity and wholeness, both in their studied resistance to brahmin power and through an assertion and practice of their 'essential' difference; that is, they could and ought to evolve into a culture and community with its own values and conventions. Theagoraya Chetty extolled the 'genius of Dravidian civilisation' and held that it 'does not recognise difference between man and man by birth'. For, 'the leaders of Dravidian thought, Thiruvalluvar, Avvai and Cumban do not claim to be born from the brain of the Godhead. The Nayanars and Alvars do not claim greatness in virtue of birth' (ibid: 139).

To attain a desired level of truly democratic practice, non-brahmin leaders suggested four lines of action. Firstly, non-brahmins were to educate themselves in vast numbers. Secondly, they were to work to their and the country's economic advancement and, thirdly, they were to come together and work to ensure proportional representation for all communities in administration and in the legislative councils. Lastly, they were to realize, through their unified interaction, a grand fraternity of peoples over whom, at some utopian hour, the doctrines of varnashrama dharma would no longer hold sway.

Some of these objectives lent themselves to immediate action more than others. For instance, the matter of non-brahmin education, with which no one, including the most prejudiced brahmin, could possibly quarrel with, proved to be an easy subject for legislation. However, the exhortation to non-brahmins to improve their economic fortunes could not be easily translated into purposive action. For one thing, a majority of non-brahmins, peasants, agricultural workers, artisans or itinerant labourers of various sorts, worked either in the rural hinterlands or in the fast growing towns. The Justice party's leaders, however much they sought to represent these masses of men and women, were too far removed from them, their daily lives and miseries even to formulate, let alone resolve, the problems the former experienced. Moreover, some of the leaders, being zamindars and landlords and merchants were, in some instances, themselves the chief cause for the problems faced by the non-brahmin poor. Secondly, as we shall see, economic growth and development were contingent on imperial trade and manufacture policies and the Justice party could not, even if it so desired, seek to effectively influence or direct these.

It was with respect to the issue of proportional (or communal) representation that the Justice party secured its greatest victories, for here it could address a generalized non-brahmin constituency, all of whose members were sensitive to the wrong done them by brahmins who had, for decades now, come to mediate non-brahmin needs and concerns. But in this instance, the Justicites had to face up to an extremely hostile brahmin press and function in a brahmin-dominated public sphere. They literally had to un-make public opinion with respect to caste and the question of representation, and their successes in this regard, constituted no mean achievement. For, they amounted to nothing less than a re-drawing of the limits of civil society in the Tamil country. As for the great non-brahmin fraternity the Justicites wished to constitute, this, again, proved more viable in theory than easy to realize in practice. The symbolic significance of such an imagined fraternity was greater than the political viability of such blocs that actually came to be constructed in Madras. Besides, given the hegemonic attractions of Brahminism, non-brahmins often found it difficult, at all times, to dissociate themselves from all things to do with brahmins and Brahminism.

THE IMPORTANCE OF EDUCATION

In an article written for *The Nineteenth Century* (reproduced in NI 23.10.18), Dr. Nair attributed the absence of a common national sentiment in India to the lopsided development of education in the country. He observed that state education policies were not only framed but executed on 'wrong premises'. For decades, secondary and higher education received greater support from the government than primary education. The neglect of the latter had been chiefly responsible for the emergence of a small literate class that came to speak for all other classes, 'though its acquaintance with the [latter's] condition is of the remotest possible description'. This class also elevated itself to represent 'a nation'. Arguing that 'a few very highly educated individuals cannot constitute a nation', Dr. Nair noted that the spread of Western education had not brought India into touch with the outside world nor helped to loosen, even gradually, the 'barriers of social and religious customs'. Instead, Western education had only helped raise the political consciousness of Indians in the narrowest possible manner, without inducing in them social and civil obligations.

Such perceptions were shared by other non-brahmin leaders as well. In his address to the First Non-Brahmin Confederation, Theagoraya Chetty noted that 'until lately education meant education in English and the greater part of the public money spent on education was spent on higher education, a very little proportion only going towards primary education, so much so that high schools and colleges sprang up on all sides, in which graduates were manufactured in thousands, while primary education was shamefully neglected' (Varadarajulu Naidu: vol 2, 135). Quoting from a resolution of the Governor-in-Council (1904), he pointed out that the rate of growth of primary education had been slowed and retarded due to the 'indifference of the more advanced and ambitious classes to the spread of primary education'. Besides,

> There is a cry everywhere and always for the extension of higher education and sufficient funds are always available for

> its encouragement and not only from government but also from district boards, municipal and devasthanam funds. The University encourages Sanskrit learning as against the living vernaculars of the masses, and chhatram funds, endowments of Dravidians are available for the encouragement of a dead language but for primary education which is of such real importance to the people, money cannot be found (ibid: 136).

Theagoraya Chetty was also highly critical of such agricultural education as existed. While he commended the work of the Agricultural College at Coimbatore and the Pusa Institute, he lamented the fact that agricultural bulletins were published only in English:

> They make good reading no doubt for the highly educated man but of what use are they for the agriculturists? Until our peasants are educated, at least in their vernaculars, unless the bulletins are published in vernacular languages, understood by the people, unless demonstration farms are established,... and unless village schools undertake to teach improved agriculture and thus create in the minds of the rising generation a love of improved methods no advance of any kind can be expected (ibid: 137).

Likewise, Theagoraya Chetty was exasperated at the state of technical education in the country. He argued that commercial autonomy was contingent on the existence of a highly skilled workforce and indicated how Japan's superior educational achievements in this respect had lead to her dumping her goods in India:

> Why is this so? In British India, with a population of 255 millions the universities have 36000 students pursuing a literary course, while only 12000 study in technical schools, which teach mostly type-writing, book-keeping, short-hand, etc. Japan on the other hand with a population of 51 millions has only 7500 students pursuing a literary course in its universities whereas 29,00,000 pupils attend technical schools (ibid).

It is clear that non-brahmin leaders envisaged a comprehensive educational model which would educate their vast but illiterate compatriots into virtues of citizenship as well as teach them a useful trade. Primary education was deemed necessary for securing the former, since a general literacy would enable learners to adopt a more extensive world-view and to ask questions and seek knowledge of matters which otherwise would be routinely denied them. But at the same time, primary education alone would not obviously be enough. Technical education was important to equip students with the means to earn a living and acquire new skills, so necessary to keep pace with and aid in the continuing transformation of a fast-changing world. Such an educational model would be in stark contrast to the existing one that produced only 'automatic quill-drivers, indifferent school masters and pettifogging lawyers' rather than competent agriculturists, technicians and tradesmen (ibid).

Almost all resolutions to do with primary education which were passed and upheld in the various Non-Brahmin conferences held in 1917, the first year of the movement's existence, demanded that it be made compulsory, at least in municipal areas. There was a further demand that the government bear two thirds of the costs incurred for making primary education available to all. It was also stipulated that any school or institution which restricted admission to pupils of particular castes or creed should not be entitled to receive any contributions from government revenues and other public funds. Besides, rules in respect of recognition of such schools as were 'intended for the children of ryots, labourers and depressed classes', were asked to be relaxed (ibid: 21; 58; 114).

At the First Non-Brahmin Confederation, it was urged that the government recognize and act on the necessity of providing free education to adi dravidas and other depressed classes in government-aided institutions. It was also resolved that immediate steps be taken to establish a sufficient number of industrial schools for the training of artisans and mechanics. A resolution was passed that asked the government to make provision for research on technical subjects. The Confederation also urged the establishment of primary and secondary agricultural schools and colleges, as had been foreshadowed in a recent Government of India resolution (ibid: 162).

More generally, it was resolved that concessions in school fees be made available to all Backward Classes. Scholarships were demanded for poor non-brahmin girls and boys, and it was suggested that district educational funds be organized by non-brahmin notables in all districts to further the cause of non-brahmin education. Non-brahmins also asked that the study of vernaculars be made compulsory in all schools (ibid: 21; 57; 99).

While Non-Brahmin conferences laid a general emphasis on women's education, this does not seem to have been enough; for, at least one woman participant at the First Non-Brahmin Confederation was moved to remark that though resolutions on education 'sought to bring light to the masses and to womankind...the emphasis on the latter was not so strong as [one] could wish' (ibid: 163).

It is significant that Dr. Nair thought it fit to measure the progress of education in India in terms of the actual figures of female literacy:

> If you eliminate from the statistics showing the spread of Western education amongst Indian women the figures showing the literacy in English of the women in Indian Christian and Parsee communities the result will show the infinitesimal progress made by English education among the women of India (NI 23.10.18).

It must be noted here though that the Justice party was the first political party in colonial India to remove those restrictions which disallowed women from voting. Besides, the Madras Council's first ever woman member, Dr. Muthulakshmi Reddi, served as a member of the legislature during the Justicites' tenure in office (Ray 1995: 192).

Non-brahmin leaders also suggested that Educational Boards comprising the collector, inspector of schools, a non-official member, one each from Taluk and Municipality Boards—these latter will have to be from all communities in the region—and not more than four nominated non-officials be formed to supervise local educational work (ibid: 58). These various resolutions were remembered and acted on, when non-brahmins under the auspices of the Justice party, assumed office in Madras in 1921 under the Montagu-Chelmsford (Montford) reform scheme. Education, a transferred subject under dyarchy, received immediate attention. By 1925, in nearly 18 out of 25 municipalities, free and compulsory education was introduced. The Education Act of 1920 was amended twice, under successive Justice ministries, with a view to keep children in school. It was held that children, once in school, could not be removed within the period of their school age and parents who attempted to do so were liable to pay a penalty fee. The Justice party revived a scheme to feed poor children in schools. This scheme was, originally, introduced by Theagoraya Chetty when he was president of the Corporation of Madras. The Justice party also attempted to accelerate the spread of education amongst adi dravidas and insisted all public schools admit adi dravida children, failing which, their managements would forfeit grants-in-aid, at present being made available to them. Adi dravida students were allowed to pay half-fees and to take their school leaving exam without paying the customary examination fee. Justicites also set up separate schools for adi dravidas, known as 'Labour Schools' (Rajaraman 1988: 236-40).

These reforms however proved to be limited in their impact. Under dyarchy, an elected government could not resolve on matters of Finance, which was a reserved subject. Further, Madras suffered a perennial revenue crunch at the best of times, and very small sums were actually available for expending on the so-called transferred subjects, amongst which Education was one. Secondly, legislation when it moved into the realm of practice, had to battle with the studied recalcitrance of a prejudiced and crafty bureaucracy whose cooperation was essential to realize good intentions into fitting acts. Thirdly, the Justice party could not very easily or effectively reverse the trend, initiated decades ago by the British, in favour of higher education. In fact, in at least one important instance, Justicites themselves had to intervene in the sphere of higher education, when they attempted to secure a greater encouragement for the study of the vernacular at the university (Nambi Arooran 1980: 88-91; 107; 117-18).

Justicites achieved a degree of modest success in their bids to secure a foothold for non-brahmins in the university's Senate. The Madras University Act of 1923 sought an enlargement of the University of Madras' Senate that would render it a more elective and representative body. The enlarged membership of the Senate allowed for the representation of various communities. The Andhra University was also created during the Justicites' term in office, as was the School of Indian Medicine (Rajaraman: 242-46).

THE PRODUCING CLASSES

For non-brahmins, education was not merely a means to gain

access to the precincts of the government. As we have seen, their educational model envisaged learning as a continuous process and as integrally linked to work and labour. It would be useful to recall, in this context, the testimony presented by Daivasikamani Achari, secretary, Vishwakarma Mahajana Conference Committee, to the Indian Industrial Commission of 1916. Citing the Census Report of 1911, Achari observed that the problem with the present educational model was that when it came to sending students to foreign countries, students from industrial and artisanal classes 'who possess the initial aptitude for manual labour' were often ignored. Since they lacked formal literacy, this class of students were deemed ineligible for technical scholarships (Visvanathan 1985: 57). The point is that non-brahmin castes had become particularly sensitive to the hiatus that existed between the demands of formal literacy, which many of them could not easily meet, and a certain kind of experiential and 'guild' knowledge which they knew they possessed. Hence, their plea that education and work, labour and knowledge cohere with each other.

This re-definition of education by non-brahmin leaders to mean action and a means to action derived from a certain kind of self-imaging. Non-brahmins, it was now said, were the toilers, the producing communities, and it was their work which made possible the riches of Indian civilization. More than once, we hear Theagoraya Chetty, Ramarayaningar and Kalingarayár and others refer to themselves and their communities as having a real, 'material' stake in the land; as being strong, capable men who did not disdain manual labour. It had also become commonplace to declare that India's future lay in a further and speedier development of her industries and commerce. It was said of Bombay, 'the premier city of India':

> A barren island becoming the premier city of India! What was the cause of this greatness? It is not Sanskrit Literature, it is not the world-admired Sankara's philosophy, it is not [even] the political greatness we are hankering [for] which had made Bombay great. It is enterprise—the enterprise of a small community—the Parsees (Varadarajulu Naidu: vol 2: 93).

This enthusiasm for 'enterprise' led some to celebrate the virtues of the European merchant. The zamindar of Telarpole argued that

European profits constituted only one aspect of the matter, the other being 'the direction of India's products to the markets where they will bring the producer the highest prices and the instruction of the Indian labourer in the best methods and the use of the most economical machinery and materials'. Telarpole declared he too was for Swadeshi but the dictates of economic commonsense could not, therefore, be overlooked. Indian capital, thus far, had proved a shy and reluctant debutante and Indian markets needed European money and resourcefulness (ibid: 108).

Not all non-brahmins were as sanguine as Telarpole in their estimation of British economic interests or as naive as regards the needs and imperatives of imperial manufacture and trade. As we have observed earlier, Theagoraya Chetty desired commercial autonomy and favoured the removal of those restrictions and rules, with regard to tariff, which served ill everybody else except British manufacturers and business houses. He was also convinced that the granting of commercial freedom and autonomy alone could propel non-brahmins onto the stage of history and render meaningful to them the ideal of Home Rule. He remarked, rather poetically, that he longed for the day,

> When every boy and girl in our community will be educated, when every peasant will be lord of his land, his hereditary knowledge of agriculture being supplemented by scientific methods and improved implements so that with heaven's blessings in the shape of timely rains his land may yield tenfold more than they do at present and he and his family will have a full meal and his status in life shall be considerably raised; and not only that he will be able to produce bumper crops of commercial products with which India can supply the requirements of other communities; when the industries of the country will be far advanced; when we shall wear clothes of our own manufacture, use our own machinery in our own workshops (ibid: 140-41).

This economically self-governing polity would prove viable and liberative in other ways as well, for now suitably armed with the powers of production, non-brahmins would seek to break free of the 'tyranny of the lawyer . . . the trammels of hereditary priesthood' and even 'put an end to varnashrama dharma with its ethics of shudra and untouchable'. Then, in this new millennium not only will 'men of all castes and creeds... live as brothers and form one nation' but 'self-government in the real sense of the word will have become an accomplished fact' (ibid).

The very limited powers granted to Ministers-in-Council under dyarchy and the logic of imperialist economics did not allow non-brahmins to exercise their political powers to create conditions which would make for the attainment of commercial autonomy, even in the long run. In this sense, the ideal of productive communities vesting in themselves political powers, adequate to their role and function in the economy, remained a rhetorical turn of phrase. Often, it served to legitimize the very limited authority available to the elected ministers. Nevertheless, the idea of 'power to the producers' proved useful and attractive to non-brahmins, since it signified a new sort of politics and one they could use as a counter to what they clearly considered the politics of a parasitic Brahminism.

Later, during the Justice party's first term in office, a department of industries was set up and we may be sure non-brahmins in the government and Justicites themselves worked for its acceptance. It is another matter that in spite of this, and in spite of the passing of the State Aid to Industries Bill, industrial growth did not pick up in Madras (Rajaraman: 246-48). The reasons, one presumes, were social and not merely political and economic. Madras' large artisanal class languished in illiteracy and, besides, was ill-served by developments in imperial manufacture and trade. In this context, the non-brahmin cry for proportional reservation of seats in the services, education and councils was but fair and signified something more than a mere desire to covet the spoils of office. This demand represented, in effect, a desire to wield power that would enable non-brahmin communities to advance their productive as well as ideological concerns.

THE STRUGGLE FOR A NEW POLITICS

The Question of Representation

The non-brahmins' desire for power and office derived from their general conviction that unless power was evenly distributed and shared amongst various communities, there could not evolve a national community or a democratic polity in India. Dr. Nair, for instance, was emphatic that 'a number of men belonging to different communities must first of all be trained in the art of Government' before Indians or the British could even contemplate the possibility of a self-governing polity for India (Varadarajulu Naidu: vol 1, 47). In a response to the Memorandum of the Nineteen, Dr. Nair suggested that, firstly, existing councils be enlarged, for 'this will enable the training of a necessary number of men and what is of equal importance the representation of various classes and communities'. Besides, if the councils remained small very few newcomers could be accommodated and many old ones would continue to be elected for successive terms. This would invariably lead to a small, fixed class of men acquiring a 'preponderate influence' in the assemblies and eventually deter and defeat the attempts to create a democratic self-governing polity (ibid: 48).

Secondly, the British ought not to transfer all subjects of governance to elected governments in a hurry. Local self-government could figure as the first of the transferred subjects, but revenue and judicial departments should be made over to Indians only after they had abdicated their clannish spirit (ibid: 49). Dr. Nair pointed out that local self-government institutions awaited drastic reform. Official intervention in municipal bodies had not only kept away from their precincts able and resourceful men but had deprived these bodies of 'that sense of responsibility and power of initiative', the exercise of which alone could have transformed them into truly democratic and representative units (ibid: 58). (Writing a few years later, Dr. Nair would argue that the authors of the Montford Report 'deliberately chose the level of provincial government to begin responsible government although responsible government has not yet been given to the sphere of local bodies' (NI 23.10.18).

Thirdly, the functions of imperial and provincial governments needed to be clearly demarcated. For, 'unless the Provincial Governments know what their exact powers are, how can they transfer any of their powers to popular control?' Dr. Nair further noted: 'It is impossible to devise a satisfactory scheme of self-government for India except on the basis of federal Home Rule and in any scheme of federal Home Rule the units of the system should be properly constituted before we can think of constructing the federal authority' (Varadarajulu Naidu: vol 1, 46-47).

While almost all these concerns, interlinked as they were, were debated in Non-Brahmin conferences, it was the principle of communal representation that lent itself easily to the purposes of political propaganda and agitation. Communal or proportional representation, as a norm for recruitment of members to government service, had existed as an aspect of English official policy from as early as 1851, when the Board of Revenue in Madras promulgated a standing order (No.128, clause 2) that laid down the means by which entry of brahmins into the revenue department could be suitably regulated. The order held that the respective collectors ought to divide the 'principal appointments in each district among several castes' and further stipulated that the proportion of the tahsildars in each district should belong to the non-brahmin castes (Irschick 1969: 220). The order also declared that the two most important officials in the revenue department, the huzur sheristadar and the 'English' head clerk, should not belong to the same caste.

The standing order was not implemented and efforts to enforce it proved largely unsuccessful. To work the order, the government resorted to other means. The Public Services Commission Report of 1886 decided to fill in the appointments to the Provincial Services through open competition rather than direct appointment, in the hope that such competition would ensure a fairer distribution of posts. However, for the years, 1893-95, the exams returned only one non-brahmin candidate to the services. The government, then, attempted to deliberately include non-brahmins in the services and, even as late as 1912, when the Second Public Services Commission held its hearings, orders were issued urging collectors and others who made government appointments to comply with Standing Order 128 (ibid: 219-21). In 1917, on the eve of the impending reforms of 1919, the spirit of Standing Order 128 was resuscitated by the Justice party to yield a new political argument.

At one level, the demand for communal representation was expressed in and through arguments against Home Rule. Home Rule was considered undesirable for four interrelated reasons. Indians possessed little or no experience in ruling themselves. Annie Besant and her coterie in Adyar might point to the example of Ireland and claim Indians ought to emulate the example of Irish Home Rulers. But India was not Ireland where, in spite of warring sectional interests, there had existed, since the eighteenth century at least, parliamentary institutions. Secondly, Indians had not, yet, cemented into a nation and were divided along sectoral and class lines. Thirdly, Indians, on the whole, lacked education and could not, therefore, be expected to use their vote wisely and well. Fourthly—and this was the most compelling reason advanced by non-brahmins for rejecting Home Rule—in the present conditions of general illiteracy and caste differences, it would only serve its chief proponents, the brahmins, well (Varadarajulu Naidu: vol 1, 11-18).

The zamindar of Telarpole, addressing himself to India's imperial rulers, summed up the non-brahmin case against Home Rule thus:

> England is responsible for the welfare and for the uplifting of the socially downtrodden silent masses who form the majority of the population of India. She cannot, in the name of fair play, make a present of them to the Home Rulers, like dakshina given to officiating brahmins in a temple. If we are to have Home Rule then it will have to be Home Rule in every sense, not Home Rule enforced by British bayonets but brahmin vakil rule enforced by a posse of litigants with full liberty to the peoples of India to deal with it and them as may seem proper.... (ibid: vol 2, 109).

Non-brahmin fears and apprehensions over Home Rule were heeded by imperialists in England and their civilian representatives in India; both of whom made use of non-brahmin objections to Home Rule to argue the merits of moderate and gradual political reform for India. Lord Islington in England, Under Secretary of State for India, reminded fellow Englishmen that political reform must necessarily be moderate, for, if in their haste and enthusiasm, India's rulers urged forward a programme to transform overnight a highly centralized bureaucracy into a set of decentralized self-governing systems, they would upset the 'essential principle of parliamentary government'. Thus, 'the effects of the proposals of the nineteen would be to place the government in a constant risk of seeing measures and resolutions carried to which it objected and whose execution could not, as in constitutional countries be placed upon those responsible for their introduction' (quoted in ibid: 43).

The Government of India had its own set of reasons for opposing political reform. In a despatch to Lord Montagu, the government wondered at the propriety of granting democracy to an eastern country which did not possess a history of steady and fair governance and where the powers of an oligarchy remained as yet unassailed and resistant to ideals of equality and fraternity (Irschick: 114).

In place of the Home Rule demand, the Justice party outlined a number of proposals within a general logic of communal representation. Most of these had already been advanced by Dr. Nair, but they were now represented as the party's official claims. The demands comprised an extension of local self-government and an enhancement of its institutional powers, a plea for adequate representation for all communities in the services, for an enlargement of the franchise and for a system of direct elections and finally the establishment of the franchise on a communal basis to enable non-brahmins secure an adequate number of places in the councils (Varadarajulu Naidu: vol 1, 63-65).

Other non-brahmin forums—various caste associations, the Madras Dravidian Association, the Madras Adi Dravida Jana Sabha—expressed their opposition to Home Rule in terms similar to those deployed by the Justice party, but not all of them urged Montagu to adopt a different approach to reform (ibid: 61-63; 70-74). Most caste associations asked for special representations in the new council for their communities while others, such as the Nadars, demanded an increase in the number of nominated members—from their own ranks—to all elective bodies (ibid: 74-76). All non-brahmin organizations called for an extension of British rule in its present form and some, like the Buddhists of South India, submitted that agitations for reform did not represent popular aspirations and demanded, instead, the abolition of the caste system and the spread of education (ibid: 76). The Justice party's ideal of communal representation served to rally together and unite various non-brahmin concerns since it represented, all at once, a resistance and a means of resistance to brahmin power, and the caste order and a novel practice of democracy; one that was not merely rhetorical in its claims but suited to the exigencies of a caste-bound polity.

Britain, as we had suggested earlier, had its own reasons for conceding the validity of the case in favour of communal representation. For civilians in Madras (and elsewhere), political reforms meant a possible shift in power, however subtle such a shift may be, from the executive to an elected and enlarged legislature. In the latter their arch foes (and one-time friends) the brahmins—Home Rulers and Congressmen—were bound to dominate and, naturally enough, Madras civilians desired to counter this imminent development. They thus came to favour communal representation. For this, they reasoned, would strike at the heart of brahmin power (Irschick: 112-22). In England the imperialists and public opinion favoured communal representation for reasons we shall soon see.

Through the better part of 1917 and for most of 1918, the Justice party's demands with respect to communal representation were discussed and debated in political circles in Madras. The tenor of these debates and the interest they aroused in Madras' public-minded citizenry produced unintended effects. For soon enough, those who until a few months ago, had characterized the Justice party as a rank communal organization, now began to propound variations on the Justice argument with regard to reform in recruitment procedures. As may be expected, *New India* played a cardinal role in mediating these debates. On the eve of Montagu's visit to India, several letters and articles were published in *New India* that drew attention to the ostensibly fallacious arguments which were being advanced by non-brahmins in their tirades against brahmins and Home Rule.

A letter described by its author as 'India's Open letter to Lord Pentland [Governor of Madras]' noted that 'all the gospel of unfitness [of India for Home Rule, that is] which Dr. Nair's school would propagate is a false gospel which no self-respecting class of people will accept. I do not think that Dr. Nair would preach such a gospel in the critical turn in the political life of his countrymen, had he not fallen victim to a hallucination that he would be taken seriously as fighting for a cause on behalf of millions of non brahmanas' (NI 7.8.17). Yet another open letter to the Governor, this time signed rather self-consciously by 'a non-brahmana Home Ruler' criticized the notion of brahmin dominance in the services and remarked that if brahmins were indeed found to be dominating, this was due to the government's own 'heaven born civilians' who make or marr appointments (NI 8.8.17).

But, in spite of these and other 'reasoned rebuttals' of non-brahmin views on Home Rule, it soon became clear that these were slowly gaining ground and acceptability. Kesava Pillay now thought it fit to remark that the Congress-Muslim League scheme ought to include provisions for guarding non-brahmin communal interests (NI 10.10.17). Lodd Govindass, one of the vice-presidents of the Madras Presidency Association (MPA)—the Congress forum for non-brahmins—noted that the idea of communal representation was certainly not new, even to Congressmen, for there already existed the practice of getting speakers from different communities for moving resolutions at Congress conferences. Thus, when 'we [MPA] ask for communal representation we are asking for recognition of a practice which is already in existence'. Govindass however made it clear that he did not endorse the Justice party's thinking on this matter, especially its demand that there be 'equal distribution of political power and official influence amongst the various communities'. He admitted he could neither see the propriety of such a demand, nor accept its logic:

> I do not know where will these communities exist for obtaining representation for them if, as proposed by them [the Justice Party] they are extinguished—the caste system is abolished, the depressed classes merged into one class. . . . In one breath they preach we are unfit for self-government, in another they want communal representation for each and every community as though all of them are eminently qualified (NI 9.1.18).

Govindass also doubted non-brahmin sympathy towards panchamas and declared it a 'sin to make promises to panchamas that cannot be fulfilled in practice'. Besides panchamas in these modern times did not require such spokespersons as the Justicites. Their cause was acknowledged to be a just one and 'surely they can neither ask for nor can be conceded to them undue prominence' (ibid). In its submission to Lord Montagu, the MPA observed that non-brahmins in the Congress were 'anxious that due and adequate representation of the varied interests and communities . . . be secured in the contemplated reforms so that no talent might rust for lack of opportunity to serve in the nation building that is proceeding apace under the British rule and no interest might suffer for want of proper representation in the councils of Empire' (Varadarajulu Naidu: vol 1, 62).

Later in 1919, when the Franchise and Function Committees were constituted by the Government of India to go into the question of franchise limits and the vexed matter of Reserved and Transferred subjects, the MPA, in its testimony, reaffirmed its position with regard to securing for non-brahmins what was due to them. In the evidence tendered before the Franchise Committee, the MPA representative observed that while his organization did not consider the granting of communal representation a necessary condition for the attainment of self-government, it desired the franchise be enlarged and a limit be placed on the number of brahmins who could enter the Legislative Council (NI 22.5.19). (The Justice party boycotted both these committees, claiming their composition was prejudicial, since neither contained a single non-brahmin member.)

Even as the MPA self-consciously came forth to represent, what its votaries claimed was the true non-brahmin spirit, Justice party leaders, especially Dr. Nair, worked hard to present their case at home and abroad. Annie Besant continued to revile their efforts and was particularly harsh on Dr. Nair who left for England in mid-1918 at a time when, claiming wartime regulations, the Government of India had refused permission to several known Indians, including Tilak, to leave the country (NI 14.5.18). Dr. Nair's visit—chiefly occasioned by an acute bout of diabetes for which he needed to be treated urgently—was viewed in Home Rule circles as a sort of advance guard action by the Non-Brahmin movement in the cause of communal representation (NI 26.6.18). Though Dr. Nair had given a written undertaking he would not discuss politics during his sojourn in London, no one was really prepared to believe him.

In a satiric editorial titled 'Dr. Nair as Passive Resister' Annie Besant observed that Dr. Nair could wilfully break his vow of silence on political matters and yet not suffer for it, since certain members of the British War cabinet—Lord Curzon and Mr. Chamberlain—were believed to have notified Lord Montagu that even if Dr. Nair were to speak politics 'they intended taking no action against him' (NI 19.9.18).

New India published an article from *The Indian Patriot*, 'The Most Advanced Politician in India' that was sharply critical of Dr. Nair. The author of this piece noted that Dr. Nair's democracy 'consists in the resistance that he offers', to every measure which will benefit the whole people of India. In a more biting vein he added:

> There is no element of selfishness or sectarianism in his politics. He stands for all because he knows that all people cannot at the same time be advanced at the same level. He is of the opinion that everybody must wait until everybody else has advanced enough to receive the measure of liberty.... He therefore goes against every law of progress. In no country is progress achieved if people have to wait until the whole is advanced to the same forward level.

The author also queried Dr. Nair's claims that he represented non-brahmin opinion:

> But how will the non-brahmins be benefitted by his politics is more than we can say... if the whole country is to be denied every advance which is not attainable by the least progressive class, the illiterate, the ignorant and the materially backward.... His followers are those who have no political view or political convictions. The panchamas of Madras who gather to hear him in large numbers in the Spur Tank may be said to follow him. But we do not attach importance to such a following. When he discusses high politics they cannot understand him. They can understand him when he hurls epithets at brahmanas.... There is no use of merely representing one class of people who are most progressive as hated beings (NI 26.9.18).

Non-brahmin leaders refused to be deterred by such outbursts of anger and contempt and pursued their task of propagandizing about communal representation with diligence. In his address to a non-brahmin conference held at Madurai, in October 1918, Thirumalai Pillay noted that though there were many amongst the non-brahmins who were 'enlightened and courageous enough to do their duty towards their less fortunate brethren', they were, yet, helpless since 'they do not count in the councils of government'. This discouraged non-brahmin attempts at reform, since nothing could be done without the 'active countenance and cooperation of Government'. Besides, for all their liberal pronouncements and programmes, non-brahmin leaders of the movement 'have been face to face with stone walls. Repeated attempts were made to destroy the movement at its birth... and they were still being continued in a more sinister form'. Even those who ought to know better, like Sir Surendranath Banerjea, had preferred to cavil at the Non-Brahmin movement, rather than try and understand its pertinence. Banerjea was known to have remarked that non-brahmins should ideally join hands with the Germans, 'against the civilisation and freedom of the world' (NI 21.10.18).

Perhaps nothing expressed as eloquently the success of the Justice party's campaign with respect to communal representation as the principled support extended to the latter idea by men such as Sir Sankaran Nair. A distinguished Madras notable and reformer and a member of the Governor's Council in Madras, Sir Sankaran Nair, whom we have encountered briefly before, disagreed with the Madras government's extremely conservative stance on the matter of political reform. But, unlike others who spoke out against the civilians' conservatism, he also registered his unease and apprehensions over a possible brahmin dominance in the reformed council.

In a dissenting minute, appended to Government of India's despatch submitted to the Franchise and Function committees, he remarked on the justness of the principle of communal representation but made it clear that he did not consider it an 'essential preliminary' to 'responsible government'. He also sought to illuminate the context in which non-brahmins originally came to advance their claims with respect to a preferential representation for themselves. He observed that in the past decades, in spite of colonial officials warning non-brahmins of the mischievous intentions of the Congress, they had joined that party and lent their support to its work during the early years of its existence. The onerous effects of ryotwari had affected labouring and artisanal classes as well as the landlords and all three segments, for different reasons, agreed with the Congress' criticisms of the British.

Non-brahmins, however, were not entirely unaware, even then, of the ambiguity which marked the brahmins' relationship to government. They knew, for instance, that the government favoured brahmins in administrative posts since that class possessed qualities 'required for a foreign ruling race who wanted good subordinates'. On the other hand, non-brahmins were told their function was to 'obey and produce wealth which should be at the disposal of their masters'. The government, even as it denounced the brahmin–non-brahmin divide and appeared to favour non-brahmins at times, did nothing that would benefit the latter and remained passive to the efforts of reformers of caste, who were either ignored or castigated as 'anglicised Indians out of touch with the masses'. Besides, several civilians were known to have remarked in private that they thought the caste system was necessary to maintain stability. Thus, non-brahmins had ever been sceptical of Congress' criticisms of the government and, likewise, had not been fooled by the latter's impatience and anger over brahmins. Gradually, non-brahmins, unhappy with the government's studied indifference to their concerns and with the persistent 'moribund and orthodox' attitude of the older generation of Congressmen, had sought to abandon the Congress for a party of their own (NI 16.5.19).

It is clear Sir Sankaran Nair desired to legitimize the non-brahmins' demand for communal representation without minimizing the importance of such reforms as may be wrung out of an imperial state which had, after all, come forward to negotiate on this matter. Besides, he also wished to de-link the justness of the non-brahmin cause from the support extended it by the Madras government, and consider it valid on its own terms. Sir Sankaran Nair was also mindful of the needs of the adi dravidas, whose material prospects, he held, had steadily deteriorated under British rule. Not only had they lost access to free house sites, materials from the forest and free pasturage, but had been left bereft of a living wage due to the ruination of Indian industry. He believed that the reforms, if implemented in the 'proper spirit' could 'enable them [panchamas] to materially influence elections or to create electorates to send their representatives to council' (ibid).

Sir Sankaran Nair's dissenting minute proved to be of catalytic significance. It emboldened men like Kesava Pillay to speak out against the Home Rulers' ambivalent stance on the question of communal representation. In her testimony to the Joint Select Committee in London—the hearings of the committee took place in London in August 1919—Annie Besant had maintained the 'Home Rule deputation did not approve of communal representation as it intensified the separatism [between brahmins and non-brahmins] by importing religious questions into politics' (NI 14.8.19). Kesava Pillay, responding to this observation, noted in pained surprise that, until now, he had laboured under a 'misconception that Mrs. Besant would not oppose communal representation as far as this Presidency was concerned'. Further, 'neither brahmana Home Rulers or Congressmen' had opposed the demand when the MPA advanced it, possibly because they wished 'to avoid an open split in the Congress camp or among the Home Rulers, that is between the large mass of non-brahmin and brahmana Congressmen'. The demand for communal representation had been raised and endorsed by C. Rajagopalachari at the Bombay Special Congress Subjects Committee as well. Further, on the advice of Congress, MPA in its submission to the Franchise and Function Committees, had deputed Kesava Pillay to argue the case for communal representation. Recalling the evidence tendered by him to the Franchise Committee, he pointed out that Lord Southborough who was its head had remarked that Kesava Pillay's testimony was offered 'in a spirit of compromise and [was] not hostile to the Brahmanas'. In this context, it seemed rather strange to Kesava Pillay that Mrs. Besant would speak of religious questions, especially 'as she knows that the bulk of non-brahmin Hindus who are agitating for communal representation or communal electorates belong more or less to the same religion or religious sects as their brahmana countrymen'. The point was that Mrs. Besant had chosen to ignore the fact that the latter who constitute the 'priestly order and who, though they be laymen, following learned professions or serving Government cannot as a class rise above their prejudices or clannishness'. Kesava Pillay ended his long explanatory note to *New India* thus:

> I little thought that she [Mrs Besant] would give communal representation such a short shrift even though such a great patriot as Sir C. Sankara Nair has supported communal representation in his dissenting minute (NI 14.8.19).

Kesava Pillay's observances provoked a heated debated in *New India.* Expressing his disenchantment with Pillay, who had argued 'like a non-brahmana' than as a patriot of India, K. Ramaswami of Pudukkottai went on to observe that Pillay's 'supreme class prejudice' would eventually incite him to call on all brahmins to tear their sacred threads and mingle with non-brahmins. Ramaswami also noted that shudras in the present day were animated by 'the mean and ill-advised spirit of the vandals' and were 'impudent and insolent' in their behaviour (NI 18.8.19). Kesava Pillay's rejoinder was sharp and unusually candid. He condemned Ramaswami's barely disguised rancour against non-brahmins, exhibited 'in the style of a person conscious of his indisputable and sacred birthright to dictate and lord it over the multitude'. He further pointed out that rather than being motivated by class prejudice, his own misgivings over Mrs. Besant had really to do with the progress of the Joint Select Committee hearings in London, where M. Ramachandra Rao had joined Mrs. Besant in demolishing non-brahmin claims and where one of the non-brahmin witnesses had broken down:

> Men like Ramaswami who love the country perhaps more than Sir Sankara Nair, with all the shudras and the panchamas in it, whom they treat as their wards if not their brothers, just like our Anglo-Indian brethren love the 'natives' of the country so long as they keep their distance, may be satisfied with the course of events in England. But it bodes no good for the immediate prospects of reconciliation between the party fighting for communal electorates and communal representation and politicians who are now condemning communal representation in London.

Kesava Pillay also reminded his critic that the latter knew nothing of Congress politics and prejudices; especially of the 'pressing events which lead to the formation of the MPA, pledging itself to secure communal representation and the solicitude and eagerness displayed by the Madras Congress politicians at that time to help in the propaganda' (NI 22.8.19).

Non-Brahmin Leaders and the London Hearings

The Joint Select Committee hearings which convinced Kesava Pillay of the uselessness of reasoning with Congress and Home Rulers on the subject of communal representation had begun in August 1919 in London. Dr. Nair, who was to represent the Justice delegation, died rather suddenly. His worsening diabetic condition had caused him to travel to England for the second time within twelve months. Unfortunately, he did not recover and died within a few days of the arrival of the Justice party's official delegation in London. In the wake of Dr. Nair's death, K. V. Reddi Naidu, Ramarayaningar, Tulsiram and A. Ramasamy Mudaliar testified on behalf of the Justice party. Among the Home Rule stalwarts who gave evidence were Annie Besant, M. Ramachandra Rao and C. P. Ramaswamy Iyer. Before his untimely death, Dr. Nair had worked hard to ensure that politicians of some standing in Britain would view the reform scheme from a 'non-brahmin point of view'. In a vivid description of the future effects of a political reform which was not sensitive to the problems specific to caste society—delivered as a speech just months before his death—Dr. Nair had noted that the new legislative council would comprise a large number of Home Rulers, most of them given to extremist views, some Moderates, who endorsed the reform proposals but who remained a minority, and a few non-brahmins hedged in between these two groups. Even if the Moderates were to form a ministry, since the Governor could send for anyone and ask him to form one, the non-brahmins would not gain much for 'the whole power must necessarily rest with the extremist Home Rulers' who did not like the reforms 'in as much they do not go far enough'. But Home Rulers would act if necessary to bring the 'whole machinery of Government...to a standstill', wherein the government will 'have no alternative but to go where the extremists drive them'.

Dr. Nair argued that it was to ward off this eventuality that the Government of India had passed the Rowlatt Acts. There were those who carped against the latter, but this was because they desired to take control over the Government of India and run it themselves and who naturally wished to 'deny to the British administrators the option of having certain weapons in their hands to govern the country against certain mischievous influences...If a citizen denied the government a necessary weapon for carrying on the government then he is not fit to be entrusted with any responsibility'.

Referring to a letter written to him by Lord Sydenham, a peer who was supportive of non-brahmin demands (who served on the Joint Select Committee which heard evidence on the Montford reforms), he noted that the latter had sought to make him wise with respect to the 'appalling situation in Russia created by a "little body of extremists"':

> If any of the reforms led to a concentration of powers in the hands of a few individuals, brahmanas, non-brahmins or panchamas, Bolshevism will be the necessary result....If in spite of their [non-brahmin] constitutional agitations, power got into the hands of the brahmana Home Rulers, Bolshevism would be the only end.

Dr. Nair was convinced that nationalists in India, especially those in the Extremist camp, were veritable Bolsheviks since they 'were with the current disturbances'. Therefore, 'at the present time if they [the government] wanted to go on a progressive scale they would have to go exceedingly cautiously and the only cautious way was to see that every community was properly represented in the Legislature' (NI 26.4.19). In his eagerness to state the non-brahmin case, we find Dr. Nair taking a rather untenable position with respect to such sensitive matters as the Rowlatt Acts. It is also curious that like other liberals of his time he would identify Annie Besant and her Home Rulers with the Bolsheviks, especially since Annie Besant was, herself, extremely critical of the latter! (Indeed Annie Besant was inclined to favour the Rowlatt Acts. In response to a query from C. P. Ramaswamy Iyer, who had expressed surprise at her alleged support of the acts, Annie Besant noted that times were such that such strong measures were required: 'In times of revolution and invasion, all good citizens should rally round the King's Government until the danger is over' [NI 21.4.19]. It is clear that for many in England and the English colonies, the word 'Bolshevik' stood in for lawlessness and the rule of the mob.)

Liberalism of the kind favoured by Dr. Nair earned the Non-Brahmin movement the scorn of Congressmen. In the wake of the Jalianwala Bagh massacre, Annie Besant, who blamed the victims of the shooting as much as she did General Dyer, accused the Justicites of not protesting enough. When Theagoraya Chetty denied allegations that he had not said anything that may be construed to be in favour of Dyer's actions, Annie Besant carped at what she considered his insincerity (NI 8.1.21). (However, the fact is that Justicites did protest the killings in the Punjab: the first time, at a Non-Brahmin conference held at Nagapattinam, where it was resolved that the government ought to take further and more serious action against those official offenders who were responsible for the massacre (NI 13.10.20); and the second time, in a resolution passed at the Fourth Non-Brahmin Confederation (Rajaraman: 199).

Though Dr. Nair had prepared the ground for his colleagues, who had to appear without him before the Joint Select Committee, they had to face up to unrelenting and tough interrogators. Besides, they had to challenge and disprove the submissions of the redoubtable Mrs. Besant and the suave and sophisticated C. P. Ramaswamy Iyer.

In the evidence she tendered the committee, Annie Besant revealed a pointed bias in favour of brahmins, as Kesava Pillay discovered to his dismay. Further, she questioned the idea of a non-brahmin community as such, and insisted that such an entity did not, in fact, exist. Answering a specific question on the origin of the present caste war, as the committee termed it, she said it could not be dated to beyond the past two years and that it was not due to political causes:

> It seems to be an artificial agitation largely fomented by the European element and favoured negatively—I will not say more than that—I cannot be quite sure—by the Government of Madras. I ought to state my reasons for saying that. Dr. Nair had carried on a very active propaganda, not non-brahmin but anti-brahmana [sic] and has attacked in his paper the class of His Majesty's subjects called brahmanas and exposed them to hatred and contempt with a violence and virulence, which compared to the Home Rule agitation against the Bureaucracy is like whisky to water.

Mrs. Besant also claimed that, were it not for the overt partiality shown to Dr. Nair and his movement by the Madras government, *Justice*, the chief newspaper of the anti-brahmin party, would surely have come in for surveillance and invited penal action under the Press Act for vilifying and inciting hatred against a particular community.

A great deal of Annie Besant's evidence had to do with the status of the Nair community and with the question of whether it was 'truly depressed'. She characterized the Nairs as 'far more oppressive than the very much smaller and less influential brahmana caste' and argued that 'the grievance of the lower castes is more against Nairs than against the Brahmanas'. The latter, she pointed out, were to be consistently found in the forefront of the reform movement for 'bringing the submerged people to a better condition of life and giving them education'. Nairs, for purely partisan reasons, she claimed, were determined to decry the brahmana caste and question its credibility and worth.

Mrs. Besant's evidence attempted to reduce the Non-Brahmin movement to a clique of upper caste non-brahmin Hindus, chief amongst whom were the Nairs of Malabar Coast. She held Dr. Nair possessed only a compact and limited notion of the non-brahmana community in contrast to the MPA that considered 'all who literally are not brahmanas, that is... Christians and Parsees and those who belong to no caste' as constituting the great non-brahmin fraternity. Dr. Nair, on the other hand, 'limited his non-brahmanas to caste Hindus, excluding brahmanas only and that of course makes a great difference because if you take in the whole of the caste or the sub-caste you have no possibility of any changes which could bring about communal representation and that is why no such scheme has been brought forward by them. They cannot do it because there is no such thing as a non-brahmana community. It does not exist. No scheme has ever been put forward because it cannot be done' (reported, NI 5.10.19).

It should be noted here that Annie Besant nursed a personal grievance against Dr. Nair, ever since the latter had criticized Charles Leadbeater of the Theosophical Society, in an article published in the famed medical journal, *Antiseptic*. Dr. Nair's article was later picked up by *The Hindu*, which used it to criticize Mrs Besant's characterization of the young J. Krishnamurthy as the next messiah (Irschick: 49-51). The point is that Annie Besant had found her match in Dr. Nair. A sort of Ibsenite figure, Dr. Nair, as civic leader and social critic, mocked at Annie Besant's curious mixture of Orientalist nostalgia and an assumed Aryan pride. Dr. Nair was sensitive to this 'Irish Brahmani's will to power and scornful of the sociology and aesthetics she invoked to express it.

C. P. Ramaswamy Iyer was even more forthright in his condemnation of the demand for communal representation. He concurred with Annie Besant's view that 'there is no such thing as a non-brahmana community in point of view of homogeneity'. He also declared that if communal representation was to be granted 'it will mean an agitation in each subsection of that community over separate representation because it would be quite open to any of these subsections to come forward and say, "our interests are not safeguarded in this particular matter"'. Ramaswamy Iyer pointed out that according to Edgar Thurston's *Castes and Tribes of South India*, there exist 153 subcommunities among the non-brahmins, 'each of whom assume superiority, religious and social, to the others. The power to the members of the non-brahmin community *qua* community would mean that the 152nd and 153rd community would say "we are swamped by the rest". Given this extremely complex and stratified social context, it would be fallacious, submitted Ramaswamy Iyer, to set up a system of communal electorates: 'I am at one with those who have pleaded that if a compromise were accepted and was going to be loyally worked on both sides of the problem by a maximum for the brahmins and a minimum for the non-brahmins that may be suggested, but that, as I say, must be a matter of compromise.'

On being questioned closely as to the origin of the brahmin–non-brahmin divide in Madras, Ramaswamy Iyer, like Annie Besant, insisted the divide emerged only very recently but added that it was not for him 'to deny that for a considerable time there has been a feeling among the non-brahmin community that they, not having taken advantage of the educational facilities as the brahmanas did, were at a disadvantage in as far as the recruitment of the services and so forth were concerned'. But he hastened to add there had been no bitterness involved and certainly 'no question of the elimination of the brahmana element'. Besides, non-brahmins had all along played prominent roles in public life in Madras and, until recently, had worked with brahmanas who supported them during elections. He also observed that 'prior to the last election in which exceptional causes supravened non-brahmins were frequently returned to the Legislative Council by all (including largely brahmin) constituencies'. He concluded his submission with the observation that the brahmana–non-brahmin problem 'has been given much more artificial importance than it deserves' (reported, NI 6.10.19).

Compared to this spectacular performance by the Home Rulers, the non-brahmin deputation's presentation of themselves and their concerns to the Joint Select Committee proved remarkably tame. K. V. Reddi Naidu, who was examined in what proved to be one of the longest interrogation sessions, submitted that general electorates would not facilitate the election of persons truly representative of the non-brahmin communities. He claimed he was not averse to a general electorate comprising Indian Christians, Mohammadans, Eurasians and Europeans but insisted the brahmins should be kept out of it: 'We cannot get on if we are linked with the brahmanas. We can never succeed against them. They are so powerful.' When asked if a gradual widening of the franchise and the present constitution of the electorate would not favour non-brahmins, he remarked that 'mere numbers do not count' and added that the Indian peasant was at the mercy of his brahmin lawyers and officials in service. Reddi Naidu also observed that if communal representation was not granted, all that non-brahmins could do was 'keep quiet and die a civil death' or else they could choose 'to oppose and obstruct Government in all possible constitutional ways and as far as the law will permit and as far as the ability and capacity and organisation of the few that could get into councils can do' (reported, NI 23.2.20).

A. Ramasamy Mudaliar perhaps put across the non-brahmin case very well and with an honesty C. P. Ramaswamy Iyer would later mock and criticize:

> Why should I come here to admit we are not educated in such large numbers, that we are not organised, that our voters are illiterate and do not understand the value of the vote, that they are coerced by the officials, that they are a poor helpless lot who can be driven about like sheep by brahmana officials?...It is because we feel that in spite of the humiliations in making these admissions especially with an adverse audience behind me it is really a vital matter for us and it is not in any spirit of lightness that we have come forward and said this is one of those things which cannot be got rid of by mere platitudes (ibid).

In spite of the Justice party delegations's persistent arguments in favour of communal representation, the Joint Select Committee refused to endorse the measure. However, members of the Joint Select Committee were beginning to see the brahmin–non-brahmin divide in Madras for what it was and, pushed onwards by the liberal Lord Montagu to grant the reforms and bring about a transformation in the governance of India, they decided to adopt a stance that would give the reforms a working chance. This, they decided, could only be done by accommodating, to an extent, at least, non-brahmin aspirations. They mooted the idea of reserved seats for non-brahmins and entreated the latter to arrive at an exact number, after consultations with their brahmin peers. This did not work out—the brahmin witnesses refused to cooperate—and the entire matter was referred for arbitration and decision to the Government of India.

But the granting of reserved seats, it must be said, did not come about easily. Home Rulers and Justicites campaigned hard amongst English liberals and others to advance their respective claims. C. P.

Ramaswamy Iyer drew attention to the conduct of the non-brahmin witnesses before the Joint Select Committee and noted that, 'inspired by timidity, prejudice and a shortsighted outlook of the national future', they lent their 'ready and willing ears to the facile counsels of those who would fain keep India as a preserve for their own ambitions'. It was as if non-brahmins were 'apprehensive of their own powers so absolutely suspicious of their own faculties and capacities' and demanded a 'perpetual kind of [British] supervision' of their activities. And this he concluded could not possibly endear them or their cause to 'the average Britisher [who] is not accustomed to obsequiousness whether overt or covert' (NI 7.11.19).

Annie Besant demanded indignantly if the reservation of seats for non-brahmins in a general electorate would, indeed, be fair: 'Is it fair to the electors to thus restrict their choice and to force them to elect a man they do not want or not to elect a man they want?...Is it good to penalise a class of citizens for their superior qualities, to deprive them of their rights of citizenship because of their education, ability and culture?' (from 'United India', published in NI 17.11.19).

But non-brahmin claims won the day due to a number of reasons: K. V. Reddi Naidu won over British liberal opinion in the Joint Select Committee. The latter were also influenced—and influenced decisively—by the fact that the MPA, while being an arm of the Congress and the Home Rule League, also demanded concessions for non-brahmins. The MPA memorandum to the Joint Select Committee was cautious in tone. It denounced the Justice Party's anti-Brahminism, argued there were no grounds to imagine non-brahmins were any more civil to panchamas than the brahmins, refused the Justicites' allegation that the Home Rule League and the Varnashrama Dharma movement had common leaders and pooh-poohed the idea that brahmin lawyers did or would exercise undue influence in the future polity. However, it concluded that to 'safeguard the interests of the non-brahmins without giving rise to communal warfare' it was necessary to accommodate non-brahmin anxieties and allay them while working the reform scheme. The MPA clarified it was not for communal representation, since the non-brahmins were not a homogeneous group and therefore communal electorates would soon become caste electorates. Besides, special electorates would deprive non-brahmins of the influence they would wield in general electorates. Reserving seats for non-brahmins in plural member constituencies would be ideal, since this would assure non-brahmins of a place and yet leave them free to contest through general electorates as well (NI 6.12.19).

The MPA was also disenchanted with the Home Rule League and the obviously partisan attitudes of Congressmen such as C. P. Ramaswamy Iyer and Ramachandra Rao towards non-brahmins and communal representation. V. Chakkarai Chetty of the MPA noted in despair of the Joint Select Committee hearings and his own testimony that 'none of the delegates of the Congress took the slightest notice of the presence of such an insignificant delegate as the representative of the MPA'. Further, 'nor did the Congress representative from Madras show any disposition to champion the demand for communal representation' (reported, NI 10.12.19).

Meanwhile, there had also occurred a shift in Congress thinking on the matter, with Kasturi Ranga Iyengar of *The Hindu* and Rangaswami Iyengar endorsing the idea of reserved seats. These men, who would latter call themselves the Swarajists, were anxious to work the reforms and were unhappy with the Home Rulers and their ostensible extremism. Besides, by this time, Annie Besant had won many enemies in the Congress who were sharply critical of her extremely ambivalent stance on the Rowlatt Acts. She had also mocked at and criticized the Congress' angry reactions to the Jalianwala Bagh massacre. As Periyar would observe later, she was inclined to blame the crowd that had gathered at Jalianwala Bagh than the general whose men opened fire on it.

Due to this complex array of reasons and motives, the Justice delegation managed to achieve a partial victory. Their case had been heard out and its significance acknowledged. While the difficult task of arriving at a viable number of seats to be reserved awaited the Justicites in Madras, it could now count on many factors to achieve its ends.

The Meston Award

The fixing of the exact number of reserved seats proved to be an extremely arduous task. The Justice party now found itself united with the MPA in a common endeavour. As soon as it became clear that brahmins and non-brahmins may not be able to hammer out a tenable compromise formula, the Madras government decided to seek the services of an arbitrator. This failure to arrive at a mutually agreeable solution was largely due to the obduracy of brahmin Congressmen who were not prepared to concede anything, except the bare minimum by way of reserved seats. Brahmin public opinion was marshalled to support the cause of brahmin legislators and the newly appointed Governor of the Madras Presidency, Lord Willingdon, was soon besieged with memoranda of various sorts. A brahmin representation categorically stated that 'the principle of reservation of seats in favour of non-brahmanas who form the majority of the electorate is unjustified'. But if such a principle was to be enforced, if only 'to allay the feeling of grievance strongly entertained among a section of the non-brahmin community and with a view to secure the goodwill and cooperation of all communities in working the reforms', not more than 50 percent of the elected seats ought to be made over to non-brahmanas (NI 9.2.20).

Other brahmin opinion makers were not prepared to concede even this. At a meeting held in Triplicane in Madras, graced by none other than the smooth-tongued C. P. Ramaswamy Iyer, it was resolved that 'any response upon a communal basis is detrimental to the best interests of the country and as regards the Hindu community, reservation of seats as proposed will prove highly injurious to the integrity of Hindu society'. It was also suggested that 'as regards deficiency of representatives of any section of the Hindu community the proper course would be to provide or supplement elections by general electorates in those areas where the deficiency is to be made good' (NI 28.2.20).

A protest against the reservation of seats was issued from Thanjavur which stated unequivocally that brahmins could not discern any merit in the non-brahmin demand for concessions. For, though Hindus recognized divisions among the higher castes pertaining to labour, such as the brahmins, vaishyas, kshatriyas and shudras, they did not acknowledge such distinctions as brahmins and non-brahmins. The protesters from Thanjavur also held that if a reservation of seats came about, this would create a cleavage amongst non-brahmins and brahmins, where none existed before. Arguing that 'there is no evidence of the vast majority of the Hindu population desiring these distinctions being made as regards elections to the council', the protesters noted haughtily that the brahmin was sought to be penalized on the grounds that he was deemed 'intellectually superior to the other sections of the Hindu community' and because he was reputed to wield a 'great influence over the masses':

> We may concede that as a class the brahmanas are superior to other classes but... there is absolutely no evidence that they will be able to influence the election so as to secure a whole or a majority of seats for themselves. The brahmana as a class is notoriously poor for one thing and he cannot bring money power to bear on voters. If he exercises intellectual and moral influence over the people and they think he will make a better representative than men from other sections of the community it will be an oppressive and tyrannical act on the part of Government to fetter the choice of voters and select a man who may not have the same number of votes as the man of his choice' (NI 28.2.20).

Lord Meston, the arbitrator, began to take evidence in March 1920 and as the various witnesses deposed before him, it was apparent that the non-brahmins were divided amongst themselves. Lodd Govindass, for instance, wondered if V. Chakkarai Chetty, an Indian Christian, could represent non-brahmins. Tulsiram, who had accompanied the Justice delegation to London, now wondered if communities such as the Saurashtras—whose representative he was—and the Nadars could be classified as non-brahmins, since the former did not accept themselves as such and the latter favoured being called kshatriyas. Though A. Ramasamy Mudaliar attempted to counter Lodd Govindass and Tulsiram by pointing out they represented nobody's views but their own, and that the Justice Party did not believe in distinctions of caste, the damage had been done (NI 2.3.20).

C. P. Ramaswamy Iyer pounced on Tulsiram's evidence and stated this was proof enough to 'dispose of the question of the possibilities of communal electorates' (ibid). T. R. Ramachandra Iyer claimed that in view of Tulsiram's evidence, one may conclude the non-brahmins did not, in fact, constitute a community. He wondered if it were not the apt moment to consider 'whether brahmanas had not hitherto represented the interests of all and would not represent as well in the future'. Besides, 'to ask for elections and at the same time say electors are fools is a contradiction in terms' and non-brahmins would do well to ponder over this obvious act of folly on their part (ibid). C. P. Ramaswamy Iyer stated that of the 60 elected seats, one seat in every district and three seats in Madras would give the non-brahmins 26 seats, and if one were to add to this the seats reserved for zamindars and landholders, some of whom would be non-brahmins, the number of seats that the latter could contest would be greater (ibid).

Non-brahmins could not hope to match either C. P. Ramaswamy Iyer's eloquence or his perverse logic, and, besides, Lord Meston seemed quite determined to disregard their apprehensions. For instance, Lord Meston rejected the non-brahmin demand that a limit be placed upon the number of brahmin candidates who may be elected to the Council. On the other hand, he appeared to favour the brahmin plan which held that a non-brahmin seat be reserved in each territorial unit. Further, Lord Meston refused to consider seriously allegations by non-brahmins of 'brahmana tyranny' and remarked thus:

> It does not appear necessary to guarantee the non-brahmins a large majority of seats or any majority. It seems sufficient to ensure them such a start in the race as will prevent them being outdistanced, if they exercise ordinary energy and intelligence. In this connection it is impossible to overlook the very great preponderance of the non-brahmins in the electoral rolls (NI 18.3.20).

Lord Meston, in all likelihood, was influenced by the results of the August 1919 elections, the last to be held under the Morley-Minto scheme, which returned a greater number of non-brahmins to the councils and by the results of the 1920 elections to the Corporation of Madras, wherein voters seemed to have voted across communities (NI 22.1.20). Thus, Lord Meston observed: 'That the non-brahmanas are already competent without special protection to secure reasonable success would appear from statistics which I obtained informally from the Madras Secretariat' (NI 18.3.20).

When the Meston Award was announced, it invoked a volley of protests from non-brahmins. At a meeting held in the office of *Justice*, non-brahmin leaders vehemently opposed the award and Theagoraya Chetty exhorted non-brahmins 'to never trust a brahmana, never help a brahmana and never vote for a brahmana'. Characterizing the award as 'atrocious', V. Chakkarai Chetty, likewise, demanded that non-brahmins return only their own in the forthcoming council elections. The MPA, following Chakkarai Chetty, called on all the non-brahmins in the Presidency 'to immediately organise, combine and carry on active propaganda' for the elections (NI 23.3.20).

As if to announce a newly consecrated solidarity, non-brahmin leaders—of the Justice party and the MPA—called for a mass meeting at Triplicane beach in Madras on 3 April 1920. Speakers at the meeting included non-brahmin notables such as Theagoraya Chetty, Ramarayaningar, V. Chakkarai Chetty, Kalyanasundara Mudaliar and Lodd Govindass, all of whom railed against the Meston Award and called for a concerted defence of non-brahmin interests. Rather than assign seats to non-brahmins in proportion to their representation in the total population of the Presidency, Lord Meston had chosen to reserve a mere 28 seats, a number that was not only inadequate to the original seven-ninths demanded by the non-brahmins, but did not amount to even 50 percent of the total seats (NI 5.4.20). Lodd Govindass, by no means a brahmin hater, pointed out the obvious injustice of the Meston Award, while T. V. Gopalasamy Mudaliar, who had earlier accused the Justicites of being prevailed upon by the Madras government, now spoke of the need for the MPA and the Justice party to come together to oppose the unfair treatment meted out by Meston to non-brahmins. He pleaded that the Justice party and the MPA bury their differences and not say or do anything to embitter their relations with one another (NI 5.4.20).

A joint memorandum was issued by the Justice party and the MPA, which protested the Meston Award and noted that the latter had created widespread resentment amongst all ranks of non-brahmins. The latter, irrespective of the political views they held, had now decided to close ranks. The memorandum also pointed to brahmin views on the matter of reserved seats, expressed at various conferences prior to the announcement of the Meston Award, and observed that earlier brahmin Congressmen had endorsed non-brahmin claims in this respect. The memorandum further noted:

> Are the non-brahmins to infer from the studied silence of Lord Meston with regard to the resolutions passed by the predominantly brahmin conferences recognising the right of non-brahmins to a reservation in proportion to their numerical strength and tax paying

> capacity, that he attaches no importance to political consistency and that brahmana politicians are free to make [any] representations they please, provided they can thereby hoodwink the gullible non-brahmin public?

The memorandum rejected Lord Meston's views on the 'high' non-brahmin representation in local and municipal boards and wondered how Lord Meston was warranted in 'drawing this inference with regard to the possibility, let alone the certainty of non-brahmins, capturing a proportion of seats which will be commensurate to their importance in the body politic?' Besides, it was a well-known fact, that only seems to have escaped Lord Meston's attention, that brahmin politicians as a rule 'do not care very much to be elected to these boards and local bodies for helping in the performance of the unromantic and dull work of municipal administration. They want to exert themselves in the larger sphere where they will have more influence and more power and where their ambitions to occupy the seat of the mighty can be gratified.' The memorandum concluded with an appeal to Lord Meston to view the problem of reserved seats from the non-brahmin point of view and not yield the non-brahmins to the 'tender mercies of one of the most clannish oligarchies in the world' (NI 7.6.20).

The exit of a substantial number of non-brahmin notables from the MPA and the Congress proved to be a momentous event, at least for men such as Kesava Pillay. Kesava Pillay was now thoroughly disenchanted with Congressmen. The latter had taken to blaming alternately the Moderates and the Home Rulers for failing to live up to non-brahmin demands. Kesava Pillay refuted the Home Rulers' allegation that the Moderates were to blame in this respect and noted that, previously, 'as a matter of fact all brahmanas (nationalists and moderates) were against a separate electorate and with the exception of a few all were openly or tacitly for communal representation by limiting the number of brahmanas to be elected in order to avoid split in the Congress ranks'. He observed that 'all the brahmanas have changed their views after the Montford Report was issued and after the pronouncements of the Southborough Committee' (NI 20.5.20).

Annie Besant was stung into her usual vituperative rhetoric by this 'turnabout' on Kesava Pillay's part and noted that he had gone over to the side of those who penalize birth. It was clear the province would very soon experience a 'non-brahmin tyranny in which rank, wealth, land and numbers would combine to crush a small minority because of their birth' (ibid). Several letters were written in defense of Kesava Pillay and Annie Besant respectively. Non-brahmin anger at Mrs Besant's insinuations with regard to an impending non-brahmin tyranny was evident in P. S. Gurusamy Naidu's response: He observed that non-brahmins were not out 'to extinguish the brahmana' but merely wanted to reduce him to 'his proper place in the body politic': 'This necessary process however unpleasant to the brahmana or to *New India* because of its brahmana associations will be found ultimately to be beneficial to the development of true democracy' (NI 21.5.20).

Kesava Pillay himself responded with a spirited defence of his earlier observations on Moderates and Nationalists. He suggested that '*New India* may do some real service to bring about harmony and goodwill between communities, if it will cease dreaming of non-brahmin tyranny over a small minority on account of their birth, and carping against communal representation which is for the present a settled fact'. He warned his brahmin comrades that it was for them, 'that have had the whiphand over others . . . to gain and retain that trust and the allegiance of the many who had hitherto accepted them trustfully and in good faith as their leaders in social, religious and political fields'. In any case non-brahmins, now awakened to a sense of their due in history, were not likely to heed brahmin privileges (NI 22.5.20).

This sense of 'an awakening' amongst non-brahmins registered by Kesava Pillay had been in evidence at the Non-Brahmin Confederation held in December 1919, soon as the Justice delegation returned from London. In addition to the usual resolutions to do with education, industry and agriculture, it was resolved that marriage and other ceremonies, as well as prayer rites in front of an idol, would be performed by enlightened members of the non-brahmin community, rather than by brahmins. The federation had further urged its participants to give up brahminical customs such as infant marriage and called for a greater mingling and intermarriage amongst different non-brahmin castes. It was also proposed that all Hindu temples, tanks, wells and roads and schools be open to all classes of Hindus. The non-brahmins at the federation vowed to form an association 'for securing the proper management of religious and charitable trusts and counteracting the diversion of funds in favour of the brahmana community' (NI 31.12.19).

The Justice Party Comes to Power

The election results of 1920 revealed the political will to power of non-brahmins in Madras. In all, 65 non-brahmins were returned to the council. To an extent, non-brahmin victory was facilitated by the Congress' decision to boycott the elections; yet it was obvious that a non-brahmin constituency with its own distinctive political claims had emerged in Madras. In 1920, this constituency had responded to the pressure of political ideologies as well as to the pull of felt existential needs. The Justice party mirrored these needs and, more important, articulated issues of non-brahmin self-respect to represent significant political concerns. Nationalism, the imperative to free oneself and society as a whole from colonial rule, could no more be deemed the only political issues of any significance to the people of Madras. Nor could the question of power, difference and subordination in the varna-jati order of things be subsumed by the larger and, by implication, more important question of nationalism.

However, the immense importance of the election results of 1920 was lost on Congress and brahmins in the Presidency. *New India* noted covertly :'It is significant that in not a single instance was the Meston Award practically operative as in every constituency where reservations had been guaranteed, the minimum of non-brahmin councillors was reached or exceeded' (NI 11.12.20).

Before the elections, *New India* had argued, as we have seen, that cross-communal voting was the norm in Madras and that conventionally brahmin councillors to the corporation and the council, had been returned by a largely non-brahmin electorate. At the same time, following a line of argument advanced by Lord Meston, it was pointed out that a large non-brahmin electorate could not be expected to return only brahmins. It is clear these mutually contradictory arguments were made to 'prove' the utter irrelevance and gratuitous nature of the non-brahmin demand for reservation of seats. What was conveniently and wilfully ignored was the fact that half a decade of intensive Justice propaganda and activity had stimulated the demand for the reservation of seats for non-brahmins.

The Justice party's victory allowed the constitution of the first non-brahmin ministry in Madras under the Montford scheme. Lord Willingdon invited Theagoraya Chetty to form a ministry but he declined on grounds of ill-health. Three others, A. Subbarayalu Reddiar, Ramarayaningar and K. V. Reddi Naidu assumed office in December 1920. This choice of ministers elicited a further round of criticisms from *New India.* On 13 December 1920 the paper carried an editorial which remarked that:

> We are decidedly of the opinion that Lord Willingdon has committed a fatal, stupendous and political blunder.... By choosing the ministry not from any political party in the proper sense of the term, having any fixed principle or policy but activated by communal feeling and prejudices the Governor has directed the flow of political activity along communal channels to the prejudice of a healthy formation and progress of political principles.... The entrusting of power at the beginning of responsible Government to a body of people who have nothing in common except communal bias would have the most damaging effect on public morals and retard the extinction of communal prejudices.

Besant had favoured C. P. Ramaswamy Iyer and Dr. Rama Rao for the ministerships and had exhorted the government not to fall prey to communal machinations but, instead, 'choose the best men, irrespective of birth' (NI 14.12.20). C. P. Ramaswamy Iyer had addressed election meetings in his usual flamboyant fashion: he had dismissed away rather airily charges of brahmin tyranny, had, in turn, charged that non-brahmins were prejudiced. He had even sported a revolver at a meeting to indicate his readiness to face the worst (NI 1.11.20). He had noted that his agents were being threatened and all this had come to pass because he had shown himself ready to 'sacrifice a lucrative practice to serve his province and his country' (NI 8.11.20). It is, of course, another matter, that after he realized he was not going to be on the ministry, he accepted the post of advocate-general! When matters seemed fluid, that is, when it was not yet clear who would be asked to constitute a ministry, he had written a pious disclaimer to *New India*, politely refuting allegations that he had been tipped for a judgeship in the Madras High Court (NI 21.8.20). But a few months later, we find him announcing to the public that, in spite of having won at the elections, he would represent the nation's interests as an advocate general rather than as a member of the council (NI 3.1.21). Annie Besant wrote an explanatory note, defending his acceptance of this post and argued that, perhaps, he had decided that he could serve his country best that way! (NI 5.1.21)

When, in spite of her strident calls to 'play fair', Lord Willingdon chose to install a non-brahmin ministry, Annie Besant naturally cavilled:

> Does His Excellency not see that the enthronement of undiluted racial bitterness will throw the body politic into confusion, retarding the growth of a healthy public opinion and national feeling?... It is a truism that a party in power can strengthen and consolidate their position in the country by... a judicious exercise of patronage in various ways. We hear that attempts are already being made to shut the mouths of anti-Justice non-brahmana members by holding out promises of a place in the new regime (NI 14.12.20).

Annie Besant was not alone in her condemnation of the Justice ministry and the communal principles that had ostensibly determined Lord Willingdon's choice. K. S. Rajagopalan writing in *New India* lamented that the Governor had chosen a 'handful of bigoted die-hards to whom the word "brahmana" itself was an anathema' and argued that the Governor ought to have divided the council along party rather than caste lines: 'This is no party government but caste government and no amount of sophistical reasoning can turn it into a popular government' (20.12.20).

What was, of course, conveniently forgotten by Annie Besant and other detractors of the Justice party was that with the Congress boycotting councils, and with brahmin Congressmen such as C. P. Ramaswamy Iyer and Rama Rao contesting as independents, the political and nationalist claims of the latter could hardly be urged as legitimate and as beyond doubt; especially, since there was no party in the Council to represent and ratify such claims. The patriotic credentials of C. P. Ramaswamy Iyer and Rama Rao rested chiefly on their always already privileged status, that is, as brahmins they could not but be patriotic. This implied all brahmins were nationalists and non-brahmins, if they were not with the nationalists, usurpers and loyalists. Annie Besant was particularly insistent in her denunciations of the new ministry in this particular regard and refused to accept that the Justice victory signified a political verdict:

> Choose any twelve men who have not been pestered with the communal wrangles of Madras but who possess a working knowledge of parliamentary government in Western countries, put before them the case of Madras and we are confident, we are certain that their verdict will be that the Governor's step is against the true parliamentary manner tending not to fit all classes of the population to take their share in public life in Government... but to discriminate and discriminate in favour of a small section of a particular class of the whole community... *Justice* prates about the people's verdict.... We protest the defeat has been misconstrued into a victory (ibid).

In spite of Annie Besant, the Justice ministry retained its hold over office, and the logic of communal representation it had sworn by came to dominate not only council politics but also influenced Justice policy in many very crucial respects.

CHAPTER 5

Legislating for Non-Brahmins: Justicites, Law and Social Change

THE PASSING OF THE COMMUNAL GOVERNMENT ORDERS

Initially, communal representation was an idea that was associated with an increased non-brahmin presence in the services. Only later was it re-defined to signify a demand for an electorate along communal lines. The Justice party, however, never lost sight of its original objective: rendering the services more accessible to non-brahmins and securing for them positions in government, commensurate with their presence in the population. The passing of the so-called Communal Government Orders thus represented a point of high achievement for the first Justice ministry.

The Madras government issued, what subsequently came to be known as the First Communal Government Order (GO), in September 1921. This marked the end of a long and tortuous series of debates, arguments and negotiations between brahmins, non-brahmins and the European members of the Madras Service. The desire to 'non-brahminize' the services in Madras possessed a double history: on one hand, it was impelled by British desire to hold brahmin administrative dominance in check (Irschick 1969: 218-20). However, and herein we may discern the 'other' history to the efforts to non-brahminize the services, the government found help forthcoming from another quarter: educated non-brahmins who felt it wrong that they were represented in so miniscule a fashion in provincial administration. Such men now began to pressurize government and several of them gave evidence before the Public Services Commission in 1913 (ibid: 222-25). Thereafter, they carried their concerns into the newly formed

Justice party, where they came to be inscribed at the heart of the Non-Brahmin Manifesto. The rest is, of course, familiar history: the persistent resolutions on the issue at various non-brahmin conferences; the pressure exerted on government by various forums and during the many depositions before committees during the Montford Report hearings.

The time between the assumption of office by Justicities in early 1921 and the actual passing of the Communal Government Order in September 1921 proved to be a period of hectic propaganda. As in earlier instances, Justicites had to heed and respond to an unconvinced, rancorous and obdurate brahmin public opinion. Justicites opened their arguments for increased non-brahmin representation in the services by drawing attention to the state of the judiciary in Madras. Since judges of the Madras High Court had the power to appoint district munsiffs and since these judges were invariably brahmins, in several instances they had appointed men of their own caste as district munsiffs. As if this were not injurious enough to non-brahmin interests (and pride), men like K. Srinivasa Iyengar, Law Member in the Governor's Council, justified such appointments on the grounds that brahmins were preferred, because they were far more efficient than others (quoted in 'Contemporary Opinion', NI 27.3.21). In this context Justicites demanded that the power to nominate district munsiffs be taken away from the Madras High Court; or that the court insist that judges heed the principle of 'due representation to all communities' in making appointments (Irschick: 234).

Responding to this instance of 'brahmana hatred', a *New India* reader lamented thus: 'There is no knowing whether similar discrimination may not be called in every department of life. Rights that are secured by the Queen's Proclamation and Government of India's plighted word are sought to be made a nullity as far as the brahmana is concerned.' The letter writer suggested that brahmins form themselves into a distinctive political party to secure their rights that were now continually being undermined (11.5.21). Another *New India* reader, P. N. Rao, disagreed with this suggestion for a brahmana political party. Noting that 'the time is not ripe to form a brahmana party and [that] forming one will only further anti-brahmana hatred', he observed that non-brahmana anger was not against brahmanas who, in any case, were 'extinct as a caste', but against the latter's brains:

'It is trade jealousy at the bottom as is everywhere in the world; when the deficiency of intellect has the upper hand over intellect, the results are obvious.... Prick the bubble and you will see the English educated shudra out for a job under false colours. It will not be long before non-shudra Hindus come to know how they have been made pawns by a scheming few' (19.5.21).

Not all brahmins were overeager to castigate the Justicites. There were men like A. Rangaswamy Iyengar who expressed the opinion that the present way of ordering lives and duties must transform itself:

> There is a new value of the individual to society.... That every man should be given all the opportunities for expression which his soul is capable of taking advantage of is a principle which will have to be realised—in every department of individual and national activity in a modern State whether of physical health or well-being, education, intellectual, athletic or moral or technical training, industries, commerce or statesmanship.

However, senior statesmen ought to make sure that

> Disabilities intended to be removed do not give rise to new disabilities... that new forms of antagonism do not come into existence... and that barriers are not placed against vital principles of the Age, viz. that every man or woman should be enabled to rise to the full height of his or her status whether it be physical, moral, intellectual or spiritual (NI 18.6.21).

But even this qualified and wily endorsement of the idea of redistributing appointments was not to be had from other brahmins. Nevertheless, the Justice party's resolution on communal representation in the services was moved by O. Thanikachalam Chetty in the Madras Legislative Council. He resolved:

> That this Council recommends to this government that a standing order be issued to every officer or Board or body of officers authorised to make appointments to the public service to give preference to candidates from the non brahmin communities including therein (Christians, Muhammadans and members of the depressed classes)

> until a proportion of at least 66 percent of officers carrying a salary of Rs 100 per mensem and upwards and a proportion of 75 percent among officers carrying a salary of less than Rs 100 are reached within a period of 7 years from this date so long as such candidates possess the minimum qualifications prescribed by the rules relating to appointments to public services although such candidates be less qualified than brahmin candidates (NI 6.8.21).

He moved a second resolution as well, that demanded all appointments to all offices in the Secretariat be made only from amongst non-brahmins to bring about equality within three years between brahmins and non-brahmins (NI 6.8.21). A. R. Knapp, the Home Member, approved of the first resolution but asked that it be amended to mean the principles prescribed for recruitment in Standing Order 128(2) be extended to all departments. But he thought the second resolution gratuitous, whereupon O. Thanikachalam Chetty remarked it was vital and necessary for non-brahmins since the Secretariat was a 'fortress within a fortress' to which non-brahmins may otherwise never hope to gain admission (ibid).

In spite of Knapp's criticism and his apprehensions over the 'loss of merit' in the Secretariat, O. Thanikachalam Chetty's position won the day and so the First Communal Government Order came to be promulgated on 16 September 1921. This was followed by the second and far more comprehensive Government Order, the Second Communal Government Order of 22 August 1922, which also demanded that Council be submitted with lists of appointees by caste in various departments, so that progress with respect to non-brahmin recruitment could be analysed (Irschick: 232-38).

But the Justice party's victory proved pyrrhic and for two reasons: for one thing, it displaced the problem of communal representation from the legislature onto the Executive and, as a consequence, removed it from the realm of debate and policy making. Secondly, the Madras civil service worked hard to scuttle all efforts to work the GOs. The inscription of communal representation into Executive fiat allowed the government to modify, supplant and retard its realization.

Under dyarchy, Indians could legislate on the transferred subjects, but they were necessarily restrained in their activity by the interference of official English members of the Executive as well as the non-official nominated members in the Executive, most of whom were brahmins. Madras civilians, anxious to prevent or at least delay an imminent 'brahminization' of its higher echelons had supported the non-brahmin demand for communal representation, though even then there were men like Knapp who worried over the possible 'sacrifice of merit' this may involve. Now, faced with the prospect of a legislation which in effect would curb their powers to make appointments, the civilians acted swiftly.

Thus, the civilians sought to banish several brahmins in the Madras Secretariat either to the mofussil or to the Central Secretariat in Calcutta and, substituted in the places and positions they had occupied, non-brahmins brought in from the mofussil. The idea was to appease Justicites whom, the civilians reasoned, merely desired to occupy front ranks in the City Services. However, the revenue department which stood to be affected by these transfers, opposed this move and it had to be dropped. The ICS cabal in the Legislative Council proved to be extremely resourceful. Thus a new GO was issued in 1923 which noted that 'no hard and fast rule can be laid down which will fetter the discretion of the secretaries to government and collectors in the matter of appointments' (Baker 1976: 51). This more or less foreclosed the working chances of the two earlier GOs.

The first GO had clearly stated 'heads of departments and other officers empowered to make appointments are requested to adhere strictly to this principle (that is, Standing Order 128(2)) which facilitated distribution of posts amongst various communities) in filling up vacancies in the future' (Irschick: 367). The Second Communal GO had stipulated that this principle be operative not only with respect to the 'number of men newly entertained in the permanent service' as stated in the First GO, but with respect to appointments 'both at the time of initial recruitment and at every point at which men are promoted wholly by selection or seniority' (ibid: 370). But, with the GO of 1923, these imperatives were rendered ineffective.

In order to further neutralize the Justice cause and render the principle of communal representation unworkable, the Madras government set up a Staff Selection Board which was empowered to conduct qualifying examinations and interviews. While the Board vowed to abide by the spirit of Standing Order 128, it was evident that the government intended, through this measure, to circumvent and retard the effects of the principle of communal representation. Since the Justice party's desire to secure a communal balance expressed itself in and through a politics of patronage, this latter served the government as a valid reason to insist on the constitution of any 'impartial body' that would oversee appointments (ibid: 238-40).

In spite of all this, the symbolic significance, for non-brahmins and adi dravidas, of the promulgation of the Communal GOs cannot be overstressed. For many decades to come, the GOs served to remind successive generations of non-brahmins that in a caste-bound polity, democratic practice would be uneven and necessarily subversive of hitherto dominant interests. For the Justicites, the GO's represented a promise fulfilled; they ratified Justice politics and legitimized the Justice politicians' love of office. The Justicites, though, were not entirely sanguine about the usefulness of the GOs. Recalling the First Justice Ministry's achievements at a Nellore District Non-Brahmin Conference held in April 1923, Theagoraya Chetty would note, with barely concealed anguish, that 'although the GO has been passed, in many cases it is treated as a scrap of paper.' But he would hasten to add 'a couple of years is but a drop in a nation's life' and call upon his partymen to put in 'persistent endeavours to rectify an age-old inequality and injustice' (NI 21.4.23).

For Congressmen and nationalists, the GOs were something of a political embarrassment, for they indicated the importance and necessity of importing social concerns into politics. In effect, they expressed an implicit critique of Congress politics, which Congressmen could afford to ignore in the early twenties, only because a section of them were caught up in the heady thrills of Non Cooperation.

Sir Sankaran Nair perhaps understood the importance of the GOs best. In an address to non-brahmins he clarified that, 'so far as the non-brahmanas are concerned... we have no spiritual gospel of our life as the basis of our government.... We want the Government to attend to our material interests. We want sufficiency of food, we want all opportunities for education and room for development along our lines' (NI 15.5.22).

The success of the 1919 reforms, whose usefulness was most evident in the instance of the communal GOs, soon began to taste sour to Justicites who came to realize gradually that non-brahmins could not exercise their authority within a political framework which constantly subordinated non-brahmin aspirations to the discretionary powers of a supremely self-centred Executive. At the Fifth Non-Brahmin Confederation, held in Madras, Natesa Mudaliar observed that several worthy schemes in respect of education, industries and irrigation cannot even be broached for fear of that monotonous reply from the Executive which commanded the finance portfolio, 'No Funds' (NI 16.1.22). The raja of Ramnad, president-elect of the confederation suggested that dyarchy ought to be abolished. Two important resolutions passed at the confederation called on non-brahmins to divest themselves of British influence and to work towards acquiring fiscal autonomy (ibid).

At a non-brahmin conference held at Kumbakonam, dyarchy was criticized vehemently, chiefly because all those vital areas of concern to non-brahmins—agriculture, industry and finance—were reserved subjects (NI 8.4.22). Similar sentiments were voiced at the Third Non-Brahmin Conference held at Coimbatore (NI 25.4.22). Thus, confronted with the limits to their own power, Justicites who sought to work dyarchy as best as they could while in office, also came to realize they needed to ask for more and this led the party into making a series of very complicated political choices. After the 1926 elections, Justicites began to seek new alliances and attempted to preserve their identity and integrity in the face of challenges posed by the Gandhian Congress as well as Periyar's Self-Respect movement. In those troubled times, their original political impulse, expressed most fitfully through their securing of the communal GOs, served them well. For it became the one factor that caused the Self-Respect movement to consider the Justice party as a serious, if somewhat seriously handicapped, alternative to the Congress.

THE QUESTION OF THE ADI DRAVIDAS

From its earliest days, the Justice party had been mindful of its duties and responsibilities to the non-brahmin community as a whole. As the resolutions passed at several of its conferences indicate, it endeavoured, in good faith, to constitute a non-brahmin fraternity. This latter comprised, for Justicites, not only caste Hindus but adi dravidas as well, and its singular attribute was to be a consistent anti-Brahminism; a studied resistance to brahmin secular and sacral power.

But the Justice party, at all times, could not represent or hold together a non-brahmin fraternity, because in Madras, as elsewhere, several contradictions underwrote the caste Hindus–adi dravidas relationship. Nor could it offer a concerted opposition to Brahminism, especially its sacral character, since several non-brahmin Hindus were reluctant to alter beliefs and practices, many of which involved the use of brahmin priests and the practice of brahmin rituals, which they considered central to their faith. Besides, non-brahmin attitudes to the adi dravidas and Brahminism were mediated through a vortex of material interests which often undermined the basis of the much desired and often imagined non-brahmin fraternity.

A Problem of Names and a Politics of Identity

The adi dravidas, comprising the so-called outcastes, had organized themselves as early as the last quarter of the nineteenth century. But the Dravida Mahajana Sangam and the Pariar Mahajana Sabha, both of which were formed in the 1890s, did not seek to attain or aspire to political power and, instead, concentrated their efforts on challenging and mitigating various practices of untouchability and on securing concessions for the adi dravidas in education and the public services. It was only when the Justice party articulated the need for an overarching non-brahmin political identity that several organizations of the adi dravidas came to subscribe to the idea of an inclusive and broad-based non-brahmin political formation. But in spite of these desired and sometimes achieved horizontal political linkages, the relationship between the adi dravidas and the non-brahmin caste Hindus remained problematic.

When on the advice of O. Kandasamy Chetty, Dr. Nair attempted to convince a gathering of the adi dravidas at Spur Tank, Madras, of the importance of building a broad-based non-brahmin movement to counter the propaganda of the Home Rulers, he found himself confronted with a rather suspicious audience. Anchas, president of the Pariar Mahajana Sabha, retorted that the adi dravidas would suffer as much under a non-brahmin caste Hindu Home Rule as under Brahmin Home Rule (Irschick: 71-72). Non-brahmin efforts to mobilize the adi dravidas to the ranks of the Justice party continued well after Dr. Nair's Spur Tank Road address and, eventually, a sizeable section of the adi dravidas represented in the Madras Adi Dravida Mahajana Sabha, of which M. C. Raja was a member, did respond favourably to the Justice party's ideological and political overtures.

Like non-brahmins, the adi dravidas endorsed the idea of communal representation. A memorandum on reforms submitted by the Madras Adi Dravida Mahajana Sabha to the government pointed out that only a separate electorate, which would return a member of their own community to the Council, would ensure their concerns were not misrepresented or distorted. The adi dravidas proclaimed their opposition to Home Rule, even as Justicites did, and on similar grounds: that it would perpetrate oligarchic and caste rule (NI 9.1.19). Non-brahmin leaders, for their part, sought to make the concerns of the adi dravidas their own. Not only did they eloquently argue the case of the adi dravidas with regard to separate electorates in their own memoranda, but also came to display a rare sensitivity to their other symbolic but hugely significant demands.

For instance, Natesa Mudaliar took up the issue of a change of names with respect to the adi dravidas in the Madras Corporation and argued that the government immediately re-classify the so-called panchamas as adi dravidas as was desired by prominent and representative members of that community. The Madras Adi Dravida Mahajana Sabha had expressed such a desire in December 1917—in a conference held by its Kolar branch—when a resolution was proposed and passed which requested the government to henceforth refer to panchamas as 'Authee Dravidas, thus bringing them into line with non-brahmana Hindus who are spoken of as Dravidians' (NI 3.1.17). Later, when M. C. Raja recommended the deletion of the terms 'paraiah and panchama', from government records and asked that the word 'adi-dravida' be substituted in their stead, his resolution was carried out unanimously in the Justice-dominated Madras Council (NI 21.1.22).

Justicites addressed the disabilities suffered by the adi dravidas in their conferences as well. The First Non-Brahmin Confederation held in Madras in December 1917 passed at least four important resolutions that related to adi dravida welfare. Two of these had to do with education, while the third and fourth had to do with abolition of caste differences. They were proposed by the zamindar of Singampatti and supported by O. Kandasamy Chetty. They read as follows:

> *(a)* 'This Confederation is strongly of the opinion that for the unification of all non-brahmin classes there should be a fusion of castes and urges the necessity of legislation for the removal of legal hindrances which stand in the way of a free social intercourse between the different classes of the Indian people.'
>
> *(b)* 'This Confederation is of the opinion that all restrictions which prevent adi-dravidas and other depressed classes from a free use of public wells and tanks and public streets should be removed' (Varadarajulu Naidu 1932: vol 2, 164).

But neither the political and historical imperative to present a united non-brahmin historic bloc, comprising caste Hindus and the adi dravidas, to counter Congress and its elite brahmin leadership, nor the enormous goodwill that leaders such as Dr. Nair, Kandasamy Chetty and Natesa Mudaliar enjoyed with the adi dravidas, proved determinate when the adi dravidas later sought to establish their own distinctive political identity. Even in the 1919 memorandum on the new reform scheme, where they had preferred a separate electorate, the members of the Madras Adi Dravida Mahajana Sabha had observed:

> We are particularly desirous of a separate electorate being created for us. Representation by nomination is no representation at all. The advisers of the Government in making these nominations will hereafter be brahmanas and non-brahmana caste Hindus and they are likely to recommend persons who play to their whims rather than speak out boldly the views of our community. Besides a communal electorate is a political school for educating the community in the effective exercise of their franchise and effect criticism of actions of representatives. A panchama who owes his seat to the kind offices of Government advised by men belonging to other communities will not feel his responsibility to the community as keenly as one returned by the community itself (NI 9.1.19).

Clearly, the adi dravidas desired to preserve for themselves a measure of political autonomy and, in some ways, their choice of the appellation, 'adi dravida' rather than 'dravida' reflected this desire for a distinctive political and social identity. While closing ranks with the Justice party was, no doubt, a conscious political gesture, it could not be taken to mean that a complete identity of interests existed at all times between non-brahmin caste Hindus and the adi dravidas. Thus, at the Third Non-Brahmin District conference held in Coimbatore in April 1922, Pettachi Chetty, president of the conference noted that if the Non-Brahmin movement was to address political, social and religious concerns simultaneously, it would only precipitate a clash of interests amongst non-brahmins. If the present conference, for instance, were to permit intermarriage and interdining amongst all non-brahmin castes and between the latter and the adi dravidas; if the conference were to address matters of religious reform, non-brahmin caste Hindus and adi dravidas would confront each other in hostility. Pettachi Chetty was convinced it was in the sphere of politics that non-brahmins, of whatever caste, and adi dravidas could come together on the basis of mutual interests (NI 25.4.22).

The relationship between the two groups which, at the best of times, was defined by a certain tautness was further sought to be maligned by Madras' brahmins and the Home Rule League. Annie Besant and her coterie of readers would thus cast aspersions on M. C. Raja's representative claims with respect to his community, chiefly because he was an enthusiastic Justicite, while self-styled reformist brahmins would often argue that non-brahmin caste Hindus were more mindful of caste prejudices and untouchability than reformed brahmins.

New India fired its first salvo against Raja when the latter was nominated as a member from the adi dravidas to the Madras Council in 1919 under the Morley-Minto scheme and later in 1920 under the Montford scheme. A report on Raja, that appeared days after he had been appointed to the council, objected to his nomination on two counts; that he was a 'declared anti-Home ruler and [did] not believe in any Indian Nation' and because he was an 'avowed brahmin hater' who held that in the olden days, Aryans had descended on the original inhabitants of the land, the 'Authee Dravidas', and attempted to impose on them the 'hated creed of Brahminism' (NI 2.8.19). Raja was not without his supporters. One Ponnusamy declared that Raja was a 'simple and sincere worker' and rebuked Annie Besant for her partisan views. He further noted: 'There are enough men in my community or outside it who are capable enough to look after our interests better than you and your brahmana advisers' (NI 5.8.19).

In 1920, *New India* proposed the name of V. G. Vasudeva Pillay, who was a Congressman, in place of Raja as adi dravida member for the Madras Council. It claimed it was merely representing the views of a section of the adi dravidas and had no real bias in the matter. That section of the adi dravidas, which owed allegiance to Congress, acknowledged Vasudeva Pillay, rather than Raja, as its leader, and even objected to being called 'Authee Dravida', as Raja was wont to address his people. The views of this section deserved to be known and *New India* was acting as its spokesperson (NI 17,23.12.20).

The problem of names and identities proved to be one that would divide opinion and men amongst the adi dravidas. For instance, R. T. Ramakrishna Pillay, writing in *New India*, observed the name adi dravida was chosen by only one section of his community and proposed in the Madras Corporation as a tenable description of his people by a non-brahmin who, at best, may be said to represent the views of this one section only. Thus,

> When there is a divided opinion on the subject and when there is a single representative in the Corporation who can advocate one of the two sides, it is unfair for the Corporation to dispose off the case without learning the other side. No non-brahmana can represent the other side unless some of the panchamas are playing into their hands.

Besides, argued Ramakrishna Pillay, the desire to preserve a distinctive caste identity, apart from not being reflective of panchama opinion as a whole, would only confirm the panchamas in their caste status and serve to isolate them. Some panchamas may argue that the assumption of a distinct identity would confer privileges on the community, but this would imply that panchamas were destined 'to be beggars, always pitifully appealing to Government for help or courting oppression from the hands of higher castes' (NI 23.7.20).

P. J. Pillay, writing in a similar vein but with a different sort of emphasis, opined:

> Tamil scholars maintain that there was no caste amongst dravidas in ancient days. If the panchama wants to elevate himself from the clutches of that baneful caste institution, he must extricate himself from it. By assuming the name 'Dravida', the panchama renounces his caste entirely. No doubt, it is somewhat tempting, nowadays, for

> panchamas to come forward professing a distinct caste on account of the communal privileges conferred by the British Government. But no useful purpose can be served by baptising the communities with new names as long as the name refers to a distinct place in the caste system. If the community is anxious to elevate its status, it must be prepared to discard the special privileges as soon as the time is ripe and assume without delay a title outside the pale of the caste distinction. Dravida is such a name. Suffixes and prefixes added to the word 'dravida' entirely miss the point. The term 'dravida' is elastic. It will include the so-called panchamas and also those Hindus who observe no caste in keeping with their present enlightenment or who have forfeited their caste by reasons of intermarriage, etc (NI 21.7.20).

It is interesting the issue of names should have generated a lively polemic. P. J. Pillay was so convinced of the import of the matter that he observed somewhat self-righteously: 'The question is a momentous one and is not to be treated lightly in a mass meeting, where generally illiterate men and women and children congregate to gratify their curiosity' (ibid).

The 're-naming' of the adi dravidas assumed significance in the eyes of the Congress and the Justice party as well. The choice of a particular name was taken to be symptomatic of the community's political affiliations and reflective of its self-image. For those adi dravidas who were Congressmen, the assumption of an identity which underscored their distinctive character and denoted a particular history was not desirable, since it privileged what Congress brahmins habitually termed 'communal feeling'. Like their peers in the MPA who, initially, at least, forsook such a 'communal' identity for an ostensible 'nationalist' one, adi dravidas in the Congress sought to claim an equality with all castes.

M. C. Raja and others in the Madras Adi Dravida Mahajana Sabha sought out a more complex politics of identity. They took caste distinctions and discriminations as given but, even as they pointed at the contradictions which existed between non-brahmin caste Hindus and themselves, undertook the politically important task of constituting a non-brahmin historic bloc. Thus, even as they retained their autonomy, they aspired towards building relationships in horizontal comradeship. In this instance, it may be seen that adi dravida loyalties were necessarily transitory and shifting: grounded in a hostility towards brahmins, which they shared with non-brahmins, adi dravidas preferred to remain vigilant with respect to their political and social allies as well. Ensnared within the terms of a complex and problematic politics of identity, the adi dravidas had to negotiate their political relationships with caution and with the least injury to themselves. It is in this context that we need to address the issue and reality of their steady alienation from the Justice party, which was arrested only gradually, and with the emergence of the Self-Respect movement.

Caste and Class: The Buckingham and Carnatic Mills Strike

No single event served to reveal the contradictions which lay at the heart of the Justice party–adi dravidas relationship than the Buckingham (or Binny) and Carnatic Mills (B & C Mills) strike which took place in Madras city in 1921, the first year of the Justice ministry's term in office. The strike revealed not only the political limits to the use and spread of the ideology of Non-Brahminism, but also the limits to political action and understanding within a dyarchic form of government.

The B & C Mills strike began as a simple enough affair. A lock-out was declared at the mills in December 1920 and was lifted after the Madras Labour Union president, B. P. Wadia, a Home Ruler and friend of Annie Besant, entered into a negotiated settlement with the management. Wadia resigned his post as union president thereafter, leaving V. Kalyanasundara Mudaliar, the union's vice-president, to pursue pending matters of discord with the director of the Binny Mills. The latter refused to grant Kalyanasundara Mudaliar an interview, and it soon dawned on the union leadership that Wadia had duped them. M. A. Jalilkhan, another vice-president of the union, wrote as much in a letter released to the press in April 1921:

> If he [Wadia] had made known his determination to give up the office we would certainly have settled the lock-out and the strike ourselves much better than what he had done. He, in fact, duped us and did not disclose the terms of the settlement agreed to by him.... Having concealed the important facts from us, he ruined

many a honest worker (SWD 1921: 237).

In this restive atmosphere, seething with discontent, mill hands at the Carnatic Mills organized by the Madras Labour Union, then under the political and ideological influence of the Congress Non-Cooperators, struck work in May 1921, following the unwarranted dismissal of an adi dravida employee in the carding section of the mill. The workers of the Binny Mills too joined them in a gesture of sympathy. The strikers were predominantly caste Hindus and Muslims, since the adi dravidas had consciously refrained from joining the strike, in spite of the fact that a majority of the workers in the Carnatic Mills were adi dravidas.

Describing the sequence of events that followed, Jalilkhan noted that it was only after the Binny Mill workers struck work, that Government and Capital decided to intervene and alter to their advantage a fairly incendiary situation. As long as the workers of Carnatic Mills alone were on strike, there was no question of the workers splitting along caste lines; that is, the government did not, at that stage, seek to separate adi dravida labourers from caste Hindus and convert them into 'blacklegs'. But once the Binny workers joined in the strike, Government and Capital acted decisively. Thus, 'a few blacklegs among adi dravidas came to be created and their leaders have taken up the work of strike-breaking, resulting in scuffles, disturbances and burning of huts and houses' (SWD 1921: 216-17).

M. C. Raja, one of those leaders referred to by Jalilkhan, noted later that the adi dravidas 'had exercised their right to give or withhold their labour as they though best in their own interests'. Previous experience had taught the adi dravidas that participation in strikes proved detrimental to their interests and they had often been forced to sell their property and pledge their jewels in the past (NI 13.10.21).

Raja's decision to keep his men away from the strike provoked interesting responses. On one hand, a significant number of adi dravida workers resented his intervening in a matter they considered theirs and theirs alone. Jalilkhan went so far as to claim that this section of the adi dravidas clashed with Raja's supporters and, in all probability, were responsible for those acts of arson that took place in adi dravida neighbourhoods in August 1921 (SWD 1921: 217). On the other hand, though, the government welcomed Raja's decision not to join the strike and a government spokesman—no less a person than the economist Gilbert Slater—claimed a labourer was free to give or exchange his labour power! (SWD 1921: 396)

However this may be, adi dravidas were drawn into the politics of the strike as violence erupted in Pulianthope—in north Madras—between adi dravida workers and the strikers. Arson, looting and destruction of property ensued and three men were knifed to death in the course of the rioting. Finally, police intervened to arrest the situation from further deterioration. This however made things worse, for six men (all caste Hindus) died when police opened fire in Perambur, also in north Madras, in August 1921 (SWD 1921: 329). To ease matters, adi dravidas were asked to leave their homes, many of which had been burnt down. They were lodged, at government expense, at camps in Vyasarpadi, north of Perambur.

The Pulianthope troubles, as they came to be called, evoked protest and concern from all quarters. Justice, Congress and adi dravida leaders flung recriminations at each other and at the government. The government, for its part, chose to exercise its discretionary executive powers and even disallowed a motion in the Madras Legislative Council that called for a debate on the troubles in the city (NI 2.9.21). The government's move angered all parties to the debate, and the Justice ministers as well as the Congress notables and Annie Besant, were equally annoyed by this reluctance on the government's part to throw the matter open to discussion.

Annie Besant observed that the government's unwillingness was particularly inappropriate, since the Justice party as well as the Congress accused it of being partial to adi dravidas and the government, of necessity, ought to try and clear its name (NI 2.9.21). The Congress resented the fact that the government and Justicites alike considered the strike an instance of Non Cooperation militancy and was particularly incensed at what it thought were government-inspired attempts to alienate the adi dravidas from the rest of the workers. Justice leaders, for their part, while blaming the politics of Non Cooperation for the effect it had ostensibly produced in the striking workers, were also inclined to blame the government for its alleged partiality to adi dravida workers (ibid).

The government, in its turn, vehemently denied allegations of partiality—both with respect to weaning away adi dravidas from the strikes and to its conciliatory and friendly attitudes to those amongst the latter who were purportedly involved in the Pulianthope troubles. A press communique issued from Fort St. George observed:

> Since disturbances commenced their [the government's] constant endeavour has been to order and as far as it lay in their power to enable all without distinction to pursue their occupations without fear of molestation and to ensure to all peaceful citizens, protection in their homes and streets.... Police and the military have been employed to avert collisions and protect property and ensure if possible general tranquillity. Persuasions and warnings have been impartially applied and wherever the use of force had been necessitated it has been directed against all delinquents to whatever community they may belong (ibid).

The government claimed that if it had attended to adi dravidas immediately this was because 3000 of these people had been rendered homeless in the course of the riots and had to be lodged in special camps. Arguing that 'no civilised Government could possibly stand aside and simply leave these sufferers to their fate', the government insisted it had to resort to making rice available to adi dravidas since the latter had been refused supplies in the bazaar. But the government had not abdicated its responsibilities to other communities and assistance had been rendered wherever necessary (ibid).

Theagoraya Chetty, O. Thanikachalam Chetty, V. Shanmughan Mudaliar and S. V. Ramasamy Mudaliar and others of the Justice party were unimpressed with this statement of intentions. They undertook a visit to the site of the troubles on their own and, based on their impressions, made a representation to the government. They noted:

> (*i*) Caste Hindus and Mohammedans have lost all faith in the impartiality of the Police; (*ii*) they distrust Inspector Hankinson, particularly; (*iii*) they believe that Mr. Sundaracharulu, the Assistant Labour Commissioner, has through the agency of Swami Desikananda and of some others set up the Authi Dravidas against the caste Hindus and Mohammedans; (*iv*) The Authi Dravidas are far more restive than any other party.

The Justice memorandum alleged that adi dravidas had armed

themselves with swords and knives; that they had inflicted false wounds on themselves to implicate caste Hindus in acts of wilful violence and that they had set fire to their own houses, so as to draw governmental attention and acquire free houses. More specifically, the Justice memorandum demanded that free feeding of adi dravidas at government camps should be stopped; that a proclamation should be issued announcing wrong-doers of all castes should be punished; that the adi dravidas should not be kept together in one camp or near each other in the affected areas. The camps should be removed outside the limits of Madras—distributed over half a dozen centres but all on the railway line—so that adi dravidas may be brought by train to the mills. In fact they should be carried to the mill premises in trains. Justicites demanded that Sundaracharulu, Assistant Commissioner of Labour, and Inspector Hankinson, responsible for the police action, and his men be transferred. The memorandum also condemned the imposition of a punitive tax on house owners of Perambur and Pulianthope and noted that this was an unfair measure that would cause discontent to spread, rather than arrest it. The memorandum concluded with the observation:

> We think the final solution to all these troubles is to influence the mill authorities to take back the large number of labourers now without employment. Even if they are taken back the strained feelings between the Audhi Dravidas on the one side and the caste Hindus and Mohammedans on the other are such that for some time to come, goodwill and amity cannot prevail. It is absolutely necessary to separate the two sections from living near each other for some time to come (NI 6.9.21; SWD 1921: 332-34).

Somewhat similar recommendations were made at a special meeting of the Madras Corporation. The councillors recommended, among other things, that the Commissioner of Police and his subordinates be transferred; that the Commissioner of Labour be directed not to take interest in one section of labourers only and provide labourers to the mills. The Corporation councillors also hinted that adi dravidas had been instigated into violence (SWD 1921: 37980).

Adi dravidas protested these demands and also the Congress' attempts to characterize them as 'blacklegs' (NI 13.9.21). In the course of a Madras Council debate on the matter, M. C. Raja presented the adi dravida case. He noted that unlike the Justicite non-brahmins and the Congress brahmins, his community possessed no newspapers to ventilate its grievances. The fact was that his people were being intimidated and subjected to violence. He himself had been driven away from his house in Royapettah while several hundreds of adi dravidas had been rendered homeless. As for the labour department that was also in charge of the welfare of the adi dravidas, it had only done its duty to his community. As for the strike itself, adi dravida workers had held a meeting in his presence on 19 June and had resolved not to join it. Subsequently, they had informed the labour union of their decision. Hence, there could be no question of treachery or pre-meditated violence, as the Congress seemed to imagine or as even the Justice party seemed to believe. Raja was particularly indignant over the Justice memorandum to the government and observed 'this campaign to excite public feeling against my community deprived non-brahmanas of their right to stand for the oppressed and the depressed' (NI 13.10.21).

Congressmen, responding to Raja, continued to revile the government. S. Srinivasa Iyengar, participating in the Madras Council debates, opined that the government ought to have been neutral. Like the Justicites, he was also inclined to blame the Commissioner for Labour for his partiality, and demanded that the office of the Commissioner of Labour be detached from that of adi dravida welfare. Speaking on behalf of the government, K. Srinivasa Iyengar, Law Member, argued that the Labour Commissioner was well within his rights to persuade the adi dravidas not to strike work and noted that the strike was initiated by obdurate workers who desired to voluntarily deny themselves food and drink! (ibid)

These arguments and counter arguments did not facilitate the emergence of a consensus as to what had really transpired and what ought to be everybody's imminent concerns. Each participant in the debate stuck to his position with tenacity and each allegation brought forth a fresh response and newer and different allegations. The government, for instance, refused to submit its actions to critical scrutiny. A press communiqué issued by the government on 6 September described the Justice memorandum as reproducing the 'fears and anxieties expressed to the signatories by members of the caste community in the Mill area' (SWD 1921: 335). The government noted that anxiety and terror were present amongst the adi dravidas as well and one could not blame them entirely for what had happened. While it was true, as was pointed out in the Justice memorandum, that adi dravidas were seen with crude swords and the like, so too were Mohammedans and caste Hindus in possession of such implements. As for the Justicites' actual recommendations, all that the government could say was that it was determined to punish wrongdoers of all classes. The government rejected the plea that adi dravidas be transferred to distant camps for that was clearly impractical. The government also dismissed the charges against Swami Desikananda and the veiled charge that M. C. Raja was actively instigating adi dravidas into violence. The government also refused to condemn its police and executive officers, 'merely because they do not appear to have been able to please all parties in the discharge of their duties'. The government decided to set up a committee of enquiry under Justice Ayling to go into the details and results of the troubles (SWD 1921: 334-35).

The Congress was critical of this move and held that the Ayling Committee did not really take into account or seek to bring within its scope of enquiry the nature and content of the B & C Mills dispute and as such would not merit its attention. V. Kalyanasundara Mudaliar declined to appear before the committee on behalf of the Madras Labour Union and noted that 'the inquiry into the disturbances that took place in the Perambur division on and after the 29th of June is a matter of concern to the general public and not the members of the Labour Union as such as it affects peace and order in the northern part of the city. The Labour Union repudiates any manner of connection with such disturbances as have taken place' (NI 14.10.21). The Congress, it is clear, was concerned only with accusations of the strike being instigated by Non Cooperators and with the machinations of the government which, it held, sought to divide workers along caste lines. When the government decided to focus chiefly on the Pulianthope disturbances and not on the strike and strikers, Congressmen lost interest in the entire affair.

Annie Besant, ranged as she was against the Non Cooperators in the provincial Congress, blamed them for their decision not to testify before the committee, but apart from repudiating the Committee of Inquiry's report when it appeared, had nothing more to say. But she did manage to hit out at the Justicites. She noted, with a barely suppressed chuckle, that the adi dravidas had taken a note out of the Justicites' book of hate and sought to set themselves against all caste Hindus. She also wondered at ministerial complicity in the executive decision to deploy the police at Pulianthope. In an editorial of 13 October, she raised the following question: 'Is there a difference of opinion between the accredited leaders of the party in Council—the Ministers—and the bulk of the party or are they quietly witnessing the whole fun on the ground that Order is a reserved subject? (NI 13.10.21).

Justicites, for their part, insisted the Assistant Labour Commissioner Sundaracharulu, a brahmin, be brought to book for his partiality to adi dravidas. Later, they would demand the labour department be divested of its other duty, which was ensuring the welfare of the adi dravidas or be reconstituted as one wholly in charge of the latter.

In this melee of arguments, counter arguments and accusations, one rather extraordinary document sought to analyse the strike and its aftermath in as unprejudiced a manner as possible. This was the dissenting minute appended to the Ayling Committee report by R. Venkatratnam Naidu. It was pointed in its criticisms of the Ayling Committee report. Agreeing with the committee's refusal to take into account the nature of disputes at the B & C Mills the minute noted, 'there exists no inherent necessity, no inevitable occasion for these serious [Pulianthope] disturbances arising out of these [Mill] disputes'. However it raised a fundamental question: 'Does the scope of this inquiry include or exclude this question, who were accountable in a substantial measure for the big fires and what moved them to these atrocities?' The minute further observed that by not raising this question, the Ayling Committee had set arbitrary limits to its scope of enquiry. The minute criticized the report's observations on the Pulianthope mob and its assault on the police: 'In a thickly populated locality a mob forms with surprising rapidity. But a vital question is what can be its cohesive and resistive power... [the mob could have only been more] disorderly than riotous, more demonstrative than defiant, more imposing than substantial'. The minute argued that individual malefactors might have attacked the police but one cannot, therefore, attribute these chance attacks to the calculated fury of a mob of restless strikers. Nor could the fires that destroyed several hutments be attributed to mob fury:

> The crime is far too enormous for the suggested motives. That even the ordinary mill hand's nature should have been so depraved... chiefly because a certain section of the expected strikers—not more than a tenth of the total body—had declined to strike work and to starve, it is not easy for me to believe.

Venkatratnam Naidu also pointed out that a good while before the projected strike in the Buckingham Mills, adi dravidas 'had distinctly fallen off from the Labour Union'. Hence the so-called 'secession of the adi dravidas' was something of a foregone conclusion; one that grew out of 'existing differences than a staggering desertion at a psychological moment'. Nor could it be alleged (as was being done in some quarters) that adi dravidas and Mohammedans were settling old scores, since their earlier feuds had been settled two months prior to the outbreak of the struggles. The question for Venkatratnam Naidu was: 'How under these circumstances, without the assumption of some other potent influence elsewhere, a large body of persons could be goaded to unkindled exasperation?'

He also characterized police action as tardy and careless, since they had allowed key witnesses who were involved in the murder of the three that died to slip away. The dissenting minute concluded with an evaluation of relief measures: of the 418 huts burnt, 269 belonged to the adi dravidas [Paraiahs], 149 to others, 67 of these being chucklers [Chakkiliyars, an adi dravida community]. However, the relief afforded by the government had been patently unequal, for over and above philanthropic contributions, nearly 20,000 government rupees had been spent on adi dravidas [Paraiahs] and only Rs.100 on the others (NI 15.10.21).

T. M. Narasimhacharulu's note appended to the Ayling report was also circumspect in its judgement with regard to the victimized adi dravidas. Narasimhacharulu observed that while the strikers might have provoked the adi dravidas these latter 'were not slow in taking the law into their own hands' and retaliating on caste Hindus and Mohammedans, strikers or not. Subsequently, when adi dravida huts were set on fire some of them took to carrying weapons and were, in all probability, responsible for the assault of the three that died. But the petition of one Satagopa Mudali which contained evidence of this could not be traced. Narasimhacharulu noted that there had been at least one instance of adi dravidas getting out of hand in response to stone throwing by the strikers, at which moment the police stood by watching. But this does not mean, concluded Narasimhacharulu, that the police were, at all times, partial to the adi dravidas (NI 15.10.21).

R. Venkatratnam Naidu's dissenting minute and Narasimhacharulu's note held that the Pulianthope troubles were perhaps precipitated by the discontent caused by the strike but were not entirely due to it. Venkatratnam Naidu was reluctant to blame either the strikers or the adi dravidas wholly for the troubles and was more inclined to suspect Congress demagoguery and the government's silent encouragement of the adi dravidas' anger and resentment. The Justicites were of course severely critical of the Non Cooperators and, on several other occasions, had reprimanded them for their deliberate attempts at sabotage and anarchy. What was new in the Justicites' perceptions was a candid and unflattering opinion of the government. It is noteworthy that O. Thanikachalam Chetty moved a motion in Council, protesting the 'malfeasance, misfeasance and non-feasance of the Madras government in its connection with the Great Strike'. Earlier, his fellow Justicites in the Madras Council had endorsed the resolutions passed in the Corporation of Madras, censuring the government for its continued apathy to the strike and its indiscretion in respect of the action it finally undertook (SWD 1921: 459).

The Pulianthope troubles revealed that in spite of the broad-based non-brahmin sensibility which inhered in non-brahmin caste Hindus and the adi dravidas alike, on occasion, the two groups could revert to traditional positions of domination and subordination respectively. Even amongst such groups as the mill workers, unified as they were by the fact of being industrial labourers, class consciousness did not automatically subsume caste feeling. For adi dravida workers the prospect of long-drawn-out industrial disputes, in all probability, conjured up images of feudal oppression and humiliation, for these most certainly awaited them were they to leave the city. Caste Hindu and Mohammedan workers, on the other hand, had a small plot of village land to return to, farm work or even an extended family. It is interesting to note, as E. L. Iyer, Secretary, Central Labour Board admitted, Adi Dravida 'blacklegs' were mostly agricultural labourers from districts adjoining the mills. Their wages were absurdly low and work at the mill fetched them a higher wage (SWD 1921: 339). Adi dravidas were also moved to abstain from the strike due to their conventional deference to colonial authority, which, after all, had constituted them as equal subjects. They were, therefore, reluctant to engage in what could be termed anarchist, or worse, seditious activities. M. C. Raja was also frankly disapproving of the Congress Non Cooperators.

As far as the strikers were concerned, they were only partially influenced by Non Cooperation propaganda. Their grievances were real and Non Cooperation propaganda merely helped to mediate these grievances. The fact that a section of the adi dravidas were used as 'blacklegs' did, perhaps, momentarily poison relationships between workers of different caste groups. Then, again, there is no evidence to suggest that the ordinary mill worker was free of caste prejudice, though it was claimed he was. Thus, it was said: 'During the first Tramway strike, the brahmin strikers cooked food for the rest and all of them dined, irrespective of caste and religion. The beginnings of the Madras Labour Union were laid out at a breakfast where brahmins and non-brahmins sat besides adi dravidas and feasted' (SWD 1921: 346).

For the Congress, the Pulianthope troubles marked yet another event in the saga of Non Cooperation troubles and there is no evidence to suggest that the problematic articulation of caste and class in the present instance invited further reflections on this matter from men such as Kalyanasundara Mudaliar. Congress attitudes to the outcome of the strike was particularly ambivalent. The party not only failed to mobilize such sums of money as had been promised for the workers' relief, but it could not even provide the strikers with the promised charkhas, with which the workers were asked to make a living. Gandhi addressed the strikers when he visited Madras in 1921. His comments bear recounting in the context of our discussions until now. Gandhi conceded the validity of the workers' demands but insisted they also perform their duties as workers, that they practice diligence, punctuality and commitment to their task. Referring to the adi dravidas and their 'desertion', he noted:

> I know that nothing is so demoralising to labourers than that they should use force against a single one of their brethren. The lowest

> one of us, the fewest of us must have the right of exercising his own free choice even though you may consider he has erred.

Gandhi added that if the adi dravida worker was left alone, in time, he would realize that his fellow workers bear him no ill-will and would, then, join them (CWMG: vol 21, 131-32).

It was the Justice party that was most affected by the Pulianthope events. As far as the Justice leaders were concerned, the strike was yet another vicious and disruptive instance of the Congress Non Cooperation struggles in Madras and seemed to them to have been engineered only to thwart the Justice ministry in its day-to-day work. When non-brahmin strikers were injured and shot at by the police and their homes destroyed, Justice leaders chose to see these workers as benighted victims of Non Cooperation propaganda, who now stood to pay for the sins of Congress. In their eagerness to represent the non-brahmin workers' case, the Justice party did not seek to understand the interplay between class and caste factors in this instance. They thus maligned the adi dravidas and, as we have seen, came to propose drastic solutions such as their temporary ghettoization outside the city. Their views in this regard were further influenced by the fact that the Assistant Labour Commissioner was a brahmin who had worked to provide succour to the affected adi dravidas.

Justicites also came to realize the limits to dyarchy in the course of these events. Even though they were elected members of the Council and were clearly in a majority, precious little could be done when the Executive arm of the government retained policing authority for itself and also possessed certain discretionary powers that could supersede ministerial demands and the councillors' concerns.

It must be said, though, that for all their support to the workers' cause, Justicites did not wish to offend the government overmuch. Though the party supported Theagoraya Chetty and O. Thanikachalam Chetty in their attempts to mediate the grievances of the striking workers, it abstained from voting on O. Thanikachalam Chetty's motion in the Madras Council with regard to the government's alleged misfeasance and malfeasance. At the last minute A. Ramasamy Mudaliar proclaimed his party would not extend official support to the motion (SWD 1921: 406).

The silent player in these events was, of course, the government, which not only placed the Justice ministry in a vulnerable position but also demonstrated, in no uncertain terms, as to who was in charge. The Justice party was thus brought face to face, albeit covertly, with the implications of its own political reluctance to engage in an anti-imperialist politics.

The 'failure' of dyarchy and the adi dravidas' growing distrust of the Justice party were two pronounced effects of the B & C Mills strike. The one revealed to the Justicites the reality of political power and the limits to its expression in a colonial context, while the other served to remind them that political power wielded by non-brahmins had to rest firmly on the concrete and well-forged political consensus of the ruled. By its own admission, the Justice party was a party of non-brahmins but now its representative claims suddenly seemed assailable and fragile. An ideology of Non-Brahminism, the Justicites were forced to admit, had to be realized in and through the practice of a demanding politics.

The Pulianthope troubles served to alienate, at least for the moment, a section of the adi dravidas leaders from the Justice party; so much so that at the South India Adi Dravida Conference, M. C. Raja launched into a frontal attack on his former colleagues and friends in the Non-Brahmin movement (NI 21.7.22). Raja charged Justice leaders with an abuse of trust and mutual goodwill and observed the casteist rancour of these leaders now stood revealed to all who would care to notice it. Raja's indignation was most forcefully expressed and directed chiefly at certain remarks made by O. Thanikachalam Chetty in his presidential address at an adi dravida conference held at Palayamkottai. Thanikachalam Chetty, as we have seen, had suggested, that the department of Commissioner of Labour be abolished along with the post of Assistant Commissioner of Labour to prevent occurrences such as had taken place at Pulianthope. He had thus recommended:

> In view of the conflicts between the duties of the Commissioner of Labour to the labourers in general and his duties towards the adi dravidas in particular and in view of the failure of the department to prevent strikes or to minimise the period of strikes when they broke out I gave notice in the Legislative Council of a resolution for the abolition of the Department of the Commissioner of Labour but owing to the exigencies of business in the Legislative Council and for want of time, the resolution was not taken up and discussed.

> These and other events lead to a scrutiny of the combining of these departments and to an investigation, whether they were run on right lines from the point of view of efficiency, economy and expediency, whether they could be re-organised and whether they could not be managed more economically, making available for the benefit of the adi dravidas and without conflict between the castemen and the adi dravidas, without bitterness of feeling and without jeopardising the feeling of friendliness and neighbourliness which must exist and has existed between the several communities (NI 23.5.22).

Arguing that this suggestion and the resolution that was moved in this connection in the Council, represented 'a veiled attempt to prevent the government from continuing the policy they had hitherto pursued of improving the condition and status of the adi dravidas', Raja went on to note that the resolution constituted a 'deliberate withdrawal from the professions of goodwill towards them made by all parties in the country in order to secure the reforms'. Raja characterized this move as an attempt to 'undo the good work of the late Dr. Nair in overcoming the prejudices of the caste Hindus and other mirasidars and landlords in securing the social economic and political rights of the adi dravidas and other depressed classes'. While both non-brahmins and brahmins had vied with each other to secure the support of the adi dravidas, the latter, pointed out Raja, had 'helped caste Hindus masquerading as non-brahmanas to secure communal representation'. Raja also noted:

> It was by our hearty cooperation with them [the non-brahmins] and by their appearing to cooperate with us that they were able to convince the democratic people of England of the undemocratic nature of political and social Brahminism.... Let not the caste Hindus forget this formula, that the caste Hindus, with the adi dravidas form the non-brahmana community and the democratic party and the caste Hindus without the adi dravidas form a mere oligarchy.

Raja and his companions were also incensed at the apparent lack of remorse on the part of the Justicites over the Pulianthope incidents. Thanikachalam Chetty had sought to impress on the adi dravida conference at Palayamkottai the importance of resisting Non Cooperation, but had not thought it fit to apologize for his party's role in the Pulianthope troubles. The adi dravidas, argued Raja, had consistently resisted Non Cooperation, whereas the Justicites had given into casteist feeling and extended support to non-cooperating caste Hindu strikers. Besides, the Justicites had resolved to abolish the one forum—the department of the Commissioner of Labour—which helped advance adi dravida needs and concerns (NI 21.7.22).

It is clear that Raja was in no mood to heed the Justicites' professions of support and solidarity and was even critical of the Elementary Education Act passed by Madras government to aid the educational progress of adi dravidas. Thanikachalam Chetty in his Palayamkottai address had dwelt at length on the salient features of this act and its significance for adi dravidas, but had dampened the effects of his observations in this respect by noting: 'It should not be understood that by reason of receiving elementary education that your community should give up your old avocations of toiling in the field or working at the ploughshare or doing similar manual labour' (NI 23.5.22).

As may be expected, Raja was stung by this admittedly ill-advised and careless remark. He wondered if Thanikachalam Chetty in spite of his Western and legal education had remained faithful to the customary avocation of the Beri chettis:

> May I ask Mr. Thanikachalam Chetty on whom I may be permitted to bestow in the absence of a better title the title of Manu of the twentieth century, what the old avocations of the Beri chetties are? Why he left his ancestral avocation and took to the study of law? Will he at least use his mighty influence and see that his children and his relations pursue their old avocations? Does he at least understand what it would be if we stick to our old avocations of toiling in the field or working at the ploughshare or doing similar other labour?

Raja also mocked at Thanikachalam Chetty's suggestion that the costly establishment of the Commissioner of Labour be abolished so as to secure funds for adi dravida welfare:

> Mr Thanikachalam Chetty as an attorney can demand fees of all sorts—fees for opening letters, reading a letter, for speaking to you face to face or by telephone but would not allow government

officials getting carriage allowances, travel allowances and duty allowances and would not like the adi dravidas give up their old avocations of toiling in the field for 2 annas a day (NI 21.7.22)

Raja was not alone in his denunciations of the Justice party. Rajarathnam Pillay who addressed the Chinglepet district adi dravida conference, likewise, accused Justicites of ingratitude and pointed out that adi dravidas figured neither in the council of ministers nor in those other posts such as secretaries to ministers. He argued that the adi dravidas had allowed themselves to be lulled by false promises but now it was clear the community had to wake up from 'this sleep of confidence and put on the girdle of self-respect' (NI 21.11.22).

Raja had also blamed Justicites for the low representation of the adi dravidas in the Madras Council and local bodies and noted they had not been nominated to any of the committees set up by the Justice ministers. Besides, claimed Raja, caste Hindus had monopolized all posts in the services to the detriment of the adi dravidas. Arguing that it was the principle of communal representation so consciously urged by Dr. Nair which had made his community cooperate with the Justice party, Raja observed rather ruefully, 'if under the influence of personal ambition or class prejudice they [the non-brahmins) deviate from the democratic principles which ought to animate their leaders, we shall not remain true to them' (NI 21.7.22).

There were adi dravidas who refused to condemn the Justice party. Madurai Pillay, who had earlier insisted the Pulianthope troubles had not caused the entire adi dravida community to suspect the Justice party's democratic credentials but only alienated a section of them from that party, now came to rebuke Raja's harsh stance with regard to Justice leaders (NI 3.10.22). The Chief Minister, Ramarayaningar, was warm in his commendation of Madurai Pillay and remarked, contrasting him with Raja as it were, that he was a 'gentleman by nature and by grace of god [and] not being pecuniarily in needy circumstances, there is no fear of his yielding to the temptation to sell his conscience to the highest bidder in the political market' (NI 3.10.22).

Such observations did not of course help to make matters better for the Justice leadership and even earned Ramarayaningar the wrath of a fellow Justicite. Thus, O. Kandasamy Chetty, half brother of

O. Thanikachalam Chetty, noted of his remarks with respect to Madurai Pillay:

> A truly democratic idea from the mouth of a hereditary Raja in trying to establish the democratic character of a movement in which he is a leader as if honesty is the monopoly of the rich and as if we have not heard in the world's history of such a thing as the buying and selling of honour and appointments among rich people (NI 5.10.22).

The adi dravida case against the Justicites was rendered credible by men such as O. Kandasamy Chetty taking the part of M. C. Raja and his men. Kandasamy Chetty was an able and committed Justice publicist. Along with J. S. Kannapar, J. N. Ramanathan and others he had propagandized the non-brahmin cause far and wide before the Justice party won elections and assumed office. But once Justicites had won the elections, men like Kandasamy Chetty had to necessarily accept secondary status within the movement. The elections and the electoral imperative to capture a place in Council had produced astonishing and pragmatic mutations in Justice ideology that was now retained more for its rhetorical appeal than for its social and political effectivity. C. R. Reddy, who left the party along with Natesa Mudaliar to form the Justice Democratic Party in 1923, remarked of the elections: 'The general politics of press and platform hardly affect the voting. The landlord, merchant and lawyer have their clientele and every man has his tribe, clan or creed behind him who follow with sheepish fidelity. In this medievalism political conviction counts for nothing' (Baker: 35). His observations, however cynical and sweeping, did possess a ring of truth, since the Justice party's official candidates for the elections comprised not those 'men of the press and platform' such as Ramanathan, Kandasamy Chetty and Kannappar. In fact in the case of Kandasamy Chetty, he was overlooked in favour of his half brother, O. Thanikachalam Chetty, leading *The Hindu* to speculate that the latter's prestige as a lawyer and the influence he wielded in the market place and over temples had determined his candidacy (ibid: 36-37).

However this may be, it is true that the Justice party's democracy had to and easily did accommodate itself to the reality of an electoral process in which the voters, for the most part, were men of property and some learning. In such a context, nepotism, favouritism and intrigue were bound to flourish and it was not long before the Chief Minister, Ramarayaningar, was accused of playing wily political games and exercising the power and influence vested in him to secure government appointments for his own men. Kandasamy Chetty was one such critic and, on two different but related occasions, he held the government, especially the ministers, accountable to the non-brahmin people and to the principles that had won them legitimacy and defined their cause as a just and honourable one.

DEBATING NON-BRAHMINISM

In his address to the First Adi Dravida Congress, Kandasamy Chetty drew attention to the vast gap that divided the Justice party's ideological professions from its actual practice and to the constitutive limits of the Non-Brahmin movement (NI 23.9.22). Like M. C. Raja, Kandasamy Chetty was troubled and anguished over the Justicites' 'breach of compact' with the adi dravidas. Pointing to the efforts of Dr. Nair in this regard he observed:

> It is clear that here was a political compact if ever there was one, unwritten like most popular compacts, a compact effected for mutual benefit [yet]...certain non-brahmana caste Hindus are very fond of taunting the adi dravidas who show any sign of independent thought and action by saying that they owe to them their present position in the Legislative Council and elsewhere. That is, M. C. Raja owes his position to Sir P. Theagoraya Chetty or Mr. Ramarayaningar is in a sense true, but is only true as Sir P. Theagoraya Chetty and Mr. Ramarayaningar owe their present position to M. C. Raja and those people of his community.

Kandasamy Chetty pointed out that the fact adi dravidas had chosen to align with the Justice party ought to indicate to its leaders that it was their principled political support which gave the Non-Brahmin movement, 'if not a democratic character, at least a democratic complexion'. He also noted that Justicites had come to travesty their own ideals. He characterized the founding principles of the Justice movement thus:

> 1. Social Justice with its antagonism to caste rule in all its manifestations and its espousal of the cause of the adi dravidas.
> 2. Democracy with its antagonism to class rule and its advocacy of an equal distribution of the benefits of Government to all classes of the people.
> 3. The redress of the grievances of the non-brahmanas against the brahmanas.

Kandasamy Chetty argued that while the third of these three ideals was included in the earlier two, 'the realisation of the third does not mean the realisation or even an attempt at realisation of the first two'. For, in their energetic tirades and action against the oppressive brahmin minority, Justicites had come to rely on the brahmin's own methods to preserve power and exclusivity at any cost. Thus, they had come to direct their authority against those whose interests clashed with theirs, in this instance, against the adi dravidas; as if to say, 'any abuse of the past may be corrected by perpetrating similar abuses in the present'.

He was convinced that the best way of vanquishing the brahmin lay in the pursuit of higher and loftier ideals: 'if we adopt his [the brahmin's] strategy and are actuated by his spirit of exclusiveness and aggressiveness how are we better than he?' These 'higher methods', entailed eschewing caste practices and the propagation of social reform ideals at every level of the Non-Brahmin movement. Justice leaders had however shown scant interest in these methods and had displayed little or no initiative in advancing progressive social legislation. Kandasamy Chetty wryly pointed out 'the only attempt at social legislation to the credit of the non-brahmana party is Mr. M. K. Reddy's bill which seeks to strengthen the position of the so-called legitimate sons with regard to inheritance and to introduce among non-brahmanas an unjust law previously prevalent among brahmanas'.

The party had also failed to challenge casteism in its own ranks, as was evident not merely in its handling of the Pulianthope troubles but in other instances as well. Kandasamy Chetty recounted that at the Thanjavur non-brahmin conference in 1918, certain mirasidars had voiced their apprehensions at a government decision to grant house sites for adi dravida labourers; whereupon Dr. Nair rose up immediately and announced he would speak on the matter the following morning. Dr. Nair's passionate espousal of the adi dravida cause had finally won over even such a recalcitrant mirasidar as Vandyar, who had initially been censorious of the government scheme. Now that Dr. Nair was dead, the cause of the adi dravidas had assumed a merely nominal importance to Justicites.

According to Kandasamy Chetty, three factors contributed to the Justice party's indifference to its own founding principles. One was the death of Dr. Nair and the waning of the influence he had commanded amongst Justicites with regard to matters of social reform. The second factor was the nature of the Justice leadership after his death and its implications for party policy. The third factor had to do with the circumstances in which the Justice ministry had come to function and over which it had imposed its own partisan agenda.

Kandasamy Chetty was convinced that with Dr. Nair's death 'reactionary landlordism' had come to the fore in the Justice party. From the days of its inception, the Justice party had attracted and relied on non-brahmin zamindars and landlords for financial support, but the influence of this class had been contained by the dynamism and forthright political approach of Dr. Nair. Besides, amongst the landlords themselves, there were men of liberal learning and progressive ideas who, according to Kandasamy Chetty, 'encouraged and supported the movement from a chivalrous and sportsmanlike feeling based on a noblesse oblige which was a source of interest in the democratic movement'. But after Dr. Nair's death, 'reactionary landlordism found its opportunity; and its views and prejudices came to be more and more respected; The support of the many was sought for less than the support of the few'.

The onset of this reactionary tendency within the party was manifest in the changes that had occurred in the functioning of the Justice party. Not only had the party not created an institutional forum where non-brahmin opinion may be debated, but its leaders had preferred to confer behind the closed but exalted doors of the Madras Cosmopolitan Club. Opinions hatched in secrecy were then imposed upon the party. Kandasamy Chetty lamented that 'as things stand, at present the length and breadth of the movement and the height and depth of the party are coterminous with the intellectual and moral dimensions of the leaders whose views and prejudices, whims and fancies have to be consulted before anything is done even as an adjunct of the movement'.

To Kandasamy Chetty the party's ambivalent attitude to matters ranging from social reform to the tacit compact effected between the adi dravidas and non-brahmins were symbolized in the personage of Theagoraya Chetty. According to Kandasamy Chetty, the latter had already earned the ill will of M. C. Raja when they were both councillors in the Madras Corporation. In his private correspondence, Raja had detailed several instances wherein Theagoraya Chetty had adopted ostensibly reactionary stances, especially with regard to adi dravida welfare and progress.

Raja's criticisms of Theagoraya Chetty were accepted and repeated by Kandasamy Chetty who attributed the failure of the Justicites with regard to social reform to what he considered the benighted beliefs of one of its most senior and venerable leaders:

> With a leader entertaining prejudices... is it any wonder that in connection with the Non-Brahmana movement there is no social reform propaganda, no attempt at social unification by bringing about intermariages even within Hindu society.... There has not been, to my knowledge, a single intermarriage which owes its inspiration to the Non-Brahmana movement.

Kandasamy Chetty also noted that a Non-Brahmin ladies conference was once held in Georgetown, in spite of Theagoraya Chetty lecturing to the organizers that if women were allowed to get out of their houses they would learn all sorts of things 'which would break up a joint family like his own'.

The effects of the 'mental paralysis' which, according to Kandasamy Chetty, had gripped the Justice movement, following the death of Dr. Nair and the assumption of the party's leadership by Theagoraya Chetty, were further compounded by the circumstances in which the Justice party had to function.

In the Madras Council, after the 1920 elections, two groups confronted each other, each determined to work its particular agenda. There were the Justicites, now clearly in the ascendant, with their faith in social justice, and there were those with pronounced nationalist affiliations who were opposed to the Justice ideology but could not claim a political identity in the Council, since, technically, the Congress had not participated in the elections. This group was, thus, chiefly distinguished by nearly all of its members being brahmins. While there were non-brahmins in the Council who had previously been Congressmen, they were considered, and in many instances, they considered themselves as political non-brahmins, that is, as men who accepted in part, or in its entirety, the Justice party's stance on matters such as communal representation. This was, of course, due to the rapprochement that had been effected between the Justice party and the MPA, following the announcement of the Meston Award.

Thus, Kandasamy Chetty was not wrong when he observed of the Madras Council that the wheel had come full circle, with Justicites who had begun their political careers and movement to resist identification of power with caste status, now being identified, chiefly, by their caste origins: 'Birth, as before has become a badge of political status'. Political distinctions had come to be mapped over caste distinctions. While this endowed the latter with a certain political weight and worth, it also served to subsume political ideologies in a welter of caste feeling.

Arguing that the principle of communal representation had been worked by the Justice party only partially, Kandasamy Chetty noted that, as a consequence, a piquant political situation existed in Madras, at present:

> The present government is not a government based purely on communal representation. It is neither party system nor communal. It is a cross between the two, possessing the virtues of neither; possessing neither the free and effective discussion of the party system nor the equal and equitable distribution of power of the communal system. While the members of the Madras Legislative Council had been elected and even nominated on communal considerations there is within the Government itself no communal representation.

Kandasamy Chetty considered the ideal of communal representation a nuanced and flexible one and insisted that assumption of political power by a non-brahmin ministry was a mere first step, a fulfilment of merely one of the many promises contained in the ideal. If communal representation were to be interpreted to mean that 'the community which has the largest members in the Council can alone constitute the ministry... it will mean that other communities will have to remain in a state of perpetual dependence on looking upon the leadership of the majority community for such favours as they choose to bestow on them'. Kandasamy Chetty agreed the Justice ministry could not be accused of betraying the interests of any non-brahmin community except that 'they have allowed their followers to trample upon the adi dravidas'. He insisted that 'it is one thing for the various communities to be treated kindly and patronisingly by a Caste Hindu Ministry and another thing for each of these communities to have its own representative in a popular and even democratic ministry'.

Kandasamy Chetty was convinced that incidents such as had taken place at Pulianthope could have been averted had there been a minister and a Council secretary from the adi dravidas. He noted that even brahmins deserved a representative in the ministry for 'surely it is no gain either to the state or the people that the brahmana... is compelled to plough the lonely furrow or to play the part of a cynical critic or to foment discontent with the existing state of things among an ignorant people over whose credulity he still exercises undoubted sway'.

Elaborating on the significance of achieving a complete ideal of communal representation, Kandasamy Chetty noted:

> Under a communal system the only form of a possible ministry is a composite ministry containing representatives [of different communities] and upon their cooperation and adjustment of mutual differences will depend the success of government. If the elements of the composition do not cohere then that communal representation which the non-brahmana leaders have sought for is proved a failure.

Kandasamy Chetty also outlined definite proposals for moving towards a complete realization of the principle of communal representation. He pointed out that originally the British had been averse to the very idea of communal representation because 'they could find no place for it in the party system of which alone they had practical knowledge'. Since then they had come to accept the inevitability of such a mode of representing in the popular interest, but they had to be told that the principle required further refinement, if it were to succeed in attaining its objectives. Thus if the British could be persuaded that a scheme be adopted that allowed for a broad-based and inclusive representation of all classes in the Council, and of the need for increasing the number of ministers, the Council as a whole and the ministry in particular would possess more of 'the popular element'.

Though Kandasamy Chetty's strictures against his party's leaders had been occasioned by the Pulianthope incidents, these latter did not figure in this address he presented to the First Adi Dravida Congress. It is clear he considered the troubles a symptom of a grave and imminent political crisis in the Justice party which needed to be understood in all its detail and complexity. Kandasamy Chetty's attack on Justice, as *New India* termed it, was repeated but with a different emphasis, when he addressed an adi Andhra conference at Mustabad in April 1923. This time, he was not so much concerned with the Justice party's specific problems and limitations. Instead, he chose to dwell on the problematic politics of communal identities (NI 23.4.23).

Kandasamy Chetty argued that the reformed constitution of 1919 revealed in its actual workings a certain anomaly. For,

> Those who had worked for securing it either found themselves denied rightly or wrongly or denied themselves wisely or unwisely the opportunity of working them; and those who had said they did not want the reforms until their interests were secured first and foremost were found only too willing to work for them for all that they were worth, for themselves first and foremost, and then for others.

This anomalous situation proved particularly complicated, since the logic of the reforms presupposed a polity where men were divided into parties on the basis of political principles and not by distinction of birth and status. The Justice party, which began its years in office with a communal rather than a political majority, thus, found itself unable to accommodate diverse political interests within its ranks or even tolerate them. Kandasamy Chetty hastened to add that he did not wish to counterpose an abstract political nationalism to a politics of communal representation. For,

> A patriotism which ignores the existing communal differences is no practical patriotism and is often a mask for sectarian and communal

> selfishness; and a communalism which is not inspired by a national ideal and zeal for the welfare of the people of all classes to the exclusion of none is nothing but organised selfishness leading towards class tyranny.

Kandasamy Chetty opined this conundrum could be resolved through securing what he termed 'intercommunal justice'. This would reconcile the communal element with the commonweal and make for a political philosophy 'better than a nationalism which ignores communal differences and would act as if none exists while all the while the fire of communal discontent burns beneath the surface of a united front'. Likewise, such a philosophy would be preferable to a communalism that allowed such a community as 'the caste Hindus of South India endowed with wealth and possessing the strength of superior numbers to pose before the world as representative of all communities but one and to direct its guns not only against that community but also against a weak community included in its pretended definition whose interests clash with its own'.

He was unrelenting in his criticism of and opposed to brahmin hegemony, but he insisted the exclusion of the brahmin had not resulted in the extinction of the brahmin spirit of exclusivity:

> It was thought by excluding the brahmana the principle of exclusiveness for which in theory he stands would be excluded from the lives of the people and that the non-brahmin classes using the term in its most comprehensive sense of Muhammadans, Christians, Anglo-Indians, adi dravidas and non-brahmana Hindus ... by a sort of politico-chemical combination become a political if not a social unity. Has this actually been done?

Kandasamy Chetty favoured an electoral system that was not anchored in particular identities but which ensured that such identities and their interests were adequately represented: 'The only hope lies in men of broad outlook and liberal sympathies transcending distinctions whether they are brahmanas or non-brahman caste Hindus or adi dravidas being returned in large numbers. Men who will not allow themselves to be bound or dictated by caste combinations of any kind.' This would lead to the 'formation of real political parties on more pertinent lines or more rational or ethical lines than the communal considerations which now divide the Council'.

His criticisms of the Justice party were pooh-poohed by that party's official paper, *Justice*. In 'The Ravings of a Rebel', written as a rejoinder to Kandasamy Chetty's September 1922 address to the adi dravidas, *Justice* questioned his credibility and noted that his contribution to the Non-Brahmin movement had not in any way been remarkable. He had never been a politician and, as a religious and social reformer, was hardly competent to lead or direct public opinion on political matters (From 'Contemporary Opinion', quoted in NI 25.9.22).

Ramarayaningar, who took it upon himself to refute Kandasamy Chetty, denied that the Non-Brahmin movement had fraternized with the adi dravidas for solely political reasons. This relationship had been marked by an exhibition of a 'brotherly and democratic spirit' on the part of the Justice movement and only the latter's detractors would want to 'misrepresent' its aims and activities. As for the Pulianthope incidents, they were brought about by a conflict between 'strikers and seceders'. The adi dravidas happened to be the seceders in this instance, but this fact ought not to deter one from acknowledging that the struggles at the Mills were essentially between 'the general body of labourers on the one hand and the capitalists and seceders on the other side'. Arguing that it may be that in the frequent collisions that had ensued in the wake of the strike, the strikers displayed greater aggression than the seceders, he remarked that this could not be taken to mean the latter were entirely blameless. Besides, his party, of necessity, had to support the strikers:

> I ask you in a struggle like this, a struggle between labour and capital with whom do you expect, generally speaking, the sympathy of the majority of the democratic party to be? Suppose the party was indifferent or sympathised with the capitalists and the seceders, will not the party in spite of the seceders in this case happening to be adi dravidas be charged with having been undemocratic?

Ramarayaningar also defended his government's decision to ask for the abolition of the post of Assistant Commissioner of Labour, since the post, with a 'few honourable exceptions', encouraged corruption.

In future, activities to do with adi dravida welfare would be supervised by the district collector himself with the help of lower grade officers who would be appointees from the adi dravidas (NI 2.10.22).

It is significant that Ramarayaningar's answers to Kandasamy Chetty's allegations skirt the major political issues and concerns raised by the latter. Besides, Ramarayaningar can also be seen refusing to acknowledge the fact that in the Pulianthope incidents class and caste issues were entangled in a very complex fashion that would allow of no glib and easy resolution. His favouring of labour against capital sounds hollow in this respect and a mere rhetorical ploy to take the sting out of Kandasamy Chetty's criticisms; especially since the Justice party had ever sought to distance itself from political as well as economic radicalism. Not only had the party been sternly critical of the Moplah Revolt of 1921, and of the left wing militants of Punjab, as it termed them, but had constantly warned its supporters against the possible eruption of Bolshevism in India. It is not surprising, then, that Kandasamy Chetty was not moved to recant on his charges against the Justice party. He reiterated his earlier views and observed that Ramarayaningr's opinions only confirmed what he had already said; that in the Non-Brahmin movement 'there is no scope for discussion and internal criticism and that there is very little passage of thought and influence to and from its people and its leaders' (NI 4.10.22).

The responses of Justice leaders to Kandasamy Chetty were necessarily perfunctory due to a number of reasons. Justicites were wary of Non Cooperation activities and apprehensive these would disrupt the functioning of the government. They preferred to work the reforms rather than enhance and consolidate their political gains. The ministers were able men but they, especially Ramarayaningar, also sought to wield to their advantage the powers of patronage and office vested in them by the reforms. It is not to be wondered at that they were short on political dissension and unmindful of the pressures currently forced on them by the alienation of the adi dravidas. In retrospect, it seems that even the latter fact, which originally motivated Kandasamy Chetty's ire and anguish over the Justice party, was but momentary, for in the years that followed we find M. C. Raja once again supporting the Justice party. In this sense, the Pulianthope troubles did not produce long-term mutations in the Justice party-adi dravidas relationship, as Kandasamy Chetty had feared they would. But, yet, for purposes of historical analysis, the troubles may be taken to mark a significant moment in the political evolution of Non-Brahminism in Madras, for it threw up an array of important questions and issues that would be foregrounded a few years hence by the Self-Respect movement.

For Annie Besant and those Madras Congressmen who were eager to capitalize on the Justice party's failures, the criticisms levelled against that party by a long-time member proved a veritable godsend. Annie Besant, for instance, wrote commending Kandasamy Chetty's analysis of the Justice movement and so did *The Hindu* and *Swarajya* (NI 25.9.22). Annie Besant and *Swarajya* however disagreed with his conclusions and proposals. Annie Besant was also annoyed that he had not dwelt at length on the sufferings imposed on brahmins by Justice rule (NI 3.10.22). Referring to Kandasamy Chetty's April 1923 address to the adi dravidas, she remarked he was mistaken in his belief that nationalism and communalism are reconcilable principles (NI 24.4.23).

Justice political activity throughout the twenties until 1926, when the party lost the elections, continued to proceed along well-worn grooves of secrecy, intrigue and, in some instances, nepotism. Dissension was rife in its ranks, with Tamil and Telugu members seeking power and prestige for themselves. Kandasamy Chetty, C. R. Reddy, Natesa Mudaliar and J. N. Ramanathan and others attempted to redeem the party's politics from its quotidian concerns but their efforts did not produce any lasting effects. In 1923, the party almost lost its most devoted and able spokespersons, when C. R. Reddy, Natesa Mudaliar and others attempted to break away from that organization and set up one of their own. While this new group proved, as may be expected, an easy prey to Congress machinations, the very emergence of a dissident group from within non-brahmin ranks signified that the Justice party was unable to sustain its ideological and political coherence.

Yet, in spite of all this, the Justice party's first two terms in office proved enormously important for it served to instil in many a non-brahmin a sense of pride and competitive worth. Ramarayaningar, for all his political ways, proved to be an enabling leader and managed to work dyarchy as well as the circumstances would allow him. Justicites were out of power for only a single term and returned to assume office in 1930. Perhaps, the singular success of the Justice party lay in the conditions it created for future political activity in Madras. It brought the communal problem to the fore and thereby raised the hugely significant question regarding the future of democracy and nationalism in a society divided along vertical lines of caste. Its own efforts at answering this question were themselves often simplistic and, worse, half-hearted, and guided by the exigencies of retaining power, but the raising of the question has earned it a well-deserved place in history.

From 1926-37, Justice leaders, though in and out of office, could not offer a viable political alternative to the Brahminism they despised. However, these decades witnessed several ideological victories for the cause of Non-Brahminism. For this period saw the rise of the Self-Respect movement that strove to detach Non-Brahminism from its associations with upper caste non-brahmins and lend it a more egalitarian and radical character. Justice leaders lent their support, sometimes grudgingly, to the new movement that often threatened to breach the limits of political legitimacy and decorum constructed by the Justice party. The Self-Respect movement addressed, in many instances quite successfully, those ideological limitations that Kandasamy Chetty had considered problematic for a successful practice of the politics of Non-Brahminism.

Kandasamy Chetty had likened the caste system to an acrobat's trick in a circus performance: 'the brahmana rode on the shoulders of the non-brahmana and the non-brahmanas rode on the shoulders of the adi dravidas'. The problem was to persuade non-brahmins to see that the latter stood in a contradictory relationship to them even as they, the non-brahmins, stood in such a relationship to the brahmins. The Self-Respect movement, on its own, and by forcing its radical concerns onto the Justice party's agenda, would secure substantial successes in this regard, as we shall shortly see.

COMPETITIVE NON-BRAHMINISM: THE MAKING OF THE HINDU RELIGIOUS ENDOWMENTS ACT

The Justice party's dream of constituting a unified non-brahmin fraternity was retarded in its realization, not only because it could not, at all times, carry the adi dravidas with it. It was also because the party's anti-Brahminism proved to be vague, half-hearted, more rhetorical than actual, and always underwritten by a competitive urge to supplant brahmin secular power with non-brahmin authority. While this will to displace brahmin dominance was in itself fair and legitimate, the terms of its (dis)engagement with Brahminism proved extremely problematic.

If one were to assess Justice social reform legislation in this context, the two communal GOs and the Hindu Religious Endowments Act of course stand out as important legislative efforts. Yet these interventions in the public realm left untouched the world of customs and conventional practices, with respect to marriage, inheritance, worship, and so on. As we shall see later, individual Justicites such as W. P. A. Soundarapandian did wield their powers to affect whatever reforms were possible, given their limited authority. Likewise, non-brahmin legislators such as Dr. Subbarayan and Muthiah Mudaliar, though not of the Justice party, were clearly inspired by a politics of Non-Brahminism when they introduced several pieces of worthwhile legislation, including the Devadasi Abolition Bill, when they were in office. But it must be said that the Justice party as a whole, in spite of its various resolutions on intermarriage, throwing open temples to adi dravidas, and so on, did not present a credible ideological alternative to Brahminism, at least, not until the advent of the Self-Respect movement. Then, Periyar literally scolded it into radicalism! Even the one instance that Justicites and their admirers cite as their most significant legislative achievement to counter brahmin secular and sacral hegemony, the Hindu Religious Endowments Act, proved problematic in its contents.

The decision to regulate temple administration and bring it under the control of the state was taken by the Justice party soon after it assumed office in 1921. Earlier in the century, a group of influential brahmins had founded the Dharma Rakshana Sabha to 'protect' temple interests and ostensibly to render unto the temple what was due to it. The Sabha was constituted in response to gross mismanagement of temple affairs by temple trustees and other officers and the Sabha's patrons claimed that they sought to correct various corrupt practices by bringing the courts to bear upon various issues of temple management and administration. The Sabha, comprising entirely brahmins, also urged the government to assume an interest in temple affairs and pleaded for the setting up of a supervisory mechanism of some kind. When the Non-Brahmin movement became active after 1916, the activities of the Dharma Rakshana Sabha came in for severe criticism. Justicites held that the Sabha existed only to transfer to brahmin lawyers and patrons such powers as had been vested in temple officers and trustees, most of whom were non-brahmins. Justicites also argued that temple funds were being appropriated for partisan purposes such as the setting up of Veda Patashalas and Sanskrit schools that were open only to brahmin students, though the endowments for these were often made by non-brahmins. But when the Justice party came to power it came to consider the question of temple administration in an entirely different light. Earlier, its leaders, many of whom were temple trustees themselves, had protested the Dharma Rakshana Sabha's highhandedness and cautioned the government that the curbing of local powers by the Executive would spell disaster for civil peace and political order. But now, from the vantage heights afforded by the Legislative Council, Justicites came to appreciate the possibilities that lay immanent in government control of temples and temple property (Baker: 25; 27; 59).

Since the early nineteenth century, the colonial government had evolved a formalized relationship with temple affairs. Even after their much publicized withdrawal from participating in religious ceremonies, and their avowals of neutrality with respect to native religious institutions and practices, state officials retained a degree of control over temple matters. While the colonial powers in London and Calcutta were keen on enforcing the neutrality clause, especially after 1857, the Madras government was unenthusiastic. Its response to the pressure to withdraw from temple matters was thus 'a mixture of resistance, reluctant accommodation and deception. In some cases the detail and intensity of control was modified; in others control was simply shifted to other agencies or buried in hidden institutional arrangements' (Presler 1987: 16). What the Madras government finally agreed to was to withdraw its officers and men from ceremonial Hindu festivals, where traditionally the state had made donations and enforced local practices such as the pulling of the temple car. But the government was not agreeable to any move that would transfer authority from British to Hindu hands in matters of temple finance and administration.

The government, however, agreed to abide by the terms of the Hindu Religious Endowments Act of 1863, and curb the activities of its Board of Revenue. It also consented to the constitution of local area committees, which, henceforth, would appoint trustees, supervise temple personnel and temple management. Area committees did not have jurisdiction over temples in zamin areas where hereditary dharmakarthas (trustees) held sole power and responsibilities. The 1863 act empowered courts to mediate in cases of succession to trusteeships and to enforce customary temple services. The jurisdiction of the courts in temple matters was further strengthened by changes in the Civil Procedure Code in 1887 and 1908 that allowed the Attorney General—acting on his own initiative—to bring suits to prevent temple mismanagement in hereditary and non-hereditary temples, and which empowered persons who had no personal grievance against the temple management in question to initiate suits. Thus after 1863, the government retained a measure of control over temple affairs through its judicial rather than executive powers. It was the judiciary with its phalanx of successful brahmin lawyers that was put to good use by the Dharma Rakshana Sabha (ibid: 16-27).

When the Justice ministry decided to move the bill for regulating temple administration in 1921, the act of 1863 was still in force. The Justicites' objectives in this instance were clear. They decided to arm the Executive with more powers and vest these powers in centrally controlled institutions that would function under the watchful eye of the minister-in-charge. The bill introduced by the Justicites, Bill 12 of 1922, was a re-working of Act 20 of 1863. The area committees that the earlier act had initiated into existence were now to comprise partially elected and partially nominated members. Under the proposed act, the area committees were granted greater discretionary powers, including the power to direct temples and other religious institutions to have their accounts audited annually by auditors certified by the local government. The committees could also make rules to facilitate and regulate intervention in the internal administration of temples. The decisions of the committees, the local government and collector were to be final in all temple-related matters. The most important clause of Bill 12 related to the use of surplus funds from religious endownments. These funds could now be used as public resources and the power to re-deploy funds for purposes, other than for which they were originally intended, was vested in the courts. The bill's most novel observations had to do with the Hindu religious mutts which, for the first time in the history of colonial legislation on temples, were included within the common purview of the bill (NI 7.12.22; Mudaliar 1976: 6768).

Before the bill was handed to the Select Committee, several criticisms were made and they emanated from brahmins as well as non-brahmins and sometimes even cut across party lines. For instance, the raja of Ramnad cautioned the government and his party men against a sweeping use of surplus temple funds (NI 18.12.23). Other criticisms of the bill objected to the inclusion of mutts within the scope of the bill and the diversion of surplus funds for secular purposes such as ensuring water supply and medical facilities to the locality in question. It was also argued that religious endowments be kept outside the pale of party politics.

A. G. Sankara Iyer, a High Court vakil, noted that 'customs and sentiments and mamool are more important in a Hindu temple or mutt than in the institutions of other religions. Any variance from immemorial custom will cause the greatest pain and heart burning among the people' (NI 20.12.23). S. Satyamurthi characterized the Bill as 'confiscatory and pernicious legislation' and compared it to Henry VIII's measures to confiscate the wealth and resources of monasteries. Admitting that the Hindu religious endowments needed to be reformed, he argued that this could be done only by 'a real awakening of the Hindu conscience' (NI 23.1.24). Several comprehensive suggestions and amendments to the bill were proposed and embodied in a memorandum by both brahmin and non-brahmins and submitted to the Governor. The memorandum brought together several sorts of criticisms against the bill and objected chiefly to the inclusion of mutts within the purview of the bill and the diversion of funds for other than the originally intended purposes.

Yet, there were some who felt the bill did not go far enough. A. Ranganatha Mudaliar insisted that temple committees should be empowered to do away with the institution of dancing girls (NI 18.12.23). M. C. Madurai Pillay supported the decision to divert funds and suggested that surplus temple funds be made available for charity towards all, irrespective of class and caste. He also utilized this opportunity to object to M. Shanmugham Mudaliar, who had questioned the propriety of including panchama leaders, such as Madurai Pillay and E. Perianaickam Pillay on the Select Committee. Madurai Pillay retorted that panchamas have as much right as any others to be on the committee. They also made offerings to temples and the scriptures did not object to panchamas worshipping at temples (NI 24.1.23).

The issue of the diversion of funds proved to be the most contested of all. Fervent appeals were made in the name of 'the feelings and susceptibilities of pious and philanthropic donors in years gone by' to leave temple funds well alone. One indignant member of the Legislative Council asked of the Justice ministry: 'May I ask how many of us will be prepared for a portion of our income being diverted for the sake of humanity?' (NI 23.12.23). The *Madras Law Journal* published an article that held the proposed bill was entirely 'out of sympathy' with the sentiments of the Hindu community. The writer went on to note that there are two ways in which this issue could have been approached:

> One to proceed merely on the principle of toleration or at best of some little sympathy for religious institutions, as though one is dealing with Trade Unions, Criminal Tribes and the like and the other to proceed on the basis of a genuine appreciation of the true value of the religious institutions. The Bill has obviously followed the first of the two methods. The Bill, by proposing to utilise surplus funds for purely material purposes will shock the majority of the Hindus, especially since Hinduism is characteristic in its disdain for material pleasures (NI 9.1.23).

The observations of Alladi Krishnaswamy Iyer, High Court vakil, in this regard, were most ingenious and reflected the carefully ambiguous stance of the moderate social reformer. He proclaimed his support to the bill as a whole, but criticized the invocation of the English precedent, the Cy Pres doctrine, to justify diversion of temple funds for secular purposes:

> The doctrine of Cy Pres allows for the substitution of another mode of carrying out charitable functions not being fulfilled for one reason or the other. The substitutions can only be made if its objects are as close as possible to the objects of the founder.... in

> case of these institutions the primary concept is that the idol as a juristic personality is the owner of all the properties and of the religious foundations and endownments vested in it...So long as the juristic personality exists and the institution as an institution is not obliterated there can be no question of failure or exhaustion of the original purpose.

The 'original purpose' may be defined, it was argued, as that deemed by 'a votary that makes an offering, the donor that makes the settlement or the King that makes the grant'. Any extension or substitution of these deemed purposes could only legitimately be those that guaranteed 'fresh services and festivals, affording medical relief to pilgrims...providing accommodation or water supply...institute courses on religious education such as *agamas, Saiva Siddhantha* or to provide instructions for *archakas*...and *prasadams* to *desantris* and pious men' (NI 25.12.23).

In spite of much vociferous and angry criticisms, the Select Committee, to which the bill had been referred to for review and re-drafting, presented a revised bill that was even more drastic than the original: a board of commissioners to be appointed by the minister-in-charge was proposed to be set up that would directly control temple committees and hear appeals from their decisions. The board was to supervise all religious institutions and was authorized to deal directly with the mutts. Temple committees were to consist of elected and nominated members and it was stated the minister for Local Self-Government would appoint these members for the first year. The minister for Local Self-Government was also given powers to fix the electoral area for the constitution of temple committees. The Select Committee announced the creation of a new category of institutions, the 'excepted temples' that included, not only those that were governed by hereditary trustees, but which belonged to and were endowed by wealthy landholders (Mudaliar: 68-70).

The Select Committee's re-drafted bill was debated vigorously in Council and at least 1200 amendments introduced. Except for allowing all temple committee members to be elected, the Justicites did not allow for any other amendment. The inclusion of mutts within the scope of the bill and the diversion of funds for other than the original purposes were upheld by the Justicites—in spite of the concerted protests of non-brahmin as well brahmin *madathipathis* (heads of mutts) (NI 8.1.23). After accepting suggestions from the Governor, the bill was amended and passed during the next Council as Act I of 1925 (Mudaliar: 71).

The Justice party's legislative efforts to reform temple administration were explained as so many attempts at regulating the secular features of temple life. The control sought to be exercised over mutts, for instance, was defended on the ground that 'it aimed at controlling only the properties of the math and not the person of the madathipathi and that it affected only the secular administration of the properties of the religious institution' (ibid: 77).

This zeal to thus correct the secular life of temples was however neither as transparent or innocent as it seemed. The zamindari segment in the Justice party made sure that the secular offices in temples endowed and controlled by zamin interests were secured from official scrutiny and intervention. Secondly, the Justice party's careful disclaimer with respect to the sacred inner life of temples, their rituals and festivals, which that party declared was beyond Executive control, revealed that its opposition to Brahminism was more competitive than ideological. Thirdly, the Justice party's attempts to distinguish secular and sacred aspects of temple life represent a failure (and perhaps a refusal) to comprehend the dialectical interplay that obtained between the two and which, in effect, rendered Brahminism a consensual ideology. Justicites declared in public they were critical of the brahmin's temporal and spiritual powers but when they had to implement legislation that would challenge this temporal-spiritual authority, they refrained from carrying out that challenge to its logical conclusion.

For our purposes, the instance of the Hindu Religious Endowments Act of 1925, serves to demonstrate the problematic nature of the Justice party's Non-Brahminism. In the final analysis, it is clear the party's greatest successes (and its greatest failure) lay in evolving institutional and executive challenges to brahmin power, rather than constituting political and social challenges to the same. Justicites could not, at all times, match precept with practice, partly due to the pressure of conflicting forces in their own ranks, and partly due to their inability to distinguish competitive from counter-hegemonic Non-Brahminism.

CHAPTER 6

The Justice Party, the Congress and the Self-Respect Movement

DURING THE EARLY years of the Justice party's existence (1916-20), Madras was witness to the debilitating effects of the Great War, which by 1919 had more or less bled India white. In 1918 food riots broke out in the city of Madras, as elsewhere, and grain shops were attacked and looted by hungry mobs (Arnold 1979). Following the publication of the Montford report in 1919, and the intensive political activity which accompanied it, the Non Cooperation struggle was launched in 1920 by the Congress under the leadership of Gandhi. Though it did not lead to broad-based agitations in this southern Presidency, as happened in Champaran and other places in the north and west of the country, it did create enough turmoil for the ruling Justice party and forced the latter into advancing sharp rebukes of nationalist ideology and agitations.

THE JUSTICE PARTY IN THE ERA OF NON COOPERATION

The Justice party's leaders were uneasy and unhappy with the Non Cooperation struggle on several counts. Most of them were cautious liberals who were antipathetic to the idea of agitational politics as such. Secondly, they were anxious to make the 1919 reforms work and naturally did not wish to be faced with systematic subversions of their attempts at running a government. In an address delivered at an anti-Non Cooperators' conference at Cocanada, Ramarayaningar thundered indignantly thus:

> What sins have they [the government] committed? Have they with

> a view to gain their selfish ends quietly excited the passion of the ignorant people and caused the slaughter of thousands of human beings? Have they been cause of the Punjab tragedy or Malegaon's horrid deeds or of the Malabar bloodshed or the burning of cloth worth crores of rupees? (NI 21.9.21)

Even though Gandhi and other Congressmen denounced the Moplah revolt in Malabar, Justice party leaders found fault with them for having activated anarchic political agitations everywhere. Commenting on the Moplah uprising, *Justice* held that it had been inspired by Non Cooperation propaganda and characterized it as 'an exhibition of unbearable hooliganism and terrorism' directed specifically against 'non-Hindus' (quoted in 'Contemporary Opinion', NI 26.8.21). Even such a leader of the Justice party as A. P. Patro, who was inclined to be soft on the Congress, and who accepted that the Non Cooperation struggle was due to 'deep seated causes which must be enquired into and remedied', felt the Non Cooperation sentiment was not to be encouraged' (NI 9.7.21).

The harshest denunciation of Non Cooperation came from Theagoraya Chetty. In an address devoted to a description of the first Non-Brahmin ministry's achievements, he remarked that brahmin Non Cooperators constantly abused the Justice ministry and sought to 'successfully hoodwink the gullible portions of our non-brahmin brethren and enmesh them in their coils'. Non Cooperators had also worked to obstruct the business of government, not because they desired to weaken colonial authority, but because they wished to create a situation that could be of pecuniary advantage to themselves. Thus,

> Under the guise of prohibition the Non Cooperators in several parts of the Presidency successfully interfered with the abkari sales [auctioning of liquor licenses] so that few were privileged to bid and the shops were knocked down for a ridiculously low price, very often for some relative or friend of the Non Cooperator himself who thus gained materially under the guise of a patriot (NI 21.4.23).

It is clear, however, that the Justice party, for all its righteous anger at this thwarting of dyarchy, was blind to the genuine problems and issues thrown up by the Non Cooperation struggle. Though the Justice party insisted on proclaiming itself to be a party of the 'producing communities', this turn of phrase was not enough to counter the lures of Non Cooperation and failed to sustain the Justice party's ideological credibility and its day to day practices. The Non-Brahminism espoused by the Justice party was rooted in and derived its political and social significance from an urban liberal commonsense, articulated by bilingual intellectuals in and through a discourse of equality and justice. These men possessed the skills and imaginative vigour to endow felt notions of deprivation and injustice with a certain ideological coherence. But, though sensitive and alive to the problems of caste, community and Brahminism, these intellectuals had little or no direct engagement with the political economy of rural India or with the world of workers. They envisaged a community of non-brahmins who, in spite of economic and social divisions amongst themselves, would come together into a common and united bloc, driven by their revulsion of brahmins and Brahminism and animated by ideals of reform and scientific progress. In their imaginings, Non-Brahminism emerged as a flexible ideology which would enthuse the radical reformer as well as his conservative peer. The latter was attracted to the idea of Non-Brahminism not because he was convinced of the pernicious nature of the caste system, or desired its early abolition, but because he found the ideology an effective weapon to brandish in the face of brahmin power, that was ever given to wily justifications of hierarchy and privilege.

Non-Brahminism, in effect, represented a split consciousness: as a counter hegemonic ideology, operative as political propaganda and social message, it possessed a radical dimension which was reflected in the work of men like W. P. A. Soundarapandian, J. N. Ramanathan, J. S. Kannappar and O. Kandasamy Chetty, K. A. P. Viswanathan, T. V. Subramanium and A. R. Sivanandan. But at the level of pragmatic, everyday politics, and in the context of rule and governance, Non-Brahminism served to legitimize the private prejudices and ambitions of zamindars, bankers, traders and men of property.

The fact that all was not well with the Justice party, after nearly six years of rule, was registered most keenly by E. V. Ramasamy Periyar. As a former president of the Tamil Nadu Congress Committee and one of the Vice-Presidents of the MPA, he was particularly well situated to assess and interpret the political mood in Madras. After having walked out of the Kanchipuram session of the Congress in 1925, in protest against its refusal to endorse the principle of proportional representation, Periyar spent a great deal of his intellect and energy in debating, what seemed to him, urgent social questions. Meanwhile, searching for a viable forum, he made use of all existing ones, including caste associations, to express his concerns.

Periyar had been attentive to the policies and practice of the Justice party since his earliest days in the Congress. When A. Rangaswamy Iyengar and S. Srinivasa Iyengar chose to speak ill of the Justice leadership, at a Congress meeting in Thiruvannamalai in 1921, Periyar expressed his misgivings and declared himself angry and dismayed (*Viduthalai* (Vi) 16.8.50; Anaimuthu 1974: 358). Later, when the Justice party introduced and campaigned for the Hindu Religious Endowments Bill, Periyar endorsed this measure and published details of the proposed act in his newspaper, *Kudi Arasu* (KA) (Sitambaranar 1971: 81-82). The very first number of *Kudi Arasu* carried a moving and gracious obituary to Theagoraya Chetty (2.5.25). An article on Dr. Nair and his contribution to the non-brahmin cause appeared in the issue dated 18 October 1925. Periyar also heeded Ramarayaningar's request to address an election meeting on the eve of the municipal elections in Madras in 1925. At that meeting, he spoke of the necessity of honest and efficient candidates irrespective of political affiliations being returned to office (KA 20.9.25).

It is clear that during this period, Periyar did not consider the Justice party to be any better or any worse than the Congress Swarajists and remarked as much on several occasions. But he was also concerned that legislative efforts undertaken by the Justice party, such as the Hindu Religious Endowments Bill and the Andhra University Bill, should not be subverted in their workings by the Swarajists' meddling and opposition. His sympathy for the Justice party was most evident in this instance, that is, in the context of the Swarajists' antipathy to that party (KA 25.10.25). When Swarajist leaders described Theagoraya Chetty as a leader who was as imperialist and resistant to Swaraj as General Dyer, Periyar condemned them in very harsh terms (KA 28.6.25).

The Swarajists had vowed to disrupt Council activities, once they had gained an entry into the Madras Council. But no sooner had they done so, they sought to hold onto their Council seats with tenacity.

We have already seen how men like A. Rangaswamy Iyengar were eager to support dyarchy and were willing to concede to non-brahmins their share of the polity. It is clear the Swarajists desired power and, in order to wield it, they were willing to consider all possible political options. As Periyar pointed out, their crying hoarse over the question of carrying Non Cooperation work in to the councils, was but a convenient piece of fiction. For the Swarajists, Non Cooperation meant 'being close to government and cooperating with those non-brahmins who are opposed to the Non-Brahmin Ministry' (KA 25.10.25).

Given this alignment of men, events and circumstances, it is not surprising that Periyar agreed to address a Justice party special conference convened in December 1925 at Coimbatore. He utilized this opportunity to espouse a radical and militant Non-Brahminism. He observed the Justice party had been unable to attract popular support because it did not have a political programme which addressed the real needs of the people. Its members and leaders seemed to labour under the illusion that an English education and a position in the services, in themselves, would bring cheer and good to the non-brahmin commonweal. Periyar assured his audience that he endorsed these objectives, but did not consider them significant achievements in themselves. For, they could very well go to constitute a non-brahmin elite which, in the days to come, could prove as oppressive as a brahmin oligarchy. Justicites would do well to re-think their options and address themselves to the travails of the rural non-brahmin poor, who were often at the mercy of unscrupulous brahmin officials and scheming brahmin lawyers. Periyar urged Justicites to adopt Gandhi's Constructive Programme and show themselves to be better than the Swarajists (KA 27.12.25). For Periyar, during this period, Gandhian Constructive Work seemed a worthwhile and fit counter to the politics of the Vote and the Council. His attempts to interest the Justice party in Constructive Work were aimed at securing for Non-Brahminism a popular constituency and endowing it with a more credible ideological resonance.

Speaking on another occasion, and only a week later, Periyar reiterated his suggestions. He added that the Justice party must work to broaden its constituency and pointed out that, at present, it comprised zamindars, mirasidars, rajas and government officials, in short, those who had the remotest possible acquaintance with ordinary non-brahmins. If these men, 'in their collars, ties, trousers and English caps' were to speak of the non-brahmin commonweal and seek to lead non-brahmins, no good could possibly accrue to the latter: 'Non-brahmins can progress only when they rise above self-interest and commit themselves in a disciplined fashion to implement Mahatma Gandhi's philosophy of Non Cooperation and his Constructive programme' (KA 3.1.26).

A year later, we find Periyar again appealing to the Justicites. Speaking at a non-brahmin conference in Madurai which was attended amongst others by former Congressmen such as George Joseph and Surendranath Arya, he observed:

> Firstly have we made the common people understand what our movement is all about? Have we done anything to win the sympathy of the common man?... We bagged posts in government for ourselves, won titles but did the people benefit from these? We utilised our power and position to retard the progress of brahmins, no doubt, but what have we done to relieve the miseries and superstitions which hold our people in thrall, which make them lead the lives of a poor coolie and worker?... I do not mean to say we need neither posts or titles, but these cannot be our only objectives.... When we speak of non-brahmins we speak of the 90 percent that are poor and deprived and not of the rajahs and zamindars... I ask this gathering if it is truly committed to the non-brahmin cause or if it is concerned only with the improvement of a select few. I hope and appeal to all leaders to act and resolve on this matter with intelligence and responsibility (KA 26.12.26; Anaimuthu: 459-61).

Periyar continued to impress upon the Justice party the merits of Gandhian Constructive Work in the months that followed. Since Congress had abandoned Constructive Work, he considered the Justice party could, and, indeed, should make the latter its own agenda (KA 26.9.26). Besides, as he remarked, rather caustically, since Gandhi had been appropriated by Congress brahmins, non-brahmins should, at least, try and appropriate Gandhian Constructive Work (KA 6.2.27; Anaimuthu: 410). His efforts seemed to have borne fruit, for, a few months later, we find him writing rather positively about the Justice party. But even then he noted that though Justicites, on the whole, had come to accept the inherent worth of Gandhian Constructive Work, yet, there were some amongst them who had no faith in Khadi or prohibition. Neither did these men seem averse to the existence of untouchability (KA 5.6.27; Anaimuthu: 755).

It is clear that, in 1925-26, Periyar found Gandhi's insistence on Spinning, Untouchability Abolition and Prohibition inspiring, and discovered in them worthwhile and useful principles of action and conduct; so much so that he desired to situate a political philosophy of radical Non-Brahminism within the terms of Constructive Work. When Periyar left the Congress to launch the Self-Respect movement in 1925, he began to propagandize on matters of caste, culture and religion with a direct and unalloyed oppositional vehemence. This signified the birth of a new political practice, one that was primarily directed at those hegemonic forces which, for over a century, had shaped colonial civil society and sought to represent their partisan interests to be universal. This new politics of society and culture required Periyar to forge alliances and cement blocs amongst various non-brahmin castes and communities. He thus came to construct a comprehensive non-brahmin historic bloc that straddled political as well as civil societies. He was not able to influence the Justice party's decisions at all times, but the historic bloc that came to be, comprising as it did, his own Self-Respecters, lovers of Tamil, itinerant sadhus, women, the adi dravidas, workers and even Congressmen, proved a far more effective and resilient political force in Madras than the Justice party.

The Self-Respect movement's subversive energy was extremely magnetic and contagious. When the Justice party held its Thanjavur district conference in May 1927, Self-Respecters thronged the conference premises, insinuated themselves with the Justice party's regular members, and persuaded them to adopt more radical postures in matters of social reform. The presence of the Self-Respecters at Thanjavur proved so overwhelming that it seemed as if it was hosting a Self-Respecters' meet rather than a Justice party conference. As a result of this fraternizing between various segments of non-brahmins, hundreds of young men and women, including adi dravidas, participated enthusiastically in several temple-entry campaigns, which were organized by the Self-Respect movement and the radicalized members of the Justice party.

Thus, in the first week of May 1927, over a thousand men and women, including adi dravidas, marched towards the Mayuranathaswamy Temple in Mayiladuthurai in Thanjavur district. On seeing the marchers heading towards the temple, the temple authorities closed the main gate. The marchers, however, managed to get in through a side entrance, only to find that the sanctum sanctorum had also been hurriedly shut on them; whereupon, in the manner of the early medieval Saivite saint, Thirunavukarasar, they began to chant songs. Legend had it that when the latter sang in front of the closed doors of a temple, the doors opened of their own accord. The Self-Respecters were fully aware of the irony of their situation and their choral chanting must have proved extremely subversive. In late 1927, J. S. Kannappar, editor of the Justicite daily *Dravidan*, led a group of adi dravidas to the temple in Thiruvannamalai (Murugesan 1990: 229-30; KA 13.2.27). On 25 June 1928 a band of young men attempted to storm the Trichy Rockfort temple premises, and were brutally attacked by men employed for this purposes by the orthodox Hindus (Kesari 1948: 73; Irschik 1969: 339).

Though these campaigns did not succeed in their ultimate objective, their rapid occurrence within months of each other, and at a time when Periyar was struggling valiantly to provoke Justicites into professing a more radical politics, signified the emergence of a popular and militant Non-Brahminism in the Tamil country. The Justice party, for its part, came to adopt—if indeed, it seriously did—Gandhian Constructive Work on other considerations. It had received a severe drubbing in the 1926 Council elections, a defeat that seemed all the more bitter, given the electoral triumph of the Swarajists. The election results had made it clear that the electorate, whether brahmin or non-brahmin, was no more swayed, as in 1920 and 1923, by merely local concerns. The aura which surrounded Gandhi, and the consistent propaganda of Congressmen, had rendered nationalism a veritable new religion. A subtle but decisive shift in the Justice party's stance with respect to nationalism was evident in the pronouncements at a party conference convened at Coimbatore in 1927, following its defeat in the elections. Several Congress non-brahmins such as Kalyanasundara Mudaliar, Varadarajulu Naidu and V. Chakkarai Chetty, who were present at Coimbatore, urged Ramarayaningar and his men to join the Congress. Chakkarai Chetty even moved a resolution that would allow Justicites to be members of the Congress. However, this was opposed by several Justicites and Periyar. A long-drawn out debate ensued, in the course of which Chakkarai's resolution was amended and passed. The amended resolution held that Justicites, if they so wished, could join the Congress (KA 17.7.27; Anaimuthu: 467; Sitambaranar 1971: 90).

Periyar was, however, not too happy even with the amended resolution. He entertained no illusions about the Congress, especially with regard to its views on the brahmin–non-brahmin question and on the subject of proportional representation. However a resolution, which forbade Justicites from assuming office, until the abolition of dyarchy had been passed, much to his relief. Periyar believed that staying out of Council would encourage Justicites to undertake such work as would extend and deepen the realm of civil society. Periyar's apprehensions regarding the fate of non-brahmins in the Congress proved to be extremely well-founded. A. Ramasamy Mudaliar joined the Congress party and took to wearing Khadi, but the expected bonhomie between non-brahmins and brahmins, that is, between Congressmen and Justicites, did not come about. Periyar alleged later that A. Ramasamy Mudaliar was not elected to the All-India Congress Committee and, worse, Tamil brahmin Congressmen even hid away his nomination papers! (Sitambaranar: 90) This seemed to him an illustrative instance of the Tamil Nadu Congress' unrepentant casteism.

It is clear the Justice party–Self-Respect movement relationship was underwritten by a tacit tension. At the level of ideology, there were no obvious problems though contradictions would surface in the tumultuous thirties. At the level of practice, however, there existed differences in emphasis. Justice party leaders interpreted Non-Brahminism in chiefly functional terms. Even their much vaunted faith in the ideal of proportional representation, when translated in practice, served narrow and even partisan ends. The Self-Respect movement's Non-Brahminism, on the other hand, was broad-based in its appeal, range and content. As a social and political philosophy, it constantly looked to fill newer and newer spaces and refused to be bound by the exigencies of the political realm. Yet, Justice party leaders such as Ramarayaningar were not entirely lulled to the attractions and significance of the Self-Respect movement. Keenly sensitive to the possible uses of Periyar's political acumen, communicative skills and insuperable powers of argument and expression, Ramarayaningar decided to avail of his services.

The Justice party executive committee offered him a high post in the party organization, which Periyar immediately refused (Murugesan 1990: 232). Ramarayaningar, then, requested him to take over and run *Dravidan*, the Justice party's Tamil daily. He accepted Ramarayaningar's offer, but insisted that Ramarayaningar honour certain conditions. Firstly, *Dravidan* would be run on the same lines as *Kudi Arasu*; that is, it would reflect the ideology of Self-Respect. Secondly, he as editor, would criticize the Justice party as well as the government and its leaders if the need arose. Periyar explained he felt obliged to specify such conditions, in view of the fact that the Justice party had allowed itself to be lured by the ideologies of nationalism and Swaraj. He did not wish to see Justicites resorting to deception and chicanery, like Congressmen, in their dealings with the public, and therefore would prefer to retain for himself the right and authority to call them to order (KA 17.7.27; Anaimuthu: 469). *Dravidan* was entrusted to Periyar in 1928, though it was the Justice party that really gained by this transfer. For now it had a daily that was bold enough to take on the brahmin press and challenge brahmin public opinion.

THE JUSTICE PARTY AND THE SIMON COMMISSION

Differences between the Justice party and the Self-Respect movement did not die away, in spite of *Dravidan*, and were most evident in their differing attitudes to the party-in-Council. The 1926 election results saw the Justicites reduced to a minority in the Council, but their arch foes, the Swarajists, refused to accept office. Though the Madras Swarajists did covet the ministerships, the All-India Congress' decision to keep out of governance had to be heeded. Lord Goschen, Governor of Madras, allowed an independent ministry, comprising Dr. Subbarayan, a former Justicite, Ranganatha Mudaliar and Arokiasamy Mudaliar to be formed. Dr. Subbarayan became the Chief Minister, while the other two, one of whom was a theosophist, and the other a man known to be close to Congress circles, became the second and third ministers respectively. This pleased the Swarajists no end, for not only had they successfully kept the Justicites out of office, but managed to get two of 'their own men' into the Council (Baker 1976: 73-74; Arnold 1977: 104).

When B. Munisamy Naidu, a Justice party member moved a cut-motion during the Council discussions on the Budget, in March 1927, the Swarajists refused to support it and the cut- motion was effectively defeated (Arnold 1977: 104). But after the Justice party resolved at its Coimbatore conference, held in July 1927, that it would not accept office so long as dyarchy was in force, the Swarajists began to adopt a wholly different attitude towards the Subbarayan ministry. Freed from the onerous task of keeping the Justicites from assuming office, they now turned their attention to subverting the new ministry. They proposed a no-confidence motion against the ministry in August 1927. A section of the Justicites supported the motion, but the Governor who was keen to work dyarchy at any cost refused to oblige the Swarajists (ibid: 107). Periyar, who found in Subbarayan a man with a certain amount of commitment to social reform, was dismayed at the Justice party's political games. When Munisamy Naidu moved his cut-motion, he warned the Justicites that such unprincipled and opportune manoeuvres would impede the progress of non-brahmins and bring upon them a great deal of public ill will (KA 24.3.27). Periyar's dismay was compounded by the events of August 1927, but perhaps what bothered him most was the Justice party's decision to boycott the Simon Commission hearings that were scheduled to take place in 1928.

The Simon Commission was constituted to work on a future political reform scheme for British India and meant to take evidence from various sections of Indians. Congress had decided to boycott the commission, claiming there was no Indian member in it. The Justice party's decision to follow Congress in this instance seemed extremely unscrupulous to Periyar, who understood they had decided to embark on this obstructionist path merely to embarrass Subbarayan. The latter had welcomed the commission and was prepared to testify before it. Periyar warned Justicites that their boycott would cost them dear in the days to come, because they would be bereft of a hearing by the government; whereas the Congress, given its capacity for caprice and cunning, in respect of its relationship with the imperial government, would manage to get the ear of the Englishman in India and England:

> In our country all political associations with which brahmins profess a relationship suffer from a singular lack of integrity. That class of men possess neither honour nor shame nor honesty... for today they will scream for boycott, but tomorrow they will agree to cooperate. Today, they will profess a policy of Non Cooperation but embark on Cooperation the very next day. Today they will seek to obstruct reform, but will themselves create the basis for further reform the day after. Today they will declare they have no confidence in government, but tomorrow will come to an agreement with it (KA 13.11.27; Anaimuthu: 420).

The Justice party, observed Periyar, was not constituted to pursue such a politics of opportunism and self-interest. It had ever averred to accept and realize whatever political reform was possible within limits. At Coimbatore, Justicites had agreed to work for the attainment of provincial autonomy and push forward the claims of proportional representation. Therefore, it was only fair they made their views known to the government and the Simon Commission (KA 27.11.27; Anaimuthu: 421-22).

Writing a few months later, Periyar took pains to explain that 'Government and posts in government are really public property just as the revenue collected by Government represent public resources that ideally ought to be expended on the public good'. Justicites, therefore, had to fight to secure their place in the government, so as to enable a fair and equitable distribution of the public good:

> It may be that those who hold high posts in government and partake in more than equal measure of common [and shared] rights, and who conspire to keep others down, consider it a slur on their self-respect to approach government—with pleas and claims—for their advancement. But for those who enjoy very few rights and wallow in low posts and are considered untouchable, acts such as seeking government assistance for their advancement in office and for working out their [social] liberation, cannot be considered demeaning to their self-respect.

Periyar observed that, in view of the Nehru Committee report the Congress had prepared and circulated widely, and the separate reports submitted by Annie Besant and the members of the Varnashrama

Dharma Sabha to the Commission, non-brahmins must outline their own agenda and refute the Nehru Committee report which had nothing to say of equal rights and opportunities to all classes of citizens (KA 24.2.29; Anaimuthu: 762-63).

The Justice party, in early 1928, however, kept its own counsel and when the Swarajists resolved in Council on 25 January 1928 that the Madras Legislature would not cooperate with Simon, Ramarayaningar abstained from voting on the resolution, which, under the circumstances, signified an endorsement of it. The Swarajists' resolution was passed and this immediately put the Subbarayan ministry at a disadvantage. Subbarayan's cabinet was deeply divided on the issue of the Simon Commission and his second and third ministers had abstained from voting on the Swarajists' resolution. This caused considerable embarrassment to Subbarayan, who offered to resign. But Goschen, Governor of Madras, desperate to save dyarchy, looked to other means to keep Subbarayan in office.

Meanwhile the Swarajists moved a vote of non-confidence against the ministry on 2 March 1928. Periyar warned the Justi-cites not to cause problems for Subbarayan, as they had done in January. He rebuked Ramarayaningar for falling into the Swarajist trap, which he noted, was designed to discredit Subbarayan in the eyes of the Justicites. If Swarajists were opposed in principle to dyarchy, that was a different matter. But since they had 'loaned' two of their own men to Subbarayan, they could not possibly be interested in principles. Their moves could only be construed to mean an instance of Congress-brahmin scheming to deter non-brahmins from stating their claims unequivocally and clearly before Simon (KA 4.3.28).

Eventually, and somewhat abashedly, Justicites did agree to support Subbarayan. Ramarayaningar made use of his good offices and shored up the ministry by arranging for Muthiah Mudaliar and Sethurathinam Iyer to join Subbarayan's cabinet. (Both these men, though they got elected to the Council as Swarajists, had voted against a boycott of Simon.) Justicites also agreed to testify before Simon, and A. P. Patro was made head of a seven-member joint committee that would prepare evidence for submission to the Simon Commission. Periyar was none too happy with the choice of Patro whom he regarded as an implacable foe of reform. Patro had voted against a motion in the Madras Council that sought to endorse a measure to raise the age of marriage of girls (KA 23.9.28). But, at least, for the moment, Subbarayan was safe and the Justicites had acted with discretion.

Periyar's attempts to interest the Justice party in testifying before the Simon Commission grew out of his displeasure over the Nehru Committee report. The report was prepared after an all-parties conference was called in 1928, after the Congress had passed its 'Purna Swaraj' resolution, and its aim was to draw up a Constitution for India. Periyar was watchful of this exercise, and when the report was ready, was critical of it. For, apart from wanting a fairly close relationship with the British Crown, and cordial ties with British merchant capital, the report had nothing to say on the question of proportional representation. Besides, it envisaged a polity that was more central than federal in its constitution. In contrast to these recommendations, the Patro committee report reflected non-brahmin aspirations. It asked for proportional representation and demanded provincial autonomy (Rajaraman 1988: 227).

In February 1929, the First Provincial Self-Respect Conference was held at Chinglepet and Dr. Subbarayan was invited to preside over it. He had endeared himself to the Self-Respecters by his principled support of proportional representation and his general pro-social reform attitudes. Justice leaders attended the conference as well and W. P. A. Soundarapandian in his speech warmly commended the Self-Respecters' creed. A resolution was passed at the conference welcoming the Simon Commission and endorsing the Justice party's decision to cooperate with it. But Periyar was annoyed by the ingrained conservatism of a section of the Justice leadership which was clearly upset by some of the resolutions passed at Chinglepet, especially with the ones that had to do with marriage and women's rights, and with the decision taken on the floor to give up the practice of saying a prayer before commencing public events. Periyar observed in consternation that 'Justicites had ever been political moderates, concerned only with grabbing plum government jobs for themselves from the brahmins' and in all other respects had created obstacles in the path of reform (KA 17.2.29). It is clear that Periyar's attitudes towards the Justice party were ambivalent, to say the least. He never lost a chance to criticize its policies, but never wholly alienated its leaders and members from those campaigns undertaken by the Self-Respect movement in the cause of a non-brahmin commonweal.

THE JUSTICE PARTY UNDER B. MUNISAMY NAIDU

Following Ramarayaningar's death, Periyar was drawn into the very vortex of Justice politics. In October 1929, the party convened at Nellore to choose a new leader. The party leadership also desired to take up the question of allowing brahmins in the Justice party. After Ramarayaningar had arranged for the inclusion of Sethurathinam Iyer in Subbarayan's ministry, the issue of non-brahmin Justicites cooperating or not cooperating with brahmins had once again come to the fore. In an editorial written before the Nellore conference, Periyar warned the Justicites that under no circumstances should brahmins be allowed to join the Justice party, for if they were allowed within its ranks, they would work to render it captive to their partisan interests. Whatever the political compulsions urged by the situation at hand and whatever reasons may be advanced by the Justicites, these ought not to be considered determinate in the last instance by the party's leaders. Periyar insisted he was not influenced in the least by communal considerations but, given their will to dominance, the onus certainly was on brahmins to prove their humanity, and not for non-brahmins to accept their professions of goodwill. As far as he was concerned, noted Periyar, he was not averse to giving brahmins their due share in the polity, as long as this did not contradict and subvert the general non-brahmin good (KA 22.9.29; Anaimuthu: 428).

When the question of admitting brahmins into the Justice party came up for discussion at a meeting of its executive committee, it was proposed that brahmins be allowed into the legislative wing of the party. Periyar welcomed the proposal but it was defeated by a single vote in the subjects committee. Periyar, now, welcomed the defeat as well. He remarked that the proposal was, in fact, a redundant one, since till such time the Justicites had secured for themselves an absolute majority in the Council, they would have to cooperate with other members, both brahmins and non-brahmins. He also clarified as to why he agreed to the resolution in the first place. Dr. Subbarayan had indicated he would like to join the Justice party, but had asked that the latter cooperate with brahmins, at least as far as the Council activities were concerned. Subbarayan and the Justicites had asked for Periyar's counsel and he had agreed to work out a solution, agreeable to all (KA 13.10.29).

At Nellore, when A. P. Patro tabled a resolution at the Justice party conference, calling for his party to admit brahmins into its ranks, Periyar opposed the resolution and observed that as long as the notion of caste inequality remained an article of faith in Hindu society brahmins ought not to be allowed to join a non-brahmin political party (ibid). (In an article written months later, Periyar would note that at Nellore it had been resolved not to allow any brahmin to become a member of the Justice party, not to support a brahmin during elections nor nominate a brahmin as an electoral candidate (KA 29.6.30). He was forced to recall the Nellore decision thus, because in June 1930, at a meeting of the Justice Party's executive committee, Munisamy Naidu had succeeded in amending the party rules to allow brahmins to join its ranks.)

At Nellore, Munisamy Naidu, a Justicite known for his pro-Congress proclivities, was elected president of the party. Periyar was critical of this choice and in an article on Naidu pointed out that the latter's presidential address at Nellore had been replete with Congress rhetoric :

> There is nothing in it that refers to those ideals which constitute the life breath of Non-Brahminism; nothing on the abolition of untouchability, eradication of caste differences, temple-entry or the removal of the horrors women endure.... [Yet] none would object that Munisamy Naidu is a responsible and broadminded leader. We are willing to abide by his leadership and cooperate with him—in the hope and desire that he would support the abolition of untouchability, enable the depressed classes enter temples and endorse the equal rights of women and work to do away with problems faced by workers and struggle against obscurantist social and cultural practices. At the same time we would like to entreat Munisamy Naidu that he should not, on any account, imagine he can get brahmins into the Justice party or use his power of office to achieve this end (KA 13.10.29).

Periyar had good reasons to suspect Munisamy Naidu's ideological good faith. For one thing, the brahmin press had welcomed the choice of Munisamy Naidu as president of the Justice party, and besides, in an earlier instance, Naidu's conduct had not been particularly impressive. When Dr. Muthulakshmi Reddi tabled the Devadasi Abolition Bill in the Council, the Justicites, on the advice of Munisamy Naidu, had sought to defer and retard its passage. Naidu had also been critical of the Self-Respect movement's so-called atheism and had been uncharitable in his references to the movement. Periyar was particularly piqued that S. Satyamurthi and S. Srinivasa Iyengar and nationalist dailies, such as *Swarajya* and *Swadesamitran*, who were openly inimical to the non-brahmin cause, were warm in their commendations of Munisamy Naidu's leadership (KA 23.3.30; 22.10.33; Anaimuthu: 176).

Munisamy Naidu's term as president of the Justice party proved to be a troubled one for himself and his detractors. Munisamy Naidu, P. T. Rajan and the raja of Bobbili were all locked in an endless tussle over the leadership of the party and, on the eve of the fourth Legislative Council elections in 1930, the party was in more or less complete disarray. Subbarayan, who had hoped that he would be welcomed into the Justice party and accepted as one of its leaders, was ranged against the Justicites as well, for at Nellore, his bid to arouse interest among the Justicites in his leadership had failed (KA 13.10.29; Viswanathan 1983: 132-35).

Writing on the eve of the elections, Periyar lamented the fact that non-brahmins were split thus into different parties. He noted that basically 'these were parties of the ministers, of those who wished to be ministers and those who would join the winning party'. As far as the Self-Respecters were concerned 'they would extend their support to whomsoever endorsed the ideals of Self-Respect' (KA 20.7.30.) Periyar also pointed out, in this context, that ideologically, the Justicites and the Ministerialists (Subbarayan and his men) were in the same camp: they had both welcomed the Simon Commission, opposed Civil Disobedience and sympathized with the innocent victims of the Civil Disobedience agitations. This being the case, voters ought, perhaps, to prefer those who would act on the principle of proportional representation, work for the destruction of caste and untouchability, work to render men coeval with women and who would put to productive use the vast wealth vested in temples and make sure religious sensibility did not permeate education (KA 3, 31.8.30).

But it is clear that Periyar was none too happy with the Justice party at this point in time. He lamented their disinterest in the cause of adi dravida welfare and progress, noted that Justicites had not worked the principle of proportional representation to secure adi dravida rights and criticized those who wanted to make Raja Sir Annamalai Chettiar the leader of the party. He wondered if the interests of the adi dravidas and the poor could be made over to the care of men like this rich banker. Periyar also pointed out that the rich were as mindful of social distinctions as the brahmins. Just as non-brahmin kings in the past had brahmin ministers, the rich men of the present time were friends of the brahmins (KA 29.6.30).

Periyar was, thus, inclined to favour Subbarayan, who, he argued, had adopted the creed of Non-Brahminism, even as the Justicites had abandoned it. Though Subbarayan lost out in the struggle for the ministry and the Justice party won handsomely—the Congress abstained from participating in the 1930 elections—Periyar continued to point to the example of Subbarayan's independent ministry. Even at the First Self-Respect Conference held at Chinglepet, Periyar had claimed that Subbarayan had achieved, in just over two years, what ten years of Justice rule and presence in politics could not (KA 17.2.29). In contrast to the Justice party's hesitancy in matters of reform, the Subbarayan ministry had conducted itself admirably. Even the brahmin member of Subbarayan's cabinet had proved his worth and been impartial and gracious in the matter of distribution of government posts amongst various castes. Muthiah Mudaliar had advanced the cause of proportional representation by extending the earlier Communal GOs to the Registration department. Subbarayan had made it possible for representatives of women and the adi dravidas to be elected to local bodies and announced that women could avail of free education up to Class 8. It was due to the efforts of the ministerialists, that W. P. A. Soundarapandian, a Self-Respecter, had been elected as president of the Ramanathapuram District Board and two adi dravidas—Swami Sahajananda and Munusamy Pillay—were nominated to the House Committee on Hindu Religious Endowments. Besides, during Subbarayan's tenure as Chief Minister, grants-in-aid to schools which refused to admit adi dravida children were stopped, and the government issued specific orders to aided schools to admit the latter (KA 2.11.30).

Periyar put down the Justice party's victory in the fourth Council elections to the underdeveloped commonsense of an ignorant electorate which, he held, had been corrupted early by nationalist rhetoric (ibid). But he also noted that the fault lay as much with the system of representation, which allowed for a very limited franchise, restricted to the rich and the landed and the educated. These sections of the populace could not be expected to represent the concerns of the poor, the outcastes, the workers and the peasants. But Periyar was pragmatic enough to realize that he had to make the best of a situation he could not alter. As he had remarked in an earlier editorial: 'However, this may be, we will have to identify individuals favourable to our cause, plead with them and persuade them to do their duty to the oppressed castes and the adi dravidas' (KA 21.9.30).

The Justice party, unmindful of these criticisms, began its term in office, preoccupied as ever with its own intra-party feuding. Munisamy Naidu became Chief Minister in 1930. His ministry comprised two Tamil notables, P. T. Rajan and Kumarasamy Reddiar. Rajan was sceptical of Naidu's concern for non-brahmins and critical of his endorsement of the Congress' policy with reference to Gandhian Constructive Work. In his bitter opposition to Subbarayan, Rajan had unwittingly helped Munisamy Naidu come to power. But it had also been decided at Nellore that the latter would remain President only for a year, at the end of which a party conference would be convened to elect a new leader. Munisamy Naidu did not convene a conference for two years and, meanwhile, opposition to his policies grew within the party (Justice Party Golden Jubilee Souvenir 1968).

Munisamy Naidu faced opposition from other sections of the party as well, especially from the zamindars grouped around the raja of Bobbili who, along with the Nattukottai Chettis (a Tamil non-brahmin caste comprising merchants and bankers), were aggrieved at not being included in the ministry. These two segments were constantly at work to dislodge him from his post as Chief Minister. Munisamy Naidu's interest in securing tenurial rights for ryots in zamin lands annoyed his zamindar colleagues, who came to oppose vehemently the amendment Naidu brought to the Madras Estates Land Act of 1908 to render the latter operative and efficient. Zamin ryots, apart from the handful that had made good due to rank absenteeism, were often ignorant of the extent, nature and duration of their tenures. Besides, tenurial rights proved to be contested ones, with tenancies and subtenancies often representing different and opposed claims.

Munisamy Naidu's amendment to the Madras Estates Land Act of 1908 sought to regulate the matter of tenurial rights and angered the zamindars no end, who conspired together to defeat the amendment. Consequent to this, Naidu's fortunes fell and he was ultimately removed from his post and Bobbili was elected in his place as Chief Minister in 1932 (Baker 1976: 239-44; *Peasant Organisations in Andhra Pradesh* 1979: 79-81).

THE JUSTICE PARTY AND THE SELF-RESPECT MOVEMENT: THE NATURE OF A RELATIONSHIP

Periyar continued to hope and work for an imminent radicalization of the Justice party, but these years were momentous ones in another sense, for they witnessed the coming of age of the Self-Respect movement. After 1929, the Justice party functioned as a party of elite non-brahmins and its interest in Periyar was, more than ever, underwritten by tactical considerations. Periyar's robust and energetic Non-Brahminism, his vituperative critique of the Congress and Gandhi, his remarkable insights into the uses of British rule and, most important, his indomitable courage and completely selfless interest in his cause rendered him a formidable ally, whose very presence and ideological pronouncements could legitimize and redeem Justice practice from the sins of its avaricious and self-centred leadership. Periyar's support for the Justice party, in turn, was qualified and conditional, and characterized by a certain critical distance which he was anxious to inscribe between himself and the Self-Respecters on the one hand, and the Justice party on the other. But Periyar was also reluctant to give up entirely on the Justicites for two interrelated and complex reasons, both of which drove him, time and again, to throw his weight and support behind a party that possessed little or no strengths in itself.

As early as 1927, in fact, after the Coimbatore conference of the Justice party, Periyar had suggested that it would be beneficial to non-brahmins if the South Indian Liberal Federation were to divide itself into two distinct organizations. One would carry out specifically political functions and assume political responsibilities, with an implicit commitment to the transformation of the social realm; the other would function as a social reform organization and work consistently in the realms of society and culture. Periyar argued that even those political parties, which professed the attainment of certain social changes as their ultimate objective, were often forced to compromise on first principles for purely political gains. Pointing to the example of the Congress, he observed that after that party had decided to enter the Legislative Councils, it had suffered a singular lack of integrity. Therefore, 'those who are engaged in independent social reform work may, if they so desire, and if it is absolutely necessary, that is, if they are convinced their political choices would not hinder their social work, choose a particular politician and recommend his merits and cause' (KA 31.7.27; Anaimuthu: 470-71).

This resistance to a sustained engagement with the political realm remained an article of faith with Periyar throughout his long life. Even when the Self-Respect–Samadharma party was launched in 1932, he and the Self-Respecters distinguished two distinctive lines of action: one would be chiefly political, having to do with contesting elections and working from within the legislature, while the other, oriented towards a future utopia, would be chiefly ideological in intent and practice. In the late twenties and during the thirties, however, his reasons for supporting and soliciting the support of the Justice party in his various endeavours were as much political as ideological. Given the historical conjuncture of events and ideologies which obtained under the sign of Gandhi and the Congress, he considered it imperative that the Justice party constitute itself into an alternative political force.

The year that Munisamy Naidu assumed office, 1930, was also the year which saw the beginning of Congress Civil Disobedience campaigns all over the country. The early thirties witnessed social and economic upheavals of various sorts, many of which were triggered off by the disastrous effects of the Great Depression of 1929 and after. The depression years in Madras saw a large scale migration of labour, not only from the villages into towns, but from Burma, Ceylon and East Asia into the Presidency. As a consequence, wages dropped even as prices rose. Widespread discontent and anger provoked a general weakening of social bonds and conventional political alignments, which in turn, created troubled zones that were well utilized by the Congress Civil Disobedience activists (Baker 1976: 211-24; Arnold 1977: 114-31). While Madras did not produce spectacular activism in this respect, even here, the attractions of agitational politics were visible.

Congressmen, with the exception of the Swarajists, who disassociated themselves from the Civil Disobedience campaigns, worked hard to tap the widespread discontent and managed to coopt to their cause various social segments: workmen, weavers, disaffected abkari contractors, subaltern castes such as the Nadars, the adi dravidas and unemployed students. Congress also worked hard to capitalize on convention and custom. The Vedaranyam satyagraha, undertaken by C. Rajagopalachari (Rajaji) on the model of Dandi, proved to be a carefully worked out political strategy that would mythicize the cause of Civil Disobedience and lend it the sanction of custom, culture and religion. Significantly enough, it was launched on the first day of the Tamil New Year and blessed by brahmin pundits, who flagged off the satyagrahis with the chanting of appropriate Sanskrit hymns (Arnold 1977: 118-19). Civil Disobedience activists achieved popularity and emerged as martyrs in the public eye when police opened fire on the satyagrahis at a meeting in Madras, where striking mill workers had also gathered (ibid).

The Justice party's responses to these events was predictably bland. It condemned the Congress agitations and proclaimed that the convening of a Round Table conference under British auspices to be the only viable solution to the present crisis. The Justice leadership also offered its assistance to the government to quell the troubles (KA 14.9.30). Periyar was singularly unhappy with the Congress agitations, as well as with the Justice party's unimaginative responses to the latter. His own responses were angry, bitter and satiric in turn. He published an article which, commenting on the speeches and observances of Congress leaders on a resolution moved at the Coimbatore district session of the Congress, noted that the speakers compared Gandhi to Rama, Patel to Lakshmana and Kasturba to Sita! Further the speakers had invoked the names of other puranic figures as well, such as Bhima, Krishna and Harischandra (KA 11.5.30). Periyar objected to the Civil Disobedience agitations on other considerations as well: He objected to the symbolic dimension of these agitations; to the fact that very few substantial issues were raised by the agitators, who were more interested in defying government, attracting public attention and courting arrest than in resolving matters of political import. He argued Gandhi's salt satyagraha was gratuitous and irrelevant. Nowhere did the satyagrahis seek to address the real economic difficulties faced by the people (KA 16.3.30; 13.4.30).

Periyar was convinced that the Civil Disobedience campaigns possessed neither consistency nor were they responsible in the actions they initiated. He indicated how the rhetoric and semantics of nationalism had become so charged with partisan political energy that virtually anyone

> [had] only to heed the nationalist call and engage in Civil Disobedience—[and he] could emerge a nationalist and a patriot, whatever else he may be in other respects. But let anyone support government or welcome the Simon Commission, and whatever his motives and intentions, he was automatically labelled a friend of government and a loyalist (KA 29.6.30).

As he had done in the past, in the wake of Gandhi's suspension of Non Cooperation and his own disenchantment with the Congress, Periyar drew attention to the double-facedness of the Congress, whose largely brahmin leadership in Madras were capable of the most amazing political somersaults. Periyar noted that nationalist brahmins were past masters in the fine art of deception and, that in the twenties, when the Justice ministry passed the Hindu Religious Endowments Act, they had initially opposed it on 'principled' grounds. But when the act had become law, they were not averse to seeking posts for themselves in the newly created Hindu Religious Endowments Board! (KA 29.6.30) He further observed that 'This nationalist agitation and government containment of it are, both, really a game in which Congress and Government are trying to outwit each other to prove who is smarter when it comes to cheating the common people'. Besides, the Congress' nationalist rhetoric was thoroughly bogus and rang hollow:

> For thousands of years this country has known no nationalists. Could anyone claim (with confidence) that this land has known complete independence in the thousands of years that are behind us? Is it not important to discover the reasons for this and set it right? It has always been the religious dharma and legal norm in this country to consign a man to perpetual unfreedom and oppress him.

Periyar observed that whose who insisted 'nationalism is all' were, in reality, those who possessed neither the skills nor the aptitude to do a day's honest labour. They were parasites, unused to physical strain and merely awaited a chance to corner posts for themselves in government (KA 3.8.30). He argued that due to the Civil Disobedience agitations, 'many may become devotees of and martyrs to the nationalist cause. Yet others may acquire a name and a place for themselves in government. But beyond this we do not expect anything to change.' For,

> The 'purna swaraj' that is expected to emerge out of these agitations and from the reform efforts of a government, intent on political reform, will both benefit only the upper castes, the rich and the educated, but for the peasants and workers who comprise 90% of our populace, there will be no relief (KA 23.11.30; Anaimuthu: 374-75).

Periyar's criticisms of Civil Disobedience, and a nationalism which drew ideological and political sustenance from it, was not merely reactive. Even as Gandhi announced his decision to conduct satyagraha, Periyar had adumbrated a very different notion of Swaraj and one that would bring about the destruction of caste and religion, the abolition of untouchability and the liberation of women (KA 16.3.30).

Periyar's expostulations against the Congress were really counter-hegemonic responses to the growing appeal of that party amongst various sections of the people. Periyar sensed in Congress propaganda and activism a decisive will to power and understood its hegemonic ambitions as perhaps no one else did, during this period and after. His support for the Justice party must be viewed in this context, that he viewed it as an alternative, however weak, ineffectual and driven by factional feuding it may be, to the Congress, at least in Madras. His own Self-Respect movement had vowed to stay away from politics and in spite of his insightful perceptions regarding the constellation of caste, class and religious interests in nationalist discourse and practice, the incipient communist movement in Madras took no note of him. True, men like M. Singaravelu were drawn to the Self-Respect creed, but there was no sustained interaction between the communists and the Self-Respecters. Besides, Periyar was himself critical, as he remarked in later years, of the communists' silence on caste and

Brahminism. However this may be, in the crucial 1932-33 period that marked the interval between the Second Round Table Conference and the suspension of Civil Disobedience, Periyar's decision to move closer to the Justicites became in more than one sense inevitable.

THE JUSTICE PARTY IN THE CRUCIAL THIRTIES

In November 1930, the First Round Table Conference was held in London, without Gandhi's participation. Congress leaders were released from prison and the Gandhi-Irwin Pact was signed the following year. The Justice party, as we have noted, was busy with its own squabbles and, except for denouncing the Civil Disobedience campaigns, was barely in touch, either politically or ideologically, with the momentous events of the period. When Congressmen accused the Justicites of abetting Madras police in the violence unleashed against satyagrahis, it was Periyar who pointed out that under dyarchy, an elected government could only wait and watch, since Law and Order were reserved subjects (KA 1.2.31).

But, as in earlier instances, neither Periyar's support of the Justice ministry, nor his relentless criticism of Congress, mattered to the Justice leadership, which remained opaque and passive to the pressures and anxieties of the period. Periyar, on the other hand, was remarkably perceptive as to the outcome of the First Round Table Conference and observed it had created the political, ideological and institutional conditions for the Congress to protect and secure its concerns and hegemony. He also noted that such a situation, which would enable and allow the Congress to exercise its dominance and crush opposing political trends, suited India's rulers. For they could now stand apart and preserve their autonomy and maintain their authority, unsullied by the business of everyday realpolitik. Britain, concluded Periyar, feared the spread of Bolshevik ideas in India, which was why it had decided to ask the princely states to federate with British India, so that Congress political sagacity and cunning on the one hand, and feudal and princely authority on the other could, in unison, stifle the imminent political struggles of the period (KA 25.1.31).

Throughout 1931, Periyar wrote and spoke out against the wiles of Congress nationalism and submitted the Gandhi-Irwin Pact to his customary penetrative criticism. Reiterating an earlier observation, that the Civil Disobedience campaigns represented a mere tug-of-war between the Hindu upper castes and the British commercial elite, in which the former relied on the average Hindu's abysmal ignorance to achieve their ends, and the latter deployed the weapon of political reform to advance theirs, he now observed, 'Mr. Gandhi and Mr. Irwin met as honorary spokesmen of their respective Chambers of Commerce.' Periyar also noted that the pact had resulted in the Congress giving up on a number of substantial political demands though it was propagandized as a great victory by Congress publicists (KA 28.6.31). But Periyar's brilliant and prophetic reading of the historic conjuncture, which marked the beginning of the early thirties, was lost on the Justicites. It was only with the Second Round Table Conference and the Communal Award of Ramsay Macdonald that Justicites woke up to the realities of Congress-brahmin hegemony and its implications for the non-brahmins and the adi dravidas.

The Poona Pact and the Justice Party

Following the announcement of Ramsay Macdonald's Communal Award and Gandhi's obdurate opposition to it, Periyar's Self-Respect movement and the Justice party, together and separately, embarked on a propagandistic mission in the cause of the adi dravidas, and upheld their right to a separate electorate. A scathing *Kudi Arasu* editorial of 25 October 1931, 'The Betrayal of the Adi Dravidas by the Hindus' condemned Gandhi's clearly expressed opinion that he would oppose unto death the granting of separate electorates to the adi dravidas and his assertion that only he ought to be considered their sole representative. Several meetings were held in Madras in support of Dr. Ambedkar and Rettamalai Srinivasan under the joint auspices of the Self-Respect movement and the Justice party.

Meanwhile, following a suggestion made at the Third Provincial Self-Respect Conference held at Virudhunagar, Periyar and S. Ramanathan had embarked on a tour of the Soviet Union and other European countries to learn of and see for themselves the practical effects and uses of atheism as a doctrine of the state. (In fact W.P.A. Soundarapandian had suggested that they undertake such a trip to learn of the political uses of atheism from the Soviet Union and

Western nations.) However, meetings supporting Dr. Ambedkar continued to be held in their absence. These meetings brought onto a common non-brahmin platform prominent adi dravida leaders such as M. C. Raja (who initially supported the Communal Award), N. Sivaraj (a member of the Madras Council and a long standing Justicite and Self-Respecter) and others. Some Congressmen and brahmins attempted to disrupt the proceedings of one such meeting and nationalist dailies made much of the fracas that subsequently ensued and came out with screaming headlines such as 'Gandhi in Danger!' and 'The Mischief of the Adi Dravidas'. Undeterred, Justicites and Self-Respecters and hundreds of adi dravidas continued to hold their protest meetings and passed resolutions which asked for the immediate implementation of the Communal Award. In one instance, a 7000 strong meeting was held in the Egmore area of Madras after which adi dravidas, returning home, were purportedly attacked by hooligans (KA 25.10.31).

The announcement of reserved seats for adi dravidas in 1932, following the conclusion of the Poona Pact between Dr. Ambedkar and Gandhi, did nothing to allay the very real anger of the adi dravidas (and non-brahmins) in Madras. *Kudi Arasu's* editorial on the pact, published on 17 July 1932, was significantly enough titled 'The Liberation of the Adi Dravidas and the Deception of the Hindus'. This, as well as several others, condemned Gandhi and the Hindu Mahasabha leader Moonje in no uncertain terms. M. C. Raja, after lending his support to the idea of separate electorates for adi dravidas initially, had endorsed Moonje's stance on this matter. Thus, he was also criticized, albeit mildly, and called to account for his sudden opposition to separate electorates (ibid).

Gandhi's 'epic fast' came in for sharp rebuke and another article posed the indignant question:

> On the advice of Mr. Gandhi and in response to a statement issued by Rajagopalachari, brahmins have resorted to prayer and fasting. But have any of them observed a fast for the cause of the untouchables? These men undertook to fast when Mr. Gandhi entreated them that the integrity of the Hindu faith must be saved at all costs, but are there any brahmins who would fast for putting an end to the misery of the untouchables?

The same article went on to ask why not even a little of that attention which was being so lavishly bestowed on Gandhi was sought to be expended on Kelappan, who had been fasting in Kerala, for a while now, for the abolition of untouchability and for securing the right to temple entry to adi dravidas (KA 2.10.32).

To underscore the Non-Brahmin movement's commitment to the cause of separate electorates for the adi dravidas, a special adi dravida conference was organized with the support of the Justice party and the Self-Respect movement and was attended by Self-Respecters, Justicites and adi dravidas, including prominent community leaders like Munusamy Pillay and Kanakaraj (KA 23.10.32).

The issues raised by the Poona Pact enabled the Self-Respecters to isolate the pro-brahmin, pro-Congress elements clustered around Munisamy Naidu in the Justice party. In any case the latter had managed to alienate Tamil Justicites such as P. T. Rajan and, worse, had not called for a party conference though it was three years since he had been elected president. When such a conference was actually convened in Thanjavur in October 1932 (Periyar had not yet returned from his continental tour), it was clear that Munisamy Naidu's days as president were over. The raja of Bobbili was elected president in his place. Bobbili was a man who was warmly commended by Periyar in the days to come as a leader free from corruption and as one not given to nepotism or jobbery. The Self-Respecters, many of whom would later criticize Bobbili for his feudal 'class' interests, gave in quietly at Thanjavur; so urgent was the imperative to free the Justice party from a possible and imminent cooptation by the Congress, and to transform it into a party that would represent and mediate the achievement of a general non-brahmin good.

Though the Self-Respecters at Thanjavur had worked hard to keep Naidu out of the Justice party's leadership, they were none too sanguine about the prospects and strengths of that party for future times. They were particularly worried about the factionalism which had almost torn the party apart at Thanjavur. A *Kudi Arasu* editorial of 16 October 1932 noted with sorrow that the Thanjavur events had shown the Justice leaders in a rather poor light. It appeared that they were more concerned in looking to their self-interest and consolidating their individual positions of authority within the party than in working to broaden and deepen the non-brahmin commonweal.

It is clear that the Self-Respecters' endorsement of Bobbili was but a tactical gesture, for surely they could not have been too happy with one whose understanding of the Self-Respect movement was rather limited and, worse, ill-informed. Speaking at a Self-Respect meeting at Trichy on 2 October 1932, Bobbili had remarked that he had come to learn the Self-Respecters were aghast at those depravities which had entered Hindu social life and wished to reform the latter. He went on to say that 'in every religion, at a particular moment in its historical existence there have been known to emerge reform movements that worked to bring about such reforms as would be acceptable to all'. The Self-Respect movement, for its part, desired to 'purify the Hindu religion' and rid it of those faults which had crept into the practice of this most ancient of faiths. Later, at Thanjavur, Bobbili returned to this theme and observed that as far as he knew the Self-Respect movement worked to enhance the nobility of the Hindu faith and rid it off those excrescences which had grown around its original glory. The Self-Respecters, he claimed, were interested in the unity of all peoples and wished to realize this unity in practice. Recalling the anti-religion, anti-caste sentiments expressed at the First Provincial Self-Respect Conference, Bobbili noted that these were articulated by impetuous young men whose misplaced zeal and enthusiasm made them cross the limits of propriety, but this impetuousity ought not to be used to damn the movement as a whole (KA 9, 16.10.32).

It is important to reiterate here that the Self-Respecters' decision to support the raja of Bobbili and endorse his claims to leadership was a purely tactical one. Younger Self-Respecters such as S. Gurusamy, for instance, had no illusions about the nature of the Justice party leadership. Gurusamy had, in fact, sought to distinguish the Self-Respect movement from the Justice party, even as the two were working in concert against the Poona Pact. In an article written in September 1931, Gurusamy observed that the Self-Respect movement and the Justice party shared certain common objectives. Both desired to secure concessions for adi dravidas, the poor and women in the proposed political reform scheme. Both were convinced that Congress was nothing but a forum of brahmins who were trying to compensate for their lost sacrality by thus working in the realm of politics. However, and Gurusamy was quick to add this, the Justice party's opposition seemed half-hearted at times, and even apprehensive of its own boldness in this regard. Further, the Self-Respect movement and the Justice party were not agreed on all matters:

> It is obvious that the leaders and newspapers of the Justice party are opposed to some of the cardinal principles and objectives of the Self-Respect movement; that is, they do not endorse the latter's stance on the need to destroy religion, faith in God, religious symbols and caste titles.

Gurusamy added that even with respect to opposing brahmins, the apparent unity of the Justice party and the Self-Respect movement belied actual differences. Both opposed the brahmin because if one were to attack and challenge the caste order, one would, necessarily, have to fire the first arrow at the brahmin. 'The arrow has to pierce through the brahmin before it can get to the others.' But this did not mean that the Self-Respecters would tolerate religious zeal and caste sentiment in non-brahmins, whether these were Justicites were not. As far as the Self-Respecters were concerned, religious frenzy and caste prejudices were to be condemned, irrespective of who articulated them (Velu 1991, 2nd ed: 324-26).

The Justice Party in the Era of Self-Respect–Samadharma

Periyar returned to India in November 1932. His visit to and sojourn in the Soviet Union had kindled in him a great and general interest in socialism. The years 1933-36 were witness to hectic and radical social reform activity, as Self-Respecters came to articulate their anti-religion, anti-caste ideas and opinions within a general logic of socialism. This socialism, at all times remained an index, but a very valuable index, of Periyar's philosophy of Self-Respect and was subsumed to the imperatives of his anti-brahmin, anti-caste ideology as well as to the exigencies and anxieties of the historical moment in question.

Periyar came back to a polity that was only slowly recovering from the ruthless and violent repression that was visited on Congress satyagrahis. In spite of the much vaunted victory for the Congress, that the Gandhi-Irwin Pact was supposed to consecrate, the British as well as the satyagrahis did not always observe the terms of peace outlined in it. Throughout 1931-32, Congress activists offering individual satyagraha met with the government's iron and often brutal resistance. The publication in March 1933 of a White Paper by the Government of India detailing the political reforms which would become law with the Government of India Act of 1935 proved to be crucial for the Congress. Having kept up its pressure on satyagrahis as well as the government, it now decided to change track and move towards a policy of reconciliation and cooperation with the latter. By mid-1933 Gandhi was ready to suspend all Civil Disobedience activities—though it was only in May 1934 at Patna that this was formally done—and look to other matters.

Already, following the Poona Pact, the Harijan Sevak Sangh had been started, and Gandhi made it clear he wished to retire, so to speak, into Constructive Work. Periyar, however, was not deceived by this shift in Congress policy. He observed that since the signing of the Gandhi-Irwin Pact, Gandhi's 'secret intentions and those of his premier disciples' had been realized, albeit, gradually. On the eve of his salt satyagraha campaign, Gandhi had stated clearly that if he had not planned for this symbolically significant agitation, Bolshevism would have taken over the public imagination. This, according to Periyar, was proof enough of Gandhi's desire to quell and coopt popular discontent. Later, with the signing of the Poona Pact, Gandhi had managed to subdue yet another sullen and angry section of the populace, the adi dravidas. Not only had he ignored their political expectations and sought to contain them within the bounds of varnadharma, but also, as if to appease them and win approval for himself in their midst, had begun the Harijan Sevak Sangh with, significantly enough, the help of G. D. Birla. A few untouchable leaders were bought out to aid the activities of the Sangh, while others were coopted through (false) promises of equality. Due to Gandhi's efforts there was now available for use by the Hindus, a complaisant and captive workforce that could be made to labour for all (KA 23.7.33; Anaimuthu: 392-93).

To Periyar the starting of the Harijan Sevak Sangh seemed a manifest expression of Gandhi's real intentions. He desired to preserve the varna-jati social order and retain for himself and the Congress the support of the wealthy. Thus, noted Periyar, the implorations to thousands of ordinary people to take up spinning only served the wealthy mill owners of Ahmedabad, while the solutions offered for the problem of untouchability only went to strengthen the norms of varnadharma and legitimized, in the eyes of its proponents, the caste-based division of labour and labourers in Hindu society (ibid).

Periyar's reading of the political situation, as it stood in 1933, proved apt, correct and relevant. For the following year was witness to hectic and consistent propaganda by Congress in the Tamil country and elsewhere, as it sought to create a broad consensus for its particular mixture of politics and piety. Gandhi himself visited Madras during this period and was accorded enthusiastic receptions wherever he went. Congressmen, now eager to project themselves as friends of the adi dravidas, had utilized the funds and services of the Harijan Sevak Sangh well; hostels for adi dravida students were built, scholarships instituted, wells opened and it was proclaimed that it was due to Congress efforts that adi dravidas had been granted reserved seats in the legislature.

Congressmen in Madras had attempted to woo adi dravidas as early as 1932, in fact had attempted to win them away from their affiliations with the Self-Respect movement. For in this year, Subbarayan who had since moved close to the Congress, on the advice of Rajagopalachari, tabled a bill that would allow adi dravidas to enter a certain temple, provided its devotees and users agreed, on the basis of a referendum, to allow them such rights of entry. Since this question pertained to civil rights and law, a provincial government could not act on it, and if it desired to do so, it had to obtain the sanction of the Governor. In this instance, pleading that the matter of adi dravidas entering temples pertained to the whole of British India, the Governor refused sanction, sent the bill to Viceroy, who refused assent to it. It was also the case that the Sanatanists in the Madras Legislative Assembly feared that with a Justice ministry in power, the bill may actually be passed, and were hence determined to ensure its swift demise (Venkatraman 1946: 7-11). Meanwhile, in the Central Legislature, Ranga Iyer tabled a bill that was similar in its details to Dr. Subbarayan's Madras bill. This measure won the approval of Gandhi and Rajagopalachari who assured Ranga Iyer of Congress support to the legislation. But when in 1934, the Central Assembly was dissolved and elections announced,

Gandhi quietly withdrew his support to the measure (BAWS 1993: vol 9, 118-25).

The point is that Congressmen made much of this abortive attempt to secure 'adi dravida rights' and sought to win adi dravida approval of their good intentions with respect to the problem of untouchability. The Congress also sought to utilize local rivalries amongst non-brahmin notables in Madras and worked on them to win as many diverse segments of non-brahmins to its cause. Thus, those angry with and jealous of the Justice leadership, those who had felt and had genuine grievances against that party and those who were moved by the Congress' wonderful rhetoric of Nation, Service, Sacrifice and Piety were drawn to and accepted within the charmed circle of nationalists.

Periyar was, of course, unmoved by these developments and observed that at the present moment both the Congress and the British were implicated in the political economy of global capitalism and had therefore decided to give up their old rivalries and animosities and 'work in concert' to shore up each other's legitimacy and authority (KA 3.9.33; Anaimuthu: 777-83). Congress had thus turned away from its habitual anti-imperialist posturing and decided to win as many hearts as possible to its 'noble' cause. Both the government and the Congress had sought out a third authority, the Indian princes, to strengthen the proposed federation of provinces. (This was an outcome of the Second and Third Round Table Conferences.)

Periyar explained, at length, the implications of such a decision. He pointed to the parasitic culture practised and encouraged by Indian princes, the admixture of political and religious power these princedoms sought to cultivate, and drew attention to those various repressive laws enforced in their states to curb seditious and anti-religious activities, with, of course, the active connivance of the British. The unholy combination of King, Priest and Law, argued Periyar, had more or less subdued the people living in these princedoms into obedience and fear. The Congress' wily leadership had obviously decided to rely on the ingrained autocracy of these princes to whip into submission a recalcitrant workforce and, besides, Congressmen could remain aloof and not 'soil' their patriotic hands in this endeavour. Hence, contrary to every principle of democracy and liberty, which they nevertheless routinely espoused, they had invited the princes to federate with the rest of India (KA 3.9.33).

Periyar's opinions of the Congress did not automatically lead him to accept the Justice party as a viable alternative. His critique of the Congress was, in effect, an admission, though, not acceptance of the party's hegemonic strengths, and it is clear Periyar expected and was apprehensive of a Congress victory in the impending elections to the Central Legislature and local bodies. He was not only acutely aware of the impact such a victory would have on non-brahmin concerns, but in more general terms, was sensitive to the specific articulation of power that would follow, subsequent to the victory.

Already in the early thirties, a series of changes had occurred in local administration in terms of electoral principles and procedures. While local officials came to be elected in more and more local bodies rather than being nominated, their powers to make and break appointments to various services and the discretionary authority vested in them came to be gradually eroded. Such powers were now concentrated in the higher bureaucracy, making the edifice of government extremely unwieldy and powerful at the top (Baker 1976: 228-37). It is possible Periyar feared this centralization of authority in the Madras secretariat. For, not only would this vest enormous powers in higher brahmin officials, but would also render the state a powerful structure which, under the political control of a party such as the Congress, could deprive ordinary non-brahmins of their hard-won victories to equality, in education and employment in the services, and, more generally, with respect to opportunities for material and social development. It is this perhaps which made Periyar determined to counterpose a political challenge to the Congress and, naturally enough, the Justice party, which from its earliest days had demonstrated an insatiable non-brahmin will to power, and which had opposed the Poona Pact and thereby dared to defy Gandhi, had to be considered and constructed to represent a serious political opposition to the Congress in Madras.

However, 1933 did not prove to be a particularly opportune year for a easy coming together of the Justice party and the Self-Respect movement. From the early months of 1933, the Self-Respect movement began to debate and propagate the virtues of socialism as desirable political and social ideals. To the movement's vigorous anti-brahmin, anti-God, anti-caste propaganda was now added an anti-class and, more specifically, anti-rich theme, which, as Periyar observed, had embarrassed his wealthy supporters:

> All those who stood by us and urged us onward when we proclaimed differences in caste, between a brahmin and a paraiah and a high caste group and a low caste group, ought to be abolished have deserted our ranks, now that we claim there ought to be no differences in wealth and ask why should some be rich and others poor, why should some be capitalists and others workers... Our former allies have also begun to find fault with us and we are creating for ourselves new enemies by the day (KA 12.3.3).

Several young men in the Self-Respect movement now took to openly criticizing the Justice leadership for comprising only the wealthy and for devoting itself to elite concerns. At a conference held at Rasipuram in Salem district to address the problems of zamin ryots, and in opposition to zamindars, K. M. Balasubramanium, a youthful Self-Respecter, launched into a direct attack on Bobbili and his party. He argued that in its early days, the Justice party had been a truly democratic party, but in recent times it had come to be controlled by a clique of zamindars and self-seekers who seemed determined to destroy their party. Commenting on Bobbili's remark that he was happy to preside over a party in which the capitalist and worker, the zamindar and ryot co-existed in harmony, peace and friendship, Balasubramanium wondered what specific measures had Bobbili undertaken to improve the conditions of existence of his ryots. He also confessed himself sorry and ashamed at having helped in electing Bobbili to the Justice leadership. Balasubramanium pleaded that at least, hence, 'those few good men left in the Justice party would extricate themselves from the selfish and treacherous hold of zamindars and re-establish democracy within the party'. Balasubramanium spoke at length on the zamindar-ryot relationship and of the duplicity resorted to by the former when the question of the redressal of ryots' grievances came up. He accused Bobbili of practising deception on his peasants and took him to task for choosing to talk of ryot indebtedness, that is, the peasants' oppression by the moneylender, rather than dwell on the inequalities which structured the zamindar-ryot relationship (KA 20.8.33).

The zamin ryots conference at which Balasubramanium delivered his stirring address did not go unnoticed. Bobbili's zamindar peers, who had successfully scuttled the amendment proposed to the Madras Estates Land Act of 1908 by Munisamy Naidu, now came to support Bobbili's amendment to the said act which sought to extend tenurial rights vested in and enjoyed by zamin ryots to ryots on inam lands. Inam lands, for the most part, were owned by brahmins whose ancestors received such lands as gifts—which meant they were revenue free—from kings, chiefs and other notables. The brahmin press, a majority of brahmins in the Madras Council and in the Governor's Executive Council resisted the passage of this amendment into law and it was returned to the Council twice by the Governor who refused to endorse it, presumably on the advice of his brahmin colleagues and advisors in the Council. *Puratchi* (Pu) (a Self-Respect weekly begun on 26.11.33), commenting on the Inam ryots Bill, admitted its scope was restricted but pointed to the fact that brahmin landlords would not accept even this extremely moderate reform (Pu 25.3.34; 29.12.35). Brahmin resistance persisted, in spite of Congress socialists such as N. G. Ranga and K. Santhanam supporting its passage. S. Satyamurthi and Venkatrama Shastry were completely opposed to this measure and they had the backing of those purveyors of public opinion, *The Hindu* and *Swadesamitran*. Eventually though the amendment was passed and became law in 1936 (*Peasant Organisations and Movements*: 111-13).

Yet men like Balasubramanium continued to be critical of the Justice party and Bobbili. Thus, referring to the discontinuation of *Dravidan* by the Justice leadership, Balasubramanium wrote to say that it seemed as if Justicites were determined to realize the Swarajist Satyamurthi's old oath—that he would not rest until he had the Justice party well and truly buried into oblivion. For, with the discontinuation of *Dravidan*, not only had the party lost a voice, but showed itself ready 'to be pronounced a corpse that could now be borne to its final dwelling place by a bevy of zamindars'. Further,

> Today in Council and out of it there is no such thing as the Justice party. There is an entity called Bobbili's party. This party ought to be condemned for doing nothing to improve the non-brahmin commonweal or to even enable non-brahmins secure jobs for

> themselves. It is clear the party had abandoned those social reform principles that were so dear to Dr. Nair's heart (Pu 8.4.34).

The Justice party was criticized by others in the Self-Respect movement as well: those ardent young men who were inspired by socialism and were most vocal and by M. Singaravelu, Buddhist scholar and a socialist by conviction, who attacked the Justice party's moribund leadership and its undisguised reliance on the feudal rich. These criticisms were aired in Self-Respect forums and in the pages of *Samadharmam* (SD) that came to be published from Jolarpettai from August 1934. The first issue of *Samadharmam* carried the photographs of Periyar and the wealthy merchant R. K. Shanmugham, a longstanding supporter of the non-brahmin cause and a Justicite. This juxtaposition of two men who represented very different interests and concerns drew an acid rebuke from Singaravelu. He wondered if this signified a fundamental contradiction which lay at the heart of the Self-Respect movement (SD 15.8.34). Singaravelu was vehemently opposed to the Self-Respecters affiliating with the Justice party in any manner whatsoever. On several occasions, he had asked Self-Respecters to address economic issues with the same ardour and attention as they did social and cultural concerns (KA 1.11.31). He had also pointed out to them that there were some in the forefront of the Self-Respect movement, who were opposed to its founding principles and ideologies and who disliked the socialism the movement had come to espouse in recent times (KA 8.10.33).

Periyar's responses to these criticisms reflected an equal measure of anger and despair. He was himself, as we have seen, prone to criticize the Justice party for its ineffectuality, its vague and tenuous Non-Brahminism and for its indecisive stance with respect to the Congress and brahmins. But in 1933-34, wise to the ways of a government that was waiting to pounce on any sort of militancy, now that the Congress was more less willing and eager to cooperate with it, Periyar naturally desired to consolidate the political and social gains garnered by the Self-Respect movement in what was increasingly becoming a no-win situation. The Justice party seemed to him a worthy ally in this regard and he was not willing to give up on it all too easily.

Throughout 1933, the Government of India had watched the activities of radical groups, trade unions and political militants. Its intelligence agencies were particularly watchful of and reported on those who carried out socialist propaganda. In Madras, *Kudi Arasu* and the Self-Respecters were under surveillance and *Kudi Arasu* was asked to furnish a surety to the government. When Periyar went to Trichy to address a gathering of Self-Respecters at a Christian marriage on 12 May 1933, prohibitory orders were issued in the city (Sitambaranar: 14). On 20 December 1933, Periyar and his sister Kannamma were arrested on charges of sedition. The article that seemed to have angered the government was one titled 'Why Must this Government Go?' which had appeared in *Kudi Arasu*, 24 October 1933. Periyar was released in May 1934 and came back to confront a hopelessly divided Justice party. During this period, *Kudi Arasu* was discontinued for a while but two other weeklies, *Puratchi* and *Paguttharivu* (Pa), were now available in its place.

In mid-1934, when Periyar was released from prison, the Justice party was riven with divisions and faction fights. The kumararaja of Chettinad, M. A. Muthiah Chettiar and Bobbili had each called for separate meetings of the Justice party in June 1934. Periyar, as may be imagined, was none too pleased and a *Puratchi* article of 3 June 1934 pointed out that the Justice party had clearly fallen foul of those ideals of social justice and equality, especially with respect to the adi dravidas, which had inspired its founders. It also remarked on the fact that the party had come to be dominated by zamindars and capitalists and become an instrument in their hands, used solely to promote and secure their interests. However, the article concluded, all was not lost and 'if ordinary non-Brahmins, that is, those who were neither zamindars nor capitalists or elites, were to come together and, in a disciplined fashion, pressurise the rich to adhere to the party's true objectives, these latter might actually come around to doing so'.

Periyar attended a meeting of Justicites convened at Bobbili's residence soon after and put forth the following suggestions: Justicites must work to correct the widely prevalent impression that they were only interested in fighting for and securing jobs and posts for themselves; secondly, they must define their principles—of belief and action—clearly and produce a political programme, for otherwise they would not be able to counter the Congress. The latter, whatever the intentions (and integrity) of its leaders, professed principles and was willing to act on them and agitate for their realization; whereas

Justicites had failed to specify their plans for political and social change. They had assumed that money and the power it embodied would help them win elections. While this may be all right for individuals, a party or movement cannot afford to work on this basis and must possess a distinctive agenda. Thirdly, Justicites would do well to expel the popular notion that they comprised only the rich and the landed. For not only was this untrue, but such notions did grave injustice to the sincerity and commitment of ordinary non-brahmins who supported the party in one way or another. Fourthly, the Justice party must move beyond its provincial concerns and henceforth send its members to the Central Legislature. Until now this lapse had cost the non-brahmins dearly, for in their absence brahmins had come to speak in the name of the commonweal. Lastly, Periyar went on to express his misgivings over the re-surfacing of the brahmin question in the Justice party. He argued that brahmins had not changed their views that drastically for him to feel sanguine about letting them join the Justice party. If one were to abide by political considerations which demanded the inclusion of brahmins, one would naturally have to forgo the idea of radical social reform. As for himself, he concluded, he was not a Justicite, was not even among the forefront of that party's members and, besides, he had not come to advice the Justice party on this score or on any other, but only desired to warn them of what lay ahead in the future polity and society (Pu 10.6.34).

Periyar's suggestions proved to be in vain. Whatever they had decided on other matters, Justicites, including such old timers as Natesa Mudaliar, had decided, even before the meeting convened at Bobbili's house, that they would press for a resolution which would allow brahmins to join the Justice party. Such a move was influenced, no doubt, by the fact that elections to the Central Legislature and local bodies were to take place soon. The Self-Respecters, including W. P. A. Soundarapandian, T. V. Subramanium, editor of *Dravidan* (while it was in publication) and others, opposed the idea, but Justicites, or at least a section of them with Annamalai Chettiar in the lead, had resolved otherwise. The Self-Respecters consoled themselves with noting that experience would teach the Justicites a bitter lesson in this regard and, since they could do very little to force a change of heart amongst the Justice party members, they allowed the resolution to be passed (ibid). (The resolution was formally approved at a Justice party conference held at Madras on 29-30 September 1934.)

Paguthariyu, a Self-Respect weekly begun on 26 August 1934, commenting on the formal acceptance of the idea of allowing brahmins into the Justice party, noted that this matter cannot be considered or evaluated in isolation. The question the Self-Respecters (and Justicites) had to resolve in this context was simply this: 'Had the time come to do away with the principle of proportional representation?' For allowing brahmins to join the party was really tantamount to giving up the demand for proportional representation, since no brahmin would ever agree to this demand (7.10.34).

Earlier, in an article on the forthcoming elections to the Central Legislature, Periyar had noted that as before, the important issue for non-brahmins was the future of proportional representation. The Congress had thus far resolutely rejected this principle, so dear to non-brahmins. Periyar had then noted, 'if only they [Congress] had worked out a way to accommodate this idea at the time when we had begun to agitate around it, today the Congress would have been the only party in the country and all of us would have been ashamed of not being its members.' Congressmen had failed the non-brahmins in this respect, but now surely Congressmen ought to recognize 'that proportional representa-tion will disappear [in practice] only when caste and religion are destroyed' (Pa 16.9.34).

Periyar, for reasons we shall soon discuss, was not completely averse to Self-Respecters joining or supporting the Congress. The *Paguthariyu* article of 16 September 1934 discussed at length the differences between the Congress and the Justice party. It is clear from this discussion that Periyar felt that the Congress and the Justice party—now that the latter had decided to admit brahmins—were bound together in a relationship of equivalence. If, in one, brahmins dominated, in the other, the rich held sway. (Besides the Justice party had opened itself to brahmins.) If Congress was completely opposed to the principle of proportional representation, the Justice party had shown itself to be somewhat reluctant to address the matter seriously. True, there were sincere trusting workers in both parties, but non-brahmins in the Congress were often willing and obedient slaves of brahmins, while the poor and the adi dravidas which supported the Justice party were, likewise, forced into obedience by the party elite. The Self-Respect movement had resolutely opposed the Congress and stoutly defended the Justice party until the present moment, but while no harm had come to the Self-Respect movement on account of the Congress, no good had been rendered it by the Justice party. In the absence of any clear-cut differences between the Congress and the Justice party, self-respecters could only apply an ideological test to ascertain the worth of either. Since the Self-Respect movement was above all concerned with the social and economic progress of the poor and the adi dravidas and since it held this progress was intimately bound up with matters of social and religious practices and caste, only a party which would, simultaneously and in equal measure, address social and economic problems could win its approval. The Self-Respect movement trusted in the processes and relevance of legal public action and desired to utilize them to achieve its ends, unless of course it was declared illegal to pursue such objectives as it had set for itself; which time it would have to make serious decisions regarding its future.

A week later, *Paguttharivu* published the Self-Respecters programme of action (23.9.34) which was meant for reading by both Congressmen and Justicites (see Appendix 2). Both parties were to confer shortly and Periyar was anxious to know which one of them would accept his proposals. Periyar's relationship with and attitudes towards Congress were rather delicately poised at this stage. It was a fundamental dictum with him, even at this point of time, that the Congress represented brahmin interest in the main. But, since he also desired to chip away as much as he could at the seemingly impenetrable hegemony wrought by the Congress, he was open to various options that would enable him in this task. He had, in fact covertly, referred to his dilemma with reference to the Congress in a letter addressed to Varadarajulu Naidu and carried in *Nagara Thootan* (NT) (29.7.34) where he had noted then that he had met C. Rajagopalachari at Erode, on his release from prison, and the latter had asked him to join the Congress. He had asked for time to consider the matter and to discuss it with his fellow Self-Respecters but had also made it known to Rajagopalachari that if he, Rajagopalachari, wanted him and the Self-Respecters to align with Congress, then the latter must, in principle, accept and work to realize the idea of proportional representation in practice. A plan of action to this effect was drawn in prison and forwarded to Gandhi but since the latter failed to respond, the matter was dropped.

At a public meeting in Jolarpet, Periyar dwelt at length on this discussion with Rajagopalachari. It is not clear whether this was the Erode discussion or an earlier one, for here, Periyar refers to talking to Rajagopalachari in prison in Coimbatore. (The Jolarpet meeting was held to mark the release of the first issue of the Self-Respect socialist weekly, *Samadharmam.*) Periyar noted that while in prison, he had been attentive to Rajagopalachari's plans, but had not entertained any illusions as to the Congress' prospective behaviour with respect to those non-brahmins from the Self-Respect movement, who might join its ranks. Congress leaders had already decided that only those who believed in the idea of Khadi would be allowed to officiate in Congress committees. Periyar pointed out that many Self-Respecters, including himself, were opposed to Khadi and, thus, would not stand a chance with those who professed such a faith and who would clamber onto positions in the Congress hierarchy. Congressmen could not be unaware of such matters and their gestures in the direction of the Self-Respecters were mere ruses to divide non-brahmins into different groupings (SD 15.8.34).

A *Pagutharivu* article of 7 October 1934 compared the recently concluded Congress and Justice party conferences, both of which were held at Coimbatore. At Coimbatore, Rajagopalachari had issued a call to Self-Respecters to join the Congress. Periyar's comments in this regard bear consideration at some length. He noted that the Justice party had allowed him to table his plan at its Madras conference, but had failed to resolve on it. It was decided then that discussion on the plan would be taken up at the Justice party's executive committee scheduled for December 1934. Periyar went on to remark that he and the Self-Respect movement considered and used the Justice party as an instrument to further their goals of doing away with hierarchy and privilege in social life and to create equal opportunities for all, irrespective of caste, to achieve their varied purposes. He had, never anywhere claimed that the Justice party could rid the body politic and society of all the ills which plagued them. He also observed that it was not for him to decry the achievements of Justicites, for they had wrought some good; yet, he desired to point to the fact that, for over five years now, the party had become captive to the rich and the selfish. The Congress, for its part, had pretended to keep its doors open to Self-

Respecters but when the decisive moment came, as when he had submitted his programme to Congressmen, had closed its doors on him. Rajagopalachari, noted Periyar, was not to be faulted on this score. He was clear in word and deed and did not obviously 'wish for brahmins to pick up a shovel and use it'; that is, Rajagopalachari could not bring himself to endorse the principle of proportional representation, which would force brahmins to look to other, less cerebral occupations. But, concluded Periyar, the Justice party and the Congress were really not all that different, and if Gandhi were to leave that party as he had threatened he would, brahmin dominance in Congress would gradually lessen and Congress might, yet, witness a radical transformation of its social and economic doctrines.

Periyar dwelt on this theme—of a Congress party without Gandhi and his hypothetical relationship to it—at a public (election) meeting at Coimbatore. He remarked that he did not object to the Congress principle of self-government, as such. But he was concerned that if the latter were to come about, under the auspices of a Congress party, indifferent to the question of caste differences and, which considered even the raising of such a question 'unpatriotic', then, in such a polity, 'the Thotti [an adi dravida scavenger caste] would continue to remain a headloader [one who carries night soil]' and may never aspire to be a minister. Periyar held that if the Justice party were to rule, this latter was at least theoretically possible. He stated quite categorically: 'I am neither an opponent nor a hater of that patriotism and self-rule which works to level down differences between the brahmin and the Paraiah and assures their equality—with one another.'

Periyar conceded that differences in class existed in every country, be it a republic or a democratic polity, but in India in addition to these divisions along class lines, there existed vertical divisions based on birth. These latter had to be erased in any self-governing polity, and a party committed to constituting the latter ought to plan for this as well. Periyar argued that in contrast to Congress, the Justice party's achievements in this regard were greater. Its persistent presence in the political life of Madras and its espousal of a creed of Non-Brahminism had enabled the political advance of non-brahmins, even in the Congress. Besides, the Justice party had managed to send non-brahmins to government service and proved they were as good and as capable as brahmins.

Periyar's explanations in defence of the Justice party elicited several sorts of criticism from his audience, one of whom asked if competing for government posts was indeed important for non-brahmins. Periyar's response was characteristically blunt:

> Yes [it is important]. Until now those who consider themselves patriots and Congressmen had been working with this objective in mind: that they should attain high office [in government]. But today, when non-brahmins seek to appropriate this objective brahmins accuse them of betraying the national cause. Let non-brahmins be appointed in government in proportion to their numbers in the population, and let them enjoy the benefits of their office for as long as brahmins had enjoyed. When such a time comes—all other things being equal—I would even venture to say there is no need for a Justice party.

But, added Periyar, such a time lay in the distant future and, meanwhile, non-brahmins must work to attain posts in the government, which alone would help them actualize their concerns. As far as he was concerned, any political work undertaken in contravention of this principle of proportional representation, even it were to be initiated by Gandhi, could not be termed just or honest. Periyar further noted that he was himself committed for life to the cause of social justice and would always stand by the backward classes and adi dravidas, even if he were to be termed a traitor, a thousand times over. It was also this commitment which had lead him to abide by the Justice party which, because of its stance on proportional representation, stood redeemed in his eyes. Periyar clarified he had nothing to lose or gain by his political choices and, in fact, these choices had caused him more hurt than gain. He had made enemies and, given the present conjuncture, could very well be arrested. His only concern was that he wished to further his creed, and whichever party chose to endorse the latter, he was not averse to joining it, be it the Congress even, for if Gandhi were to leave that party, as he had threatened to do, the influence of brahmins in Congress would decline and that party may yet heed Periyar's concerns (Pa 21.10.34).

It is clear Periyar's attempts to create new political alignments, make fresh political energy flow through old and tried channels, were bound to fail. Neither the Congress nor the Justice party, for different reasons, were ready for that political and ideological struggle which Periyar's programme required them to wage. The 1934 elections to the Central Legislature was uppermost on their minds, and besides, the Congress was rehearsing for future times when it could rule the entire subcontinent with far greater powers at its disposal.

Periyar's attempt to interest it and the Justice party in his plan drew sharp criticism from M. Singaravelu and the young socialists who wrote and debated in *Samadharmam*. Singaravelu's criticisms and Periyar's rejoinder to the same were both published in *Pagutharivu* (30.9.34). Singaravelu objected to Periyar wooing the Justice party and held this action to be most unbecoming of a *samadharmi* (socialist). He argued that the Self-Respect movement ought to abide by its own working plan, accepted by Self-Respecters at Erode in December 1932, for not only was that plan progressive in its content, but also reflected their socialist beliefs (see Appendix 1). Besides, the Congress and the Justice party were both pro-capitalist in their leanings and could not be considered allies of the Self-Respect movement. Even if Justicites such as Bobbili and R. K. Shanmugham, both of whom were rich and representative of feudal and mercantile interests respectively, were to agree to Periyar's proposals, would they be able to legislate on any of the measures contained in the latter? For instance, an elected legislature could not possibly decree that salaries of government personnel be reduced, because they did not possess such discretionary powers in the first place, and, secondly, these powers were vested in an imperial institution, the British Parliament. Unless the present constitution of the Government of India was drastically altered, such a demand could not be realized, and to insist on its fulfilment without asking for a simultaneous re-constitution of the Government of India was irrelevant.

Singaravelu also took issue with the plan's suggestion that essential industries such as transport be taken over and run by the government and argued that no party, especially a capitalist one, would assent to such an idea, for if it did, it would not win any votes. Likewise a capitalist government would never agree to the formation of workers' cooperatives for a fair and equitable distribution of essential goods and nor would it be particularly interested in solving the problem of rural indebtedness. As for other suggestions in the plan, such as the idea that universal primary education must be realized, there was nothing noteworthy about it, since even S. Satyamurthi had spoken of its desirability. Singaravelu was most dismayed by the demand that religion be treated—in any future plan of government—as a matter pertaining to the private realm and to the related demand that government ought to make special provisions for the protection of particular religions. He held that such a proposal was retrograde and would never really help to lessen the influence of religion in daily life. Besides, during its earlier term in office, the Justice party had arrogated to itself the authority to regulate religious life by creating the Hindu Religious Endowments Board and hence it could hardly be expected to lessen the hold of religion on everyday life.

Periyar's rejoinder to this string of criticisms was polite and reasonable. He noted:

> For better or for worse, the Self-Respect Movement has been associated with the Justice party for six or seven years. Besides, the Justice party is not all that worse off, when compared with Congress. Congress desires caste domination and the Justice party prefers class domination. Congress leaders are extremely reluctant to divest themselves off their sacred thread and Justicites are equally reluctant to sacrifice their wealth for a higher cause.

Periyar added, 'I, for one, think that the oppression embodied in the sacred thread is far worse than the oppression of the rich...Bobbili is an extremely rich man and so is R. K. Shanmugham. Let us assume they are interested in acquiring wealth for themselves. (After all, they have not renounced the world!) But is this such a bad thing?...anyway, are these men worse than Congress leaders, than say, the Satyamurthies, the satyagrahis and the ahimsa-vadis? Are they as deceiving or as false?' Besides, clarified Periyar, 'My proposals are meant for the Justice party to adopt and are not meant to affect the [already framed] objectives of our movement'.

Periyar also reminded Singaravelu that the plan he had submitted to the Justicites signified only a change in tactics. He and his Self-Respecters were still committed to the Self-Respect–Samadharma plan that had been accepted at Erode. They had only re-worked the tactical aspects of the Erode decisions and not interfered with its fundamental objectives. Periyar was fairly certain, even convinced, that the conjuncture at hand allowed him to ask for only such changes as he had specified, and foreclosed other options. Singaravelu, on the other hand, inspired by the oppositional rhetoric of socialism and forgetful of the legalistic electoral premises on which the earlier Erode programme was based and to which he had assented, clearly demanded the impossible: that Periyar await his time for the true revolutionary moment when socialist ideals would be realized, presumably by an autonomous socialist party. Till that hallowed dawn, Periyar was not to do or say anything which would interfere with the progress of revolution!

Singaravelu's invocation of a revolutionary moment of change must be seen in the context of his earlier statements. In an article written in early 1934 (Pu 4.3.34), he had stressed the importance of Self-Respecters entering the Council and implored them to transform the latter into a fitful arena of Self-Respect propaganda and action. He had remarked that in a situation where the bourgeoisie were powerful it was not possible to establish socialism through recourse to force. He had also suggested that Self-Respecters make use of whatever space was available to them. In an earlier article, written in 1933, he had explicated at length on the relationship which obtained between parliamentary politics and revolutionary action in specific historical contexts, as during the French Revolution, the Long Revolution in England and in Russia in October 1917 (Pu 24.12.33).

Singaravelu's changed attitudes, barely a year later, are thus puzzling. What or who caused this change? It could be that his socialist principles responded to two rather distinct anxieties that he entertained: the one had to do with caste, religion and untouchability, all of which were not merely abstract categories of thought and analysis but which, together, comprised a specific and identifiable social and historical reality. The other had to do with more abstract notions such as class, bourgeoisie and revolution, none of which could be said to possess precise historical referents in the Madras province of those days. In the first instance, Singaravelu's socialism addressed problems much as the Self-Respect movement did and was in fact influenced by the latter. But with respect to the second instance, Singaravelu's observations were almost entirely influenced by the discursive imperatives of socialism and did not heed the specificities of history and context. Thus in an article 'Socialist Leagues' (Pu 20.5.34), we find Singaravelu driving a hard theoretical and practical wedge between the political and social objectives of the Self-Respect movement. He claimed that workers needed land and peace and bread rather than a reform of their values and habits. Quoting from Lenin, he held that workers ought not to split along sectarian lines of caste and religion.

Periyar, however, was not fettered by the limits of a self-validating discourse as Singaravelu and, besides, he was convinced that after the elections, he would be arrested and the Self-Respect movement forcibly disbanded. For, following his arrest, and even before that, as we have remarked, his movement came under intense surveillance by the Home department and the secret police. A ban order on communist groups issued in July 1934 confirmed his worst fears and he did not, as he remarked a couple of years later, wish to become a martyr to the idiosyncrasies of imperial government. He desired to preserve for his movement (and non-brahmins) whatever freedom he had wrested and to go on working in whatever political space was actually available.

Periyar's younger colleagues clustered around *Samadharmam* (Sd) were somewhat more sympathetic to his dilemma than Singaravelu. Responding to his 16 September 1934 *Pagutharivu* article, where he had stated his attitudes to the Congress and Justice party, a *Samadharmam* article noted that, however much it understood the complexity of the situation at hand, it did not wish the gains of the Self-Respect movement to be compromised at any cost:

> For the past ten years due to the persistent efforts of Comrade E. V. R., S. Ramanathan and others, who braved the opposition of the orthodox, the rich, the madathipathis, the priests [of the church], the mullahs and brahmins and refused to yield even an inch on their principles, the Self-Respect creed has come to be accepted by men of all parties.... But today, when the founder of the movement states he would not object to his men joining Congress, were the Justice party not to accept his plans...many a young man feels sceptical.... Whenever the Justice party has been in trouble, the Self-Respect movement has helped it tide over its moment of crisis, but the Justice party has not helped the Self-Respect movement in any manner whatsoever. If our leaders...have to await the Justice party's

> approval of Periyar's plan, then we are surely right in asking if the Self-Respect movement is indeed an independent movement. If, in the forthcoming Justice party conference, the plan is not accepted why must we join Congress?...Can we not continue to work as we have done so far, adopting such plans as may be realistically fulfilled at the present juncture?
>
> If the Justice party were to adopt or work out a programme for the progress of the poor, we will not object to work in earnest for its realisation. . . . But, meanwhile, we would like to ask Comrade E. V. R. why cannot he continue to work alone, as he had done for these past ten years and keep intact the integrity of a movement that is after all a principled one? (19.9.34).

When the Justice party did not resolve immediately on Periyar's plan, *Samadharmam* condemned its indecisive stance (3.10.34). But a week later, its editorial noted that in the forthcoming elections the Justice party, rather than the Congress, deserved to be voted to office, for at least Justicites had worked to enhance the material and political status of adi dravidas (10.10.34). *Samadharmam* was, however, critical of elections as such, and an editorial of 14 November 1934 noted that the Self-Respecters were themselves deeply divided on this matter. Periyar had asked the Self-Respecters to stand by the Justice party, while Ramanathan had observed that the Self-Respect movement had really nothing to do with the coming elections. He had further noted that the Self-Respecters were generally supportive of the Congress. Singaravelu, for his part, had observed that a socialist could not possibly be interested in elections. The editorial confessed its inability to distinguish what could be termed a Self-Respecters' point of view in these various observations and noted it was unable to see how the Self-Respect movement's concerns would be fulfilled by parties winning or losing elections. It added that dissent within a movement was a sign of its growth, but if matters were allowed to rest there, only confusion would abound. The editorial concluded with a plea that a Self-Respect conference be convened without delay to sort out these and other matters and, until then, urged samadharmists to carry out their propaganda in a disciplined fashion, isolate and banish the selfish and the opportunists from their ranks and work to build support for their creed amongst the people.

The Decline of the Justice Party

On the eve of the elections to the Central Legislature, the Self-Respecters were more or less in concert and did, after all, support the Justice party. In their election propaganda, they attempted to bring to the fore those issues central to their movement. But the results of these elections were determined by causes and circumstances which had nothing to do with their concerns. The elections witnessed muckraking propaganda, defections, the play of avarice and the sacrifice of principles. The Self-Respecters' propaganda could have hardly served to influence the largely elitist and thin electorate to heed their claims of social and economic justice. Besides, the Congress' electoral strategy proved superior in every respect to those employed by the Justicites: Not only did Congress candidates seek the support of local notables, zamindars, merchants and important office holders in local bodies, but also it had its national leaders tour the Madras province and address the voters on its behalf.

For some time now, Congressmen had consciously wooed different segments of the populace and the party's well-wrought consensus enabled its candidates to win easily. The Justice party was handicapped on several counts. Its internal wrangles which had led to a more or less complete neglect of organizational work, the support of the Self-Respecters whose atheism and general irreverence proved irksome to some of the party notables, the power and appeal of Congress propaganda and the vast resources spent on the latter contributed to an easy Congress victory. Even though the Justicites had fielded only two candidates, R.K. Shanmugham and A. Ramaswamy Mudaliar, both lost. The other non-Congress non-brahmin candidate, Dr. Varadarajulu Naidu, who had contested the elections with the help of the Self-Respecters also lost.

Prior to the elections, the Self-Respecters had roundly condemned the Congress' attempts at false and misleading propaganda and criticized that party's doublespeak with respect to the Justicites. A *Pagutharivu* editorial of 21 October 1934, 'Are the Elections an Exercise in Communal Representation or a Traffic in Falsehood and Foolery?' pointed out that Congressmen may claim to be martyrs and patriots, yet they were mindful of and critical towards the violence inflicted on them alone. Not only did they not oppose the repression unleashed by the government on others, but in several instances, were known to have encouraged it. Secondly, Gandhi considered Civil Disobedience and Satyagraha undertaken by others, on their own initiative, violent and even supported measures taken against such satyagrahis. Thirdly, no Congressman had thought it fit to oppose the ban on socialist organizations and many of them were, in fact, waiting for the government to declare the Self-Respect movement illegal. Besides, noted the editorial wryly, not much could be expected of those who held their own socialist wing—the Congress Socialist Party (CSP)—to be violent. Fourthly, Congressmen had indulged in the most malicious sort of propaganda. For instance, a well-known Congressman speaking in support of Satyamurthi, had entreated the voters not to vote for the Justice party, for it only desired to destroy temples! This, in spite of the fact that one of the official Justice party candidates, A. Ramasamy Mudaliar, was steeped in ritual observances and religious faith. Lastly, Congressmen canvassed for votes, not on the basis of the merits or otherwise of their candidates, but instead invoked the name of Gandhi and took advantage of the aura which surrounded him to persuade voters to vote for the Congress candidate in question, as if Gandhi's was a magic name and required only to be uttered to render the Congress cause a legitimate one.

An article in *Nagara Thoothan* had pointed out how venomous Congressmen were in their attacks on V. O. Chidambaram Pillay, who addressed the voters in support of Dr. Varadarajulu Naidu. The former was described as indulging in 'poisonous' and 'foolish' rhetoric and his patriotic credentials were called into question (12.8.34).

In his election addresses, Periyar had dwelt on his reasons for supporting the Justice party. He had pointed to the persistence of caste divisions and argued that the Congress proponents of Swaraj had nothing to say on this matter. Congress leaders had no plans, indeed, never had any, to widen and broaden the basis of political representation. The Congress was also indifferent to the fact that in Hindu society, caste divisions underwrote economic divisions. Periyar had further argued that it was only with the advent of the Justice party that non-brahmins had been able to secure posts in the government and enter the Legislature in large numbers. However it may have erred in other respects, the Justice party had redeemed itself of its various sins and limitations by thus urging forth the political rights of the non-brahmins and the adi dravidas. It was in this respect that it had surpassed parties and governments in other provinces and had to be commended. Periyar had also made it clear he was not afraid of repression and noted that in all probability he would be arrested once the elections were over (Pa 21.10.34).

Periyar had good reasons to fear such an eventuality. During his visit to Kolar, in mid-October 1934, to preside over the marriage of Jayaraman, son of G. Appaduraiar, the editor of Tamizhan, with Indrani, he was greeted with rumours of his imminent arrest and was told that but for the intervention of Gopalasamy Iyer (a brahmin reformer), who assured the government that Periyar had come to solemnize a wedding and not to address the adi dravidas at a meeting, he would have been arrested (ibid).

But neither such denunciations of Congress falsehood, nor the indignant responses of Justicites and Self-Respecters to Congress malice, proved determinate in the final instance. The terms under which elections were held were defined, as we have pointed out, by money, social status and local rivalries. Besides the determination of the Madras Congress to oust the Justice party from office, the average Madras Congressman's unabashed love of power, together with the successful organization of consent by Congressmen, enabled that party to win. Gandhi's *Harijan* had played a particularly important role in rendering Congress nationalism consensual. One particular instance bears recounting in this respect. Following the Central Legislature's rejection of Subbarayan's temple-entry bill, as we have noted earlier, Ranga Iyer tabled in the Central Assembly yet another bill which would allow adi dravidas to enter temples. While this measure earned the opprobrium of Dr. Ambedkar, who felt the bill did not go far enough, and the criticism of Periyar, Gandhi enlisted Rajagopalachari and Birla to propagate its contents widely and secure the approval of Congress legislators for its passage. Of course, this proved none too easy and the bill, though tabled in early 1933, was taken up for discussion in the Central Assembly only in August 1934. Immediately thereafter, it was decided to gather public opinion on the bill. A frustrated Ranga Iyer finally moved a resolution to have the bill forwarded to a Select Committee. Precisely, at this moment, the Government of India announced its decision to dissolve the Central Legislature and hold elections, whereupon, Congress with an eye on the voters, amongst whom were a number of orthodox Hindus, decided to withdraw its support to the bill (BAWS: vol.9, 119-25).

Rajagopalachari made it clear that in its election propaganda, the Congress would limits its concerns to constitutional matters. This volte face did not serve the Congress well for the adi dravida leaders expressed resentment at this sudden and clearly opportunistic turnabout on its part. Meanwhile, Congressmen went ahead to proclaim their concern for adi dravidas and cleverly elided in their addresses the 'slip' they had engineered between sentiment and practice with regard to temple entry.

Periyar wrote a scathing editorial condemning Congress (KA 27.1.35). Blaming Gandhi and Rajagopalachari for 'consigning Ranga Iyer's bill to the abyss and burying it there', he pointed out that the money collected by the Harijan Sevak Sangh had gone to fill Congress party coffers. The editorial further remarked that for all its purported concern for adi dravidas, the Congress in Madras had actually fielded a brahmin candidate against V. I. Munusamy Pillay, the adi dravida leader, who contested the elections to the Central Legislature as an independent candidate, and defeated him. A fair recompense, indeed, concluded the editorial, to those who had saved Gandhi's life during his 'epic' fast! Yet another *Kudi Arasu* editorial noted that, in spite of having ostensibly withdrawn from the Congress, Gandhi thought it fit to instruct Congressmen to withdraw support for Ranga Iyer's bill. *Kudi Arasu* carried Dr. Ambedkar's condemnation of Gandhi and expressed its own support for the opinions expressed by the latter (3.2.35).

The Justice party's failure to win the elections elicited several sorts of criticisms. A *Paguttharivu* editorial of 18 November 1934 noted that the Justice party had been deserted in its moment of crisis by those it had groomed and whose interests it had advanced. In contrast to the unity displayed by the Congress brahmins, who buried all differences among themselves to rally behind Satyamurthi, non-brahmins in the Justice party had failed to back A. Ramasamy Mudaliar and R. K. Shanmugham. Jeevanandham recalled in this context Satyamurthi's election address at Erode, where he had boasted that Rajagopalachari would soon become the Governor of Madras and that he, Satyamurthi, would become Chief Secretary to the government! Not only did this reflect that clannishness so visible amongst brahmins, but also indicated that brahmin Congressmen stood for elections chiefly to garner posts for themselves (KA 13.1.35). Another *Paguthariuu* editorial of 25 November 1934 advised that Dr. Subbarayan and even Munisamy Naidu be wooed back into the party. It also commended the former's achievements while in office, even as it condemned the opportunism of the Justice leaders. Another article in its 9 December 1934 issue warned Justicites of the ill effects of party disunity and remarked that the Self-Respecters desired the party free itself from the clutches of the rich and the zamindars.

Periyar, writing in *Paguthaviru*, argued, in yet another variation of a favoured theme, that the Justice party compared favourably with the Congress, if only because it had enabled non-brahmins and the adi dravidas to acquire posts in such hallowed and exclusive brahmin enclaves as the police, revenue and judicial departments. Eleven adi dravidas had been appointed subinspectors of police and, generally speaking, the Justice party had nominated adi dravidas to various posts. It was all very well to say Justice leaders had availed of their powers, while in office, to their advantage, but the fact was they utilized their authority to people various institutions—district, taluq boards and temple committees—with representatives of the adi dravida and other deprived non-brahmin communities (23.12.34).

The socialists' critique of the Justicites' defeat was scathing. A series of impassioned articles titled 'Politics and Commoners' was published in *Samadharmam* (28.11.34 to 26.12.34) on the matter of elections, the Congress, the Justice party and the Self-Respect movement. In the second of these articles, their author took the Justice party to task for its various sins. He observed that, at present, the party did not possess any leader of the stature of Dr. Nair, and one cannot consider Bobbili or the kumararaja of Chettinadu as representatives of the people. If Congress functioned as an enclave devoted to the protection of the rich, the educated and the brahmins, the Justice party existed to serve the concerns of the rich and the educated. In his eagerness and anxiety to counter Congress' characterization of the Justice party as a communal party, the author argued, Periyar had resorted, as only he could, to brilliant and sparkling sophistry. But the point was simply this:

> We have come to the conclusion that Brahmins and the rule of the rich would have to be eliminated simultaneously... We would like our comrades to consider—in a spirit of friendship—whether or not the move to turn to the rich and the elitist Justice party and seek its help in the fight against Brahminism, is not a regressive one, considering that, in these past ten years, society has come to accept the necessity of our philosophy of self-respect and samadharma?

The author of these articles proclaimed categorically that the need of the moment was a firm re-assertion of the self-respect, samadharmic creed and not the wooing of the Justice party. The fourth of this series of articles (19.12.34) interrogated the socialist claims of Congressmen and declared that the boasts of Raja-gopalachari, Giri and Santhanam in this regard were vain and false. It characterized the Congress Socialist party (formed in 1934) as pro-bourgeois and social democratic, and noted that as far as this southern presidency was concerned the Congress Socialist party really had no support or standing, even amongst Congressmen. The article concluded with the suggestion that a new political party, which would comprise workers and which would simultaneously 'educate, legislate and agitate' be constituted.

This plea for a new party represented an ideal and an utopian dream more than anything else. Given the socio-political context of 1934, a year which witnessed the suspension of Civil Disobedience and the ban on Communist groups, very little space was available for manoeuvre and use by agitational parties and movements, for they could all be termed anti-imperialist and seditious.

After the elections to the Central Legislature, Periyar returned to speaking, writing and debating on the themes of caste, gender, Brahminism and untouchability and continued to subject Congress to his critical gaze. The question of the Self-Respect movement's association with the Justice party arose time and again in the years 1935-36 and was debated by the Self-Respecters. A section of the latter remained critical of the Justice party leadership, its ideological credibility and its intentions. At the Fourth Thanjavur District Self-

Respect Conference, T. A. Ekambaram, who addressed the gathering on behalf of the Self-Respecters, stated quite unequivocally, that the Justice party had shown little or no interest in the working plan given it by Periyar and not discussed it, either at its conferences, nor taken it up for discussion in the party's executive committee, as it had originally announced. In this context, would it be possible or even desirable for Self-Respecters to associate themselves with that party? (KA 27.1.35)

Kunjitham Gurusamy in her presidential address struck an altogether different note. She granted that the Justice party had not kept its word by the Self-Respect movement; nor did it seem particularly keen on working to realize the latter's ideologies. Several Justicites worked for brahmins, accepted the services of a priesthood, remained distant from the ordinary non-brahmin masses and exercised great control over their women. Yet, observed Kunjitham, if the Self-Respect movement and the Justice party were to appear to the world at large as warring groups, and if they began to propagandize against each other, ordinary non-brahmins would stand to suffer and, more important, this would prove advantageous to the brahmins, who were biding their time to conspire against the non-brahmins as whole. While there were Self-Respecters in the Congress, they possessed no standing in that party and were often used by the leadership for particular propagandistic purposes and then discarded. Self-Respecters in either camp could and would doubtless come together on matters of common concern, but if they had to choose between the Congress and the Justice party, in the event of a conflict between the two, the Self-Respect movement will act in a consistent and disciplined fashion (ibid).

Periyar, in his address at Thanjavur, commented on various points of doubt raised at the conference and noted he was aware of and welcomed different points of view, but surely there must be common ground for Self-Respecters to meet and work out a programme of action. Criticisms of the Self-Respecters working plan had persisted since the day the latter was framed and were not entirely new. Such criticisms were, perhaps, motivated by considerations which had nothing to do with the plan. The Self-Respect movement was diverse in its constituency and comprised the rich, the caste Hindus, the adi dravidas and government officials and some interests among these were bound to suffer, even as some others were advanced (ibid).

It is clear Periyar did not wish his movement to split on the question of support being extended to the Justice party. But he was also aware criticisms against that party were not too wide off the mark. Justicites, for their part, needed the Self-Respect movement to secure consensus for their Non-Brahminism and there were old timers like R. K. Shanmugham and others, who in their own ways, were committed to the non-brahmin commonweal. The Justice party–Self-Respect movement relationship persisted as before, an exercise in uneasy alignment, though in times of crisis, as when the general non-brahmin good was at stake, Periyar, and to some extent other Self-Respecters, buried their differences with the Justice party's leadership and rallied around it. Thus when Muthiah Chettiar, Subbarayan and others attempted to move a no-confidence motion against the Bobbili ministry, *Kudi Arasu* attacked the two for their want of principle and opportunism in no uncertain terms (17, 24.3.35). Periyar remarked, however, that he suspected a Congress conspiracy in this instance and suggested that Justicites undertake efforts to get both Muthiah Chettiar and Subbarayan into the Justice party (KA 24.3.35).

It soon became clear to the Self-Respecters that the Justice party had not learnt its lessons well. It took its time to approve of Periyar's plan, submitted to it in October 1934. *Kudi Arasu* reported that, at a meeting convened at Bobbili's residence, the plan had been slightly amended and it now rested with the executive committee to approve of it (see Appendix 1). The committee, for its part, promised to accept and ratify the resolutions before March 1935, when the party's district conferences would be held (10.2.35). During this time Bobbili was busy trying to see if Justicites could win a bye election to the Madras Legislature. His speech at an election meeting is worth a description, if only to draw attention to its utter vacuity. After outlining the Justice party's achievements in the Council, and criticizing Congress at length for its failure to convene to decide on a future constitution for India, he proposed the following as the primary constituents of the Justice party's working plan for the future: The Justice party would attend to the needs of the hitherto ignored villages and undertake a village reconstruction programme to solve the problems of the rural poor; within ten years, it would endeavour to secure compulsory primary education for all; it would attend to water supply needs of the villages, provide these with good roads and transport facilities and work to develop local handicrafts; the party would also attempt to save the ryots from the horrors of rural indebtedness and make available to them such loans as they desired at a low interest; the government would also make available to ryots the means to store their grain, so that they could sell them when market conditions were good and a cash advance on future sales would also be made to ryots. Finally, the present (and useless) education system would be transformed and a new system with an emphasis on learning a skill or a vocation would come into existence (KA 31.3.35.). It is noteworthy that some of these proposals had been part of the Justice lexicon for nearly two decades now and that Bobbili had nothing new to say. Besides, these were less comprehensive in their scope and emphasis than those proposals outlined in Periyar's plan.

Meanwhile, at the Ramanathapuram District Justice Party Conference at Virudhunagar, a Nadar enclave, Periyar's plan had been accepted wholeheartedly. In his address at Virudhunagar, Periyar (a special invitee) observed that conferences in the future should not be obssessed so much with questions of leadership and, instead, ought to devote their attention to what they could do in respect of their resolutions. Justice ministers should consent to a lowering of their salaries or give away a substantial portion of it to party funds. For pecuniary gains could very well force men to compromise on principles. Periyar also stressed the need for the Justice party to evolve institutional means to choose people to party posts and keep in touch with its members on the ground (KA 7.4.35; Anaimuthi: 634). In Virudhunagar, it was decided that Justicites would urge Dominion Status for India and favour a federation of provinces.

Even as Justicites remained indecisive over Periyar's plan, he continued to reason with them and his own Self-Respecters and, at all times, adopted a careful measured tone. He did not desire to antagonize the Self-Respecters and did not want the Justicites to take him for granted. As ever, driven by a contempt for the Congress, he was desperate not to let go of the one foothold non-brahmins possessed in a polity that was spellbound by the Congress' rhetoric of nationalism on the one hand and Gandhi's anti-untouchability propaganda on the other. Writing in April 1935 in response to those who were unhappy with the Justice party and the Self-Respect movement's continuing association with it, Periyar observed that such men should perhaps do well to heed the fact that for all its 'backwardness' the Justice party was considered a threat by Congressmen; so much so that a prominent Congressman had observed he preferred British rule to Justice rule:

> What could this mean? Only that Justicites had managed to achieve what 200 years of English rule could not! What have the Justicites achieved? Comrade Prakasam has pointed this out very clearly. 'The Justice party has arranged for the implementation of proportional representation and hence must be destroyed' (ibid).

Of course, Periyar never lost a chance to upbraid Justicites for not doing enough for non-brahmins and, in one particularly harsh article, rebuked them for their tardiness in implementing the principle of proportional representation. He noted that non-brahmins such as Mohammed Usman, K. V. Reddi Naidu and A. T. Paneerselvam had not utilized their powers in cabinet and Council to advance non-brahmin interests. Brahmins such as C. P. Ramaswamy Iyer, on the other hand, had always managed to convert a department under their control into veritable agraharams. But, added Periyar, in spite of the very low percentage of non-brahmins and adi dravidas in the services, in comparison to brahmins, the idea of proportional representation had now been inscribed into the rules of the government and this, to him, was the single most important contribution of the Justice party (KA 19.5.35).

The Justice party and the Self-Respect movement appeared to be working in concert once again on the eve of the 1935-36 elections to the local bodies. This time too, Periyar's decision to support the Justicites in these elections met with resistance from the Self-Respecters. At a Self-Respect meeting held at Trichy, Jeevanandham and Vallatharusu—the latter was from Puddukottai and a fiery publicist—proclaimed there was nothing in common between the Justice party and the Self-Respect movement, especially with respect to a programme for future action. Jeevanandham accused the Justicites of being loyalists, while Vallatharasu observed Justicites were not only bourgeois in their attributes, but had not shown great interest in the Self-Respecters' critique of brahmins and religion. Jeevanandham wondered what could the Self-Respecters possibly hope to achieve by propagandizing for 'these wretched elections'. The Self-Respect movement, declared Vallatharasu, had to decide whether it would remain content with a statement of its principles, or, whether it desired to realize these in practice. The Justice party, for its part, could not claim it had all along encouraged the Self-Respect movement. Whether the present leadership remained, or, whether another was installed in its place, the Self-Respecters had to ask themselves if it was indeed possible for them to work with the Justice party (KA 27.10.35).

Periyar in his address countered these criticisms with his own logical arguments. He pointed out that rash and impetuous criticisms of the Justice party were unfair, for had it not been for the legislative presence of that party, the Madras Council would have never countenanced and approved of the Devadasi Abolition Bill, the many welfare measures instituted for adi dravidas and against untouchability and the abolition of such practices as child marriages. Most important, but for the continued presence in Madras politics of the Justice party and the Justicites' work in the Council and out of it, non-brahmins would not have found a place in government service in even such numbers as they existed at present. The Justice party comprised the rich, yet it had enabled thousands of non-brahmins attain a measure of self-respect. Besides, in the present historical circumstances, the influence of the rich in political life could hardly be lessened or subverted, especially since Brahminism continued to exert its hold over the rich and confirmed them in their power.

Periyar agreed that elections were indeed a wretched business, but it was only those who managed to win them that acquired powers and were respected by government. 'If,' noted Periyar, 'the Council was to come under the control of our enemies—though they may not use the Council to our advantage—in all likelihood, they would undertake measures which may be detrimental to us. For it is the law the Councillors make which come to regulate our lives. [Besides] it is only through an election that we may send our representative to Council.' For over a decade, the Justicites had worked to make sure that the Madras Council did not fall into the hands of casteist and arrogant brahmins and unprincipled Congressmen and their contribution to the non-brahmin commonweal in this regard cannot be overlooked.

As for the socialism his younger colleagues swore by, it could not be realized in a day. Even in Russia this had not happened. Firstly, there ought to be socialism in the social sphere. Secondly the Self-Respecters could not, at this juncture, when their very movement was in crisis, afford to be rash. Circumstances were such that they had to review their situation, make sure their working plan was not compromised and bide their time. Periyar reminded his audience that he was no less enthusiastic and eager than they were with respect to the principles of socialism, but he was also aware of the need to be careful and disciplined. He did not wish to cross the limits of legality, but if such a contingency did arise the Self-Respect movement would resolve the problem, keeping all factors in mind. Thirdly, as far as the question of religion was concerned, one cannot abolish it or merely wish it away. This required long and sustained work and a continual radicalization of social and individual consciousness. One cannot, at any time, afford to please or satisfy the popular demands of the common people nor can one afford to follow where they lead. The idea was to revolutionize their thoughts and attitudes and the Self-Respect Movement was committed to this objective (ibid).

Yet dissident Self-Respecters continued to disapprove of the influence of the rich in the Justice party and the fact that its concerns were almost always determined by the ministerialists in the party. Another set of dissidents opined that this was an opportune moment to join the Congress and 'capture' it and thereby bring it around to the non-brahmin, samadharmic point of view (KA 5.1.36). The attractions of the Congress party at this juncture cannot be understimated: its electoral successes had been substantial, it had managed to coopt into its ranks varied segments of the population, and the mid-thirties had been years flush with ideological victories for the party, achieved in most instances, by the anti-untouchability programmes of the Harijan Sevak Sangh. Besides the constitution of the Congress Socialist party in 1934 had lent to the Congress pronouncements a certain radical resonance.

Periyar, who at all times understood in all its nuances, the Congress' leadership's insatiable will to power, was not at all moved by these gestures. He thus continued to support the Justice party and reminded his Self-Respecters that, as far as he was concerned, the brahmin-non brahmin contradiction was paramount in the present instance and he considered a fair and just resolution of this contradiction to be an index of true nationalism and socialism (KA 5.1.36). Meanwhile the Justice party had ratified Periyar's plan (KA 17.11.35; see Appendix 2).

Along with W. P. A. Soundarapandian, Periyar issued an appeal to the supporters of the non-brahmin good and commonweal, in which the two entreated their constituency not to identify the non-brahmin cause and the movement merely with the Justice party's elite leadership. The appeal also pointed out that public antipathy to the Justice party was on account of its leadership, that was querulous, indecisive, selfish and thoroughly indisciplined, but it was important to keep in mind that there were several party men who had remained sincere and consistent in their commitment to Non-Brahminism. Thus, at present, some of them were weary with inner party feuding and unhappy with the leadership's reluctance to mend its ways, but matters could be remedied by disciplined and systematic party work. Periyar and Pandian were both convinced that the Justice party suffered from a singular lack of effective and good communicators and suggested that non-brahmins everywhere come forward to offer their services in the cause of an intensive propaganda exercise. The appeal also insisted that only those who could devote their complete attention to the party and those who were willing to forsake their careers should come forward to perform this task (KA 26.1.36).

Even as the joint appeal was widely circulated in the Tamil districts of Madras province, Periyar persisted in his efforts to distinguish the 'true' ideals and objectives of the Justice party from the false promises and deviant actions of its leaders. *Kudi Arasu* carried an extensive critique of the party's slovenly attitude in organizational matters and its indifference to principles. Titled, 'The Stable Was Bolted after the Horses Were Stolen', this article took issue with the Justice party's decision to constitute a panchayat (tribunal) committee (to arbitrate disputes amongst Justicites at the district levels) and a propaganda committee.

Periyar, who wrote the article, condemned the Justice party's inactivity over these past few months and noted that all of Bobbili's efforts to bestir his collegues had proved to be in vain. The election results had indicated very clearly that the Justice party lost, not because its ideals were unacceptable or disagreeable to the voters, but because the party's publicists possessed no propaganda skills and sections of the Justice leadership were indifferent to the crisis that had beset the party in recent times. Periyar objected to the constitution of the committees for the arbitration of disputes and propaganda on well-reasoned premises: Justice party leaders had lost the elections due to the competitive rancour they exhibited against each other—Periyar pointed to instance of the Tirunelveli and Trichy Zillah Board elections—and an arbitration committee at this stage could not really function very effectively, now that the basis for the conflicts, the elections, were over. If this measure had been undertaken a year ago, the sorry spectacle of last minute crossovers and betrayals could have been avoided. As for propaganda, for quite some time now, he had been asking for the resumption of *Dravidan* but no Justicite seemed sensitive to the matter of a party having its own vernacular newspaper. Whereas Congress ran three newspapers at half an anna each, and two at a quarter of an anna each, the Justice party did not possess even one. As a result, news of party activities, speeches of its leaders and the achievements of the Justice ministry were not only not made known to the public, but these were routinely misreported by Congress papers (KA 22.3.36).

Periyar's criticisms were not heeded. The party blundered along in its usual ambling fashion. Periyar, for his part, continued to speak and write on the need for all non-brahmins, whether Self-Respecters or others to join hands to strengthen the Justice party. In response to the joint appeal, meetings were organized through the middle and late months of 1936 at various places in the Tamil country. Periyar undertook several propaganda tours on his own, entreated overseas Tamils to give generously to the party cause. A Central Propaganda Committee was constituted and Periyar and others not only spoke in favour of Justicites, but, at all times, pointed to the hypocritical and inconsistent politics of the Congress party. Only two weeks before the elections to the Madras Council under the Government of India Act of 1935, Periyar's plea for a Tamil daily was heeded and Viduthalai was launched.

In contrast to the unpreparedness of the Justice party, the Congress was well equipped to tackle the electorate. The widening of the franchise (from 4.5 to nearly 14 percent) allowed more people to vote than before and, emboldened by its electoral successes in the Central Assembly and local elections, Congress worked hard to broaden and deepen its sphere of dominance. Several former Justicites and non-brahmin leaders who, in earlier elections, had rallied around the Justice party now joined Congress. Varadarajulu Naidu, S. Ramanathan, V. I. Munusamy Pillai and a host of others—liberals, zamindars, Muslims, caste Hindu leaders adi dravidas—now joined a party that was fast coming to be viewed as the victor at the polls (Baker: 297-98). As before, Congress propaganda won the day: proclaimed in temple premises, in meetings of caste organizations, merchants' associations and, raised to an appropriately attractive if somewhat hysterical pitch in newspapers run by Congressmen, this propaganda served to discredit the Justicites, castigate the Self-Respect movement and underscore the Congress' representative character.

The Justice party not only had to face up to the loss of its eminent leaders—the raja of Pithapuram started his own party and roped in Muthiah Mudaliar—but had to cope with the strategic absence of other party notables. R. K. Shanmugham went on to take up the post of dewan in the former Cochin state, while A. Ramasamy Mudaliar had found a place in the Viceroy's Executive Council (ibid: 309-10). The Justicites lost the provincial elections. The 1937 elections signalled the demise of the Justice party as it had evolved over three decades. Of course, a substantial section of the party would join Periyar in the anti-Hindi agitations of 1937-39 but after 1938, when Periyar took over its leadership, the Justice party as it had existed until then, began to undergo a major transformation.

From 1938-1944 Periyar and his Self-Respecters worked hard to rid the party of self-seekers, time-servers and opportunists and to re-establish it on a firm political and ideological basis. With the Salem resolutions of 1942, when the party committed itself to the cause of a Dravidian nation, it was born anew and rechristened the Dravidar Kazhagam in 1944. But that belongs to another history, the history of the anti-Hindi struggles which convulsed the Tamil country in the late thirties. We shall return to this history at a later moment, but for now we will have to examine at close quarters, and in some detail, the Self-Respect movement, which played such a vital role in imparting to political Non-Brahminism—in the Justice party and out of it—a certain militancy, a sense of purpose and which opened up the spaces of civil society.

CHAPTER 7

Countering Gandhi: The Emergence of Self-Respect

THE YEAR 1925 is of immense significance in the history of modern Tamil society. On 22 September 1925, the All-India Congress Committee met at Patna to resolve, among other things, the vexed question of Council entry. This matter had assumed a certain importance: both in view of the relentless propaganda in favour of entering Councils carried out by the Swarajist faction of the Congress, and the impending elections to the provincial councils that were to take place in 1926. At Patna, it was resolved Swarajists may contest the 1926 elections, and, yet, Gandhian Constructive Work was to constitute the mainstay of Congress activity on the ground. Sceptical of the Swarajists' intent and aware of their lack of interest and faith in Khadi, Untouchability Abolition and Spinning, Gandhi yet insisted that the Swarajists should not be hampered in their politics by those malcontents who felt unhappy over the events that had transpired at Patna. Such dissidents, advised Gandhi, would do well to leave the party (KA 11.10.25; Anaimuthu 1974: 341-42).

Gandhi's studied ambivalence with regard to the Patna resolutions troubled at least one prominent Congressman in Madras. In an article written in *Kudi Arasu* Periyar noted with dismay that apart from giving the Swarajists a free hand, these resolutions had more or less consigned Constructive Work to the margins of Congress activity. Already, at an earlier Congress session, Prohibition as Congress policy had received short shrift and, for a while now, Swarajists had agitated against the advocacy of Khadi and openly resisted making contributions to the Khadi fund. The Patna mandate would make it impossible for anti-untouchability work to progress, since the

Swarajists were arch conservatives (at least in Madras), and would not consent to expend their energies and resources on what to them was insignificant work. In this context, remarked Periyar, when it was as yet difficult to determine who in Congress would go with the Swarajists, and who would devote their energies to Constructive Work, those who were convinced of the efficacy of the latter and of the usefulness of Non Cooperation, ought perhaps to heed the Mahatma's words and leave the Congress and constitute a separate forum to devote all their energies to Constructive Work (ibid).

Periyar's discomfort and barely concealed ire over the Patna resolutions were due to a complex of interrelated reasons. Periyar had joined the Congress on the advice of Rajagopalachari in 1920. The latter, at that time, was looking to start a Non Cooperation forum in Madras. Congressmen in Madras during this period either belonged to the moderate segment of lawyers and civilians who lived chiefly in Madras city, or to that clique of publicists, journalists and teachers—the Madras nationalists—who gathered around Kasturi Ranga Iyengar (of *The Hindu*) and S. Satyamurthi. Neither of these two groups were even mildly interested in Non Cooperation. An older type of politics prevailed in Madras, veering between the modest constitutionalism of the Moderates and the aggressive but largely rhetorical nationalism of the Madras nationalists. Non Cooperation demanded a different sort of leader, one with an ability and a desire to communicate with various sections of the populace, who commanded a felicitous talent for speaking in Tamil and who, above all, possessed the political will and acumen to set precedents and organize agitations. Periyar, with his roots firmly in the moffusil, seemed just the sort of person who could help Rajagopalachari counter the men of Madras. Periyar's wealth and status in local society, his proven capabilities as a man of public affairs rendered him an almost natural choice as leader.

In later years, Periyar would recall how non-brahmins like him, Kalyanasundara Mudaliar, V. O. Chidambaram Pillay and Varadarajulu Naidu, helped Congress grow in the Tamil country. For, in contrast to the old school of Congressmen, who spoke English, they would address meetings in Tamil. Crowds would throng to listen to these Tamil speakers, whereas a brahmin Congressman could barely interest an audience in what he had to say (Vi 26.4.61; Anaimuthu: 362).

PERIYAR AND GANDHIAN CONSTRUCTIVE WORK

Periyar was drawn to the struggles of Non Cooperation chiefly because he felt inspired by Gandhi. As he was wont to remark in later years, until the advent of Gandhi, Congress had remained an exclusive preserve of the educated upper classes and professionals such as lawyers. These men had literally 'preyed on the blood of the land (and its peoples)' but their time was now clearly past, for with Gandhi's entry into Indian political life, politics itself had undergone a transformation. It had become an activity 'common to all and which could be understood by all' (KA 31.5.25).

Periyar's commitment to the cause of Khadi, Prohibition and Untouchability Abolition and his energetic organizing of funds, men and events to secure these objectives in Erode and elsewhere in the Tamil country were truly extraordinary. For instance, his entire family plunged into temperance work and it is said that he ordered more than 1000 coconut palms—primary source of liquor—on his lands to be cut. Periyar, like Gandhi, was convinced that Khadi, rather the spinning of it, could enable people attain a level of general morality. Untouchability, he held, had to go for otherwise the essential one-ness of humanity could not ever be realized. Prohibition was obviously important if the populace was not to fall prey to degeneracy and moral laxity (KA 5.7.25).

The very first issue of *Kudi Arasu* endorsed Periyar's intentions with regard to Constructive Work and indicated he had managed to inflect the Gandhian message in very specific terms:

> A sense of self-respect and fraternity must arise within human society. Notions of high and low amongst men should disappear. A sense of the unity of all humankind must dawn (in each one of us). Communal confrontations must cease to be. In the course of propagating these ideals we will not hesitate to take on friend or foe if they range themselves against us and criticize us through word and deed (Anaimuthu: xxiv).

Kudi Arasu was the brainchild of Thangaperumal Pillay who, along with Periyar, was originally in Congress. When he fell ill, he entrusted *Kudi Arasu* to Periyar and requested him to run it (KA 7.3.26).

Initially, the weekly reflected Periyar's interest in Gandhi and Constructive Work but, gradually, it assumed a character of its own and began to debate issues of faith, ethics, politics, caste, Brahminism, untouchability, social justice and equality.

What seemed particularly significant and relevant to Periyar about Gandhian Constructive Work was that it existed in a dialectical relationship to Non Cooperation. The latter, essentially a political and moral philosophy of conscious disengagement with the world of power and politics, was redeemed of its negativity, being aligned to the positive programme of Constructive Work. Disengagement represented not a turning away but a 'turning towards', a change in direction as well. This turning towards the life of ordinary people of rural India represented, on the one hand, a fundamental shift in the political priorities of Congress and, on the other hand, indicated the limits to habitual and agitational political activity. For this latter could not be sustained at all times and had to give into the patient work of constructing new modes of living and interacting amongst the common people. Such molecular changes as would occur as a result of long hours of unseen labour would, in turn, create the conditions for further and more energetic political work (KA 17, 31.5.25).

In spite of his respect for and interest in Gandhi, Periyar was wary of those sections of the Tamil Nadu Congress that were prone to conservative and reactionary behaviour. His iconoclasm and spirit of relentless enquiry could not, at all times, reconcile to the Congress' attitudes to caste and religion. At the 1922 Tiruppur Congress, he had demanded that the *Manusmriti* and *Ramayana* be burnt since they sanctioned and justified the subordination and oppression of non-brahmin peoples (Vi 17.8.56, 30.7.56; Anaimuthu: 1455; 1842-43). When the Justice party drew up the Hindu Religious Endowments Bill, Periyar was vocal and assertive in his support of the measure, though Congressmen in Madras were on the whole opposed to its passage.

On another occasion, speaking at Rajagopalachari's ashram at Tiruchengode, Periyar observed:

> Men should not touch each other, see each other; men cannot enter temples, fetch water from the village pond: in a land where such inhuman practices are rife, it is a wonder that earthquakes have not destroyed us, volcanes not burnt us; it is a wonder that the earth

> has not split at its heart and plunged this land into an abyss, that a typhoon has not shattered us. I leave it to you to decide if you would still like to trust to a divinity that has not punished us thus; if you would still consider that God a just God, a merciful being. How long do you desire this vast section of the oppressed, the depressed classes, to remain patient, peaceful and quiet? Would you consider it wrong if these oppressed were to choose death rather than lead such a life as they do now? (Sitambaranar 1971: 65)

PERIYAR AND THE SWARAJISTS

While Periyar found the ingrained caste spirit of the average brahmin Congressman repellent, he was particularly unhappy with the Swarajists. In them he discovered not only a spirit of rancour and bile, but also a substantial measure of deception and political opportunism. Much of Periyar's energy in 1925 and 1926 were expended in railing against these wily and intelligent men who exhibited quite a blatant love of power and an even greater determination to wield it, often at the cost of principles, whether the ones they habitually professed, or the ones that were believed to direct Congress activity. Periyar was particularly incensed that men like Motilal Nehru who proclaimed their nationalist credentials far and wide should succumb to the lure of office. For, no sooner had the senior Nehru entered the Council, he had secured for himself a post in the Military Advisory Committee. In this instance, as in others, argued Periyar, the Swarajists sought to redeem their various sins by invoking the name of the Mahatma rather unjustly:

> Just as how a cat with its eyes closed laps up stolen milk, these men, the Swarajists, arrogant in the knowledge that they have the Mahatma on their side, imagine that whatever they say will be accepted as scriptural truth and that they can act as they will (KA 2.8.25).

The municipal and local board elections in Madras which were held during this time confirmed Periyar in his opinion of the Swarajists. He noted that they were driven to contest the elections only because they were envious and resentful of those non-brahmins who, since the advent of the Justice Party to power in 1921, were found in substantial numbers in the local bodies. The brahmin press, observed Periyar, served the Swarajists well in this regard, for it actively worked to defame non-brahmins, and reporters were specially employed to 'discover' stories which would discredit, in the eyes of the voters, those non-brahmins who were either already serving in local institutions, or were ready to contest the impending elections. In several articles and addresses written and delivered on the eve of the elections, Periyar railed against the ideological bankruptcy of the Swarajist candidates, wrote against the extant mode of canvassing votes through lure of money and superior communicative skills, and observed that in reality Swarajists were no better or no worse than the Justice candidates they claimed to despise and oppose (KA 19.7.25; 23.8.25).

If the local elections served to reveal to Periyar the Swarajists' insatiable will to power and their determination to wield it, the Cheranmahadevi gurukulam incidents showed prominent Swarajists such as S. Srinivasa Iyengar in a rather poor light. The question of allowing or not allowing brahmin and non-brahmin inmates at the gurukulam (run by V.V.S. Iyer with the help of the Congress) to dine together had almost split the Tamil Nadu Congress into two, with brahmins and non-brahmins ranged against each other over this vital issue. Even mild mannered non-brahmins such as Kalyanasundara Mudaliar and sagacious politicians such as Dr. Varadarajulu Naidu, neither of whom had been directly critical of brahmin power and influence in Congress before, were bewildered and hurt in this particular instance.

But even as non-brahmins protested the turn of events at Cheranmahadevi, Congress brahmins expressed their dismay at what they termed an unwarranted display of partisan sentiment. Srinivasa Iyengar, foremost amongst Swarajists, rebuked non-brahmin Congressmen for their warmth of feeling on this matter and catalogued a list of complaints against all non-brahmins, including Periyar, who had dared characterize the Congress party as brahminical in its intent and objectives (KA 12.7.25).

Periyar in his turn lashed out at Srinivasa Iyengar in what turned out in reality to be a harsh and purposive indictment of the Swarajists as a whole. Srinivasa Iyengar had criticized Periyar for not supporting a resolution on Swaraj at the Thiruvannamalai session of the Congress. Periyar now questioned his nationalist credentials and that of his Swarajist colleagues. Arguing that neither Srinivasa Iyengar nor his men deserved to be referred to as lovers of Swaraj, he went on to note that the term 'Swarajist' was actually a misnomer and an euphemism:

> To refer to these men as Swarjaists is somewhat akin to referring to prostitutes as devadasis; to oppressors as brahmins; to the present-day courts and lawyers as sites of justice and lovers of equity (respectively) and to government employees as public servants; to the gang of shopkeepers and traders who have come to loot our land of its wealth as men of Government.

Srinivas Iyengar, Periyar went on to say, could not possibly qualify as a patriot, since he was ever given to negotiating favours for himself with the government and had consistently opposed and criticized Non Cooperation—he had even asked that Non Cooperation be declared illegal and punished—and had pronounced the Mahatma mad when the latter urged lawyers to give up their lucrative practice (KA 20.9.25).

PERIYAR AND THE RE-DEFINITION OF UNTOUCHABILITY

What perhaps enabled Periyar to forge a robust philosophy of social action was his imaginative re-rendering of the terms of Constructive Work, especially his understanding of untouchability and his proposals for its abolition. Congressmen everywhere, particularly those who were personally drawn to Gandhi, were anxious to carry out anti-untouchability work. But it is doubtful if any of them, in Madras, at any rate, brought to their practice that degree of sociological clarity and ethical resonance which Periyar possessed in abundance. For instance, Rajagopalachari, though a conscious and sincere proponent of anti-untouchability work, was not particularly clear (or chose not to be clear) as to what this work was all about. His sense of what such work required and implied was often beclouded and overwhelmed by that curious self-regard, by a sort of beleaguered sensibility, which, however misguided in its intent, was experienced as real by many a Tamil brahmin. Thus, speaking of the importance of anti-untouchability work at a meeting at Gobichettipalayam, Rajagopalachari could not refrain from commenting on the present-day brahmin's alienation from society, which, he insisted, was similar to that experienced by the untouchable:

> Unable to carry out the onerous duties [prescribed by convention] they [the brahmins] are now fallen. Other castes more or less carry out their duties and tasks enjoined them. But the brahmins today have become an outcast group and are in the same position as the untouchables.

Rajagopalachari concluded his address by emphasizing the importance of abolishing untouchability but added one need not baulk at this task, or imagine that 'because we hope to abolish untouchability, we also hope to put an end to caste divisions, observances and practices' (KA 24.5.25).

In contrast to Rajagopalachari and a host of other reformers to whom the untouchability issue was important chiefly as an index of their own sense of the self, to Periyar, the abolition of untouchability signified and required nothing more or less than the abolition of the caste system itself. Speaking on an abolition resolution tabled at the Karaikudi District First Political (Congress) Conference, Periyar stated that neither the Manusmriti nor its constituent terms and references such as 'jati' and 'varnashrama' could be held to apply to Tamils. The qualities associated conventionally with the various jatis possessed no material correlates, no identifiable referents in the lives of Tamils. The term 'shudra', if considered in its original semantic import, characterized the Tamils as born to *dasis* (slave women) and, as such, was a marker of scorn and humiliation and worse, in some respects, than even the term 'panchama' which was routinely used to refer to the outcastes. Periyar went on to point out how a logic of graded inequality kept the caste system in place:

> In our country no one is spared the horrors of untouchability, unseeability, unspeakability and unapproachability. It is customary for a caste to consider the one below it [in the hierarchy] to be untouchable and unseeable, whereas the same caste is viewed as untouchable and unseeable by the caste above it. Besides this, today, all these castes are together considered untouchable and

> unapproachable by the caste that rules us—the European caste. Thus the abolition of untouchability does not merely imply the progress of the panchamas, or the mere doing away with the cruelties they currently endure. The philosophy of abolition desires to do away not only with the cruelty all of us experience, but also to cleanse us of the degradation and horror we carry within ourselves (KA 21.6.25).

Periyar held that the granting of proportional (communal) representation would go a long way in mitigating the misery of the untouchables and observed that it was not merely the brahmin Congressman who refused to consider this suggestion as a worthwhile one, but the British civilian who also seemed reluctant to advance this measure:

> If the untouchables had been granted proportional representation fifty years ago, would they suffer as they do today . . . If we, as non-brahmin Hindus, yet refuse to grant proportional representation to these seven million people, we will, undoubtedly [be forced to] extend the concession to them when [out of despair], they convert to Islam or Christianity (KA 16.8.25).

If, on the one hand, the abolition of untouchability required the implementation by the Executive of the principle of proportional representation, on the other hand, it required a struggle against brahminic arrogance and caste spirit. Adumbrating on the objectives for which *Kudi Arasu* had been started, Periyar noted that he and his peers objected chiefly to the idea which proclaimed brahmins superior, and considered the rest 'untouchable, unseeable, unapproachable and denied them even such rights as were granted to animals'. What they resisted was the partisan sentiment which desired to see brahmins progress in every field, but which insisted all others remain bound in subordination to this one caste. For such a sentiment sought 'to conspire against and use others', advancing, as it did the exclusive claims of its proponents, and this served the good of brahmins alone (KA 1.11.25).

The struggle against the rancorous spirit of caste and the exclusive privileges of the brahmin, which were sustained by this spirit, had to be one waged by non-brahmins and untouchables working in concert. Commenting on the term 'non-brahmin' Periyar remarked that, essentially, it was a comprehensive category, a veritable genus, into which could be packed all those South Indians who were 'not-brahmin'. Thus,

> Even Christians, Mohammedans, Anglo-Indians and other non-Hindus are non-brahmins. Amongst the Hindus all those, excepting those of the brahmin caste, even if they are considered comprising different jatis . . . are non-brahmins. Those referred to as untouchables and who therefore are marginalized as unseeable and unapproachable are also non-brahmins. If all these communities are to escape ensnarement by the magic web of Brahminism, and live in self-respect, they have to transcend minor sectarian differences, shed their self-interest and cease to be the brahmin's spies . . . They need to trust in universal progress and unite to achieve this objective and meanwhile should eschew prejudice and falsehood (KA 8.11.25).

Periyar also stressed, as he had done on earlier occasions, the importance of securing proportional representation for all non-brahmins, but especially for the untouchables. As he wrote in a related instance, if the untouchables had been granted posts in government and assumed positions of authority they could have acted to prevent the infliction of such ignominies on their brethren, as had happened at Kalpathi (in Palghat), where they were forbidden by the local brahmins to walk the streets of that brahmin dominated village (KA 22.11.25).

In an invitation issued to non-brahmins and members of the adi dravidas, which called for their coming together at a special non-brahmin conclave that was to be oraganized alongside the Congress conference at Kanchipuram, Periyar noted:

> The abolition of untouchability is one of the most important duties of non-brahmins. Not only is the progress of non-brahmins ultimately linked to the progress achieved by the untouchables, but the sorrows of the latter are a matter of concern and feeling to non-brahmins as well . . . [Besides] self-rule is possible only through the abolition of untouchability. Therefore, we request those who are intent on the abolition of untouchability and those who are referred to as 'untouchables' to attend the Kanchipuram conference, of necessity, and convene to discuss and plan on this vital issue (KA 15.11.25; Anaimuthu: 404).

Periyar's address at the Kanchipuram Congress conference was remarkable for its candour. He proposed a resolution on proportional representation that was defeated by his fellow non-brahmin Kalyanasundara Mudaliar. In the same address, Periyar also dwelt on the problem of untouchability and called for its abolition. He noted that true Swaraj was contingent on the granting of proportional representation, for otherwise the fruits of Swaraj would be appropriated by brahmin Congressmen and, worse, denied to the untouchables and other non-brahmins:

> In our present situation many fear that Swaraj if granted will only usher in Brahmana Raj. If, in these days of British rule, it is possible for some to prevent others from walking down certain streets and to prevent them from having access to water from village wells and ponds... what would not they—this particular community—do if they come to wield [political] authority? What horrors would they not perpetrate? People fear this eventuality... We see seven crores of innocent men and women being treated worse than animals. Why must this be so? If we were to grant each community political and other rights, in proportion to their numbers in the populace, the innocent would not have to lead an animal existence; nor would the wicked be able to pass themselves off as holy men (KA 6.12.25; Anaimuthu: 907).

Periyar's interventions at Kanchipuram, occasioned as they were by the Patna Congress decisions and the imminent Swarajist takeover of Congress, proved to be in vain. He had earlier imagined he could bring together a band of men committed to Constructive Work and to the cause of Untouchability Abolition, so that the Gandhian inspiration could be preserved and realized on its own, far away from the noise and confusion of a Congress politics dominated by the Swarajists. But the events at Kanchipuram made it clear to him that, not only were the Tamil Swarajists unrelenting in their opposition to Constructive Work, but that all Tamil brahmin Congressmen had proved themselves hostile to proportional representation.

THE IMPORTANCE OF PROPORTIONAL REPRESENTATION

For Periyar in 1925-26, proportional representation represented a veritable civil right that non-brahmins, especially the adi dravidas, had to claim and uphold. As he observed in his Kanchipuram address, society in the Tamil country—and elsewhere —was characterized by a lack of mutual trust and solidarity amongst various castes:

> While one class is constantly looking to advance its claims through any means whatsoever, other classes are anxious to avoid being victims of deception. . . . This lack of mutual goodwill on the one hand and competitive resentment on the other had forced certain classes to become spies and slaves [of Government]. . . . The body politic thus stood to be poisoned by hatred and malice (KA 6, 13.12.25; Anaimuthu: 907; 929).

Periyar conceded the idea of proportional representation was infinitely extendable and would facilitate rather than resolve the eruption of further claims and counter claims, but he felt the problem of representation through communal identities could not, therefore, be evaded or rejected for lack of a durable solution (KA 22.11.25; Anaimuthu: 902). Periyar also pointed out the details of the flawed logic which informed protestations of the demand for social justice through proportional representation: if Congress brahmins could assent to a sharing of power with Muslims and yet remain united with the latter, so as to constitute a single political bloc, why must they consider the sharing of power with fellow Hindus to hold divisive implications? Secondly, the Congress' attitude towards non-brahmins in general, and adi dravidas in particular, was as problematic as that perverse logic which sustained the caste hierarchy. This logic refused to allow the lower castes to redeem themselves or heal their wounds, nor would it enable or allow the upper castes to initiate a healing process themselves. It was inevitable therefore that the oppressed would seek to shatter this logic and exercise their rights to resist domination (KA 13.12.25; Anaimuthu: 929).

Till the end of his life, Periyar was firm in his conviction that a large and proportional non-brahmin presence in the government and administration constituted a necessary condition for the deployment of non-brahmin counter hegemony. As he argued, in one of his earliest articles on the subject, an M. C. Raja or a Veeraiyan—both were adi dravida leaders from Madras—could fulfil governmental duties as well as a C. P. Ramaswamy Iyer or a B. N. Sharma, and, moreover, would function with a keen awareness of non-brahmin concerns, that it would be virtually impossible then, as it was easily possible now, to thwart legislation which would throw open temples to men and women of all castes (KA 22.11.25; Anaimuthu: 902).

RECKONING WITH GANDHI

Conventional scholarship on the Self-Respect movement holds that Periyar was provoked to launch it following a series of incidents in the Madras Congress—the Vaikkom satyagraha, the Cheranmahadevi gurukulam incidents and the Kanchipuram debacle. These events, it is argued, proved to him the irredeemable Brahminism which structured the policy and practice of the Congress and, in the wake of such happenings, he decided to leave that party. Periyar was himself given to adducing these three instances as reasons for his decision to leave the Congress, but it must not be forgotten that such arguments and reasons were advanced in retrospect, months after the decision to distance himself from the Congress had already been made.

Though Periyar was none too happy with the Congress during this time, and even later on, he remained in that party. When he was asked why he persisted in doing so, he remarked:

> I have chosen to stay on, because I desire to change the present-day Congress, that is only concerned with getting posts in government for brahmins, so that it would resemble once again the Mahatma's Congress of two, three four years ago; when true Non Cooperation was practised and the good of all communities sought to be realised. If such a transformation of the Congress does take place, the selfish are bound to disappear. Sometimes when I hear the Mahatma speak, it seems to me he too would like to work for such a change. If I were to lose my faith in him, that is, in his will to transform the present situation, I will not stay on in the party (KA 3.6.26; Murugesan 1990: 189-90).

During the years 1926-27, when he did stay on in the Congress, that is, when he had not formally severed links with either that party or with Gandhi, Periyar remained faithful to the principles of Constructive Work. He even argued that the Mahatma's vision of Swaraj was premised on 'the self-respect and equality of the oppressed'. He also declared that the rich, the upper castes and the educated were basically opposed to the Mahatma, because he desired the poor and the depressed classes to progress (KA 18.4.26).

What is significant, though, about Periyar's reading of Gandhi (we have referred to this before but will consider it in greater detail here) are the specific inflections he brought to his interpretations of Gandhian Constructive Work. It is in Periyar's addresses to the adi dravidas that we find the most creative and astonishing mutations of the habitual Congress anti-abolition propaganda. Whereas Congressmen would exhort adi dravidas to practise cleanliness, give up alcohol and take to spinning, Periyar would exhort them to be assertive:

> Why must you unnecessarily address other castemen as Swami? The sense of being a low caste person seems to have mingled completely with your blood. But you must endeavour to change this. Whenever you see a person—of another caste—you must ask yourselves, if in reality there exists any difference between him and you. One cannot help a caste that is not concerned about its own self-respect to progress. Each one of you must recognise and be conscious of the fact that you are human (KA 25.4.26; Anaimuthu: 56).

But even as Periyar urged the adi dravidas to free themselves of their internalized oppression, he made it clear that they had been condemned to a life of un-cleanness and were not to be blamed for the execrable conditions in which they lived:

> If your clothes are dirty and you appear unwashed, who is responsible for this state of affairs? When you do not have access to drinking water, how can you possibly bathe? It is not as if you were born smelly and dirty...If mahants and shankaracharyas were denied access to water to bathe, wash their clothes and brush their teeth and were to be locked up in a house for days, would their clothes remain spotless? Would their bodies smell fragrant?

Periyar also considered it utterly fallacious that some should point to the untouchables' habit of eating the flesh of dead animals and drinking liquor and hold them inferior on that account. He observed that poverty drove the untouchable to consume the flesh of dead cows and, anyway, why should the eating of cow meat be held sacrilegous and demeaning than, say, the eating of lamb, fish or chicken? Also, not all those who partook of cow flesh were considered unapproachable or unseeable. As for liquor, would it be fair, right and truthful to maintain the untouchables alone consumed alcohol? Surely their consumption of it did not account for the stupendous abkari revenue, often amounting to crores of rupees, that was garnered by the government annually? (KA 25.4.26)

The abolition of untouchability and the problems posed by caste were foremost in Periyar's mind even on those occasions when his audience was multi-caste and variegated in its origins. For instance, in his addresses to striking workers, he would dwell on brahmin duplicity and entreat them to think through the power wielded in the present hour by brahmins in almost every walk of life, even those with whom they had no direct contact, such as, for example, the sphere of labour (KA 24.4.27; Anaimuthu 1721-22). During this period, when Periyar was not yet out of the Congress but not entirely in it either, several other crucial issues to do with caste and status were addressed with the same fervour by him. His treatment of these matters indicate how far he had travelled from Gandhian Constructive Work, though he continued to swear by the Gandhian creed. His speech at the Sengunthar (a caste of weavers) conference held at Avinashi is a fine illustration of his flexible and creative approach to the problems and practices of caste.

After noting that the Sengunthar community practised the ritual of pledging its girls to temple service—consecrating them as devadasis—he drew attention to the problems faced by Sengunthar men. Though adept at playing the nadaswaram (a wind instrument played on auspicious occasions), they were considered disreputable, and, over a period of time, these artistes themselves had come to believe in their essential lowness. There were innumberable incidents of well-known *vidwans* (artists) being forbidden to wear the upper cloth across their shoulders by their patrons, since they were perceived as being too 'low' in the jati hierarchy to aspire to such a mark of honour. On the other hand, argued Periyar, all that a brahmin had to do was to play the harmonium or sing, while a dancing girl performed, and he was acclaimed a master of his craft. Thus, 'even if a brahmin were to mediate between a dasi and her prospective patron (and lover) he was addressed as "swami". It has happened that the patron (if he is a non-brahmin) who receives a missive from the dasi (through a brahmin courier) often stands up to receive it' (KA 10.1.26).

It is obvious that those concerns and principles which would animate and inform the activities of the Self-Respect movement in its later years were already present in Periyar's thought and action. A relentless criticism of brahmins and Brahminism—visible even in the early *Kudi Arasu* articles—was advanced during this time. Such critiques not only pointed to the brahmin's role in maintaining, perpetrating and re-producing the caste hierarchy, but also drew attention to non-brahmins' complicity in thus ensuring their own subordination:

> Not only do brahmins refer to us who constitute 97 out of every 100 persons as shudras and low born, but they set themselves up as our benefactors. They possess the ear of government and have, thus, managed to appropriate all appointments and powers in government for themselves...But we, who protest this nepotism, do so merely because we wish to corner a few of those posts for ourselves....You are jealous and prejudiced against the brahmins only with regard to the matter of government posts, but with regard to religious rituals you continue to consider them superior. However well educated you are and whatever position of authority you wield, you, yet, fall at the brahmin's feet—all he has to do is to come to your house, carrying his customary darba grass and wearing on his forehead the symbols of his sacrality, and you are willing to please him (KA 15.8.26; Anaimuthu: 11).

That the self-respect idea on the basis of which he sought to oppose the brahmins was intimately linked to an anti-caste programme appears evident from Periyar's own references to his adoption of this ideal:

> The Self-Respect movement which I began and worked at with the goodwill of friends has as its objective the destruction of Brahminism which has ever encouraged the growth of superstitious practices—through its patronage of politics, god, Shastra, Dharma. Such superstitions constitute the very warp and woof of the philosophies of god, religion and caste, which in turn exist as the fountainhead of brahmin dominance (KA 1.11.26).

It is clear that self-respect, as precept and practice, was to be considered a political and ethical counter to the ideal of self-rule. In fact, the premise of one of the earliest definitions of self-respect was precisely such a distinction—to be understood to exist between self-respect and self-rule. A *Kudi Arasu* editorial, essentially a manifesto and explanation of intent, took its cue from Gandhi's purported statement: 'If I do not possess the means to preserve my self-respect, then I cannot really fight for Swaraj.' Characteristically enough, Periyar chose to explore the implications of this statement in the context of untouchability:

> Is not a man...who does not have the right to see and worship his god lacking in self-respect? Why do those who deny their fellow men such rights need Swaraj? Or any other Raj, for that matter? If such a monstrous group that has thus condemned a segment of its own society to eternal oppression were to attain Swaraj, how would this benefit others in that society?...[Further], if the citizens of a nation are found lacking in self-respect, then all attempts to win Swaraj remain nothing more than opportune attempts aimed at individual well-being and at strengthening individual interest. Besides such attempts [undertaken without a sense of self-respect] will also serve to reinforce those conditions which make for an absence of self-respect (KA 24.1.26; Anaimuthu: 449).

An even bolder definition of self-respect was offered by Periyar in an appeal addressed to the public, requesting them to support, through their generosity, the Suchindram Temple satyagraha. He remarked on this occasion on the hypocrisy of those who would rail against racial discrimination in South Africa but would yet overlook the existence in their midst of the despised and marginalized adi dravidas: 'We refuse to grant [to the untouchables] even those rights we readily grant to dogs and pigs. In our context is Swaraj a necessity? The public must ask itself what is important, Swaraj or the progress of and the attainment of self-respect by the untouchables?' (KA 31.1.26; Anaimuthu: 450).

Perhaps the most categorical and definitive description of self-respect which was advanced during this period was the one that drew a sharp distinction between Tilak's famous invocation of Swaraj as his birthright and the non-brahmins' will to self-respect:

> Tilak claimed that Swaraj was his birthright, but since he was a varnashrama brahmin, and since such men hold that others are inferior to brahmins, this sentiment, in itself, becomes their birthright. It is, on this account, that Tilak was forced to use a term 'Swaraj'—useless for this purpose and dubious in its implications for practice—drawn from the field of politics to refer to his birthright. But we are not constrained to survive by deceiving others. Instead, we are intent on discovering humanity in its truest sense. Therefore we maintain 'self-respect is a man's birthright'. We must realise that Swaraj is possible only where there is already a measure of self-respect and is otherwise not a discernible entity in itself (KA 9.1.27; Anaimuthu: 3-4).

Periyar's decision to completely sever all ties with Congress and, more important, with Gandhi occurred in 1927. A constellation of events seems to have persuaded him to abandon the politics of nationalism and Constructive Work.

Firstly, at the Kanpur Congress held in December 1926, the Swarajists carried the day and won a mandate from the Congress to contest the general elections of 1926. This not only meant that henceforth Congress would openly and completely endorse the Swarajists' constitutionalism, but that it would forego its lukewarm commitment to Constructive Work. Secondly, the Kanpur resolutions served to strengthen the Swarajists' hand in Madras and signified the triumph of what Periyar would habitually refer to as political Brahminism. Thirdly, as the year 1926 advanced, elections to the provincial councils were held which saw a handsome Swarajist victory. Though the Tamil Swarajists were eager to form a ministry, the All-India Congress Committee resolved against acceptance of office. But to Periyar the victory itself seemed ominous and he naturally desired to mitigate those dangerous consequences which were sure to follow in the wake of a possible Swarajists' takeover of the Madras Council. Fourthly, and this proved to be crucial, as far as Periyar's reading of the situation was concerned, 1926 saw the election of S. Srinivasa Iyengar as the All-India Congress president (Baker 1976: 164). The election of one whom Periyar considered a timeserver and an enemy of social progress to the highest post in the Congress, no doubt troubled him deeply.

This constellation of events and ideas signified the end of an era—

of a certain kind of Gandhian politics—and more important threatened to usher in a new dangerous one. Periyar wrote in great anger and even greater insight thus in mid-1927:

> No sooner had Congress decided to abandon its principles for the sake of a spurious 'unity', than the Mahatma disengaged himself from politics and, like a hooded shankaracharya, retired to a corner. And then began all those rituals one witnesses in a religious cult; just as how devotees throng the premises of a mutt, now several 'shastris' visit the Gandhi Mutt, sit at his feet, sing his praise and thereby enhance their prestige. The reason why Gandhian Constuctive principles have lost all value is because, in the name of a fraudulent unity, they were abandoned and in their place a Gandhi Mutt established. Since madness is characteristic of all mahatmas, our own is no exception to this general rule. Perhaps, he still hopes he may be able to alter the situation. But we do not harbour any such faith. As far as I understand the situation, no man or institution or nation which compromises on its principles has been known to prosper (KA 12.6.27; Anaimuthu: 761).

Yet, even this does not constitute a 'break' with the Mahatma. The 'break' with Gandhi came two months later. Gandhi visited Mysore in July 1927 and at a public meeting remarked on his faith in the salience of varnashrama dharma (Sitambaranar: 92). At about the same time, a 'Brahmana Sammelan' organized at Tuvar in the district of Thanjavur, acknowledged the continued validity of varnadharma in very clear terms. But, it also observed that at present there were only two varnas, the brahmana and the shudra and it behoved either to practise their vocation with sincerity and responsibility (KA 26.6.27; 7.8.27; Anaimuthu: 76, 466). Periyar read Gandhi's remarks in this context and, naturally enough, interpreted them to mean that particular castes should persist in their assigned callings and seek none other. He also noted, in an editorial that if the Mahatma were to repeat such observations during his forthcoming visit to Madras, this would only help the enemies of Self-Respect, and went on point out that the Mahatma's ideas needed to be countered:

> Though the public believes that Mahatma Gandhi wishes to abolish untouchability and reform religion and society, the Mahatma's

> utterances and thought reveal him to hold exactly the opposite views on this matter...Though he claims openly enough that untouchability should be abolished, he interprets his own words in this regard in such a manner as will enable the persistence of untouchability... [Thus] if we are to follow the Mahatma's untouchability creed, we will slip into the very abyss of that untouchability we are attempting to abolish. We have been patient, very patient and tight-lipped but today in the interests of abolition and self-respect we are, sadly enough, forced to confront and oppose the Mahatma.

The editorial also pointed out that 'If the body of varnashrama dharma did not exist, untouchability which constitutes the very life of this body would not be alive today.'

Gandhi's views, the editorial went on to say, were akin to those routinely mouthed by brahmins and he had nowhere sought to refute the latter's defence of caste privileges. Besides, both the Mahatma and the brahmins were agreed on the existence of the four varnas, both agreed that each varna should carry out those duties enjoined it by convention. The Mahatma in his Mysore address had remarked that a brahmin's dharma was to render public service and had drawn on the scriptures to uphold his claims. By the same token, though he did not say it in so many words, it could be said the Mahatma desired the shudras likewise do their duty, which was, of course, serving the brahmins! The logic of the Mahatma's varnadharma, noted the editorial, does not work otherwise. The Mahatma had insisted that no varna was superior to any other but, if this were so, why had he not sought to interrogate the matter of specific duties as assigned to specific castes? Why had he not raised the question of what was likely to happen if a man were to abandon his own duties and pursue another's? (KA 7.8.27; Anaimuthu: 76-77).

The editorial earned Periyar and his men great public ire, but as the former pointed out, such carpers, critics and baffled patriots had not cared to find out if the Mahatma indeed said this and not that, whether he had indeed not maintained certain opinions and denounced others. Instead, parrot-like, they were given to repeating such tautological observations such as 'He meant this, not that' or 'He did not intend to be understood thus'. Periyar observed that he and S. Ramanathan had spoken to Gandhi at Mysore on the need for the abolition of the Congress, Hinduism and brahmin hegemony but Gandhi had refused to consider their arguments in this regard as valid. At the end of it all, it had become clear to Periyar and Ramanathan that Gandhi did indeed endorse varnadharma. However, since it was decided then not to divulge the details of this meeting without Gandhi's approval, *Kudi Arasu* had been silent. But now with matters out in the open, one could easily see Gandhi for what he was: a crucial player in the construction and deployment of Congress-brahmin hegemony, and declared Periyar, he had no wish to meet Gandhi once again. Therefore, 'we have resolved that the creed of varnashrama dharma signifies our death-knell, and we consider it our duty to work for its destruction, for only in the wake of its demise will we attain freedom and self-respect.' (KA 28.8.27; Anaimuthu: 79-81).

It is important to note here that though this was the first forthright denunciation of Gandhi and his creed to appear in *Kudi Arasu,* Periyar had not been averse to publishing criticisms of the Mahatma even earlier. In 1925, he had reproduced an article from *Vedic Magazine* by one Pandit Dharma Deva Siddhantha Alangarar. The latter had remarked that, by endorsing caste differences, Gandhi was creating obstacles in the way of the one objective dear to his heart, the abolition of untouchability (KA 13.9.25). Periyar's differences with Gandhi had surfaced in an even earlier instance, during the Vaikkom satyagraha, with Gandhi adopting a flexible, 'soft' approach to the question of the rights of lower castes to walk the temple streets (Sitambaranar: 63-78). The Vaikkom satyagraha, in fact, marked an important moment in Periyar's political life, defining as it did his inexorable difference from his peers in the Tamil Nadu Congress. Periyar's support for the cause of the lower castes earned him a special and radical reputation, especially since he did not give into pressures from the All-India Congress leadership.

The Self-Respect movement after 1927 carried out its activities and refined its ideologies in a socio-political context that was more or less overdetermined by the progress of Congress politics in Madras and in the country at large. Yet, the various moments in the evolution of Congress politics enabled the Self-Respect movement to come into its own, so that its criticisms of the situation at hand and the conjuncture in question were not merely negative in their intent, but contained in them the seeds of a radical theory of community and politics.

CHAPTER 8

The Self-Respecters' Critique of Religion

THE SELF RESPECT MOVEMENT

The Self-Respect movement as we receive it in history does not possess a singular moment of origin. It comes to us, already, as it were, in process, as an ideological impulse, an energetic mobilizing of men and women across castes and classes, a vision of a society that had erupted into rebellion, into acts of defiance, daring and, finally, as a time of great churning, when all things were subject to doubt and enquiry, when all matters, however sacred and inviolate, were relentlessly interrogated; when women ignored the claims of family and the bonds of community; when young men willingly forsook personal fortunes and defied elders; a time when scores of hitherto despised and ignored peoples, until then, mere objects of charity, pity and paternalist benevolence, were asked to play protagonists in a struggle which, above all, was committed to turning their world upside down. From 1925-39, for nearly a decade and a half, the Tamil country was witness to such happenings and changes, that the proponents of these changes described them as millennial in their significance.

Through the critique of religion, caste and gender emerged a rational atheistic world-view, articulated overtly, in some circumstances, as an alternative way of imagining community and nation. In other instances, the relevance and uses of atheism were subtly underscored, but never imposed. Atheism in this sense constituted a mode of critique, a viable counterpoint that would help deconstruct received practices of faith, culture and custom. The oppositional rhetoric and critical energy of the Self-Respect movement was balanced and sustained in its negative significance by an alternative theory and practice which made it clear the movement's agents sought to destroy only to rebuild. Anti-religious attitudes, acts and ideologies were often accompanied by exhortations to rationality and upheld by an abiding faith in the powers of humanity to remake itself. Deconstructions of scripture were made at the behest of a radical empiricist world-view which trusted nothing and desired no certainties, except the material reality of the here and now. The priest's services were done away with, so that rituals that marked rites of passage could be secularized and conducted as community observances.

While the mystification of politics through the invocation of religion was attacked for its dissembling intent and for subserving partisan concerns, a new practice of politics, rooted in the quotidian reality of thousands of people, which demanded transformations in modes of being and living, in diet, clothes, forms of address, conduct of rituals, acts of prayer, was inaugurated. In place of affective bonds forged by kinship and a shared faith and community, new kinds of bonds of a horizontal nature, implying comradeship in the widest sense of the term, were sought to be woven; such that men and women in their workaday roles and functions may interact on the basis of mutuality and self-respect.

The politics of the every day possessed a correlate in the world outside the micro community as well. The larger community came to be defined, not in and through large and overarching categories, as with nationalism, where the partisan import of the term 'Hindu' was succesfully elided in its articulation with an imagined Indian community. Now, the nation was made coeval with the good society, a transformed social order, constructed in its otherness, so to speak, in its irreducible difference, in its alterity with the Indian nation. Whereas the latter had been elevated to represent a norm, a given, much like God, whose sanctity could not be ever questioned, this other nation, the Dravidian (Tamil) community was assumed as a construct, as a conscious expression of those who were committed to self-respect, social justice and a caste-free society.

It is clear that the Self-Respect movement was fundamentally opposed to the holy alliance of religion, caste and nationalism, an alliance, which it understood as embodying a social and political order that was inherently inegalitarian. The movement's ideologues and members, leaders and workers, men and women expended their intellectual and emotional energies in disarticulating the terms of this alliance; in indicating how and through what means—discursive, political, social—and for what partisan purposes this alliance had been forged. Such indictments of the holy threesome were never merely verbal. They were often accompanied by acts of defiance, transgression and destruction; acts which attempted to demystify religion, castigate and denounce caste with its hierarchical logic of dominance, subordination and graded inequality; and which sought to relieve nationalism of its mythic aura and locate nationalist heroes and practices in their constitutive context, where greed, avarice and self-regard as well as the lures of ideology held sway.

Let us consider the Self-Respect movement's responses to each of these issues. Though it is near impossible to separate its critique of religion from its understanding of caste, and separate its critique of nationalism from its views on religion, for heuristic purposes, we have to work with a somewhat schematic approach in order to unravel the very many strands that comprised the movement's textured and rich discourse and practice.

FIVE ASPECTS OF THE SELF-RESPECTERS' CRITIQUE OF RELIGION

The statues and busts of Periyar which adorn many a road, bye lane and dirt track in Tamil Nadu carry beneath them, inscribed on the pedestal, the following phrases: 'There is no God. Whoever believes in God is a fool.' Periyar is remembered thus, by his admirers as well as his detractors, both of whom associate him chiefly with his famous acts of iconoclasm: the breaking of the Ganapathi idol, and the garlanding of the portrait of Rama with slippers. This image of Periyar, so deeply etched in public memory, does not, in any manner whatsoever, do justice either to the many sided critique of religion, or the radical social content of the anti-clerical and anti-religious agitations launched by the Self-Respect movement. These agitations were propelled and influenced by a subversive rage against an unjust social order and were meant to shock a people out of deadening faith and degrading habits. The Self-Respect movement's pronouncements and actions with regard to religion spanned a range of ideologies and purposes. Questionings of religious dogma, faith and convention by the movement's leading ideologues owed their inspiration to Periyar himself. For Periyar set precedents in this matter, practising in his everyday life the atheism and irreverence he preached.

Periyar's irreverence and impiety, his biographer, Sami Sitambaranar tells us, were manifest in his early youth and was probably provoked by household conventions that valued and fussed over religious observances. In contrast to the highly Sanskritized lifestyle of his father, a self-made but wealthy merchant named Venkatappa Naicker, who often welcomed saintly men of learning, sanyasins and brahmins well versed in the scriptures to his house and organized religious discourses, Periyar Ramasamy's boyhood seems to have been spent in a sort of liminal space and time. Raised by an elderly aunt, he grew to defy authority and prescriptive behavioural norms and was particularly transgressive in the breaking of caste taboos, even during that very short period, when he was actually at school. Periyar did not get beyond the first few grades of primary school! (Sitambaranar 1971: 12-25)

Two sets of descriptions stand out from Sitambaranar's account of Periyar's youth, both of which are germane to our enquiry. The one has to do with his early married life and the other with a`pilgrimage' Periyar undertook a few years after marriage. Sitambaranar's account of Periyar's married life reveals Periyar to be a prankster husband, ever wont to disrupt the orthodox lifestyle, a conventional caste Hindu wife was expected to observe. Sitambaranar suggests that through the practice of a variety of tricks, schemes and audacious jokes on his wife Nagammal, Periyar, in fact, sought to disengage his young bride from the rigours of an orthodox Hindu household. These curious biographical details demonstrate a salient aspect of the young Periyar's mindset. In contrast to the great Maharashtrian reformers such as Ranade and Waman Rao Tilak, who attempted to 'educate' their wives into accepting a new role for themselves in the changed context of the times and, who, in fact, schooled their young brides into a lifestyle that demanded a judicious interpretation of custom and a tolerable familiarity with Western learning, Periyar demanded his wife free herself from custom and be a fit helpmeet to his subversive activities (ibid: 27-35).

The second set of descriptions which are somewhat pertinent to our concerns have to do with Periyar's 'pilgrimage'. His biographer tells us that a few years after his marriage, ostensibly bored with his affluent circumstances, and restless with his cloistered life at Erode, Periyar decided to leave home, in fact, ran away. The decision to leave seems to have been occasioned by a quarrel with his father. Sitambaranar's narration, enchanting in itself, deserves close attention, for it demonstrates the essentially parodic nature of the events which followed from Periyar's decision to leave home.

Periyar's pilgrimage, in the course of which he assumed the garb of a sanyasin, took him to Bezawada, Hyderabad, Calcutta, Puri, Kashi and finally Ellore. Initially, he was accompanied by two of his townsmen, who, however, abandoned their journey midway, leaving the ever adventurous Ramasamy to proceed on his 'quest'. Periyar's sojourn in Hyderabad was undertaken in the company of two Tamil brahmins, one, a Sanskrit pundit and the other a professional expositor of puranic lore. While these men engaged in lofty discussions and debates over the Hindu scriptures, Periyar indulged in his youthful habit of questioning the veracity, consistency and rationality of scriptural lore and message. The trio proved so vastly entertaining that they were invited by a Tamil clerk in the service of the Nizam of Hyderabad to reside in his house and conduct religious discourses! These discourses would be given in Tamil and then translated into Telugu by Periyar. Sitambaranar notes that the translations were actually free adaptations of the original Tamil and were liberally interspersed with puns, anecdotes and jokes. The crowds which gathered to hear these 'holy' men were naturally drawn to listen by Periyar's creative and, one suspects, sardonic retelling of Puranic tales. The holy threesome would wander in the streets, seek alms by day and harangue the devout with their expositions by night.

Later, the trio moved to Kashi where Periyar's brahmin associates left him. Sitambaranar tells us that Kashi and its mendicant inmates confirmed Periyar in his disdain, contempt and rejection of the Hindu faith. Periyar, it seems, was refused food at many a choultry because he was not a brahmin and he took to living off the food offered to dead ancestors by those who came to perform funeral rites on the banks of the Ganga. Periyar discovered to his horror that men and women freely indulged in drinking and meat eating and debauchery in Kashi. The greed, cupidity and degeneracy of mind and body he witnessed in Kashi caused him to leave the place, but not before he served as an assistant at a Shiva temple, where he was wont to pick bilva leaves for the morning prayers at the temple without taking the customary purificatory bath. This proved to be his undoing and soon he left Kashi to arrive in Ellore to be reunited with his father (ibid: 27-35; 41-51).

If one were to place this period of his life in the context of his latter-day critiques of Hinduism, which were, often, satiric and provocative, it is possible to see in such matters as his relationship to his two brahmin mendicant companions, the play of a carnivalesque energy; one that eternally delights in invoking subversion and irreverence alongside and within structures and modes of authority and power. It was this ludic element in Periyar's criticisms of religion which sustained and rendered attractive his debunking of religion and Gods and his scornful, but informed, rejections of scripture. Guided by Periyar and inspired by his transparent iconoclasm, many a Self-Respecter came to advance a theory and practice of atheism and irreverence, which reflected not only great anger and indignation, but also a saturnalian urge to debunk, parody and stand the world on its head.

The Self-Respecters' and Periyar's views on religion comprised at least five major aspects. There was the critique of the Brahmin Priest and his ideology of privilege, rule and command, in short, a critique of brahmins and Brahminism. Then, there was the critique of scripture; of Vedas, *Itihasas* and *Puranas*, at once rationalist and subversive. Thirdly, there was the criticism of religion as world-view, an ethos that determined the believer's views on sacred, profane and secular matters. Fourthly, we have an exposition and critique of religious doctrine, of the principles that sustain belief and direct action and, lastly, there was the critque of religious practices, of festivals and rituals and happenings.

While the Self-Respect movement's most vituperative and relentless attacks were focussed on Hinduism, other religions were not spared. Christianity, especially Catholicism, was severely condemned for its observance of hierarchy, for the compromises it had struck with caste, for the various sins of its priests and for the superstitions it encouraged (KA 30.4.33). Islam fared better with the Self-Respecters, who were appreciative of its call to brotherhood and its invocations of equality, but even here certain practices, such as those which enjoined the subjugation of women, were singled out for rebuke (KA 9.8.31; Anaimuthu 1974: 1378-79). Periyar was drawn to Buddhism, attracted to its rational, egalitarian anti-brahmin, anti-caste creed, but his relationship to it, unlike that of Dr. Ambedkar, was largely symbolic. That is, while defending the principles of Buddhism, he upheld its rationality and was opposed to the worshipping of the Buddha as God (Vi 26.5.54, 19.4.56; Anaimuthu: 303-07). Likewise, Periyar's and the Self-Respect movement's engagement with the mystic Ramalinga's Sanmarga creed was entirely formal. The Self-Respecters were content to note the social radicalism in the mystic's message and endorsed the spirit of fraternity he upheld, but did not, on that account, seek to spread his lore.

Atheism constituted Periyar's—and the Self-Respect movement's—mainstay with regard to matters of faith. But this was no sterile atheism: redefined and re-signified to reflect the critcal and iconoclastic tenor of the Self-Respect movement, atheism emerged as a creative mode of engagement with the problems of faith in a society ruled by caste. Like all other ideas and principles, the movement's attitudes and opinions with respect to religion were never singular or definitive in their expressions and content. Ideas emerged out of and were responsive to changes in political and social conditions and situations and, given a particular conjuncture, would constellate into definitive statements. Subsequently, as we shall see in any number of instances, were a different situation to emerge, such statements, without losing the validity they had gained in one instance, would get accentuated differently in the second instance. The Self-Respect movement's agitations, while at all times directed against the ill effects of religious belief and the cupidity and avarice of priests, proved to be as adaptive to transformed situations as its ideologies.

BRAHMINS AND BRAHMINISM

Constructing Hegemony

The Self-Respect movement mounted a radical opposition to brahmins and Brahminism. It took issue not merely with priestly misbehaviour and cunning but with the idea of priesthood as such. The brahmin was reviled on two counts: for his privileged birth, which he used to advantage; he was ever given to insisting on his priestly prerogatives, on his right to intervene in the life cycles of all individuals and demanded obesiance from them during those rites of passage he enjoined them to observe (KA 9.1.27; Anaimuthu: 7). Secondly, he was criticized for extending his medial and sacral role in society to shore up his own position of power and authority; for he had come to devise an elaborate hierarchical system that assigned places, roles and functions to all individuals, who were graded low and high by virtue of their proximity to the brahmin and by the power they could wield over those below them. In this hierarchical system power was unevenly distributed—some were allowed the use of arms, while others were allowed to amass wealth. Some were condemned to serve and labour for others. Determinate authority in this social order rested with the brahmin, who wielded it exclusively, on account of his 'sacral' birth and prowess, his knowledge of the sacred language of the gods and, most important, his appropriation of all learning to himself and the denial of it to others (KA 15.8.26; Anaimuthu: 11). As Periyar observed:

> According to the Hindu creed, only a small class, the brahmins, may exercise their rights to knowledge. Hindus have been enjoined not to ask for or know about the basis of their faith... That is, besides these brahmins, who constitute a mere two percent of the populace, all others are denied the right to put their minds to use, to enquire, to distinguish between good and evil, between what is relevant and irrelevant.

As if this were not enough, that non-brahmins should be thus prevented from acquiring knowledge of their religion, the religion of the Hindus had sought to assign particular forms of labour to particular groups such that they may perform these and none other. This system had been put in place through law, custom and the coercion of kings who, throughout history, exercised their powers in these matters at the behest of the brahmins (KA 14.4.29; Anaimuthu: 255). In a long article, published across several issues of *Kudi Arasu*, Kaivalyam Swamigal, a sadhu and a man of immense learning and erudition, who was closely associated with the Self-Respect movement from its earliest days, and who wrote regular columns in *Kudi Arasu*, explained why Self-Respecters were critical of brahmins and Brahminism. His observations bear consideration since they are emblematic of the Self-Respecters' views on how brahmins had managed to sustain their dominance and hegemony over others.

Firstly, brahmins had been granted sole custody over knowledge by the scriptures, but, contrary to scriptural dictum, they had come to use this knowledge ill. They had proved themselves masters of an ingenious hermeneutical art and fabricated arguments and interpretations of the scriptures, outlined notions of purity and pollution, sin and error. In the present hour, noted Kaivalyam, this fine art was most in evidence in the writings of those brahmins who had gathered around Annie Besant at the Theosophical Society and who were hard at work, using their interpretative skills and received wisdom, to 'divinize' the young man (J. Krishnamurthy) Annie Besant considered 'chosen' for a spiritual mission in these ungodly times.

Secondly, brahmins, ever given to deception and falsification of religious doctrine, had come to arrogate to themselves spiritual pretensions and power, even though they had long ceased to abide by those injunctions the Smritis enjoined them to observe and practise. Brahmins had, thus, come to disengage their intellect from purposeful ethical action. That is, they had come to rework successfully the rules of scripture to suit their secular and profane purposes, but had not effected in themselves a change of attitudes and opinions, as demanded by these modern times. The Shankaracharya, for instance, whose mutt had long since given up practices of asceticism, allowed the wealthy to pass themselves off as pious, and would not issue injunctions against the mutt's extravagant displays of piety. Yet he would not do or say anything to enable non-brahmins to be fed in the mutt's premises. While he would defend the brahmin's spiritual prerogatives at all times, he would not comment on or criticize their caste rancour and pride. When Tamil brahmins in the Travancore state were found guilty of this or that misdemeanour, he would plead on their behalf, that being alien to Travancore's customs, they ought not to be punished by the laws of Travancore. But, he would not comment on their observance of Travancore conventions with respect to the so-called unseeable and unapproachable Pulayas and other outcastes.

Thirdly, brahmins were inconsistent in their professions of doctrine. They would argue that true brahminic faith did not require temples or idols, but, yet, would guard their rights to enter the inner sanctum of temples, and their rights to decide who should enter and worship at temples and who should not. Alladi Krishnaswami Iyer, the famous advocate; would entreat brahmin boys to learn to eat meat, for were they to travel to foreign places, they may need to survive on animal flesh, but it would never occur to this famed lawyer to entreat brahmins to relax their rules with respect to adi dravidas and their rights of access to roads, especially those which ran through brahmin settlements.

Fourthly, brahmins had shown themselves to be impervious to criticism. Very few of them, in fact, dared criticize themselves. The educated English-speaking brahmins maintained a judicious silence, rather than comment on matters of reform, or, if they spoke at all, were hedged and careful in their responses. If, by chance, a brahmin dared speak his mind and expressed a contrary opinion, he was immediately and mercilessly damned by his peers. Thus, when Justice Sadasiva Iyer dared speak critically of the brahmin priest, he was denounced as a non-believer by S. Satyamurthi, a description that rendered Sadasiva Iyer's criticism automatically irrelevant, and marked it as prejudicial and unjust.

Drawing on the observations of Swami Vivekananda and Rabindranath Tagore, Kaivalyam observed that the poison injected into Hindu society by the brahmin could only be drawn out by the brahmin himself; but given that community's intemperate and unregenerate pride, he wondered if this would happen at all (Kaivalyam 1931: 27-44; 108-17; 129).

Symbols and Strategies

Through what means did the brahmin secure for himself a position of privilege and authority? Periyar and other Self-Respecters detailed innumerable instances—in religion, politics and the arts—in and through which brahmins sought to demonstrate their 'difference' from all others and, on that basis, uphold their supremacy. These instances had to do with birth, death, puberty, marriage and community celebrations and temple festivals. What angered Periyar and others most was the spectacle of the brahmin professing himself lord of life and death. Time and again, Periyar would draw attention to the seminal role essayed by the brahmin priest in funeral rites observed by non-brahmin communties. This role seemed most insidious to the Self-Respecters, because it sought to make a living out of death and, worse, played upon people's fears, sentiments and apprehensions. The funeral rite constituted the brahmin as a guarantor of identity, since it was his ritual presence that linked the living with the long departed. He thus secured for the living their patrilineage, constituting them as links in a chain of being which held together generations of a family. He also presided over the passage of the dead into the netherworld and thereby redeemed them of their mortal sins and follies. Periyar was particularly annoyed that it was the brahmin priest who thus assured the shudra of the reality of his being, of his identity and who, for such a service, secured for himself a handsome pecuniary compensation. Thus, here existed a strange reversal of values: contrary to custom, the alms receiver was honoured, while the alms giver, the generous patron of priests, was deemed a supplicant! (KA 27.11.43; Anaimuthu: 1525-28)

Gurusamy, whose wit and sarcasm, as well as learning and erudition, was unmatched amongst Self-Respecters, writing in the English journal *Revolt* (R) noted that the brahmin community had secured for itself a 'hereditary monopoly' over the all important function of navigating the dead to 'their heavenly homes':

> This spiritual post office has no permanent building anywhere. There is not any limit in the amount to be paid for the transactions... When an individual is dead the postmaster... arrives voluntarily with a bundle of dried grass. This powerful grass though found in plenty on the banks of rivers and tanks has a peculiar fascination for the armpit of the postmaster, for only in his hands can it effectively do the transacting business... A single grass carries to the homes of the departed loads of rice, vegetables and cloth... Ye Westerners, there is no use envying us... You cannot compete with us, for you should know that we are guided by bhoo-suras, who are directly born even today from the face of Brahma. They are not human beings like you who are too much materialised. They are spiritual ones, eating spiritual food, sleeping spiritual sleep and living a spiritual life (R 1.5.29; Velu 1991: 147-49).

The navigators of the dead also proclaimed themselves lords of time, since they considered themselves capable of dividing up time into good and bad, auspicious and inauspicious moments. Periyar remarked at a later date that it was indeed remarkable that brahmins would thus seek to sacralize time even in this modern age by calling for the performance of rituals that required to be conducted at the 'right' moment. By thus arrogating to themselves the right to sanctify time, even when the rigours of modern life do not allow for such a possibility—for instance, one cannot not attend a case at court because it was scheduled for an inopportune hour—brahmins had sought to maintain their sacral supremacy (Vi 4.1.60; Anaimuthu: 1537).

Such powers as the brahmins possessed in these matters were vested in language and gesture. By merely raising their hands to bless and appearing as if they dispensed grace—though only in return for material gifts—and by uttering a few incomprehensible Sanskrit verses, brahmins had managed to successfully separate themselves from the rest of society even in these days of democracy (KA 13.7.30; Anaimuthu: 1537).

The brahmin had managed to preserve and draw attention to his essential difference through a simple physical sign which he sported almost nonchalantly: the sacred thread. Commenting on the enormous significance vested in the latter, Periyar once wrote:

> The sacred thread is one of the several markers of caste differences in India... It is considered a sign of a man's achieved maturity. Just as how a child born into one of the so-called depressed classes, even if 'pure' and 'clean' becomes 'impure' as it grows—because it lacks the means to bathe or wear clean clothes—and is, therefore, considered untouchable, so is a brahmin child, though in all respects like other children, considered 'pure' and is believed to attain a so-called high status, soon as he starts to sport a sacred thread. Yet if a child of any other community, that is not of the depressed classes, were to grow up dirty, unwashed and adorned only in rags, yet, it does not acquire a 'depressed' or 'low' status. Likewise such children, even if born and raised in 'purity', come to wear a sacred thread at the right age and appear to be mature, they do not therefore attain an exalted high status. Today, several non-brahmins wear the sacred thread but they continue to be considered shudras and chandalas... those who wear the thread imagine they are of an exalted rank and consider others as being lowly. But in reality,... a

> brahmin, whether he wears a sacred thread or not, considers himself superior, and a depressed classes person, whether 'impure' or not, imagines himself low...Some brahmins profess no faith, either in the sacred thread or the *sandhya* ritual and have abandoned either. Yet, others wear the thread but do not perform the rituals required of them. Either one of them is, however, considered a brahmin, both by brahmins and others (KA 27.12.25).

Periyar makes it clear, that while the sacred thread is a obvious marker of identity, its significance exceeds its form. That is, in itself, the thread has no meaning. Only when a brahmin, already marked 'high' by birth, wears it, does it acquire a certain worth, for now it serves to distinguish him from others. But if others, non-brahmins, were to wear the self-same thread nothing happens, no transmutation of the self occurs; that is, the thread does not represent brahminhood, it only indicates its presence, points to what is there already. Or, as in the case of the non-brahmin who sports the thread, it indicates what is not there, to that which is being assumed and appropriated. In a caste society, as Periyar very well understood, such physical markers of hierarchy and difference signify through being gratuitous. The meaning they attempt to mediate exceeds all modalites of expression, being given, normative and entirely dependent on the accident of birth. Thus a brahmin may or may not wear a sacred thread, yet he will never cease to be a brahmin. Nevertheless, implies Periyar, Brahminism needs its markers to validate in its eyes what is already law, prove, what in its view, is already truth. Through their being ultimately irrelevant, by being there, if only as an expression of the brahmin's whim and power, objects such as the sacred thread came to secrete value in caste society.

Periyar's exposition on the sacred thread was offered in the context of the Arya Samaj's shuddhi ceremonies and at a time when some adi dravida leaders were set on 'upgrading' their lifestyles. Men like Sahajananda of Chidambaram renounced meat eating, took to smearing their foreheads with sacred ash and embraced monkhood. Periyar was convinced that none of these would help advance the emancipation of the adi dravidas, and he saw such measures as perpetrating the very Brahminism they sought to challenge. Drawing on a homely analogy in this regard, he noted: 'If a seer of stones had got mixed in a sack of rice, would we sift the rice grains and separate the stones or would we sift the stones and separate the rice grains?' (KA 27.12.25).

The Self-Respecters identified non-sacral markers of Brah-minism as well and explicated on their relevance and importance for the sustained existence of brahminical hegemony. As far as the Self-Respecters were concerned, the singlemost secular index of brahmin power in these modern times was the newspaper. Writing of the press in Madras in 1925 Periyar observed that the power of the former was such that even if non-brahmins wished to make their point of view known or desired to discuss their concerns, they invariably turned to brahmin-run newspapers and weeklies. The Madras journalist was powerful not only because he shaped public opinion and commonsense, but because he inflected these in particular ways. Thus he was given to inflating tales of brahmin political heroism and sagacity and ignoring all other instances of suffering or success. When V. Bashyam Iyengar suffered violence at the hands of the city police during the second phase of the civil disobedience agitations, the brahmin press and that community's leaders in general made it seem as if the blows that had been laid on Bashyam Iyengar's back 'had reached the skies, rent the oceans and bruised the divine backs of Brahma, Vishnu and Shiva'. But when one Eswaran (he was originally with the Self-Respecters) was beaten, bruised and left alone in a forest, during the civil disobedience agitations, newspapers in Madras had been silent (KA 1.2.31). Writing a few years later in *Samadharmam* (SD), one 'Bandhu' would note that, Congressmen were, likewise, silent when N. Muthuranga Mudaliar was beaten. Bandhu pointed out that Muthuranga Mudaliar was as rich and as much a notable of Madras as Bashyam Iyengar, but, yet, Brahmins had not thought it fit to protest the hurt that was inflicted on him (SD 12.9.34).

The Self-Respecters were determined to make an example of the hue and cry raised over Bashyam Iyengar's hurt, since, to them, this seemed such a patent instance of brahmin exclusivity and clannishness. Their point of view appears entirely reasonable when we consider that in his negotiations with Irwin, Gandhi referred to British repression using the instance of the beating endured by Bashyam Iyengar!

The Self-Respecters were so convinced of the links between the power of the written (newspaper) word and the authority of the brahmins that they began newspapers and weeklies of their own, whenever they could. This was also the reason why Periyar was insistent the Justice party have its own Tamil paper. From as early as 1922, when he was still in the Congress, Periyar entertained thoughts of starting a paper that would reflect what he would later characterize as salient non-brahmin concerns. *Kudi Arasu* began in 1925 was envisaged as such a paper, committed to Self-Respect as much as Swaraj and, in many ways, existed as a sort of nucleus for the constitution and progress of the Self-Respect idea and the movement that was inspired by it.

A Protean Sensibility

Periyar's objections to such efforts at Sanskritization by non-brahmins derived from another of his remarkable insights regarding mobility and status in the caste order. He remarked on several occasions that brahmins retained their privileges by remaining open to change and by adopting a winning flexibility. Thus, however much others attempted to emulate them and literally 'be like them', they proved to be nimble and swift in constructing their hegemony in newer realms and through novel means. This was possible because, as far as there existed a religious code of conduct for brahmins, this was through brahminical interpretations of scripture. Thus brahmins could, and often did, interpret and re-interpret the sacred texts and norms of Hinduism at their will and pleasure. In contrast to Islam and Christianity, those religions of the book, Hinduism lacked a singular sacred text, a founder or prophet and could not really be said to belong to a particular group or community:

> What does it mean to be a Hindu? Other religions refer to themselves through names of persons; hence we speak of the faith of Christ, the God of Mohammed, the Buddhist religion... In this sense to whom does Hinduism belong? Whose doctrines give it a name? Is it not the case that we refer to our religion using a name that is mere sound but which signifies nothing? Secondly, who created Hinduism? How old is it? What proof do we have of its truth? (KA11.9.27; Anaimuthu: 1353).

The utterly vacuous and amorphous character of Hinduism had been redeemed chiefly by its brahmin interlocutors, whom Periyar held, had devised its doctrines and granted it a certain coherence. Thus, Hinduism not only owed its existence to brahminical ingenuity, but enjoyed a varied and protean existence, contingent on place and time and amenable to change at every opportune moment, but only 'in accordance with brahmin power and the gullibility of and the indignity tolerated by non-brahmins'. For Periyar, writing many years later,

> Brahminism and Hinduism are that which work, produce results. Today, brahmins do not mind losing anything, as long as they may claim the status, title and influence which accrue to only the highest caste. To possess this status, they do not mind doing anything, will behave in any which way and yet consider such acts the highest forms of dharma.

Thus,

> Rajaji will eat at a panchama's house; Shankaracharya will bathe on seeing a panchama; some will bathe if a panchama's shadow falls on them, others if a panchama touches them. Yet others will marry a panchama man or woman—but all of them will still remain brahmanas...Brahmin orthodoxy in 1940 was of a different kind than what obtained in 1900. After 1940 this orthodoxy has changed form again (Vi 4.3.69; Anaimuthu:1392).

Writing of this self-same orthodoxy in the late twenties, Kaivalyam had observed:

> The brahmin son would prostrate himself before a [panchama] butler [in service at an Englishman's house] and accept to drink the coffee or soda the latter serves him...The brahmin father, on the other hand, would enjoin panchamas move away and make room for him. The son would reside in a Christian hostel, whereas the father would swear by the tenets of varnadharma. The son would go to medical college and sit down to dine with those very hands he had used to cut up corpses earlier [for his anatomy class]. The father, on the other hand, would not allow anyone to watch him dine.

Yet, father and son would be united in their caste pride and refine and redefine their respective identities to render these worthy of this pride (Kaivalyam: 36).

It is clear that, in their continual reworking of orthodoxy, Brahmins revoked certain traditions, for instance, with respect to their attire and even food, but retained certain others, such as locating norms of conduct and action in the *Manusmriti*. Periyar pointed out that in the present time, given the relentless anti-brahmin propaganda of the Self-Respect movement and the advent of non-brahmins in politics, brahmins had come to realize they needed to defend their exclusivity through other means and in other realms. Otherwise why would those brahmins, who had always disdained to study Tamil or acknowledge its genius and antiquity, seek to celebrate the sixtieth birthday of the Tamil scholar and antiquarian U. V. Swaminatha Iyer? Such brahmins had been loath to accept the work of men such as Swami Vedachalam, Somasundara Bharathy, Namasivaya Mudaliar and others (all non-brahmins), but in recent years had come to praise and extol the work of Tamil brahmin scholars such as Mu. Raghava Iyengar, Swaminatha Iyer and others. This, according to Periyar, was not because they desired to honour Tamil men of learning as such, but because they desired to appropriate the contested site of Tamil studies and establish their dominance there as well. Forced to reckon with challenges in the realm of politics, they had now turned to the cultural sphere to engage it in a fruitful hegemonic relationship. And, as was the usual practice with them, they came to posit their own as learned and great, to the consequent neglect of others who, of course, were non-brahmins (KA 10.3.35).

In the late twenties, Periyar had been critical of brahmin attempts at appropriating all honours in the field of music to themselves. He had, then, argued that non-brahmin musicians were deliberately undervalued, denied respect and honours and humiliated while their brahmin peers, even if younger in years and lacking in talent, had been encouraged by the brahmin press. The Self-Respect movement had taken up the cause of non-brahmin musicians as its own and organized music conferences alongside its own conferences to honour and encourage artistes. Even then Periyar had pointed out that brahmin attempts to dishonour non-brahmin achievements in music were undertaken to render the field of music an arena for the demonstration of a brahmin will to dominance (KA 20.4.30).

To Periyar and the Self-Respecters, the flexibility of brahmins and Brahminism was manifest in all its subtlety in brahmin constructions of the self. When asked, who is a brahmin, brahmins would answer loftily, 'he who controls his mind and leads a righteous life'. But at other times, when the question of identity was not forced on them, they would not remember this dictum and live and act as any other—indulge in falsehood, practise deception and heed their selfish concerns to the detriment of the good of others. But, at all times, whether they identified brahmin worth with good character or with birth and in all instances—as Periyar remarked, 'from the whorehouse to the temple'—they would claim special privileges for themselves (KA 26.8.28; Anaimuthu: 248).

Further, when questioned about their incursions into the profane realm, brahmins would feign disinterest in politics and insist they had no real stake in it. When criticized for their exclusivity, they would throw up their hands in dismay, and ask if the law indeed accorded them special rights. But, as Periyar noted, such assertions flew in the face of facts. For brahmins were keenly political in their intent and they did possess special privileges, as was evident from the observations of the Vedas, Smritis, shastras and even the tenets of Hindu law. Besides, observed Periyar, what about those coffee houses and restaurants reserved for them? Was this an instance of priestly privilege turned to advantage or not? He went on to note:

> When it comes to seeking alms and practising their priestcraft, brahmins feign ignorance of politics, but when it comes to securing high positions for themselves in government, they tell the white man that brahmins alone are eminently suited to man these posts and that they alone qualify as good political leaders and reformers (KA 26.8.28; Anaimuthu: 249).

Political Brahminism

The Self-Respecters were particularly wary and fearful of the secular expressions and transformations, the uses and effects of sacral power; of the political and social dominance exerted in the name of religion and at the behest of an authority derived from birth. As Periyar often noted, the brahmin's resistance to social reform was grounded, less in religious orthodoxy and faith, and more in the political proclivities, intents and ambitions of those, who, whether they lived by it or not, swore by this orthodoxy. While the Self-Respecters were aware that many brahmins (as well as some non-brahmins) held onto norms of caste and practised untoucability in good faith, in the belief that these were practices and principles ordered by divinity, they were nevertheless insensitive to the gross and intentional misuse of faith, the deliberate acts of discrimination and injustice, which many a brahmin, though schooled in Western thought and learned in the scriptures, routinely carried out.

The most complete expression of political Brahminism for Periyar was nationalism. His critique of nationalism possessed many aspects to it, but generally it may be said he pointed at and objected to the religious zeal implicit in professions of nationalism. To him, nationalism signified, first and foremost, an atavistic desire to endow the Hindu past on a more durable and contemporary basis. He observed that in contrast to other 'modern' nations which were striving hard to leave their pasts behind, India held on to its traditions and sought to revive them in all their imagined original glory. Not only were there forums for the safeguarding of varnadharma and disseminating puranic lore, but also these regarded their work as of national importance. There were men who considered it a mark of nationalist self-pride to 'die for their religion, for dharmic norms' and who would actually set up institutes for the advance of theism and claim they were doing so in the 'national' interest. The term 'nationalism' had thus come to acquire a veritable sanctity and invoked in its adherents the same response that words such as 'god', 'salvation' and 'heaven' would kindle in the believer. These specifically religious words had, over time, lent themselves to endlessly flexible interpretations and been used to mesmerize and exploit the gullible. Periyar argued that just as the language and discursive power of religion and faith served to rationalize and justify exploitation in past times, the discourse of nationalism was now being deployed to hide and mystify the play of self-interest, of a trade in ideas and sentiment. (KA 19.5.29; Anaimuthu: 371-72). (We will consider this theme in detail later.)

Periyar's strongest and most pointed critiques of nationalism aimed at its Gandhian inner core, especially, Gandhi's careful and judicious importation of notions of faith and conscience into the political realm and the reconstitution of custom, convention and belief to subserve political ends. To Periyar, Gandhi was the exemplar of political Brahminism and its most sincere and 'therefore' dangerous practitioner.

The Nature of a Critique

Periyar and the Self-Respect movement's understanding of Brahminism and the brahmin's role in caste society was, for the most part, rich in detail and incisive in its analysis. The Self-Respecters understood better than most the symbolism which made Brah-minism a powerful and durable ideology; they grasped its metaphors, the modalities of its expression; the sinuous and slippery language it deployed with felicity and ease. Yet, at times, Periyar and others would seek to characterize Brahminism as a sort of social and cultural conspiracy, hatched by self-seekers and timeservers to their own advantage. Periyar, for instance, would refer to the various ways and means through which brahmins duped, cheated and denied non-brahmins their rights and prevented them from making a honest living; he would speak of the devious strategies employed by brahmins to damn the non-brahmins, should they prove insouciant, outspoken or merely truthful. In such instances, we find Periyar reverting to a caste essentialism: that brahmins could not be otherwise. For instance, while intervening in a court case, where a brahmin judge had passed severe strictures against a non-brahmin collector for undertaking an ostensibly arbitrary action in a land dispute, Periyar remarked that given the composition of the judiciary, which comprised with one or two exceptions only brahmins, and given the fact that public opinion with regard to the case was mediated through *The Hindu* editorials, the condemnation of the collector was to be expected. That is the concerned judge, being a brahmin, could not have acted otherwise, since his religion urged him, in fact, enjoined him to demean and defame shudras. Periyar further noted that people may say he should not thus condemn brahmins as a whole and consider them inherently prejudicial, but, what could he say of a class whose most revered representative and one whose integrity and fame were beyond reproach, Rajagopalachari, maintained his faith in varnadharma—in public—

and expressed his concern that the latter may suffer unprecedented challenges in the days to come?

Periyar's argument was that brahmins, at least in Tamil Nadu, had not said or done anything for non-brahmins to consider them unbiased. On the contrary they had taken extreme umbrage at any and every criticism levelled at them, whether mild or harsh, and had done their best to obstruct and retard the Self-Respect movement and later the Dravidar Kazhagam in their functionings (Vi 23.4.57; Anaimuthu: 270-80).

On the whole, Periyar and the Self-Respecters did not bear any particular ill will towards individual brahmins. As is well known, Periyar cultivated and preserved a lifelong friendship with Rajagopalachari, his arch political foe. But more generally he did not countenance any show of obvious disrespect by his Self-Respecters towards even such men as S. Satyamurthi against whom the Self-Respecters waged a relentless battle, and for whom they reserved their most merciless and biting criticism. When during a certain public meeting addressed by Satyamurthi, Self-Respecters reacted angrily to the latter's hostile and ill-founded description of the Self-Respect movement, Periyar condemned their indignant response. He rebuked them for their lack of rectitude and reminded them they ought to maintain decorum even in the face of the most obnoxious criticism of their actions (Pa 30.12.34).

Nothing illustrates the nature of Periyar's principled anger against brahmins and Brahminism better than the obituary he wrote for Gandhi. Condemning the assassination in the strongest of terms, he went on to observe that there was no point in baying for Godse's blood, since the assassination was but an illustration of the fiendish power of religion. In other words, it was not the individual brahmin, Godse, and his bullet which killed Gandhi, but the political Brahminism that Gandhi so assiduously cultivated and nurtured all his life which claimed him, its most prized victim (Vi 22.2.48; Anaimuthu: 1404-05).

Moments of a Critique

The Self-Respect movement's critique of brahmins and Brahminism was fairly consistent and directed at all times against the secular and sacral expressions of brahmin power. Yet there were shifts in emphasis and in the tenor and intensity of this critique. In the thirties, when the Self-Respect movement preached a militant atheism, criticisms of brahmins and Brahminism were subsumed in a comprehensive critique of religion as such. But the thirties also saw the Self-Respecters and particularly Periyar lash out at political Brahminism, in its conjunctural guise of Congress civil disobedience propaganda. This made for a critical exposition of nationalism as well, which gathered weight and resonance with the anti-Hindi agitations of 1937-39.

The assumption of office by Congressmen after they won the 1937 elections to the provincial assembly proved somewhat of a godsend to the Self-Respecters, for it enabled them to reveal to the public the nature of what they described as 'purohit rule'. The Congress government of Rajagopalachari not only imposed the learning of Hindi on an unwilling Tamil public but came to counter the opposition to this move with a substantial measure of brutality and invoked against the agitators those laws—such as Indian Penal Code 117, 124A, 153A, 505C, Criminal Law Amendment Act, 1932, Section 7—which the colonial government had earlier used against Congressmen! The forties saw a continuation of this critique of nationalism that culminated in Periyar and the Dravidar Kazhagam rejecting the promises held out by 15 August 1947.

Periyar sought to identify the brahminical core of independent India in his painstaking descriptions and interrogations of the proceedings of the Constituent Assembly. He agonized over Dr. Ambedkar's decision to sustain whatever marginal gains he could notch up for the scheduled castes and his consequent neglect of the interests of other backward classes. It culminated finally in Periyar's rejection of the Constitution of India, which he regarded as enabling and legitimizing the persistence of caste (Vi 22.9.51).

Constructing an Alternative

The Self-Respect movement's rejection of Brahminism and its priesthood was not merely negative. This rejection was accompanied by various acts of re-building and re-constituting social and cultural life of Tamil society on radically different foundations. For instance, the movement urged non-brahmins to give up the time honoured habit of seeking brahmin priests to officiate at various family rituals and, for many years, *Kudi Arasu* announced proudly the names of those who had sought to conduct marriage and death rites on their own, without calling a priest.

It is signifcant that Kaivalyam who denounced brahminic funeral rituals invoked, in his discourses on the subject, an ancient Tamil practice—still extant, he claimed in the rites observed by the Vellala Gounders of the Kongu country—who remembered the dead in a wholly different way. On the day of remembrance, the concerned household would invite ten friends of the family, pledge them gifts of food and silk and pray to the household deity. Thereafter, they would feed the crows—in memory of the departed—and dispense food to the needy. Kaivalyam exhorted his fellow non-brahmins to pursue rituals such as these and advised them to get the women of their households to understand the folly and extravagance of feeding brahmin purohits who, anyway, spoke a language of faith which no one, including the priests, really understood (Kaivalyam: 47).

Self-Respecters also called for a boycott of brahmin priests at non-brahmin weddings and instead organized marriages of their own. They came to evolve a simple contractual ritual, where the marriage vows were uttered, either by a community elder, or a Self-Respecter or other distinguished non-brahmins, and were repeated by bride and groom. In several marriages, women served as 'modern' priestesses. Marriages were deliberately conducted during the so-called inauspicious hours and on un-holy days. It was perhaps with respect to the marriage ceremony that the Self-Respect movement scored its greatest victories. For not only did it delink marriage from family and caste honour, but also refused to grant it the status of a sacrament. Most important, the movement arrested a growing tendency among many non-brahmins to replace their own community marriage rituals with brahminical ones.

The ritual dishonouring of non-brahmins and the adi dravidas by brahmins, who denied them access to education and scriptural knowledge on the one hand and forbade them using public tanks, wells and temples on the other, were challenged at every turn by the Self-Respecters. *Kudi Arasu*, as if in defiance of the age-old taboo against the shudras reading the scriptures, carried articles on Itihasas and the Puranas, all of which interrogated and deconstructed the text in question, laying bare its various illogicalities, the perversities such texts usually upheld in matters of sexuality and women, and the questionable character and motives of the divine protagonists of any particular text. Periyar himself wrote many such articles, Gurusamy mimicked the solemn tone adopted by expositors of puranic lore in his efforts at parodying their art, and many others displayed great wit and sarcasm in recounting and exposing to public scorn and entertainment the various absurdities contained in the scriptures—the absurdities of character, events and morals.

The movement's most studied challenge to Brahminism was that embodied in the various temple-entry agitations it pioneered. For Periyar and the Self-Respecters, temple-entry was a significant right that had to be won and retained by the adi dravidas, since, as Periyar often argued, the temple was the locus of the brahmin's authority and it was in its hallowed precincts that his sole rights to priesthood were effectively upheld and denied to others. To Periyar such a right, as upheld by the brahmins, was not sustainable anymore, not merely because it had provoked adverse attention and objections, but also because the temple had literally become a public place. At times, Periyar argued that temples as houses of God ought to be open to all, especially if one believed God to be kind, benign and fair-minded. But more often than not, he considered the adi dravidas' rights to enter temples represented strategic civil, rather than religious, concerns. His interest in temple-entry derived from his conviction that rights such as these and others, which had to be claimed and won by adi dravidas and other marginal social segments, were universal and inalienable. As he noted, he did not imagine adi dravidas (or others) would gain materially or even spiritually by entering temples and offering worship there. Yet they had to stake and realize their claims to enter and use a public space. As he reminded the adi dravidas, their labour had made the very existence of temples possible, while the endowments of non-brahmins had ensured their survival (KA 22.11.25; Anaimuthu: 1506).

For Periyar, the right to enter temples was a step forward in the struggle of non-brahmins and the adi dravidas for self-respect. This right contained within itself other rights which may also be rightfully claimed by non-brahmins and the adi dravidas:

> If one has the right to enter the temple, does not one have the right to worship God? If one had the right to worship God does one not

> have the right to break coconuts in front of the deity and offer it fruits? (KA 13.2.27; Anaimuthu: 1507).

It was another matter that Periyar as well as other Self-Respecters, such as Gurusamy, who were in the forefront of temple-entry struggles also simultaneously reminded non-brahmins and the adi dravidas of the uselessness of faith and the folly of worship. The final assault on Brahminism required more than an appropriation of symbols and claiming of forbidden rights and honours. Brahminism, with all its cunning, protean ways of being, had to be consciously renounced and this meant, either the acceptance of a religious world-view that was consistent and rational and committed to securing for all men and women a life of self-respect and dignity, or it required the practice of atheism. If one were to choose the first option, the religions one could possibly adopt were Buddhism and Islam. For both these religions, in their own ways, were antithetical to Brahminism. Islam with its power of community and notions of equality, and Buddhism with its doctrines of love and its repudiation of caste and brahminic ritual, were considered by Periyar as serious alternatives to Brahminism. The one would help consecrate a fraternity of peoples; for if an adi dravida were to convert to Islam he or she would immediately become one of the faithful and, hence, would be defended and protected from opponents at all times (KA 2.8.31; Anaimuthu: 1379). The other would instil in the believer a rational, egalitarian world-view and enable him to question and think matters out for himself (Vi 19.4.56; Anaimuthu: 307).

Atheism as propounded by the Self-Respecters signified a critical openness; a refusal to be bound by dogma or principle and a desire to accept nothing and be sure of nothing. Atheism would thus allow for a critical and vigilant engagement with the world and history, and in this regard represented the very opposite of Brahminism, which, too, was alive to changes in space and time, but which always sought to adapt and re-mould its priorities to the advantage of the brahmin and for the singular objective of confirming him in his exclusivity.

Since Periyar understood Brahminism as a protean ideology that was active in one instance as a political option, and present in several other instances as belief, ritual, tradition, in short, as an aspect of commonsense, he envisaged the struggles against it as taking place at different levels. As he remarked, the enemies of Self-Respect had a greater opportunity for propagating their ideas. 'Temples, Puranas, art, festivals, religious discourses, bhajans, conventions, school education, textbooks facilitate the communication of reactionary ideas easily and without anyone having to put in any particular effort.' Besides, there were 'those stupendously rich religious institutions' with 'their host of lazy and jobless vagrants' who helped spread the brahminic creed (KA 9.12.28; Anaimuthu: 329).

It is not surprising, then, that Periyar explicitly delinked matters of civil, religious and social import from the political realm and insisted struggles over these issues had very little to do with the struggle against the white man or with the attainment of nationalism. These were matters that were specific to caste Hindu society and had to be addressed as such. In later years, following the anti-Hindi agitations of 1937-39, Periyar and the Self-Respecters envisaged their struggle against Brahminism, whether in its political guise or otherwise, as a struggle for a new community, rather than a polity. This community was described as a samadharmic society, where rights, claims and responsibilities would be equal, and where there existed a measure of shared public or community experience. Further, this society would be distinguished from the brahminic caste order by its civilizational and cultural difference. Thus, it would be 'Dravidian' in its ethos and animated by a desire to build a world free of caste. The term 'Dravidian', while the opposite of Aryan, also signified an openness, an acceptance within its fold of all those who consented to the destruction of caste and who wished to found a rational egalitarian order. Thus Dr. Ambedkar claimed, after a meeting with Periyar in 1944, that the idea of Dravidasthan was, in reality, applicable to the entire subcontinent, since Brahminism was a problem which afflicted India as a whole (KA 30.9.44). Periyar, in turn, expressed similar views in his discussions with the Hindu Mahasabha leader, Moonje (KA 7.10.44).

RELIGION AS WORLD-VIEW

The Self-Respect movement understood religion in its broadest sense to represent a world-view, an ethos or informing principle which mediated the individual and the community's perceptions of everyday reality and which structured their attitudes and responses to matters ranging from art, literature and music on the one hand to sexuality, work and labour on the other. For Periyar and the Self-Respecters, it was not so much what a particular religion meant or what were considered its founding principles that mattered; they were concerned essentially with religion as social practice and with religion as ideology:

> Do not imagine that when I talk about Hinduism or Islam, I talk after having examined their 'truth claims'. Leave that to a student taking his exams. I am not concerned with what is actually present in these religions. I talk of the manifest ideas and related practices that a majority of the practitioners of religions indulge and of the manifest gains that accrue to them as a result of these religious practices (KA 2.8.31; Anaimuthu: 1375).

Periyar was inclined to consider Hinduism, rather than Islam or Christianity, as embodying in itself and in its various practices an entire way of being that directed its adherents to think and act in particular ways. Thus, whether they were actors in the political realm or in the social sphere, whether they were concerned with particular problems, arising out of the contingent, or worried about problems of a more universal nature, such as to do with faith and knowledge, Hindus were clearly influenced by their religion. It determined what they ate, how they dressed, whom they married, their choice of a profession, their relationships with each other, their behaviour in public places, their political choices, their modes of worship, in short, a religious sensibility was manifest in the Hindu's each and every actions. Religion was fundamental to the very organization of caste society and had to be viewed not merely in terms of beliefs, faith and the succour it offered to the believer, but in terms of its material quotidian existence (KA 9.11.46; Anaimuthu: 1197-98).

It was because Hinduism constituted an entire ethos that religions radically different from it, and even opposed to it in certain aspects, such as Islam and Christianity, had come to be affected by its power. Thus Christianity in India had come to exist in tandem with caste (KA 19.5.29; Anaimuthu: 1369; Velu: 235). Islam had managed to retain its antithetical character, but particular practices of Islam, the various festivals, forms of worship and blind devotion to tradition, which characterized its existence in India, were clearly the result of its engagement with an all pervasive Hindu ethos (KA 9.8.31; Anaimuthu: 1379).

The Self-Respecters argued that not merely other religions, but even ideologies that were patently non-religious, assumed, in the Indian context, a religious resonance, as with nationalism; or if they happened to be anti-religious, like socialism, were upheld by those who continued to observe caste and religious norms. The Self-Respect movement was never tired of pointing to the example of Jawaharlal Nehru who, for all his fiery agnosticism and verbal adherence to socialism, yet performed, wearing a sacred thread, as befitting the brahmin that he was, the last rites, as demanded by his religion, for his father (KA 29.5.32). In 1938-39, when the socialists in keeping with their pro-Congress policy, opposed the anti-Hindi agitations in Madras, several articles were written in *Kudi Arasu* and other Self-Respect journals on the compromises essayed by the socialists in their dalliance with Congress and nationalism. In one such article it was pointed out that, at least, as far as the Madras Presidency was concerned, the socialists had managed to accomplish the near impossible and grotesque feat of reconciling a religious world-view with their vision for an egalitarian free society:

> In Madras one may count on the fingers of one's hand the number of socialists who have actually renounced religion; one would have to really search hard for those socialists who have abandoned caste. Among the socialists here are many who fear their caste norms would be violated, if they were to merely snip away at their 'sacred' tuft; there are yet others who fear their religiosity would suffer, were they not to smear their foreheads with sacred ash. Then there are those socialists who consider themselves highborn and sport a sacred thread (KA 5.2.39).

The critique of religion as world-view was inflected in particular ways, depending on the specific objective, as well as intent of the critique. In such instances as music, where, as mentioned earlier, the Self-Respecters were sharply critical of the play of caste in determining the quantum of respect paid to a musician, they would target such things as tone of voice and gesture, as being emblematic of an inherently flawed world-view, underwritten by religious custom. Thus Periyar would point out how non-brahmin musicians, however advanced in age and talent they may be, were expected to assume subservient postures in front of and speak in hushed tones to their patrons; how a brahmin vocalist, even if he were a mere child, would treat his non-brahmin fellow musicians with contempt and condescend to bless them, as it were, by languidly raising his left hand in a barely visible gesture; how the brahmin press and audience were given to systematically ignoring non-brahmin performers (KA 20.4.30).

In criticizing literature, more specifically Tamil literature, the movement was wont to dwell on other details: Periyar would note, for instance, that this literature, though inexorably religious in content, failed even as exemplum, because the morality enjoined by the Puranas was objectionable. For instance, in the story of the Paraiah saint Nandan, the latter ultimately burns in a purifying fire, but while he is thus etherealized, his untouchability survives, inflicting his fellow Paraiahs (Pa 16.9.34; Anaimuthu: 1283). In another context, commenting on temple paintings, Periyar remarked that these puranic themes may be seen for what they are, in all their irrelevance, if one were to compare them to Western realist art that is true to life, self-explanatory and bound to a place, a context, in short, to a history (KA 26.4.31; Anaimuthu: 1271).

S. Ramanathan, referring to puranic texts observed that criticisms of the aesthetic value of these texts were often mediated through explicatory theories and philosophies that expounded symbolic meanings for any and everything: for statues, numbers, trees, rivers. Puranic heroes were shown to be repositories of particular qualities and attributes and were often mere formal expressions of specific and singular emotions and ideas. Referring to the devadasi system, Ramanathan wondered if one could not have systems of music and dance that were not implicated in a system of sanctified debauchery: 'If Indian culture is dependant for its growth on our temples and Puranas, it is best that our arts are destroyed.' Ramanathan observed that above all he desired to see the dawning of an era of realist aesthetics, completely free of religious fervour (KA 12.4.31).

Writing in a similar vein and four years later, a Self-Respecter observed of the new art of cinema that, while in the West, cinema signified a fruition of that culture's growth into intelligence, progress and confidence and represented their spirit of relentless endeavour and rationality, in India, cinema had come to serve as yet another modality for the expression of a religious world-view. Films were thus replete with puranic themes, chiefly Hindu in character and it was small wonder that Muslims had objected to the cinematic version of Sant Ramdas. Besides, if tales such as those of Nandan, were reproduced for a large audience, these were bound to confirm the deprived adi dravidas in their lowliness, so to speak. For the film screen would not merely return to them unflattering images of themselves, but would actually facilitate the reification of such images. At a time when adi dravidas were fighting for rights to temple-entry—Ranga Iyer's bill was still fresh in public memory—it was surely not right to portray Nandan as burning in front of a deity:

> Does it mean that just as the philosophy of socialism is invoked by socialists [the writer has in mind the members of the Congress Socialist party] to justify the deferral of the question of temple-entry, that, henceforth, a baptism of fire would be deemed an essential ritual before adi dravidas could enter temples? (KA 30.6.35)

Apart from such imprecations against the religious sensibility as such, Self-Respecters also undertook to challenge and destroy completely, if this was indeed possible, the rule of this sensibility in public life. The Third Self-Respect Provincial Conference held at Virudhunagar in 1931 explicitly committed itself to the abolition of religion and even passed a resolution to this effect. This was mainly due to the Congress' resolution at its Karachi conference, where it was declared that in independent India the freedom of various people to observe and practise their faith would be honoured and that no attempt would be made by Congress to impose regulations on the populace in matters of belief and practice. But the Virudhunagar conference reflected other anxieties as well.

The first phase of Congress Civil Disobedience campaign, which reached a nadir with Gandhi's salt satyagraha agitations, had revealed to the Self-Respecters the power and appeal of religious motifs and sentiments in a society that was largely illiterate. Further, within the Self-Respect movement itself, atheism as a viable, communicable creed was being upheld and propounded with enthusaism by men such as Gurusamy. In a series of articles written for the paper *Puduvai Murasu* (PM), published from Pondicherry, Gurusamy criticized and mocked the religious pretensions of nationalism, the dangers inherent in the Gandhian creed with its admixture of religion and politics and, more important, upheld the Self-Respecters' right to propagate atheism. Responding to an unnamed editorial in a local magazine, that had called for a destruction of the Self-Respect movement, Gurusamy remarked that if the corrosive and poisonous core of Hindu society were to be destroyed, then, automatically, the Self-Respect movement would cease to exist. But this required, among other things, the discarding of the religious world-view:

> It should be seen that people cease being concerned about God. All religions should be destroyed at their roots. Temples, churches, mosques should be converted into either schools or factories. Not a single paise should be spent on religion. Varnashrama, caste, notions of high and low must be destroyed. The Puranas, Vedas, Agamas, songs in praise of god, religious texts, Vedantic texts—all these should be destroyed as well.

After outlining the need for widespread education, equality and justice, Gurusamy went on to enumerate various other things he would like to see destroyed: 'Astrology... Palmistry... Festivals... religious mutts, funeral obsequies... atavism... notions of heaven and hell, ghosts, phantoms, sorcery... religious and caste symbols' (PM 2.2.31; Velu: 255-57).

Besides such programmatic statements, the papers of the Self-Respect movement also carried, during this period, in fact throughout the thirties and even after, articles on the atheistic way of life in the Soviet Union and projected this as an alternative to a life informed by a religious world-view. It was also during this time that the claims of Islam as an alternative to Hinduism were advanced and endorsed by the Self-Respecters, especially Periyar. In the early thirties, when Gandhi and Congress were keen on 'representing' the adi dravidas and other depressed classes, and in coopting them into the gigantic caste Hindu family, the Self-Respect movement opposed this stealthy but clever political ruse and prevailed upon adi dravidas to consider conversion to Islam, if only to falsify and prove hollow Gandhi's claim that adi dravidas too were Hindus.

Religious sensibility was attacked in specific instances as well, as when Gandhi was assassinated and, earlier, during the anti-Hindi agitations, when criticizing the Rajagopalachari government as exercising 'purohit rule', Self-Respecters drew attention to the essentially religious nature of the mindset which would thus seek to quell the agitations. The Self-Respecters argued that in order to counter the influence of their movement, which was fast gaining ground, the Congress government of Rajagopalachari had sought to smuggle religion into the lives of the people through the imposition of an Aryan-brahmin language, Hindi (KA 15.5.38; Anaimuthu: 1766).

Periyar's resistance to religion as world-view, to the fundamental religious substratum of all experience and activity in Hindu society, represented a consistent challenge to the way Hindus lived, thought and acted. This rejection of a religious ethos went beyond atheism, beyond disavowals of divinity, and asked for nothing less than a complete remaking of the Hindu consciousness, for a re-fashioning of Hindu subjectivity. Whether partial, insconsistent or amorphous, any and every attempt at such a remaking was hailed by the Self-Respecters as a significant move forward in the evolution of a politically sound 'good' sense in Hindu society. Non-brahmin theists, atheists, Self-Respecters, anti-Aryan Dravidianists, Buddhists, Muslims, Christians (who had given up caste)—all of these, in one way or another, were encouraged in their efforts at transforming the Hindu mindset. Likewise, organizations and parties professing different aims, won the Self-Respecters', more specifically, Periyar's approval, if they challenged, in however, mild a manner, a Hindu view of life: the Justice party, the socialists, the Tamil Nadu Congress under Kamaraj's leadership, even J. Krishnamurthy, were all, at one time or another, hailed as allies in this respect.

The rejection of religion as world-view by the Self-Respecters was somewhat tempered by the writings and ideas of men like Kaivalyam, who were themselves keen scholars of scripture, and who felt it necessary to separate the wisdom contained in the Vedas and Brahmanas from the lore of the brahmin priesthood, which comprised chiefly puranic texts and elaborate and complicated moral codes. Periyar was aware of the uses of such a stance as assumed by critical religionists such as Kaivalyam. As he explained in his introduction to a collection of Kaivalyam's articles, all of which had appeared orignally in *Kudi Arasu*, Kaivalyam's learning and undoubted scholarship helped fortify the Self-Respecters' commonsensical observations with respect to religious texts, customs, practices and priests (Kaivalyam: 3-14).

Kaivalyam, even as he wrote regularly for *Kudi Arasu*, refused to abandon his essentially spiritual world-view, but endowed it with a certain social worth. Thus, for him, the practice of true faith required the practitioner to eschew prejudice, hatred and all notions of high and low. Kaivalyam was insistent on distinguishing and rescuing a true religious core out of the dross that had come to pass off as the Hindu faith for some centuries now. He was convinced such inquiries into religion would make for the emergence of a genuine religious sensibility and one that would encourage rather than retard the material and mental progress of non-brahmins (ibid: 14951). In an article on the duties required of the devout, Kaivalyam argued that the devout ought to prove their worth, not through acts and rituals of obeisance and penance to the Gods and their priests, but by exercising their minds to probe into the complexities of action and duty. These latter were to be understood, not as abstract virtues, but in the context of the individual's responsibilities to the society he or she lived in. Interestingly enough, Kaivalyam drew upon the karma yoga doctrines of the Bhagavad Gita to exhort non-brahmins to act on their own spiritual and moral initiative rather than heed the advice of a selfish priesthood (ibid: 113-14).

CRITIQUE OF SCRIPTURE: PURANAS, ITIHASAS AND THE EPICS

The Self-Respect movement's diatribes against the sacred texts of Hinduism were shot through with a certain recklessness of language and analysis. Irreverent and subversive, earnest and indignant in turn, the criticisms of the Puranas and the Itihasas proceeded along two intertwined axes. One read these texts as manifest testimonies to a thoroughly barbaric and debauched culture and civilization, whose depravity was abundantly evident in the sexual mores these preached, in tales of divine birth and marriage and in their constructions of womanhood, invariably demeaning and humiliating, if considered from a woman's point of view. The other interpretative model, while linked by virtue of its concerns with the first, yet, proceeded along its own trajectory: it chose to read the puranic tales as tales of war and conquest, waged between invading Aryan brahmins and the local Dravidians.

Of the Itihasas, the *Ramayana* was singled out for attack. Cong-ress nationalism, after Gandhi, had rendered the Ramayana emblematic of all that was wise and valorous in ancient India. Gandhi himself spoke of future India as an anticipated Ramrajya and, in his writings and addresses, resorted to metaphors and analogies drawn from the epic to illustrate or explicate an idea. The Self-Respect movement's earliest criticisms of the epic were voiced first in the late twenties, when Chandrasekhara Pavalar began a series of essays in *Kudi Arasu* on the problems of meaning and value in the epic. But the hostility towards Rama was muted because he had not yet attained the cultic status of a national hero then. Thus, Kaivalyam in one of his articles, would image divine grace in the Rama who befriended Guha. And, Periyar writing of the epic in 1928, was merely content to note that several versions of the tale existed and that the morality enjoined by Valmiki's text could at best be considered arbitrary and contingent. But it must be pointed out that, as early as 1922, Periyar demanded at the Congress conference in Tiruppur, that the *Ramayana* be burnt, since it contained several degrading references to shudras and explicitly condemned the shudra, Shambukha, to death for having dared perform a penance (Vi 30.7.56; 17.8.56; 13.9.56; Anaimuthu: 1842-43; 1455).

Subsequently, the earlier leniency with respect to Rama was abandoned and the Self-Respecters came to advance a virulent and angry denunciation of the epic, especially during the thirties. But even then, men like Kaivalyam were oblique in their criticisms. In an article, informed by a delightful play of irony, Kaivalyam observed that the *Ramayana* held no lessons for modern times because the morals it spoke of were meant to be realized by Gods in mortal guise and, as such, could not be emulated by the merely human souls of the present era. Besides, noted Kaivalyam, the morals preached by the epic were clearly contradictory. For, while Parashurama was directed by his father to kill his mother, Rama accepted banishment on the plea of one who was not even his natural mother. In this day and age, the first act would be deemed criminal, while the second was clearly a matter of state concern. In fact, British jurisprudence and imperial authority would explicitly forbid the pursuit of many of the practices found in the Itihasas. If, today, a king of a princely state were to abdicate his responsibilities, imperial authority would prevail upon him to act in a manner it considered just and right. If, today, a man were to abduct a woman who was married to another, British law would take care of him. Such were the powers vested in His Majesty's minions and, in view of the extraordinary power he wielded, wrote Kaivalyam, it would only be fair to consider King George an avatar of Mahavishnu, and abide by the rules he had outlined and not seek to invoke the moral codes of a dim, distant past! (Kaivalyam: 164-71)

Commenting on the Self-Respecters' animosity towards the *Ramayana*—and writing in a totally different vein—Gurusamy observed in 1929:

> The evils of present-day Hindu society draw nourishment from the teaching of the *Ramayana*. Caste, untouchability, suppression of women, husband worship, brother worship and every other impediment to progress have their origin within the crevices of the epic's edifice...Our young men will not learn to sacrifice at the altar of Rama. They will not follow the example of Rama, worship their father and abandon their country. The teaching of *Ramayana* therefore is a menace to Indian nationalism. The patriot should protect the masses from the nefarious influence of the Itihasas and save the children of the land from being lead astray by the debasing doctrines which undermine national life.

Objecting to the privileging of the *Ramayana* as a quasi-national myth, and to the various attempts that were being undertaken in the present time to posit Rama as a hero for all seasons and cultures in the subcontinent, Gurusamy remarked:

> It is often said that we should retain the good things in the *Ramayana* and eschew the bad. We do not desire to be unnecesarily offensive and would gladly undertake the task were it possible. Let us illustrate our difficulty. Rama killed a 'shudra' for the sin of having dared to perform religious austerities to which only the twice-born were entitled. The defender of the *Ramayana* ejaculates, 'This incident may have been authentic but my Rama never did it.

> I feature to myself a Rama who was not of such inhumanity'. We are willing to venture on a process of elimination of such incidents in the story, if there were a possibility of a skeleton of the main plot surviving a process of such wholesale operations. There is no such possibility (R 13.2.29; Velu: 139-40).

In contrast to those who upheld the liberative and inspiring lessons the *Ramayana* purportedly offered to the modern Hindu, the Self-Respecters set about systematically to desconstruct the epic. They worked with English translations, sometimes with the original text, compared the latter and Kamban's Ramayanam, discussed the non-canonical versions of *Ramayana*, undertook analyses of characters, motifs, plot—in short, they produced meticulously argued and well-informed criticisms; some of which mimicked the style of expositors of the Itihasas, who were wont to give impromptu oral recitals of the tale and who often produced ingenious variations on the original story. Periyar was particularly good at thus capturing the tone and the style of the 'harikatha' exponent and his articles on the *Ramayana*, for the better part, communicate their subversive intent through the sheer parodic energy that sustains his text. The parody worked at several levels: it produced for the reader a bland set of observations, facts culled from the epic, and either left the reader to draw her own conclusions from these, or appended a commentary that 'demystified' character and denounced the morality of the tale.

Thus, in an article on Valmiki's Sita, Periyar gathered from the epic, references to Sita as wife and mother, and asked his readers to determine, if the picture which emerged out of these references was indeed the woman Valmiki meant to uphold as the chaste, ideal wife or if she was not just another character in a plot, that narrated the story of people who were really ordinary and as vulnerable to folly, prejudice, sin and error as anyone else. Periyar's argument in this instance, of course, left one in no doubt as to what he imagined Sita to have been: she emerged in his narrative as a less than exemplary heroine and was shown to be human, all too flawed and inconstant. For she rebukes Rama, is defiant at the moment of the Fire test and leaves him to bear her children alone in the forest (Vi 13.1.51; Anaimuthu: 1444-50). Thus, not only was Sita relieved of the aura which attaches to the silent, suffering wife, but Valmiki's text was also shown to be less a moral fable and more a story in the manner of the *Arabian Nights*. Periyar in fact compares it to the *Arabian Nights*! (Vi 5.11.48; Anaimuthu: 1460).

What did the Self-Respecters' object to exactly in the *Ramayana*? Periyar, in his reading, 'inverted' the epic such that Vali, Kaikeyi, Ravana, Mandodari (and the rakshasas in general) were hailed as righteous, while Dasaratha, Rama, Lakshmana, Hanuman and Bharatha were damned. Dasaratha was berated for his entourage of 60,000 wives and for having broken his promise to Kaikeyi. Rama was shown to be the very antithesis of a hero: he was shown to be not really righteous, merely circumspect and cunning; he gave into Bharatha's claims, only when he knew he had no choice. Further, Rama's monogamous intents were queried, his claims to being an ideal son interrogated and his affection for his brothers criticized, because if he really trusted to brotherly love, why did he set brother against brother in the case of Sugriva and later Vibishana? On the other hand, Vali's bravery, Kaikeyi's presence of mind, Ravana's rule and Mandodari's love for her husband were commended (KA 18.12.43; 8.1.44; 15.1.44; Anaimuthu: 1433-41) For Periyar, writing on the epic in the forties, the *Ramayana* was an 'Aryan' text, a fit testimony to the vulgar, depraved culture of the Aryans. But it was a text which was also history, for the victory of Rama over the rakshasas signified an Aryan conquest. The rakshasas, Periyar was convinced, were indigenes, Dravidians, who were lured into war by the Aryans, who used Sita as a bait to draw out and destroy Ravana (KA 20.9.47; Anaimuthu: 1441-44).

What seems particularly problematic in Periyar's reading of the *Ramayana* is his handling of the character of Sita. In his eagerness to deny the worth of the ideal—of the chaste, loyal *pativrata* —Sita had come to represent, he dwells at length, in fact, devotes a great deal of his critical attention to Sita's 'origins', her sexuality and character. This, at times, borders on the prurient.

As far as other epics were concerned, the Self-Respecters' criticisms were limited to particular sorts of critique. Men like Gurusamy were given to mocking the Tamil Puranas, especially those that narrated the life histories of the Saivite men of piety. Saivites claimed their faith owed nothing to brahminical Hinduism and held the Saiva Siddhantha to be a wholly local philosophical system that was distinctive from both the Advaitic and Vedantic schools of thought. But Gurusamy (and Periyar) considered such a position anomalous and untenable. Thus, Periyar and others would mock at canonical Saivite texts such as *Kandapuranam, Thirutondar Puranam* and *Periyapuranam* and would mercilessly interrogate these tales for their illogicality, absurdities and falsehood.

Gurusamy not only wrote of these texts in his usual satiric and vituperative fashion, but took to attending conferences convened by the Saivite faithful, where he would ask questions, advance audacious explanations and seek to disrupt conference proceedings (Velu: 357-62). Gurusamy was given to parodying the pietistic and solemn tone of Saivites, such as Kalyanasundara Mudaliar, who were drawn to the Self-Respect creed but felt clearly embarrassed and perturbed by its adherents' atheism and irreverence. When Kalyanasundara Mudaliar objected to Periyar's atheistic and anti-brahmin speeches, Gurusamy took it upon himself to defend his mentor. In a style that mimicked Kalyanasundara Mudaliar's mannered discourse, Gurusamy wrote back a fitting reply that pointed out the differences which existed between the epics of other nations and the epics which were held dear by the Hindus. Regarding the Hindu epics Gurusamy observed, 'Nowhere except in India are the epics an obstacle in the path of social progress' (KA 8.7.28; Velu: 100-01).

There existed another dimension to the Self-Respecters' critique of the Puranas: one that was gendered in its approach as well as its concerns. Periyar, for instance, selected for ridicule certain notions of feminine worth and honour that were to be found in the Puranas. He thus came to query the moral pretensions of the five satis whom puranic lore considered exemplary: Tara, Ahalya, Sita, Draupadi and Mandodari. His expositions of their 'true' morality served not merely to demystify them, but also called into question their essential integrity (KA 11.12.27; Anaimuthu: 1473-77), As with his critique of Valmiki's Sita, his comments in this instance seem somewhat problematic: for one thing, it is not clear whether Periyar wishes to denounce the Aryans' claims to moral superiority or, whether he is critical of Aryan notions of womanhood. However this may be, in his critique, the chaste (or unchaste) status of the Aryan puranic heroine becomes symbolic of the decay that had eaten into (or was inherent in) the core of Aryan civilization and culture. This concern with the sexually depraved element in Aryan culture got written into other contexts as well: as when Periyar dwelt on the 'vulgar' content of the Puranas. Here, he detailed the various instances of licit and illicit love, of love that is taboo and love that is 'unnatural', such as that of Narada for Vishnu, of Brahma for his daughter (Vi 14.5.90; 19.4.52; Anaimuthu: 1499-1501).

This insistence on condemning the Puranas for their tales of explicit lust, incest and perversity spawned an entire tradition of critique that revelled in thus 'exposing' the various Hindu epics to a public, which, in turn, was drawn to listen to these outpourings of an imagination that was part subversive and part prurient. Herein we may discern a curious politics of sexuality, where the concern over woman's status in caste society is expressed in and through expressions of horror at deviant love, practised by the Gods, for which the women in question, being Aryan, are blamed. But one must note in this context that Periyar's criticisms of the puranic heroines was extended to folk figures such as Nallathangal—the quintessential suffering wife of Tamil lore—as well. The uses of chastity as expressed and urged through such tales, argued Periyar, were not only spurious but irrelevant. For what did Nallathangal achieve for all that suffering, sacrifice and pain? Did her chastity being her happiness or help her in preserving her and her children's lives? Or consider Savithri's feat, as it was extolled by the Puranas: is a woman to be tested for her chastity, thus? Does she have to fight Death to prove her virtues? Does it therefore mean that women who let their husbands die are unchaste? (Anaimuthu: 1480)

Periyar (and the Self-Respecters') objections to the Puranas were of course directed against the actions and practices of non-brahmins who seemed so eager to accept, on faith, these fabulous tales as their own and who expended vaste sums of money in remembering them through song, dance, play and performance. (Anaimuthu: 1480-81). Periyar produced extremely creative readings of the puranic godheads to indicate to his non-brahmin readers the implicit content of the tales and symbols associated with them. Thus, writing of the ten avatars of Vishnu, he suggested that the tale of each of these avatars represented a crucial moment in the Aryan-Dravidian conflict. Referring to Matsya, Narasimha and Varaha, he noted that in the first instance the Asuras (the Dravidians) attempt to 'hear' the Vedas and to destroy them, and Vishnu donned the guise of a giant fish. In the second instance,

Hiranya was attacked and killed for being anti-brahmin, anti-vedic and a spoiler of yagnas. In the third instance, the Asuras had managed to defeat the Devas (the Aryans), and hence the tale of the boar that spirited away the earth, for to the Aryan brahmins, their defeat signifed nothing less than a loss of the whole world! (Vi 20.12.58; Anaimuthu: 1336-38). More generally Periyar placed Puranas and Itihasas within an evolutionary-historic logic. The *Sivapurana* and *Kandapurana* were considered narratives of physical conquest of the Dravidians by the Aryans, while the *Ramayana* was shown to represent the intellectual conquest of the indigenes through Aryan brahmin scheming and cunning (Anaimuthu: 1485-91).

The Self-Respecters' critique of scripture was influenced considerably by the insistence of Islam and Christianity on their own historicity. These religions possessed origin tales, definitive texts and codified laws and stood in stark contrast to Hinduism that was formless, vacuous and bereft of founding fathers and, more significantly, a sense of history. It was not that the Self-Respecters held that historicity and codified laws redeemed Islam and Christianty in themselves. As we have noted earlier, they did direct their critical attention to these religions as well. But Hinduism was their chief target, convinced as they were, that it directed, justified and encouraged all those obnoxious and repressive practices characteristic of caste society.

CRITIQUE OF RELIGION AS DOCTRINE

The strictures and imprecations uttered against varnadharma were not only numerous but expressed in several Self-Respect forums by both men and women. Unlike Gandhi and the Arya Samajists who were wont to re-define and humanize varnadharma, the Self-Respecters chose to demand its complete destruction. They were convinced that varnadharma could not be construed to mean a mere division of labour. Firstly, even if one may presume varnadharma in its original days referred to functional divisions in work and did not connote notions of high and low, in later years, it had come to sanction differences and hierarchy amongst peoples on the basis of an individual's birth. Secondly, as Periyar argued, even the idea of thus assigning particular work to particular groups was problematic and arbitrary since one could choose 'to be a carpenter by day, a merchant in the evening and a teacher by night' (KA 11.1.31; Anaimuthu: 1602). Thirdly, varna divisions now possessed the sanction of religion, of texts such as the Bhagavad Gita and unless these texts were declared irrelevant and pernicious, varnadharma would continue to represent and justify notions of high and low derived from birth (KA 28.7.35; Anaimuthu: 1603).

What the Self-Respecters found most distasteful about varnadharma doctrine was the privileges it accorded brahmins, however mean of temperament and vicious in their practice they may be. The supremacy granted to the brahmin, as Kaivalyam argued, demanded and was, in fact, enabled by the subordination required of non-brahmins and panchamas. Believers might argue and point to any number of examples from puranic lore to indicate how, many a time, non-brahmin piety and bhakthi had triumphed over the learning and wisdom of brahmin priests and spiritual leaders: They would thus point to the stories of Nandan and Kannappan (lower caste bhakthins who were redeemed in their lowness by the love they bore for Siva), to the incident of Siva and Parvathi appearing as Pallas (a Tamil untouchable caste) to bless the brahmin devotee Sundara; they would refer to the time when Siva appeared as a chandala to teach the great Adi Shankara a lesson; Vaishnavites would point to the example of Ramanuja who declared the secret of the scriptures from atop a temple tower. But, argued Kaivalyam, none of these instances altered or reformed priestly behaviour or the rules of caste society. Siva might choose to represent himself as a Palla but the fact remained that Pallas, to this day, were not allowed anywhere near the precincts of a temple. Brahmins in spite of Ramanuja guarded their sacral books jealously and, worse, interpreted them as it pleased them, thus mystifying meaning and obfuscating the minds of the devout (Kaivalyam: 138-40).

Kaivalyam, Periyar and Gurusamy and others took great pains to explain that the term 'shudra' denoted a 'son of a slave', that according to the great sages of yore, it referred to one who revelled in Untruth and Violence and was *tamasaic* in temperament and therefore a prey to desire, greed and passion. But in spite of being labelled thus, the shudras of the Tamil country had continued to assent to a faith that demeaned them. The Saivites who considered their faith indigenous to the Tamil country and who tried to elevate themselves as 'sat shudras' had lent ideological credence to brahminical Hinduism, though they claimed the contrary. Their worship of Siva and the philosophy of faith they defined as Saivism allowed non-brahmins to trust to the illusion that they possessed a religion and spirituality of their own which could be advanced as a counter to brahminical Hinduism. Periyar, Gurusamy and C. D. Nayagam were unrelenting in their attacks on the Saivites, since they believed that this sort of an internalized oppression, revered as faith, was most damaging to non-brahmin morale and self-respect.

Kaivalyam too challenged the Saivite non-brahmins to re-examine their religion, but being a believer, his criticisms were of a different order. He entreated them to rid themselves of superstitions and brahminical influences and practise a creed that was inspired by the famous spiritual aphorism 'Love is Siva' (ibid: 125). The Self-Respecters were aware that classical Saivism had little popular appeal, being a 'high' faith, but yet felt it to be a dangerous influence, since it could and had in fact captivated the imagination of the non-brahmin intelligentsia.

The Self-Respect movement's anti-Saivite utterances came to exist as regular aspects of their propaganda from the late twenties onwards. From March 1928 (and in some instances even earlier), *Kudi Arasu* carried articles which attacked the Saivite classics. *Revolt* and *Puduvai Murasu* (PM) too raised a clamour against these revered texts, with Gurusamy writing at his satiric best on the grotesque and depraved context of these stories of God and his faithful. The movement did not spare such renowned Tamil scholars as Maraimalai Adigal and Kalyanasundara Mudaliar. The Saivites, for their part, were either hostile and angry, or attempted, in a few instances, to strike a conciliatory note. Though Saivite opinion ranged from being conservative to reformist, their concerted efforts at upholding their own against Self-Respect attacks proved to be conservative in the main. Several Saivite journals—*Kumaran, Sivanesan, Siddhantam*—responded to the Self-Respect movement's criticisms with defenses of their creed. (But *Kumaran* also carried approving reports on the Self-Respecters and on at least on one occasion was generous in its praise of *Kudi Arasu* (KA 13.5.28).

The Saivites' opposition to the Self-Respect movement possessed varying resonances: from principled refutations published in *Kumaran* and *Siddhantam* to scurrilous attacks on Periyar and others that were routinely carried in the Saivite-nationalist *Desabandhu* (DB), this opposition only served to provoke the Self-Respecters into greater vituperation. *Desabandhu* was begun explicitly to counter the atheism and the 'godless' propaganda of the Self-Respecters and was harsh and even vile in its denunciations of Periyar. He was constantly referred to as Ramasamy 'Siriyar' (in contrast to 'Periyar', the great man, 'Siriyar' means a small—and mean—personage), the idea of Self-Respect was ridiculed and held to be a mere excuse to indulge in debauchery, the claims to rationality by the Self-Respecters were debunked, the Self-Respect movement's reform work was attacked for being hypocritical and a justification for social anarchy and its commitment to the cause of the adi dravidas was questioned and dismissed as smacking of insincerity. Kaivalyam was also attacked, several refutations of his views published, and *Desabandhu's* journalism justified its often libellious writings by claiming its efforts in this regard were meant to fortify the cause of theism and more specifically Saivism. Likewise, protests ensued regularly from Thanjavur and we find Kaivalyam often answering, debating and rebutting charges of godlessness and anarchy brought by the Saivites (Kaivalyam: 123-24).

What did the Saivites object to in Periyar's (and the Self-Respect movement's) propaganda, that is, apart from their tasteless and barely concealed ill-will towards the movement, what other ideas did the Saivites possess in their critical arsenal? Saivites objected to the movement on general grounds. As S. Somasundaram Pillay from Tuticorin noted in his article titled 'Hinduism and the Hero of Vaikkom', Periyar's speeches and writings were recklessly critical of Hinduism and Hindu sentiments; he was unnecessarily abusive of temples, in fact, had referred to them as dance halls; was sceptical of the power of faith and miracles; he was merely destructive in his intent and would not propose an alternative faith or suggest the means to reform the present religious systems of the Hindus. Somasundaram Pillay also noted that the Self-Respecters were ill-informed about the scriptures, that their efforts only served to alienate the non-brahmin faithful from the Self-Respect creed, that they did not seek to understand the inner core, rather, the hidden truths of Saivism, especially the invocations of bhakthi it had inspired (KA 25.12.27).

Periyar's responses to such criticisms were characteristically blunt, though courteous. In his lengthy riposte to Somasundaram Pillay, he objected to the use of the term 'Hinduism', as such; he refused to accept Swami Vivekananda's definition of 'Hindu'—Somasundaram Pillay had suggested this definition as valid—and argued the term referred to a geographical space, and not to a particular faith to which one can, automatically and unquestioningly, owe allegiance. Even if the term 'Hindu' had been used with reference to the Vedas, shastras and the Puranas, these latter were themselves foreign and even alien to the Tamil country and, besides, no evidence could be adduced from the Tamil classics to prove the existence of the 'Hindu' faith in this part of the world. Periyar also refused to accept, as Somasundaram Pillay had alleged, that his attacks on Hinduism were meant to hurt the devout. If the latter were content in their religious beliefs and did not seek to impose these on others, his criticisms would not mean anything to them, for he addressed himself chiefly to those who made a living out of and who worked to cheat others in the name of religion. As for being critical of temples, he could speak with authority on the subject, considering he had himself been a temple trustee for over thirty years at Erode. Periyar upheld his objections to miracles and his scepticism with respect to matters of faith, since many a time these were based on hearsay and did not merit acceptance by one who thought through matters rationally. As for his so-called destructive rage, he only meant to do away with falsehood, not at the behest of a truth he alone knew, but because he believed that with the withering away of the religions of old, men will discover newer and better principles of thought and action that would not enable a man to mistreat and humiliate his fellow human beings. Periyar also remarked that his iconoclasm will not render the non-brahmin an inert and sterile creature, as Somasundaram Pillay had feared it would, but on the contrary, would instill in him a considerable measure of self-respect (KA 25.12.27).

Gurusamy's responses to the Saivites were markedly different. He was at all times mocking, satiric and savage in his attacks and, moreover, as we have remarked earlier, would make a nuisance of himself at Saivite conferences by questioning, hectoring and arguing with those present. For instance, he addressed 79 questions to the Saivites (that were published in *Kudi Arasu*, 24.3.29) when the latter held a conference at Tirunelveli in March 1929. These questions were meant to draw public attention to the contradictions in Saivism and interrogate its claims to being a non-Aryan religion. Some of the questions read as follows:

QUESTION 5: What distinctive features does Saivism possess that are not found in other religions?

QUESTION 14: Why do Gods in the Saivite pantheon bear Sanskrit names?

QUESTION 17: Do Saivites accept or reject the Aryan Vedas and sacrifices?

QUESTION 25: If one were to eliminate from the Saivite canon Sanskriticw tales and Puranas, would Saivites have any texts to call their own?

QUESTION 53: From which language is the term 'lingam' derived?

QUESTION 63: Does Saivism accept the category 'brahmins'?

Gurusamy also asked of the Saivites whether they possessed rituals and rites of passage which could be deemed patently and indisputably un-Aryan; if they could reconcile their notion, 'Love is Siva' with the diatribes the Saivite saints had addressed to the Jainas, the Buddhists and the Vaishnavites and, finally, whether they accepted, did not accept or denounced caste and varnadharma (KA 24.3.29; Velu: 122-27).

It should not be forgotten though that neither Periyar nor other Self-Respecters sought wilfully to keep Saivites away from the non-brahmin fold. During the anti-Hindi agitations and during such times when Saivite scholars were berated or ignored by brahmins, they worked with and took the part of Saivites. In this sense, the latter were an integral part of the non-brahmin historic bloc. But at the level of doctrine and ideology, Saivites were at odds with the Self-Respect movement, whose young men and women were vociferous in their condemnation of either.

CRITIQUE OF RELIGIOUS PRACTICES

The Self-Respect movement's criticisms of religion as ideology, doctrine, as an instance of brahminical sophistry, were undertaken in the service of the intertwined ideals of self-respect, rationality and freedom. Religious practices—rituals performed during rites of passage, temple festivals, festivals observed in honour of particular deities and on auspicious days, pilgrimages, sacred baths—embodied most completely that folly and ignorance, illogicality and absurdity, extravagance and bad taste, which were consistently railed against and considered characteristic of a religious world-view.

The critique of religious practices may be considered to represent the Self-Respecters' understanding of the political economy of religion in the Tamil country. This critique drew attention to the sheer waste involved in the celebration of festivals, to the extraordinary amount of energy and wealth that were invested in these celebrations and suggested that the money expended thus be utilized for civic activities, for propagating scientific knowledge, for holding exhibitions on modern technology and its uses, for education, better sanitation and health care. Self-Respecters also pointed out how such perfomances of faith, festivals and feast days filled the brahmin priest's coffer and held it extremely demeaning to non-brahmin self-respect that they should thus throw away their hard-earned wealth on activities which confirmed them in their shudrahood.

Kaivalyam, for instance, pointed out that the non-brahmin rich would rather make a temple endowment—for feeding brahmins, perfomance of regular pujas—rather than pay a mite extra to their farmhands and workers. He also remarked on the cupidity, of not merely the priest who thus amassed wealth, but of the merchants and the brothel keepers, who profited from this truly unholy alliance of commerce and religion (49-56).

To indicate the utter irrelevance of religious rituals, the Self-Respecters probed into the various stories woven around these rituals and indicated these tales were improbable and an affront to one's self-respect and intelligence. Festivals and other such holidays were considered a veritable waste of workdays, occasions for unmitigated gluttony and excess. Periyar was, as ever, pointed in his criticisms and argued that such a festival as Saraswathi Puja—observed during the last three days of Dusshera—was a particularly ironic event since the society which celebrated it with piety was, for the large part, illiterate! Besides, he asked angrily, what could be sacrosanct about paper, that was ritually and religiously worshipped during this time, when in the modern world, paper was used for even sanitary purposes! (KA 20.10.29; Anaimuthu: 1560). As for such local festivals such as the Mariamman Thiruvizha, he reminded his readers (and listeners) that according to Hindu puranic lore, Mariamman was but the transmuted form of Renuka, the sexually unchaste mother of Parashurama who, on his father's command, killed his 'fallen' mother. How could public morality be benefitted by thus celebrating what was clearly a symbol of sexual depravity? (Vi 25.3.60; Anaimuthu: 1594-95).

Not only festivals, but the plethora of beliefs and superstitions encouraged and demanded by religious faith, such as the casting of horoscopes, or spirit possession were castigated by the Self-Respecters. Kaivalyam noted that except for the mapping out of planetary positions through mathematical formulae, astrology comprised patent absurdities. He was especially severe on the notion of 'recompense' cultivated by astrologers, that is, astrologers would often enjoin their clients to perform this or that ritual, undertake a pilgrimage or make a monetary or other sort of offerings to appease the evil and malefic planets that were believed to govern the life of the individual in question. In a 1935 article, Periyar observed that a horoscope was in reality a universe of symbols to which astrologers were wont to assign arbitrary meaning and significance. Could astrology predict the fate of non-human beings? Of stones, for instance? Could it explain and forsee the fate of a single piece of stone, from which is carved out a deity as well as a toilet seat? Could it indeed indicate that the same piece of rock would be used for two very different purposes even before the rock is cut up? (Anaimuthu: 1532).

Self-Respecters were also apt to scoff at so called faith rituals such as 'fire walks' during Amman (Mother Goddess) festivals in villages and would demonstrate that even a non-believer could do this and that the so-called powers of faith or the grace of God were mere fictions! Kaivalyam sought to explain the causes and circumstances of spirit possession to his readers. He noted that women, rather than men, were likely to be possessed and, combining a keen sociological sensibility with the knowledge gleaned from contemporary studies in hysteria, hypnotism and mesmerism, suggested that commonplace and material factors may be adduced as explantions for this phenomenon. For one thing, there existed in every village and hamlet, priests and magicians who stood to gain by such 'unnatural' events; secondly, not aware of the true import of religion and lacking the means to education, the common man or woman was prone to believe whatever he or she was told. Besides, as far as the ordinary believer was concerned, his (and her) deities are iconically represented as fearsome, vengeful and all powerful and given to demanding gory and cruel sacrifices. Thirdly, local priests would work themselves into a frenzy during festivals, burst into song and dance—matters which were calculated to instil fear and awe in the devotees. Growing up in such a cultural context, girls who conventionally are less stout-hearted than men may be expected to suffer from delusions and in all probability would 'see' and 'hear' sounds and voices. Kaivalyam also noted that girls and women had other reasons to be thus 'possessed'. For many of them, marriage, if it proved a loveless one and if it was consummated when the girl was very young, signified a traumatic experience that would tell on her senses and mind. Moreover women, if they happened to be childless, were forced to listen to much abuse and forced to visit temples and mortify themselves. This naturally lead them to assume unnatural identities and speak through 'other' voices the trauma they experienced. Kaivalyam also pointed out that the mind possessed immense and unknown powers, as does the psyche of an individual, that one may retain sounds and images at a subliminal level, which one cannot and does not routinely access, but which come to the fore when the mind was exceptionally sensitive or receptive (Kaivalyam: 77-93).

As if to counter superstitious practices and beliefs, Self-Respecters converted their own conferences into vast pedagogical sessions and developed extremely creative modes of communication. Speakers drawing upon everyday experiences and resting their arguments on commonsense would take great pains to explain their points of view patiently and even answer queries and doubts. As if to impress upon the audience the inherent folly of religious practices, speakers would resort to metaphors and analogies which demystifed these practices and rendered them funny, absurd and instances of venality and power. These rhetorical devices derived their force of appeal from their discursive context that was, often times, shaped by scatological and sexual references. As we had remarked in a related context, such forms of communication appealed to conventionally prurient and repressed sensibilities. Now, by being spoken about, the 'repressed' acquired certain subversive and even liberative possibilities, since such elements in consciousness, as are normally subsumed to heed the imperatives of decorum, are now invoked in the service of a thoroughgoing iconoclasm. Thus, scatological and sexual images fired with a transgressive intent served to disrupt the 'religious commonsense' of the average believer and forced her and him to rethink the terms of their faith and their practice of it.

CHAPTER 9

Problems of Caste and the New Order

WRITING IN SEPTEMBER 1971 two years before his death, Periyar observed:

> Though I have endeavoured all along to abolish caste, as far as this country is concerned, this has meant I carry out propaganda for the abolition of God, Religion, the Shastras and Brahmins. For caste will disappear only when these four disappear. Even if one of these were to remain, caste will not be abolished in its entirety... because caste has been constructed out of these four... only after man had been made a slave and a fool would caste have thus been imposed on society. One cannot abolish caste without instilling a taste for freedom and knowledge [in the people]. God, religion, the Shastras and Brahmins make for the growth and spread of slavery and folly and strengthen the existence of caste (Periyar: Ninety-third Birthday Souvenir 17.9.71; Anaimuthu 1974).

To Periyar, caste was, simultaneouly, system and ideology; it comprised a complex set of social relations, as well as those principles which informed, sustained and justified these relations. As a system, caste served the interests of brahmins who were its favoured agents and existed chiefly to gratify and perpetrate their sense of their own superiority. As an ideology, caste worked to ensure that notions of 'high' and 'low' birth were accepted as given by the peoples who were marked thus. The ideology of caste—referred to by Periyar as Brahminism, varnadharma and Hinduism—held that society could not have been divided otherwise, and offered a range of explanations and arguments as to why this hierarchy had come to be and why it was desirable.

Following Periyar, the Self-Respect movement's ideologues and publicists not only considered the abolition of untouchability and the emancipation of non-brahmin shudras as absolutely indispensable for the destruction of caste, but also insisted that these two differently oppressed segments come together into a new relationship of mutuality and reciprocity. Untouchability was understood, both as an instance of a general inhumanity and arrogance derived from notions of 'high' birth, and as a condition that was fundamental to the very existence of caste society. The Self-Respecters never tired of pointing out that all imprecations to freedom, equality and justice were in vain, if they did not address this extremely crucial problem, and not merely from a religious and moral point of view. Untouchables were, first and foremost, workers whose labour through the centuries had made possible and ensured the wealth and welfare of caste society as a whole. Unless the untouchables were freed from servitude and fear, all talk of freedom and self rule could only be construed as partisan and narrow in its concerns.

The Self-Respecters considered the problems of the shudras as being of a different order altogether. They saw the shudra's position as particularly vulnerable and discouraging since the community of castes that came under the broad category of 'shudra' was, at all times, unsure of its own identity. That is, shudras habitually deferred to brahmins, observed the norms of varnadharma judiciously, perpetrated untouchability and were often the direct cause of the misery that was the lot of the adi dravidas. So much so that they revelled in their 'shudrahood' and did not deem it fit to rid themselves of it. The liberation of shudras from the lowness they seemed eager to own, argued the Self-Respecters, was contingent on the abolition of untouchability. That is, it was not enough if the shudra non-brahmins rebelled against the brahmin's authority and asserted their rights to a dignified existence. They had to abandon untouchability consciously and work for the freedom of the adi dravidas from bondage.

As against the principles that underwrote caste hierarchy, Self-Respecters upheld the norms of what they defined as 'samadharma'. At its simplest, samadharma connoted equal rights, but, when used in the context of the logic of caste, it denoted new and radical ways of imagining social interaction and suggested that social relationships may actually be instituted on the basis of mutuality, self-respect and equality between and amongst all human beings. Samadharma then sought to completely subvert the norms of the caste order and expressed a veritable new sensibility, in fact, came to propose an entire new structure of feeling.

Samadharma, when translated as a set of political demands, came to signify and represent a range of non-brahmin concerns and needs. Thus, it underwrote the non-brahmin plea for proportional representation of all castes and communities in the services, legislature and educaton. It proved to be instrumental to the Self-Respecters' discovery of socialism in the thirties and came to inform those mutations of socialist principles that Periyar and others achieved as they worked to realize socialist ideals in a caste-bound society and polity. At a third level, samadharma came to stand in for a civilizational and cultural alternative: a social order based on radically different principles from the present, which needed to rest on premises derived from a non-Aryan, non-Sanskritic ethos.

ADI DRAVIDAS

The Self Respecters' Constituency

Self-Respect propaganda meetings were held regularly in several parts of the Tamil country from 1926 onwards. *Kudi Arasu's* reports of these meetings invariably noted that such meetings drew a large number of adi dravidas and women (reports of meetings at Lalgudi, KA 6.5.28; Poovalur and Komangudi, KA 13.5.28 may be cited as instances). The presence of adi dravidas in substantial numbers at Self-Respect meetings seemed to have caused palpable tension in the various towns where such meetings were organized. For instance, when it was announced that a Self-Respect meeting would be held at Poovalur, rumours circulated, wide and thick, that 'Ramasamy Naicker proposed to enter the local temple with adi dravidas!' This caused no small confusion and panic amongst the orthodox residents who gathered together a group of local adi dravidas to remonstrate against Periyar and the Self-Respect movement (KA 18.12.27).

Desabandhu (Db), published from Tuticorin, remarked on several occasions that the Self-Respect movement deliberately gathered together rowdies and low sorts of people to create tension and fear amongst good citizens (29.6.29; 17.8.29). One particularly vicious report observed 'Naicker's favoured haunts are dustbins and roadside seats', that is, places where the most 'common' and 'vulgar' elements of the populace were wont to congregate (Db 29.6.29).There is enough evidence to suggest that the movement was eagerly and curiously sought out by various subaltern caste groups, of whom, the adi dravida castes were of course the most conspicuous in terms of sheer numbers. Singaravelu, writing of the Self-Respect movement in the eighth year of its existence, observed that Gandhi had merely sought to oppose untouchability verbally, whereas the Self-Resepcters had made this abolition an aspect of their practical politics. Thus, argued Singaravelu, the Self-Respect movement had become a 'veritable protective umbrella in whose generous shade thousands of members of the depressed classes had taken refuge' (KA 1.5.32).

Castes such as the Nadars, who also suffered ritual humiliation of the kind that was routinely inflicted on the adi dravidas, were vociferous in their support of this new and radical movement, whose proponents refused to patronize them, but who, instead, spoke directly, harshly and with passion, of their rights to resist a degradation of their persons. *Desabandhu* was so incensed (and threatened) by this show of subaltern support to a movement it sought to deride, that it warned Nadars not to be taken in by the machinations of a few Self-Respecters (3.8.29).

Responding to Periyar's address to the Third Nadar Youth conference at Porayar, one C. V. Duraikannu Gramini remarked in a long piece, titled 'The Arrogance of the Self-Respect Movement' that Periyar had entreated Nadar youth to stop sporting the marks and signs of religion, only because he did not desire them to enter temples and stake their claims to worship! Gramini also noted that Periyar and his men belonged to that class of timeservers who would sell their nation for the fishes and loaves of office. Periyar's concern for the Nadars, he claimed, was false, and just as how in the past the Nadars had been cheated of their rights by Thirumalai Naicker (the Nayaka ruler of Madurai), so in the present day, they were being duped by the 'Naicker from Erode'! (Db 11.5.29)

Such diatribes against Periyar and the Self-Respect movement did not influence the Nadars, who emerged as one of the staunchest supporters of the Self-Respect movement through the decades which saw it mature into the Dravidar Kazhagam. The fact that the Self-Respecters' avowed constituency proved somewhat embarrassing to those who wished to dismiss the movement as disruptive and anarchic, serves to remind us that, from its earliest days, the Self-Respect platform was essentially a space for the articulation of demands and concerns by the despised communities.

The Self-Respecters' Rejection of Untouchability

Periyar's robust and indignant rejections of untouchability were anything but sentimental. He remarked at a valedictory function of the Gandhi Reading Room in Siravayal, where he was asked to declare open a well for exclusive use by the adi dravidas, he was actually ashamed to be involved in this event. As far as he was concerned, he did not want adi dravidas to be thus assigned 'separate' utilities, for that would only further alienate them from the mainstream (KA 18.4.26; 25.4.26). On another occasion, when he was addressing a meeting at Komangudi, an old man in the audience interrupted him to observe that he and his fellow villagers had gathered to hear Periyar speak, because they were told he would talk of brahmin tyranny. But now it seemed Periyar wanted to unite and consider as one, the caste Hindu peasant and the agricultural (untouchable) labourer. The old man was nonplussed as to the 'rightness' of this latter suggestion. Whereupon Periyar was visibly angered, and noted that the non-brahmin caste Hindus and adi dravidas had to necessarily unite to liberate themselves from caste and the brahmin's power. Whoever objected to this, concluded Periyar, cannot really fight against the brahmins (or the British) for, in effect, they would be fighting for merely a partial emancipation of their selves (KA 13.5.28).

From 1926 to 1939, in and through various conjunctural shifts, the Self-Respect movement never lost sight of its untouchability abolition campaign and sought to refine and re-define it to suit the anxieties of the moment. When the First Self-Respect Provincial Conference was held at Chinglepet in 1929, untouchability abolition figured as an urgent concern in the debates and discussions. Likewise, at the Second and Third Provincial Self-Respect Conferences, held at Erode in 1930 and Virudhunagar in 1931 respectively, this concern was manifest in the debates as well as resolutions which transpired there. In the early and mid-thirties, the Self-Respect movement's campaigns were guided chiefly by adi dravida concerns: whether it was opposing Gandhi, or the Poona Pact or reviewing Dr. Subbarayan's temple-entry bill, or evaluating critically the activities of the Harijan Sevak Sangh, or advancing the rights to equal dignity of adi dravida Christians, and asserting these rights in the face of stiff and obdurate opposition from the Catholic clergy in Madras—in all of these instances, the question of adi dravida rights and progress constituted the modality through which the concerns of the movement as a whole were mediated, expressed and addressed.

In Public Solidarity with Adi Dravidas

Kudi Arasu carried lengthy reports of adi dravida conferences, whether these were organized by the movement or one or the other of the adi dravida organizations (KA 15, 22.1.28; 11.3.28; 20.6.28; 25.5.29; 16.6.29; 25.8.29; 19.4.31). Whenever the nationalist press sought to misreport the events that unfolded at these conferences, *Kudi Arasu* immediately refuted such distortions. Thus, when *Swadesamitran* and *Tamil Nadu* described an adi dravida conference held in Madras on 8 January 1928 as a meeting of 'selfish "pro-government" peoples' Periyar wrote a scathing reply, in which he took the Swarajists (who were the critics in this instance) and Annie Besant (who endorsed the Swarajists' point of view) to task for thus maligning the adi dravidas: 'Have those who conventionally...begged for a living...but who are now in government posts that fetch them fat salaries ever done anything by way of enabling adi dravidas to find even a coolie's job?' In such a context, thundered Periyar, what could adi dravidas do but turn to government for help and assistance? (KA 22.1.28).

The Self-Respecters applauded those who undertook measures that would benefit the adi dravidas, such as, when the Pachaiappa's Trust in Madras decided to admit adi dravidas into the Pachaiappa College in Madras city. Conversely they criticized those who were careless of adi dravida rights or downright hostile to them, as the brahmins of Kalpathi were when they refused the adi dravidas of the village permission to walk through the streets where brahmins lived (KA 11.12.27).

The victory of an adi dravida—at a local election or his or her nomination to a post in the executive proved to be an occasion for not only the Self-Respecters, but also the Justice party to celebrate. Often the adi dravida notable in question would be carried in procession through the town or village where he resided and later felicitated at a public meeting. When J. Sivashanmugham Pillay was nominated to the Madras corporation, Justicites held a meeting in his honour and spoke warmly of his talents and character (KA 31.7.32). When Dr. Subbarayan who became Chief Minister of Madras in 1926 nominated two adi dravidas to a devasthanam committee, *Kudi Arasu* was fulsome in its praise and at Erode where the Second Self-Respect Provincial Conference was held, Subbarayan was hailed and admired for his initiative. *Kudi Arasu* remarked, in this context, on the appropriateness of adi dravidas officiating on such committees, for now they were placed in a position from where they could observe and regulate, if neccesary, those sacral activities to which they had hitherto been denied access and the language of which was considered too exalted for them to learn (KA 25.5.30). Writing on what he would do, were he to be made Viceroy, Gurusamy declared that he would make Dr. Ambedkar Minister of Law and M. C. Raja the Chief Minister of Madras (PM 7.12.31; Velu 1991: 309).

During his term as president of the Ramanathapuram Zillah Board, the Self-Respecter and Justice party notable, W. P. A. Soundarapandian warned owners of bus fleets that they would not be allowed to ply their vehicles if they did not immediately end the practice of not allowing adi dravidas on their buses and of issuing tickets which carried the message, 'Adi dravidas will not be allowed to travel on this bus' (KA 4.5.30). The Ramanatha-puram Zillah Devasthanam Committee, under pressure from Soundarapandian, passed a resolution that allowed adi dravidas and others unrestricted access to ponds, wells, schools and roads under its jurisdiction (KA 24.8.30).

Self-Respecters also raised a clamour at Congress meetings where untouchability was discussed and insisted that untouchability abolition and granting of access to all public places to adi dravidas be immediately achieved. At a Congress meeting chaired by T. S. S. Rajan at Coimbatore, Kovai Ayyamuthu, a Self-Respecter, opposed the Congress' habitual resolution on untouchability. Referring to another resolution on salt and satyagraha, Ayyamuthu noted, 'a man may live without salt for days but cannot do so without drinking water even for a day' and demanded that adi dravidas be granted access to public wells. Ayyamuthu pointed out that in Coimbatore alone there were lakhs of adi dravidas who could not drink at public wells, whose children were not allowed into schools where caste Hindu children studied, and even where they were allowed, were seated separately. In this context, Congress' lofty resolutions would not serve any purpose, unless they served to address these specific disabilities and concerns of adi dravidas (KA 11.5.30).

Kudi Arasu carried regular reports of the educational achievements of adi dravidas and also advertisements which advertised for an adi dravida spouse. Several adi dravidas chose to get married the Self-Respect way and one such marriage, the first of its kind in the Arundathiar (an adi dravida caste) community presided over by J. S. Kannapar, was described in elaborate detail (KA 27.4.30). Two of *Kudi Arasu's* most regular columnists in the thirties were the couple, Rathinasabapathy (a Saiva Vellala) and Annapoorani (an adi dravida), whose marriage was considered an important achievement of the movement (KA 17.4.32). Their writings and speeches at several conferences appeared in all their detail in *Kudi Arasu* and their life together was considered by Self-Respecters a fine instance of a non-caste, self-respecting existence. *Kudi Arasu* carried untouchability abolition songs and poems from as early as 1925, though they appeared regularly only in the thirties.

Besides Periyar, several other Self-Respect publicists and speakers wrote and spoke their way into the hearts of the adi dravidas. J. S. Kannapar, Gurusamy, Kunjitham (Gurusamy), A. Raghavan, Jeevanandham, Vallatharasu, Ponnambalam, Azhagirisamy, Nagai Murugesan, Neelavathi and many others addressed or presided over adi dravida conferences, proposed resolutions on the abolition of untouchability, advocated commensuality, intercaste marriages, fought for temple entry (for adi dravidas), took on Congressmen and others who were wont to sentimentalize the adi dravida cause and railed against violence inflicted on the adi dravidas. The Self-Respecters took very seriously Periyar's dictum that the liberation of the shudra was contingent on and would be complete only with the liberation of the panchama.

Adi Dravidas and Temple-Entry

Besides, working to realize adi dravida rights in any number of particular contexts, the Self-Respect movement also mounted systematic campaigns with respect to temple-entry. As we had remarked in an earlier section, they drew into this venturesome act Justice party notables as well. Apart from supporting temple-entry legislation—with reservations, of course, as to the intent of those who framed these bills—Self-Respecters pioneered several temple-entry attempts themselves. The Suchindram Temple satyagraha which took place when Periyar was still in Congress may be reckoned as one of the earliest of these attempts (KA 31.1.26; 14.2.26). There were many others in the years that followed. J. S. Kannapar was implicated in a court case when he attempted to enter the Thiruvannamalai Temple with a group of adi dravidas in 1928 (KA 6.5.28). (The case was subsequently decided in Kannapar's favour.) Gurusamy and A. Ponnambalam, along with a few adi dravidas, entered Eswaran Temple at Erode in April 1929, though Periyar had advised them to be circumspect in his action. The temple priests took the matter to court. The conviction of the adi dravidas in the lower court was nullified on appeal to the higher court (Velu: 159-61).

Apart from these well-publicized and well-known campaigns with respect to temple-entry, which were duly reported and celebrated in *Kudi Arasu*, the latter also reported numerous routine instances of adi dravidas urged by Self-Respecters at times, and at other times acting on their own, attempting to enter temples. *Kudi Arasu*, for instance, carried the story of an adi dravida girl who made a bid to enter a temple while the men of her community waited outside to make sure no harm befell her (18.3.28). In another instance, Self-Respecters extended their support to the temple-entry movement launched by the Pune depressed classes leaders, Shivram Kamble and Rajbhoj (KA 27.10.29). Of course, for Self-Respecters, temple-entry pertained to the realm of civil rights, and even as they urged it as a right to be claimed and won, castigated the existence of temples, gods, proclaimed the uselesness of worship and exhorted the adi dravidas to renounce Hinduism! (KA 2, 22.1.32; 30.10.32; 20.11.32). Gurusamy, even as he urged adi dravidas to exercise their right to temple-entry, wrote with disarming candour of the sites of oppression and the caste order that temples essentially were.

In yet another show of anger against caste and the horrors it had reserved for adi dravidas, the Self-Respecters took to burning copies of the *Manusmriti*. J. S. Kannappar, for instance, burnt a copy of this text at a public meeting in North Arcot (KA 11.12.27). A *Kudi Arasu* article reported several earlier instances of the burning of the Manusmriti by the Self-Respecters (4.12.27). It is clear that the Self-Resepcters support for the adi dravida cause ranged from urging their rights to a dignified existence in any number of of quotidian instances to arguing for their free existence as equal and valued citizens of civil society. However, when it came to the question of politics and the political rights of adi dravidas, the Self-Respecters reverted to a different discourse: they demanded separate electorates for adi dravidas, insisted that adi dravidas could not really afford to quarrel with and antagonize the imperial government and that they must seek to work political reforms, however minimal and cosmetic these may be, to their advantage and counselled their adi dravida constituency not to get distracted by the Congress agitational campaigns.

Self-Respecters, Adi Dravidas and the Question of Politics

In fact, the Self-Respecters evaluated political reforms, agitations for or against reforms and the effects of reforms by testing their use value against the touchstone of adi dravida welfare. If a scheme or reform or support (or opposition) to a scheme served adi dravidas well, they welcomed it. If it served them ill or did not benefit adi dravidas enough, they criticized it, but exercised restraint while doing so, since they preferred negotiation and persuasion to confrontation and disavowal; except, of course, when an agitation seemed disruptive and inimical to the non-brahmin (and adi dravida) commonweal as a whole, which made them condemn it altogether. For instance, with respect to the Civil Disobedience campaigns that began in March 1930 and were carried on with a greater or lesser degree of intensity till 1933, the Self-Respecters maintained a consistent critical and oppositional distance. Commenting on the Congress' Purna Swaraj resolution and the agitations launched in support of the latter, Periyar observed that Purna Swaraj will become a reality only when 'the dominance of religion and the blind faith responsible for this dominance are destroyed; untouchability abolished, the oppression of women ended and brahmin hegemony displaced' (KA 16.3.30).

It is clear—and we have remarked on this before—the Self-Respecters identified Swaraj with social justice and progress and often made the abolition of untouchability an index of justice and progress. Thus R. K. Shanmugham, speaking at Erode during the Second Self-Respect Provincial Conference, noted that the abolition of untouchability was a matter of greater import and urgency than the struggle for greater political rights for Indians. Further, the Self-Respect movement was concerned with social reform, noted Shanmugham, not because it was embarrassed and provoked to do so by European criticisms of the backwardness of Hindu life and manners, but because it desired to stir the minds and hearts of the depressed classes and draw them into militant social action. The Self-Respecters were not in the least averse to political reform; nor did they imagine social and political reforms could be pursued independently of each other. But as long as nationalist politicians did not feel impelled to protest untouchability, Self-Respecters would not seek to endorse the claims of nationalism (KA 11.5.30).

It is not surprising then that the Self-Respecters chose to pass a resolution calling for the destruction of religions at the Third Self-Respect Provincial Conference at Virudhunagar in August 1931. It was then argued that religions deterred humanity from realizing itself and that religious norms and customs militated against the realization of the ideals of fraternity and equality amongst all peoples. Through this important political statement, the Self-Respecters made it clear that they were determined to shake the Hindu social order to its very roots and would be happy with a nationalism which endorsed their determination to do so. Needless to say, this 'shaking up' was held to be desirable chiefly because it would destroy untouchability (KA 23.8.31).

In at least three well marked instances, the Self-Respect movement adopted a proactive policy with respect to adi dravida political rights: during the Simon Commisssion boycott campaign; the Second Round Table Conference and the Poona Pact. When the Simon Commission held its hearings in Madras, *Kudi Arasu* explained in several of its editorials why adi dravidas ought to disregard the Congress' call to boycott the commission. In a long article titled, 'A Necessary Word of Advice to Adi Dravidas', Kaivalyam urged adi dravida leaders to reflect on the good done them by the white man and remarked they ought to make known to the latter the adi dravidas' loyalty was to them at all times. Adi dravidas had to also impress upon the Simon Commission that their demands for political concessions be conceded, since 'from Arcot to Mesopotamia they had fought the white man's battles' and besides had helped raise the white man's children. Kaivalyam also reminded his adi dravida readers that brahmins might claim that, as Congressmen, they will boycott the commission but would utilize other occasions and forums—such as a tea party here, a dinner there—with the members of the commission to press forward their claims (KA 29.1.28).

When the Simon Commission's report on the proposed reforms was finally published, the Self-Respecters welcomed its recommendations. The report had observed that if there was to be one representative at least for a population of 10,000 caste Hindus, there ought to be one representative at least for a population of 100,000 adi dravidas. Periyar noted in this context that adi dravidas were under-represented, but at least their political rights had been acknowledged as valid and legitimate and accepted in principle (KA 29.6.30).

The second specific instance when Self-Respecters came to support adi dravida political claims was occasioned by the Second Round Table Conference, when Gandhi proclaimed himself the sole representative of the adi dravidas and pooh-poohed and ridiculed the right of Ambedkar to represent his people. Congress had already earned the disapprobation of adi dravidas for its stance on the question of separate electorates. At a Madras Adi Dravida Mahajana Sangam meeting held in Thirupadiripuliyur, V. I. Munusamy Pillay had noted in despair that caste Hindus were driving his brethren to the camp of the Mohammedans (KA 19.4.31). When at London, Gandhi insisted on his rights to speak for them, adi dravida anger knew no bounds. *Kudi Arasu* played a singularly important role in channelizing and directing this rage. Articles, editorials and protests were published condemning Gandhi. Protest meetings were held throughout the Tamil country and attended by prominent Self-Respecters.

When Congressmen were debating the possible benefits they may derive from the Second Round Table Conference well before it had begun, Periyar had noted that Congressmen, including Gandhi, who clamoured for political reforms, desired to enthrone Manudharma and thereby secure their own (and brahmin, upper caste) hegemony (KA 17.5.31; Anaimuthu: 776-77). The happenings in London confirmed Periyar in his opinion. A *Kudi Arasu* editorial (18.10.31) observed 'Just as how Mr. Malaviya was concerned about protecting Brahminism, so are Dr. Ambedkar and Mr. Rettamalai Srinivasan committed to its destruction' and went on to condemn Gandhi for his implacable resistance to accepting Ambedkar and Srinivasan as legitimate representatives of the depressed classes. Yet another editorial (25.10.31) titled 'The Betrayal of the Adi Dravidas by the Hindus' rebuked Gandhi for maintaining that the so-called adi dravida leaders who had come to London were not really adi dravida leaders, and went on to denounce Gandhi's purported request to adi dravida students to support him and thereby humiliate Srinivasan and Ambedkar. *Kudi Arasu* also reproduced an article from the Justice party's *Dravidan* that supported the adi dravida leaders' demand for a separate electorate for depressed classes.

The third and, perhaps, the most important instance of support for adi dravida political aspirations was the concerted campaign the Self-Respect movement carried out to protest the Poona Pact. Gandhi's fast was criticized, his inordinate political cunning held up for ridicule, and the entire body of conservative Congressmen who stood behind Gandhi and ensured he would carry out their behest were attacked in the bitterest of terms. *Kudi Arasu* and the Self-Respect movement launched a massive campaign to build non-brahmin public opinion against Gandhi's epic fast and its supporters. M. C. Raja, who in league with the Hindu Mahasabha leader, Moonje, endorsed Gandhi's position, was criticized and *Kudi Arasu* warned him and his followers not to fall prey to the machinations of the caste Hindus. A *Kudi Arasu* editorial titled 'The Liberation of the Adi Dravidas and the Deception of the Hindus' returned to an earlier argument: that Gandhi and Congress were intent on wresting political control from the British only to enthrone the authority of varnadharma. The editorial further noted that caste Hindus feared adi dravida political power and autonomy on this account, that it would undermine the basis for the desired brahminical dominance in a future, free polity (KA 17.7.32).

Meetings supporting Dr Ambedkar and Srinivasan and denouncing Raja were even held in Kolar. In May 1932, at the First Kolar Self-Respect Conference, where separate sessions on Self-Respect, Buddhism and adi dravidas were organized and attended by Self-Respect and adi dravida leaders, such as V. P. S. Maniar, G. Annapoorani and her father, G. Appaduraiar (editor of *Tamizhan*, founded by Iyothee Thass), a resolution was passed, calling for a separate electorate for adi dravidas and condemning the Moonje-Raja accord (KA 29.5.32).

Several articles written on the subject in *Kudi Arasu* drew attention to Gandhi's sophistry. *Dravidan* in a satiric vein, remarked that Gandhi had come forward to 'sacrifice his life' only because 'over 7 crore corpses had dared to seek a separate representation for themselves' (reproduced KA 18.9.32). Gurusamy, wrote of 'Gandhi's Suicide' and recalled that Gandhi had once declared he did not desire Swaraj unless untouchability was abolished, which earned him the wrath and calumny of orthodox Hindus. But now he was one with these very same Hindus, with those who, in Devakottai, had demonstrated recently the 'worth' of their Hindu faith by setting adi dravida houses on fire and butchering adi dravida men and women (KA 18.9.32). An editorial of the same date, also written by Gurusamy and titled 'Gandhi's Orthodox Fury', examined in detail the correspondence between Ramsay Macdonald and Gandhi on the question of separate electorates; discussed the merits of separate as against joint electorates; argued the 'fairness' of Macdonald's final award and condemned Gandhi's fast as being directed explicitly against the adi dravidas. (In many ways the arguments put forth in this article bear a striking resemblance to Dr. Ambedkar's observations in 'What Congress and Gandhi did to the Untouchables' published in 1946.)

Finally, when Dr. Ambedkar did sign the Poona Pact, albeit, with great reluctance, *Kudi Arasu* examined the conditions and circumstances in which the pact had come to be forged, noted the marginal gains that had accrued to the adi dravidas but did not fail to remark on the effects of Gandhi's fast which, it declared, was undertaken to gain the sympathy of the caste Hindus. It also reproduced Dr. Ambedkar's statement of intent and explanation with respect to the Poona Pact (KA 2.10.32). From Kolar, Appaduraiar wrote in his paper on the 'uses' of Gandhi's fast for the adi dravidas.

Since Gandhi was an avowed sanatanist and one who believed in the Smritis and the Bhagavad Gita, who desired to build a future Ramrajya and who wanted that each person should labour at the task he or she was born to, could one reasonably expect him to work out a scheme for the equal and peaceful coexistence of adi dravidas and caste Hindus? (reproduced KA 25.9.32)

In the years 1933-36, when the Self-Respect movement announced its affiliations to socialism, adi dravidas were seen as not merely victims of a vicious order sanctioned by religion, but of an order of economic exploitation as well. However, it must be kept in mind that from very early on, Periyar insisted that all non-brahmins were workers: the shudras were deemed slaves by Hindu convention and the outcastes condemned to be slaves by Hindu faith. Adi dravidas were thus always already workers in the Self-Respecters' lexicon. But whereas, formerly, labour was deployed less as a category of political economy and more as a moral category of analysis, now, that is, in the thirties, labour as a category was anchored in the context of political economy. Thus addressing a meeting of adi dravida Christians in May 1933 at a village near Lalgudi, Periyar observed:

> If you desire true freedom you must have courage to destroy that which validates and constitutes the basis of your abject and enslaved existence...No one had ever told you the real reason for your low and degraded status because they know if you were to know of this you would pounce on them that very minute and tear them to pieces; which is why they concocted stories about God, religion and custom...If you were to bring together a brahmin and a Paraiah and consider how they are constituted high and low you will see a high caste man is one who shuns labour, is lazy and lives off the work of others; whereas a low caste man is one who labours but yields the fruits of his labour to others and lives as an animal does—without a home, without proper clothes, without a regular morsel of food and without education.

Periyar went on to argue that as far as caste society was concerned, its only interest in the untouchables (and the shudras) was to keep them alive at subsistence levels so that they may live to labour (KA 7.5.33; Anaimuthu: 72-73).

The Nature of a Relationship

The relationship between adi dravidas and the Self-Respect movement was reciprocal and equal at all times. Adi dravida leaders commended the work of the movement and urged adi dravidas to support it. The Tirunelveli Zillah Adi Dravida Mahajana Sabha passed a resolution urging adi dravidas to read *Kudi Arasu*, *Dravidan*, *Tamizhan*, and *Adi Dravida Kavalan* (KA 11.3.28). Adi Dravidas wrote regularly for *Kudi Arasu* and the writings of adi dravida intellectuals of an earlier generation, such as Iyothee Thass were advertised as worthy reading in *Kudi Arasu* and recommended as useful reading for all non-brahmins.

One particularly felicitous instance of how adi dravidas chose to interpret and apply the ideal of Self-Respect as a norm and as a category of analysis was a piece that appeared in *Kudi Arasu* (18.12.27). Titled 'Nandanar Charitiram: The "Elder Brother" of Manusmriti', this article noted the fable of Nandan, the famous untouchable Tamil saint, was really an apologia for caste, since it was premised on notions which held birth to be decisive in determining status and character, considered untouchability permissible and enjoined that only brahmins may have close access to God. The author of this article, clearly an adi dravida, went on to identify specific textual references to illustrate his claims. In the fable, Adanur, Nandan's cheri, is described as foul smelling. Bones are seen strewn everywhere and men and women, it seems, were found drunk at all times. The fable also describes miracles such as a rich old man acquiring scriptural wisdom, as soon as Nandan anoints him with sacred ash. This mixture of realism and fantasy notwithstanding, the fable makes it clear that Nandan and his people were slaves by birth and vocation. So much so that to attain salvation, Nandan has to shed his 'slave' status—through fire baptism—and thus, suitably 'refined', meet with God. The author of the article makes it clear that not only were such notions demeaning to adi dravida self-respect, but also that these served to persuade his people to accept slavery as their destiny and to rid themselves of it, they had literally to consign their bodies to fire!

The Nandan fable was performed as a play, in fact, it was very popular during the early decades of our century. But the play with its mixture of paternalism, sentimentality and piety, irked adi dravida self-pride to a considerable extent. Thus, some adi dravidas demanded that the play be banned altogether, while others held that all derogatory references to 'Paraiahs' must be deleted from the play (KA 18.12.27).

Adi dravidas, then, constituted the Self-Respect movement in very many crucial ways and were in the forefront of all the major struggles launched by that movement. Even during the anti-Hindi agitations they played a major role and one of the martyrs to the anti-Hindi cause was a young adi dravida who died in prison. Periyar and the Self-Respecters were warmly supportive of Dr. Ambedkar. The conference of the depressed classes of Central Provinces and Berar was held in Jalgaon on 29 May 1929 and was addressed by Dr. Ambedkar. *Kudi Arasu* in its report noted that this was the First Self-Respect Conference of Bombay Province. It was also reported that Periyar had sent his greetings to the conference, which were duly read out after Dr. Ambedkar's address (KA 16.6.29). Ambedkar's views on caste, separate electorates for adi dravidas, Gandhi, the Harijan Sevak Sangh and other concerns were regularly published in *Kudi Arasu*, which also translated and serialized Ambedkar's 'The Annihilation of Caste' (from 24.7.36). This was subsequently brought out as a book in February 1937 (KA 14.2.37). Almost every number of *Kudi Arasu* in 1937 carried advertisements for the book.

Self-Respecters did not spare non-brahmins when they hurt, humiliated or indulged in wilful violence against adi dravidas. When, in 1930, Kallars (a middle non-brahmin caste, conventionally associated with policing and warfare), convened a caste conference at Devakkottai and passed resolutions which commanded adi dravidas to refrain from wearing jewellery and adi dravida men from wearing shirts, vests or coats and from wearing dhoties that reached below their knees and which held that adi dravidas, men and women, should not cut their hair, should not use any but mud vessels and that adi dravida women should not sport flowers in their hair, Gurusamy wrote a furious editorial in *Puduvai Murasu*. He noted that the Kallars in their attempts to 'upgrade' themselves into pious Saivites had come to be beset by the latter's religious zeal and frenzy as well. Gurusamy pointed out that the Kallars had exhibited a cruelty and an inhumanity which put to shame General Dyer's atrocities! (PM 5.1.31; Velu: 229-31). When violent clashes ensued between Kallars and adi dravidas at Devakottai a few months later, Gurusamy wrote yet another indignant editorial. This time, he painted a moving picture of adi dravida misery and, additionally, utilized this occasion to draw attention to the effects of political Brahminism that had rendered the political uses of caste and religious morality legitimate (PM 16.3.31; Velu: 279-82).

W. P. A. Soundarapandian also intervened in the cause of the adi dravidas of Devakottai. He tried to make local government act decisively and put an end to the violence that had been inflicted on the adi dravidas. A resolution to this effect was moved in the Madras Council on 30 January 1931 but the government chose not to respond to it. A second resolution was moved by Soundarapandian a few months later and was passed, in spite of the nominated members, brahmins and the Justice ministers not supporting it (KA 23.8.31). Later, at the Third Self-Respect Provincial Conference at Virudhunagar, a resolution was passed that demanded an enquiry committee be constituted to go into the details of the atrocities against the adi dravidas (KA 16.8.31). More generally, during this period, a great deal of the Self-Respecters' energy came to be expended in explaining the concept of shudrahood and how closely it was tied to the idea of untouchability.

SHUDRAS

Periyar and the Self-Respecters held that the brahmin-non brahmin division was fundamental to the constitution of Hindu caste society. Untouchability was viewed as a necessary condition of this division and, as Periyar observed once, untouchability, like steps in a ladder, characterized all human relationships within the caste order (KA 12.4.31; Anaimuthu: 60). For the Self-Respecters, being non-brahmin or characterized as one meant two things. A non-brahmin by his constitutive status was opposed to, in fact, through centuries, had been considered as antithetical to all things brahmin. But in contemporary society, the non-brahmin existed, not merely as a despised shudra, but as the primary constituent of a grand fraternity comprising all those whom brahmins and Brahminism held to be low, depraved and less than human. The Self-Respecters were anxious that non-brahmins free themselves from shudrahood and come together with the adi dravidas to realize a social utopia in which caste would have no place. This, then, was a catholic, political non-Brahminism, which bound Self-Respecters in filiative relationships with all non-brahmins, irrespective of their political affiliations.

Fighting Brahmins and Brahminism

Just as men like Iyothee Thass had been concerned with the semantic import of the term 'Paraiah', so were Periyar, Kaivalyam, Gurusamy and others concerned with the origins and history of the term 'shudra'. Self-Respecters, taking their cue from the Smritis, Dharmashastras, Itihasas and Puranas understood the term 'shudra' to refer to one who was the 'son of a dasi'. The word, 'dasi' was interpreted by them to mean not merely a slave woman, but one who had been forced into concubinage with invading Aryan brahmins. Thus a shudra, the Self-Respecters reasoned, was deemed low and despicable on account of his 'flawed' birth, because he was not considered to be born into honour. 'Shudra' thus denoted bondage as well as dishonour and the Self-Respecters were quick to point at the various ways and means through which bondage and dishonour had been imposed on shudras and perpetrated as a neccessary condition of their existence through the centuries of Aryan brahmin rule (Kaivalyam: 63-66).

Firstly, shudras were ordained to labour. Secondly, they were forbidden to read of, hear or study the brahmin's scriptural lore. Thirdly, they were told that whatever wealth they may earn ought to be spent in ways that would please the brahmins (and therefore the Gods). Fourthly, they were confirmed in and made to accept their shudrahood through various rituals and rites which they were coerced to perform, and which ensured their continual deference to brahmin sacral authority. Fifthly, they were persuaded to accept and practise untouchability, so that they would be consoled in their inferior non-brahmin status by looking down on the outcastes. Lastly, shudras were allowed to command wealth and men so long as they did not seek to aspire to sacral prowess, in keeping with their secular prowess (KA 13.9.31; Anaimuthu: 1640-43; Kaivalyam: 93-104).

Self-Respecters urged the large non-brahmin populace to stir itself into knowledge and action and thereby renounce their shudrahood in the name of their self-respect. Imprecations, denunciations, pleas and requests to non-brahmins appeared daily in *Kudi Arasu* which also carried slogans such as 'If anyone calls you a shudra, get enraged and beat him'; 'if you are a shudra then it means you are the son of a concubine.' At public meetings, in caste gatherings, at Tamil literary forums and Saivite conclaves—Self-Respecters were to be found in any and all of these, raising a clamour against shudrahood; asking non-brahmins to give up the practice of inviting brahmin priests to officiate at marriages and funerals; pleading for interdining and intermarriage between all non-brahmin castes.

At the First Self-Respect Provincial Conference held at Chinglepet in February 1929, it was resolved that henceforth non-brahmins would drop their caste suffixes. *Kudi Arasu* regularly carried names of those who had given up inviting brahmin purohits to their households. Almanacs were produced that carried slogans against caste and shudrahood. Calendars with photographs of those who had made intercaste marriages or had married widows were published. Kaivalyam and others incessantly warned non-brahmins against expending their wealth on what were termed useless and barbaric customs and festivals. *Kudi Arasu* carried special reports commending such reforms in marriage and funeral ceremonies that were carried out in the homes of non-brahmin zamindars and merchants (even while pointing out that such reforms had not gone far enough!).

Shudras and Adi Dravidas: Building a Historic Bloc

Imprecations directed against what Self-Respecters characterized as non-brahmin passivity and foolishness comprised certain familiar themes. When invited to address caste conferences, Periyar would warn non-brahmins of the dangers inherent in any process of upgrading, in the practice of any set of activities that non-brahmins believed would make them more like brahmins. Thus, speaking at a Devendra Kula Vellala conference (the Devendra Kula Vellalas, in spite of their exalted name, were in reality a caste of untouchable agricultural labourers, the Pallas of Tamil Nadu) he noted in an address:

> You desire to call yourselves Devendrakula Vellalas. The Vanniyars want to call themselves kshatriyas while Chettiars refer to themselves as vaishyas. Why must you do this? If someone were to point out

to you that this [upgrading] is really a kind of self-degrading act, you claim,`how can you say this? we have only now succeeded in reforming our parents'...(Dravidan: 5.10.29; Anaimuthu: 1607).

In another instance Periyar observed:

> Each caste group may discover and produce proofs of its own superiority but yet such proofs will only serve to illustrate the fact that all castes are inferior to those who call themselves brahmins (KA 30.11.30; Anaimuthu: 1599).

But, Periyar, it must be noted was also aware of the uses and importance of caste associations and the sodalities they brought forth. When asked once as to how he could denounce caste and yet address caste gatherings, he replied that he saw caste organizations as forums for debate on matters of reform and change within particular castes and he believed that by interacting with such forums he would be able to persuade them of the importance of abandoning particular identities for the identity of a commonweal:

> All castes should progress in education, in intelligence and in culture and achieve parity with each other. All castes should attain an equal share of government posts...All castes should come together and attain a common level of culture, a common educational status, should experience a common morality (KA 24.1.32).

Another recurrent theme in Self-Respect discourses on shudrahood had to do with achieving a non-brahmin solidarity that would unite caste Hindus and adi dravidas. Writing of the non-brahmin castes' proclivity to imitate and subserve brahmins, Periyar noted:

> Amongst the non-brahmins there are many who observe caste differences. But if you wish the upper castes to consider you their equals then you must grant that the caste below you is equal to yourselves. Sometimes it seems to me that the caste oppression we perpetrate is greater than that practised by brahmins.

For, 'the Nattukottai Chettis who have amassed such immense wealth choose to spend it on the study of Vedas, a vocation that prepares one for lifelong beggary! They thus not only feed brahmins but encourage them to study. If they were to use this money to educate a few adi dravida children the latter would not be forced to undertake a coolie's job at such a tender age' (KA 9.12.28; Anaimuthu: 332).

On another occasion, Periyar wrote in exasperation of his own non-brahmin constituency:

> When we speak of adi dravidas, it is understandable that brahmins get annoyed. But it is incomprehensible to me that non-brahmins too should be dismayed. This is but foolish and dishonourable. If you feel really humiliated by the fact you are considered 'shudras' would you even for a moment feel uneasy when we claim that paraiah-hood should be abolished? (KA 11.10.31; Anaimuthu: 60).

When it came to addressing the adi dravidas and impressing on them the necessity of viewing the shudra castes as their comrades-in-struggle, Periyar adopted a different discursive strategy. He argued that shudras were not very different from panchamas, were as worse off, and as humiliated by the Hindu upper castes:

> As far as the philosophy of our social life is concerned, there is no difference between us. Just as you are considered untouchable, we who are supposed to be superior to you are likewise considered untouchable by those who claim to be born from the face of God, those who consider themselves gods on earth, that is, by the brahmins.

Further brahminical scripture had constituted the shudra as a veritable criminal, much in the same way the British government had designated certain communities as 'criminal tribes'. Just as criminal tribes are hounded out and punished in British India, so in the past and in the present too, shudras continue to be deemed slaves, sons of concubines and thieves (KA 30.11.30; Anaimuthu: 1600).

Periyar also observed that the term 'shudra' was meant to provoke and cause offence and the negative significance attached to it was even greater than what was implied by the terms 'Paraiah' and 'Palla': For,

> At least the terms 'Palla' and 'Paraiah' refer to the task one performs and to one's residence. Those terms do not denigrate or seek to enslave the Paraiahs and Pallas. But the term by which we are known, that is the term 'shudra', denotes one who is a slave and the son of a concubine...at least a Paraiah is born to his own parents, that is the term does not dishonour his parents, but a shudra means one who is the son of a slave, prostitute, a concubine, a born slave, one who has been raised as a slave.

Even the term 'chandala' was not as demeaning as the term 'shudra'. For the class of chandalas came into being due to sexual unions between members of the four varnas, the emergence of this class reflected the norms observed (or not observed) by the people of the four varnas and did not indicate dishonour at the very moment of birth. Besides, given the racial mix in the subcontinent nearly 99.5 percent of the populace must qualify as chandalas! So the chandalas theoretically at least escape the ignominy of a disreputable birth, which option was not open to the shudras (KA 16.6.29; Anaimuthu: 57). Such reminders of their 'low status' served to shame shudras in their assumed superiority over adi dravidas.

This does not of course mean that Periyar or the other Self-Respecters ever believed or acted as if the adi dravidas were in some way better off than the non-brahmins. In fact, on several occasions, as we have noted, Periyar pointed to Justicites as well as to Subbarayan that adi dravidas needed to be included in greater numbers in the government and the services (KA 9.3.30).

The Community of Self-Respect

The Self-Respect movement's efforts to wrest non-brahmins from the varna-jati fold and their internalized shudrahood and to bring them into a new and creative relationship with adi dravidas made for the existence of a new community of Self-Respect. Comprising thousands of young men and women, bound to each other by ties of ideological (and personal) affiliation, this community eschewed custom and convention, trusted to reason, practised the virtues of freedom and egalitarianism and organized itself into hundreds of Self-Respect clubs all over the Tamil country. Several hundreds of men and women who forsook family, kinship ties and their inheritance rights to propagate their philosophy of Self-Respect and the destruction of caste made up this community. These men and women hailed from various castes, some of them made intercaste marriages, others married widows, while yet others broke free of earlier relationships to enter into new romantic associations. Romance itself was, of course, re-defined in the process and came to signify companionship and compatibility.

Nadars and adi dravidas, as C. N. Annadurai would remark years later, constituted the movement's mainstay, so to speak. Nadars, in spite of having attained a high economic status, were yet plagued with the vestiges of untouchability and ritual impurity and the Self-Respect movement was seen by them as a forum where they could advance their claims to dignity and self-worth. Prominent Self-Respecters such as S. Ramanathan, Gurusamy and Rathinasabapathy were Vellalas by birth, but they were all too happy to renounce and rail against their sat shudra status. Vallatharasu, an intelligent lawyer from Pudukottai and a member of the Mukkulathavar community was also not averse to leaving his caste and class origins behind him. Then there were women like Neelavathi from the Naidu caste who braved community scorn and anger to work with the Self-Respecters. Every major non-brahmin caste yielded its young to the Self-Respect movement, which also became the context for the emergence of a new generation of non-brahmin organic intellectuals. These could be men like Gurusamy, learned, bilingual, erudite and brilliant in their expressions or they could be like Azhagirisamy who were untaught, unschooled, but who went on to become some of the movement's much loved and sought after publicists and speakers; men such as C. D. Nayagam, Ponnambalam, S. V. Lingam, Mayuram Natarajan, Nagai Murugesan, Jeevanandham, A. Raghavan and many others. The movement also served as a school for women intellectuals and Neelavathi, Annapoorani, Girija Devi, Minakshi and others learnt to express a range of ideas, concerns and practise the virtues of citizenhood through their participation and involvement in its struggles.

The Self-Respect movement was active outside the Madras Presidency as well. In Kolar the adi dravidas, prominent among whom was G. Appaduraiar, were in the forefront of the Self-Respect movement. In Pondicherry there existed Self-Respect forums as well as newspapers. Gurusamy wrote for *Puduvai Murasu* from here and attracted to Self-Respect propaganda work, men such as Sivaprakasam, Noel, the poet Kanakasuburathinam, who later adopted the name, Bharathidasan, and a host of others. Typically, these men were from different caste backgrounds and some of them were active amongst Pondicherry's working population as well. On the occasion of the Third Self-Respect Provincial Conference held at Virudhunagar, *Puduvai Murasu* published a special supplementary number to which several of these young people wrote articles and songs (Siva Illango 1991: 79-84). Self-Respect forums were also to be found in Ceylon and Malaysia and *Kudi Arasu* carried greetings from Tamilians in South Africa, the Fiji islands, Burma, Malaya and even Saigon! Periyar of course undertook extensive propaganda tours in both Ceylon and Malaya.

Being as flexible as it was, in terms of the people it attracted, the Self-Respect movement naturally enough received the attention of wealthy non-brahmins such as R. K. Shanmugham, W. P. A. Soundarapandian, the raja of Bobbili and the scions of prominent Nattukottai Chetti families. Yet these men, though they were respected and allowed to play gracious hosts and patrons, never exercised any decisive influence within the movement which, at all times, remained bound in fealty to Periyar.

The presence of young Self-Respecters in any small town or in the moffusil was enough to provoke the pride and ire of not only the brahmin but the non-brahmin orthodoxy in those places, and as several articles published in *Desabandhu* indicate, the latter did all they could to obstruct Self-Respect meetings, often employing adi dravidas to do this work (Db 28.9.28). On one occasion, an effigy of Periyar, after being garlanded with slippers, was burnt and *Desabandhu* covertly indicated that the miscreants, of whose behaviour in this instance it evidently approved, were possibly adi dravidas (Db 13.7.29). On another occasion, a *Desabandhu* correspondent addressed a satiric and vicious note to J. S. Kannapar who had taken the initiative in several adi dravida struggles. Titled, 'Kannapar's Wedding', this short note suggested that if Kannapar had not married, perhaps, he would consider marrying an adi dravida girl from the same village as the correspondent. The implication was that Kannapar may talk about the importance of making inter-caste marriages but would not marry a woman out of his caste himself (Db 29.6.29). Such taunts are to be found in almost every issue of *Desabandhu*, if one were to consider at random its numbers of 1928 and 1929.

Shudras: Theorizing Oppression

The Self-Respect movement's characterization of the shudra's role and place in the caste order was based, as we have seen, on the notion of a dishonoured birth. This theft of one's birthright by an exclusive priesthood and its sacred books, seemed to Periyar and others cruel and irreversible, unless one voluntarily struggled against and opted out of shudrahood. This was why time and again the Self-Respecters insisted it was the brahmin's lore which had enslaved the shudras (and the adi dravidas). Various shudra castes through their wealth, control over land and labour may oppress the labouring outcastes, but this contradiction between the shudras and the outcastes was not central to the caste order. The shudra's wealth did not redeem him in the eyes of a caste-ridden divinity and its voracious priests; neither did it grant him those natural inalienable rights which ought to be common to all of humanity. Thus,

> Raja Sir Annamalai Chettiar is a crorepathi. Sir R. K. Shanmugham Chetty possesses immense wealth. They are both men of property. But they will both admit that they do not possess those common rights that even a brahmin beggar assumes as due to him. A lowly brahmin who is privileged [on account of his birth] even if he has no property does not suffer from want of wealth and comfort. Thus, without working for it, without investment, because he is specially privileged, he can educate his son to enter the ICS, make him a zillah collector, a zillah judge, why, even a high court judge, a Shankaracharya or a Seer (KA 25.3.44; Anaimuthu: 1712).

The Self-Respecters were moved to criticize and comprehend in this and other instances, the production and the reproduction of knowledge in Hindu society rather than the production and reproduction of wealth. Much as the two kinds of production were integrated within an economy that relied on and was sustained by caste divisions, the production and circulation of knowledge possessed a certain relative autonomy. The owners of knowledge guarded their wares jealously and for centuries had derived their authority from the moral and spiritual surplus which accrued to them as a result of their hoarding of knowledge and living off it and their using it to demand and retain the labour of others. The owners of knowledge, unlike the owners of wealth, were not subject to contingencies arising out of trade, famine, marauding kings and wars and at all times could mediate and construct their authority as supreme. The brahmin's sacred thread was thus a more potent symbol of power than all the wealth of the non-brahmin merchant or landlord.

The denial of rights to an entire mass of people at birth, the systematic erosion of the non-brahmins' self-respect, achieved often with his consent, seemed particularly unfair and galling to the Self-Respecters because of the role assigned to the so-called shudra mother. Characterizing the shudra woman as a *dasi*, brahminical scripture had pronounced her sexually unfree. In these modern times, she may not be forced into sexual slavery as Self-Respecters believed she was in the past, but a caste of non-brahmin women, the devadasis, still eked out an existence by selling their sexual labour—in temples and to the rich and the famous. In the Self-Respecters' semantic universe the word 'dasi' often carried connotations of and slipped into the semantic space marked out by the Tamil word, *vesi* or prostitute. The devadasi thus came to be viewed as a reminder of an original shame and bondage, as the carrier of a memory of an original dishonour. This memory had all but been lost to non-brahmin consciousness, as Periyar so often remarked, since no non-brahmin sought to enquire into the origins of the word, 'shudra'. However, this memory of the non-brahmin woman as a sexual slave had been preserved elsewhere, in the dharmashastras and had since served to 'fix' the shudra in his lowness.

The vehemence with which the Self-Respecters supported the Devadasi Abolition Bill cannot be accounted for, unless we situate it in the context of a discourse that was structured around the notion of an original dishonour whose effects had marked the shudra, scarred him and her for eternity and consigned him and her to a perpetual and ritual degradation. What is significant about these various remonstrances against the dedication of girls to temples is that they embody a split sensibility: on the one hand the proponents of devadasi abolition were moved to protest the practice because it encouraged licentiousness, undermined and strained marital relationships and, besides, endorsed and legitimized 'dishonourable' behaviour in women. On the other hand, the abolitionists were influenced in their anger by the inhumanity of a system that enjoined only certain castes of (always non-brahmin) women to be sexual slaves of upper caste men. The fact that devadasis were attached to temples and were often at the mercy of the temple priests as well as the local notables pointed to the role of brahmin agency and interest in keeping alive the devadasi system. The Self-Respecters saw in the plight of the devadasi yet another instance of brahmin power and rapacity. It seemed to them that in her dishonour lay the collective dishonour of all shudra women and in her abject surrender to her vocation they discovered the loss of chastity of the shudra woman.

While the shudra woman was not explicitly denounced, a patriarchal semantics of honour and dishonour underwrote the Self-Respecters' perceptions in this regard. Though they wished to focus on brahmin cunning and hypocrisy in keeping an entire community of women bound to sexual slavery, their somewhat uncritical use of a semantics handed them down by history deflected their criticism from its ostensible target and relocated it in the space of the female body.

CHAPTER 10

Women: Coeval with Men

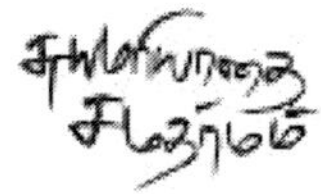

VOICES AND RESPONSES

A two-part article,`Women's Depressed Status', by one who called herself Penn-ina-nallar appeared in *Kudi Arasu* (22, 29.4.28) Written in logical, incisive and ironic prose the article recounted various travails endured by women. The author touched on a variety of themes: female education, Tamil culture, marriage, widowhood, Brahminism. She observed that the cause of women's education was being urged by many at present but those women who dared to go to college were vilified, teased, harassed and subjected to petty and mean tribulations. In almost all instances whether it be marriage or love, women stood to be blamed; but while the world was always eager to blame an erring woman, a man was allowed to get away with the vilest of crimes. Women were not free to choose their husbands, not allowed to get acquainted with them, in fact, marriages were arranged in such a way that neither man nor woman could speak or get to know each other before marriage. As for the Hindu widow, her plight was most pathetic. Her every movement and gesture was closely scrutinized, her dress, bearing, her talk criticized and if perchance her husband died, society was prone to suspect her character, her chastity and worth. On the other hand were a man to be widowed, the convention was that he could (and often did) marry 'before his wife's body had grown cold in her grave'. While the widow was enjoined to commit sati, no norms or strictures applied to the widower who was not required, like the widow, to discipline, deny or destroy himself.

Penn-ina-nallar noted that culture and custom had conspired to thus humiliate and destroy a woman's sense of self-worth. Brahminical rituals not only served to reinforce her secondary status but denied her the right to seek redress for the multiple ills that beset her. That is, she was forbidden to seek peace and penance through religious means. Commenting on Tamil cultural norms which defined ideal female behaviour, Penn-ina-nallar referred to the female poet and wise woman of yore, Avvaiyar, who, in spite of being a woman herself, wrote and railed against her own sex (possibly due to her long association with men). Taking exception to Avvaiyar's statement that 'if a wife is unbecoming [in her conduct] and is not able to perform her duties, her husband may take refuge in renunciation', Penn-ina-nallar observed that the poet did not deem it fit to allow women such an option; though it was men who often committed unspeakable deeds against women.

In the second part of her article, she defined what seemed to her, the ideal terms of marriage and existence for a woman. She noted that the husband-wife relationship ought to be based on love and nothing else and exist as an instance of comradeship. Men ought not to mistreat or beat their wives but must, instead, accord them the greatest affection and respect. She concluded her observations by drawing attention to Periyar's efforts in this regard; to his various entreaties to men not to subjugate women, to his endorsement of their rights to love and marriage with one of their choice and his encouragement of female education. She remarked that if this sort of persuasive propaganda were to proceed for a while the oppression of women by men would eventually cease. But, she added, such men that came forward to urge the cause of women must 'like Sriman Naicker [Periyar] be transparent in word and deed and cooperate with women in their forward movement, towards progress' (KA 29.4.28).

We find Penn-ina-nallar writing often enough in *Kudi Arasu* in 1928 and her opinions on matters related to women's life and well-being were expressed with a firm candour. Thus, in an article on women's education, we find her arguing that rich or poor, a woman is forced to fend for herself were her husband to die, and education would come in handy at such moments. Besides, a woman had no other means at her disposal than work to acquire income. For even *stridhan* that is given her at the time of her wedding is never hers to use at her discretion. A fond father may set aside the customary *manjakani* land for her at the time of marriage, but the income from it would come to her only during his lifetime; for unlike Islamic law, Hindu Law did not grant property rights to women. While Islamic law too did not offer women equal rights, it at least conceded partial rights. Thus for women to be economically secure, work and an education that would enable her to earn a living were important. And, of course, added Penn-ina-nallar, for women to thus pursue learning, the age of marriage had to be necessarily raised to at least 18, if not 20 years of age. Besides, she concluded, physiologically and emotionally a woman can handle marriage only at that age (KA 3.6.28).

Articles such as these would appear regularly in *Kudi Arasu* from 1928-29 onwards written by both women and men. Prior to this, we do not find as much space being devoted to gender concerns in *Kudi Arasu*, though from 1926 onwards the paper carried occasional articles on women's education, reports of Periyar's addresses on widow remarriage, Self-Respect marriages and on the need for women to assert their equality. The constituent germs of the Self-Respect ideology of gender are to be found in Periyar's addresses of this period. Full-fledged essays by Self-Respecters on the question of women, femininity, gender rights and responsibilities followed much later.

The year 1928-29 seems to have marked a new beginning, for throughout this time, we find Periyar and others writing, remonstrating, arguing, persuading and compelling their readers to heed gender concerns. It is evident from Penn-ina-nallar's affectionate reference to 'Sriman Naicker's' work in the cause of her sex's progress, that Periyar had already set the tone for debates on this matter, indeed, been doing so systematically for a while. In 1935, when the Self-Respect movement decided to set up a women's centre in Erode, Periyar would refer to his earliest undertakings in this respect; of how he, in 1929, started an informal association for women in his house in Erode and of how women would visit him for learning about various matters with regard to their personal and social lives (KA 28.4.35). Periyar also seems to have run a sort of home for deserted and unhappy wives who had left home. For at the Third Thanjavur Self-Respect Conference, we find an appeal being made on behalf of one Chinna-ramayammal, a 22-year-old woman who had been forced into marriage with a 50-year-old man, as his third wife. She had attempted to leave him, but her mother's family would not have her, while her husband was determined to make her bear his child. He had in fact tried to coerce her into doing so and when she refused, had tried to 'prostitute' her, whereupon, she had taken refuge in Periyar's *chattiram* (choultry) (KA 12.3.33).

However this may be, we may safely conclude that from 1928 onwards, the Self-Respecters possessed a coherent understanding of gender, for otherwise we cannot account for the clarity and sharpness that informed Penn-ina-nallar's articles during this period. Unless a discursive and social context that could accommodate, refine and advance women's concerns as pertinent had evolved, women writers would not have been able to thus write and agitate their way into the public sphere. Conversely, of course, it was women such as Penn-ina-nallar, drawn to the Self-Respect movement and its subversive intent and ideology and who adapted the latter to interpret and re-define gender concerns, who contributed in substantial measure to the making of a Self-Respect ideology of gender.

THE SELF-RESPECT MARRIAGE: A CATALYST FOR CHANGE

It was the Self-Respect marriage form and all that it implied which emboldened women to speak out their minds. Such marriages were conducted by Periyar and other Self-Respecters and were unique in several respects. They eschewed the services of a brahmin priest as well as the chanting of ceremonial mantras in Sanskrit, which, as Periyar pointed out, neither bride nor groom nor the attending public understood; they discarded custom and convention since these were often practised without a sense of what they signified and only because 'elders' held these rituals sacrosanct. (If the bride and groom desired to retain some of the rituals, such as the tying of the mangalsutra, the Self-Respecters were not averse to the idea. Their chief concern was that practices such as inviting an officiating brahmin priest and the uttering of Sanksrit mantras should be given up.) Moreover, Self-Respect marriages held that the bride and groom's approval (and not the consent of their parents) was absolutely necessary and central to the securing of the marital relationship (KA 3.6.28).

Periyar went so far as to honour the bride's wishes even when these proved to be somewhat problematic. Thus, in June 1928, he presided over the marriage of Nagammal and Rathinatayammal with Arangasamy, and explained this instance of 'bigamy' as having happened because the girls in question were inseparable, being friends, and did not want to be parted or married to different men! (KA 3.6.28)

Several Self-Respect marriages openly defied orthodoxy and, not merely the brahmin priest but the so-called clean non-brahmins were aghast at these performances. The marriage of Neelavathi (of the Naidu caste) and Ramasubramanium (of the influential Nattukottai Chetti community), when conducted in the Self-Respect fashion, drew the latter community's ire and its chief newspaper, *Sivanesan*, not only jeered at the marriage but also remarked that the marriage was attended by none but 'jutkawallahs, paupers, "temporaries", frauds and other such nonentities' (KA 19.10.30). Other Self-Respect marriages such as Ponnambalam's with Sulochana provoked caustic comments of a different kind, because Sulochana was already married to another man but had left him because she desired to wed Ponnambalam, an intrepid Self-Respecter. *Kudi Arasu* reported that Sulochana's first husband consented to her marrying a second time (31.5.31). Even zamindars and merchants came to break taboos regarding marriage and *Kudi Arasu* (24.7.32) reported that the zamindar of Singavanam had married a woman from a devadasi family.

The Self-Respect marriage vow required man and woman to abide by each other's views, needs and concerns. At the wedding of Sivagami a widow, with Sitambaranar, a Self-Respecter and Periyar's biographer, the following vow was proclaimed:

> Today our conjugal life that is based on love begins. From today I accept you my dear and beloved comrade as my spouse, so that I may consecrate my love and cooperation for the cause of social progress in such a manner as would not contradict your desires (KA 11.5.29).

The Self-Respect marriage vow thus allowed and enabled man and woman to come together on an equal basis and thereby indicated that the family that, after all, functions and is built on the basis of the conjugal relationship may be re-imagined. Marriages which defied the norms of caste, community and what was considered 'proper' or 'respectable' sexuality thus made for families which were outward in their orientation; they came to be less concerned with domestic virtues and worries and notions of privacy, honour and pride and were more interested in activities deemed public (as opposed to the private). Thus many a Self-Respect couple worked as full time propagandists and movement-builders, did not mind travel, dislocations of home and family that happened from time to time, and committed as several hundreds of them were to the cause of Self-Respect, they did not seek to build careers or fortunes. The life of Gurusamy and Kunjitham bear testimony to the near spartan existence that must have been the lot of many a penurious Self-Respect family in those days. Yet this penury was endured and in spite of a hectic public life, children were born and reared, educated and cared for. But neither conjugal love nor motherhood seemed to have played as significant a role in the life of women Self-Respecters as the demands of a public life. Women such as Kunjitham, Neelavathi, Annapoorani and Minakshi were first and foremost citizens and comrades and only then wives and mothers.

The catalytic significance of Self-Respect marriages was understood and opposed by those who were hostile to the movement as such. The burden of *Desabandhu's* argument against the movement was simply this: that by conceding to women's desire with respect to matrimony, Self-Respecters were encouraging licentiousness! Various sorts of objections were put forth to the Self-Respect mode of marriage, all of which make it clear the objectors feared such marriages would bring about the imminent destruction of caste and the consequent emancipation of women. It was claimed that Self-Respect weddings were deceptions practised on a gullible public; that not all non-brahmins associated with the movement forswore the services of the brahmin priests (P. T. Rajan, a Justicite, celebrated his daughter's wedding on a grand scale and called on brahmin priests to officiate at the ceremony); that in spite of the Self-Respecters' denunciations of caste, very few non-brahmins would actually consent to marry or marry into an adi dravida family (Db 28.9.29). A 'Student' writing in *Desabandhu* wondered how far the Self-Respecters would go in their practice of a new culture of matrimony. Would they, just to be 'radical,' marry their girls off to men within the family? Would they consider it an insult to their self-respect to marry their daughters to strangers, where they would have to heed and work for the happiness of others, and therefore would rather keep them within the families they were born into? (ibid).

A *Desabandhu* correspondent asked if, in the Self-Respect lexicon, the attainment of self-respect by women required that they be transformed into witches; for that was what the promised freedom—for women—would bring about. He further argued that women had always been accorded the greatest respect in Hindu society, had been imaged as goddesses, of wealth and learning, were celebrated as the divinities of the household. The Self-Respecters were not only unmindul of this but seemed to want to deliberately travesty time-honoured ideals of femininity, such as modesty, chastity, rectitude and courtesy (17.8.29).

Yet another *Desabandhu* correspondent took exception to what seemed to him the Self-Respecters' utter disregard for notions of female honour and character. He observed that if women were to be educated and employed and came to work (and compete) with men, they would surely shatter the peace of the household. He also disagreed with the Self-Respecters' insistence on 'choice' and 'preference' in matters of matrimony. He confessed that he was unable to see what place love was assigned in a Self-Respect marriage, though the Self-Respecters clamied they encouraged unions based on love. But could it be real love that cemented such unions, shorn as it was of modesty and restraint? (20.7.29; 17.8.29). Several other *Desabandhu* correspondents implied in their articles and reports, all of which denounced Self-Respect marriages, that the Self-Respecters were in essence propagating and encouraging debauchery. One P. V. Kannappa Mudaliar opined that if women were to be granted equal rights, especially rights to property, they would not hesitate to desert their husbands, were the latter not able to give them children (3.8.29). E. V. Rajagopal warned his countrymen on the pernicious effects of a philosophy of Self-Respect and remarked that this creed would force society as a whole into prostitution (20.7.29).

The re-definition of marriage by the Self-Respecters as instances of a 'social contract' forged between two individuals who could therefore break the contract if either of them so desired, no doubt, irked those who held marriages to be sacred unions. The idea that marriage could be considered a revocable contract suddenly made the caste Hindu family vulnerable and laid it open to disruption and disintegration. With women now deemed free to marry men of their choice, the integrity of caste too stood to be challenged, since after all caste honour, identity and pride were centred in the woman's body and being and consecrated in and through strategies of control and regulation imposed on women by patriarchal family heads. S. Ramanathan's observations in this instance bear repeating: 'To control their women Aryans devised a system which would characterize their enemies as untouchable and which would ensure that [the women] do not even touch [these other] men.'

Ramanathan held that transgressions of such a norm had led to the profusion of castes and as each caste segment constituted itself into an integral whole, it came to practise untouchability against the caste that came after it. Untouchability, according to Ramanathan, as precept and practice, was closely bound to notions of ideological and actual control over women. Thus, 'because our forebears held women as property they had to create the phenomenon of untouchability to safeguard this property.' Ramanathan also noted that because women were held to be property, they were automatically constituted as objects of suspicion and paranoia (KA 12.4.31).

For the women who were drawn to the Self-Respect movement, either through marriage or due to a fascination with the promises of freedom and knowledge, implicit in its creed, the world opened up in unprecedented ways. Participation in a Self-Respect marriage, conference and other public events brought the woman out of her home and family space and integrated her into a community of like-minded citizens, who did not abide so much by ascriptive rules of conduct and interaction, as they did by those norms of civil virtue which required men and women to mingle freely, across castes and creed, in a spirit of equality and mutuality. (Periyar often pointed out how the Self-Respect movement had actually ensured that women could travel, that is, made them mobile and visible.) Distinctions between home and the world, the private and public realms were thus gradually erased or reduced to near nothing as women Self-Respecters came to cogitate, speak and write on a range of personal and social concerns, often defining the one in the terms of the other.

THEMES IN GENDER AND SELF-RESPECT

As we have discussed earlier, every other *Kudi Arasu* published in the years 1928-29, carried articles on women, whose contents taken together, may be said to constitute the theoretical core of the Self-

Respect ideology of gender. Here are to be found articles on chastity, including Periyar's famous denunciation of this false and deceptive ideal; criticisms of what Periyar termed 'manhood' or masculinity and his famous critique of beauty; discussions on sexuality occasioned by the Devadasi Abolition Bill, the Sarda Act and the publication of Katherine Mayo's *Mother India* (1931); articles on purdah, on Hindu law and the rights it granted and withheld from women, and on men and women in contemporary Russia.

Periyar's remonstrances against the stranglehold of the ideal of chastity on women's lives and his plea for equal rights for women provoked a Saivite, P. R. Paramasiva Mudaliar, to respond angrily and derisively, and both these articles were duly carried in *Kudi Arasu.* In a remarkable essay that was passionate in its defence of a woman's right to desire as it was candid in its refutation of the myth of chastity that had been woven around female sexuality, Periyar discussed those principles which structured the quintessentially Tamil concept of *karpu* (chastity).

Tracing the etymology of the word, he argued that originally the term must have referred to qualities of firmness, steadfastness and honesty. Early in human history, karpu was probably considered a universal human quality that was believed to inhere in the human body prior to coitus; for after coitus the body becomes marked, comes to bear the trace of an other. However, after Aryan Hinduism entered the Tamil country, karpu came to denote wifely chastity and was associated with and considered an index of selfless, pure wifeliness. Periyar argued that the Sanskritic term *pativrata* denoted subjugation, surrender and control whereas terms such as *manaivi* (wife, woman of the household) and *nayaki* were connotative of equality, at least in the realm of love and desire.

Yet, observed Periyar, this did not mean the Tamil language and culture were any less culpable with respect to women in this regard, for Tamil poets, time and again, had resorted to a rhetoric of karpu in their works. Even the poet Thiruvalluvar, who was otherwise given to a rational and egalitarian world-view, was not averse to lyricizing the quality of karpu. For had he not said 'if a chaste woman who worships not God but her Husband wills the heavens to rain, it will'? Periyar further noted that had Valluvar been a woman he may not have written the way he did with reference to marriage and conjugality. Likewise, if women had written the dharmashastras, they would, perhaps, have not defined chastity in those terms that were commonplace in the present day. However this may be, given the unequal world of the sexes that we inhabit today, concluded Periyar, women had been coerced and persuaded, in turn, to accept their bondage, consent to an idea that stifled their desire and distorted their very being. Periyar also pointed out that women had come to assent to this state of affairs, convinced that they were chattels of men and wary of provoking their husbands' anger. This was not to be wondered at, considering that in Hindu society for centuries now, a set of communities had come to view themselves as low and outcaste, had in fact accepted their own subordination. Women too had come to consent to their oppression in a like manner and to practise a mortification of their selves, all on account of a false ideal (Anaimuthu 1974: 115-17).

Paramasiva Mudaliar in his turn argued that contrary to what the Self-Respecters (and Periyar) seemed to believe, ancient Tamil culture had educated and honoured its women. Thiruvalluvar had not erred in this respect and it was sheer folly on Periyar's part to imagine a woman in those times would have thought differently. (That is, even if Thiruvalluvar had been a woman he/she would not have written differently.) For one thing, women in the past had actually consented to their status and role in society and it was strange that Periyar should thus humiliate women by comparing them to the outcastes and refusing them their intelligence. The outcastes did not have access to knowledge but women were not handicapped in this sense. Tamil society had known women such as Avvaiyar who not only did not think differently from Valluvar, but in fact approved of him. Paramasiva Mudaliar also objected to what seemed to him curious, irrational and arbitrary about the Self-Respecters exhortations to equality. He disagreed with the Self-Respecters' demand that women be accorded a status, equal to and coeval with that enjoyed by men. He observed that not only could no living being be absolutely equal to any other, but equality of persons might be deemed a virtue only if an individual's claims to equality did not come in the way of fulfilment of another person's needs. If women were to claim such rights to equality as would not infringe on the needs of men and if men were to exercise similar rights, as would not hinder women, the promises inherent in the doctrine of equality would be realized. But for this one ought to grant and recognize that female and male needs are different, though not hostile, and that they arise from different attributes possessed by men and women. Thus men, known for their courage, valour, anger, power and desire to rule obviously differed from women who, as a rule, were merciful, loving, patient and given to nurture. The needs of the two sexes in keeping with their differing attributes were therefore distinctive (KA 12.2.28).

Periyar's riposte, as may be expected, was sharp and scathing. He refuted every one of Paramasiva Mudaliar's comments. He disagreed that women had actively assented to the secondary role assigned them and observed that this was because they did not know any better that they persisted in their quiescence. Besides if women were to truly believe they were inferior to men or that femininity denoted a set of lesser qualities than those associated with masculinity, they were unworthy of their sex. Periyar dismissed the idea that Avvaiyar could be considered an ideal woman of her times, and noted that a single Avvaiyar's learning does not redeem a general female illiteracy. As for the supposed congruity between Valluvar and Avvaiyar, one cannot refer to the latter's ideas to excuse the former's culpability. If anything, both were equally culpable, since both held unfavourable opinions of women. Besides, argued Periyar, it did not matter to him as to who said what. Nor was it useful or relevant to produce or comb through exegetical tomes on the writings of these poets. As far as he was concerned, there was enough, and palpable injustice in their manifest observations and he had no use for endless interpretations. Such attempts at exegesis were all too anxious to prove an idea was true for all times and this, for Periyar, betrayed a brahminical will to control knowledge.

Periyar also took great exception to Paramasiva Mudaliar's misreading of his comparison of women and the outcastes. He clarified that not only did he deem the comparison relevant and fair, but had made it because it was clear that 'at about the same time when a community of the depressed classes was created and denied access to the means of knowledge, women were also prevented from acquiring learning and thereby oppressed and consigned to servitude'. Paramasiva Mudaliar might consider such a comparison odious and demeaning to women, but for himself the subordination of women and the depressed classes were closely interwined and served a similar purpose.

Periyar was also scornful and dismissive of Paramasiva Mudaliar's theory of separate needs and rights. He refuted the notion that men women were innately different and remarked, 'Though women get pregnant and carry children in their wombs for ten months this does not make them different from men. With respect to qualities such as courage, anger, the power to command and the will to violence, women are like men [that is they too possess these attributes]...On the other hand just because men do not bear children it cannot be said they differ from women in respect of love, peace and the ability to nurture' (KA 12.2.28).

Periyar's views on karpu were particularly original for, in effect, they represented an implicit critique of masculinity. Such a critique was made quite explicitly in a related article titled 'Masculinity Must Be Destroyed', where Periyar observed that the very term 'masculinity' degraded women. As long as masculinity persisted as a norm, women could not expect to be, indeed, would not be respected. He reasoned that men, whose selves were bound to and constituted by this norm, naturally enough believed courage and freedom inhered solely in the male subject. Further, society as a whole had come to accept this division of qualities into male and female as God-given. But, warned Periyar, unless masculinity and its obverse femininity (which always already implied subservience), were destroyed there could be no genuine freedom for women. For this, women must consent to re-think their roles, must give up thinking they could not ever live without men. Periyar however granted that women were often constrained into accepting dependence on a man as their lot, because even if all other things proved equal—'even if a husband was to be had for hire'—the fact that women require help and support in childbirth nullified their autonomy. Thus, unless the burden of reproduction was shrugged off consciously by women, their emancipation would always remain fragile and vulnerable to attack (KA 12.8.28; Anaimuthu: 106-07).

Periyar's views on karpu, as they emerged in the course of his debates with Paramasiva Mudaliar and his re-reading of gender roles and functions, encapsulate an interrelated set of themes. Periyar would return to these themes many a time or explicate on any or all of them in other related contexts. In his denunciations of male privilege in the realm of sexuality, he would refer to the partisan use of the ideal of chastity. In his writings on motherhood, he would point out that a culture which negates and refuses women the right to desire also robs them of their right over their bodies. While commenting on conventional ideas of beauty he would indicate how such ideas were intrinsically linked to notions of chastity and how, together, they restrict a woman's progress. In his writings on Self-Respect marriages and on marriages in general, he would often revert to the theme of an unregenerate Tamil past, which like the past of the Aryans, sought to enslave women through injunctions to them to observe decorum and morality. In his varied and detailed discussions on female sexuality, he would demonstrate how chastity and promiscuity were really intertwined notions, two parts of a semantic whole that denied female desire and sexual autonomy.

Such imprecations to men and women to re-examine critically the codes they lived by produced astonishing results. As an irate *Desabandhu* correspondent pointed out, women had become bold and insolent and actually wished to do unto men what had been done unto women for centuries now. For at a meeting held in Erode, one 'Srimathi' said in public that she wished to see men suffer even as widows did; wished that they were submitted to ritual tonsure, veiling and consigned to the kitchen and the hearth (Db 4.5.29). Women also began to write of the importance of criticism, of the necessity for women to cultivate rationality and an enquiring mind. One Dharmu Ammal, writing on the (mis)use of religion in practice, pointed out that women must seek to ask questions rather than accept the conventional and customary tales and stories (KA 15.7.28). Periyar of course egged women on in their defiance, both during these early years of the Self-Respect movement and later on as well. He insisted that men too deserved to be judged in their conduct by standards of chastity; he enjoined women to take lovers, if only to demonstrate to men the injustice they inflicted on women, when they abandoned their wives and lovers for other women. He encouraged women to prove that they were as capable of earning money and taking on familial responsibilites as men (KA 8.2.31; 1.3.36; Anaimuthu: 108, 109).

Not only women but also men began to speak and write of the need for men to re-conceptualize and re-make their selves. For instance, at a Self-Respect marriage conducted by Nagammal, Gurusamy suggested that perhaps henceforth men should sport the mangalsutra, just so they realize the power and weight of restrictive symbols (KA 12.5.29). (In fact at a Self-Respect wedding held in 1935 the groom actually consented to wearing a mangalsutra [KA 14.7.35]). The Self-Respecters asked that men, at least symbolically and imaginatively, 'become' women to understand the horror of their own misdeeds.

A. Rathinasabapathy (who married Annapoorani) wrote a novelette on this theme, *Yezhai Azhutha Kanneer* (The Tears of the Poor) (1932). This amazing piece of fiction sought to lay bear the travails of the Hindu widow. A young widow subjected to harrassment and humiliation is killed by her own brother who is aghast that she should dare break the codes of widowhood and actually look out of the window of her room. The author comes to know of her fate and while reflecting on the dead woman's sad life drifts into deep sleep and thereby chances to enter a dream world where women rule. Here, the author discovers men in chains, in dungeons and in abject despair and is horrified to find a friend of his subjected to various sorts of torture as would be usually inflicted on a young widow on earth. The author then comes to learn that men such as his friend and all others who opposed widow re-marriage and other schemes for women's progress were subject to such punishment in this Un-Real world. He also learns that escape from this woman's city is impossible for the place was surrounded by a vast stretch of water that cannot be crossed. This stretch of water comprised the tears of all those wronged women, especially young widows, and unless the tears dried up, there would be no reprieve for men. Even as the author is struck by the poetic justice of it all, he wakes up.

Such exhortations to men to 'imagine' womanhood in all its despair and indignation no doubt proved to be extraordinarily effective. Several men came to query notions of masculinity, honour and chastity. Besides, women, now free to criticize and cast aside conventional ideas of manhood, family and female subservience and, free to demand their tormentors be tormented, came to experience, as mentioned earlier, an exhilarating freedom. For some, this freedom translated as a will to knowledge. When Periyar came to address a non-brahmin youth conference in North Arcot, he was pressed to speak to women, several of whom gathered on their own initiative to listen to him. Periyar spoke to at least three hundred women on this occasion and dwelt in his talk on the culture of masculinity and how it was complicitous with religion and caste and how together they worked to degrade and oppress women (KA 13.1.29). For yet others the fact that they were free to upbraid men served as an opportunity to address the latter on their own terms. Thus Penang Janaki Ammal, writing in *Kudi Arasu*, asked of men why they persisted in considering women as somewhat less than human. Were not women sentient creatures, even as men were? Why must men berate women and thus prove to themselves their own 'prowess'? In spite of proclaiming themselves valorous and wise, men were given to deception and crime, for had not many of them lured women to the Straits settlements under false pretences and then sold them off? Women, insisted Janaki Ammal, would never do such things! (25.11.28)

The decade 1928-37 witnessed a remarkable outpouring of female anger, desire, talent, intelligence, sensitivity and social concern. Women came to write on all and sundry matters as we shall soon see.

CONTENTIOUS MATTERS: WOMEN, THE ORTHODOX AND THE SELF-RESPECTERS

While on the one hand Self-Respecters desired to re-define gender roles and disentangle the complexities that lay at the heart of the sex-gender system, on the other hand they had to countenance, refute and challenge those who objected to their project of female emancipation. Objectors were of several sorts: those who resisted all and any attempt at reforming marriage customs and the status of women; those who resisted the Self-Respecters' creed with regard to these and other related matters, and those who possessed very different ideas about female progress.

Of those who resisted reform of marriage practices, the opponents of the Age of Consent Bill and the Child Marriage Abolition measure were the most vociferous in their protests. M. K. Acharya, a Tamil brahmin Congress leader, speaking in the Central Legislature against the proposed measure, opined that unless girls were married off before puberty, their chastity could not be ensured, that morality in marriage would suffer and conjugal life would invariably become corrupt (KA 23.9.28). T. R. Ramachandra Iyer, echoing Acharya's views, remarked that once girls attained puberty, they developed sexual desires, to regulate which they needed to be married early (KA 25.11.28).

Periyar was struck by the perverse intent of these arguments and observed caustically that if brahminical scripture could devise elaborate safeguards for containing the sexuality of widows, surely their modern-day interpreters could do the same for children who are after all pliable and easier to manage. He also pointed out Acharya's remarks implied he could not possibly guarantee the chastity of the women of his community, should they remain unmarried after attaining puberty (KA 23.9.28; Anaimuthu: 132). Periyar confessed himself aghast that these men, in such an obviously unjust manner, should invoke the authority of the scriptures to justify their oppression of women. He noted that no rational arguments could persuade such men of the folly and error of their ways and concluded that the iron laws of an authoritarian state were required to force them to think differently. Or else those who desired change should shatter all social norms, violate convention and thereby bring forth a new world (KA 25.11.28).

Neelavathi, writing on the Sarda Act, pleaded that the orthodox mend their ways and simultaneously assailed them for wanting the state to refrain from interference in religious custom. She observed that such men who railed against state intervention swore by their conscience, as if to say they willed the persistence of injustice. The Sarda Act, she concluded was even more urgent and necessary than the act which abolished sati, for, at least, the so-called sati died only once whereas the hapless widow died every day! To prevent the horrors that befall many a child widow the postponement of the age of marriage for women was thus very important (KA 10.8.30).

There were others amongst the orthodox who were very angry and critical of the Self-Respecters' attitudes to reform in marital customs and sexual mores. When Muthulakshmi Reddi proposed an amendment to the existing Hindu Religious Endowment Act, which would strike at the economic basis to the devadasi system, in the Madras Council in 1927, prominent Congressmen such as S. Satyamurthi and Swami Venkatachalam Chetty opposed it. The Justicites who were in the opposition were timorous in their support of the bill. The Self-

Respecters of course carried out an impassioned campaign in favour of the abolition measure. They denounced Satyamurthi's opposition to the bill, expressed dismay and anger over the Justicites' nervous stance in this matter, wrote and spoke of the degrading lives of the devadasi and condemned the inhuman and insidious system which thus condemned a class of women to perpetual and hereditary sexual slavery.

The Self-Respecters' campaign for the abolition of the practice of dedicating entire families of women to 'the pleasure of the Gods' was supported by several women from that community. The most famous of these women was Ramamrithammal who wrote a novel with the explicit pedagogic intention of upbraiding rich young men who spoilt their youth and wealth and squandered their riches on those 'shameless' women who seduced them into waywardness. The novel also addressed the devadasis, urging them to reflect on their existence and change their vocation. This semi-autobiographical work focussed on two devadasi sisters who opted out of the profession ultimately. Ramamrithammal herself left behind her despised and imposed vocation, married her music teacher and worked to propagate the ideals of the Self-Respect movement (Ramamrithammal 1936).

As we have discussed earlier, the Self-Respecters' attitudes towards the devadasi were ambiguous. She represented the quintessential shudra woman, ordained to serve the upper caste, largely brahmin interlopers who had come into the Tamil country centuries ago. The injustice wrought against her (and her progeny) had to be redeemed and set right. Yet, in herself, she was a 'fallen' woman, whose debauched existence constituted the rotten and corrupt core of a social and sexual order of things that was thoroughly degenerate. In either sense, though, she was a mere player in what was essentially a brahminical system of sexual oppression; one who ought to be pitied as well as despised.

However, it must be pointed out here that Periyar was only rarely inclined to blame the devadasi for her seductive powers, and even then only because she was a participant in what he considered a structure of sanctified debauchery. At other times, he criticized those social codes that were so ready to call a woman a prostitute but demurred from judging male promiscuity. In an article on prostitution, he observed that the Tamil language did not possess a word for the male debauch and added that even if a man was held to be lascivious, neither he nor society was likely to consider this amiss. In fact, argued Periyar, men considered it a matter of sexual pride that they should thus be characterized, since, after all, conventional morality considered debauchery an important aspect of masculinity. Periyar also remarked that while men did not mind being referred to as sons of debauched fathers, they expressed great ire when told their wives, mothers or lovers were promiscuous or when they were mocked at for letting them 'go astray' (KA 26.10.30; Anaimuthu: 170-73). To Periyar, karpu and debauchery were two dissimilar constituents of the same sexual ethic and he refused to consider them as given or sacrosanct moral categories. Both terms referred to degrees of male ownership of female sexuality. The one insisted a woman could be possessed by only one man while the other sought to make woman an object of public lust.

In an appeal to devadasis published in *Kudi Arasu,* one Ti. Si. Masilamani Pillay entreated them to renounce their profession and asked them to divest themselves of the hated *pottu* (the symbol of their initiation as devasasis) which marked them as objects of male sexual pleasure:

> The pottu casts into shame [you] innocent little girls, pushes you into an abyss and keeps you there, brings upon you dishonour—you are referred to as a slave and a prostitute—it is necessary that this degrading pottu is burnt and reduced to ashes.

Masilamani Pillay agreed that devadasis may not be able to, were not, perhaps, ready to thus abandon their profession but yet they must surely be aware of how their own children, their sisters and brothers often turned against them and disowned them. Surely they would not want such a state of affairs to continue? He suggested that devadasis join the Isai Vellala sangams that were being organized everywhere and express their support for abolition through *Kudi Arasu* and *Dravidan* (KA 17.6.28).

Devadasis were not unanimous in their response to Muthulakshmi Reddi's bill. Some like Ramamrithammal openly denounced the system of temple dedication. Their example fired many others to leave the profession but some others resisted the bill, disclaimed they were 'prostitutes' and sought to safeguard their claims on certain rites of passage, especially funerary rites, which had conventionally been granted them as a token of recognition of their service to the temple and in view of the fact that they were considered *nityasumangalis* (the eternally married).

The Self-Respecters continued in their tireless propagation of abolition, convened meetings, passed resolutions and published stirring articles on the subject in *Dravidan* and *Kudi Arasu*. Periyar reasoned that no one could possibly object to the Devadasi Abolition Bill: for one thing, legislation in this regard had long been in the making. In 1913 the government had proposed a bill on its own volition which was subsequently rejected because objectors to the bill claimed no clear guidelines as to the rehabilitation of former devadasis were entertained by the framers of the bill. In 1922, yet another bill was introduced in the Central Legislature to raise the age of girls to be dedicated to the temples. This measure became law in 1925. Periyar argued that Dr. Muthulakshmi Reddi's bill was merely seeking to improve on existing legislation and did not deserve to be contested. If yet certain persons persisted in their opposition and invoked the shastras to validate their point of view, this could be due to one of two reasons: either they were abysmally ignorant of what the scriptures actually say on this matter, or else they stood to profit by the devadasi system in several ways and did not wish to see it destroyed (KA 23.3.30; Anaimuthu: 173-76). Muthulakshmi Reddi's bill was finally passed. Initially, though, as Periyar pointed out, a section of the non-brahmin members in the Council—those in the Justice party—had exhibited a reprehensible hostility to it and voted to circulate it for public discussion, which, of course, would ensure its passage would be deferred (KA 23.3.30).

The debates over the Sarda Act and the amendment to the Hindu Religious Endowment Act proved acrimonious for two reasons: the Self-Respecters' support of these proposed measures provoked anger and derision in those who detested their reckless candour and transgressive energy. Secondly, the Self-Respecters' debates took place at a time Katherine Mayo's book *Mother India* was being discussed and denounced in public forums. Mayo, as is well known, argued that the barbaric and regressive social life of the Hindus was most in evidence in those offensive and unnatural sexual practices they encouraged and institutionalized through various customs, conventions and traditions. Mayo also dwelt on practices of motherhood and childbearing to indicate Hindu society was callous towards its women and unmindful of their welfare. Mayo's views angered Congressmen and, more generally, nationalists of every variety, and she was denounced as a conscious agent of British imperial interests which wished to prove to the world Indians were as yet unready for and unworthy of freedom. The anger of patriots and nationalists in the Tamil country was further fuelled by the Self-Respecters' endorsement of Mayo's opinions.

For the Self-Respecters, Mayo's book, detailing, as it did, all those social practices they considered vile and an affront to one's self-worth and rationality, served as an effective instrument to badger the orthodox. Besides Mayo's fascination with what she considered depraved, licentious and corrupt aspects of Hindu society served them well in their own iconoclasm. Mayo's text, sustained by an imaginative vigour that was part prurient, part righteous and part horrified inspired them to play out their drama of subversion with great gusto.

Kovai Ayyamuthu, a Self-Respecter, undertook a systematic defense of Mayo and sought to answer those specific objections nationalists and others had made to her work. *Kudi Arasu* carried (intermittently from 14.10.28–24.3.29) Ayyamuthu's observations on Mayo's work. Ayyamuthu argued at the outset that Mayo's Mother India assumed it was Hindu scripture which degraded women, an idea that was not new to the Self-Respecters. He then went on to consider Mayo's comments on the devadasi system; her remarks on the Hindu wife; her description of the Hindu widow and finally her critique of brahmins and Brahminism.

In each of these instances, Ayyamuthu pointed out that Mayo was right and justified in her criticisms. The devadasi system was unjust, the devadasis did not, as brahmins claimed, belong to God but were ensnared at an early age. The system that deemed them sexual slaves was particularly perverse for, while it allowed women to adorn themselves in bright clothes and entice men with their glitter in the precincts of the temple, it yet disallowed 'our panchama brothers, the Nadars and the Ezhavas to enter the temple'. As if such debauchery was not enough, there existed even more deplorable practices; as in Kerala where it was customary for many a rich man to force poor young men who came to them as supplicants into having sex with them. (Mayo had indicated the existence of such a practice, which, of course, the nationalist press had disowned and claimed did not exist.) (KA 14.10.28)

Ayyamuthu observed that Mayo was surely right in her description of the Hindu wife: that she was often ignorant before she got married; that she was made to perform endless rituals along with her husband and condemned to serve him for life; that Hindu wives were unaware of their rights and hence were given to schooling their children into servility as well. Rather than refute such criticisms by pointing to the isolated examples set by Avvaiyar, Asalambigai, Sarojini, Kamaladevi, Saraladebi and others, nationalists would do well to educate women into a knowledge of their condition. As for the Hindu widow, Mayo's criticisms of Hindu society's attitudes towards her were entirely fair and just. For, asked Ayyamuthu, does not the Hindu widow suffer in her loneliness, is she not vulnerable to illicit desire and sexual violence, is she not unfree and cannot act as she wishes, is she not forced to abort children she conceives but cannot raise? Besides does not society consider widows even more degrading and even less auspicious than even the much despised shudras and panchamas? (KA 16.12.28). Such defences of Mayo did not endear the Self-Respecters to nationalists or even to moderate reformers who were either given to subsuming social concerns in national ones, or who preferred such reform as would preserve the varna-jati order while effecting changes within its confines.

It is not surprising that faced with such an implacable and resolute oppostion to their efforts at upgrading the status and life of women and convinced that their opponents desired, at all times, to shore up their authority and that of varnadharma, the Self-Respecters came to query and challenge the gendered nature of caste and the brahminical basis to patriarchy in Hindu caste society. The Self-Respecters' formulations in this respect were influenced by a constellation of ideas and events: their own readings in the history and anthropology of several cultures; the Russian experience with respect to family and religion (which Periyar observed at close quarters during his visit to the Soviet Union in 1931-32). Ideologies of birth control and contraception that were in vogue in the late twenties and early thirties in several parts of the world and even here had a major impact on them, as did political events at home that convinced them the question of reform, of which the woman's question was a crucial aspect, was critical to the resolution of the problems of justice in caste society. Finally the participation of several hundreds of women in the Self-Respect movement's activities and their writings and speeches brought to its ideology of gender the authenticity of lived and felt experience.

THEORIZING BRAHMINICAL PATRIARCHY

As we have seen, Periyar's ideas on brahminical patriarchy drew sustenance from his original and robust rejection of the conventional feminine ideal of chastity. Linking up the pressure on women to remain chaste with the social imperative which held she must prove fertile and reproduce, Periyar enunciated a theory of motherhood in caste society. He then went on to describe and interrogate those values and ideologies which valorized motherhood and those material processes which ensured the reproduction of motherhood and mothering.

As pointed out, earlier, Periyar did not confuse biological difference with gender roles. He did not imagine that because men's bodies were different from women's bodies, men and women were different in their attributes and temperament:

> To make strength, anger and ruling ability solely male attributes and calm, patience and the ability to nurture life female ones is to say that bravery, strength and ruling prowess are characteristic of the tiger while the ability to care characterises the lamb (Anaimuthu: 121).

Such worthy pieces of fiction, reasoned Periyar, were not only misplaced in their intent but arbitrary in their choice of attributes, for masculine and feminine qualities were in reality produced by acts of history and practices of culture. Therefore, male and female roles were interchangeable:

> We maintain that while it is the case women possess the attribute of bearing a child in their womb for ten months and eventually giving birth to it, this, in itself, does not make them different from men with respect to [qualities such as] anger, ruling prowess and strength. Likewise we think that though men do not possess the [biological] means to get pregnant, it cannot be said that they possess qualities

> different from women in respect of love, calm and the power of nurture. If we are to value true equality—if there exists true love between man and woman—it is certain that all responsibilities except that of bearing a child should be considered common to both (ibid).

By making parenthood rather than motherhood the decisive factor in the nurture and care of human life, Periyar liberated the female body from the oppressive and suffocating realm of eternal fertility and thus granted the female person a will and subjecthood. Having done this, he next turned his attention to conventional modes of fetishization of the female body. He refused to accept the argument that women needed to and desired to look beautiful and that this was why they eagerly took to an adornment of their selves. He wrote in exasperation that literary descriptions of women were always given to hyperbolic celebrations of their bodies, while almost nothing was said of their minds, their reasoning and thinking abilities and their intellect. He exclaimed that women were seen as no more than 'pegs' on which one hangs jewellery and lamented that such notions of beauty which almost always stressed the seductive and glamourous appeal of feminine good looks were internalized by women themselves (KA 21.9.46; Anaimuthu: 127-30). He observed that from childhood girls were thought to feel simultaneously proud and vulnerable about their bodies and that this led to their transformation in adult life into icons of desire and pride:

> We allow girl children to play and prance about from infancy to childhood, shower them with kisses, nurture them without the least hint of discrimination on our part. But when such creatures attain maturity and intelligence we worry about them in an unnatural fashion, distinguish them from the rest of humanity and finally constitute them as useless dolls and come to consider them a burden to parents; women become a matter of concern to themselves and others and having thus made them objects of worry we then strive to protect them, satisfy their every whim, decorate them so that they become inert, lifeless dolls which need to be pampered and praised (KA 21.9.46; Anaimuthu: 127).

It was Periyar's contention that conventional notions of female beauty served to foster a pattern of expectations and needs in the woman which, she assumed, may be fulfilled only by the attaining of motherhood. Having been told to cultivate their bodies and look beautiful, women, naturally, expected to use their bodies honourably and the ideology of motherhood allowed for a play of female desire within safe bounds. Periyar saw motherhood as a carefully and ingeniously designed idea that had historically been used to secure women's bodies with their reproductive capabilities as the natural property of men.

Periyar traced the valorization of motherhood to those early historical times when private property first came into existence. He noted that until the genesis of private property, there could not have existed a need or an imperative for children to know their father's name. Only after Man sought to secure property in his name would he have felt the need to safeguard it; likewise only after 'ownership' and 'home' came to imply each other, would Man have desired a Woman to attend to his needs and protect his property and home. First, Woman was brought into the male household as a protector of property and soon enough she herself came to be viewed as Man's property. This, to Periyar, was a significant development in human history, for even as women came to be viewed as possessions, the system of marriage was instituted to underwrite male ownership of women. When, later, men wanted heirs to inherit their wealth and name, they perceived themselves as progenitors, and to preserve this mark of definitive male parentage came to enforce on women a code of monogamy. Further, it was held that property would accrue only to men and this resulted in a greater enslavement of women. Women thus came to be regarded as worthy only in their role as mothers and by honourably fulfilling this 'destined' role, they not only reproduced the oppressive system of which they were a part, but also their own oppression as well (Vi 11.10.48; Anaimuthu: 159-66).

Periyar's narrative of the history of women's subordination possessed a further dimension in that he placed the logic of reproduction in the context of Hindu caste society, presided over by a brahmin priesthood. He noted that the desire to have children for the inheritance of one's name and wealth would not have assumed such immense significance in Hindu society, if it had not been for the religious and cultural reasons that were advanced in justification of this desire:

> After it had become the norm for people to want children to safeguard property, brahmins who had invented fictions of heaven and hell to keep the poor from stealing from the wealthy and to secure some of that wealth for themselves now sought to argue that...man must have a [male] child who would keep alive his name after death and perform his yearly obsequies (Vi 11.10.48; Anaimuthu: 163)

Thus even as the real reason for wanting children faded into the recesses of communal memory, the fictitious reasons invented by brahmins came to take hold of the Hindu male imagination. Women were now to bear children not only to produce heirs but also to facilitate the passage of the mortal soul form this world to the next. Motherhood came under increasing pressure, for now it was significant for the reproduction of the patriarchal caste order in this world and also for its existence in the next as well.

Periyar thus demonstrated how private property, sexuality and caste were invariably interlinked so as to form a structure of which they were the constituents. To him not one of these constituents could be detached from the structure and considered the basis of an oppressive system; for it was in and through their interaction, so manifest in the realm of conjugality, that the social and sexual order reproduced itself.

Periyar considered marriage the ultimate badge of a woman's enslaved status, for it was marriage that thrust upon her, in the most decisive manner possible, the burden of motherhood. He often said that marriage, usually considered necessary for the ordered propagation of the species or for the good life was, in reality, a deception practised on women, a conspiracy that had been hatched very early in history to keep women submissive. Of whatever caste, class she was, the bond of marriage invariably rendered woman a property and slave of her husband. Periyar characterized the entire marriage ritual as it existed as an Aryan-brahmin imposition on the Dravidian South. The presence of a purohit even at non-brahmin weddings—a practice which he pointed out was becoming all too fashionable—signified that the former possessed certain superior and exclusive powers of sanction and legitimacy and this of course only served to confirm the non-brahmins in their low conceptions of themselves and the brahmin in his smug and complacent hegemony (Anaimuthu: 207-08).

While Periyar sometimes argued for a return to 'original' Dravidian rituals, at other times he insisted there were no such rituals. For, in the Hindu scriptural tradition, the various *samskaras* or rites of passage including the marriage sacrament could only be properly observed in a brahmin's life cycle. Periyar declared that Dravidians who were shudras had no rituals of their own, which was why some of the shudra castes took to wearing the sacred thread during rites of passage as marriage and childbirth so that for that period of the rite they may claim brahmin status and privilege (ibid: 216-19).

Periyar rejected brahminical rituals such as *kanyadana*—the giving away of the bride as a gift—and *Tara Muhurtam* that consecrated the act of gifting the bride, because these reduced women to mere objects and denied their autonomy and subjectivity. Besides, the purohit's Sanskrit mantras were degrading, for they described the bride as the wife of the gods, the *gandharvas*, the *devas* and *kinaras* before constituting her as a mortal bride. Periyar wondered how a woman's sense of her self could be enhanced if her sexuality was thus reified and displaced from her being onto rites of which she understood nothing (ibid: 206).

Implicit in Periyar's rejection of marriage was his rejection of what he perceived as a brahminical system of values which negated female selfhood on the one hand, even as they obfuscated and confused non-brahmins on the other. As he remarked, 'just as how Brahminism condemns a very large portion of the working population to shudrahood so it has condemned women to the servitude of marriage…To the extent that a woman lives up to the norms of a chaste and ideal wife to that extent she accepts and revels in her slavery' (Vi 28.6.73; Anaimuthu: 178).

How was woman to be liberated from brahminical patriarchy? Periyar saw his Self-Respect marriages as part of the solution and in his several speeches at such marriages outlined his theories of conjugality, love, marriage and divorce. By making private ceremonies into occasions for public homilies, Periyar effectively delinked marriage from domesticity and, more important, laid open domesticity itself to public scrutiny. Since Self-Respect marriages were voluntary unions, Periyar insisted they implicitly endorsed divorce (KA 29.12.29; Anaimuthu: 146). Arguing that the absence of a provision of divorce affects women more adversely than men, he said that if divorce was not made a realistic option for women, the only way out for them was the practice of polygamy. Thus, 'if the right to divorce is not granted, polygamy and polyandry should become norms. To bear in silence and patience the travails of an unhappy marriage is a slur on one's humanity, self-respect and an act of clear folly' (Anaimuthu: 148).

Periyar encouraged a second marriage for those men and women who had fallen out of love or singly or mutually decided they were not good enough for each other, for whatever reason: 'To discipline love and desire and direct it along particular channels and orient it towards particular persons does not seem to us to have any justification. To desire is human. To control it is to practise a kind of slavery' (Anaimuthu: 153).

The chief virtue of Self-Respect marriages lay in the fact that they defined women as persons rather than as wives or potential mothers. Besides, such marriages constructed women as equal subjects with equal rights to property and power in the household and outside of it. Hence women did not have to consider themselves as mere adjuncts of men and bearers of their seed. Self-Respect marriages were thus of tremendous political importance in that they prepared women to view motherhood as a choice rather than as their destiny.

As we have seen, Periyar considered motherhood the crucial link which held a caste-bound patriarchy together, since it ensured the reproduction of the system on the latter's own terms. He noted:

> Men's responsibilities end with getting women pregnant but all other responsibilities beginning with the moment of pregnancy through the time the women experience labour pains (including the dangers accruing to women's health) are thereafter women's alone. Even after a child is born it is the mother who nourishes it with her blood now transformed into milk. If the child falls sick it is the mother who observes the requisite diet (KA 1.3.31; Anaimuthu: 159).

Periyar's devaluing of motherhood was, on the one hand, a response to the nationalist argument that women had to be liberated only to be returned as more intelligent and efficient members of their sex to the kitchen and the hearth. On the other hand, it was a carefully articulated argument against the naturalization of the idea of motherhood in caste

Hindu society. Against this seemingly self-evident idea, he advanced a radical counter idea, chiefly, to help women come to terms with their overdetermined status as mothers. In this context he invoked other arguments as well: produced Malthusian images of hunger and poverty (on account of the ever growing population); constructed images of human sweat and toil (suggesting such hard labour has become imperative in view of the number of mouths to feed) (KA 6.4.30; 1.3.31; Anaimuthu: 155-56; 157).

Periyar advocated birth control as an effective means that would help women relieve themselves of the fear and responsibilities of childbirth. He also pointed out that birth control afforded physically weak and sick women a means out of the trauma of pregnancy. It is interesting to note that he opposed abortion, convinced as he was that it affected women's health most adversely. His concern for women and their well-being, as in this instance, bordered on tenderness—which seems so striking a quality in one who was rarely given to any display of sentiment (KA 1.3.31; Anaimuthu: 158).

Periyar's advocacy of Self-Respect marriages and his rejection of motherhood constituted important aspects of his principled critique of brahminical patriarchy. Another important ideological counterpoint to patriarchy was to be had in the general philosophy of Self-Respect, constructed as it was on the basis of an enquiring and curious Reason which was sure of nothing but its own probity. In the last instance, though, patriarchy was to be countered by the rebellion of women and, more important, by their unified challenge to the ways of men.

Women were to realize their new subjectivity and work in concert with each other (and with men who had attained a measure of self-respect and who valued equality) so that they could undertake tasks and responsibilities conventionally denied them and thereby project novel role models to each other and to successive generations. A *Kudi Arasu* editorial (22.1.33) indicated how this may be done. Commenting on a meeting of 'Indian Women', presumably held under the auspices of the Congress, the editorial observed that it was indeed odd that the conference resolved to teach little girls 'music, *kolattum* [a Tamil folk dance], home science'. How could educated upper class women forget the fact of their secondary and subordinate existence and thus seek to perpetrate it by invoking conventional symbols of feminine learning and worse, hold up role models—such as Sita,

Nalayini, Chandramathi and Vasugi—whose husband-worship was certainly not worthy of emulation? The editorial concluded by noting new role models and heroines, those who had made their mark in education, the sciences, the art, in sports and other feats of endurance and who were recognizably modern, had to be upheld and celebrated to facilitate the gradual emergence of a new female subjectivity.

The making of the modern woman required among other things that she be equipped with information and knowledge, especially as regards her own body and her self. *Kudi Arasu* carried regular articles on birth control and contraception in the thirties, all of which urged that women learn to take control over their reproductive capabilities. It published a translation of a survey conducted by an (unnamed) American university on contemporary American women students' attitudes to marriage, sexuality and childbirth (18.1.31). The results of the survey indicated that most women favoured birth control, pre-marital sex and stressed the need for sex education. The translator, who preferred to remain anonymous, observed, as if satisfied, that 'not only were the women at the university aware of birth control methods but they feel and seem to consider it necessary that in today's increasingly complex world they should possess the rights to and control over their pregnancies'.

A series of articles on contraception by one T. D. Gopalan appeared that year (3, 17.5.31; 5.7.31). Gopalan reviewed various scientific and pseudo-scientific modes of birth control and at the end of it all upheld a woman's rights to desire and conversely to say no to unwelcome sex. Periyar in one of his articles on the subject referred to the pioneering work of Marie Stopes and her clinics in this regard and argued forcefully that when childbirth ceases to be a matter of choice but a condition to be endured at all costs, it not only traps women into loveless marriages but prevents them from seeking out other male friendships or from forsaking a husband they dislike for another (KA 1.3.31; Anaimuthu: 159). *Kudi Arasu* even carried a short appreciatory note on Gandhi's views on contraception. A report published in *Nagara Thoothan* (NT), a weekly that was close to the Self-Respecters, on an adi dravida Christian conference held at Trichy, observed that participants at the conference had entreated government to frame a bill which would grant them rights to avoid unwanted pregnancies. They had also noted birth control was of particular importance to adi dravidas since being mostly poor, they stood to suffer if families were large. Adi dravidas had counselled the government not to heed the Catholic clergy who might protest this demand. For the latter, being single and without families, did not and could not understand the problems of poor adi dravidas who after all constituted 75 percent of the Christian community (12.11.33).

A PLACE FOR WOMEN

Apart from such articles that sought to provide women with a knowledge of their own bodies, there were other articles written during this period—by women—on any number of themes: women wrote on rationality, the uses of science, on the irrelevance of religion, the effects of Manudharma on women and on the parasitic nature of brahmins. Gender concerns were debated furiously by the Self-Respecters and there is evidence to suggest that some women (and a few men) desired a partially autonomous forum for women that would function independently of the movement, even while it remained aligned to it. The emergence of such a demand points to two things: one that the movement had come of age and was willing to submit itself to self-criticism and two, for all of the movement and Periyar's interest in the woman's question, women felt the need to function independently and to commune together as women, even as they did as Self-Respecters or citizens.

A. Raghavan, a regular contributor to *Kudi Arasu*, in an article (13.3.35) observed that the Self-Respect movement had acquired a certain worth in the public eye, that even its staunchest opponents were now inclined to view it with a degree of approbation. Yet all was not well with the Self-Respecters. While women had contributed substantially to its success, Self-Respecters had slackened in their efforts to involve women in the movement's work on a sustained basis. Women, to an extent, were responsible, too, because those who professed defiance and claimed they would change the world, when married to a man of their choice, did precious little and 'were content to be seen in the company of their husbands. They play cards, bear children or else take to complaining incessantly of ill-health, of toothache, headache... Whenever there is a conference they appear dressed in a doll-like fashion and if they can speak... do so for half an hour and then leave.' This situation could be remedied, argued Raghavan, if the movement were to create conditions and opportunities for women to talk to each other and evolve certain objectives that they may collectively pursue and address. One could perhaps begin this process by setting up a women's centre at Trichy or Erode: a centre which could serve as a retreat for widows, destitute and deserted women and children; where women could learn a few skills and be educated in the philosophy of Self-Respect. Raghavan considered this task of setting up a centre so urgent that he felt the movement's atheistic and socialistic propaganda should be deferred for a while so that Self-Respecters could devote all their energies to this endeavour.

Neelavathi endorsed Raghavan's proposal and pointed out that such a centre as he had envisaged would enable women meet and discuss matters of common concern. At present only upper caste women had access to such forums, but the Self-Respecters' forum would bring together women from different castes and communities (KA 24.3.35).

Raghavan went ahead to frame rules for the proposed centre. He suggested the centre could be called the Rationalists Women's Association and noted that its objectives could be the following: to educate, cultivate intelligence and rationality in women; teach them the arts of painting, music, various crafts and exercises for bodily well-being; to propagate and encourage widow re-marriage, love marriages and inter-caste marriages. As for the rules, children and destitute women would be admitted as inmates, but once they were taken in, their parents would forfeit all claims on them. The centre would undertake to feed, clothe and marry off children when they grew up. The centre would also take in, within limits, widows and women who wished to marry outside their castes or those who wanted to educate themselves or learn a craft. Money for running the centre would be accepted from those who could pay for their keep. Women, once admitted, would have to stay for a year at least and if they desired to leave in the middle ought to compensate the centre by paying up a small amount. While all women, irrespective of caste or creed would be admitted, and their religious affiliations be considered their business, the centre would yet frame common norms of behaviour which would be binding on all women (KA 31.3.35).

Neelavathi was enthusiastic about these plans and remarked these would go a long way in extending women's participation in the movement. She added that perhaps women should have their own magazine as well, for as a fellow woman Self-Respecter had remarked ruefully, at present the Self-Respect magazines asked for and carried articles on gender 'only when there is a paucity of articles on samadharma' (KA 21.4.35).

Periyar lent his support to these plans but cautioned Raghavan, Neelavathi and others to be circumspect in their approach: they ought to identify women's needs precisely and address these within the limits of the possible. Periyar recalled his own efforts at setting up an informal association for women in Erode in 1929 but admitted that on the whole the Self-Respect movement had undertaken only piecemeal programmes with respect to women. However, now that plans had been hatched for a more systematic intervention in the cause of women, it was important that Self-Respecters carried out their task in this regard with a sense of responsibility and not give room for gossip and cheap talk; since at all times they ought to be sensitive to public opinion, for otherwise they would lose the ear of the commoner (KA 28.4.35).

Neelavathi agreed with Periyar and added that lately she herself had felt the need for such a centre. Initially, she had imagined that if women organized themselves separately they would be alienated from men but she had seen, these past years, that women were reluctant and scared to speak in mixed company and had come to feel the importance of a space for women all their own (KA 28.4.35). Following a meeting held in Vai. Su. Shanmugham's house (he was a prominent and well-known Self-Respecter), Raghavan's idea finally acquired shape and the Tamil Nadu Women's Progressive Association was formed and Shanmugham and Neelavathi elected secretaries (KA 26.5.35).

The formation of a women's centre at Erode must be seen as the logical result of nearly a decade of hectic propaganda about women and women's problems. Even a cursory glance at *Kudi Arasu* from 1928-1937 will reveal the extremely wide range of gender concerns the Self-Respect movement sought to address. We give a sample of these concerns.

ADDITIONAL THEMES IN GENDER AND SELF-RESPECT

An article on the horrors of purdah—republished (and translated from the *Indian Daily Mail*)—by one Laila Banu Begum appeared in *Kudi Arasu* (14.10.28). The writer observed there was no sanction in Islam for purdah and hence no punishment for its non-observance. The practice was in all likelihood extrapolated into the Islamic world from Persia and later came to India as well, where it had taken firm root. Laila Banu observed rather satirically that in the past when kings ruled and subjects had no rights and the practice was observed amongst the rich, men could at least afford to—and often did—build lovely gardens for their veiled wives. But now in these days of democracy and rampant poverty, what joy could women possibly experience in the secrecy of their veils? Several Islamic nations had abolished the practice and women no longer wore scarves and veils in Turkey, Bosnia, Herzegovina and Albania. Several other countries—Egypt and Afghanistan amongst them—were considering abolition. What was deemed good for Muslims in one instance surely ought to be good for Muslims anywhere! Laila Bano Begum pointed out that the Muslim community had to address the problem of purdah from the point of view of women's health. Not only were a majority of Muslims—men and women—poor and lived in bad, unhealthy environs but for every Muslim boy who survived, six Muslim girls died, usually of tuberculosis. To ensure that women survive in good health, practices such as the observance of purdah ought to be abolished and women educated. Another article on purdah by S. Abdul Azeez was published in *Kudi Arasu* (25.11.28).

A critique of Hindu law as framed by the British and with reference to the rights of women was published in *Kudi Arasu* (2.9.28). The author of this lucid article pointed out that while men had rights to polygamy, it was near impossible for women to seek and obtain a divorce. Moreover, women possessed no rights to property, which strengthened male familial control over her. Women had no right to a faith of their choice and often had to practise their husbands' faith. The Hindu widow's access to her dead husband's property was severely limited; besides, she could not alienate it at her discretion nor will it to anyone. She had no rights in ancestral property. Men had greater rights to guardianship than women and though courts theoretically could exercise discretionary power in this regard and allow the mother rights to guardianship if the child was small, very rarely did this come to pass. The author, after a brief comparison of Hindu and Islamic law, remarked that Islamic women possessed relatively more rights than their Hindu counterparts with respect to property and guardianship.

Kudi Arasu carried articles on marriage, the Sarda Act and divorce throughout 1930. C. K. Pitchandi wrote of how caste would be destroyed in its entirety were intercaste marriages to become a norm (KA 6.7.30). Neeelavathi wrote an impassioned article on the Sarda Act that was addressed chiefly to what she characterized as the orthodox mindset (KA 10.8.30). *Kudi Arasu* ran an editorial on the right of conjugal partners to divorce which in all likelihood was written by Periyar (17.8.30). An editorial on re-marriage also appeared (KA 12.10.30). There were other articles too written during this period: Sami Sitambaranar wrote on the extraordinary strengths of women (KA 25.5.30); Penang Janaki Ammal wrote on the uses of atheism for women (KA 28.9.30). Neelavathi commended the Travancore state's decision to abolish the devadasi system in an article addressed to the Queen Regent Sethulakshmiammal (KA 24.8.30). Yet another article on law and women, but this time devoted entirely to the question of property rights, was carried in *Kudi Arasu* (26.10.30). Several articles on Russia and the policies of the new Soviet state with respect to women and the family appeared regularly in *Kudi Arasu* in the mid-thirties. One of the earliest articles on the subject was a translation of an article by W. J. Brown, 'The Conduct of Man and Woman in Russia' (KA 19.8-28). An article, 'Russian Women' was also published (KA 18.11.29) and one on 'Socialism and Women' by M. Singaravelu appeared as well (KA 15.11.31).

Nagai Murugesan, who joined the Communist Party of India, later wrote a brilliant piece on the sex-gender complex. Titled 'Man-Woman Differences: They Are Artificial Not Natural' (KA 8.10.33), this article was obviously inspired by Marxist theories of state and society. He pointed out that it was an original division of labour between man and woman that created the sex-gender system. Differences in work engendered differences in perceptions, attitudes and even behaviour and eventually these came to be viewed as differences in character and temperament and were located in biology rather than in the social context. Referring extensively to the researches carried out by Bachofen and Humboldt, Murugesan detailed the varied roles and functions performed by women in different societies. He also pointed out that the devaluation of domestic work was probably an important reason for the historical subordination of women. He argued that if the division of labour which, at present, organized work and its perfomance was to be abolished, men would automatically lose their privileges and distinctions.

Not merely Murugesan, but several other Self-Respecters seem to have read widely in anthropology. Periyar himself was conversant with the findings of contemporary research on tribal societies and used these as illustrative instances to discuss the problem of sexual morality; whether one may legislate universal norms in this respect or consider morality in love, marriage, sex a wholly relative affair, considering the variety of human practices with respect to conjugality.

Puratchi carried an article on women and samadharma and Jeyasekari, wrote of women in the socialist world (KA 29.4.34). Two articles on domestic work appeared in *Kudi Arasu*. One suggested that cooking be simplified to ease women's burden and urged the Self-Respect movement undertake a campaign in this regard (26.5.35). The author added that because brahmins ate only one elaborate meal for the entire day they, especially the modern brahmin woman, had time to spend on other things such as educating themselves. He urged non-brahmins to devise simple but nutritive diets that would leave them with enough time and energy to pursue more cerebral activities! The other article demanded that housewives be paid salaries for cooking, raising children and for keeping a home (23.2.36).

Besides articles on marriage, family, socialism and labour, which constituted a staple of Self-Respect discourses during the thirties (in addition to the usual articles by women and men on religion, custom and convention), there appeared well-argued articles by women on political matters. These included their addresses at conferences and were concerned chiefly with appropriating political ideologies towards serving gender concerns. We shall consider in some detail a few such strategies of appropriation.

APPROPRIATING POLITICS

The attitudes of women Self-Respecters to politics were influenced by the movement's general reluctance to engage directly with the political realm. Women too accepted the claims of civil society as urgent and immediate and considered the struggle against brahmins, Brahminism, caste and religion, whether Hindu or otherwise, to be paramount. This did not of course stop them from critically interrogating the politics of nationalism and situating it in the context of not merely an anti-imperialist logic, but an anti-brahminic and anti-caste logic as well.

At the very first women's conference held under the auspices of the Self-Respect movement (along with the Second Self-Respect Provincial Conference which took place at Erode in May 1930), the chairperson of the reception committee, Lakshmi Ammal observed in her welcome address that 'those books [shastraic texts] written by selfish men' and those 'religions which divide people and which are an affront to one's rationality' are the chief cause of women's degraded and secondary status in Hindu society. She pointed out that this degradation was further compounded by women's lack of choice in the matter of marriage and the denial of property rights to them. Women, she observed, must fight against obscure and superstitious custom and work to rid men of their masculinity and their inordinate selfishness. Lakshmi Ammal warned that 'if men were to persist thus in not giving into women's demands for freedom and if they were to persist in their belief that women were their playthings', women will have no choice but to practise a policy of 'Non Cooperation with respect to the men in their lives' (KA 11.5.30).

Such an easy and felicitous re-use of that charged phrase 'Non Cooperation' is of course not accidental. Gandhi had launched his first phase of Civil Disobedience in March 1930 and managed to capture the imagination of thousands of people with his grand and solemn march to Dandi. In Madras, as we have seen, Civil Disobedience campaigns began on a modest note, but the power of appeal of Gandhi's rhetoric of civil disobedience and resistance was, as yet, immense. The Self-Respecters, while critical of the entire Dandi campaign, were nevertheless alive to the semantic possibilities that lay immanent in the idea of Civil Disobedience and brought to their uses of the term (and concept) an ironic and critical resonance. Lakshmi Ammal's deft re-interpretation of the term in the context of home and family may be taken as a fitful instance of the Self-Respecters' command over language and their undoubted skills at dislocating words into a meaning that was at once startling and entirely relevant.

Writing nearly two years later but in a related context, when following the Gandhi-Irwin Pact, Congress agreed to pursue a policy of peaceful picketing of liquor shops and those which sold foreign cloth, Minakshi questioned her protesting sisters thus:

> Today I hear my sisters are engaged in a boycott of stores selling foreign cloth and in a picketing of liquor shops; that they are breaking the Law and going to jail. Whenever I hear of this my heart sinks; not because I think one ought not to serve the nation; neither do I dislike such [exhibitions] of patriotism. But if we, as women, were to reflect on our conditions of existence, are we not forced to ask ourselves if the need of the hour for us is political freedom or social freedom?... it is indeed astonishing that we who are steeped in folly, convention and [given to performance] of obscene rituals, we who give in to religious hysteria, to a faith in God bordering on madness and to blind superstition, should... engage in this boycott and picketing... Sisters, reflect for a moment on the horrors you endure in your day to day life. You borrow money—because you wish to observe a custom, practice a ritual; you borrow for a funeral, for a pilgrimage... Consequently poverty, humiliation, debt, police warrant, mortgage, the misery that visits your children, unbearable sadness, the rebuke of others—one follows the other. Why must you do this? To preserve a convention, an orthodox custom? To appear virtuous in the eyes of others? Do you not realize your [minds]) are diseased... stricken with barbarity and afflicted with degenerate rituals....

Minakshi's passionate expostulations were however tempered with the appeal of reason. She argued that she wished to awaken women to their responsibilities, convince them of the folly of remaining bound to custom. Therefore,

> We need to picket and boycott. But not the liquor shops and those which sell foreign goods, schoolrooms and courts. At a time when

> such resolutions [on reform] as have been accepted by government are being framed into law, we need to picket the homes of those fanatically orthodox men who seek to obstruct reform and conspire to defeat it; we heed to picket the homes of the foolish, of those who are ostentatious, of those orthodox men who wish to prevent young widows from marrying again. You may offer satyagraha—why, your very life—for the sake of our devadasi sisters who are being coerced by their parents into the profession of their forebears. Offer satyagraha in front of the homes of your sisters who disdain to grant our adi dravida sisters' rights of access to the common well. During election times, picket the homes of those who are opposed to our development... commit satyagraha to impress upon men in whose homes the women cannot go out on their own nor see any one (KA 6.3.32).

Such exhortations by women Self-Respecters to their sisters to remember and act on their sorrows, with a view to ending them, served to re-define not merely the nationalists' terms of discourse but also political activity and agitation as well. Girija Devi, speaking at the Madras Self-Respect Conference (KA 10.1.32), noted that the woman's question was as important as any other political question. Specific institutional solutions needed to be evolved to tackle the needs and concerns of women. Girija Devi suggested that perhaps a separate department for women's development ought to exist with a woman as its head. The women members of this department would take charge of and attend to all matters concerning women. Initially these women could be nominated but in due time they must be elected to their posts and solely by an all woman electorate. Further, women officers ought to be appointed in all institutions of local government; in panchayats, municipalities, taluks and districts.

What issues would these women officers consider pertinent to women's welfare? Girija Devi observed that from helping to mitigate the travails of poor women, especially pregnant women, who suffer ill health and live on a poor diet, to holding meetings in villages every month that would serve as general pedagogical forums, where women would be addressed on a variety of issues—women officers could assume charge over a range of functions. To Girija Devi, two functions seemed to have been the most important: education and employment. She noted that whatever its financial constraints, the government must invest in female primary education and make sure all women, from the adi dravida girl working in the fields to those who imagine they are progressive, being of the upper classes, are compulsorily educated at least up to Class Eight. Secondly, all efforts should be undertaken to ensure women become economically independent. Whatever jobs they seem to be able to do must be reserved for them and them alone.

Girija Devi concluded her address by noting that at the present hour women need to be protected because their own powerlessness and men's irresponsibility rendered them vulnerable to assault. But this situation could not persist forever and could and must be transformed. This could be done if women were taught to defend themselves and if they worked to change those conditions of existence which left them powerless. Perhaps, noted Girija Devi, women, like the Sikhs, should be allowed to carry a knife, should, in fact, be ashamed to be seen anywhere without it! Some women may consider the carrying of a weapon by women a reversion to barbarism, but if they desired to move about freely and without the help of men they will surely see the wisdom of this.

The re-centring of political work in the particular context of women's lives and the re-definition of political tasks and responsibilities which followed may be reckoned as perhaps one of the most original, compelling and radical attempts at re-drawing the limits of political society. Not only the matter of rights but the all important question of power is addressed here and resolved with great clarity and insight. Here we find those first intimations of an autonomy to the women's question that would gather into a demand for a women's centre in 1935.

If Girija Devi sought to 'feminize' politics in a general sort of way, Neelavathi sought to make out an explicit argument for what we today recognize as an incipient feminist socialism. Writing in 1934, on the eve of the impending May Day celebrations in Madras province, Neelavathi produced an amazing treatise, 'Women and Work', whose purpose was to call men's attention to the fact that women were also workers (Pu 29.4.34). Neelavathi began by observing that not only did women work hard but their work was systematically devalued and they were themselves scorned and humiliated for all their labour. If one were to leave aside the very rich amongst women, who lolled about all day long and idled their time away, one would easily see that the remaining 90 percent worked night and day. Neelavathi went on to say:

> It is often asked how women who have been born to housework may be called workers. It is said that women have nothing to do with work and that they are fit to perform only certain tasks such as child bearing [that is, housework is reduced to child bearing]. It is also said that women may not aspire to be considered a part of the labour force as men. Those who say these things refer to the oft-repeated maxim, 'Work is the mark of a man!' But no rationalist can accept this, that there is something about work that it could thus be considered essentially male.

Neelavathi added that such maxims and beliefs, had been concocted by the rich ruling class, by 'those who have instituted the present order of things'; so that 'women may be kept away [at home] from the eyes of the world'. But what women desired was something different. They desired to see that dawn when it shall be said, 'Labour is the mark not of a man but of humankind'. Neelavathi went on to detail how women's work—performed in the course of a single day—ought to be granted the dignity of labour, though it may be largely confined to the kitchen and the hearth:

> From dawn to night... women labour with their bodies... they have been condemned to household tasks and in reality ought to be known as kitchen workers. Women labour thus through the year without respite... One cannot claim they are not labourers on the argument that cooking is not work.

Besides women's lot was no different from that of the exploited worker and in many ways worse, since at all times women had to remain 'composed and balanced': 'More than any other social segment that has been deprived and marginalised and enslaved, women suffer and suffer such wrongs.' Yet, women's work, even as it exhausted her 'refines existence as such; is a necessity for society'. Neelavathi pointed out that currently women's workloads had multiplied, because, today, women worked besides men in all spheres, 'in factories, hospitals, in the countryside', in 'tailoring, weaving, construction, vending, trading'. Women were also doctors and teachers and journalists.

While this expanded workload no doubt tired women out, the continuous expansion of their arena of work enabled them to labour at all those tasks men performed and therefore, argued Neelavathi, one may expect that in the decades to come women may actually be coeval with men and preside over the disintegration of the system that subordinated women to men. However, warned Neelavathi, one could not always assume men would allow or want women to labour thus, at all and sundry tasks. She pointed to the example of Hitler's Germany in this instance and noted that his regime had withdrawn German women from the workforce and returned them to their kitchens and thus laid the basis for an uncontrolled dominance of women by men. Men, concluded Neelavathi, should not give into the silly and defensive temptation to prevent women from working on the ground that even men have no jobs. Instead they should learn to see women as co-workers who had as much stake in a future ruled by samadharmic (socialist) values even as men did.

This plea for recognition of women as workers may be considered an adjunct to that demand, voiced in different ways and in varied instances by Self-Respecters, to view women as fellow citizens, equal to and coeval with men in every way. Neelavathi's defence of women's work and her emphasis on its productive quality is of singular significance, in that she showed that a woman did reproduce the conditions of production, and, most important, refined these conditions to resemble a 'life' and not a regimen of labour and leisure. Neelavathi in fact suggests that not merely the working class, but that the category 'work' itself, needed to be re-interpreted, so that the struggle for socialism could be located inside the home and outside of it as well. The alienation of the labourer as well as that of woman had to be overcome for the coming of socialism.

Given such creative and original interventions in the political realm by women Self-Respecters, it is not surprising that, like their male counterparts, they came to engage with those conjunctural crises and problems faced by the larger non-brahmin movement quite effectively. Neelavathi, for instance, was scathing in her condemnation of the Justice party for its decision to admit brahmins into its ranks and proposed mockingly that the Justi-cites pick a cabinet that would reflect their latest political pro-clivities: Why should not they, argued Neelavathi, work to make Satyamurthi a law member, M. K.

Acharya the Council member in charge of women's affairs and T. R. Ramachandra Iyer and A. Rangasamy Iyengar ministers for social reform? (KA 8.6.30) Neelavathi was also sharply critical of the Harijan Sevak Sangh and Gandhi. She noted in an address delivered at the Kovilpatti Taluk Third Self-Respect Conference that whatever sacrifices Gandhi influenced would always be in vain, for they would be placed at the altar of varnadharma. 'Gandhi asks women to remove the jewels they sport on their person and hand it over to him', noted Neelavathi and added, 'we do not object to this. But the women who heed him are blind, in spite of having eyes, deaf in spite of possessing ears ... What is Gandhi going to do about this ... Gandhi says Bihar is the birthplace of "my Janaki" ... That may all be very well but what about the Janakis of the present day who languish in misery?' (Pu 11.2.34).

Periyar's dream of a community of women Self-Respecters who would unite in solidarity with their male peers in a spirit of horizontal comradeship and citizenhood was partially fulfilled by women who came to the fore in the Self-Respect movement, and who thus clarified the relationship between social reform, gender and politics. The women's question through the thirties and forties did not devolve onto the rarified inner world of culture, tradition and community but continued to haunt civil society at large.

CHAPTER 11

Samadharma

THE SELF-RESPECTERS' desire to found a community of rational, fraternal, freedom-loving citizens, equal and coeval with each other in every imaginable way was propelled forward by their conviction in the principle of what they habitually termed *samadharma*. Samadharma constituted the founding principle of the new republic they imagined and was conceived as a refutation of Manudharma. Samadharma assumed equality amongst men and between men and women as a given but, more important, it required that this equality be realized in and through an affirmation of each individual's self-respect.

The Self-Respecters were aware of the difficulties that stood in their way of achieving a social utopia animated by samadharma. For, the idea of samadharma was not available as a norm or a given towards which one may move; neither was it a pre-defined value that could be assumed at will by those who wished to live by it. It was an ideal that had to be constructed in and through acts of defiance and subversion—of caste, religion—and reflections on these acts. In almost every instance, the Self-Respecters had to interpret and re-interpret the significance of these acts, and propose to an eager but bewildered constituency new ideas, new notions, different ways of seeing, hearing and being; in short they had to cultivate and nurture a veritable new structure of feeling.

The Self-Respecters' ideal of samadharma then may be best understood as an idea-in-process; one that was never entirely grounded, either on the basis of a simple contradiction, such as, for instance, between brahmins and non-brahmins, or in antagonisms between rich and poor, capitalist and labourer, or landlord and worker. However, the fact that the principle of samadharma was left theoretically open-ended does not, of course, mean the application of this principle in practice was vague or ineffectual. The Self-Respecters at different times and contexts identified the ideal of samadharma with a set of clearly defined material attributes which they held ought to characterize the good society. Thus the achievement of proportional (communal) representation in the services, the evolution of common and shared rights of access—to public and sacral spaces, to property, education, employment—to all sections of the populace and the reorganization of society's social and economic life on the basis of socialist principles came to be acknowledged as valuable and desired material correlates of the principle of samadharma.

It must be noted here that for the Self-Respecters, samadharma was not merely the Tamil, local equivalent of socialism, both as a term of reference and as a concept. On the other hand, though, socialism existed as an aspect, an inalienable aspect of samadharma. The equality and self-worth the Self-Respecters desired to instil and cultivate in countless non-brahmin hearts and minds required not merely the dawning of a new age of economic equality and public ownership of property, but the fulfilment of a millennarian dream, whereby caste society in its entirety and in all its complex ways of being, would be transformed.

The Self-Respecters' deployment of the term 'samadharma' was distinctive and differed, for instance, from M. Singaravelu's use and interpretation of the word. Singaravelu noted that only in the Tamil country had the word 'samadharma' been endowed with a socialist resonance and edge. He pointed out that in the context of Hindu thought, dharma, as defined in the Gita, for example, implied the performance of duties assigned to the caste of one's birth. The Buddha had however used the term to refer to a thing, to sheer materiality (*vastu*). If one were to understand the present import of the term in the context of the Buddha's use, one would see how it meant the 'ownership of property in common' (Pu 4.3.34). Amongst others who sought out Buddhist origins for samadharma, as a word and as an ideal, was the Buddhist scholar and long-time friend of the Non-Brahmin movement, Professor Lakshminarasu. In an address delivered at a meeting of the South Indian Buddhist Association, he noted that the moral-spiritual basis for countering Hinduism 'which is inseparable from the brahmin (and who, in turn, is plagued by untouchability)' can be had only in the creed of the Buddha, which, he declared, was the oldest samadharmic creed in existence. Buddha dharma which, historically, had resisted Hinduism and its brahmin priesthood, would alone enable Self-Respecters attain their ideals of self-respect and samadharma, in this instance socialism (KA 29.3.31).

Adi dravida intellectuals, especially those associated with *Tamizhan* and the Sri Siddhartha Puthagasalai in Kolar, identified a caste-free society as a samadharmic society. Their publications were advertised as samadharma books. P. M. Maduriar, whose *In and Out Religions* was one such text, used the terms 'non-brahmin', 'atheist', 'working-class person', 'rationalist' and 'samadharmist' interchangeably. Further, he defined Brahminism as a creed that ran contrary to the principles of universal justice and used the term 'capitalist' to refer to the class of priests (1935: ii-iii).

To understand the play of the principle of samadharma in Self-Respect discourses and practices, in all its nuances, we need to consider a whole host of related concepts and activities: the definitions (always provisional, flexible) of samadharma; its material correlates; and, finally, the possibilites that existed in the thirties and after, for a political practice of this ideal in all its complexity.

DEFINITIONS

Kudi Arasu published an article, 'The Self-Respect Movement Is a World Movement' (7.10.28). Written by Gurusamy, its purpose was to counter those believers and brahmins who found the movement's propagation of atheism offensive and who therefore consistently denounced the Self-Respecters. Gurusamy observed that the Self-Respect creed was not a lone and partisan ideology that had been evolved by a few men in the Tamil country. For at the present hour, 'all over the world workers and labourers were doing precisely this: that is, everywhere they were engaged in a fight for their self-respect. It is because of this struggle that workers have been able to liberate their respective nations from bondage.' Such an affirmation of one's self-respect, noted Gurusamy, may be witnessed elsewhere in the Indian subcontinent, in Bombay, for instance, where a whole set of radical demands related to the abolition of religion and priestcraft had been raised in several forums. Two years ago, several resolutions were passed in the Bombay Legislative Council that demanded an abolition of the much despised tyranny of the priesthood. At several youth conferences held in Bombay province, it was declared that the authority of mullahs and the Christian clergy ought to be challenged and overthrown. Everywhere in that province, service castes such as the dhobis and the barbers had vowed to withhold their services to those who professed caste arrogance. It had been resolved that children of different castes be allowed to drink from a common water point in their schools. Gurusamy went on to recount other instances of defiance by young people everywhere—in the Central Provinces, in Punjab and Calcutta—and their abjuration of custom. He was particularly impressed by Subhas Chandra Bose's efforts at countering caste, creed and social hierarchy and noted that the latter had proclaimed caste differences and superstitious practices as well as the authority of gurus must be abolished and the importance of reason emphasized; that the subjugation of women must end and inter-caste marriages encouraged; that the control wielded by capitalists over labour must be done away with and the power of landlords over agricultural labourers countered; and, finally, that all differences, between rich and poor, upper castes and lower castes, men and women must cease to be and that equality govern social relations (Velu 1991: 105-07).

For the young Gurusamy, this programmatic statement of intent by Bose encapsulated those ideals which he felt ought to animate and constitute the core of Self-Respect activity. Several others during this period felt likewise and looked to the example and inspiration of the Soviet Union which had done away with its priesthood and ensured a modicum of social and economic justice in its vast regions. As early as 1927, Kaivalyam had pointed out how the modern Russian and Turkish states had achieved substantial victories in their rejection of religion (KA 25.12.27). An article on how the Soviet state had decreed that Christmas and Easter not be observed and celebrated and on the success and salutary effects on the general populace of the propagation of atheism in the Soviet Union was published in *Kudi Arasu* (13.1.29). Gurusamy pointed out that the Russians were so serious in their atheism that even their playing cards carried anti-religious messages (KA 26.5.29). Penang Marudhamuthu argued that the destruction of caste and religion alone would signify and mark the advent of socialism or samadharma (KA 29.9.29). At a Self-Respecters conference held at Pattukottai, Gurusamy spoke of the relevance of anti-clericalism and its success in Russia. Gurusamy also warned his audience that in view of the tyranny and oppression that was being routinely and habitually visited on the adi dravidas, it would not at all surprise him if a revolution, as had taken place in Russia, were to erupt here (KA 26.5.29). An article on the Russian Revolution noted that the people had rebelled against the hated triumvirate of Lords, Kings and the Clergy (KA 1.6.30). Yet another article referred extensively to the various laws relating to the abolition of religion which had been passed in the Soviet Union. Interestingly enough, the arbitrative functions which such laws served and represented were described by the author of this article as constituting in themselves a 'samadharma panchayat' (KA 5.10.30).

From 1926 onwards Periyar had advocated a theory of Self-Respect and adumbrated a comprehensive critique of caste and Brahminism. But Self-Respecters were especially thrilled and excited when they discovered that this home-grown philosophy of equality and justice possessed resonances that were truly cosmopolitan. The 'success' of the Soviet experience in realizing equality, fraternity and justice 'proved' to the Self-Respecters the inherent worth of their own convictions, both in their own eyes and in the eyes of the world. What is, of course, noteworthy is that it was not Soviet socialism, as it is commonly understood, which attracted the Self-Respecters, but Soviet experiments in abolishing religion (Gurusamy was likewise attracted to Bose because the latter opposed caste and the clergy).

When Periyar and S. Ramanathan visited the Soviet Union they registered themselves as honorary members of the Atheists' Association, and on their return to India in December 1932 they published a series of articles in translation in *Kudi Arasu* that contained Lenin's views on religion (KA 11, 18, 25.12.32; 8.1.33; 15.1.33; 22.1.33) Later when *Kudi Arasu* ceased publication and *Puratchi* was begun in its place, the very first editorial of this new weekly proclaimed that the present capitalist state was held captive by a clutch of priests. It further declared that 'this class of priests ought to be destroyed before the capitalist class could be destroyed' (26.11.33).

In an article that spanned several issues of *Kudi Arasu* (4.10.30

to 25.1.31) which introduced the *Communist Manifesto* to the Tamil reader, Periyar noted that logically a revolution should have occurred in Indian society as in Russia; for here were to be found such horrors and deprivations, such poverty, illiteracy and ignorance and, worse, such a perversion of the human spirit. Centuries of bondage to religion and a priesthood had crushed people into mental and physical submission; yet, the anticipated and necessary revolt of peoples had not taken place because, unlike in Russia 'the caste system functions as a protective fort and helps to preserve and perpetrate the notion of economic inequality' (KA 4.10.31; V. Anaimuthu 1974: 1677-80; 1678).

Moreover, there had come to exist in modern Hindu society a vicious philosophy of religion and politics advocated by Gandhi. Periyar would argue thus a few years hence, and at a time when Gandhi's hold over the political life and imagination in the Tamil country and elsewhere was complete and hegemonic. Gandhism, according to Periyar, was akin to Tolstoyism, that gospel of charity which held the poor and the meek ought to be revered and served and that politics ought to be spiritualized. Both Tolstoy and Gandhi claimed they were engaged in a spiritual mission and that they desired to 'cleanse' public life. Both had done enormous disservice to the poor, since their ideas held these latter in thrall and prevented them from rationally and critically examining their lives and fortunes. Gandhi and Tolstoy had confirmed the poor in their misfortune and actually convinced them of the inherent beauty and goodness that attended a life lived in poverty and misery! Periyar remarked that just as the destruction of Tolstoyism had constituted a necessary condition for the emergence of communism in the Soviet Union, so in India the destruction of Gandhism was required before once could usher in socialism (KA 30.7.33; Anaimuthu: 1681-82).

It is clear the Self-Respecters inflected their creed of subversion and revolt in a manner that would affiliate their ideas and activities with the great Russian Revolution and the promises of freedom and equality which underwrote it. A *Revolt* editorial thus observed:

> It was on the 7th of November 1928 that memorable day in the history of nations, the anniversary of the immortal revolution in Russia, the day which is looked upon as the violent explosion of

> human liberty, the day which is memorialised by millions in Russia for the mighty mixing of monarchs and masses—it was on that day that *Revolt* saw the light of day at Erode. Even as we pointed out at the outset we unfurled the flag of revolt to destroy tyrannies and to befriend man and woman. Our aim, as we declared, was to put before our people and humanity in general how social injustice is at the root of our economic bondage and political subjugation (17.11.29; Velu: 155).

An earlier *Revolt* editorial, written on the eve of the First Self-Respect Provincial Conference held at Chinglepet in February 1929, had argued in defence of its dictum that social injustice was fundamental to the economic and political bondage of the Hindus. It had remarked that above all Self-Respecters ought to struggle to destroy brahmin parasitism and ensure employment for all; that they should see all work and jobs were equally distributed and that all special rights and privileges, such as those which accrued to particular social groups, were abolished ([translation from Revolt] KA 17.2.29).

This marriage of Self-Respect and socialism, as A. Raghavan characterized it (KA 30.4.33), took place during those momentous years which saw the signing of the Poona Pact and the subsequent eruptions of adi dravida anger and discontent with the Gandhian Congress. In the Tamil country, the Self-Respecters were in the forefront of those denunciatory campaigns against Gandhi which convulsed political life in the Presidency. Their critique of religion served them well in their condemnation of Gandhi's paternalism, which seemed to them not only dangerous in its religiousity, but which they felt would strengthen the material basis of caste and varnadharma. A *Kudi Arasu* article (20.11.32), written as a critique of Congress' sudden interest in temple-entry struggles, observed that economic disparities constituted the basis for the practice of untouchability, and that to preserve the subjugation of labour and the labourer, religious strictures, norms and texts had been evolved. The editorial also pointed out that untouchability was indissolubly linked to economic oppression and hence required not merely the abolition of caste and religion, but also the institution of economic equality. Adi dravidas, warned the editorial, ought not to be seduced by exhortations to temple-entry, for while these may be necessary rights that they should exercise, these rights in themselves could not facilitate their emancipation.

Such an approach to problems of religion, caste and untouchability, was clearly mediated through a consciousness newly awakened to the economic aspects of social bondage and oppression, but yet to the Self-Respecters, it constituted a moment merely in a discourse that desired to counter at all costs and in whatever way it could the power and appeal of Gandhi's politics. For the Self-Respecters, this appeal derived chiefly from Gandhi's association of politics with piety. Thus, A. Rathinasabapathy wrote on the pernicious influence of religion on people's minds and observed that it was not merely the dominance of the rich that must be challenged, but also the power of the priest that needed to be contained, if samadharma was to become a reality (KA 6 and 13.11.32).

One can understand this desire to counter the lures of religion in its Gandhian expressive forms as well as its habitual manifestations better, if one considers the fact that not merely Hinduism, but Catholicism was attacked by the Self-Respecters during this period—1932-33— in the name of samadharma. In this instance the Self-Respecters deployed their samadharmic notions to two interlinked purposes: they articulated an anti-clericalism which was obviously inspired by Russian diatribes against the church, but which addressed, in pointed terms, the casteism rampant in the Catholic Church in India. Secondly, the Self-Respecters resorted to invoking socialism as a desirable ideal in their dialogue with adi dravida Christians to point out to them that the church, which rested on their membership and support, was really not a haven for them as it claimed to be, but that it was, as any other religious insitution in Hindu society, implicated in practices of caste. Self-Respecters pointed out to the adi dravidas that the Catholic religion had not really enhanced their status nor could it do so, for the oppression they suffered possessed a material basis in caste society and the Catholic Church had proved itself unwilling to counter and destroy this basis (KA 30.4.33; 7.5.33).

Gurusamy was one of the earliest and perhaps the most bitter and unrelenting of those critics who attacked the Catholic Church. As early as 1931, he had observed that the non-brahmins or any Self-Respecter for that matter, could not possibly approve of a religion that assigned separate pews and churches to members of different castes (Velu: 235). His translations of Jean Meslier's observations and criticisms of the Catholic Church appeared regularly in *Kudi Arasu* from June 1931 (Velu: 249). (Interestingly enough, Meslier was one of the radical proponents of enlightenment and supported the French revolution, when it happened. He was an early advocate of a sort of utopian communism, arguing, as he did, for the rights of the workers and the poor peasantry. He was also firm in his conviction that religion was one of the chief causes for the ignorance of the poor.) Gurusamy also translated Bertrand Russell's *Why I Am Not a Christian* (Velu: 250). In April 1933 wrote an article, 'Catholic Fury', inspired by a Catholic conference held in Madras and attended by several high-ranking priests in the church hierarchy. The purpose of the conference was to assess the damage caused to the Christian faith by Self-Respect propaganda and publicly denounce the Self-Respecters. The assembled priests not only spoke out furiously against Periyar, *Kudi Arasu* and the socialism they espoused, but passed two resolutions condemning the Self-Respect movement. Gurusamy in his well-reasoned article pointed out that the Self-Respect movement's critique of Catholicism was based on a careful study and review of church history, policies and practices. Referring, among others, to the ideas of John Huss, Bernard Shaw and Bertrand Russell, he observed that while all churches were 'instruments of bondage', the Catholic Church, as befitting its status as a hoary and great institution, was perhaps an extremely powerful one (KA 30.4.33; Velu: 332-34). Besides the church, the Catholic faithful also demanded a ban on the Self-Respect movement. Thus, J. A. Lane, a Catholic from Ceylon, demanded that the Self-Respecters be put in their place (KA 29.10.33).

The Self-Respecters' anti-clerical, pro-socialist sentiments had angered not only the church but the *Madras Mail* as well. In one of its editorials (11.2.33), it cautioned its readers of the possible ill-effects of the Self-Respecters' anti-religiousity. Noting that the latter's propaganda has been particularly successful it observed that it had virtually banished from public forums all discussions of religion and questions of faith. The *Mail* concluded by noting that if this situation was to continue, all religions would be destroyed, as had happened in Russia. Responding to all these remonstrances, a *Kudi Arasu* editorial (30.4.33) noted that, for all their purported interest in the poor and the meek, and in spite of the fact that adi dravidas constituted the majority of the Christian faithful, precious little had been done for them by way of education and employment by the Church. The clergy had spent most of its time dividing up its congregation into Paraiahs, Pallas, Udayars, Vellalas and Chakkiliyans and thus preserved intact the varna-jati order of society. The Catholic Church, implied the editorial, had much to answer for and the Self-Respecters were entirely justified in their criticisms.

The propaganda against Catholicism existed as an important aspect of samadharmic propaganda and contributed substantially to the general anti-clericalism which characterized the Self-Respecters' pronouncments on samadharma. It is significant that Muslim Self-Respecters sought to re-interpret samadharma in terms of a 'true' Islam as preached and lived out by the Prophet from a 'false' Islam that was deployed by mullahs, maulvis and other religious heads to dupe the devout. A. K. Rahman observed in this context that praying together and dining together cannot be taken to be instances of an Islamic samadharma. What was needed instead was to rescue the samadharmic tenets of Islam from the Muslim clergy and align Islam to the poor and the deprived rather than to let it become an instrument in the hands of the priesthood. Rahman also pointed out that Self-Respecters were critical of the 'false' Islam of the clergy and did not seek to confound this with the practice of the Prophet (Pu 4.3.34).

The point is the Russian example in all those instances we have just discussed proved enabling and educative to the Self-Respecters in a very specific sense: it sharpened their critique of religion, validated their iconoclasm and atheism and, most important, aligned their creed to the communist creed of universal human liberation.

THE CASTE-CLASS RIDDLE AND THE SELF-RESPECT MOVEMENT

Because Self-Respecters attacked religions and religious institutions for justifying hierarchy and injustice does not of course mean that they ignored the economic aspects to socialism, or that they were disinterested in comprehending how economic facts and ideology are related to each other. After all, they were constantly reminded of the necessity to address economic problems by M. Singaravelu. The latter was euphoric in his endorsement of their social radicalism, but held that it was imperative they practise samadharma in the economic sphere as well. Singaravelu granted that the Self-Respecters had worked hard to bring to public attention the problems of oppression specific to a caste society and at revivifying the question of adi dravida rights, as perhaps no other politcial or social reform movement had done. Yet, they had to heed more seriously the problems of the economy and could not afford to subsume these to social imperatives and concerns (KA 1.11.31; 8.5.32).

As we have remarked earlier, for the Self-Respecters, economic oppression could not be more than a moment in their practice of Self-Respect and socialism. Even when they entreated adi dravidas to abandon a church that was not really interested in them, their descriptions of the economic basis of untouchability possessed a symbolic rather than a substantial value. As always, the cunning of priests and the deceptions of religion which justified social injustice were abhorrent to them. The reasons for this very important decision to grant primacy to their struggle against social injustice rather than economic oppression are complex and worth discussing in some detail. For this we need to attend a little closely to that 'marriage of Self-Respect and socialism' which was effected in the Tamil country in the thirties. What were the terms of articulation and integration of concepts and how were these effected?

Firstly, the Self-Respecters vision of equality and justice had taken shape and acquired relevance in the very specific context of caste Hindu society and, as we had noted earlier, demanded the fulfilment of three interrelated and equally important demands: the realization of rights to education, employment and of access to public and sacral places to all, irrespective of birth and status; the destruction of priestly privilege and the ideas, norms and practices which had been instituted to consecrate these privileges as given and indestructible; and, finally, the re-constitution of the family and a re-organization of gender roles and functions. Secondly, the Self-Respecters understood the organization of production and labour as these existed within the terms of the varna-jati order. Their understanding of the relations of production drew heavily on and was influenced by their critique of Gandhian economics. Thirdly, the Self-Respecters' options, both in theory and practice, were determined at least partially by the extremely complex conjunctures in which they had to function. They had to counter the hegemony of Gandhi, negotiate skilfully with the colonial state that was simultaneously coercive and persuasive in its exercise and use of authority, and finally they had to strike a fairly isolated path in their social radicalism. The limitations of the Left alternative in colonial India deprived the movement of an effective catalyst, and its economic agenda, at the best of times, comprised a set of objectives whose significance was more rhetorical than real.

It is clear the Self-Respecters' vision of justice and equality was complex and that it possessed several levels to it, each of which signified the attainment of a certain right or the redressal of a particular wrong. While all these levels were interrelated, they were not easily reducible to a common determining instance. The Self-Respecters did not assume, for example, that the achievement of a measure of economic equality would lead to the dissolution of caste differences. They knew the varna-jati order was cunning in its workings and would survive in one form or another, unless it was completely dismantled. Therefore, they carried out their propaganda work at all levels, determined to make mankind 'unlearn many things' before it could 'store up new stock' (R 17.11.29; Velu: 155-56).

It is worth recalling here Periyar's defence of the Self-Respect movement's interest in holding conferences of the 'non' variety, such as conferences of non-zamindars, non-moneylenders, non-capitalists, and so on. The idea was to exclude the oppressor in each specific instance and not in any other because, as Periyar often argued, the oppressor in one instance becomes the oppressed in another. Of course, added Periyar, this does not mean the Self-Respect movement was opportune in the constituencies it sought: at all times it was opposed to the triumvirate of the rich, the educated and the brahmins (this was of course an ingenious re-reading of the Russian triumvirate, the Kings, Lords and Clergy) (KA 27.8.33; Anaimuthu: 1682-85).

A Question of Rights and Power

In 'Common Rights or Common Property', an article written in 1944, Periyar pointed out that caste society disallows its citizens from experiencing in common, shared and indivisible rights. Even wealth fails to be the great equalizer here, as it is in other societies, since the wealthiest non-brahmin may lack and, indeed, be denied those rights possessed and exercised to his partisan advantage by the humblest brahmin. Therefore, the most urgent task for the Self-Respecters was to work towards the immediate abolition of social differences, which would require that the rights arrogated by some as their exclusive property be destroyed. In other words, 'rights' should be made universally applicable and available to all. Otherwise, it might not be possible to persuade the populace to hold property in common. That is, if as some desired, socialism was to take root in India, it could only happen in a context where exclusivity in respect of status, privileges and persons are destroyed in their entirety (KA 25.3.44; Anaimuthu: 1711-13).

For Periyar and the Self-Respect movement, the holding of rights in common, rather the creation of an egalitarian civil society, required, as we had remarked, the fulfilment of certain conditions. Some of the movement's most sustained campaigns were devoted to the securing of these conditions: temple-entry struggles, campaigns to render public spaces and institutions accessible to all, untouchability abolition struggles, campaigns undertaken to secure equality between the sexes and the emancipation of women from the bondage of family and community, anti-brahminic and anti-caste crusades. In and through these various challenges to an unequal and unjust society, the Self-Respecters articulated a theory and practice of rights. As we have seen with respect to the temple-entry struggles, the 'rights' the Self-Respecters sought possessed a double resonance: on the one hand, these were merely civil rights, that is, the rights of every citizen to enter a temple had to be honoured, irrespective of the desire and intention of the citizen in question. On the other hand, the obtaining of these 'rights' did not in themselves signify an achievement. Their relevance was only partial: for instance the right of adi dravidas to enter temples, if granted, did not mean that they were therefore freed from the lures of the brahmin's faith, for, unless they consciously abjured the practice of religion, they would remain captive to the mysteries of the priest's religious lore. Likewise, as Gurusamy argued, an adi dravida might secure rights of admission to schools and educate himself. But, as Dr. Ambedkar had pointed out, this education did not really divest him off his untouchability, so to speak. Gurusamy pointed to the instance of the Madras adi dravida leader, N. Sivaraj, who for all his learning had been refused membership and admission in the Madras Cosmopolitan Club (Velu: 234-35).

What did the realization of civil rights then really mean? For the Self-Respecters, civil rights were significant because they enabled adi dravidas and other subordinate castes to participate in, deepen and extend the frontiers of civil society. As Periyar remarked of the nomination of Swami Sahajananda of Chidambaram and Munusamy Pillai to the Devasthanam Board, the very fact that they were members of an institution, whose exalted (Sanskrit) name they were held unfit to pronounce, was significant. For it implied that adi dravidas were finally in the 'know' of an experience denied them for centuries. Likewise the very fact that women were deemed free to attend conferences, make speeches, exercise rights of control over their bodies and sexuality meant that an entire new world, together with novel ways of seeing, relating and interacting, were now available to them. Women too were thus brought into the realm of a social experience which until then had excluded them.

The Self-Respecters' complex understanding and use of an original theory of rights was best symbolized in the consistent support they extended to the idea of proportional representation. The right of all communities to their rightful share of public resources—of governance and education—was interpreted by Periyar in very many subtle ways; so that it ceased to be a mere civil right and instead came to express a will to power, knowledge and justice.

The demand for proportional representation, did not derive, as is commonly understood, from a non-brahmin desire to have their due share of the 'fishes and loaves of office'. As Periyar argued, it was absolutely vital and necessary that various communities were adequately represented in the legislature and services, for otherwise the body politic would become prey to avarice, jealousy and social cannibalism. Besides, in caste society, mutual trust between people and a public spirit did not exist naturally, as it were, and had to be consciously invoked and realized (KA 6.12.25; 18.4.26; Anaimuthu: 907-08).

Periyar also argued that the demand for proportional representation was in essence a political demand and did not derive from partisan caste considerations. After the advent of the Congress in the political life of the country, opportunities for employment in the services and places in education had more or less come to be monopolized by those who traded on their brains and learning. These men were almost all brahmins and they had come to constitute a solid phalanx in the bureaucracy. These men felt legitimized in their lust for power by their ritual invocation of patriotic and nationalistic ideologies (KA 13.6.26; Anaimuthu: 910-12). To ensure, that non-brahmins were not altogether left out, their leaders had advanced in turn a social philosophy—of rights—and sought the assistance of the colonial state to push forward their demand for proportional representation (KA 19.4.31; Anaimuthu: 916-17). Periyar argued that as long as caste and community existed as the basis on which social identities rested, and which made for social cohesion, the demand for equality would necessarily express itself in and through the voices of community. Besides such a demand also represented a claim on the nation, a claim on wealth and resources and could not therefore be termed partisan (KA 8.11.31; Anaimuthu: 917-19). Periyar agreed that diiferences and prejudices marked human relations in every culture and that each particular community considered every other community as its 'other'. Thus for Muslims, non-Muslims were kaffirs; for brahmins, all non-brahmins were 'sons of dasis' and for Christians all non-Christians were the 'heathen'. Proportional representation if granted would do away with the menace of exclusivity, and bring into the political realm a whole range of peoples who could now successfully intervene in the affairs of the state (KA 13.12.25; Anaimuthu: 92729).

Proportional representation then signified a right, a righteous claim on the state and a subversive will to power. What was most important, it represented a refusal of the tyranny of caste, for by laying claims to hitherto denied privileges—non-menial specialist service functions, which for long, had remained the preserve of the upper castes—Self-Respecters attempted to disarticulate caste and labour. In one of his earliest writings on the subject, Periyar made it clear that he objected not merely to the brahmin monopoly of the services, but to the fact that brahmins monopolized those posts which brought with them the largest salaries and the greatest powers. The point was not that there were no non-brahmins in the services or that they were represented in too meagre a fashion—in relation to their presence in the population—but that they were almost entirely packed into the lower and to an extent the middle-level services. Periyar objected to the principle which underwrote this division of labour, to the idea that intelligence was founded on birth and caste and to the related notion that non-intellectual labour was demeaning (KA 18.4.26; Anaimuthu: 908-09). As he wrote in a different context, he longed to see the day when all forms of labour would be considered interchangeable; when brahmins would labour in the fields and brahmin women perform domestic labour in others' homes (Vi 10.8.56; Anaimuthu: 1750).

Labour, Caste and Self-Respect

The Self-Respecters' understanding of rights and their invocation of common and public rights in place of those special privileges claimed by brahmins derived from a discursive context framed by Gandhian economics. Periyar was drawn to Gandhi's Constructive Work because he sincerely and truly believed that spinning would provide succour to countless poor families and thus urged all his followers to take to spinning and the wearing of Khadi. But subsequently, as he broke faith with Gandhi, and became one of his most bitter and consistent critics, he subjected Gandhi's prescriptions for the revival of rural economic life and industry to a searching and ideologically powerful critique. Thus he came to question Gandhi's views on technology, his justifications of the divison of labour as it existed in the varna-jati order and his support for the brahmin-bania class.

Periyar divided economic activity into two kinds: productive and unproductive. In his view economic life in India was fundamentally unproductive. He observed that in Hindu society vast amounts of money were spent on rituals, festivals, pilgrimages and in appeasing gods and brahmins. Such wasteful expenditure not only inhibited economic growth and progress, but also acted as a deterrent to production itself, since rather than make rational economic decisions, people were wont to act on considerations of convention and religion. Moreover, though peoples' consumerist needs were ever on the increase—since, following the mores of the West, people had begun to spend more on personal comfort and pleasure—levels of productive economic activity had not arisen or grown as in the West. Those who were rich had managed to grow richer while others remained in penury (KA 18.1.31; Anaimuthu: 1637-39).

Periyar further argued that this economic disparity was founded on caste: that is, the rich and the privileged comprised 'purohits, officials, lawyers, merchants, capitalists, zamindars and mirasidars', all of whom were destined by virtue of their 'high' birth to cultivate wealth and prosperity; whereas others, by the same token, were cursed to labour (KA 6.9.31; Anaimuthu: 1640). It is not that the land was lacking in natural wealth and resources. On the contrary, pointed out Periyar, it was rich in its acreage and water systems. Yet, the wealth that accrued from it was made over, indeed, appropriated by an exclusive class of people who felt justified in their prosperity and exaction because the sacred books they lived by ordained 'a shudra has no right to possess property' and 'if a shudra has property the brahmins have every right to take it away from him by force'. Thus there existed religious sanction for the idea that the poor shall remain poor and, worse, be robbed as well! Periyar pointed out that such conventional ideas had acquired a certain worth and weight in these modern times because of Gandhi's adroit re-definition of varnadharma ideas. Gandhi had enjoined that the village poor should not 'seek to hoard wealth like the Bombay bania' but should instead 'continue to labour honourably—grazing cows, making footwear' (KA 13.9.31; Anaimuthu: 1640-43).

Periyar, as may be expected, was sharply critical of this varna-jati economics and argued eloquently against the Khadi campaigns of the Congress and Gandhi. He observed that in the Congress lexicon, the spinning of Khadi was construed to represent a penance and a sacrifice (KA 7.6.31; Anaimuthu: 1656). So much so that Khadi had acquired all the characteristics of a new superstition: 'Just as religion and religious texts inform cultural and social commonsense so has the economics of Khadi come to inform political and economic commonsense'. Besides notions of freedom and liberation had come to be magically associated with the spinning of Khadi; such that the hard and tireless labour of the labourers was subsumed in a rhetoric of Swadeshi and Swaraj. Besides,

> Just as how the food dedicated to the souls of the dead is supposed to transmute itself as if magically into air and replenish the hungry stomachs of the departed so is the hard labour that goes into spinning expected to generate wealth for the poor (KA 16.7.33; Anaimuthu: 1663).

Periyar also pointed out that the advocates of Khadi were not the workers so much as those who were interested in keeping intact the division of labour (and labourers) by caste. Such men spoke highly of the virtues of occupational self-sufficiency and insisted each individual take up his caste occupation. Periyar argued that this was a most pernicious conviction for, divided thus by caste, workers were separated from each other and prevented from cooperating with one another. They were not allowed 'to ease their way out of their "condition of being a worker" or from their traditional caste duty' (KA 7.6.31; Anaimuthu: 1657-58)

> Who benefits by this extollation of traditional ways? By this revival of tradition? None other but the brahmins who deceive the people and lead lazy lives themselves; the rich who reap the labour of the poor; the educated who wish to lead their lives without the least physical effort; in short the powerful who advocate a politics which would strenghten their dominance.

Periyar further added,

> To those who for generations have remained poor and who have always laboured to live and to the original inhabitants of this land who are considered no better than donkeys, pigs, dogs and who are deemed unworthy to walk in the streets and drink at the village pond, can Mr. Gandhi seem anything but a veritable 'Yama'? (KA 7.6.31; Anaimuthu: 1658)

Periyar held that Gandhi's distaste for technology was but emblematic of that romantic nostalgia for the past expressed by those who consider labour in itself praiseworthy, having never laboured themselves. Periyar's argument was that in a society organized around varnadharma, labour possessed no inherent worth or dignity. He observed that labour, even if necessary for survival, proved demeaning when one had to labour at this particular task and not at any other and when the privileged refused to work but insisted on living off the fruits of others' labour (KA 14.6.31; Anaimuthu: 1658-60).

The Self-Respecters' returned to this critique of Gandhian economics in the late thirties when they responded to Gandhi's Wardha Plan for education which envisaged teaching the child a vocation, preferably one that was his caste occupation, while still in school. Periyar then argued that this proposal which sought to promote what was coming to be known as the 'handicrafts' sector was somewhat anachronistic. For the world was changing fast and with machines being increasingly used in manufacture, transport and construction, he did not foresee any meaningful productive future for a child who was schooled in his caste occupation. Periyar noted that the Congress was interested in the Wardha Plan because it desired to keep the entire labouring population in bondage to its dominance. If non-brahmins and adi dravidas were to acquire technological skills, they would grow into a consciousness of their own status as productive labourers and rebel against the conditions of their existence which were, after all, unjust. To forestall such an eventuality, Congress had decided to oppose all modern technological innovations and education and dismiss these away as imperialist in intent (KA 21.11.37; Anaimuthu: 1674-75).

Periyar reiterated these ideas in 1940 in a letter he wrote to Deivasigamany Achary, the secretary of the South Indian Vishwakarma Conference. He noted that 'the workers' question in our country unlike in Western countries is a very complex one'. Generally it was assumed that only those who worked with machines and in capitalist production were workers. Thus, 'neither the artisan nor the craftsman who accepts work on contract or those who are casual day labourers' were considered workers and there existed no organization to mediate and represent their concerns and interests. This, according to Periyar, was tragic because at the present moment, weaving, smithy and carpentry were on the decline. These workers, unlike the factory workers were labourers by birth. That is, they were caste workers who were born to and inherited a particular skill or form of labour. In the varna-jati scheme of things such forms of labour were considered demeaning and therefore 'rather than concern themselves with upgrading their skills and economic status, artisans were anxious to upgrade their caste status'.

But artisans, reasoned Periyar, cannot remain thus forever, for with the advent of the machine in all spheres of manufacture and production, they needed to enhance their skills. If they failed to mechanize their production processes, they would be left behind to suffer in outmoded and inefficient forms of production. Besides, technology, apart from enhancing the workman's skills, would also help him overcome the drudgery, tedium and exhaustion that were often the lot of many an artisan. Technology would also make available to him a certain amount of leisure and workmen could utilize this to better their life in ever so many ways. But, noted Periyar, if artisans desired to thus embrace the machine, they would have to consciously reject Gandhi's Wardha Plan and seek to press their claims for an enhanced work status in forums such as the Justice party. (Periyar pointed out that in its testimony before the Simon Commission, the Justice party had sought to represent workers' concerns and demanded workers have their own representative in Council.) (KA 18.2.40)

In yet another article on the same theme, published this time in *Viduthalai* (16.2.40; Anaimuthu: 1748-50), Periyar elaborated on the theme of the 'Caste Worker and the Wage Worker'. Here he argued how caste divided labourers into high and low and preserved these divisions through the elaborate injunctions and rules of commensuality and marriage. Though a weaver, a blacksmith, an agricultural labourer were equal in themeselves, and equally indispensable to a nation's economic life, yet each, in their lives, observed caste. Thus, 'if a blacksmith or a weaver attempted to brahminize himself, an artisan would attempt to outdo him and covet the status of a "rishi" '. This competitive envy amongst workers, argued Periyar, should cease and workers think through the terms of reference which constituted all of them as caste workers or shudras.

In and through all of these arguments, Periyar wished to demonstrate how caste was determinate in the last instance, when it came to questions of social honour and identity and the workers' own perceptions of these latter and, more important, of themselves. He also wished to (and did) show that class divisions in Hindu society were inscribed within caste divisions, such that brahmins as a whole resisted labour, while non-brahmins, by virtue of their birth, were deemed workers and slaves. Besides, brahmins lived off their intellectual capital and spiritual surplus while non-brahmins, denied easy access to either, had to labour to live. The division of labour into intellectual and manual labour and the elaborate religious and cultural codes devised to validate this division were considered by the Self-Respecters to be fundamental to the problems of justice and equality in caste society.

The Self-Respecters, then, insisted on locating problems of class and economic exploitation on the one hand and problems of democracy and socialism on the other within the varna-jati order. As early as 1933, Periyar distinguished *podhu udaimai* or social ownership of wealth from 'samadharma' or the creed of Self-Respect and mutuality. According to him, the former, involving as it did, the issue of equal distribution of wealth was a 'mathematical problem'; whereas the latter constituted a veritable existential problem (KA 10.9.33; Anaimuthu: 1707).

This marked the point of departure for Self-Respecters from socialists and communists. The latter, as Periyar noted, were often given to repeating the observations of Marx, Engels and Lenin, as if these were given normative ideas and, worse, had dragged these latter down to the level of 'revealed' truth. But this, argued Periyar, could not enable socialists to understand their particular social totality for there were specificities to this society that neither Marx nor Lenin could be expected to know of in all its detail. Thus, 'would Marx have known of the dominance exerted by the brahmins of this country, of how they conspire to keep their authority intact? Would he have known that the native inhabitants of this land are considered shudras—sons of slaves—by birth? That there exist here religious and shastraic lore to validate all this? Marx spoke of capitalism and its dominance, of how religion justifies capitalist exploitation in a particular context and really, it is neither fair nor just to expect him to have known of our situation' (Vi 20.9.52; Anaimuthu: 1746).

Periyar also pointed out that existing socialist and communist movements were not sensitive to the deceptions of religion and the power of caste, whereas his own movement was committted to ending the influence of either. Besides, as far as the Self-Respecters were concerned, no movement could be termed socialist or communist, if it did not address the problem of social hierarchy and injustice and which did not deem it fit to press for proportional representation for all communities in education and the services (KA 6.12.36).

The Self-Respecters theorized religion as an economic determinant in such a manner that the non-productive basis to much of the economic activity in Hindu society stood revealed to all who cared to see it. Thus, a mock economics text comprising the following exercises was published in *Kudi Arasu*:

> Indicate with the help of statistics the wealth that is vested in Indian

> temples and explain how it is being wasted rather than being put to good indus Since a great deal of Indian gold serves as adornment for people and deities in temples, gold, as such, has lost its value in the country and India therefore deserves to be taken off the gold standard—examine the significance of this statement.
>
> Enumerate the economic reasons that have lead to the increasing wealth of the brahmin. How may this situation be remedied?
>
> Write on the economic use of converting temples into hospitals and schools and of appropriating the wealth of mutts for industrial growth (KA trial use.17.4.33).

The Self-Respecters at all times, both when they were a movement with a radical social agenda, and when they captured the Justice party and reconstituted it into the militant Dravidar Kazhagam, considered themselves to be workers and their organizations to be workers' organizations. For, as Periyar argued, time and again, all shudras condemned to labour as they were, by definition (if not by social and economic status), were workers, and to work for the abolition of shudrahood was as necessary a task in the struggle for workers rights as the struggle against Capital (Vi 1.7.46; Anaimuthu: 1732-33).

What was the economic content, if any, of the Self-Respecters' campaigns against the brahmins, the rich and the educated? Periyar had addressed workers' meetings from the late twenties onwards and he and other Self-Respecters courted arrest during the Great Railway Strike of 1928-29. But even in such forums he was wont to stress on the social import and relevance of his message. In the early thirties Self-Respecters organized anti-landlord, anti-moneylender conferences and addressed the problems of caste and economic deprivation as interlinked matters. In early 1933 it was decided to constitute a Self-Respect–Samadharma party—as a political adjunct to the Self-Respect movement—whose agenda was fairly modest. But it must be remembered that even the Congress' economic demands, during this period, were extremely modest and did not go beyond asking for rent remissions, writing off rural indebtedness, better working conditions for workers, and so on. In the mid-thirties when Congress attempted to take the part of those landlords who protested in Madras against the government's decision to import rice from Burma, the Self-Respecters argued eloquently in favour of the decision. Periyar pointed out that the demand for rice had far outstripped its production, since for the past hundred years more and more people had taken to eating rice, substituting this for their earlier coarse (but healthy) diet of dry grains. If rice was not imported to meet this rise in demand, prices would remain high and beyond the reach of most workers and even small farmers. The landlords were therefore extremely unjust in demanding that imports ought to cease or be regulated. It is noteworthy that in this instance, Periyar and the Self-Respecters sought to represent what seemed to them a common, popular interest rather than a partisan one. Their sense of workers, it must be kept in mind, was at all times mediated by this sense of a popular good that went beyond mere divisions of caste or even class (KA 17.2.35).

Generally it may be said that the Self-Respecters' economic agenda was limited in its objectives. Periyar himself spoke chiefly of the virtues of workers' cooperatives when he discussed alternative and more egalitarian economic structures, and visualized economic democracy as a sharing of profits between workers and capitalists. In a striking metaphor he described social ownership of property as akin to the property rights held in common by members in a Hindu joint family (KA 10.9.33; Anaimuthu: 1707). Later in life, Periyar spoke of the need for the capitalist and the worker to resolve their conflicts amicably. He remarked that the capitalist and worker were locked in a relationship that was akin to the husband-wife relationship. They had to understand that the terms of their union could be strengthened and rendered equal only if they practised trust, mutual respect and comradeship towards each other (Vi 9.5.61; Anaimuthu: 1757).

What was of course missing in Periyar's understanding of capital and labour was the idea of class conflict; he did not perceive this relationship as antagonistic and contradictory by the very terms of their constitution and articulation with one another. Though he understood the hold of the bania in modern India and the terms of the bania's engagement with Gandhi and the Congress, as he understood the role essayed by landlords in nationalist politics, his prescriptions for an anti-bania, anti-landlord struggle were almost always conceived within the terms of an anti-brahmin struggle. The anti-brahmin struggle unlike the struggle against Capital could be conducted—and, indeed, was—at the level of ideology and consciousness, whereas the latter required organized political assaults on property and property rights. The Dravida Vivasaya Thozhilalar Sangam in the fifties did undertake such struggles chiefly against landlords, but effective as they may have been in particular instances, they were restricted to local agitations and were on the whole neither substantial nor consistent. In pre-independent India, though, a radical economic and political agenda was consciously deferred and discarded by the Self-Respecters for reasons we shall now examine.

PROBLEMS OF SITUATION AND CONJUNCTURE

Periyar returned from his tour of Europe and Soviet Union in November 1932, flushed with enthusiasm for the socialism he had discovered in the institutions and ideologies of the Soviet Union. His immediate concerns, however, had to do with the adi dravidas and their situation; for in the wake of the Poona Pact, nationalism had come to proclaim its 'victory' in securing a consensus for its Gandhian inner core. Gandhi's epic fast, his starting the Harijan Sevak Sangh, his purported withdrawal from politics into the activities of the sangh, in short, the transformation (in Jeevanandham's words) of the 'political Gandhi' into 'the harijan Gandhi' rendered him almost mythical in the eyes of those adoring multitudes who were convinced of his mahatmahood (Pu 11.2.34). To Periyar and the Self-Respecters, this shift in Gandhi's political stance seemed ominous. Periyar lost no time in thinking through a series of political and ideological strategies which would help him constitute an oppositional bloc to counter Congress dominance, at least in Madras.

Kudi Arasu announced that on 28-29 December 1932 a meeting of the Self-Respect movement would he held at Erode to decide on a future plan of action for the Self-Respecters. It was also proclaimed that the meeting would consider two suggestions which had been put forth by various comrades. One had to do with what had, provisionally, been termed the Self-Respect Samadharma party plan,while the other had to do with what were considered the long-term and permanent concerns of the Self-Respect movement, namely, its desire to found a social order based on rationality, fraternity and mutuality. The Self-Respect Samadharma party would contest elections and enter Councils to promote and realize the movement's permanent objectives.

After a long drawn out debate at Erode, where a host of Self-Respecters had convened to discuss the plan proposed by M. Singaravelu and Periyar, it was decided that a Self-Respect–Samadharma party would be formed to function as the movement's legislative wing. It was also decided that the Self-Respect–Samadharma Action Plan drawn up by Periyar and Singaravelu would be disseminated widely, and a provincial conference convened after a period of time, at which the plan would be formally accepted and ratified (see Appendix 3). Referring to the apprehensions voiced by some, that the movement would be termed a socialist one and thereby come to incur the wrath and displeasure of the government, Periyar observed that from the day of its inception it had been characterized thus. Besides, while explaining the objectives of their movement, the Self-Respecters had at all times assumed their ideas were essentially socialist in character and intent. The socialism of the Self-Respecters could not possibly anger anyone, argued Periyar, save those who lived off the labour of others, the capitalists, parasites, zamindars, kings and maharajas (KA 1.1.33; Anaimuthu: 506-07).

From 1933 onwards the movement was riven by debates on the possible uses (and distractions) of a socialist agenda. As we have seen, for the Self-Respecters 'samadharma' was a conceptually rich term which helped them grapple with and make sense of multiple inequities and injustices. These latter could now be grouped under the common rubric of an oppression, which would end when the rule of the priest, the rich and the educated was overthrown and replaced by the rule of citizens committed to the ideals of a republic founded on liberty, justice, equality and fraternity. In the thirties, the Self-Respecters identified this oppression with the imminent rule of a Congress under the leadership of Gandhi and all their remonstrances, arguments and interventions in the cause of samadharma (and socialism) during this period were urged forth chiefly to counter its dominance in the political sphere. The release of a White Paper by the British in 1933 proved to be an opportune event for Periyar and the Self-Respecters to consider the Congress' political strategies, even as these unfolded.

The White Paper released in March 1933 outlined the terms of constitution of a future Indian polity. In a long article which discussed the implications of this gesture for social and political movements, Periyar observed that it was clear that in the days to come, one would witness the curious but not entirely unexpected phenomenon of the Congress cooperating with the government. For one thing, the government had come to understand that the Congress, 'which functioned on the basis of a capitalist world-view', stood between real emancipation for the people of India and British imperial dominance. If the Congress could be appeased or made to re-consider and re-formulate its demands, Britian and the Congress could together retain their respective authorities and, more important, function entirely within the logic of imperial governance. Periyar noted that colonial government was, in essence, a capitalist government, an adjunct of an empire founded on the profits of capital, and would really have no difficulty in associating itself with a party that was pronoun-cedly pro-capitalist in its concerns. Periyar also pointed out that given this politico-economic logic, the government and the Congress would, in the future, direct their concerted strength against the communists and socialists and seek to crush them into obedience. The fact that Gandhi had signalled to the government and the public his readiness to suspend Civil Disobedience and agree to contest elections constituted further proof that the Congress was willing to mend fences with imperialism. 'All that remains,' noted Periyar, 'is for Gandhi to instruct Rajagopalachari to prepare to send Congressmen to the Legislature and for the nationalist press to advertise this in bold letters' (Pu 5.3.33).

Periyar's political forecast proved prophetic. From May 1933 when he began his 21-day fast to express his anguish over the persistence of untouchability, till the Patna Congress session held in April of the following year, Gandhi undertook to cajole, entreat, threaten and force the government into accepting his plan for the suspension of Civil Disobedience and for the revival of the Swarajist party. As Gandhi wrote in separate letters to Birla and Patel, he now desired the Swarajists to take over the Congress, contest elections and enter Councils (Ghosh 1995, vol 2: 74-81). As if to underscore its willingness to renounce agitational politics, the All-India Congress Commitee which met in June 1934 resolved that confiscation of property and class war were antithetical to its creed of non-violence. (Gandhi had made it clear that he did not believe in class conflict and was opposed to the abolition of zamindari, the commutation of loans incurred by workers and peasants and to the nationalization of the means of production.) The Congress also noted it was unhappy with the details outlined in the White Paper and desired instead the formation of a constituent assembly on the basis of a universal franchise, with safeguards for the minorities. A Congress election manifesto, released to make its policies well known to voters who would exercise their votes in the November 1934 elections to the Central Legislature, reiterated the demand for a constituent assembly. It noted covertly that except in those situations where such an assembly was constituted after a revolution, a constituent assembly was usually convened on the basis of an agreement between the rulers and the ruled. Obviously the Congress, in spite of its earlier Purna Swaraj resolution, desired the latter, that is, it did not wish for revolution but only for an honourable gentleman's agreement between the government and itself (ibid: 82-83).

In the context of the Madras Presidency, Periyar's fears regarding Congress' lust for power were extremely well founded. The various phases of Civil Disobedience had resulted in a gradual but systematic and solid consolidation of the Congress' influence amongst various sections of the populace. As we had pointed out earlier, Subbarayan's temple-entry bill of 1932 and the activities of the Harijan Sevak Sangh, together with Congress' general propaganda regarding its concern and regard for the adi dravidas, were calculated to woo sections of the adi dravida leadership to its cause. In 1933 when there was gloom and despair on the agricultural front, caused largely by a fall in the price of food grains, the Congress decided to plead with the government for a reduction in land revenue rates. S. Satyamurthi was in the forefront of this campaign which earned Congress the grateful support of not merely landlords and rich peasants but of ordinary ryots as well (Arnold 1977: 147; Baker 1976: 265). Congress' influence was also consciously sought to be enhanced amongst castes such as the Nadars (Baker 1976: 219).

To further extend its sphere of influence, the Congress decided to send its candidates to local bodies and participated in the elections to the latter held in mid-1932. As we have seen, with the widening of the franchise in 1931-35, local government stood to become more representative and its offices were transformed into bitterly contested sites of power. Congressmen then appealed to the various real and imagined grievances entertained by disgruntled Justicites and envious local notables who had not won positions for themselves, and won handsomely in the various elections to the local bodies that were held intermittently in the thirties. It is against the immediate objective of countering Congress, which the Self-Respecters set for themselves that one ought to evaluate those various debates on socialism which raged in the movement in the years 1933-36. It is also in this context that one ought to view the movement's decision to distance itself from an overt engagement with socialism.

It would be useful to recall here the criticisms aired by S. Ramanathan to the decisions taken at Erode in late 1932, where he had not been present. His objections were listed by Singaravelu, who took it upon himself to justify the constitution of a Self-Respect–Samadharma party. Ramanathan had noted that the Erode plans reflected the opinions of only a section of the Self-Respecters who had somehow managed to constitute themselves into a well-knit group at Erode. As far as he was concerned, the objectives enunciated in these plans were not entirely in consonance with the founding ideals of the movement. Ramanathan was particularly unhappy with the decision to contest elections and enter Councils. This seemed to him a regressive step, since from its earliest days, the Self-Respect movement had consciously renounced the politics of the vote and had chosen to work in the realm of civil society. Besides, given the perils of social democracy, whose effects were most visible in the politics of Europe, could the movement afford to engage with a political practice that was social-democratic in character? (Pu 24.12.33)

Singaravelu defended the Erode decisions but his response did not really address the issues posed by Ramanathan. For instance, Singaravelu refused to accept Ramanathan's criticisms of social democracy as valid and, instead, in a tone redolent with righteous ire, called into question Ramanathan's politics. Thus, Singaravelu ventured to ask caustically if Ramanathan had, indeed, anything better to suggest (Pu 24.12.33). Singaravelu's reading was not only completely misplaced but unfair as well. Ramanathan, as is evident from his translations of and articles on Lenin, which appeared regularly in *Kudi Arasu* and *Puratchi* in the thirties, was familiar with the theories and practice of socialism and, besides, had sought to understand Hindu caste society in the light of those theories. He brought to his intellectual tasks a certain imaginative vigour and his descriptions of the modes of class-caste articulations in Hindu society were highly original. Speaking at a meeting at Sivaganga, he had remarked that the enemies of Self-Respect comprised two sorts of social groups. The one consisted of men who believed in the principles, practices and institutions of Hinduism and caste. These men (and women) could, at best, be persuaded of the inherent worth of the Self-Respect mode of living, thinking and being, but they could not be coerced into accepting it. The second class of men and women comprised those who lived off religion and caste. They naturally would be and were averse to the Self-Respecters. These men were the merchants of faith, whose power could never really be destroyed, unless the devout, on their own and convinced of the uselesness and dishonesty which structured religion, assented to breaking faith with their priests. At the present moment, however, the power of the brahmin priest was immense, for not only did he exploit the gullible through his cunning, but he had come to exercise financial control over them as well. In his new avatar as moneylender, the brahmin was a veritable capitalist. Ramanthan pointed out that, polarized though society was along antagonistic axes, of rich and poor, there existed sections that could align with either. These sections, he held, were akin to the petit-bourgeoisie and would be proletarianized in the days to come, but, at present, they functioned as mediators of capitalist power and brahminical ideology.

Ramanathan also pointed out that the class-caste system removed brahmins from the actual sites of oppression and exploitation—the Indian villages and towns—where the peasant and trading castes practised untouchability with impunity. But the brahmin remained at the apex of this order, the overturning of which could be achieved only by the adi dravidas. The latter 'possessed those qualities required of a revolutionary vanguard. They were not bound by property. Since they were not allowed into temples, they were not intoxicated with the experience of religion. Neither are they under an obligation to render their thanks to a God who had been responsible for them being treated worse than animals for over thousands of years' (Pu 10.12.33).

It is clear then that Ramanathan's objections to the Erode decisions did not stem from an ignorance of or an antipathy to socialism, but derived from his apprehensions regarding the future of social radicalism in the Self-Respect movement. The events of the thirties proved that his fears were well founded.

Even after the Self-Respect–Samadharma party was formed, the movement continued to work at cementing and holding together the non-brahmin historic bloc it had so painstakingly constructed. Periyar persisted in his anti-untouchability campaigns, was as concerned as ever with issues of gender equality and justice, and as before sought to induct non-brahmins—of whatever political creed or standing—into the forums of the Self-Respect movement.

When Periyar invited Somasundra Bharathy, Saivite scholar, Tamil enthusiast and Congressman, to preside over an untouchability abolition conference, young Self-Respecters such as Vallatharasu, Jeevanandham and Gupta were visibly annoyed and attempted to interrupt and jeer Bharathy while the latter was delivering his address. Bharathy's references to religion and his observations that no religion can possibly oppose the abolition of untouchability and his invocation of the Vaishnavite Ramanujacharya's example in this context, provoked young Self-Respecters to ask him why the famed Vaishnavite teacher had sent his wife away. Periyar felt that such interruptions betrayed a want of propriety and tolerance on their part. However, he had to answer his young critics who clearly disapproved the seeking out of rich and influential non-brahmins to preside over Self-Respect conferences. In a passionate defense of his choice of Bharathy, Periyar made the following observations: the rich and the powerful amongst Justicites were involved in the Self-Respect movement, but neither he nor anyone else sought to derive pecuniary advantage from this; referring specifically to the clamour raised against Bharathy, Periyar noted, 'My responsibilities [as a leader] are greater. At least my colleagues possess the excuse of youth and can get away with rashness but not me.' He also remarked that an organization such as the movement needed to be disciplined and members had to give into consensus. This was especially required in the present hour, observed Periyar, when even Congressmen were being attracted to Self-Respect ideals. In the past, such men as Bharathy had been invited to address conferences; while their presence had enhanced the stature and prestige of the Self-Respect movement, the latter had, at no time, compromised on principles.

Periyar opined that if such intolerance and impudence were to be expressed once more, he would not mind leaving the movement and would even propagate his ideas on his own at every street corner. For the behaviour of his younger colleagues had saddened him and made him wonder if there was any point in even continuing with the movement and 'whether the Self-Respecters deserved to conduct any such conferences in the future' (KA 1.10.33).

Periyar's remarks provoked a lengthy response from Singaravelu. In 'The Future of the Self-Respect Movement and Its Present-Day Crisis' (KA 8.10.33), he began by noting that the movement had proved itself to be a considerable force in Madras. Its activities were wide ranging and influential in enabling social change. A few Self-Respecters had even been elected to local bodies. Given its strengths and character, why should the movement seek out those who were not samadharmists and who, in fact, were opposed to samadharmic ideas, to preside over its conferences? Why should it keep company with those opposed to the Self-Respect-Samadharmic working plan and who were given to opportunistic behaviour? Singaravelu argued that it was this very vagueness in defining supporters and allies which had diluted Congress' original ideological power and wrought a destruction of its integral core. Referring to the example of the Soviet Communist party which, 'once a year purged itself off its undesirable members' and thereby retained its purity, Singaravelu suggested that the Self-Respect movement identify its friends (and enemies) and include supporters and exclude detractors of samadharma. He pointed to Self-Respect clubs being formed all over the Tamil country and suggested that the movement discipline its ranks and grant these clubs a degree of coherence. He further observed:

> There is nothing as obscene as inviting a theist to address a conference of atheists and asking a capitalist to preside over a workers' conference... If our movement has [therefore] to split let that happen. Such things are anyway common... It will not do anymore to invite those, who, however esteemed they are, do not acknowledge our samadharma [socialist] ideals to preside over our conferences.

In complete contrast to Singaravelu's line of argument, that identified 'samadharma' exclusively with 'socialism', A. Ponnambalam argued that the Self-Respect movement had fallen foul of some of its original anti-Brahminism and urged his comrades to work for the destruction of the priest's creed, since 'the destruction of Brahminism was a condition that had to be fulfilled if socialism was to be achieved'.

Ponnambalam noted that brahmins had turned particularly insolent in the recent past and taken to denunciations of the Self-Respecters and non-brahmin leaders. Earlier, when the brahmin press had dared criticize Dr. Muthulakshmi Reddi by referring to her caste origins, *Kudi Arasu* had sprung to her defence, forcing the former to recant and apologize. But now it seemed as if the Self-Respect movement could not defend its own against such wilful calumny of its ideals, practices and leaders. The Self-Respecters must work to consolidate its gains (KA 22.10.33).

Periyar responded to Singaravelu and Ponnambalam in *Kudi Arasu* (22.10.33). To Singaravelu, he pointed out the limits of the samadharmists' working plan and reminded him the Self-Respecters had resolved to press for such changes as they required through peaceful, constitutional means and had vowed to enter Councils to represent and seek a redressal of their demands. In addition to their working plan, the Self-Respecters possessed a set of permanent and broad-based objectives which existed independently of the former, and even non-socialists could work to realize the latter. The movement comprised a vast constituency and not all of its members could be said to abide by even either of these two plans and objectives. Indeed, even at present there were many in the movement who were opposed to and were, in fact, active against the Self-Respecters' working plan. Periyar conceded these segments had a right to their opinions, and anyway the Self-Respect movement possessed no means—no list of members, no specific test of affiliation and identity—to ascertain who had accepted the socialist ideals and who had not. Periyar further noted:

> A believer can be a member of the Self-Respect movement. Our movement will not be affected or compromised if a theist and non-samadharmist were to participate and address our conferences... We will not object even if the Shankaracharya were to accept to preside over our conferences. Because before he comes to us he will naturally acquaint himself with our principles and objectives. Even if he does not, we need not fear that his propaganda and advice will win over our ideals; nor need we fear our men will undergo a change of heart.

He added that it was because of this conviction and this faith in themselves that Self-Respecters had invited, in the past, even theists and men of wealth to address their meetings and neither of these had sought to or succeeded in subverting the ideals of Self-Respect. Moreover those who had accepted the Self-Respecters' invitation and participated in their conferences were appreciative of and had assented to its objectives.

Referring to Singaravelu's misgivings over the rich and the powerful being called to address Self-Respect meetings, Periyar remarked that having accepted to enter Councils, one cannot really baulk at affiliating with the rich and the propertied, for under the existing political conditions only these segments of the populace could vote and afford to send men to the Council. The Self-Respect movement had forsworn violence and hatred and could not therefore be negative in its attitudes to the rich.

It is clear that while Singaravelu attempted to collapse the Self-Respect movement's varied and nuanced responses to an unjust social order to the terms of a simplistic, unilinear (and imitative) socialism, Periyar desired to locate samadharmic objectives within the context of the movement's permanent objectives. But in his response to Ponnambalam we find Periyar arguing for the importance of agitating around issues of economic injustice. Thus he assured Ponnambalam that while he was well aware of the importance of the anti-brahminic struggle, he was impelled to challenge the rich as well. Due to the Self-Respect movement's systematic propaganda, brahmins had begun to waver in their convictions and Brahminism was now unsure of itself. But now some non-brahmins had come to take the place of brahmins and, like the latter, had shown themselves willing to suppress the poor and the depressed classes. The Justice party had also proved itself unreliable and lacking in initiative with respect to non-brahmin needs. Its ministers who, at one time, had praised the Self-Respect movement had all but forgotten it. 'It would make sense,' noted Periyar, 'to work towards achieving non-brahmin political dominance if non-brahmins had shown themselves worthy [of it] and if they had proved to be intelligent, self-respecting people.' But non-brahmins had not shown themselves interested or worthy of this objective and therefore he did not wish to substitute brahmins in power with those non-brahmins who were no better than and were, in fact, slaves of brahmins.

It must be noted here that Periyar's invocation of the Self-Respect movement's 'permanent objectives' was more symbolic than anything else. While the Self-Respect-Samadharma party possessed a working plan and a set of permanent objectives, these latter did not comprise what Self-Respecters and Periyar himself considered their movement's fundamental concerns: the abolition of caste, the priesthood and brahminical patriarchy. The defined permanent objectives of the party were modest and more or less economistic in content. Hence, whenever Periyar referred to the movement's permanent concerns, he was clearly not referring to these spelt-out details but to those ideals which, since 1925-26, had guided the practice of Self-Respect.

Balancing ideals and possible practice, negotiating contrary ideological positions and at all times striving to preserve the integrity of the non-brahmin historic bloc, even while acknowledging the contradictions which seemed ready to tear it apart, Periyar had a difficult time holding the Self-Respect movement together. When he was arrested in December 1933, his worst fears regarding the government and its readiness to construct other 'enemies'—to justify its rule and power—now that the Congress was ready to cooperate, were confirmed. Periyar realized he had to change his strategies. In a context where confrontation with the government would only serve to undo the good work of the past decade, he decided to beat a tactical retreat and consolidate his gains. Besides he had always maintained Brahminism was as powerful and dangerous an enemy to non-brahmins and adi dravidas as imperialism. In 1935 he remarked as much in the addresses he delivered at various adi dravida conferences held that year (KA 10.2.35; 10.3.35; 28.7.35; 6 and 13.10.35). He had reiterated these arguments in another context as well. Commenting on the Jubilee celebrations that were to be held to mark the successful conclusion of King George V's rule, Periyar wrote that if at all the British presence in India had been useful, this was due to the fact, that unlike the kings of old, the British, even if they had not helped resolve the miseries of the poor, had assured women and the depressed classes certain rights and promoted, to an extent, their concerns. In future too, he hoped this would continue to be the case (KA 12.5.35).

Even those 'impetuous' men who had earned Periyar's rebuke for having interrupted Somasundara Bharathy's address, were convinced that it was imperative to challenge Brahminism rather than imperialism. More important, they recognized that 'samadharma' had to be defined contextually, keeping in mind particular forms of exploitation and oppression. The very first issue of *Samadharmam* (launched by V. Parthasarathi in Jolarpet in August 1934) carried an editorial 'Samadharma' which argued thus:

> The term 'samadharma' which today is resonant throughout the world is used in each nation and by people professing different religions and belonging to different castes with an emphasis peculiar to their context. However this may be we wish to explain the exact sense in which we use the word. We hold that people in all walks of life must exist in equality and eschew differences based on birth and we wish to see humankind lead a life free from worry and discontent that we have begun *Samadharmam* (8.8.34).

Even as regular articles on the Russian Revolution, Lenin, New Economic Policy appeared in *Samadharmam*, the paper ran anti-caste, anti-brahminic articles and reports. It carried Jeevanandham's speech delivered at a Self-Respect Conference held in North Arcot. Jeevanandham had railed against brahmin tyranny, their appropriation of modern learning and posts and their exploitation of non-brahmin labour and intelligence (31.10.34). Yet, as we have seen earlier, he and others like him were none too happy with Periyar's decision to support the Justice party against Congress and Brahminism during the 1934 elections. Jeevanandham had then issued a call for a new party to be formed to propagate the ideals of socialism. He was, of course, not the only one to entreat Periyar to wed his anti-Brahminism to a rigorous anti-class and anti-imperialist politics. We find Periyar responding to one such appeal sent in by an 'unnamed comrade' in *Pagutharivu* (9.12.34).

His critic had maintained that samadharmists in India could not hope to imitate the Russian model and, besides, the Russians were themselves re-defining their principles. However this may be, the Self-Respect movement ought not to ally with any party. The Justice party was as careful of caste distinctions as Congress and as 'bourgeois' in its attributes. Periyar ought not to have allied himself with that party and besides he had referred once again to the brahmin–non-brahmin problem, and this implied he had not gained full confidence in the principles of socialism. Periyar and the movement should indirectly work for uniting all socialists—in the Congress and out of it—and evolve a common working plan.

Periyar defended his privileging of the brahmin–non-brahmin contradiction as central to the samadharmists' agenda. He observed that if one were to examine the ills that plague the poor with an unjaundiced eye, freed from the prejudices of caste and religion, one would identify this contradiction as germane to the problem at hand. The brahmin-non-brahmin contradiction was not one which depended on or was structured by what brahmins and non-brahmins said about themselves. On the contrary, 'irrespective of what a so-called brahmin or non-brahmin feels and how he acts', the contradiction existed and had to do with 'the rights enjoyed by the brahmin'. It rested on 'what a so-called non-brahmin perceived his rights to be and on the rights and status of the so-called brahmin as enjoined by the shastras and as available in experience'. 'A samadharmist,' noted Periyar, 'is one who, in his heart, considers others equal to him and holds himself equal to others.' Any others (he refers here covertly to Congress socialists) even if they professed socialism, but did not experience this equality with all their heart, cannot be deemed samadharmists. In this sense the Justice party was 'samadharmic', for it upheld the rights to equality of non-brahmins and at the very least did not oppose the demand for equality. Periyar further observed:

> I understand the antonym 'rich-poor' to mean one that exists between one who does not work with his hands for a living, that is, one who holds it sinful and wrong to labour thus and considers it his right to not labour, and one who is condemned to work and who considers it his 'right' to work for another and who suffers physical distress on that account.

Periyar added that he considered it important that samadharmists work to transform this condition. Finally, he refused to accept that the Justice party practised caste distinctions. Even if Justicites did observe such differences, this could be put down to a residual Brahminism in their hearts and to an ingrained competitive envy that made them uphold the privileges of one caste over another. Periyar concluded his remarks by noting that he was at all times aware of and faithful to the Self-Respect movement's permanent concerns, but did not think it wrong for a movement to change its tactics and strategies from time to time.

It is in this context that we should locate Periyar's statement of intent and the apology he made Jeevanandham write, when the later was arrested for translating Bhagat Singh's article on atheism. E. V. Krishnasamy, Periyar's elder brother, who published the translation was arrested as well (KA 24.2.35). The statement of intent as well as the apology make it clear that for Periyar, the Congress was the primary enemy, emblematic as it was of brahmin power and committed to preserving the varna order. Periyar noted that he had always considered the British more sensitive to and willing to work with the principles of samadharma than the Congress (KA 10, 31.3.35; Anaimuthu: 515-21). He also clarified that he had ever sought to abjure violence and always his Self-Respect movement had abided by the law. Hence there was no question of the movement posing a threat to the government or to society.

Periyar's statement of intent was occasioned not merely by his desire to change tactics in the wake of imminent and very real government repression. Since 1933, the government had been watchful of the Self-Respect movement and awaited every chance to persuade Periyar not to indulge in socialistic propaganda. (As we have seen, Periyar had been arrested and incarcerated in December 1993). Jeevanandham's translation of Bhagat Singh's testimony to atheism enabled them to accuse Periyar and the Self-Respect movement of harbouring seditious motives. Periyar, quick to sense trouble and mindful of the fact that the movement was too important a social phenomenon to be sacrificed, immediately apologized (as he said) on the advice of friends and well wishers.

As he remarked later, of his decision not to confront government, at the Thanjavur District Self-Respect Conference in March 1936:

> When I realised that Government was determined to repress the Self-Respect movement and that our movement had already suffered [as a consequence of Government's surveillance and interference] and when I saw that even Congress had retreated into indirect action, not able to countenance Government repression... I decided to put a halt to socialist propaganda by the Self-Respecters. If I had not done so even the Self-Respect movement would have been destroyed... Already I have had to pay Rs 2000 as surety for Jeevanandham's article. My sister and I had been imprisoned earlier on... Many of our books have been confiscated... we have had to

> pay sureties for our other newspapers...Would it have helped if I had chosen to become a hero and had gone to jail and allowed the Self-Respect movement to be slowly destroyed? This being the case, I beg you to consider if it was not for the best that I forswore socialist propaganda and decided to devote attention to the other activities of the Self-Respect movement (KA 29.3.36; republished, Vi 17.6.88).

Though Periyar's decision to 'moderate' his stance was not entirely acceptable to his younger colleagues, men like Jeevanandham and Vallatharusu continued to work with him and the movement. Besides, articles on socialism continued to appear in the movement's journals. Jeevanandham accompanied Periyar on a tour of the Tamil country undertaken to prepare Self-Respecters for the Fourth Provincial Self-Respecters conference that was to he held at Nagapattinam shortly (KA 9.6.35). Jeevanandham entreated Self-Respecters to assess the developments of the past years and decide on a future course of action. He also requested them to assemble in as great a number as possible at Nagapattinam for the conference (which was never held) to make their views known (KA 30.6.35). Others too wrote and spoke of the future prospects of the Self-Respect movement, the nature of its relationship to the Justice party and of their expectations. Thus Mayilvahananar (14.4.35), M. M. Chidambaram (21.4.35), Poluran (26.5.35), S. R. Samy (18.8.35). V. M. Vellaiyan (20.10.35), P. Minakshi (10.11.35), L. Muthusamy Pillay (24.11.35), Sitaram (5.1.36) and Udumalai Kanakaraj (15.3.36; 2.4.36) were some of those Self-Respecters whose views were carried in *Kudi Arasu*.

However, in spite of the enthusiasm shown by the Self-Respecters in evolving a future plan, it became clear the young samadharmists would persist in their critique of the Justice party and would continue to insist the Self-Respect movement realize its samadharmic ideals and to re-think its relationship to the Justice party. Vallatharasu, for instance, returned to this theme at the Ramanathapuram District Fourth Self-Respect Conference (KA 14.7.35). Periyar, for his part, remarked that in spite of the movement having given up on its socialist propaganda, the government continued to scrutinize its activities carefully (KA 18.8.35). In early 1935, the offices of *Kudi Arasu* were raided by the police (KA 27.1.35). An anthology of essays selected from *Kudi Arasu,*

Jeevanandham's translation of Bhagat Singh and another publication were seized (KA 23.6.35). The police also refused to grant permission to both the Congress and the Justice party to hold meetings at Salem and Vellore (KA 7.7.35). Periyar also added that the Self-Respect movement had decided to halt its socialist propaganda because 'it was dependent (for its existence) on the opinions, sympathies and support of different sorts of people and, moreover, it wished to bring about such changes in society that were fundamental. It had therefore always been careful not to let itself be labelled a seditious organization and had sought to carry out its activities within legal limits.' Periyar pointed out that there may be people in the movement who had their own opinions on these matters, but as a responsible and older member, he was duty bound to define and place within certain limits the activities of the Self-Respect movement (KA 18.8.35).

Differences between Jeevanandham and Vallatharasu on the one hand and Periyar on the other surfaced once again at the Trichy District Self-Respect Conference held in October 1935. Periyar had to once against define his position and justify his choice of a politics of restraint over a politics of agitation and confrontation. He also had to heed other concerns during this period.

The Government of India Act of 1935 had become law and with elections to the provisional legislature imminent, he had to once again contend with a Congress party that was eagerly awaiting its chance to enter the Madras Council and wrest authority from the non-brahmin Justicites. Periyar, as we have seen, had worked hard through the difficult months of 1935 to strengthen the Justice party. While his working plan was finally approved by the Justicites, this decision drew the opprobrium of Congress leaders in Madras who accused Periyar of modelling his plan on the Congress' Karachi Plan which had remained their gospel for action since 1931, when it was formally adopted by the Congress. Periyar went to great length to distinguish his 'socialism' from that entertained by Congressmen. He now noted that the Self-Respecters were opposed to the idea of non-intervention in matters of religion, which Congressmen had adopted as policy at Karachi, and that unlike the Congress the Self-Respect movement and the Justice party were committed to the ideal of proportional representation (Anaimuthu: 434-37). In 1934, Jeevanandham too produced brilliant and penetrative critiques of Congress socialism and its Gandhian matrix. He had observed, for instance, that Gandhi was willing to allow Congress socialists to proclaim their principles out aloud, as long as this did not interfere with his and Congress' affiliations with the bania class (Pu 11.2.34; 12.9.34).

In spite of Periyar's gallant and tenacious defense of his political and social creed, he lost some of his most trustworthy and reliable colleagues to the Congress: Jeevanandham, Vallatharasu, and many others joined the Congress on the eve of the 1937 elections. Periyar, as we have seen, was not moved by this desertion and *Kudi Arasu* published a long article explaining why this desertion had taken place (29.3.36).

This desertion by the young samadharmists is in a sense inexplicable. For almost all of them to the last man joined the Congress Socialist party and submitted themselves to a leadership, whose cunning had drawn their greatest ire and contempt in the past. Jeevanandham, who at one time, had declared Brahminism was as great an evil as imperialism and who had railed against the inhumanity of caste, now came to accept and argue that the primary contradiction in Hindu society was between the rich and the poor! Though the samadharmists who left the Self-Respect movement for the Congress Socialist party noted that the Self-Respect movement had reneged on its socialist principles and capitulated to the rich, we find that *Kudi Arasu* in 1935 and after continued to carry articles on socialism. An appeal to observe May Day was published (28.4.35) when Jevanandham and others were still in the movement, and it noted that samadharmists and Self-Respecters ought to impress upon the workers the need to 'eschew differences of nationality, religion and caste and feel themselves part of the international working class'. The appeal concluded by noting that May Day should be celebrated with a view to assure to all 'their rights to equality and equal opportunity'.

In this context, it would be useful to consider the nature of the Self-Respect movement's relationship to the imperial state. It is clear the movement was simultaneously critical and appreciative of colonial governance. Periyar, at one time declared that he preferred British rule to Brahmin rule and would exchange the former only for socialist rule! (Sd 15.8.34) On the other hand, Self-Respecters also argued that it was the coming of the white man that had catapulted brahmins into positions of authority and vastly enhanced and multiplied their strengths. Yet they were willing to acknowledge it was colonial government that had enabled adi dravidas and women to come into their own, encouraged their education and helped lessen at least some of the burden custom and convention had imposed on them. The government was here, not merely to govern, but also to process the profits of colonial trade and exploitation and ensure their passage into imperial hands. Artisans, agricultural workers and peasants had suffered as a consequence. But the government had also made available to non-brahmins as a whole education and technology—as Periyar pointed out to the secretary of the South Indian Vishwakarma Conference—and this had enabled some to rid themselves of their caste-ordained occupations. The rule of the white man had brought with it those intimations of a modern sensibility, rationality, science and notions of progress which the ordinary masses could use to challenge brahminical authority and the hold of religion. Like Phule, Periyar sought to affiliate himself and his Self-Respect movement with the idea of progress implicit, by his understanding, in colonial rule and with the promises of freedom which this rule in spite of itself seemed to hold. More generally, it may be said that Periyar felt compelled to endorse the colonial state in its role as a sort of bulwark against the hated tyranny of a hereditary priesthood and for tactical purposes he saw it fit to even remark that colonial government could not possibly be considered an enemy of samadharma! (Sd 15.8.34)

It is clear that given the complexities of situation and conjuncture, as these obtained in the mid-thirties, Periyar and the Self-Respect movement were faced with choices that were not easy to make. They could not possibly have given up on their anti-brahminic, anti-caste propaganda and agitations, for these now possessed a momentum and logic of their own and had to be pursued at any cost. As for socialism, it had always existed as an adjunct, no doubt a crucial adjunct, but an adjunct, nevertheless, of their ideology of self-respect and anyway the movement did not possess the organizational strength or the ideological singularity to function as a socialist forum. It was, in essence, a popular-national forum (in the Gramscian sense) and not a class organization. However this may be, the difficulties it encountered are symptomatic of that larger and still unresolved problem of articulating anti-caste struggles with class war in a society that is divided on the basis of multiple inequities.

CHAPTER 12

The Ideal Society: Imagining Dravida Nadu

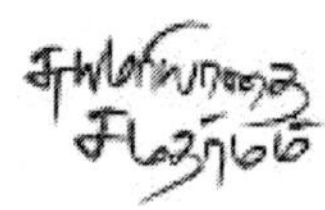

THE SEMANTICS OF NATIONALISM

Periyar's critique of nationalism has several moments to it, each of which refers to a particular phase in the history of nationalist politics and its progress. His earliest pronouncements against nationalism were directed against the misuse and travesty of a political idea he associated with Gandhi's Non Cooperation and Constructive Work. Thus he was concerned, not so much with the semantics of nationalism, as he was with the crass opportunism which underwrote a certain political practice, which he identified with the Swarajists. During this period, from 1925-27, Periyar was convinced nationalism possessed a pure and integral Gandhian inner core which had to be disengaged from Swarajist rhetoric and practice and constituted as the basis for the evolution of an authentic nationalism. His disenchantment with Gandhi in late 1927 and his criticisms of the Congress' Simon Commission boycott propaganda together constituted the second important moment in Periyar's critique.

The period 1928-30 thus brought forth a denunciation of Congress duplicity and hypocrisy and helped Periyar grasp the symbolic power and significance of Congress politics: its clever use of tradition, myths and rituals; its carefully constructed rhetoric of Civil Disobedience which drew heavily on notions of sacrifice, moral rectitude and patient suffering, and finally its supreme indifference to the vast distance that separated its professed ideologies from its actual practice. Periyar's critique of nationalism in the second instance had moved from a condemnation of the misuse of nationalist ideals to a critique of those ideals themselves.

Ramsay Macdonald's Communal Award, and the events which followed in the wake of its announcement, provoked Periyar and others in the Self-Respect movement to mount a direct and fierce attack against Gandhi and his attempts to inscribe the nationalist agenda within the logic of varnadharma. Ranging from relentless interrogations of the Poona Pact to a condemnation of the activities of the Harijan Sevak Sangh, this third moment of critique was intense, bitter and indignant in its expressions. Yet, this critique was informed by a very nuanced understanding of the 'class' basis of nationalism and of the complex terms of its articulation with imperialism. In 1934 the Congress Socialist party was formed as a left nuclei within the Congress. This marriage of a nationalism, hatched within the confines of caste, to a socialism, which promised to free the labouring classes, was criticized by the Self-Respecters in no uncertain terms. This remarkable fourth moment in the Self-Respect movement's condemnation of nationalism not only exposed the hollow socialism of Congress, but also demonstrated the socialist construction of nationalism and their posing of the national question in India to be problematic. The year 1937 brought forth the moment of Dravidian (Tamil) nationalism: beginning with the anti-Hindi agitations of 1937-39, this moment of critique spanned very nearly the whole of the following decade which witnessed the birth of the Dravidar Kazhagam and the evolution of a Tamil alternative to a pan-Indian nationalism.

Each of these moments of critique proved to be not merely negative in their significance; in each instance, a different mode of imagining the nation was offered and adumbrated, along with condemnations and denunciations. To understand better the evolution and progress of the Self-Respecters' critique of nationalism we may isolate a few instances, drawn from each moment of the critique. Of the first moment of critique, we have said enough earlier: the criticisms levelled against the Swarajists. In various contexts, we have also dealt with the movement's observations on the Congress and the Simon boycott, Gandhi, the Poona Pact, and the activities of the Harijan Sevak Sangh. Yet, we need to interrogate in some detail the developments which followed the conclusion of the Gandhi-Irwin

Pact and the resolutions that were made at the Karachi session of the Congress which concluded in March 1931.

Responding to the Congress' Karachi Resolutions

The year 1931 was a momentous one by any reckoning for nationalists. It witnessed the signing of the pact between Viceroy Irwin and Gandhi which signified a truce after the first phase of Civil Disobedience activism. This was also the year when the government hanged Bhagat Singh and his comrades after an exceptionally unfair trial. It was also in 1931 that the Karachi session of the Congress took place. Self-Respecters understood these various events as constellating into a conjuncture which would bring forth a new kind of nationalist politics. Commenting on the Gandhi-Irwin Pact and the hanging of Bhagat Singh, *Kudi Arasu* observed that these were actually interconnected events; in the pact he eventually made with the Viceroy, Gandhi had refrained from seeking a reprieve for Bhagat Singh and his comrades. His silence in this respect was strategic and helped Gandhi and the Congress to interpret the pact as a victory. Behind this victory, though, lay the implacable opposition of the Gandhian Congress to those samadharmic ideals which had animated the short, but, remarkable life of Bhagat Singh. Self-Respecters, at this moment in time, were convinced that Congress' betrayal of Bhagat Singh would not go unchallenged and would incur the wrath of the people. However, Congressmen seemed determined to trumpet aloud their victory in the manner of those 'who possess a lamp but would yet fall into a dark well'. That is, they would rather own the victory than dwell on and pay attention to those criticisms of Gandhi by those who were convinced of the worth and relevance of the ideals of samadharma (29.3.31).

Here, as elsewhere, Self-Respecters understood samadharma to mean not merely socialism but an anti-brahminic and anti-caste ideology as well. Referring to Bhagat Singh's socialism, *Kudi Arasu* noted: 'The philosophy that desires to end poverty is akin to the philosophy that wishes to abolish untouchability.' Further, 'just as how notions of high and low [castes] have to be abolished for untouchability to be destroyed, so must the division of society into capitalists and labourers be ended for the abolition of poverty' (KA 29.3.31). The 'essence' of Gandhian nationalism stood revealed for the Self-Respecters in the death of Bhagat Singh, while the truths of samadharma acquired a particular importance and relevance in the wilful travesty of those ideals in the practice of the nationalists.

Such a critique of the Congress was enhanced and sharpened as Self-Respecters took stock of the goings-on at the Karachi session of the Congress where several important decisions, which would direct and influence Congress policy in the future decades, were passed. *Kudi Arasu* carried detailed reports of the Karachi Congress, soon after its conclusion and these were chiefly critical in tone. For several months following Karachi, Periyar and others spoke and wrote of the Karachi decisions in several forums. Speaking at a meeting at Kottaru, where Self-Respecters had gathered to observe the anniversary of their sangam, Periyar discussed the Karachi resolutions at some length in what turned out, in reality, to be a dissection of nationalism as such. Thus Periyar observed, in the course of his speech, that nationalism acquired an anti-imperialist resonance only after non-brahmins, Mohammedans and adi dravidas came to stake their claims to their share of government posts and seats in the Councils. As soon as the largely brahmin leadership of the Congress sensed the imminent spread of disunity in the party, it came to proclaim it was no longer particularly interested in government jobs and denounced those who wanted these and who were not averse to heeding and obeying the government, as 'backwards', 'betrayers' and 'communalists'. Thus, noted Periyar, 'if a few caste associations had not come forward to ask their share of what had until then been the Congress' cake, "loyalty to the Raj" would have been a quality patented by Congress and flaunted as its trade mark by right'. But once it resolved to turn nationalist, Congress came to propose its own distinctive plans for a future polity.

At the Kottaru meeting, Periyar also dwelt at length on the powers of those patriotic Congressmen who constituted a veritable 'secular priesthood'. He remarked that for them Swaraj signified the advent of Ramrajya, and to realize their chosen utopia, they had sought to define a charter of rights at the Congress session at Karachi. There (among other things) it had been resolved that in a future free polity, Congressmen would 'remain neutral with respect to religions, preserve varnashrama dharma and not do or say anything which would harm the rights of particular communities, in short, not seek to hurt another's sentiments by professing an opinion that might be baneful to them'. Periyar drew attention to Section 14 of the charter of rights discussed at Karachi, which stated quite clearly that 'the State will not interfere in religious matters' and to Section 17 which stated that 'Government will not wound the susceptibilities of any of its citizens who profess opinions or a creed different from its own'. Periyar noted that non-brahmins would have no use for such a government or a polity governed by such principles, for either would not, and indeed could not, by the terms of their constitution, bring about a reform of caste or even help to abolish untouchability (KA 12.7.31; Anaimuthu 1974: 345-51). Referring specifically to the rights guaranteed in Sections 14 and 17 he demanded indignantly whose rights were thus sought to be advanced and protected:

> Are these rights guaranteed by religion? Rights enjoined by the shastras? Or else rights that have come about as a result of experience, out of custom and habits? Or are they rights which guarantee 'nationhood' or are they natural and universal rights? Besides, if there were to ensue a clash of rights as between Hindus and Mohammedans, brahmins and adi dravidas, whose rights would be considered sacrosanct and on what basis? (KA 12.7.31; Anaimuthu: 348).

Commenting on the Karachi decisions immediately after these had been made public, *Kudi Arasu* had remarked that the pious resolve to respect individual conscience would only enable men like S. Satyamurthi and M. K. Acharya to justify their hidebound attitudes to women, for now they would claim their conscience was clear on such matters and they could not therefore be forced to reconsider their opinions. It had also pointed out the ambiguity that marked the resolutions on temple-entry, which spoke of the need to preserve ancient cultures and languages. It observed that such general sentiments concealed a very definite desire on the part of Congressmen to retain the varnadharmic basis of Hindu society. *Kudi Arasu* had also faulted the Congress' economic resolutions on securing better working conditions for workers and rationalizing the terms of their employment and income. It noted these would only confirm the workers in their present status and conditions of existence (5.4.31).

Kudi Arasu had been particularly incisive in its criticisms of the Congress' stance on untouchability as reflected in the Karachi resolutions. Two resolutions had been urged which held no discrimination be observed and practised in respect of access of all peoples to jobs, positions of power, status and public places. However, since the definition of public places had been left (purposely) vague, Congressmen such as Satyamurthi had insisted that places under the control of particular social groups and temples did not qualify as public places! *Kudi Arasu* damned this treacherous reading of the Karachi resolve and condemned the Congress for practising a deliberate politics of doublespeak with respect to the untouchables (19.4.31). It is clear that Periyar and the Self-Respecters grasped the significance of the Karachi Congress resolutions as no other leader of this period did, then or afterwards. The acceptance of these resolutions by even the socialist-minded Nehru convinced Periyar that Congress (and Gandhi) were embarking on a new and historically important path, one from which they would not henceforth turn back.

The Karachi resolutions directed Congress behaviour well into the thirties. Periyar enunciated with a brilliant display of both logic and passion the important third moment of the Self-Respecters' critique of nationalism to be its most crucial. For, in essence, this moment of critique occasioned a demystification, if one may call it that, of Gandhi and of that potent and heady mix of faith and politics that the Mahatma exemplified.

Reading Gandhi

In July 1931, after the Karachi resolutions had come to take firm root in the political commonsense of the people, Periyar observed that Gandhi was a veritable friend of brahmins and a proponent of Brahminism; and that it would be extremely foolish if one were to expect him to be a friend of samadharma:

> Gandhi considers only the northern merchants and the southern brahmins to be human. He keeps company with them and considers their problems to be universal problems. Thus his plans will always

> keep their concerns in mind and not those of the poor and the depressed classes. As far as the latter are concerned, Gandhi entreats them to take to spinning and assures them that he considers the practice of untouchability a sin. But even with respect to these matters, interpretations vary and are contingent on what the mill owners and brahmins say (KA 26.7.31; Anaimuthu: 351).

Yet in spite of this, Gandhi's was a name that thrilled many a heart into rapturous devotion. How could this be? Periyar pointed out that Gandhi had come to be so closely associated with Indian nationhood that 'were anyone to call him a fool or consider him an ordinary man like the rest of us, this, in itself, is enough to brand a man a betrayer of the nation...and becomes in fact a touchstone on which one's love of the nation could be tested' (KA 29.9.35; Anaimuthu: 386).

The identification of the nation with Gandhi had come about chiefly because of his construction and characterization of the nationalist cause as a deeply felt, quasi-religious and personal one that required the devotion and sacrifice of millions of hearts and minds. To Periyar, such a quasi-religious, semi-mystical resonance which the 'Mahatma' had brought to politics and nationalism was mediated through his bearing, demeanour and ways of being and talking. Thus,

> His religious guise, god-related talk, his constant references to Truth, Non-Violence, Satyagraha, cleansing of the heart, the power of the spirit, sacrifice and penance on the one hand and the propaganda his disciples and others—nationalists and journalists—who in the name of politics and the nation consider him a rishi, a sage, Christ, the Prophet, a Mahatma...and a veritable avatar of Vishnu on the other, along with the opportune use of Gandhi's name by the rich and the educated...have together made Gandhi a political dictator' (KA 23.7.33; Anaimuthu: 389-90).

Periyar compared Gandhi to Annie Besant and pointed out that like Gandhi she had dominated nationalist politics by talking of the Bhagavad Gita, by claiming she communed with gods and mahatmas and by professing to know peoples' previous and future births. The popularity of people such as Besant and Gandhi, noted Periyar, derived from their habit of putting their religious sensibilities to political use and endowing their political acumen with a mystical aura (ibid).

Writing a couple of months later, on the death of Annie Besant, a *Kudi Arasu* obituary noted that the waning of Besant's influence in the Congress coincided with the entry of Gandhi and the growth of his influence in that party. The obituary suggested that in many significant ways, Gandhi was a fit substitute to Mrs. Besant (even as he was presented as an antidote to her powers and influence in the Congress), combining as he did matters of the spirit and issues of political import (24.9.33).

The Gandhian conundrum for Periyar was best represented in the Gandhian ideal of satyagraha. In an article titled 'Satyagraha', he dwelt at great length on the meaning and relevance attached to this ideal in the Gandhian lexicon. He noted that the Self-Respecters could not possibly wage this 'war of truth'. For those against whom this war would be waged would consider opposing the Self-Respecters in name of a 'truth' of which they were convinced. Periyar went on to detail the nature of the Self-Respecters' struggle and their achievements in respect of their anti-caste and anti-untouchability campaigns. He argued, that as opposed to claiming to speak and act in the name of an ineffable truth, Self-Respecters had sought to persuade rather than force a change of opinion. They had travelled from town to town, from village to village, holding meetings, prevailing upon the public to listen and if convinced, heed their words. But they had not sought to explain and interpret their ideas to suit the occasion or the context. This mode of public debate, implied Periyar, was in stark contrast to the habitual Congress mode of conducting its public and political campaigns. Congress was interested in displays of power and sentiment, it was given to shows of defiance against India's imperial rulers and was clearly interested in rousing rather than educating people's sentiments and feelings on matters of import to them.

Periyar also pointed out that the appeal of satyagraha of the Congress variety derived from its semantic associations. Congressmen were wont to attribute to the ideal of satyagraha notions of dharma, sacrifice and divine will. Satyagraha, it was claimed, being morally and spiritually right, could not but succeed, could not but win its victories. By rendering satyagraha as an ideal and a mode of protest naturally and inevitably successful, Congressmen had come to interest the people in its causes. Whether these causes actually succeeded or not, the aura associated with these latter, on account of their inherent 'truth', sustained and redeemed them in the eyes of thousands of ordinary Congressmen. Yet, pointed out Periyar, 'there need be no truth in a particular cause (for which one conducts satyagraha) nor need a winning cause need to be a particularly truthful one'. This was because Truth was never singular in character and could be interpreted differently and understood in a number of ways. Besides, what appeared true to one need not necessarily be true to another. 'What is Truth? Untruth? For which may one conduct satyagraha? Is there indeed a way of testing these things? What appeared as truth to, say, Pandit Madan Mohan Malaviya need not be true as far as the Self-Respecters were concerned.'

Periyar's problem with the Gandhian notion of satyagraha was simply this: It rested on faulty premises in that its relevance and worth could not be measured, except in and through its own forms of expression. Secondly, were one to interrogate its truth claims, one would have to admit that these were arbitrary and relative. Thirdly, and this proved particularly bothersome to Periyar, one could never be sure if the efficacy of satyagraha was due to its inherent worth, or due to the fact that its proponents, by claiming they were 'acting in Truth', had coerced their opponents or those whom they addressed, into heeding their claims. Thus, he wondered if it was because the satyagrahis' arguments and ideas were persuasive and convincing that they were heeded, or because those who were forced to confront their obduracy had to give in to their claims, not being able to find a way out of a situation forced on them by the satyagrahis. It was because the ethical effects of satyagraha seemed to escape definition that Periyar held the practice of satyagraha demanded and required the simultaneous practice of manipulation, deception and falsehood.

Periyar also argued that, desirous as the Self-Respecters were of building a samadharmic society where property will be held in common, they could not possibly expect or hope that the conduct of satyagrahas will enable adi dravidas to acquire land or a share of the wealth that was held by religious institutions and temples. Neither would satyagraha prove successful against zamindars and merchants and kings who were determined to keep their working population captive to their interest and who gave them enough only so that they may live to labour. What satyagraha could do and had indeed achieved for all its pains (and for all the impetus given it by

Gandhi and the Congress) was that it had forced the common people to trust to the divine powers of truth and instilled in them a false faith as to what could possibly be achieved to ameliorate their conditions of existence (KA 6.9.31). For Periyar, then, satyagraha served as an expressive modality in and through which the discourses of Gandhian nationalism had habitually been made available to the world at large. The moral ambiguity which lay at the heart of discourses and practices of satyagraha were interpreted by him to represent the problematic nature of a politics that attempted to subsume its partisan concerns in a universal rhetoric of truth, patriotism and sacrifice. Satyagraha in this sense represented the favoured mode of expression of nationalism and one that rendered the latter an appealing idea.

Gandhi was criticized by other Self-Respecters as well. Gurusamy proved to be one of Gandhi's most consistent critics and drew attention time and again to his extremely contradictory stand on untouchability, which he characterized as devious and a clever ruse that would enable nationalists to secure a widespread consensus for their ideology. M. Singaravelu, though he was drawn to Gandhi during the Non Cooperation phase of Congress, produced a most penetrative critique of Gandhian nationalism in the early thirties. Jeevanandham understood, even as Periyar did, the enormous significance of Gandhi's relationship to the bania class and explained this as one of the most crucial constituents of Congress hegemony. The views of Jeevanandham and Singaravelu bear consideration—and we shall attempt here a brief description—if only because these men later joined Congress and were forced to adhere to Gandhi's decisions.

In an article written in 1932 on Gandhi's epic fast, Singaravelu argued that Gandhi's life represented a 'series of contradictions'; that he was ever given to initiating actions and movements that he would abandon midway. During the Non Cooperation struggles he had abruptly and arbitrarily suspended all action, following the Chauri Chaura incidents, leaving thousands of people to suffer in prisons. Earlier, during his life in South Africa, he had maintained a strategic silence during the British operation against the Zulus and had cultivated a carefully ambiguous stance during the Boer War. Later in the thirties, after he had undertaken a thoroughly useless march to Dandi and involved thousands of people in his satyagraha, he had surrendered the gains he had notched up, in terms of enthusing the people into opposing the British, to the extremely modest and restrained directives of the pact he signed with Viceroy Irwin. Subsequently, he had launched massive Civil Disobedience struggles all over the country, but after having raised popular anger and expectations to feverishly high levels, had, characteristically enough, failed to consecrate this popular rage at the altar of a sustained strategy of challenge to imperialism. Instead he had chosen to deflect public attention to his own fast. This latter, argued Singaravelu, was thoroughly agreeable to the British who were awaiting their time to scotch the Civil Disobedience agitations.

Describing the epic fast as an instance of 'claptrap', Singaravelu dismissed Gandhi's arguments in respect of adi dravida/caste Hindu unity which the 'Mahatma' had insisted was under threat in the wake of the adi dravidas' demand for separate electorates. This, noted Singaravleu, 'is akin to the wolf crying because he discovered the lamb wet in the rain'. For what had these caste Hindus done for the adi dravidas? How many wells, schools, hospitals had they constructed? How many scholarships had they instituted? Singaravelu could not understand the fuss over separate electorates, considering the fact that under the present circumstances, no real political gain for Indians awaited them, either in the shape of political concessions the British might grant or what they might reasonably expect from an imperial government; especially when the colonial state was determined to outmanoeuvre the Congress at every turn (KA 25.9.32).

Singaravelu's stance on Gandhi and nationalism, in this as in other contexts, was modelled on the opinions of the Communist International. The Comintern had chosen to describe the Yeravada fast as a distraction, a cover for the political compromises Congress wished to accomplish with its British rulers (Ghosh 1995: vol 2: 158). Singaravelu accepted these formulations and chose to subsume other observations and insights as regards the Indian political scene, such as were advanced by Self-Respecters with respect to Gandhi. Thus, though he conceded the adi dravidas should have their separate electorate, he refused to endorse the Self-Respecters' reasons for supporting this demand.

Writing of Gandhi in 1934, Jeevanandham noted that samadharmists were opposed to Gandhi because constantly and on all occasions he inflected his theories of society and culture with a religious sensibility.

Thus Gandhi had carefully cultivated that very tree of sanatanadharma that was responsible for the practice of untouchability, which he claimed he abhorred: 'Gandhi, the friend of the poor, yet hails the capitalist class; Gandhi who professes himself the emissary of this country's poor [the *daridra narayanas*] yet describes wealth as a gift of God and desires that property remain with the capitalists' (Pu 11.2.34).

To Periyar and the Self-Respecters, then, the Gandhi phenomenon expressed best the 'truth' about nationalism and embodied the deceptions and contradictions which lay at the heart of this truth. In many ways, Periyar's own responses to questions of nationalism and to matters of caste and religion were provoked by Gandhi's observations on these matters. However, they were also informed by Periyar's conviction that Gandhi wielded enormous influence over the psyche of the ordinary Indian. For Periyar, the 'nation' was coeval with the 'good society' and was not grounded in religious, cultural or ethnic sentiment. In fact, as he often remarked, the example of the new nations of his time, Turkey, Egypt, Afghanistan and the nations that made up the Soviet Union proved to him that national progress was possible and in fact based on a negation of the past and a refusal of its arcane glory. For Periyar nationalism could be a viable ideal only 'if a nation's citizens could realize it, without having to forgo or compromise on their dignity and sensibilities.' Besides, for a nation to exist as such, there would have to be an 'all round growth of knowledge; spread of education; the cultivation of rational thought, work, industry, equality, unity, initiative and honesty and the abolition of poverty, injustice and untouchability' (KA 19.5.29; Anaimuthu: 372).

Like Periyar, several others defined nationalism along these terms. Unlike Congressmen, Self-Respecters rarely referred to the history of India or its civilizational strengths. For them India was a geopolitical entity whose freedom was contingent, not so much on a promise of self-rule held out by imperialists, but on the possibilities of self-respect and samadharma which they held ought to animate every Indian's imagination. It is noteworthy that even after the utopia the Self-Respecters wished to create assumed a Dravidian-Tamil countenance, its proponents defined it in terms of shared ideologies and convictions rather than in terms of language, ethnicity and geography. To better understand this sense of a nation, we need to look at how and through what discursive and practical means the Self-Respecters came to imagine a nation.

Posing the National Question: The Self Respecters and the Left

In 1934 the Congress Socialist party was formed and soon after the government banned all communist organizations and proscribed individuals, newspapers and groups from propagating communism. As we have seen, the years 1934-36 witnessed dissensions in the Self-Respect movement, as several young socialists chose to interrogate Periyar's decision to align the Self-Respect movement with the Justice party in the forthcoming elections to the Central Legislature and the local bodies. Periyar's argument was that given the Self-Respect movement's constitution it could not directly engage in politics. It needed affiliates, and the Justice party, for all its various ills and limitations, was the only available party with which it could align and work. Moreover, Justicites were at least committed to the ideal of proportional (communal) representation and had struggled against the lures of Brahminism. Congress with its rhetoric of nationhood and unity, and Gandhi with his stated belief in varnadharma (and his friendship with the bania class of merchants and industrialists) represented infinitely worse choices. It was also imperative to halt both in their triumphant march towards a self-governing polity carved within the confines of varnadharma.

Unconvinced by such arguments the young socialists left the Self-Respect movement and joined the Congress Socialist party. Following instructions from the Comintern, they attempted to bring about a radicalization of the Congress. But they completely misjudged and undervalued the strength of the Congress' hegemony, sustained as this was by the charisma of Gandhi. Now, men like Jeevanandham were forced to defend those leaders they had denounced as casteist and bourgeois until recently, and had to endorse those ideologies, which until then, had spelt anathema to them. *Kudi Arasu* and *Viduthalai* of course lost no time in pointing out these inconsistencies. T. S. S. Manian writing in *Viduthalai* observed, 'those who had loudly proclaimed they desired to "Russianise" India are now to be seen propagandising on behalf of Congressmen in the forthcoming elections' (6.12.36).

Kudi Arasu noted that Jeevanandham, Neelavathi and Ramasubramanium who had argued against the ostensible domination of the rich in the Justice party and had objected the loudest to the Self-Respect movement affiliating with Justicites, had not only joined Congress with its bevy of zamindars and industrialists, but also actually dared to criticise a Justice candidate in a local election as being a wealthy man! (20.12.36)

Men like T. S. S. Manian, T. N. Raman and Lakshmiratan Bharathy left the Self-Respect movement in the hope that an autonomous samadharmists' forum would be constituted. However, at the Tamil Provincial Self-Respect–Samadharma Conference, which was convened at Trichy on 1 November 1936, to resolve on the question of the strategy to be adopted by samadharmists, it was decided to merge the forum of Tamil samadharmists who had left the Self-Respect movement with the Congress Socialist party. This measure caused a dissension in the ranks of the samadharmists and some of them decided to return to the Self-Respect movement rather than join the Congress. T. N. Raman, who subsequently came back to the movement, pointed out that though the Congress socialists were earnest in defining their socialist politics and its attributes, the rules of the Congress Socialist party insisted that one had to first of all enrol as a member of the Congress, before one could join the former. This meant that one accepted Congress policies as well. Raman wondered whether one could hope to achieve anything, by way of transforming the Congress from within, in such circumstances (KA 29.11.36). *Kudi Arasu* pointed out in a related context that all Congressmen, including the samadharmists who were now implicated in a race for power were, to the last man, loyalists; for having decided to contest elections, Congressmen had to agree (and many did wholeheartedly) to swear fealty to India's rulers (27.12.36).

S. C. Baran, writing in *Kudi Arasu* in 1939, after Congress won the elections, conducted under the Government of India Act of 1935, and formed ministries in several provinces, asked of the socialists in the Congress Socialist party, whether they deserved to be considered socialists at all, now that they had to support those who were willing slaves to imperialism. He pointed out that socialists in the Congress were placed in an unenviable position. Their intent in joining that party had been thoroughly compromised: not only were they not able to divest the Congress of the influence of capitalists as they had hoped they would, but they were also now forced to defend the indefensible, praise those who were ever ready to humiliate them and destroy whatever influence they had managed to wield amongst the ill-defined Congress Left. Rajagopalachari, Patel and Rajendra Prasad were openly hostile to the socialists and had made no secret of their desire to destroy and discredit socialism. Gandhi had covertly made known that there was no place in Congress for those who did not wear Khadi and did not believe in those principles which underwrote the philosophy of Khadi. Socialists had also been forced to abandon their radicalism in respect of workers' rights. For instance, when the Industrial Disputes Bill was sought to be passed in the Bombay Council—the bill was framed to limit workers' rights to strike work—socialists and trade unions resisted its passage. But soon their militancy was held in leash by the Congress leadership and many succumbed to the pressure exerted on them.

Baran went on to note that this bill was but a prototype and soon several others, along the same lines, would be introduced in other Councils. Baran also observed that Congress policy with respect to ryots had proved to be equally repressive and fights had broken out between Congressmen and socialists in the United and Central Provinces. But in Madras, socialists were careful of their caste and religious identity and were not quite as militant; which was why they had carefully distanced themselves from the anti-Hindi agitations and even denounced them. For instance, Jeevanandham's *Janasakthi* carried editorials supporting Hindi. But even this had not endeared socialists and communists to the Congress, and cases had been registered against the communist Batliwala. If it had not been for the personal intervention of Rajagopalachari, Jeevanadham would have fallen prey to the repression the Congress had set loose (KA 15.2.39). S. C. Baran's long article addressed to Congress socialists was intended less to rebuke them and aimed more to lay before them the consequences of the choices they had made when they decided to join the Congress. The article was also a tacit critique of the socialist understanding of the idea of nationalism. For, we find Baran linking the Congress socialists' refusal to support the anti-Hindi protests with their limited and imitative understanding of nationalism.

Even as they denounced the Congress socialists in the 1936-37 period and afterwards, Self-Respecters did not desist from writing and speaking about socialism. Indeed *Kudi Arasu* carried articles on socialism and on the Soviet Union with surprising regularity in 1937. For instance, an article on Lenin appeared on 25 July 1937. Articles on developments in China were published fairly regularly right through the late thirties. R. H. Nathan wrote an article condemning Chiang-Kai-shek and supporting the Chinese communists (5.9.37). An article on Chinese students and their role in advancing the cause of China also appeared (15.5.38). A biography of Karl Marx was published in several parts and eventually published as a book (20.2.38). J. K. Velan wrote an article 'What Is Marxism?' which was also published in several parts in *Kudi Arasu* (the first part appeared on 29.5.38).

It is not surprising that the Self-Respecters were particularly anguished with Jeevanandham, especially since the latter did not seem to have learnt his socialist lessons well. As Lakshmiratan Bharathy argued brilliantly in 'The Congress Socialists and the Tamil Agitations' (KA 29.1.39), Jeevanandham and his mentors—Jayaprakash and Jawaharlal—had proved their interest in the Soviet Union to be of the most tenuous kind. For they had failed to learn any lessons from the Soviet experience with respect to questions of language and nationality. Quoting at length from Leon Trotsky's *History of the Russian Revolution*, Bharathy pointed to the importance granted by Russian revolutionaries to language and observed that socialists in Congress ought to read their Russian history seriously and, if they chose to still swear by it, lend their support to those peoples such as the Tamils, who were agitating at present for their linguistic rights. Socialists, concluded Bharathy ought to evolve plans for the preservation and encouragement of different languages in a future polity and also grant the right of self-determination to citizens of different language groups.

Bharathy's choice of text to illustrate his argument and uphold the validity and significance of the anti-Hindi agitations was the chapter 'The Problem of Nationalities' found in volume three of Trotsky's. Trotsky's arguments on the rights of nationalities to self-determination follows the Bolshevik, more specifically, Lenin's formulations in this respect. Bharathy takes his cue from Trotsky's opening remarks in this chapter: 'Language is the most important instrument of human communication and consequently of industry. It becomes national... with the triumph of commodity exchange which integrates nations' (Trotsky 1980, vol 3: 36). Bharathy quotes with approval Trotsky's dictum that 'for the oppressed nations of Russia the overthrow of the monarchy inevitably meant also their own national revolution' (ibid: 38). Through his selective use of Trotsky's text, Bharathy suggests that the constitution of a government after the February revolution, may be considered analogous to the formation of the Congress governments, following the suspension of Civil Disobedience and the holding of the elections on the basis of the Government of India Act of 1935. The implications of this analogy are obvious. Trotsky says of the 'official democracy' ushered in, in February 1917: 'Holding inviolate its right to settle the fate of all other nations, it continued jealously to guard those sources of wealth, power and influence which had given the Great Russian bourgeoisie its dominant position' (ibid: 38-39).

Drawing on Trotsky's definitions of the Russian language at this stage in history as the 'language of the possessing classes' (ibid: 40) which was sought to be imposed on non-Russians, Bharathy notes—in a parenthetical aside—that at present, English and Hindi are to the Indian masses what Russian was to the non-Russian nationalists! Likewise, quoting Trotsky again, Bharathy remarks, in another aside, that just as in areas like the Ukraine where a dominant minority, comprising different nationalities, and living mostly in cities was separated from the 'fundamental mass of the people not only by their level of life and culture but also by language' (ibid: 44), so in Tamil Nadu, the British, the brahmins, the Marwaris and the Sheths were separated from and pursued interests that were fundamentally different from those professed by the Tamils.

Finally, Bharathy refers to Trotsky's reading of the significance of February 1917 and glosses it thus: 'The chief service of the February revolution, perhaps its only service but one amply sufficient lay exactly in this, that it gave the oppressed and the nations of Russia at last an opportunity to speak out. This political awakening of the peasantry [Bharathy translates this as 'people'] could not have taken place otherwise however than through their own native language with all the consequences ensuing in regard to schools, courts, self-administration.' Here again the analogy is obvious. Rajagopalachari's Congress government is likened to the liberal government that was formed under Kerensky in February 1917. Just as how Kerensky, acting on the logic of a situation his party had created, catalysed into emergence the struggle of nationalities, Rajagopalachari, propelled forward by the logic of his politics, which was but the logic of the varna order, sought to impose Hindi on the Tamil country, but provoked instead a fierce Tamil nationalism.

Bharathy's use of Trotsky was not only ingenious but was calculated to force Congress socialists to come to terms with their own avowed socialism. Bharathy indicated to the Congress Socialist party how the national question in India could be understood and posed, given the constellation of forces, conditions and ideologies in the Indian context. It is significant that he entreats socialists in the Congress to grant the right to self-determination to various language groups at a time when this was not even considered germane by the Indian Left.

The Self-Respect movement's stand on nationality emerged with greater clarity, in a theoretical sense, that is, in the forties. The Self-Respecters constituted now as members of the Dravidar Kazhagam (in 1944), had already rejected 15 August 1947. In the late forties, they explained their position to the Left and entreated them to support the cause of Dravidian-Tamil nationalism. These debates are significant because they proposed an understanding and definition of nationalism which was novel, creative and radical. In addition, they carried forward the argument advanced by men like Bharathy in the late thirties, and thus we have here an implicit critique of the communist appropriation and resolution of the national question.

On 30 September 1946, *Viduthalai* carried an appeal to 'Dravidian merchants' which requested them to heed the example of Muslim merchants who had formed a Muslim Chamber of Commerce, affiliated themselves to the Muslim League, and lent their support to the cause of Pakistan. Jeevanandham, writing in *Janasakthi*, chose to misinterpret the appeal, criticized it as partisan in its intent, and wondered aloud whether the Dravidar Kazhagam was a ladder for the rich to climb up and advance their cause, or an organization which had the interests of the poor in mind. His remarks sparked off a debate and a four-part article by S. Gurusamy appeared in *Viduthalai* (21-25.8.47) which enumerated those principles of Dravidian nationalism which *Janasakthi* had either ignored or overlooked, but which were really not very different from and which represented an interesting inflection of the communists' position on the question of nationalities in the Indian Union.

Viduthalai began by noting that while communists had supported the rights of Muslims to self-determination, they were uneasy about extending that support to the Dravidian cause, though Dravidian-Tamils had proved themselves distinctive from the Aryan North in respect of 'religion, race, language, culture and mode of life'. While *Janasakthi* had not asked itself whether Pakistan's future polity would be socialist, or even sought to criticize such a body as the Muslim Chamber of Commerce, it seemed ready to attack the cause of the Dravidian Tamils on the ground that this cause was not sufficiently socialist and because it was (ostensibly) eager to claim support from even the enemies of the working class!

The article went on to say that just as the Dravidar Kazhagam had called on Dravidian students and Dravidian government officials to affiliate their organizations with the Dravidar Kazhagam, it had asked Dravidian merchants to do so. It further noted that it was aware there were some amongst the latter who were wealthy capitalists, but the Dravidar Kazhagam was equally sensitive to the importance of taking on the northern bania-brahmin complex and therefore desired to build as wide a political bloc as possible to counter it. Besides, unlike the communists, the Dravidar Kazhagam had ever endeavoured to counsel workers of the pernicious influence of religion in their lives, of the manner in which religious customs and practices 'drained their hard-earned earning' and several times had drawn the attention of the working class to the rule of those 'stone capitalists' who ruled in state in the temples. For instance, it had asked that workers agitate to 'convert temples into hospitals, use the riches amassed in religious institutions [mutts] for the cause of education' (Vi 21.8.47).

In the subsequent part of its lengthy response *Viduthalai* explained why it considered the Aryan-bania exploitative and alien to the Tamil country and how it believed capitalists' existed in non-productive spheres as well. 'Though capitalism does not heed differences in caste, religion, geographic limits and national sentiment, capitalists are divided by differences, competition and envy. Thus the capitalists of one nation constantly endeavour to cheat the capitalists of another nation. For instance, today a distinctive national sentiment has emerged amongst the northern capitalists which unites them against any others' (23.8.47). *Viduthalai* further argued that such differences amongst capitalists were not only due to the uneven development of capitalism in colonial conditions, but also due to the uneven spread of education. While almost all brahmins were educated, not even 5 percent of non-brahmin Dravidians were literate. British imperialism had encouraged and sustained the growth of Aryan-brahmin hegemony by shoring up the authority of the brahmins in government and out of it, on the one hand, and by supporting the Aryan-bania capitalist class on the other; which was why a Congress minister in Madras did not think twice about allowing Birla and Dalmia to start their industries in Madras. 'One cannot afford to forget that the Congress today is supportive of the exploitation of the Aryan capitalists' (ibid).

Viduthalai hastened to add that it did not seek to promote the Dravidian-Tamil capitalist in place of his peers from the North. For one thing, no Dravidian Tamil capitalist was with the Dravidar Kazhagam, and, besides, the journal had always been critical of capitalist speculation and hoarding. Moreover, and this was important, *Viduthalai* had sought to oppose not merely the capitalists but his gods as well; especially those Hindu gods whose vast wealth and resources could rival the possessions of any capitalist. *Viduthalai* desired that 'a future socialist rule should not be given away as a gift to the Aryan brahmins nor should it be consecrated at the feet of Lord Venkateshwara'. The Dravidar Kazhagam was committed to cleanse the social sphere of those dangers to socialism which lurked in the thickets of faith and custom (ibid).

Viduthalai defended its references to 'stone capitalists' (*Janasakthi* had criticized this formulation). It noted that these capitalists, by merely sitting in state in their temples, 'exploit the poor, live off their blood. They are capitalists without capital. Dangerous and parasitic in their attributes; leeches that suck the blood of the working class.' Moreover, in the past the 'stone capitalists' had vanquished greater enemies such as the Buddha. Brahminism had even deceived its interlocutors, assumed a variety of guises:

> It would taunt you with the mask of nationalism . . . implore you in the guise of Sahajananda [of Chidambaram], flaunt itself as Ramana Maharishi, seduce you with its invocations of Saivism, implore your

> attention as Vaishnavism...It could assume the countenance of a rishi and demand the thumb of the communist Ekalavya.

Thus, the Dravidar Kazhagam was saddled with a huge responsibility and one it could not afford to treat lightly. It had to counter Brahminism (Aryanism), and uphold the Dravidians' right of self-determination (ibid).

Janasakthi replied saying that it too considered the issue of self-determination pertinent, but it desired to struggle in the cause of a genuine unity of working peoples and was not interested in encouraging or endorsing separatism. In the last of its four-part article, *Viduthalai* responded to the communist position on the struggles for self-determination. It noted that one could not ignore social differences, since these existed and were important in defining and distinguishing the rulers from the ruled, the oppressor from the oppressed. The Dravidar Kazhagam was firm in its conviction that 'if Dravidians were to be allowed the right to determine their national status, they must necessarily oppose the exploitation of the northern bania and his Aryan [brahmin] mentors'. The Dravidar Kazhagam did not disagree with *Janasakthi's* claim that 'the success of the right to self-determination of nationalists rested on the successful conclusion of revolution in the countryside and on the nationalization of industry'. But the Kazhagam also insisted that 'the social order and Hindu religion which are closely interwoven with and into an exploitative economic order' must be destroyed. The Dravidar Kazhagam, concluded *Viduthalai* emphatically, was not a haven for the rich. It was a party of the labouring shudras and the despised adi dravidas and it was committed as the communist party to end capitalism. But it also had its own agenda and one which no communist could ignore (25.8.47).

The Dravidar Kazhagam was born out of the anti-Hindi agitations and its vision of a Dravidian-Tamil nation as well as its rejection of India were alike shaped by the experiences garnered by Self-Respecters in the course of these agitations. To better understand the logic of Dravidar Kazhagam's argument with respect to self-determination we heed to enquire in some detail into the nature of the anti-Hindi struggles.

LANGUAGE AND THE QUEST FOR COMMUNITY

Modernizing Tamil

Two sorts of figures dominated the Tamil intellectual sphere in the early decades of our century: the antiquarian and the publicist, each in their respective ways and in their chosen spheres, came to articulate a Tamil sensibility that was recognizably modern. Tamil antiquarians extolled the past but their relationship to this past was modern in its profound self-consciousness. Publicists in the Tamil country, of whatever political persuasion, attempted to bring to their invocations of a Tamil past a certain communicative worth and power and thereby indicated that the strength of a language and culture lay in their ability to respond to, absorb and express contemporary concerns and anxieties. The Self-Respect movement produced some of the Tamil country's best and brilliant publicists, men and women of immense talent and imagination who sought to render the Tamil language simple, elegant and lively in its expressions. They were keenly aware of and sensitive to the strategic uses of history and literature. They sought to rescue from the antiquarian that sense of the past which had come to be inscribed in discourses of Tamil literature and Tamil history, and redeem this mixture of nostalgia, reverence and awe by placing history within an evolutionary logic. As Periyar argued, in the course of a debate on reforming the Tamil script, the Self-Respecters did not imagine that those who lived in the days of the past were fools or were wilfully ignorant. But every generation, naturally and inevitably, as it were, seeks to improve on the efforts of the previous generation. Thus, what are commonly regarded as 'classical' and 'antique' were themselves the result of conscious changes effected by our predecessors, who naturally, considered the time before them as being of a 'classical' nature (KA 20.1.35; Anaimuthu: 961).

The Self-Respecters' understanding of language and its functions was based then on two related notions: one, that a language naturally develops, grows and modernizes over time, unless human agency intervened to arrest or retard this progress, and, two, that language, therefore, is to be judged by its contemporary worth, communicative vigour, rationality and its power to express ideas and opinions which are useful to humankind. Conversely, if a language refused to adapt itself to transformed political, social and economic conditions, or if a section of its users were to insist on its antiquity and use this as an excuse to defer change, or if they were to invoke the language's divine origins to refrain from a reform of its script and forms of expression, the Self-Respecters proclaimed they had no use for it.

The Self-Respecters viewed their own use of language as modern and were careful at all times to unlearn received wisdom. Gurusamy who was considered (and considered himself) a scourge of antiquarians—of Tamil pundits, Saivites and classicists conversant with Saivite scriptures—could recite hundreds of verses from Kamban's *Ramayanam* and was familiar with elaborate interpretative modes and conventions adopted by those who sought to expostulate on what they held to be the inner truth of scripture. But once Gurusamy turned a Self-Respecter, he came to write a simple, incisive and logical Tamil prose (Velu 1991: 180). As we have remarked elsewhere, he possessed the gift of parody and on many occasions produced brilliant and hilarious expositions of puranic myths, in the manner of the conventional *harikatha* exponent. His attitude towards old Tamil and its literary texts was, likewise, recognizably modern. Responding to Tamil scholars and Saivites who had proclaimed the Self-Respecters' propaganda was destroying literary sensibilities and denying the value of aesthetics, Gurusamy observed that the Self-Respecters were merely reading texts differently in the manner of Western critics:

How do Westerners encourage the learning of their ancient texts? How do those who are considered Hindus develop their languages? In the West, if one were to discover a rare manuscript, they would at once seek to correct its errors and publish it after analysing it using modern critical methods. They would seek to separate truth and fiction and indicate where and for what reasons the editors chose to disagree with the ideas expressed in the manuscript—and all this through notes and appendices. Further they would demonstrate how and why the author had written thus and not otherwise, how he was a product of his times and milieu (KA 7.7.29; Velu: 177-78).

Writing in a related context, S. Ramanathan observed how the refusal to detach art from religion had resulted in a truncated development of the aesthetic sensibility. This insistence on developing the arts—music, literature and dance—in the context of a religious world-view, he argued, had resulted in a mystification of meaning in the arts. As far as literature was concerned, this had caused a lopsided development of the critical faculty, which was rather wont to dwell on the intricacies of metaphor and interpretation, than on problems of relevance and communication (KA 12.4.31). The Self-Respecters' exhortations to demystify texts were then expressed in the cause of restoring a substantial measure of expressive and communicative worth to them. Even men like Kaivalyam who wrote a rather dense style of Tamil prose brought to their use of language a critical and modern sensibility. In his exegesis on puranic texts, Kaivalyam made it clear that nothing was so sacrosanct that it could not be examined for its absurdities and inconsistencies.

Such a radical linguistic sensibility was cultivated in the course of the movement's various campaigns and, as the Self-Respecters came to address vaster and vaster numbers of people and an ever wider range of issues, they enhanced the vocabulary of the Tamil language, rendered it flexible and conceptually rich. During the days when socialist ideas and themes were spoken of and addressed in public forums and in the movement's journals, Tamil developed categories of thoughts and ideas which were entirely novel, or, if drawn from an existing repertoire of concepts, endowed with a certain analytical vigour.

The term 'samadharma', for instance, while a referent for socialism, and in this sense a novel category, yet carried accretions of an older meaning: the Self-Respecters had used it initially to refer to a much desired equality and equal justice for all in caste society. The term *suyamariyathai* or self-respect recalled the Tamil notions of dignity (*maanam*), but was disengaged from its conventional context of personal or community honour, and affiliated with the natural, universal, individual subject of history, who possessed natural, universal, indivisible and inalienable rights. Or if we were to consider the term 'capitalist': though the term came to stand in, generally speaking, for the rich and the powerful, it was inflected in Self-Respect discourses to refer to brahmins, not all of whom were rich or propertied. Thus Self-Respecters would refer to brahmins as 'birth capitalists', as those who sought to capitalize on their already sacral and pure birth. Extending the meaning of the term 'capitalist' in another context, Gurusamy, as we saw earlier, used the term, 'stone capitalist', to refer to the deity in a temple. In the first instance, the Marxist notion of the capitalist as one who extracts surplus from labour suffered a mutation and was invoked to signify one, who by virtue of his birth, refused to labour, in fact, lived off the labour of others. The term 'stone capitalist' referred to the chief deity in a temple and was equally novel and rich in its significance. Periyar often argued he considered temples as favoured sites for the distribution and consumption of surplus in pre-colonial Hindu society. He therefore viewed Gods as capitalists and temples as important economic institutions which, together, extracted surplus by way of offerings, during festivals, rituals and through pilgrimages and sacrifices.

The most felicitous use of language by Self-Respecters had to do with gender concerns. Not only did Self-Respecters deconstruct terms such as 'chastity', 'beauty' and 'motherhood' but introduced new terms and notions. Their discourse on gender made constant references to women's rights to contraception, reproductive rights, and to a sexually satisfying existence of their choice. These were essentially new ideas which drastically and dramatically altered the terms of reference in the debates regarding women's rights and their emancipation from patriarchy. Self-Respecters also wondered why the Tamil language did not possess any (male) equivalents for terms such as vidavai (widow) and vibachari (female prostitute). In this context the singlemost important achievement was the re-naming and the re-definition of marriage and the consequent transformation of its meaning and significance. Marriage was divested of sacrality and deemed a contract, an agreement—an *oppandam*—entered into by consenting adults. The conventional Tamil word for marriage, *Thirumanam* connoted a sacred or at least a hallowed event. The Self-Respecters substituted in its stead the term *Vazhkai Oppandam* (agreement/contract for life, that is, for conducting the business of life).

The Self-Respecters were so sensitive to the use of terms, that they took to referring to each other as 'comrades', dropped caste suffixes, gave their children conspicuously modern names—names of famous leaders and places such as Lenin, Stalin, Bernard Shaw, London, Russia—since, to them, these names betokened pride and existed as affirmations of rationality and egalitarianism.

The Self-Respecters attempts to 'purge' Tamil of its brahminical influences took them to Tamil conferences where, though uninvited and clearly unwelcome, they made their point of view known. A Tamil conference was held on 6-7 August 1932 at Trichy and advertised widely as having been planned 'to answer the charges hurled at Tamil scholars by the Self-Respecters and to put an end to their insolence'. Gurusamy, Jeevanandham, Kunjitham Gurusamy, Neelavathi, Indrani, Sami Sitambaranar and several others attended the conference and made their presence felt. The entrance to the conference hall was decorated with arches which carried slogans, calculated to insult the Self-Respecters. Even as they entered, the Self-Respecters tore away at the offending decorations. After this initial confusion, the conference began with a musical invocation to the God Shiva. Gurusamy protested and said either the devotional song must not be sung or if the scholars insisted on singing it, the Self-Respecters should be allowed to sing one of their songs. When one of the Tamil pundits objected to this, saying that the Self-Respecters could not possibly know much Tamil, Gurusamy retorted by noting that the Self-Respecters were Tamilians as well and as concerned with the development of Tamil as the Saivites and the pundits. Finally, due to the mediatory efforts of V. Kalyanasundara Mudaliar, the Self-Respecters were allowed to sing their song.

The Self-Respecters proposed their own resolutions at the conference (Velu: 351-52). Gurusamy had, for some time now, spoken of the need to reform and simplify the Tamil script to make it easy for learners to use and, more important, ease the irksome task of typing and type-setting Tamil letters (KA 16.11.30; Velu: 366-70). He now suggested that henceforth a reformed script be adopted by Tamil users, which did not prove acceptable to the assembled scholars. (*Kudi Arasu* began to use the reformed script from January 1935; KA 13.1.35; Velu: 368-69.) However, two other resolutions, one on using the vast wealth and endowments that were vested with temples for the cause of development of the Tamil language and another on women's education were accepted without demur by the pundits and Saivities. A. Ponnambalam sent his own resolutions to the conference: he wanted the abolition of caste and religion, especially those religious markers, which spelt out differences between faiths. He also wanted the study of those Tamil Puranas which were offensive to one's sense of self-respect and rationality to cease, and all derogatory references to Jainas and Buddhists in Tamil puranic literature to be deleted. One of Ponnambalam's most important resolutions opposed and condemned the attempts to impose the study of Hindi on Tamilians

(KA 31.7.32). All these resolutions were rejected.

In 1933, a Tamil-lovers' conference was held in Madras on 23 and 24 December. The conference was attended in large numbers by Madras brahmin notables and scholars (as well as non-brahmins). Once again, through uninvited, the Self-Respecters attended the conference and occupied seats in front. Once again they insisted on singing Self-Respect songs and proclaimed that since this was not a Saivite or a Hindu conference, but a conference of Tamil-lovers, and that all Tamils, atheists, Mohammedans, Christians and others, should be allowed to sing songs of their choice. Later, as the conference progressed, the Self-Respecters demanded that a resolution which would henceforth disallow or prevent the singing of devotional songs at such conferences be considered. While the conference was thrown into confusion and tumult by such goings-on, the Self-Respecters yet managed to get their resolution on the need for reforming and rationalizing the Tamil script passed (Pu 31.12.33; Velu 355-57).

But much as they criticized the romantic nostalgia of Tamil Saivites and their pietistic attitudes towards language, the Self-Respecters jumped to their defence at those times when their scholarship was doubted or berated by brahmin scholars of Tamil. Likewise when brahmin intellectuals and scholars of Tamil expressed opinions which were deemed derogatory to Tamil culture and history, Self-Respecters turned into defenders of their past! When there ensued a furore over Maraimalai Adigal's critique of the *Ramayana* in his book, *Arivurai Kothu*, prescribed as a textbook for study at the Intermediate Level at the Madras University, the Self-Respecters defended him and his opinions (KA 15, 22, 29.8.35). In another instance, when the Tamil scholar Mu. Raghava Iyengar drew attention to what he considered certain retrograde aspects in ancient Tamil culture, Self-Respecters, along with the Saivites and Tamil pundits, condemned him (KA 16.2.36).

The Imposition of Hindi and Its Aftermath

Those very reasons which made the Self-Respecters attempt to purify the Tamil language, its association with religion and scripture, its inscription in a discourse of unwarranted and gratuitous pietism, and, finally, the awe and aura which surrounded its study and scholarship, proved germane and determinate when they came to oppose Hindi in the late thirties. (Periyar had opposed attempts by Congressmen to promote Hindi as the national language even in the twenties (KA 7.3.26). Thus Hindi was to be opposed, not only because it was an alien tongue, but also because it was closely allied to Sanskrit and therefore corrupt at its very core. Besides, the proponents of Hindi in the Tamil country (and elsewhere) urged the learning of Hindi for this very reason, that it would enable one to get acquainted with Hindu religious lore. Rajagopalachari who became prime minister of the Madras province, after a Congress ministry assumed charge in 1937 following that party's victory in the provincial elections, suggested that a knowledge of Hindi would enable Hindus to read Tulsidas' *Ramayana*! (KA 22.8.37).

For the Self-Respecters, such invocations to unity and oneness seemed inexorably brahminical in their intent, since they represented a refusal of difference, and it is not surprising that Periyar preferred Tamilians to learn English, which, as he pointed out, was a world language, the language of commerce and science, the official language of the government of India and, most important, it was a language free of Brahminism and its superstitions (KA 15.5.38; 26.9.37; Anaimuthu: 1766-67).

In an address he delivered at Kollampalayam, Periyar argued that it was impossible to ordain a common language for India, for India's geopolitical context was constitutively diverse. Besides, even in the socialist Soviet Union, where all things were held in common, there was no single, unifying, official language. Periyar's contention was that in British India, the lines of political and administrative demarcation were necessarily federal and that it was the provinces, as units of the federation, rather than the federal whole, which possessed specific cultural identities. Periyar also pointed out that, unlike in the countries of western Europe, here existed differences of caste and community which made the problem of unity and the possibility of a single national language an insuperable one. He was convinced that 'our freedom lies in secession (from the brahmin-bania North); we owe our self-respect and our freedom to our identity as Tamils, as those who are not familiar with Hindi or the backwardness which is intrinsic to the culture it embodies' (KA 26.9.37; Anaimuthu: 649-55).

Initially, the Congress claimed it was not interested in assuming office, since the British would not agree to a restriction of the Governor's discretionary powers. Thus, an interim government, comprising former Justicites, K. V. Reddy Naidu and M. C. Raja was constituted. Periyar was unhappy with this development and insisted that the interim ministry had nothing to do with the Justice party (KA 4.4.37). Later, Congressmen returned to claim their place in office, though their plea for a restriction of the Governor's powers had not really been heeded. The 1937 provincial council elections, which ushered in to power a Congress government, saw Rajagopalachari pick a cabinet packed with his trusted brahmin peers and a few non-brahmins. Dr. Subbarayan was made Minister for Education and S. Ramanathan, Minister for Information and Publicity. Almost within months of its functioning, and for the entire period of its existence, the Congress ministry was criticized by the Self-Respecters, and not only because of its attempts to make the learning of Hindi compulsory in schools. Rajagopalachari's maneouvres over the Temple-Entry Bill tabled by M. C. Raja, his half-hearted implementation of prohibition, his education policy and his determination to discredit and diminish the influence the Self-Respect movement had come to wield in civil society, angered the Self-Respecters and, more generally, the non-brahmins, who came to refer to his rule as 'Purohit Rule'. *Kudi Arasu* even called for the constitution of an anti-purohit association that would defeat the Rajagopalachari ministry's covert intents and attempts to enthrone the rule of Manu. An angry editorial demanded that the Self-Respecters write in blood their resolve to do away with purohit rule (12.9.37).

The imposition of Hindi of course proved to be the undoing of the Congress in Madras during this period. For this measure served to unite Tamil speakers of all political and ideological hues. Moreover, as Lakshmiratan Bharathy remarked, referring to the example of the Ukraine in 1917, it provoked a profound and deeply felt national sentiment into existence. Periyar and the Self-Respect movement viewed the anti-Hindi agitations as a concerted fitting response to Congress brahmin hegemony, now underwritten by the Northern bania's economic interests. They came to espouse a Tamil-Dravidian nationalism to counter, retard and deflect the lures of an 'India' and the (false) unity of people it embodied.

The anger and indignation against the Congress ministry's decision to make compulsory the teaching and learning of Hindi in Classes 6, 7 and 8 were due to a number of reasons. The clamour against Hindi was loud and vociferous and ensued from a cross-section of the populace: the Tamil literati—poets, songsters, teachers, scholars—the Self-Respecters, Mohammedans and Christians, youth organizations, adi dravida sangams, caste associations, the Justice party, women and even a few brahmins. The compelling of non-Hindi people to learn Hindi was resented because, as a *Kudi Arasu* editorial put it, a majority of the populace was not even literate in their mother tongue. At least a case may be made out for the compulsory study of English, for learning that language would acquaint the learner with rational, progressive ideas and help her or him communicate with the rest of the world. But even here, noted the editorial, brahmins had taken a lead over others and not only were they proficient in English but in Tamil as well. In matters of 'the intellect, social control and public life' brahmins had come to exercise much authority. Even if it were decided that only Tamil and English would be taught for the next twenty-five years or so, the current situation of widespread non-brahmin illiteracy and powerlessness, and brahmin intellectual and political dominance would not alter or suffer drastic change. In this context and at a time 'when there existed a general feeling that all sections of the populace must be educated and granted opportunities to thus educate themselves' the forced study of Hindi would not only produce baneful effects but scuttle all chances of non-brahmin educational progress (22.8.37).

These sentiments found an echo in a resolution passed by the Karanthai Tamil Sangam which, at a meeting held at Thanjavur on 27 August 1937, strongly condemned the imposition of Hindi. A resolution to this effect moved by the Tamil scholar U. V. Uma Maheswaran Pillai noted that 'at present children suffer from having to study a range of subjects such as English, Mathematics and Science. The compulsory study of Hindi will only add to their burden'. He recalled how the Karanthai Tamil Sangam had stoutly resisted the imposition of Hindi even in the past and fought to make Tamil the language of instruction in schools. At a time when attempts were under way to use Tamil in the teaching of logic and the sciences, the forcing of an alien language on children would retard the progress of Tamil. Pillai pointed out that Gandhi and Nehru addressed their audiences in the South in English and it seemed as if they would rather not learn Tamil. He declared that 'Hindi was a potpourri of many languages' and that it was the language of 'primitive, wandering gypsies' and would only serve a person well in his old age and that too only if he decided to go on pilgrimage to Varanasi! For then he would need to know Hindi 'to bargain with the shopkeeper over tobacco and to talk to jutkawallahs'! (KA 29.8.37)

Somasundara Bharathy, whom we have encountered before, remarked at a meeting called to protest the imposition of Hindi, that he was a Congressman, continued to be one and besides was a member of the Hindi Prachar Sabha. (Thus he could not be accused of being unpatriotic or an enemy of Congress.) He further noted that the current decision to impose Hindi was nothing but a 'brahminical ruse to destroy the Tamil language and arts and make the Tamils perpetual slaves to their masters, the Northern Aryans'. Besides, 'why must Tamil be sacrificed for the unity of India? Tamil is the only language in India which has rejected Sanskrit and remained distinctive.' Uma Maheswaran Pillai who also spoke on the occasion pointed out the reasons advanced for compelling students to learn Hindi were dubious and there could not but be a secret motive to all of this: 'Through Hindi they desire to impose Sanskrit and thereby obstruct all progress in education.' (KA 12.9.37).

It is noteworthy that almost all the Tamil scholars who opposed Hindi upheld the use and relevance of a study of English (besides Tamil). Suddhanandha Bharathy, for instance, noted that Tamils would benefit vastly from a study of English, just as the Japanese in the present hour had, for English would help them communicate with the rest of the world and help them resolve the problems specific to their society (KA 31.10.37). Maraimalai Adigal too agreed that English had its uses, but noted that at present the teaching of English and Tamil was faulty and had only produced a muddled consciousness in learners (KA 12.9.37). Sivananda Adigal (from Ceylon) condemned the imposition of Hindi for similar reasons and pleaded that the Tamils be instructed in their mother tongue (KA 19.9.37).

Such arguments against Hindi bore fruitful action, as protest meetings were held at several places in the Tamil country. Jathas were organized, anti-Hindi songs composed and sung at public meetings and a Provincial Anti-Hindi Committee was formed to concentrate the protesters' efforts and direct their action. Every issue of *Kudi Arasu* from 22 August 1937 onwards carried reports of protest meetings by Tamil scholars and others. Protests ensued from overseas Tamil settlements, from Singapore, Malaya, Burma (23.1.38; 1.7.38; 14.8.38). Of the various protest meetings, some turned out to be particularly significant. At the Third Provincial Tamil Conference held at Trichy, it was decided to send a delegation to the Governor comprising Periyar and a few others. Periyar declined to meet the Governor, convinced as he was that nothing would come of this. He instead moved a resolution requesting the Government of India to recall the Governor of Madras Province in view of his indifference in the matter of Hindi. This was not acceptable to the others (KA 2.1.38). They went ahead with their plan, but the Governor refused to intercede in the matter of Hindi (KA 23.1.38).

At a protest meeting at Tiruvaiyaru, Somasundara Bharathy reiterated Periyar's suggestions at Kollampalayam that perhaps the freedom of Tamils could be ensured only by their insistence on an autonomous Tamil Nadu. He noted that 'just as how Congress had decided to separate the Andhra province it must allow for the separation of the Tamil province' (KA 21.11.37). Not merely Self-Respecters, but non-brahmins of various sorts, Arya Samajists, even a few brahmins—U. V. Swaminatha Aiyar, Venkatrama Shastri—and men like Dr. Arundale were opposed to Hindi (KA 5.12.37). A massive anti-Hindi conference was organized at Kanchipuram and attended by even non-Tamils such as M. Krishnan Nair and K. V. Reddi Naidu. Reddi Naidu in his address pointed out that not only Tamils, but all Dravidians were against the imposition of Hindi. Quoting Caldwell and Burnell, he spoke of the antiquity, beauty and richness of the Tamil language. Krishnan Nair praised Tamil as being 'sweeter than our Mother' and urged his audience to accord respect to English 'our honoured Guest' rather than Hindi (KA 27.2.38).

In spite of these meetings, and determined to disregard these protests, the government announced its decision to experiment with Hindi in 125 schools on the conclusion of the summer holidays (KA 8.5.38). This resolve accelerated and lent a certain urgency to the anti-Hindi campaigns. *Kudi Arasu's* editorial (29.5.38) titled 'The War Has Begun' appraised this latest decision of the Congress ministry in the context of the overall retardation in educational progress that had occurred in the province. It observed that the number of schools had come down, in spite of the government acquiring a massive loan to meet its budgetary commitments. (An earlier editorial had remarked that the Justice party had allocated far greater sums of money than the Congress towards education. Moreover, the latter had caused the closing down of English schools at the middle and high school levels if they had an enrolment of less than 60 students. (KA 19.12.37). The May editorial went on to point at the pernicious effects Hindi was likely to produce in Tamil learners. It called to account the Saivites who had ever mediated Aryan Sanskrit influence in the Tamil country and asked them to repent for their former sins and support the battle against Hindi. The editorial betrayed an apprehension, which would be amply justified in the months to come, that the Congress ministry would seek to crush the anti-Hindi protests violently.

A concerted and systematic protest plan was sought to be drawn up at a meeting convened under the auspices of the Provincial Tamil Sangam and the Provincial Anti-Hindi Committee. A supervisory group comprising Uma Maheswaran Pillay, Somasundara Bharathy, W. P. A. Soundarapandian, K. M. Balasubramanium, K. A. P. Vishwanathan and Periyar was formed. It was decided that a volunteer corps of protesters would be formed to march throughout the Tamil districts, propagating the cause of Tamil and denouncing Hindi. Parents were asked not to send their children to schools teaching Hindi (KA 29.5.38).

Even as plans for a comprehensive anti-Hindi agitation were being framed, the government turned repressive. A Congress worker Ponnusamy, who had been fasting since June in front of the Prime Minister's house, protesting the imposition of Hindi, was arrested. So were C. D. Nayagam (a Self-Respecter) and Swami Shanmughananda. The latter had led a procession of protesters to the Prime Minister's residence. C. D. Nayagam and Swami Shanmuganandha were released on bail after they gave an undertaking that they would refrain from anti-Hindi propaganda until their trial was over. Ponnusamy threatened to continue his fast until mid-June and was promptly remanded (KA 5.6.38). Meanwhile, from 1 May, one Stalin Jagadeesan had been fasting, protesting against the imposition of Hindi, and his condition provoked a lot of anxiety (KA 8.5.38). The fast drew Gandhi's disapproval. Gandhi declared that Jagadeesan was fasting on a non-issue, for imagined wrongs! (KA 29.5.38) The Self-Respecters were also uneasy with Jagadeesan, and Periyar, while praising his heroism, albeit guardedly, refused to endorse the idea of a fast as such (KA 10.7.38). The Self-Respecters seemed to have doubted the authenticity of the fast and perhaps suspected a local conspiracy behind it. Stalin Jagadeesan was finally persuaded to give up his fast and the issue ended quietly. (In fact it was the adi dravida leaders, Sivaraj and Minambal Sivaraj, who were responsible for its conclusion in a more or less honourable fashion.) (KA 10.7.38) The arrests, incarcerations, the mistreatment in jail and the registering of cases however continued. Satyamurthi even proclaimed the anti-Hindi agitators ought to be tried for preaching sedition and declared that, if found guilty, they ought to be hanged! (KA 3.7.38; Anaimuthu: 1780)

Penal action against the anti-Hindi protesters was intensified, as huge volunteer corps started forming in various towns. It had been decided that protesters would gather at Trichy and march towards Madras in two or three batches, taking different routes (KA 26.6.38). They were to march for at least 10 miles a day, hold meetings at their halting places and then move on. Even as these plans were under way, a huge meeting attended among others, by over 1000 women, was held on the Madras beach on 26 June 1938 (KA 10.7.38).It lasted for over five hours, from 5.30 p.m to 11 p.m. Periyar and others addressed a restive and enthusiastic audience. Periyar pointed out that in the face of protests, Rajagopalachari had suggested that students learn Hindustani, instead of Hindi and if the protest continued, this idea would be dropped as well! Periyar by now had the support of former friends such as Varadarajulu Naidu and Singaravelu. The latter, much to the consternation of his younger colleagues in the Congress Socialist party, had come out strongly against the imposition of Hindi and refuted every one of the reasons advanced in favour of compulsory learning of Hindi in his characteristic logical fashion (KA 26.6.38).

Even those the Self-Respect movement had criticised in the past—V. S. Srinvasa Iyengar, K. Bashyam Iyengar, V. Bashyam Iyengar, V. V.Srinivasa Iyengar—endorsed the anti-Hindi protests (KA 7.8.38). Brahmins such as Paravasthu Rajagopalachari went to jail and his writings on Hindi were publicised in *Kudi Arasu*. Among the anti-protesters was a brahmin woman, Thulasibhai, whose protest was duly recorded in *Kudi Arasu* (29.1.39). Jinnah agreed with Periyar that Hindi should not be imposed on non-Hindi speakers and Kalifullah Sahib, a Muslim notable from Trichy, joined in many a protest (KA 26.6.38; 3, 10.7.38; 8.12.38). A Muslim League volunteer corps was formed, and as they sought to proceed to Madras from Dindigul, some of them were arrested (KA 9.10.38). Likewise, several adi dravida leaders such as M. C. Raja, N. Sivaraj, and Minambal Sivaraj were particularly visible and vocal in the several protest campaigns. Scores of women Self-Respecters held conferences of their own and agitated to have Hindi removed from the school curriculum (KA 31.7.38; 20.11.38). A women's conference attended by over 2000 women was held in Madras on 24 July 1938 and one Pushpavathi Ammal spoke movingly at the meeting of the plight of the anti-Hindi protesters in prison. Jalajakshi Ammal (who later Tamilized her name and came to be known as Tamaraikanni Ammaiyar) praised the courage of the prisoners, while Minambal argued as to why she considered the learning of Hindi useless as far as women were concerned, for a majority of them were illiterate. Such conferences continued to be held throughout 1938, at which, in addition to specifically women's concerns the problem of Hindi was also addressed.

The Justice party, whose members were part of the protesters, had not however lent its formal support to the agitations. When the anti-Hindi protests began, Periyar remarked rather caustically that the Justice party was indifferent to the events of the day (KA 26.4.37; Anaimuthu: 655). Later on, he remarked that not much may be expected of Justicites such as M. A. Muthaiah Chettiar and Mohammed Usman, who were at one with their brahmin compatriots in the Council on several matters (KA 7.3.38). Bobbili, who had returned from Europe just then, issued a statement asking the government and the agitators to conduct a referendum on the question of Hindi. He also condemned the repression let loose on the agitators (KA 11,18.9.38) The government of course paid no attention to this demand. A meeting of the Justice party's executive committee resolved at last that the imposition of Hindi was unnecessary and calculated to produce ill effects in Tamil society and urged its members to undertake and join in legal agitations for the repeal of Hindi (KA 23.1.38). The Self-Respecters resolve against Hindi was strengthened at the famous Madras beach meeting held on 11 September 1938, when volunteer corps of protesters from

Trichy assembled in Madras to hear it proclaimed that henceforth 'Tamil Nadu was only for Tamilians' (KA 18.9.38).

As the protests gathered strength, the repression of rights and the mistreatment of the anti-Hindi protesters worsened. So much so that the Madras branch of the Civil Liberties Union (founded by Jawaharlal Nehru) was moved to issue a statement of condemnation and protest (KA 24.7.38). Ponnusamy who had been in prison since June 1938 wrote in *Kudi Arasu* of the horrors suffered by prisoners (28.8.38). Several women were arrested and some went to prison with babes in their arms (KA 29.1.39). The government also compelled *Kudi Arasu, Viduthalai* and *Paguttharivu* to pay sureties or face penal action, while the editors of these papers, E. V. Krishnasamy and Pandit Muthusamy Pillay were arrested on charges of sedition. On one occasion copies of *Kudi Arasu* and *Viduthalai* were confiscated (KA 9.10.38). Singaravelu wrote a long article on the nature of the repression practised by the Congress ministry and compared it to the treatment meted out to Congressmen by the British when they had been arrested in the past. He pointed out that Madras' Indian rulers had exhibited a will to power and authority and a determination to practise violence that exceeded anything done unto Congressmen in the past by the British (KA 31.7.38).

Apart from the repression, which was systematically practised on the anti-Hindi protesters, these latter were subject to taunts of various kinds by Congressmen. A *Kudi Arasu* report (24.10.37) recalled Rajagopalachari's remarks made at a public meeting that he had promised Jamanlal Bajaj he would make the learning of Hindi in Madras compulsory, were he to be made the premier of this southern province. Rajagopalachari had also noted then that Tamil was like a pair of human feet. It could only travel that far and no further, while Hindi was like a cart. English, of course was like the train. Further, at yet another public meeting held in Madras, Rajagopalachari and T. S. S. Rajan had attempted to discredit the anti-Hindi agitators and accused them of being under tutelage from the Justicites! (KA 21.8.38) Satyamurthi had observed arrogantly that if he had the authority to do so, he would not only make the learning of Hindi compulsory but would also insist that a knowledge of Sanskrit was a prerequisite for a post in the services. He had also remarked he would do his best to usher in Ramrajya and ensure that each social group did its duty and performed the task assigned it by birth and tradition (KA 30.7.39).

Yet in spite of these taunts and the repression (the latter reached such proportions that T. T. Krishnamachari even considered framing a bill that would enable a recall of repressive legislation (KA 24.7.38), the protests continued. The huge volunteer corps assembled at Trichy was flagged off on its march onward to Madras by Periyar (KA 7.8.38). Earlier, Hindi Opposition Day had been observed throughout the Tamil country. Organizations as different and disparate as the Muslim League, the Beedi Rollers associations, barbers' associations, adi dravida welfare associations, Christian and non-brahmin youth groups participated in the observance of this day of protest (KA 3.7.38).

A public meeting to celebrate the arrival of the volunteer corps from Trichy was held at Triplicane in Madras city on 11 September 1938. The crowds were large and it was estimated that over 1,50,000 had gathered to hear their leaders speak (KA 18.9.38). The meeting brought together Justice party men such as K. V. Reddy Naidu, P. T. Rajan, Saivite pietists such as Maraimalai Adigal, the Congressman Somasundara Bharathy, Dr. Dharmambal who had led many a women protester to rallies and presided over and participated in several anti-Hindi conferences, Periyar, Ponnambalam, Azhagirisamy, and other Self-Respecters, Paravasthu Rajagopalachari, the brahmin scholar from Kanchipuram, Maulana Moulvi Shahabuddin Sahib from Vellore, Swami Shanmuga-nandha, N. Sivaraj and Minambal Sivaraj. *Viduthalai*, reporting on the meeting, noted (reproduced, KA 25.9.38) the three great leaders of the Tamil country, Somasundara Bharathy, representing Congress, Periyar representing the rationalists and Self-Respecters, and Maraimalai Adigal representing the Saivites, were present, representing Tamils and Tamil society and its concerns, raising the cry 'Tamil Nadu is for Tamilians' and thereby announced the emergence of a Tamil sensibility, 'beyond party limits, beyond limits of caste, religion and colour'. They had named a new movement into being, a movement which would enable Tamils realize their identity. The editorial went on to note:

> Henceforth 'Tamil Nadu for Tamilians' should be an article of faith with Tamils. It should forever be inscribed in their memory and help strengthen their movement. It should be printed in thousands and every Tamilian must carve such an inscription on his wall...This

> cry should be heard all over Tamil Nadu. It should animate our very being. When we eat, when we sleep, walk, work... It has now been proved beyond doubt that when their shared traditions are under threat, Tamilians will eschew differences which separate them and close ranks, irrespective of differences in party, creed and faith.

The editorial argued that in the past, Tamilians, even as they had sought to resist brahminical hegemony, had been held captive to it. In the present hour nationalism had tried its best to hold Tamilians in thrall, but the current agitations had turned the nationalists' dream of unity into a nightmare; 'As Comrade Ramasamy had observed at the Madras Beach meeting of 11 September 1938, Tamilians must agitate for a separate Tamil Nadu. The anti-Hindi agitations are but initial moves that would eventually lead to the separation of the Tamil districts.' After extolling the usefulness, relevance and strengths of the Tamil language, the editorial suggested that Tamil needed to acquire a modern resonance, become supple enough to express the truths of science. But for this, it would need to borrow freely from other languages and become the language of use and communication in all walks of life. The editorial concluded by noting that this would become a possibility only when Tamil became an official language which, in turn, required the constitution of a separate Tamil nation.

The Madras Beach meeting had marked a significant moment in anti-Hindi agitations, linking as it did the cause of Tamil with the cause of a beleaguered nation. At various times during the agitations, speakers and writers who dwelt on the problem of cultural diversity had pointed to the examples of the Soviet Union, Canada and Switzerland and argued that a political resolution of the language question was in order. They had pointed out that in all these instances, the autonomy of particular languages within a union or a federation had been ensured through political means, that is, by defining this autonomy precisely, and with a view to assuring that different languages and cultures are accorded respect within larger political formations which included them (KA 27.2.38; 26.6.38).

The agitations proceeded apace, claiming its first victim in an adi dravida youth, Natarajan, who died on 15 January 1939 while serving his sentence in prison (KA 22.1.39). His funeral became a huge sorrowful public event and was ceremoniously performed and

Ponnambalam, Albert Jesudasan, Paravasthu Rajagopalchari, Dhanapal and others spoke. Periyar meanwhile had been arrested. The reason cited by the government for thus apprehending him was ridiculously tame. The government held that in his address at a Madras women's conference and at an anti-Hindi conference held two days later, he had made incendiary and provocative observations (KA 27.11.38). Periyar was sentenced to three years rigorous imprisonment and asked to pay a fine of Rs.2000 (KA 11.12.38). The agitations however continued as did the repression. Another young man, Thalamuthu (a Nadar) died on 13 February 1939 and like Natarajan was accorded a hero's funeral. C. N. Annadurai (who became Chief Minister of Madras in 1967), speaking on the occasion, condemned the Congress government's callous and brutal handling of the agitations and called on Tamils to remember their martyrs and fight on. Annadurai concluded his address by noting that, whenever the Self-Respect movement had been in crisis, 'the adi dravidas and Nadars had stood by Periyar and helped him' (KA 19.3.39).

Periyar's sentence was commuted and he was released in May 1939. While in prison he had been elected president of the Justice party, Bobbili having resigned this post. Periyar's presidential address to the party conference, sent from prison, was read out by A. T. Paneerselvam. The address was replete with familiar themes: the resilience of the Aryan brahmins in holding onto their power, their capacity for scheming and conspiracy, the horrors of purohit rule, the notion that all non-brahmins, being shudras, constituted the working people and that the authority derived from birth was far more insidious and determinate that the power associated with and expressed through wealth (KA 1.1.39).

What was novel and striking about the address, though, was its observations regarding the relationship between the class of priest-intellectuals represented by the brahmins and the non-brahmin rich, be they zamindars, merchants or, simply, the rich and the powerful. Periyar argued that the caste order perpetrated itself by consigning a vast section of the populace to eternal shudrahood and unrelieved labour. To gather assent for this unequal social order, brahmins had, at all times, sought the help of the rich and the powerful. These latter served this purpose adequately and, in their turn, held those who were bound to them in thrall and fear.

Periyar's argument was that given a situation where the rich cannot be wished away and where their resources were necessary for even movements such as his own and for parties such as the Justice party to survive, there was no point in merely railing against zamindars. One had to understand their position, role and function in the social totality and consider if their power and influence was as great or as insidious as that of the brahmin who was committed to the sustained existence of the varna order. Periyar at this point in time desired Bobbili to continue as president of the Justice party. More generally, though, he was addressing those apprehensions the Self-Respecters were given to voicing against the rich and their influence in the Justice party. In spite of Periyar's gracious gesture towards Bobbili, that wily and intelligent zamindar resigned his post as president of the party. Thus, on his release, Periyar found himself with the responsibility of re-organizing and running the Justice party.

On his release, Periyar gave an interview to the *Madras Mail,* where he spelt out his future course of action (KA 28.5.39). He noted that, were the Congress ministry in Madras to resign, Justicites would not seek to step into their place but would instead devote their time to winning the people's confidence and weaning them away from the Congress. The Justice party would abide by the plan of action (prepared by Periyar and accepted by the Justice party in 1935). Periyar pointed out that there were changes to be made in party organizational matters and even a change of name was being suggested. As for the anti-Hindi agitations, these would continue until the Congress repealed its earlier imposition order. Periyar conceded the validity of the separate Andhra demand and pointed out that both Andhra and Tamil provinces needed to be separate and granted autonomous status.

In a response to the *Madras Mail* (which had criticized the demand for a separate state of Tamil Nadu), published a few months later, Periyar defended his demand for a separate state. The term 'Tamil Nadu', he noted, referred but to Dravida Nadu and its geographical area corresponded to the Madras province, and its people were those whose spoken and native languages (besides Tamil) were Telugu, Kannada and Malayalam. Dravidians comprised all non-brahmins including adi dravidas, Christians, Mohammedans and Hindus, who lived within the limits of the said Dravida Nadu. Periyar also clarified that in a future Dravida Nadu, the rights and concerns of non-Tamils would be accorded due respect and protected and advanced. If necessary, Dravida Nadu would even be divided into linguistic provinces on the model of Great Britain, which comprised as Wales, Scotland and Ireland. Dravida Nadu would remain under British protection till such time it was acknowledged as independent and autonomous by the League of Nations (KA 26.11.39; Anaimuthu: 656-58).

There is of course a subtle but nevertheless important difference in Periyar's opinions and views on a future Dravida Nadu and a future Tamil Nadu, as these emerge from statements he granted to the *Madras Mail.* In the first instance, which was an interview, he seems to argue his case for a separate Tamil Nadu from a point of view which accepts the unity and integrity of a Tamil nation as a pre-given, normative premise. In the second set of observations, however, Periyar seeks to interrogate and explicate this premise, and here we find his ideas somewhat ambiguous. In the first instance, he had stated clearly that he recognized the rights to separate and autonomous existence(s) of both the Andhra and Tamil provinces. In the second instance, though, he seems to want to maintain that not only Andhra and Tamil provinces, but the other southern provinces constituted together an entity called 'Dravidam'. In his second set of observations, the idea of an autonomous Tamil province slides into the idea of 'Dravidam' quite unproblematically. As we have seen, in the discourses of the Non-Brahmin movement, the term 'Dravidian' stood in for a whole host of meanings, existed in many contexts as a veritable category of analysis, which sought to mark out and celebrate a civilization and culture that was different from Aryan-brahmin culture and society. When the *Madras Mail* sought to criticize the demand for a separate Tamil Nadu, Periyar, naturally enough and in the manner of Tamil antiquarians, came to locate the distinctive nature of Tamil culture and society in their Dravidian attributes and characteristics.

As if to consecrate a new and achieved solidarity of the non-brahmin peoples of Madras, a 'South Indian Leaders' Appeal', signed, among others, by Periyar, Patro, Kumara Rajah of Chettinad, K. V. Reddi Naidu, A. T. Paneerselvam, Rettamalai Srinivasan, M. C. Raja, N. Sivaraj, Appadurai, the trade unionist C. Basudev, W. P. A. Soundarapandian, K. A. P. Vishwanathan, Albert Jesudasan, S. Muthaiah Mudaliar and several others was released to public

(KA 15.10.39). The appeal made it clear that the Congress could not arrogate to itself the status of the sole representative of the Indian people. The Appeal noted that the Congress was one amongst several political organizations in the country and that in Madras, Muslims, adi dravidas, Indian Christians and non-brahmins were opposed to the Congress. The appeal then dwelt on the nature of Congress politics in Madras and on the nature of brahmin power and authority in this southern presidency. It also pointed out how the Congress had succeeded in cowing the adi dravida leaders within its ranks and how the promises of autonomy, as these were present in the Poona Pact, had been unfulfilled, for in reality all reserved seats had been peopled with (adi dravida) friends of Congress, all of whom, out of fear of breaking party discipline, had desisted from supporting M. C. Raja's Temple Entry Bill in Madras. (Only two adi dravidas supported the bill.) The appeal also reviewed two years of Congress rule and argued that, given the experience of its signatories and given the example of governance set by Congress ministries in the various provinces, it was clear that the Congress was not only not representative of the peoples of India but also that it was unfit to rule, for its rule, until now, and at all times in the past, had signified only partisan caste rule, that allowed a minuscule group of men to hold the majority in thrall.

In many ways, the South Indian leaders' appeal represented non-brahmin, Dravidian resistance to Congress and its brahmin-bania power, and in it one may discover the fitful effects of two years of sustained anti-Hindi propaganda, when the claims to superiority and representative worth of not merely Hindi but also of 'Hindu' and 'Hindustan' were called into question.

THE NATURE OF A STRUGGLE: CONJUNCTURE AND CONTENT

The imposition of Hindi occurred at a conjuncture when Gandhi's political efforts to stymie oppositional and even vaguely socialist dissension within the Congress had proved mostly successful. Due to Gandhi's obduracy, and as a result of that convoluted reasoning he was capable of, Subhas Chandra Bose had been prevented from becoming president of the Congress for another term. As Periyar and the Self-Respecters pointed out, Gandhi's bania patrons and supporters were anxious that Gandhi's hold over the vast constituency of the patriotic devout that he had created must remain as firm as it had been. For this reason, Bose, who was opposed to the business communities of Bombay and Ahmedabad, had to be marginalized and cast away. For Periyar, who keenly followed Congress activities during this period, the fallen fortunes of Bose and Gandhi's tightening hold over the Congress, signified the successful achievement of capitalist dominance in the party. The fact that all Congress ministries that were elected to power in 1937 had proved to be uniformly repressive of workers' rights revealed that Periyar was correct in his reading of the situation (KA 5.2.39; 12, 26.3.39).

Periyar was of course particularly critical of the Congress ministry in Madras. Periyar discovered that Rajagopalachari was a political leader who was determined to wield power at any cost. The Congress ministers were keen on cooperating with the executive and Rajagopalachari had remarked that he trusted British civilians rather than his own Congressmen! (Suranjan Das 1994: 280) Further he had made it clear to Lord Erskine that his sojourn in office afforded the Congress and the British an opportunity to crush the unruly Civil Disobedience spirit (Ghosh 1989: vol 1, 219).

In addition, the Congress ministry had served adi dravidas ill by pretending an interest in M. C. Raja's Temple-Entry Bill, but had desisted from lending their support for its passage, on the argument that Raja really ought to wait until public opinion was in favour of such legislation. Citing the instance of Travancore, where an initiative had been taken in this regard, Rajagopalachari had suggested that such a bill may be introduced within the limits of the Malabar region, where it may be expected that the example of Travancore would be heeded, than elsewhere in the Madras province. This, in spite of the fact that the demand for temple-entry had been consistently gaining ground in the Tamil regions of the Presidency. (Later, Rajagopalachari had allowed one Vaidyanatha Iyer to enter the Madurai Minakshi temple, along with a few adi dravidas, and sought to protect the temple trustees and Executive officers who were nonplussed by this 'organized' protest by passing hurriedly—and when the Assembly was not in session—an Indemnity Ordinance [Venkatraman 1946: 50-56].) Raja had been pained by this turnabout on the part of Rajagopalachari, and had remarked in an interview he granted to the *Madras Mail*, that if radical legislation had to await the approval of public opinion and precedents set elsewhere, it would never become law. In certain other instances, such as with respect to prohibition and rural indebtedness, the Congress had not awaited the approval of the public, but created laws that would bind even a recalcitrant public to abide by it. If, yet, Rajagopalachari and his men were anxious to defer the temple-entry legislation, this could only mean they did not wish to make enemies of and offend their orthodox friends in and out of the Congress (KA 21.8.38).

Periyar was also extremely unhappy with the Congress ministry's educational policy. Modelled on Gandhi's Wardha Plan, this latter held that children should be prepared for a vocation even while in school. According to the Wardha scheme, primary education ought to be made compulsory for the first seven years and the vernacular made the language of instruction. But the children, it was suggested, ought simultaneously to be taught the practice of a trade, for the present educational model did not enable them acquire skills. Thus, it was argued that 'most... boys were lost to parents and to the occupations to which they were born. In this age those born to certain professions had forgotten them, taken to clerical careers and were lost to the country since' (KA 9.1.38) To redeem the situation, students were to be instructed in the specific craft of their communities, even while at school. Periyar saw in the Wardha scheme a justification for the perpetration of varnadharma and the division of mental and physical tasks that followed from the norms of jati and varna. He located the desire to impose Hindi in this scheme of things and, naturally enough, brought to the opposition of Hindi a sociological, political and cultural resonance.

It is clear that the anti-Hindi agitations were fought on multiple levels, and not all of those who joined the protests felt equally or as intensely about the Tamil language or its hoary past. The Self-Respecters themselves were wary of plunging the anti-Hindi movement into an abyss of atavism and romantic nostalgia. However, they realized the importance, as we have seen, of counterpoising Tamil to Hindi, of defining the language to signify a form of resistance in itself. Tamil ceased to be a mere instrument of a cultural opposition but came to embody a non-brahmin will to power and counter-hegemony. The focusing of resistance to Northern Sanskritic dominance in and through the Tamil language possessed a long history, as discussed earlier. This history assumed a distinctive form and coherence for modern times in the anti-Hindi agitations. What was the meaning of Tamil for the Self-Respecters? Periyar was quite clear as to what Tamil did not mean, as far as he as concerned:

> I love Tamil not because it is my mother tongue or because it is the national language; or because it is a language that can stand on its own. Neither is my love of Tamil due to its antiquity, to the fact it was the language spoken by the god Siva or the language created by the sage Agasthya...I love a particular thing for its quality, for its usefulness. I do not extol a thing just because it happens to be my language, my nation, my religion...If ever I am convinced that Tamil cannot help me realise my ideals, if I cannot make it serve my purposes, I will move on and leave it behind me. Likewise if ever I think my language will not serve my ideals, will not help my people live with honour nor help them progress, I will give up on Tamil...If I love Tamil it is because I have weighed the good I expect to come out of it against the ill effects of its disappearance from public life...I oppose Hindi too on this basis, on account of the ill effects it may cause...I have understood the nature of these effects and unable to tolerate their existence have decided to resist Hindi, but not because I will not be able to understand Hindi or that it is an alien language (Sitambaranar 1971: 213-15).

Periyar's functionalist views on language, however utilitarian these may sound, helped him assess a language's ideological resonance and distinguish its usefulness from the irrelevant and worthless dross which often rendered a language opaque and unfit for rational, intelligible communication: 'It is my opinion that the Tamil language can help its people progress in all fields, liberate them and help them lead a rational and honourable life. Of course, some may ask, if Tamil is indeed capable of all this. Tamil may not help its speakers to achieve all these purposes but I do know that of all the Indian languages, Tamil possesses those arts, manner of speech and custom as well as the words requisite for people's progress (ibid).

Periyar was no purist and advocated that the Tamil language borrow from all other languages, except Sanskrit. This is not to be wondered at, since to Periyar and in the general discourse of Self-Respect, Sanskrit embodied an entire system of values through which the Tamil people had been enslaved in times past. Thus, for Tamil to thus serve as a kind of liberative energy, that would rid Tamil society of Aryan brahmin excrescences, the tongue of the commoner and the patterned Tamil speech and writing revered by the antiquarian had to fuse together to constitute a marker of a new national identity. The anti-Hindi agitations achieved just this: they made Tamil a carrier of a new political spirit; one that was sustained by a creed of social justice and animated by a cultural desire to preserve and render durable a sense of historical difference. For the Self-Respecters, this difference was less a matter of glory than of ideological worth. For Tamil enthusiasts of various persuasions, the Self-Respecters' philosophy of language and society was less important than their political will and determination to resist Hindi. For the thousands of men and women, who eagerly joined the campaigns against Hindi, Tamil, Self-Respect and the future prospects for their liberation from caste were all at stake. For all concerned with the struggle, neither caste not class nor even gender distinctions mattered, since the imagined community of free self-respecting Dravidians made possible for the moment of struggle at least a horizontal comradeship.

Horizontal Comradeship: Some Questions and Problems

The invocation and celebration of a horizontal comradeship was underwritten by a subtle but extremely significant shift in the terms of discourse about culture and community, as these had evolved in and through the various struggles launched in the previous decades by the Self-Respect movement. As we have shown, the movement had located the basis for comradeship and citizenry in shared notions of rationality, equality, especially between the sexes and social justice in respect of caste. The movement's observations, proclamations, reports, articles, in short its mode of expression, was, for the most part, free of derogatory references to women and consciously refused an objectification of the female body.

But with the anti-Hindi struggles, the Self-Respecters found themselves having to forge as wide a bloc of peoples as possible. The non-brahmin historic bloc they had always attempted to build was forged in the heat of the struggle, as Self-Respecters came to align and work with all sorts of non-brahmins. The specific details and attributes of Self-Respect ideology were now subsumed in a layered and complex discourse of Tamil culture, history and community. This discourse rested on a wholly different set of premises: it invoked notions of honour and pride (rather than self-respect) and, more often than not, imaged the beleaguered Tamil community and society as a woman. Even during their most virulent campaigns against brahmins and Brahminism, Self-Respecters had been logical, rational and would, in fact, insist they were motivated to say and do what they said and did, not out of prejudice and communal considerations, but out of a deep sense of justice. But the protest over the imposition of Hindi transgressed such epistemological limits and the bounds of decorum Self-Respecters had set for themselves and sometimes bordered on linguistic chauvinism.

Thus, Hindi was reviled as we have seen with Uma Maheswaran Pillay, as the language of barbarians; Tamils, in several instances, were asked to remember the injustice visited on their 'mother'. Self-Respecters were critical of the concept of Bharat Mata, but this iconizing of Tamil during this period was neither criticized nor disallowed. Tamils were asked to defend their (and their beleaguered mother's) honour and demonstrate their courage in the face of this most trying of challenges and this most terrible of crises. An exhortation to Tamils urged them 'not to betray future generations' (KA 26.10.37). An earlier call for battle to Tamils had entreated them to remember their mother 'who wishes to be delivered from Aryan cruelty. Are they men who are ungrateful to their Mothers and who refuse to honour their wishes?' (KA 29.8.37) *Kudi Arasu* carried a rebuke addressed to Tamils which asked them 'if they yet desired to live' now that their honour had been destroyed (KA 19.12.37). A cartoon that seemed to have been drawn by K. A. P. Vishwanathan was published in *Kudi Arasu* (19.12.37), which showed a woman, ostensibly Mother Tamil, being disrobed, in the manner of Draupadi. The robe carried the inscription 'Tamil Arts' while Rajagopal-achari was portrayed as a veritable Dushasana! Tamil scholars and pundits were portrayed in the somewhat unlikely role of Krishna, who help to preserve and guard the honour of Mother Tamil. A *Kudi Arasu* appeal (22.5.38) calling on Tamils to march to Madras, to express their protest read thus: 'The War against Hindi had begun. This is going to be a long drawn-out war. Mother Tamil calls you to perform your duty by her. Don't give in to cowardice. Demonstrate your heroism in public. Contribute to this noble cause and gather in strength.' A variation of this appeal appeared again (29.5.38): 'The Tamils' War is on. This is a War for the sake of Tamil; for Tamil Honour, for the Tamil Arts. For Heroism.'

Though during this time Self-Respecters voiced their protests and opinions in their usual sardonic manner, the expressive energy of their discourse was often coopted and subsumed to the terms of a larger and rather uneven discourse of protest, that combined atavism, notions of wounded male pride and honour and which reified womanhood. This latter aspect bears consideration in itself, because while there occurred a gendering of discourses of protest during the anti-Hindi agitations, this was also accompanied by a political coming out of women. As we have noted, women were prominent in the anti-Hindi campaigns, several of them courted arrests, while others addressed meetings, organized conferences and worked hard to make the cause of Hindi a deeply personal one to every self-respecting Tamil woman. But yet the gains notched up by women in a political sense signified sometimes nothing more or less than a pyrrhic victory.

If we are to consider critically the women's conferences that were held during this time, we find that apart from routine resolutions on widow re-marriage and women's rights to education, very few reform questions were actually raised or discussed at these conferences, most of which were resonant with anti-Hindi rhetoric. The famous women's conference that was held in Madras, at which it was decided that, henceforth E. V. Ramasamy would be referred to only through his honorific Periyar, was unremarkable in other respects, except of course that it witnessed angry denunciations of Hindi (KA 20.11.38). At a meeting held in Vellore, Tamaraikanni Ammaiyar condemned the Malayalam poet Vallathol who had spoken ill of the anti-Hindi agitations and also called to order Sarojini Naidu who had remarked that she did not see the point of these protests. Tamaraikanni Ammaiyar also took issue with Kovai Ayyamuthu, a Self-Respecter turned Congressman, who had said that the anti-Hindi struggles had revealed Tamil women to be 'mere grain to the pestle wielded by Tamil men', that is, little more than appendages to their men. She criticized his tasteless remarks, as she did his ironic references to her singing the nationalist poet Subramania Bharathi's songs. She noted that while Periyar and others might disapprove of Bharathi, she liked and respected the poet and would sing his songs (KA 8.1.39). Such defiance, though, was rare and by its constitutive terms limited. Women like Minambal Sivaraj did speak in a compelling fashion about the ill effects of Hindi, but given the gendered basis of the emergent Tamil nationalism, such intelligent defiance came to be easily overlooked or, worse, coopted.

It is noteworthy women (and of course men) themselves referred to the problem of Hindi in specifically gendered terms. For instance, Neelambigai Ammaiyar presiding over the Tamil Women's Conference at Madras, in her address, compared Tamil to the nurturing mother who had sadly enough been left to go hungry, while an alien woman, a mere 'servant' (signifying, of course Hindi) had been allowed to come into the Tamil country and partake freely of the people's generosity and good will (KA 20.11.38). A *Kudi Arasu* appeal called upon the Tamil people to resist the imposition of Hindi, because this was but a prelude to a sordid drama of seduction and betrayal (21.8.38). The appeal recalled in this context the fate that had overtaken Malayalam:

> For no sooner had Malayalam come under the spell of Sanskrit, than Malayali women, especially those belonging to the upper castes, were taken as mistresses by brahmins. Some women in fact desired to be the mistresses of brahmins. If Sanskrit were to achieve dominance in the Tamil country such a fate will surely befall the Tamil people...If Sanskrit had not originally extended its influence in the Tamil country, would Tamil families have bound their daughters to sexual slavery?...Sanskrit is definitely a means to enslave Tamilians to Aryans, to degrade Tamil women.

In another instance, when women gathered to greet anti-Hindi agitators they performed *arthi* in the traditional way, in the manner of women welcoming soldiers of war! (KA 18.9.38). In such proclamations and expressions of honour and solidarity, we find a feminization, in a conventional sense, of the terms of discourse. Tamil becomes the site of female (and male) honour and conversely, the female body, rather its chaste status, comes to stand in for and mediate the worth of Tamil! Tamil-as-Mother, in whose person is invested the Tamil community's honour, also becomes a sexually vulnerable, though desirable figure, whose chastity then must be preserved at all costs!

Periyar was critical of this gendering of language. On one occasion, while replying to charges of non-brahmin virulence, he remarked that if, as brahmins claimed, their women had been degraded by anti-Hindi protesters, who had made unpleasant references to them, he was willing to condemn the crime:

> To speak ill of women thus is wrong; it ought not to be done. This ought to be held wrong not only with reference to brahmin women but also with regard to prostitutes, to those who have been ordained by custom to be sexual entertainers. We do not think brahmin women to be different from our women. If one of them . . . is humiliated, we will consider it a shame.

But, argued Periyar, brahmins who took umbrage when their women's name was thus wantonly or otherwise besmirched, were themselves given to malice. While brahmins objected to non-brahmins treating the brahmin's sacred thread with contempt in the present instance of the anti-Hindi struggles, they had, in the past, indulged in much mischief themselves, as when they announced in public that Ramarayaningar was dead, when the latter had lost an election. Brahmins were even known to have ceremoniously distributed tobacco to fellow brahmins on the occasion! (KA 28.8.38) However this may be, Periyar, in all likelihood, could not prevent the gendering of the terms of public debate concerning language, caste and identity. Differing voices had to be accommodated, however distasteful to Self-Respecters some of their expressions and ideas. Besides, the invocations to honour and male pride were infectious and we find that in some instance Self-Respecters resorting to such rhetoric!

The anti-Hindi protests concluded with Rajagopalachari's announcement that Hindi will not henceforth be a compulsory subject of study. But the pan-Tamil identity which had emerged in the context of these protests would provoke yet another mutation in Self-Respect ideologies. When Periyar became president of the Justice party, his Self-Respect movement was transformed from being a radical social movement to one interested in a politics of nation and community. The demand for a separate Tamil (Dravida) Nadu was heard throughout the forties, and in 1944 the Justice party was renamed the Dravidar

Kazhagam. Though at all times it was the Tamil people who were interested in the cause of a Dravidian nation, Periyar insisted on referring to this nation of Tamils as 'Dravidian' in its attributes. As we have remarked earlier, the term denoted for him, both a distinctive linguistic and cultural identity as well a philosophy of Self-Respect, equality and social justice. He and the Self-Respecters had caused it to evolve as a counter to the brahminical logic of varnadharma. Thus the Tamil language while an important site of struggle was not, indeed, could not, in Periyar's political lexicon, constitute the sole term of the struggle.

With the anti-Hindi struggles, a new generation of publicists and intellectuals appeared in the Tamil public sphere. Symbolized most aptly in the person of C. N. Annadurai, this group of (mostly) young men were gifted with the power of oratory and, rather than persuade their listeners, learnt to seduce them into accepting certain political ideas and notions as valid and significant. Annadurai was erudite, intelligent and had a way with words and his inexorably gendered discourse, which, even when it spoke of women's freedom, objectified them as creatures of beauty and desire, proved alluring and therefore curiously educative. Drawn to his wonderful rhetoric, part prurient, but always well informed, an entire generation of youth came to be schooled in politics, history and culture. When Annadurai left the Dravidar Kazhagam to form the Dravida Munnetra Kazhagam in 1949 along with several others, he worked to render the idea of Dravida Nadu consensual. But meanwhile, the non-brahmin, Self-Respect sensibility, as we have seen it grow through three decades from 1916 to 1939 acquired new attributes and resonances.

Throughout the forties Periyar's control over the Dravidar Kazhagam never loosened and even as he tirelessly criticized the making of 'free' India during those crucial years which led to 15 August 1947, his party continued to propagandize on religion, caste, untouchability and gender concerns. Alongside this, grew another impulse, nurtured by the younger intellectuals, that fed on notions of honour, fealty to community and culture and which imaged the Dravidian-Tamil nation as a virginal young woman, whose chastity had to be jealously protected. In 1949 this impulse would fructify into the creation of a patterned, elaborate and rhetorical Tamil nationalist discourse, perfected to a fine art by those men of the stage and the theatre who came to head the Dravida Munnetra Kazhagam. But that belongs to a different history. The end of the thirties marked the end of an era of tumultous heady and exciting social radicalism. The beginnings of this radicalism were, as we have seen, modest, though startling. From Iyothee Thass through the Justicites to Periyar, the progress of social radicalism in the Tamil country mounted in intensity, as the years rolled by, and made for a non-brahmin commonsense that one hopes will survive until the dawn of that millenium anticipated by Iyothee Thass and Periyar.

CHAPTER 13

Awaiting the Millennium

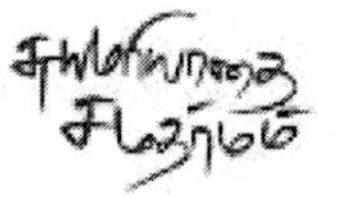

FIRST THE IMPORTANCE OF SELF-RESPECT

Non-Brahminism—as ideology, faith and structure of feeling—emerged out of a time and a place, when differences of birth, status and privileges were defined and interpreted in terms of a logic of inequality, oppression and subordination. This logic emerged into history during the moment of colonialism, and was characterized by violence, disruption, impoverishment on the one hand and by intimations of utopia, promises of infinite freedom and equality on the other.

In a context when brahmins claimed that birth was no more a badge of status and then went ahead to act and speak as if it was, non-brahmins, comprising a range of castes and communities, including both those who owned land and those who laboured on it, claimed the contrary. They called attention to practices of discrimination, humiliation and negation suffered on account of their always already lowly birth, and came to articulate a philosophy and practice of rights which would help them combat inequality and humiliation.

The question of rights soon assumed political significance and non-brahmins, who had assumed a constituency and community derived from birth, as their own, realized the importance of transforming their communal agenda into a hegemonic political programme. The Justice party was thus forced to work through the enormously difficult problem of constructing a political bloc out of its disparate caste and community segments.

They were not lacking in signs and portents to guide them in their work. Iyothee Thass had indicated at the beginning of the twentieth cenury that the task awaiting all those opposed to brahmin prowess and authority required the making of a grand fraternity of peoples, which would be animated by ethical and philosophical ideals that guaranteed freedom, mutuality, equality and self-worth. The Justice party brought to the task it had set for itself considerable political acumen. But it could not and, at times, would not work at creating the necessary social and cultural conditions which would enable them realize their vision of rule and community.

It was Periyar and his Self-Respecters, young men and women of unbounded energy and imagination who realized—in idea and practice—the historic responsibility that non-brahmins had decided to assume. The Justice party had defined the non-brahmin agenda in chiefly political terms, that is, in terms of governance and rule. Justicites wanted non-brahmins to educate themselves in vast numbers, populate state services, and claim what was due to them by virtue of their being the producing and labouring communities. But Justicites did not, at all times, seem averse to the sacral brahmin, as they were to the political brahmin. Even when they did identify the brahmin's sacrality and the knowledge which underwrote his political and social dominance, they seldom called into question the phenomenon of the sacred itself. Nor did they seek to unravel those moral and spiritual sophistries that lay at the heart of the sacred in caste society and which replicated the logic of the sacred realm in all other spheres—from the civil to the political.

The Self-Respect movement then had very few precedents in Indian history; Mahatma Phule was a forebear, no doubt, but he lived at a time when the nation had not been sufficiently and passionately imagined. Living in the heyday of nationalism and having to work within a conjuncture defined by nationalist politics, Self-Respecters found themselves face to face with a hegemony that exacted from them the most difficult and consistent of challenges. Yet they not only countered Gandhi but also proposed a theory of rights, power and justice and a definition of community which brought forth a new subject of history: rational, committed to reciprocity, equal, yet desirous of fraternity and, above all free, bound only by the ideal of self-respect.

This 'subject' was fashioned in the tumult of struggle and resistance. The social and economic forces (which propelled the subject of Self-Respect discourses and activism to claim her/his rights) derived their strength from old injustices—caste, the tyranny of the household and family and the power of religion. The Self-Respecter, more often than not, was a woman, an adi dravida, a rickshaw puller, a weaver, a peasant, a factory worker. As we have shown they comprised the very 'dregs' of society, men and women of no consequence whatsoever. The movement constituted them into knowing, desiring subjects. Self-Respect platforms were turned into schools and publicists became pedagogues as meetings turned into lectures, explications, remonstrances.

From contraception to Hindu law, from atheism to Russian history—a range of concerns was discussed, debated and made known to vast assemblies of people. Homely metaphors and analogies, rivetting descriptions, ironic and satiric observations—the Self-Respecters managed to communicate their weighty ideas through an ingenious and creative use of language. Periyar's addresses were remarkable in this respect: not only did they breathe a sincerity and transparency of intent, but they revealed a ludic imagination at work. This imagination revelled in standing the world on its head, laughing, sometimes bitterly and angrily, at ignorance, folly and the naked play of power and greed in public life. Periyar's addresses and writings also possessed an oracular power of utterance: he cajoled, persuaded, threatened and warned his listeners all at once, resorted to sexual and scatological metaphors to endow his irreverence with vigour. Yet, at all times he was eager to be understood and not merely accepted. His public addresses often ended on a note of entreaty: he would request his audience to think, analyse and judge the truth of what they had heard. But he could also be a raging prophet, especially when he was roused by a particularly vicious instance of Brahminism or roused into anger by an injustice whose grossness shocked and baffled him.

There were other communicators in the movement besides Periyar, of course: men and women of immense learning who could argue their points of view with skill. They could write and discuss a range of subjects: from Boccaciao's *Decameron* to the writings of Lenin; from religious history to the travails faced by weavers and sanitary workers; from the suffragette debate to the sociology of cooking. There were songsters, poets, theatre persons: the movement yielded to modern Tamil culture one of its most prolific and talented poets, Bharathidasan, whose youth was spent in Pondicherry. Bharathidasan's verse was part oratory, part lyric and at all times suffused by a passion for the cause of, first, Self-Respect, and later, Tamil nationalism. There were others who wrote as felicitously. Jeevanandham was himself a song writer, as was Gurusamy.

These publicists and writers enunciated a new structure of feeling and one that would help the Self-Respecters define their concerns as different from those habitually espoused as being of national pertinence by the Congress. Though Periyar was himself into his middle years when the Self-Respect movement was launched, it remained, in its constitutive years, a movement of the young. For the young were easily attracted to the movement's impatience with custom and tradition and its celebration of defiance. The new structure of feeling that grew out of the philosophy of Self-Respect was most evident in the speeches, writings and public actions of these young women and men, who were curious, cosmopolitan and entirely free in their concourse with each other and their elders. They were ready for any and every from of subversion, provided it served the cause of the radical objectives they held dear: whether it was the burning of the *Manusmriti*, leading adi dravidas to enter a temple, calling old and renowned Tamil scholars to order, or taking on well-known Congressmen in public debates, the Self-Respecters were enthusiastic and eager to demonstrate their newly acquired subjectivity.

Many of them took on pseudonyms such as 'Wanderer', 'Madman', 'One Who Could Be Anyone', 'Comrade', when they wrote for Self-Respect journals. By wilfully claiming a marginal identity they made it clear that knowledge in modern times was available as commonsense, a complex of ideas and opinions that Everyman and Everywoman could avail and use at will. Many a Self-Respecter, as we have noted, was willing to forego personal fortunes, community goodwill, professional careers and throw themselves into propaganda work. Self-Respecters often worked with the barest of resources and Self-Respect clubs that sprang up at several places in the Tamil country were organizations that emerged spontaneously, as it were. (At one time, there were nearly 118 Self-Respect Clubs functioning in the province.) These clubs could comprise Justicites, Congressmen, Hindus, Muslims, that is, any and every non-brahmin who felt moved by the injustices of the caste order and who was determined to oppose religious orthodoxy and priesthood.

Even when the Self-Respect–Samadharma party was formed in 1933 and a formal work programme was adopted for purposes of propaganda, the Self-Respecters did not seek out a formal organizational structure. True, there were men like Gurusamy who argued that the work of the Self-Respecters ought to be regulated and located in a defined institutional space. Thus, Gurusamy once requested Periyar to work out the modalities for registering the Self-Respect movement and discover means to support young publicists through the payment of a modest honorarium, since many sacrificed lucrative careers to undertake propaganda work (Velu 1991: 310-11). Gurusamy's point was that without an organizational matrix, Self-Respect work would always be improvised. Gurusamy's biographer recounts how in Madras, the Self-Respecters would often hold meetings on the beach. A rickety old table, a borrowed lantern, an impromptu drum which would be struck periodically to attract public attention—all the elements of drama and carnival were present in these efforts to woo people to listen to their views on God, temples, brahmins, caste, and so forth (Velu: 245-46). Though the moments of activity proved exhilarating, they obviously drained a great deal of their energy and Gurusamy's plea for an organization was not without reasons. However, nothing came of this.

The question, of course, is whether the Self-Respecters' multivalent and diverse concerns could have been accommodated within an organizational scheme. For instance, Self-Respect activities in nearby Pondicherry were undertaken on an almost wholly autonomous basis and did not really await instructions from Madras or Erode. Likewise, Self-Respect propaganda amongst overseas Tamils proceeded along its own trajectory and was almost entirely determined by local conditions. This does not of course mean there were no links between the various Self-Respect forums or that things were random and inchoate. Self-Respecters were, everywhere, bound in fealty to Periyar, and he defined in very broad terms what sort of propaganda work needed to be undertaken in a particular conjuncture. Of course, Self-Respecters were free to disagree and debate matters, and as we have shown, such debates occurred often in the pages of journals such as *Kudi Arasu, Paguttharivu, Puratchi* and *Samadharmam*. Periyar was civil and decorous to his opponents and was not given to using his age and experience to advantage to score points against his younger colleagues. Thus, in spite of his youth, Gurusamy was asked to assist S. Ramanathan in editing *Revolt*, while others such as Ponnambalam and Azhagirisamy and Jeevanandham were recognized as foremost and talented publicists.

We have to keep in mind that the Self-Respect movement's organizational needs, to an extent at least, were met by the Justice party. However, tense and uneven the relationship between the two, the agitational energy of the Self-Respecters assumed form and coherence in the legislative efforts of the Justice party. Besides, Justicites helped Self-Respecters conduct their conferences and were generous patrons. But this did not mean they were indispensable or could dictate terms on account of their support. Periyar could be ruthless in his criticisms of even trusted friends. He once observed sardonically that as long as Self-Respecters stayed clear from criticizing Christianity, A. T. Paneerselvam was willing to go along with them (KA 19.5.35; Anaimuthu: 942).

In the final analysis, it must be acknowledged, though, that the Self-Respect movement derived its energy, strength and resilience from Periyar, and it is in this context that we need to look a little more closely at Periyar's perceptions of himself, his role and vocation. Periyar was clearly moved by a millennarian vision of the future, a vision inspired, in part, by his own anger over varnadharma and a profound sense of justice. But he also partook of and trusted to an ideology of progress which marked rationalist thought during this time and which was voiced with great conviction by the publications of the Rationalist Press Association (whose pamphlets and books were eagerly bought and read by the Self-Respecters).

However, Periyar's millennial dream was sustained not by a totalizing vision of truth but by an existential foreboding about the powers and possibilities of human thought and action. Even as he sounded like an angry prophet, Periyar did not consider his work and movement exceptional or prophetic. He did not believe that he had disentangled the mysteries of human thought and endeavour; nor did he imagine the Self-Respect movement had completed the process of revolution. He held that change, decay and revolution inhered in the very nature of human institutions and observed on several occasions that this moment in history too would pass and other novelties and developments take over. The important thing for him was to attempt what the moment required and demanded. He saw himself as having no real, material stake in progress as such. As he said of himself, both in his middle age and after, he was a barren tree, a *Thuravi* (one who had renounced the world). In his re-tellings of his life—he would do this in the course of his public addresses, locating his actions in time and delineating their different contexts—he did not dwell on his crises of conviction or on his moments of doubt; nor did he share the agonies of his soul, as for instance, Gandhi would. He re-lived his moments of action and struggle, detailed the travails and victories of the Self-Respecters and emerged as a raconteur who wished to revivify public memory so that the challenges to an unjust social order may continue.

Since Periyar did not feel impelled to claim the voice of Truth, he did not also wish people to suffer and die for it. This was one of the reasons why he abjured violence. Violence to him represented gratuitous disorder, a waste of energy and a betrayal of reason. He was a committed pacifist and it was this aspect of his politics that made him keep company with the Justice party. Justicites, as we have shown, were liberal constitutionalists and their vision of social change, though it stood in dire contrast to the radicalism of the Self-Respecters, appealed to Periyar's sense of decorum and his antipathy to violence.

While Periyar refused to be bound by a singular Truth, this does not mean he was a relativist. His sense of the wrong wrought by unjust human institutions was too strong and powerful for him to reconcile to relativism, whether in politics or in ethics. But his ethical sensibility was not grounded in imperatives; it drew its strength from his love and respect for his fellow beings.

Periyar and Gandhi, it must be clear, were held together in a relationship of alterity. Both were great transitional figures, straddling several times and places, both were convinced of the need to transform and revolutionize consciousness, either was convinced of the need to address questions of caste, rights and faith and equally moved to reinscribe politics within quotidian acts. The matter of gender relations and the related question of the body and sexuality were central to the task they felt awaited them, as they dreamed of utopia. They were both aware of the universal dimension to the work they had assumed as their lifetime vocation and the thought of each was resonant with multiple and criss-crossing influences from, literally, all over the world. Both were, of course, consistent practitioners of an ethics of the self, whose actions were inspired by a deep sense of personal responsibility and conviction. And then, for either of them, the world was a capacious and large space and they were concerned with all of its variegated ways of being—from food to sex to death to everyday details.

What divided them was their differing conceptions of society and the positions they chose to occupy in the body politic. Gandhi spoke the language of and practised a lone faith that relied on highly experiential and convoluted notions of truth and piety; whereas, Periyar expressed himself in a language that was essentially dialogic, open-ended, critical and which demanded a mutuality constructed on reason and desire, rather than belief and suffering. Varnadharma, Satyagraha and Tapas were keywords in Gandhi's lexicon; Samadharma, Reason and Self-Respect in Periyar's.

Determined to carve out a community that would be resolutely anti-brahmin in all its aspects and in all realms—from the political to the epistemological, from the social to the ontological—the Self-Respecters transformed the original non-brahmin project into a project for Utopia. Their problem, as we have demonstrated in any number of instances, was that their visionary dream had to contend with the realities and anxieties posed by history and their genius, especially, Periyar's, lay in advancing a practice of politics that would be adequate to the moment at hand, but whose significance clearly transcended the 'normal', the here and now. The anti-Hindi agitations exemplified this simultaneity—in vision and practice—and marked a rare moment in contemporary Tamil history, when it seemed as if a world turned upside down for a while would, actually, stay that way!

PERIYAR'S LAST STRUGGLE

In the decades that followed, the energies of the Self-Respect movement were absorbed by political imperatives. The era of prophecy and action soon gave way to times of consolidation and growth. Non-Brahminism moved away from being a millennarian dream to representing the concrete needs and aspirations of those subordinate communities who were eager to render productive their engagement with power and authority.

However, that indomitable will to bear witness to the new century, to Utopia, so characteristic of Periyar's thought and action at all times, resurfaced, as he refused to assent to the fact of India. His argument was an old one, but after 1947 it acquired a certain poignancy. 'Bharath that is India' seemed to Periyar to have been conceived in the spirit of the Karachi resolutions of 1931. He held that the Indian Constitution, guaranteeing as it did, the free practice of religion and the neutrality of the Indian state with respect to different religions, was but a revamped dharmashastra for modern times. It is not surprising, then, that he resorted to symbolic acts, such as the burning of the Constitution, of the map of India and the garlanding of the portrait of Rama with slippers, as the Indian nation gradully consolidated its powers.

It is entirely logical that his last struggle should have been provoked by what he characterized as the brahminic logic of the modern Indian nation. In 1970, the Government of Tamil Nadu, then under the rule of the Dravida Munnetra Kazhagam (DMK) with M. Karunanidhi as Chief Minister, passed amendments to the Hindu Religious and Charitable Endowments Act—Tamil Nadu Act 2 of 1971—to do away with the practice of appointing *archakas* (temple priests) on a hereditary basis in over 10,000 temples, permitting persons from all castes to be eligible for the posts of priests. For Periyar, this seemed a matter of urgent import, for he had all his life held that it was the brahmin's time-honoured relationship to sacrality that granted him his exclusive identity and prowess. This act that was passed by the Tamil Nadu Legislature was, however, challenged in the Supreme Court.

The five-judge bench of the Supreme Court upheld the DMK government's reasoning in respect of the appointment of non-hereditary priests: it accepted that the matter of appointing priests had evolved out of secular imperatives and there was nothing sacred about this practice. But the Bench refused to accept the consequent argument that priests could henceforth be appointed from all castes. It was argued that such a practice, if instituted, would be a clear violation of *agamic* injunctions which were very severe with respect to the conduct demanded of a prospective priest. Further, if such injunctions were to be wilfully ignored, this would mean a direct interference with the Hindu worshipper's practice of his faith. The Bench observed that for the Hindu, the idol was a sacred object of immense significance. The devout Hindu would not countenance anyone but a traditional priest to touch the idol, for his faith was clear on this matter. Further, 'any

State action which permits the defilement or pollution of the image by the touch of an Archaka not authorised by Agamas would violently interfere with the religious faith and practices of the Hindu worshipper in a vital respect and would therefore be prima facie invalid under Act 25(1) of the Constitution'(AIR 1972: 1592-93).

Needless to say, such sentiments angered Periyar and confirmed him in his opinion that the Indian nation was not interested in all those who were condemned by the Hindu religion to be less than human simply because they were not brahmins. The circularity of this kind of reasoning proved particularly bothersome to Periyar, who sensed there was really no way out of it. The learned judges of the Supreme Court had, after all, quoted without demur P. V. Kane's reference to Brahma Purana: 'when an image . . . is touched by beasts like donkeys . . . or is rendered impure by the touch of outcastes and the like . . . God ceases to dwell therein.' Further, the Bench had unequivocally stated they were duty-bound to protect the freedoms guaranteed under Articles 25 and 26 of the Constitution:

> The protection of these articles is not limited to matters of doctrine or belief, they extend also to acts done in pursuance of religion and therefore contained a guarantee of rituals and observances, ceremonies and modes of worship which are integral parts of religion . . . what constitutes an essential part of a religion or religious practices has to be decided by the Court with reference to the doctrines of a particular religion and include practices which are regarded by the community as part of its religion (AIR 1972: 1593).

Under these circumstances, damned to eternal shudrahood, by both law, custom, precedent and practice, Periyar could not but dream of Utopia again. Thus, in 1972, he revived with vigour the demand for a separate Tamil Nadu, for a state of being and a community where touch may not defile and where angst and despair would not torment those unlucky millions who had been born as shudras and panchamas. Perhaps he cursed and laughed bitterly all the way to his grave, fuming at an injustice that seems to have been mandated by the 'Gods' themselves. But, then this is the laughter of prophecy, which dares to dream again, and yet again, and which points to the necessity of struggle, even as it anticipates utopia.

Appendices

1: THE ORIGINAL ACTION PLAN SUBMITTED BY PERIYAR TO THE JUSTICE PARTY

(*i*) Salaries of Government officials must be reduced since high salaries compromise their integrity, increase their avarice and are a drain on the financial resources of the country.

(*ii*) Industries that manufacture goods to fulfil public needs and comforts as well as transport facilities meant for public good ought to be run by the Government.

(*iii*) There should be no middlemen or creditors between agricultural producers and consumers. Cooperative societies should be set up to distribute produce in a way that ameliorates the lives of the peasant and cuts down the losses of the consumer.

(*iv*) The ryot's current indebtedness must be resolved and steps should be taken to ensure he does not get indebted in the future.

(*v*) All efforts must be undertaken to see that to an extent as many people as possible benefit from education; to ensure prohibition and to secure to the best extent possible, an equitable distribution of posts and services in the Government amongst all castes. Efforts should be made to monitor the progress of these objectives.

(*vi*) Religion should be defined as a private matter and no reference to it must be present in politics or in governance. No special concessions should be made to communities on the basis of religion (and caste), no special status conferred and Government must not spend its resources on such objectives.

(*vii*) Taxing should be regulated so that the self-employed person as well as a section of the salaried class is relieved of the tax burden. Only those who possess an income beyond their needs and whose lands are worked on by others ought to pay income tax and land revenue respectively.

(*viii*) Additional powers should be made over to local and municipal boards and cooperatives. Likewise their responsibilities ought to be multiplied and responsible and honest salaried officers appointed to the latter to help them carry out their tasks.

(*ix*) Litigation must be decreased.

(*x*) We will endeavour to fulfil these objectives through legal means, through laws that we make in the Councils, and wherever legal options are not available, we will agitate to have such legal powers conferred on us.

Source: *Pagutharivu* 23.9.1934.

The Amendments to the Plan as Made by the Justice Party

ECONOMIC

(*i*) To relieve the ryots of their present debt distress and to prevent them getting indebted in future; to prevent distress mortgage of lands to the creditors, sufficient measures should be taken.

(*ii*) The number of cooperative and land mortgage banks should be increased so that ryots do not fall into the clutches of creditors who charge very high rates of interest. Such banks should be run by Government officials themselves.

(*iii*) To prevent unnecessary litigation, especially with respect to property, Government should maintain proper records. The *benami* clause with respect to property must be declared legally invalid.

(*iv*) Middlemen who come in the way of ryots enjoying the benefits of their produce ought to be done away with and institutional arrangements must be made for ryots and the buyers of produce to interact directly so that ryots get a good remunerative price.

(*v*) Just as how the Government at present runs the Railways, Telegraphs and Posts, Water Supply and Electricity, so in the future should it endeavour to run other industries as well.

(*vi*) The concessions granted to Government servants with respect to insurance should be extended to other sections of the populace as well.

SOCIAL

(*i*) Within a specific time limit, universal literacy must be secured.
(*ii*) Consumption of liquour should be ended by law within a given time-frame.
(*iii*) Untouchability should not find a place in law and administration.
(*iv*) All efforts should be made to secure resources and opportunities for women who should also be appointed to Government posts just as men are.
(*v*) The time spent at work by a worker should be reduced, unemployment reduced and a salary that meets his complete needs should be offered to him.

POLITICAL

(*i*) All communities should be represented in Government service in the province in proportion to their numbers in the population.
(*ii*) Since the present mode of administration constitutes a financial burden on the people, efforts should be made to cut down administration expenses, provide a fair administration. Efforts should also be made to cut down salaries of officials in such a manner that is adequate and suitable to an Indian lifestyle.
(iii) To relieve people of the burden of taxation, a gradient should be fixed which takes into account the revenue from land and other incomes. For those who earn a fixed low salary, tax on land and income should be abolished.
(*iv*) More tasks ought to be assigned to municipalities and local boards as well as cooperatives and their administration should be left to officials of the state.
(v) To achieve these ends, laws may be framed, whenever necessary and these objectives should be made known to the public through effective propaganda.

Source: *Kudi Arasu*, 10 February 1935.

2: PERIYAR'S PLAN AS FINALLY ACCEPTED BY THE JUSTICE PARTY

1. To relieve the ryots of their present debt distress and to prevent them from getting indebted in future, and to prevent distress mortgage of lands to the creditors, sufficient legal and other measures should be undertaken.
2. The number of Cooperative and Land Mortgage banks should be increased so that ryots do not fall into the clutches of creditors who charge very high rates of interest. Such banks should be set up throughout the Presidency and run by Government officials themselves.
3. To prevent unnecessary ltitigation, especially with respect to property, Government should maintain proper land records. The *benami* clause with respect to property should be declared legally invalid and not accepted as a valid counter-argument in court.
4. Middlemen and traders who come in the way of ryots enjoying the benefits of their produce ought to be done away with. Institutional arrangements must be made for ryots and buyers of their produce to interact directly so that ryots get a good remunerative price for their produce.
5. Just as how Government at present runs Railways, Telegraph and Posts, Water Supply and Eletricity, so in future should it endeavour to run other industries and undertake other responsibilities.
6. The concessions granted to Government servants with respect to insurance should be extended to other sections of the population.
7. Efforts must be undertaken to raise the nation's standard of living and to ensure people wages which would help them attain this standard of living.
8. Universal literacy must be achieved within a specified time limit.
9. Legal and other efforts to end consumption of liquor should be undertaken.
10. Untouchability and other oppressive differences based on birth which exist in society at present must be abolished.
11. All posts in Government must be made available to people of

all groups on the basis of their proportion in the population and keeping in mind the requirements of government.

12. The burden of taxation on land should be shared equally by all people and tax remission should be made available to poor ryots.
13. More tasks ought to be assigned to municipalities, local boards and cooperatives. They should be given the freedom to undertake more tasks than at present and should be supervised by Government officials.
14. Since the present mode of administration constitutes a financial burden on the people, efforts should be made to cut down salaries of officials in such a manner that is adequate and suitable to an Indian lifestyle and Indian economic conditions.
15. To achieve these objectives, laws may be framed, wherever necessary, and these objectives should be made known to the public through effective propaganda.

3: THE ERODE PROGRAMME

The Aims and Ideals of the Self-Respect Party of South India

1. The statement of complete independence from the British and other forms of capitalist governments.
2. The cancellation of all national debts.
3. Public ownership of railways, banks, shipping and other transport services and waters and lands, etc.
4. Public ownership without compensation of all agricultural lands, forests and lands, etc.
5. Cancellation of all private debts and other obligations incurred by the workers and peasants.
6. Changing of all Native States into one common Indian Federation under the rule of the workers and peasants of India.
7. Improving the lives of the workers and peasants of the land by securing for them more than seven hours labour, increased wages, State aid for their unemployed, health resorts, free libraries and other cultural facilities.
8. These shall form the main ideals of the Self-Respect Party.

Self-Respect League: Samadharma Party of South India: Proposals

PREAMBLE

Whereas, the Self-Respect Party during the past eight years has very largely succeeded in rousing the attention of the mass of people to the enormity of their superstitious habits, customs and practices of their religion and caste and of their degraded economic conditions of life.

Whereas, it is becoming increasingly evident that such irrational religious and caste habits and customs and their low economic conditions of life, cannot be done away with, except through the State action, and

Whereas, it is further evident that the various political, social and religious bodies and institutions are even more determined to hold the masses in social, religious and economic bondage and degradation, through their political organization all over the country, and

Whereas, the safeguards adopted by the Round Table Conference for the perpetuation of pernicious religious practices of inhuman caste distinctions are inimical to and destructive of all rational life of the masses.

OBJECTS

It is hereby proposed to form from the body of Self-Respecters, a political party called the Samadharma Party of South India to carry out the following main objects, namely,

(*i*) To obtain by consitutional means and methods, the repeal of all irrational safeguards for the private enjoyment of public utilities, for all harmful religious and caste practices and habits, and thereby free the masses from their degrading religious and caste superstitions and habits and improve their economic life.

(*ii*) To obtain the adoption of adult suffrage for election of members to all Government, Legislative and Municipal bodies, Local, Provincial and Central.

(*iii*) To obtain security of service and minimum wage, to all workers in public and private utility services, such as factories, workshops, Railways, Shipping, Transport, Posts and Telegraph, etc.

(*iv*) To get for the landless workers and agricultural labourers working in cultivable lands, estates, and waters, a reasonable share in the produce of such lands, estates and waters.

(*v*) To obtain State sanction for utilizing temple, church, mosque and religious funds and incomes, for the education, both literary and vocational, for sanitation and housing of the mass population in the country, and for the maintenance of destitute children and orphans.

(*vi*) To obtain the removal of all caste distinctions among all castes, sects and classes of the Indian community, by removing all caste titles, from all public records and making such retention of caste ties as a disability to hold any kind of public service.

(*vii*) To secure through State action, municipalization of housing, transport, milk and medical service and establishment of nurseries in Municipalities, Taluks and District Boards and Village Unions.

(*viii*) To set up party candidates to the Legislative Councils, Taluk, District and Village Boards and Unions and Panchayats, to secure the aforesaid objects of the Party.

(*ix*) Party candidates pledged to these various objects of the Party will be elected for the various Legislative Councils, Taluk and District Boards, Village Unions, etc.

(*x*) These various measures, acts and reforms shall be obtained through all constitutional means and methods such as Council entry and propaganda by means of lectures, discussions and discourses as well as through the press. Rules and regulations for party funds and organisations, etc., will be made by a Provisional Committee of the Party called for the purpose.

Source: *Kudi Arasu*, 1 January 1933; reprinted in E. Sa Viswanathan, 1983.

Bibliography

BOOKS IN ENGLISH

'An Admirer', 1992. *Periyar E. V. Ramasamy: A Pen Portrait.* Madras: The Periyar Self-Respect Propaganda Institution, 1992.

Aiyar, Chandrasekhara N. 1959. *Mayne's Treatise on Hindu Law and Usage*, 11th ed. Madras: Higginbothams, 1950.

Alosiyus. G. *Iyothee Thassar and the Tamil Buddhist Movement,* Delhi: Critical Quest, 2015

Ambedkar, B. R.,1993. *us,* vols 9, 12. Bombay: Department of Education, Government of Maharashtra, 1993.

Appadurai, Arjun, 1981.*Worship and Conflict under Colonial Rule: A South Indian Case.* Cambridge: Cambridge University Press, 1981.

Arnold, David, 1977. *The Congress in Tamil Nadu: Nationalist Politics in South India, 1919-1937.* Delhi: Manohar, 1977.

, [Ayyathurai thesis—— 2011' Foundations of Anti-Caste Consciousness: Pandit Iyothee Thass, Tamil Buddhism and the Marginalised in South India', PhD diss, Columbia University]

Baker, Christopher John, 1984a. *The Politics of South India, 1920-1937*. Bombay: Vikas, 1976.

——. 1984b. *An Indian Rural Economy, 1880-1955: The Tamil Countryside.* Delhi: Oxford University Press, 1984.

Baker, Christopher John, and David Washbrook, 1975. *South India: Political Institutions and Social Change.* Delhi: Vikas.

Bakshi, S. R., 1977. *Simon Commission and Indian Nationalism.* Delhi: Munshiram Manoharlal.

Chandrababu, B. S 1993 *Social Protest in Tamil Nadu.* Madras: Emerald, 1993.

Chatterjee, Partha. 1993. *The Nation and Its Fragments: Colonial and Postcolonial Histories.* Princeton: Princeton University Press, 1993.

Cohn, Bernard.1987. *An Anthropologist amongst Historians and Other Essays.* Delhi: Oxford University Press..

Karthick Ram Manoharan, 2022. *Periyar: A Study in Political Atheism.* Hyderabad: Orient BlackSwan.

Copley, Anthony, 1978. T*he Political Career of C. Rajagopalachari: 1937-1954: A Moralist in Politics*. Madras: Macmillan.

Das, Suranjan, 1994.'The Indian National Congress and the Dynamics of Nation Building: Aspects of Continuity and Change'. In *State and Nation in the Context of Social Change*, edited by T. V. Satyamurthy. Delhi: Oxford University Press,.

Diehl, Anita, 1978. *Periyar E. V. Ramasamy—A Study of the Influence of Personality in Contemporary India.* Delhi: BI.

Dirks, Nicholas, B.1987. *The Hollow Crown: Ethnohistory of an Indian Kingdom.* Cambridge: Cambridge University Press.

Francis, Dayanandan T. 1990. *The Mission and the Message of Ramalinga Swamy.* Delhi: Motilal Banarasidass.

Frykenberg, R.E., ed., 1969. *Land Control and Social Structure in Indian History.* Madison: University of Wisconsin Press.

Ghosh, Suniti Kumar, 1989; 1995. India and the Raj 1919-1947: Glory, Shame and Bondage, vol 1, Calcutta: Prachi, 1989; vol 2, Bombay: Research Unit for Political Economy, 1995.

Gopalakrishnan, M. B., 1991. P*eriyar, Father of the Tamil Race.* Madras: Emerald.

Hardgrave, Robert,1969. *The Nadars of Tamil Nadu: The Political Culture of a Community in Change.* Berkeley: University of California Press.

Heimsath, Charles, 1964. Indian Nationalism and Hindu Social Reform. Princeton: Princeton University Press.

Hill, Christopher, 1972. The World Turned Upside Down: Radical Ideas during the English Revolution. London: Temple Smith.

Houghton, Graham,1983. The Impoverishment of Dependency: The History of the Protestant Church in Madras, 1870-1920. Madras: Christian Literature Society.

Irschick, Eugene, 1986. *Tamil Revivalism in 1930s*. Madras: Crea-A.

——.1969. *Politics and Social Conflict in South India: The Non-Brahmin Movement and Tamil Separatism, 1916-1929.* Berkeley: University of California Press.

Iyer, Gopal, and R. Vidyasagar (unpublished)., A Study in Agrarian Structures and Peasant Movements in Tamil Nadu, vol 1

Joshi, Sashi, *1992. The Strugggle for Hegemony in India, 1920-1947*: The Colonial State, the Left and the National Movement, vol 1, 1920-1934; vol 2, 1934-1941. Delhi: Sage.

Kavlekar, Kashinath, 1979. *Non-Brahmin Movement in South India.* Kolhapur: Shivaji University Press, 1979.

Kamalanathan, T. P. 1985. *K. Veeramani, BA, BL, Is Refuted and the Historical Facts about the Scheduled Castes' Struggle for Emancipation in India,* North Arcot: Ambedkar Self-Respect Movement, Tiruppathur.

Keer, Dhananjay. 1991. *Dr. Ambedkar: Life and Mission.* Bombay: Popular Prakashan..

Karat, Prakash, 1973. Language and Nationality Politics in India. Hyderabad: Orient Longman,.

Karthick Ram Manoharan, 2022. *Periyar: A Study in Political Atheism.* Hyderabad: Orient BlackSwan.

Kumar, Dharma, 1965. *Land and Caste in South India—Agricultural Labour in the Madras Presidency during the Nineteenth Century.* Cambridge: Cambridge University Press,

Ludden, David, 1985. *Peasant History in South India.* Princeton: Princeton University Press, 1985.

Manickam, Sunderraj, 1992. *Reflections and Themes in History.* School of Historical Studies, Madurai Kamaraj University, Madurai..

___, 1990. *Nandanar the Dalit Martyr: A Historical Reconstruction of His Times.* Madras: Christian Literature Society..

___, 1988. *Studies in Missionary Activity: Reflections on a Culture Contact.* Madras: The Christian Literature Society.

Mudaliar, Chandra, 1976. *The State and Religious Endowments in Madras.* Madras: University of Madras.

Murugesan, K., and C. S. Subramaniam, 1975. *Singaravelu—First Communist in South India.* Delhi: People's Publishing House.

Nagaraj, D.R 1993. *The Flaming Feet: A Study of Dalit Movements in India.* Bangalore: South Forum Press.

Nambi Arooran, 1980. *Tamil Renaissance and Dravidian Nationalism, 1905-1944.* Madurai: Koodal Publishers.

O'Hanlan, Rosalind, 1985. *Caste, Conflict and Ideology: Mahatma Joti Rao Phule and Low Caste Protest in Nineteenth Century Western India.* Cambridge: Cambridge University Press.

Omvedt, Gail, 1995. *Dalit Visions.* Hyderabad: Orient Longman, 1995.

——.1994. *Dalits and the Democratic Revolution: Dr Ambedkhar and the Dalit Movement in Colonial India.* Delhi: Sage.

——.1976. *Cultural Revolt in a Colonial Society: The Non-Brahmin Movement in Western India, 1870-1930.* Scientific Socialist Education Trust.

,Pandey, Gyanendra, 1988. *The Indian Nation in 1942.* Calcutta: K.P.Bagchi, 1988.

Patnaik, Utsa, and Manjari Dingawaney, eds. 1985. *Chains of Servitude: Bondage and Slavery in India.* Hyderabad: Sangam.

Periyar, E. V. R. nd, *Man and Religion,* translated by R. Sunderraj. Madras:

Rationalist Publishers.

Phillips, C. H., and M. D. Wainwright, eds. 1976. I*ndian Society and the Beginning of Modernisation*. London: SOAS.

Presler, Franklin A. 1987. *Religion under Bureaucracy: Policy and Administration for Hindu Temples in South India.* Cambridge: Cambridge University Press.

Rajaraman, P. 1988. *The Justice Party: A Historical Perspective, 1917-1937.* Madras: Poompozhil Publishers, 1988.

Rajendran, N. 1994. *National Movement in Tamil Nadu, 1905-1914.* Delhi: Oxford University Press.

Ramamurthy, P.1987. *The Freedom Movement and the Dravidian Movement.* Hyderabad: Orient Longman.

Ray, Bharati, 1995.'The Freedom Movement and Feminist Consciousness'. In *The Seams of History*, edited by Bharati Ray. Delhi: Oxford University Press.

Ryerson, Charles A. 1988. *Regionalism and Religion: The Tamil Renaissance and Popular Hinduism.* Madras: The Christian Literature Society.

Rudolph, Lloyd I., and Susan H. Rudolph, 1987. *The Modernity of Tradition—Political Development in India.* Hyderabad: Orient Longman.

S. Saraswathi,1994. *Towards Self-Respect: Periyar on a New World.* Institute of South Indian Studies, Madras.

Sarkar, Tanika, 1985. 'Bondage in the Colonial Context'. In *Chains of Servitude: Bondage and Slavery in India,* edited by Utsa Patnaik and Manjari Dingwaney. Hyderabad: Sangam.

Sesha Iyengar, K. V. 1932. *The Passing Away of Untouchability.* Madras.

Sivathamby, K. 1995. *Understanding the Dravidian Movement: Problems and Perspectives*. Madras: New Century Book House.

Stein, Burton,1980. *Peasant State and Society in Medieval South India.* Delhi: Oxford University Press.

___, 1969. 'Integration of the Agrarian Systems of South India'. In *Land Control and Social Structure in Indian History,* edited by R. E. Frykenberg. Madison: University of Wisconsin Press.

Subramanian, N. 1989. *The Brahmin in the Tamil Country.* Madurai: Ennes.

___, 1988. *Tamilian Historiography,* Madurai: Ennes.

Sundaram Pillay, P. [1909] rpt 1985. *Some Milestones in the History of Tamil Literature.* Madras: Pioneer Book Services.

Suntharalingam, R. 1974. *Politics and Nationalist Awakening in South India, 1852-1891.* Tucson: University of Arizona Press.

Varadarajulu Naidu, Diwan Bahadur T., 1991. *The Justice Movement 1917* (A Detailed Account of the Justice Party in the First Year of Its Existence). Madras: Dravidar Kazhagam Publications..

Veeramani, K. 1992a. *The History of the Struggle for Social Justice in Tamil Nadu.* Madras: Dravidar Kazhagam Publications, 1992.

___, 1992 b.*Periyar on Women's Rights,* translated by R. Sunderraju. Madras: Emerald.

Veeramani, K.; S. Selvanathan; B. S. Chandrababu; and N. Muthumohan.1990. Festschrift in honour of G. Thangavelu. *Social Justice in Tamil Nadu.* School of Historical Research, Madurai-Kamaraj University.

Vellore Senthamizhkko, 1987. *Periyar in History.* Vellore: Periyar-Gora-Kovoor Atheist Centre.

Venkatraman, S. R., *Temple Entry Legislation Reviewed: With Acts and Bills.* Madras: Bharathi Devi Publishers, 1946.

Visvanathan, Shiv 1985. *Organizing for Science.* Delhi: Oxford University Press.

Viswanathan, E. Sa. 1983. *The Political Career of E. V. Ramasamy Naicker: A Study in the Politics of Tamil Nadu, 1929-1949.* Madras: Ravi & Vasanth Publishers.

Wagle, N. K., ed.1980. *Images of Maharashtra.* London: Curzon Press.

Washbrook, David, 1976. *The Emergence of Provincial Politics.* Delhi: Vikas.

ARTICLES IN ENGLISH

Arnold, David, Aug 1979.'Looting, Grain Riots and Government Policy in South India, 1918'. *Past and Present* 84.

Arulalan. May 1971. 'The Relevance of Periyar—Caste and Class Struggle'. *The Radical Review* (Madras) 2, 2.

Ayyathurai, Gajendran, 2023. ' Memory, 'History, and Casteless Consciousness: Tamil Buddhists in Modern South India', *South Asian History and Culture* 14, 3:1-18.

—, 2020. 'Living Buddhism: Migration, Memory, and Castelessness in South India'. *History and Anthropology* 34, 3: 1-19.

Geetha, V., and S. V. Rajadurai, 15 July 1995. 'One Hundred Years of Brahminitude: Arrival of Annie Besan't. Economic and Political Weekly.

___. 25 Sept 1993. 'Dalits and Non-Brahmin Consciousness in Colonial Tamil Nadu'. *Economic and Political Weekly.*

___. 16 Jan 1993. 'Neo-Brahminism: An Intentional Fallacy?' *Economic and Political Weekly.*

___. Oct 1992. 'Towards a Re-Appraisal of the Dravidian–Non-Brahmin Movement'. *MIDS Bulletin 22,.* 10.

___, Tamil Nadu Claims Its Linguistic Heritage. *Media Development* (London) 1.

___. Nov 1991. Interrogating `India'—Dravidian Viewpoint. *Seminar* 387.

Geetha, V. (Oct 1994-June 1995). Periyar and the Women's Question. *Periyar Era* (Madras) 1, 1-9

___. December 1993. 'Re-Writing History in the Brahmin's Shadow'. *Journal of Arts and Ideas* 25-26.

Hjejle, Benedict, year? 'Slavery and Agrestic Bondage in South India in the Nineteenth Century'. *Scandinavian Economic Review* 11, 1-2.

Leonard, D., 2023. 'Sarithiram as Interpretative Pedagogy: IyotheeThass's Casteless Community and *History, Critical Philosophy of Race'* 11(1), 94-119.

___, 2021. 'Caste-Less Tamils and Early Print Public Sphere: Remembering IyotheeThass (1845-1914', *South Asia Research* 41, 3, 1-20.

___, 2017. 'One Step Inside *Tamilian:* On the Anti-Caste Writing of Language', *Social Scientist* 45, 1/2,, 19-32..

Menon, Saraswathi,1982. 'Caste and Land Control: Some Historic Aspects of Rural Labour', *MIDS Bulletin.*

O'Hanlan, Rosalind, and David Washbrook, Autumn 1991. 'History in Transition: Approaches to the Study of Colonialism and Culture in India', History Workshop. *Journal of Socialist and Feminist Studies* 32.

Pandian, M. S. S., 18-25 February 1995. 'Beyond Colonial Crumbs: Cambridge School, Identity Politics and Dravidian Movement'. *Economic and Political Weekly.*

—. 21-23 March 1994 'Notes on the Transformation of Dravidian Ideology: Tamil Nadu c.1900-1940'. Paper presented for seminar on Ethnicity and Nation Building, Centre for South and South East Asian Studies, University of Madras,

Patil, Sharad, 4 Nov 1995.' Problems of Indian Democratic Revolution'. Mainstream.

Pickering, Natalie, May-June 1993. 'Recasting the Indian Nation: Dravidian Nationalism Replies to the Women's Question'. Thatched Patio, International Centre for Ethnic Studies, Colombo.

___. 1990. 'Dravidian Movement in Its Pre-Independence Phases' *Economic and Political Review* annual number.

Swaminathan, Padmini, March 1992. 'Technical Education and Industrial Development in the Madras Presidency'. Occasional paper no. 106, *MIDS*, Madras.

___, September, 1991. 'Evolution of Industrial Policy in the Madras Presidency, 1900-1947'.

Occasional paper, no. 105, *MIDS*, Madras.

___, State Intervention in Industrialisation: A Case Study of the Madras Province, South India. Occasional paper no. 99, *MIDS*, Madras, 1991.

Venkatachalapathy, A.R. 2017. From Erode to Volga: Periyar EVR's Soviet and European Tour, 1932. In *India and the World in the First Half of the Twentieth Century*. Edited by Madhavan K. Palat. London and New York: Routledge, 2017, 102-133.

OTHER SOURCES

All India Report of Judicial Decisions, 1972.

Justice Party Golden Jubilee Souvenir, Madras, 1968.

Pesant Organisations and Movements in Andhra Pradesh. Mimeographed, Andhra University, Waltair, 1979.

Report of the Royal Commission on Labour in India, Calcutta, Government of India Central Publication Branch, 1931.

JOURNALS AND NEWSPAPERS

English

New India

Swadharma

Tamil

Desabandhu (Db)

Dravida Nadu

Kudi Arasu (KA)

Nagara Thoothan (NT)

Oru Paisa Tamizhan (Tamizhan)

Paguthariyu (Pa)

Puduvai Murasu (PM)

Puratchi (Pu)

Samadharmam (Sd)

Viduthalai (Vi)

BOOKS, TRACTS AND ARTICLES IN TAMIL

Aadalarasan, Thanjai, 1992. *Thanthai Periyarum Thazhthappattorum* (Periyar and the Dalits), Periyar Self-Respect Propaganda Institution, Madras.

Aasaan, K. V. K. 1989. *Mannitha Uriamaip Poril Periyar Peniya Adayala*m (A Socio-Historical Survey of the Identity Problem in Periyar E. V. R.'s Struggle for Human Rights), Periyar Self-Respect Propaganda Institution, Madras.

Anaimuthu, V., ed. 1974. *Periyar E. Ve. Ra. Sithanaikal* (Thoughts of Periyar), 3 vols. Trichy: Sinthanaiyalar Pathippagam.

Balakrishnan, Purasu, 1991. *Gnanakavi Ramalingar* (The Saint-Poet Ramalinga). Delhi: NBT.

Chandra, Bipin, Amalesh Tripathi, and Barun De, 1987. *Suthanthirap Porattum* (Freedom Struggle), translation. Delhi: NBT.

Ezhilarasu, K. V. 1989. *Needhik Katchit Thalaivar Dr. T M Nair: Vazhvum Thondum* (The Life and Work of Dr. Nair, Justice Party Leader). Madras: Paari NiIlayam.

Gurusamy, Kuthoosi, 1984. *Poduvudaimai* (Communism). Vellore: Kuthoosi Gurusamy Pathippagam,

Hyderkhan, Ameer,1989. *Thenninthiyavaik Kanden* (South India Discovered). Madras: New Century Book House.

___, *Then Indiyavil Communist Katchiyin Thuvakkam* (The Origin of the Communist Party in South India). Madras: Chennai Books, 1990.

Iyothee Thass Pandithar, 1957. *Indirar Desa Charitram* The History of Indirar Nation), 2nd ed. Andersonpet: SSPS, KGF.

——.1950. *Buddha Marga Vina Vidai* (Questions and Answers on Buddhism), 5th ed. Andersonpet: SSPS, KGF.

___. 1950b. *Hirikural Kadavul Vazhthy* (The Invocation in Thirikural), 3rd ed. Andersonpet: SSPS, KGF

——.1932a. *Kabaleesan Charithra Aaraychi* (The Inquiry of the Skull-Bearer's Story), 3rd ed. Andersonpet: Sri Siddhartha Puthagasalai (SSPS), KGF.

___.1932b *Vibuthi Aaraychi*. (The Inquiry of the Holy Ash), 3rd ed. Andersonpet: SSPS, KGF, 1932.

——.1932c.*Yathartha Brahmana Vedanta Vivarum* (History of the Real Brahmanas), 2nd ed. Andersonpet: SSPS, KGF.

___. 1932d. *Vesha Brahmana Vedanta Vivarum* (History of the False Brahmanas), 2nd ed. Andersonpet: SSPS, KGF.

___.1930a *Sri Muruga Kadavul Varalaru* (The History of Lord Sri Muruga), 3rd ed. Andersonpet: SSPS, KGF.

___, 1930b, *Thiruvalluvar Varalaru* (History of Thiruvalluvar), 4th ed. Andersonpet: SSPS, KGF.

...___. 1927. *Auvayar Ennum Sri Ambikaiamman Aruliya Tirivasakam* (The Tirivasakam Bestowed by Sri Ambikaiamman called Auvayar). Andersonpet: SSPS, KGF.

Iyothee Thass Pandithar, and Arangasamy Pandithar, 1950.*Arichandran Poykal* (Harischandra's Lies), 5th ed. Andersonpet: SSPS, KGF.

Jerry, Dr,1994. *Manitham: Thanthai Periyarin Madha Ethirupppu Nilaippadu Oru Arasiyal Seyalppadu* (Humanism: Periyar's Anti-Religious Atttitude: A Political Activity). Madras: Needhi Pathippagam..

Kaivalyam, Swamigal, [1931] rpt 1983. *Kaivalyam Katturaikal* (Essays of Kaivalyam). Madras: Periyar Self-Respect Propaganda Institution.

Kesari. 1948. *August 15*. Trichy: Noble Printers.

Krishnan, P. 1984. *Thamzih Noolkalil Thamizh Mozhi, Thamizhinam Thamizhnadu*

(Tamil Language, Tamil Nationality and Tamil Nadu in Tamil Literature). Madras.

Kumarasamy, Ko.,1985. *Dravidap Perunthagai Sir Pitti Theagorayar* (Sir Pitti Theagorayar the Dravidian Leader). Tirunelveli: The South India Saiva Siddhantha Works Publishing Society.

Manoharan, Karuna, 1991. *Sadhiya Samooka Amaipum Thamizh Thesa Inap Pirachinayam* (Casteist Social Structure and the Tamil Nationality Question). Tiruppur: Sammoka Needhip Pathippagam.

___, 1995. *Diravidathal Veezhuntoma? Sadhiyathal Veezhntoma?* (Is Our Fall Caused by Dravidianism or Casteism?) Tiruppur: Samooka Needhip Pathippagam.

Marx. A, Po. Velsamy, and Rav Kumar, eds. 1995. *Periyariyam* (Periyarism). Coimbatore: Vidiyal Pathippakam.

Masilamaniar, M. 1929. *Varuna Bedha Vilakkam* (The Example of the Caste Difference), 2nd ed. Andersonpet: SSPS, KGF.

Murugesan, Mangala N. K 1990. *Suyamariyadai Iyakkam* (Self-Respect Movement). Madras: Paari Nilayam.

Packiamuthu, Sarojini, 1990. *Viviliyamum Thamizhum* (The Bible and Tamil). Madras: The Department of Research and Publications, Gurukul Lutheran Theological College and Research Institute.

Paramasivam, K. 1968. *Needhik Katchiyin Thotrammum Valrchiyum* (Origin and Growth of the Justice Party). Madras: published by author.

Ponneelan, 1982. *Jeeva Enroru Manudan* (A Man Called Jeeva). Madras: New Century Book House.

Rajadurai, P. 1992. *Suyamariyathai Iyakkathil Nadarkal Aatriya Pangu* (The Role of Nadars in the Self-Respect Movement). Virudhunagar: Illamaran Pathippakam.

___,.991. *Sattamandrathil Soundrapandian* (Soundarapandian in the Legislature). Virudhunagar: Illamaran Pathippagam..

Rajadurai, S. V. 1998. August 15. Coimbatore: Vidiyal Pathippagam.98.

Rajadurai, S. V., and V. Geetha, 1996. *Periyar: Suyamariyathai Samadharmam* (Periyar: Self-Respect Samadharma) Coimbatore: Vidiyal Pathippagam, 1996.

___, 1992. *Diravida Dinamaniyin Paarpaneeyam* ('Dravida' Dinamani's Brahminism). Vridhachalam: Kavitha Nilayam.

Raj Gowthaman, 1995a. *A.Madavaiah, 1872-1925*. Madras: Kavya.

___, 1995b. *Poi + Abatham = Unmai (Lies + Absurdity = Truth).* Coimbatore: Vilimbu Trust.

___. 1993. *Dalit Panppadu* (Dalit Culture). Pondicherry: Gouri Pathippagam.

Ramamrithammal, 1936. *Dasigalin Mosavalai.*

Raju, S. A. K. K 1983, *Neelavathi Subramanium Vazhkai* Varalaru (Biography of Neelavathi Subramanium). Madras: Vanathi Pathippagam.

Rathinasabapathy, A. 1932. *Ezhai Azhutha Kaneer* (The Tears Shed by the Poor). Andersonpet: SSPS, KGH.

Samy, Aa. Maa. 1992. *Pathonpathaam Nootrandin Tamizh Ithazhkal* (Nineteenth-Century Tamil Magazines) Madras: Navamani Pathippagam.

Samy, Sitambaranar, 1971. *Thamizhar Talaivar Periyar E Ve Ra Vazhkai Varalaru* (The LIfe of the Leader of the Tamils, E. V. R.). Trichy: Periyar Self-Respect Propaganda Institute., .

Siva Illango, 1991. *B1991. Harathidasan.* Madras: Madras: Bharathi Pathippagam.

Sivathambi, Karthigesu.1988. *Thamizhil Illakiya Varalaru—Varalaru Ezhuduiyal Aayvu* (An Enquiry into the History of Tamil Literature and Historiography), Madras: New Century Book House.

Thirunavukkarasu, K. *Kalathil Ninra Kavalrkal* (The Fighters in the Battlefield). Madras: Nakkeran Pathipakkam.

—.1991. *Diravida Iyakka Verkal* (The Roots of the Dravidian Movement). Madras: Manivachakar Pathippagam.

Vasanthakumar, 1991.*Diravida Iyakka Kalacharam* (The Culture of the Dravidian Movement). Madras: Makkal Kalachara Kazhagam.

Vedanayagam Pillay, rpt. *Mayuram Munsiff Pirathaba Mudaliar Charitram* (The History of Prataba Mudaliar). Madras: New Century Book House..

Veeramani, K.1986. *Congress Varalaaru: Maraikappadum Unmaigalum Karaipadintha Athiyayangalum* (Congress History: Concealed Truth and Tainted Chapters). Madras: Periyar Self-Respect Propaganda Institute..

___. 1985. *Viduthalaip Porum Diravidar Iyakkamum—Unmai Varalaru* (The Freedom Struggle and the Dravidian Movement—A True History). Madras: Dravidar Kazhagam Pulblications.

Venkatachalapathy, A. R. 1994. *Diravida Iyakamum Velalarum—Suyamariyathai Iyakkak Kattam, 1927-1942* (Dravidian Movement and the Vellalas— Self-Respect Phase, 1927-1942). Madras: South Asia Books.

___. *Binny Aalai Velai Nirutham 1921* (The Binny Mills Strike 1921). Madras: Ponni Publications..

Velu, Kuruvikarambai,1991. *Kuthoosi Gurusamy,* 2nd ed. Madras: Valavan Pathippagam..

'Viduthalai' Rajendran, *1995. Kochaip Paduthum Kuzhappavadhikal* (The Confused Who Vulgarise Periyar). Madras: Dravidar Kazhagam Publications.

Index